Political Sociology

Political Sociology

Robert E. Dowse
University of Exeter

and

John A. Hughes
University of Lancaster

JOHN WILEY & SONS
London · New York · Sydney · Toronto

Library of Congress catalog card number
76-39229

ISBN 0 471 22145 7

Printed in Great Britain by Butler & Tanner Ltd
Frome and London

To Patricia Ann

(*R. E. D.*)

To my parents

(*J. A. H.*)

INTRODUCTION

THIS BOOK arises out of three years of collaboration in the teaching of political sociology in the University of Exeter. Having volunteered to teach such a course the authors quickly realized that no sustained attempt had been made to present the subject as a whole, although there was no shortage of compilations of more or less edited articles. As we began thinking about the framework and content of a political sociology course, we appreciated why the editing of readers was such a difficult task: there is no clear framework for selection and, hence, no criteria for exclusion. We are by no means happy that we have succeeded in drawing a clear outline, but we do believe that we have touched upon most substantive areas of interest to the political sociologist. No attempt has been made to be totally comprehensive, nor to conceal the very real problems posed by the subject. For example, we might have included a much larger section in Chapter 1 on method, but have preferred to indicate the general persuasion of the authors, leaving it to the reader to enquire further by following up some of the references.

References in this volume are of two types:

(1) Locations for quotations and allusions in the text, indicated by a raised number in the text [2] and listed in numerical order at the end of each chapter under the heading 'References'.
(2) Suggestions for further reading, and additional information about points discussed in the text, indicated by an italic number in square brackets in the text [*2*]. These also are listed in numerical order at the end of each chapter under the heading 'Notes and Further Reading'.

Various colleagues and friends have read sections, typed them and have stimulated us when called upon: Teresa Baggs, Anthony Birch, Elizabeth Brown, Jacky Jowett, John Lee, Ken Newton, Edith Revesz, Virginia Richards, Susan Ridler, Jeffrey Stanyer and Jackie West.

July 1969–May 1971

ROBERT E. DOWSE, University of Exeter
JOHN A. HUGHES, University of Lancaster

CONTENTS

1

THE SCOPE OF POLITICAL SOCIOLOGY

1.1. Introduction

IT IS FAIRLY normal practice among textbook writers to begin their endeavour by defining the subject matter they intend to introduce to the prospective student. The trouble with following tradition in this instance is the particular institutional status of political sociology: in some cases it is taught within political science departments and in other cases within sociology departments. This might not itself seem a serious difficulty except that neither sociology nor political science is noted for any clear-cut consensus concerning scope and method. Within sociology, for example, debate is enjoined about the relative merits of conflict or consensus theories of society, so-called 'grand' theorizing *versus* 'raw' empiricism, quantitative *versus* qualitative methods, and so on. Similarly, within political science a debate ranges over such matters as the behaviourist *versus* more traditional modes of political enquiry, the status of comparative study, the meaning of the term 'political' and the current relevance of classical political theory and philosophy. Clearly a subject so ambiguous in its status *vis à vis* political science and sociology is likely to defy uncontroversial elucidation.

The difficulty is not wholly a conceptual one but is in large part a product of the historical development of the social sciences, in particular sociology and political science. The early social scientists, if we may call them that, were extremely catholic both in their interests and in their methods of examining social behaviour. They were committed to neither political science nor sociology and perhaps would not have understood the distinction. To them society was an entity to be studied holistically. The names of Tocqueville, Marx, Pareto, Mosca, Spencer and Weber stand out as the intellectual heroes of both political science and sociology. What was ultimately responsible for the present uneasy separation of the social sciences was a process which has marked academic development in industrial societies for the last century, namely the professionalization of the academic role and the institutionalized differentiation of scholarly activities. No longer is it possible for scholars to receive much the same classical education. Instead specialization begins early and full professional academic licence requires many years of apprenticeship within the chosen 'field'. This tendency has its organizational reflection in the increased size and complexity of the institutions of higher learning. They no longer, or rarely, correspond to the image of the cosy commonroom we associate with, say, early nineteenth-century scholarship. Instead, they are large, federally organized institutions, with considerable budgets, and accounting and managerial problems common to extensive business firms. As part of these processes, sociology and political science began to develop a separateness based not so much on conceptual and analytical differences in their foci as on professional criteria.[*1*]

Of course this is not the whole story. Discussions on the 'proper' focus of political science and sociology are not entirely matters of professional self-justification. Such discussions can and do serve a purpose of orienting the subject towards significant problems. None the less, the social context of a discipline is a factor of more than passing interest. Social scientists easily forget that they and the subjects they teach are every bit part and parcel of the society which they study. While we would not necessarily argue that this renders them 'invalid', it does have important repercussions on the nature of the disciplines concerned. For one thing, the compartmentalization of the social sciences has meant the separate self-development of each. This is most clearly seen in the case of economics, which has developed largely without cognizance of the insights of psychology, sociology, political science or anthropology. In addition, it has meant that some areas of the social sciences, like political sociology, stand uneasily upon academically separated disciplines.

Fortunately, there are signs that the compartmentalization is breaking down. Social scientists generally are becoming more receptive to the ideas and conclusions of their colleagues from the different areas. Witness the historians' use of formal models of economic development, the social psychologists who concern themselves with the psychological predispositions conducive to economic growth, the development of interest amongst some economists in the psychological basis of consumer behaviour, and so on. Similarly, in political science dissatisfaction with the traditional interest in law, constitutional history and political theory is also evident. In the last decade the teaching curriculum of most departments of political science has been fundamentally changed. Briefly, but not too inaccurately, there has been a move towards the so-called 'behavioural' style of political enquiry.

The Behavioural Movement in Political Science

The 'behavioural movement' emphasizes the necessity of looking at and explaining the 'observed' political behaviour underlying particular institutional–legal arrangements. To give a rather obvious example: knowledge about all the details of the American Constitution does not tell us very much about the American political process as such. It does not tell us how political decisions are made in practice, or about the particular nature of the social bond between a congressman and his constituents, and so on. None of this means abandoning attention to law, constitutional arrangements and the like, but rather seeing these as one kind of variable among a host of others which could be used to explain those aspects of the political process in which we might be interested.

Of course none of this is entirely new. As early as the 1900's studies to investigate voting behaviour, party identification and attitudes and opinions were being undertaken. Developments in techniques of survey design, sampling, interviewing, questionnaire design and personality measurement during the 1930's and 1940's further accelerated the trend.[*2*] The current extent of this change was pointedly demonstrated by a survey of American academic political scientists. Asked to specify the area within which the most significant work in political science was taking place, they gave more weight to 'comparative government' and 'political behaviour' than to the more traditional 'public law' and 'political theory'. The political scientists most frequently mentioned as making the more important contribution to the subject since the Second World War were the behaviouralists Robert Dahl, Harold Lasswell, Herbert Simon, David Truman and V. O. Key.[1] While there is no comparable evidence for Britain and elsewhere, it is quite clear that there has been a similar if not as extensive a change as in the United States.

However, while this so-called behavioural movement has become the dominant force in political science, its success has not gone unchallenged. There are many political scientists who question the idea that 'behavioural' political science reflects the 'proper' focus of the subject.[2] It is not for us to go into the pros and cons of this debate here, but simply to note the effect of 'behaviouralism' on political science, and to note especially the willingness among political scientists to seek new theories and methods of enquiry from the other social sciences, including sociology.

Sociology and Political Science

While political science may have found a new openness and receptivity to what is going on in allied subjects, the case of sociology is somewhat different. For one thing, it has not needed to reach outside itself for new ideas, techniques and inspirations to anything like the extent of political science. This is not to say that the subject is better or worse off for this, but simply that its ethos, by and large, has been to regard itself as something like a universal science of social life embracing all aspects of social relations. In other words, sociology has tended to regard all social phenomena as its province; studies of economic behaviour, deviance, stratification, political life, family life, urban life, and so on, have all been undertaken in a way that would not have been possible by political scientists, economists or psychologists. As a result, sociologists have tended to see the other social sciences, in a sense, as 'derivatives' of sociology. One sociologist, for example, when writing of the relationship between sociology and political science, claimed that 'were it not for the historical fact that the behavioural approach to politics grew up in the context of existing departments of political science there is little reason to believe that it would not be a special sub-division of sociology similar to stratification or to the sociology of religion'.[3]

However, due to the compartmentalization of political science and sociology, there is little to suggest a corpus of political sociological knowledge exists in the way that there is one about the family, stratification, industry, and so on. This is not to say that one does not exist, simply that it has not been brought together. To do this, of course, it is necessary to provide a conceptual rationale to form the basis for enquiry and the ordering of knowledge. It is to this we now turn.

1.2. What is Political Sociology?

We have already suggested that, because of the historical development of political science and sociology into two disciplines with different traditions of intellectual activity, there arises a problem of definition. By and large, at this level the problem hinges on the word 'political' and its scope, a term about which there is disagreement and, as an added difficulty, a veritable mountain of writing. To begin, let us take what is perhaps an extreme definition of the term, that of Crick, who argues that 'politics depends on some settled order. Small groups are part of that order. They may help to create politics, but their internal behaviour is not political simply because their individual function is different from that of the state itself'.[4] Politics then is about the conditions of order, and Crick later makes it plain that this refers to a conciliation process *within states.* The problem here is that if this conception is accepted then it make no sense to refer to the politics of a stateless society, the politics of the business firm, or to the politics of any other non-state organization. Thus, the job of political sociology would be the analysis of the institutions of the state. As Greer and Crleans put it (but less strongly than Crick), 'The major empirical problem of political sociology today would seem, then, to be the description, analysis and sociological explanation of the peculiar social structure called the state'.[5]

There is a long tradition behind this view. But there is an equally ancient and persuasive alternative viewpoint that stresses the presence of politics in almost all social relations. This is the view which emphasizes the idea of politics being about the utilization and the development of power, and since power is generated in almost every social group and institution, politics is thus more pervasive than is granted on the first view. This opposite extreme to Crick is perhaps illustrated by Harold Lasswell, who suggests that 'the unifying frame of reference for the special student of politics is the rich and variable meaning of "influence and the influential", "power and the powerful" '.[6] This viewpoint is within the sociological tradition which tends to understand power, authority and influence as characteristic social control processes, and not unique to any particular type of social group. Fathers can exercise power in the family just as foremen and supervisors can exercise it over workers in a factory. As Dahl defines it, 'A political system is any persistent pattern of human relationship that involves, to a significant extent, power, rule or authority'.[7] This is not to say that there are no differences in the way power is used in different social groups, simply that in some form or another it is a potential feature of almost any kind of social relationship. Max Weber, for example, sees power as simply the ability of one group (or individual) to enforce its preferences on others. He defines power as 'the chance of a man or a number of men to realise their own will in a communal action even against the resistance of others who are participating in the action'.[8] To him the state is a special kind of institution that successfully possesses a monopoly of the legitimate use of power within a given territory.

The advantage of this view is its greater analytical spread, allowing one to examine under the aegis of politics a variety of structures and institutions which might otherwise be missed. The so-called 'stateless' societies are an obvious example; private governments and socialization patterns within the family and the work situation which have implications for political life are other examples. In other words, the wider-ranging conception of politics encourages an awareness of the *potential* political relevance of almost all aspects of social life not obviously to do with government and the state.[*3*] Thus all structures and processes having an impact, intended or otherwise, on the political system become of interest to the student of political life.

But, this advantage could also be a weakness in that it is too broad to exclude anything. This difficulty is well brought out by Bendix: 'if we define the political without regard to socially defined institutions—for instance if we analyse the "political" aspect of the family or the business corporation—the scope of our comparison may become so large that nothing can be legitimately excluded from our consideration and we are left without analytical guidelines'.[9] Bendix's own solution to the problem is to take the political as that which is socially defined as relating to the state as the single legitimate centre of authority. At once this begins to narrow the definition down by effectively making the political coterminous with the nation-state. The difficulty is that in a sense the process of development of the nation-state, about which political scientists are intimately concerned, becomes pre-political. In other words, the process of changing from a social-political form 'preceding' the nation-state, a process going on in most of the world, is not political development but some other unspecified thing moving towards the political until it becomes political with the formation of a nation-state (assuming it reaches that point) having a single recognized and legitimate central government.

It is not necessary to labour the point much more, but it may be remarked that single legitimate centres of authority are extremely rare in the 1970's. Both Britain and America, considered to be examples of very stable political societies, are currently experiencing a phase where sectors of their populations begin to question the legitimacy of the so-called centres of authority. In the United States, the Black Panthers, the Weathermen, student disturbances against the Vietnam war, are all movements or events which may well reflect a questioning of governmental legitimacy. In Britain, student disturbances and the recent wave of strikes may well point to a similar process. The same is true in Latin America and most of Africa and Asia. Whatever the reasons for this questioning, it does serve to point out the difficulties attached to this notion of centres of legitimate authority.

Unfortunately this kind of definitional bantering is an endless task, and a short convenient way out is simply to stipulate what we intend to mean by the term, and to state our justifications for this meaning. So, for our purposes politics has to do with the exercise of power in social situations. The study of politics, then, is concerned with understanding all the problems pertaining to power and its use in societal contexts, its relative 'amounts', its structuring and legitimation within groups of various kinds, and so on. Clearly, this leans towards the definition of Lasswell and Dahl cited earlier and we offer it for much the same reasons. In other words, there seems little convincing *analytical* reason why attention should be confined to purely state or governmental institutions, although as *a matter of fact* political sociologists do tend to concentrate on seeing in what ways society affects the state. As Bendix and Lipset say, 'political sociology starts with society and examines how it affects the state'.[10] This is an inclination supported by tradition and personal interest, not by any definition. We do not necessarily want to restrict the attention of political sociology, except on good practical grounds, to purely state institutions. Instead we want to accept the very varied nature of the material relevant to understanding human behaviour and its subclass, political behaviour. In other words, what we are doing is trying to understand 'power behaviour' whenever it occurs and with whatever tools exist to help us. But as we said before, this practically makes political sociology coterminous with the whole of sociology. In practice, however, political sociologists tend to concentrate their attention on 'power behaviour' in so far as it is relevant to understanding the way political systems work. In short, we are adopting the position that political sociology is a branch of sociology that is mainly concerned with the analysis of the interaction between politics and society. Inevitably this specification will be prone to various ambiguities. But, in spite of these, we want roughly to designate the kind of things with which this text is concerned. What we want to do is define politics in terms of a class of actions, not in terms of a set of institutions or organizations. In other words, we do not want to equate politics with some particular organizational form definitionally, as Crick does with the state, but rather to see politics as a special set of social acts, reflected or formed in many varied organizational contexts.

We have already offered a definition of politics which comes close to what we want to offer here, that is, politics is about 'power'; politics occurs when there are differentials in power or authority. Power occurs in all societies and if we equate politics with power relations then politics also is endemic to social life. This is the position we arrived at earlier. What we want to do now is specify a set of relations which is the main concern of political sociology. To do this let us go to the idea of organization. If people are organized in some way, that presupposes that there are rules which govern the relationships between the members of the group. If the group is highly organized, like an army, business firm or a school, these rules would specify positions and define who does what, when and how.

If, on the other hand, the group is relatively loosely organized the rules would be less specific, less strictly enforced and less regularized. In both cases the rules may have evolved through course of time or have been specially enacted to cover particular situations. For a great deal of the time these rules may be adequate and cover most eventualities that arise. But, sooner or later, one may expect that disagreements occur about interpretation of the rules, whether particular sets of rules are valid or adequate, whether or not a particular rule covers this or that problem, and so on. Once we reach this state of affairs then the problem of 'rule-setting' or 'rule adjudication' arises. Thus in a sense we have to make rules about rules.

This process of 'rule-making' is a fairly common one embracing a considerable part of social life. Families decide to formulate rules about behaviour at mealtimes, juvenile gangs decide on rules about who shall be leader and his rights and duties, governments make rules we call laws to govern the behaviour of the citizens of a society, and so on. These 'rule-making' activities occur when the situation demands the formulation of guide lines not previously covered by existing rules.

One particular kind of rule-making activity is that of specifying rules within relatively self-contained units for which the rules are intended to be absolute. This is what we mean by government. This particular rule-making activity need not be the special province of any particular concrete institution; the only criterion is that they are rules to govern the members of a particular self-contained social unit, whether a tribe, a village or a nation-state. Of course, this is only one kind of rule-making activity. Business firms and other organizations are just as involved in the process of rule-making as are governments. But their activities do not have the intended all-embracing quality of governmental rule-making. Political sociology looked at from this angle is concerned with the processes underlying this societal rule-making fact. This necessarily involves a consideration of the problem of social order, which roughly means that rules made, in whatever way, are obeyed. The reason why the rules made in different contexts by different authorities are obeyed is a large and fundamental question for political sociology. In turn, this interest necessarily involves the political sociologist in an examination of the social structures, and their development, within which the rules are made. Throughout the book we shall be discussing the social origins and styles of different forms of societal rule-making, the various levels and modes of involvement in the rule-making activity, and the impact of rule-making authorities on the rest of society. But to reiterate what was said earlier, political sociologists need not solely be concerned with what we have called societal rule-making, or government. They may be equally interested in rule-making activities and all that this implies in various organizations within the society, such as trade unions, business firms, armies, and the like. Indeed, study of such forms may well be illuminating for the understanding of the impact and forms of governmental activity.

So, having sketched what we see as the major focus of political sociology, it might be as well to say a few words on how this study is generally carried out.

Here again we enter what is a well-discussed field, namely the status of the methods used by the social sciences. As we understand it, the intention of any behavioural science is to try to put forward empirically verifiable theories which explain why human beings behave in particular ways. There is a great deal of argument concerning whether or not this can be done and if so, how.[*4*] The perspective of this book is that this can be done though we are a long way from knowing in detail how, or, indeed, building a body of theory at all comparable with that available in the physical sciences. None the less, we see this as the goal towards which behavioural scientists are working. As sociologists interested in political activity we are trying to explain how and in what ways the social and the political are interrelated. How, for example, are so-called democratic forms of government rule-making related to other social factors such as the level of economic development, literacy, patterns of land ownership, social stratification, socialization patterns, and so on?

It is important to stress that this is not an activity of social reductionism which reduces political events to by-products of the social, but one which sees the problem as one of interaction between the social and the political. Later we shall discuss a great deal the effect various social factors have on political life, but it is also clear that political institutions, like government bureaucracies, parliaments and so on, while they are embedded in a social network in their turn, influence the social system of which they are a part. It is a major defect of the field that very little work has been done taking traditional political organizations and procedures (for example administrations, legislatures—electoral and constitutional rules) and tracing the impact that these have on the host society. In this respect the most useful work has been done in looking at the process of 'institutional transfer', ie transplanting Western bureaucracies and legislatures into non-Western societies.

It would seem self-evident from what has been said that fundamental to this activity are regularities for which explanations are required. Thus, in political sociology the regularities between social class and voting choice, between economic development and political stability, or between single-member constituencies and two-party systems, illuminate the kind of things which need explaining. To do this, it has to be shown how these regularities could be predicted or deducted from a set of more general theoretical propositions. The relationship noted between social class and voting preference is explained (though this begs the question of how *well* it is explained) by showing how the relationship could be deduced from a theory of social class. Such a theory may be formulated as a somewhat simplified version of Marx's theory of social class: that position in the economic structure leads the individual to develop interests in common with others in a similar position, which in turn forms the basis of solidary groupings intent on political action. Now in physics, or some other equally well-developed science, such a theory would be strictly worked out with the aid of mathematics so that each element and proposition in the theory was logically connected with the others.[11] In the social sciences, however, for the moment we must rest content with much less strictly formulated theories. None the less, the point is that the connections between the events and things with which we are concerned are explained by relating them to general propositions of a theoretical nature.

So, the position we take here is that facts are of interest only in so far as they are relevant to some theory. To know that *x* per cent of the working-class regularly vote for party P is relatively uninformative, *from a political-sociological point of view*, unless it is related to some theory, say, about social class and voting preference, or about the social sources of a political party's appeal. In other words, the political sociologist is interested in building theories about events rather than in the events themselves. In a sense, he is the opposite of the historian who, on the whole, tends to be concerned with particular events, such as the French Revolution, the resignation of Sir Alec Douglas-Home as Prime Minister of Britain, the American Civil War, and so on.[*5*] This is not to say that the political sociologist is not interested in the past. On the contrary, many excellent studies have been concerned to explain past political life and, in addition, to give historical explanations of current political configurations.[*6*] In many cases an account of contemporary political life is likely to be the weaker without such an historical perspective.[*7*] Nevertheless, the political sociologist, or any social scientist, is more likely to see events in the past as a mine of data, more or less accessible, against which his general propositions are to be tested. He may be interested in nation-building, and thus is required to extract data about the past so that he can formulate a model of the process of nation-building. Some well-known examples of this historical activity are to be found in Marx's second volume of *Das Kapital*, the corpus of Max Weber's sociological studies, in Mosca's wide-ranging volume on elites, and Lipset's study of the nation-building process in the United States.[12]

Facts, then, are of interest only in so far as they are relevant to some theory. But what theory? The trouble is that many of the so-called 'facts' in social sciences are capable of explanation by more than one theory, and to develop this more fully let us take an example. Suppose we were to find that as societies become more industrialized they also become more pluralistic in that the centres of power and influence in the society become more diffuse and less concentrated at the centre. Suppose also we agreed on our measures of the variables of 'industrialization' and 'pluralism'. The problem is, then, to formulate a theory which could explain this. Figure 1 sets out the relationship found among a sample of societies, some industrialized, some not, and we find that those which are industrialized are also pluralistic.

In practice, we would not expect to find such a close correlation as illustrated here, however strong the relationship. Measurement errors for

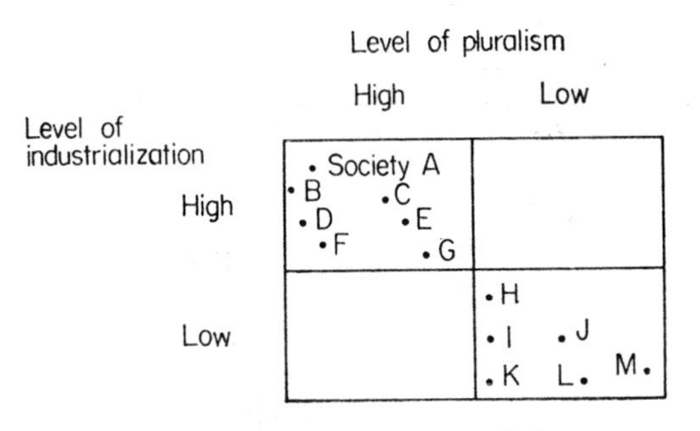

FIGURE 1. Hypothetical relationships between level of industrialization and pluralism.

one thing might place some societies in the bottom left- and top right-hand cells. Also, we would be fortunate indeed, at this stage of the social scientific game, to hit upon such an invariant relationship as this.

However, putting these points to one side, one explanation we might offer of the relationship is a theory of structural constraint, that is, as societies become industrialized the values and structures associated with industrialization, such as efficiency, rationality, reinvestment of surplus, development of large corporations, etc., etc., create alternative centres of power leading to an erosion of the power and prerogatives of the central government. In other words, the theory here suggests some kind of functional relationship between industrialization and pluralism. (Note that to fully work the theory we would have to specify clearly the propositions only sketchily implied above, moving from the most general to the specific, each step logically following from the others. Such a theory would be very complex.)

However, it could be argued that this relationship is consistent with another theory. Suppose, so the argument might run, we suggested that a precondition of industrialization is an increase in the educational standards of the population and that the same increase in educational levels is also responsible for increased political pluralism. This would lead to the same relationship, *viz.* between industrialization and pluralism, but offers a quite different explanation. In this theory industrialization and pluralism are linked only because they are caused by a third factor, namely, an increase in educational levels, and they have no other link apart from this (see Figure 2).[13]

Given these two theories, both equally consistent in explaining the relationship we found between industrialization and pluralism, the problem

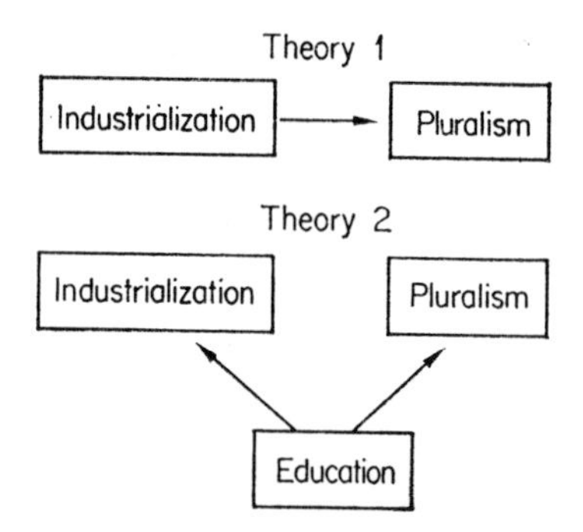

FIGURE 2. Causal links implied by two theories explaining the hypothetical relationship between industrialization and pluralism.

is to decide between them. The only way at this stage is to make further observations. The second theory specifies a crucial additional observation, namely, educational level, and if it can be shown with appropriate analytical techniques that the causal model implied in the second theory is a more accurate representation of the data, then we have grounds for rejecting the first theory.

Now, we have taken a rather simplified and hypothetical example of the theory-testing process. There are many ways in which the procedure can be and is carried out.[*8*] For our purposes the major point is the extent to which we can make crucial observations to test our theories. In the more formally developed sciences, such as physics, the set of crucial observations are normally derived in a strict logical manner from the premises and propositions of the theory, so that disconfirming observations require changes in the appropriate premises or theory. In the social sciences we have not yet reached this level. Theories are often vaguely and inadequately formulated and their links with the 'real world' are often somewhat remote. Thus, throughout this book we shall not only be discussing many varieties of 'theory' but also many alternative theoretical explanations of the same set of data. This state of near theoretical anarchy is characteristic of the social sciences at the present time. However, this should not be taken as a reason for despair, but instead, to be moralistic, as an encouragement to further endeavour. In the spirit of Pitt Rivers' comment to a concourse of archaeologists following the publication of Darwin's *Origins of Species*, 'the thought of our humble origins may be an incentive to industry and respectability'.

A great many of the theories we shall be discussing are fairly narrow in scope, what Merton terms 'theories of the middle range'.[14] These are theories about a narrow range of phenomena, such as voting choice, degree of hierarchy in political parties, revolutions, and so on: theories which claim to refer only to a small segment of social life. Other theories we shall discuss make larger claims to be general theories about a much wider range of social reality. Unfortunately the status of many of this latter type of theory leave a lot to be desired.

Thus the political sociologist is likely to take his conceptual apparatus from the sociologist; basically this includes the idea of a network of social relationships, to be explored with concepts such as role, norm, values, social structure and allocation, the transmission of these over generations and the concept of organization. These concepts are held together within theories of more or less complexity and logical rigour. The substantive area of the political sociologist's concern is less easily identifiable, but we favour a broad definition of the political such that arbitrary foreclosure of interest is not inherent in the definition. However, we suggest that an area of substantive concern for the political sociologist is the problem of social order and political obedience. Political sociology is therefore the study of political behaviour within a sociological perspective or framework. We fully realize the looseness of such a 'definition', but hope that the contents of this textbook will illuminate the discipline for the reader to the extent of making him or her realize that its foreclosure at this time would be of no service.

References

1. A. Somit and J. Tanenhaus, 'Trends in American Political Science', *American Political Science Review*, **62,** 933–947 (1963).
2. B. Crick, *The American Science of Politics*, Routledge and Kegan Paul,

London, 1959; M. Q. Sibley in J. C. Charlesworth (ed.), *Contemporary Political Analysis*, Free Press, New York, 1967, pp. 51–71; S. Wolin, *Politics and Vision*, Little, Brown, Boston, 1960, pp. 352–434.

3. N. J. Smelser, *Essays in Sociological Explanation*, Prentice-Hall, Englewood Cliffs, 1968, p. 31; L. Coser (ed.), *Political Sociology*, Harper & Row, New York, 1966, p. 1: 'Political sociology is that branch of sociology . . .'.
4. B. Crick, *In Defence of Politics*, Penguin, London, 1964, p. 30.
5. S. Greer and P. Orleans, 'Political Sociology', in R. L. Faris (ed.), *Handbook of Modern Sociology*, Rand McNally, Chicago, 1964, p. 810.
6. H. Lasswell, *Politics: Who Gets What, When, How*, Meridian Books, New York, 1958, p. 23.
7. R. A. Dahl, *Modern Political Analysis*, Prentice-Hall, Englewood Cliffs, 1963, p. 6.
8. M. Weber, 'Class, Status, Party', in M. Gerth and C. W. Mills, *From Max Weber*, Routledge and Kegan Paul, London, 1948, p. 180.
9. R. Bendix (ed.), *State and Society: A Reader in Comparative Political Sociology*, Little, Brown, Boston, 1968, p. 6.
10. R. Bendix and S. M. Lipset, 'Political Sociology: An Essay and Bibliography', *Current Sociology*, vol. 6, UNESCO, Paris, 1957, p. 87.
11. See E. Nagel, *The Structure of Science*, Routledge and Kegan Paul, London, 1961.
12. R. Bendix, *Max Weber: An Intellectual Portrait*, Heinemann, London, 1960; G. Mosca, *The Ruling Class*, McGraw-Hill, New York, 1939; S. M. Lipset, *The First New Nation*, Heinemann, London, 1964.
13. H. M. Blalock, *Theory Construction*, Prentice-Hall, Englewood Cliffs, 1969; H. A. Simon, 'Spurious Correlation: A Causal Interpretation', *Journal of the American Statistical Association*, **49,** 467–479 (1954).
14. R. K. Merton, *Social Theory and Social Structure*, 2nd ed., Free Press, Glencoe, 1968, pp. 39–72.

Notes and Further Reading

1. See, for example, A. Lepawsky, 'The Politics of Epistemology , *Proceedings of the Western Political Science Association* (supplement 15), *Western Political Quarterly*, **17** (1964). The author calls attention to the 'politics' of disciplinary differentiation between sociology and politics in the United States at the beginning of this century.
2. Some of the earliest and better known of these efforts are, S. A. Rice, *Quantitative Methods in Politics*, Knopf, New York, 1928; H. Tingsten, *Political Behaviour: Studies in Election Statistics*, P. S. King, London, 1937; C. E. Merriam and H. F. Gosnell, *Non-Voting*, University of Chicago Press, Chicago, 1924. See also P. H. Rossi, 'Four Landmarks in Voting Research', in E. Burdick and A. J. Brodbeck (eds.), *American Voting Behaviour*, Free Press, Glencoe, 1959.
3. For a very convincing argument on this point see P. Worsley, 'The Distribution of Power in Industrial Societies', *Sociological Review Monograph*, **8,** 15–34 (1964).
4. For formal discussions of these problems, see P. Winch, *The Idea of a Social Science*, Routledge and Kegan Paul, London, 1958; E. Nagel, *The Structure*

of Science, Routledge and Kegan Paul, London, 1961; A. Ryan, *Philosophy of the Social Sciences*, Macmillan, London, 1970.

5. This difference should not be overdrawn, since it highlights trends rather than describes actual practice. For a discussion of the difference between historical and scientific studies, see J. Galtung, *Theory and Methods of Social Research*, George Allen & Unwin, London, 1967, p. 22.
6. A recent and splendid example is B. Moore, *The Social Origins of Dictatorship and Democracy*, Penguin, London, 1967.
7. For example, in the case of the Soviet politics, for an otherwise valuable and illuminating study of Soviet positions but one which lacks an historical perspective see F. C. Barghoorn, *Politics in the U.S.S.R.*, Little, Brown, Boston, 1966, and contrast it with M. Fainsod, *How Russia is Ruled*, Harvard University Press, Cambridge, Mass., 1963.
8. See J. Galtung, *Theory and Methods of Social Research*, George Allen & Unwin, London, 1967, for a review of these.

2

SOME INTELLECTUAL FOUNDATIONS OF POLITICAL SOCIOLOGY

2.1. The Problem of Order

IN THIS CHAPTER we shall set out and examine a number of different theories or perspectives on the nature and working of social processes. Political sociologists place themselves within a number of traditions of thought which go back almost to the origins of self-conscious reflection about man and his social relationships. What we shall do in this chapter is to spell out some of the contributions these various traditions make to a discussion of the problem of order, a problem we think of as being central to the concern of political sociology. Briefly, what we understand by social order is that process whereby the interactions of members of social groups become patterned, that is to say the interactions are relatively stable over time and the form which they take from time to time is relatively predictable.

Social order, the problem of endurance and change, has always been seen as problematic, as something that needs to be understood either for its own sake or because it was felt that enquiry was likely to lead to controlled change. Perhaps the major difference between Plato and Aristotle was concerned with detached observation. Whatever the case, it is certainly true that the problem of order is not necessarily one which is the sole concern of the more conservative-minded theorist. Social order can hardly be imagined without its opposite, social disorder, and any useful explanation of the one will contain, at least implicitly, an explanation of the other although, as in the cases of functional analysis and conflict theory, some theoretical perspectives are biased towards order and breakdown respectively. However, the traditional emphasis on order has a strong, if rather imprecise, empirical content since it is 'obviously' true that most societies most of the time display order rather than chaos! If, then, we begin with the assumption of order we are not making a prescriptive judgement (lest the philosophical heavens fall) but we are simply beginning the discussion on the basis of a rather commonplace observation.

It is easy to explain why the concern with order has been a central question in the history of social thought: if society is to persist for any length of time the people making up that society must live without undue threat or likelihood of death. Perhaps the tag line from Hobbes, familiar to all students of the history of ideas, that in the state of nature the life of man is 'solitary, poor, nasty, brutish and short', brings out this concept most vividly. The fact that the human frame is fragile and easily destroyed makes norms or laws prohibiting violence, except under special circumstances, a necessity for any type of social order. Again, social order is almost certainly necessary so that social life may continue, in the sense that without it, people may reproduce, but they will not be able to train or induct children since there will be nothing into which they can be inducted; in other words, there would be no society. Although this is very little more than the most glaring of truisms, it is still true that the problem of producing and maintaining order is a real one. Order is not something that the social scientist can take as a 'given', the product, say, of man's biological or genetic make-up, and hence a problem for the biologist or biochemist but not for the sociologist. It is, to repeat ourselves, problematic in at least the practical sense that all societies at some time display symptoms of a breakdown of order.

Broadly speaking, social thought has suggested three lines of attack on the problem of order which we shall present in a slightly abbreviated and exaggerated form in order to isolate the main themes of the three arguments. We shall also attempt to outline the defects and strengths of each perspective and outline the kind of image of man and society upon which they are founded. We shall investigate the intellectual problem areas connected with each of these three perspectives that have been brought out by the various proponents. Coercion theories of one sort or another have from the beginning of systematic thinking about society stressed the primacy of force as the agency underlying social order and obedience. Secondly, society has been envisaged as some sort of mutual interest organization within which a sensible or rational (that is in terms of calculating) appraisal of the costs and benefits of social actions lead men to remain peaceful members of society. Equally venerable is the tradition that argues the priority of some sort of popular commitment to the norms or goals of the state or society.

2.2. Coercion as a Solution to the Problem of Order

As in all the other theories of societal cohesion or order, the coercion theory implies a concept of man. In general, coercion theorists underpin their ideas by suggesting a view of man as a somewhat selfish, short-sighted, power-seeking individual. Such a view is clearly evident in Machiavelli's: 'men have less scruple in offending one who makes himself loved than one who makes himself feared; for love is held by a chain of obligation which, men being selfish, is broken whenever it serves their purpose; but fear is maintained by a dread of punishment which never fails'.[1] A very similar view of human nature was held by Thomas Hobbes, who put as man's first characteristic or 'general inclination of all mankind, a perpetual and restless desire of power after power, that ceaseth only in death . . . because he cannot assure the power and means to live well, which he hath at present, without the acquisition of more'.[2] In this 'selfish' view of human nature the origins of the drives are variously conceived: in the cases of Hobbes and Machiavelli they are simply human nature (Hobbes invites those who do not believe him to look into themselves for a moment). Human nature is *not* changed by living in society. *Behaviour* may well be changed since man can reasonably be prudent and plan with some confidence yet his personality or drives predate society and remain unaltered by it. In later versions the drives are socially derived or, more accurately, socially shaped. Thus with Freud children are born with strong aggressive and sexual drives whose unlimited expression, if allowed to develop in a majority, would endanger the stability of society: 'men are . . . creatures among whose instinctual endowments is to be reckoned a powerful share of aggressiveness. As a result, their neighbour is for them not only a potential helper or sexual object, but also someone who tempts them to satisfy their aggressiveness on him, to exploit his capacity for work without compensation, to use him sexually without his consent, to seize his possessions, to humiliate him, to cause him pain, to torture and kill him'.[*1*] There are anti-social monsters lurking in the Freudian id. Such monsters are controlled, albeit sometimes precariously, by the socially induced superego which is the representative in the child or adult personality of the values and constraints of the society within which the person matures. And if the superego fails to control the individual from following his deepest desires—for example to commit incest—then the law will punish him since the law is some sort of agreement amongst men 'that the satisfaction of these natural instincts is detrimental to the general interests of society'.[*2*] Society as a whole is a coercive mechanism, obtained at the price of personal happiness, which leads to a frustration-aggression pattern which in turn necessitates control. Post-Freudian and Freudian-influenced social science tends to stress the displacement of personality disturbances, etc., on to the social and political systems, and it also stresses that there is a relationship between political-economic configurations and personality types. This relationship can be thought of as running in either direction: Freud saw personality types as determining economic-political types, whilst a mass of modern socialization studies tends to stress the environmental determination of personality traits.[3]

Within the coercion tradition just outlined there is an underlying psychology which emphasizes that force is needed or at least applied as a 'corrective' to the basic anti-social nature of men. But it is in no sense logically necessary for coercion or conflict theories to be underpinned by psychological propositions about human nature. All of the works mentioned in reference 3 at the end of this chapter under 'References' stress the primacy of social structure over personality types as the most important focus of study and interest; the best-known example of this position is Karl Marx. He has, it is true, a psychology—his ideas on perception, for example, are derived from his 'materialism'—but psychology was by no means his major strength, nor does an autonomous psychological view of human personality *underlie* any of his major theories. This assertion is true not only of Marx's post-1844 works but also of the more psychologically orientated 1844 manuscripts where he criticizes Hegel for failing to realize that 'consciousness of alienation is an "expression in thought and knowing of the *real* alienation of man's being", its alienation in the labour process'. [*3*] The relationship in Marx between consciousness and society is not, as it was in Engels, a simple one-way process (from society to consciousness) but a more dialectical relationship of interpenetration: 'The materialist doctrine that men are the products of circumstances and upbringing, and that, therefore, changed men are products of other circumstances and changed upbringings forgets that it is men that change circumstances and that the educator himself needs educating. Hence, this doctrine necessarily arrives at dividing society into two parts, of which one is superior to the other.'[4] Before this state of affairs could be rectified, society had to be structurally altered, and it is with this task that Marx entrusts the proletariat, and the proletariat is defined by its relationship of dependence on the means of production. Oppressed and dependent upon its own expropriated labour which has produced the factories, machines, capital, etc., by which and within which he is oppressed, the proletarian eventually becomes a force aware of himself as part of a class, or as Marx puts it as part of a 'class for itself'. That is, the proletariat, as a revolutionary force, is conscious of its common predicament and historical destiny of overthrowing the capitalist system. For Marx, the capitalist system generates conflict, a conflict which may be more or less overt but one which the whole legal apparatus and official ideology controls in the interests of one class, that of the bourgeoisie.[*4*]

Whatever the source of conflict in the force theories, whether it is a product of man's original psychological make-up or a product of societally generated consciousness, the conflict has to be constrained and force theories emphasize the fact of force as the ultimate producer of social order. According to this view, order exists in society largely as a result of the employment or threat of employment of the power that some men possess and can use to command compliance. Men do what is expected of them because if they fail to comply they may be threatened with some sort of physical punishment, deprivation or sanction. Men obey because failure to do so may result in punishment; in this view the basis of social order is force.

> 'Do you see, my son,' he exclaimed, 'that madman who with his teeth is biting the nose of the adversary he has overthrown and that other one who is pounding a woman's head with a huge stone?'
>
> 'I see them,' said Bulloch, 'They are creating law, they are founding property; they are establishing the principles of civilisation, the basis of society and the foundation of the state.'[*5*]

Force theory must base itself upon an elementary proposition about the distribution of power in society, ie that power is differentially distributed: some men have more power than others. Force theories must, therefore, involve some sort of elite theory as subcategories of the more general theory. The proposition that unequal distribution of power is necessary to force theories can be seen most clearly in Hobbes who is quite unequivocal that so long as men are broadly equal in terms of force and guile a society is impossible. It is only when men set up Leviathan, who (which) monopolizes power, that society comes into being. This is the simplest possible version of an elite theory. It suggests an elite of one (Hobbes favoured a monarchy) with the rest of society staying in much the same selfish state of mind: potentially clashing 'possessive individualists' who are controlled by the force monopolist. Such a version tells us very little about the way the monopolist will use his power or the social conditions upon which it rests. For Hobbes the matter could be settled by reference to the alternative to monopoly, which was anarchy: society reverts to barbarism, the 'war of all against all'. Thus Hobbes is profoundly a-sociological in his approach to force since neither the ruled nor the ruler change in any way as a consequence of the relationship between them, remaining an individual in the case of the ruler and a congerie of individuals in the case of the ruled.

Modern elite theories reject this individualism in favour of an interactive system.

Interaction between rulers and ruled, however, implies a dilution of the pure force theory since it suggests a measure of compromise between the two parties or that the position of the elite depends upon some sort of bargain. This can be easily demonstrated by reference to a slightly more complex case of power monopoly than Hobbes' monopoly of one. In the more complex case, power is still monopolized by a few rulers (the ruled having no power), who then need to agree upon the rewards of exercising power. Such is the case of many societies controlled by, say, an army or a navy or a combination of armed forces and police who would have to agree amongst themselves, as a minimum condition of control, as to how prestige, status, income, etc., would be divided. Failure to agree would mean that the partners would eventually start quarrelling about division of rewards. Even if we still assume a single power monopolist it is intuitively obvious that he cannot rule alone and will need as a bare minimum the support or assent of the armed forces; the inference from this is that the power monopolist will have to meet certain minimal expectations from those who control the armed forces. The same point was made by Mosca in the 1880's when he wrote that 'the man who is at the head of the state would certainly not be able to govern without the support of a numerous class to enforce respect for his orders and have them carried out; and granting that he can make one individual, or indeed many individuals, in the ruling class feel the weight of his power, he certainly cannot be at odds with the class as a whole or do away with it'.[5] The implication of this is that the pure force theory with a single power monopolist is an empirical impossibility: at the very least it must be diluted with some element of coalition based upon minimum reward for a minimum of support.

If it is true that elite theories imply a coalition of some sort then it is empirically possible that, say, the army commanders who are in coalition with the force monopolist have themselves to meet certain expectations amongst the officer corps, such as rapid promotion, better conditions, better weaponry, a larger army, etc., etc. The briefest glance at the expansion of armed forces and the promotion revolution following military intervention in Latin America, Asia and Africa will confirm this. It is therefore theoretically and empirically possible that elite coalitions are dependent upon non-elite expectations, and such a consideration represents a considerable dilution of the pure force theory towards theories based upon interest or upon some form of consensus. In order to demonstrate that this is the case we shall very briefly examine a number of elite theories.

2.3. The Relationship Between Elite Theory and Coercion

The coercion model posits force as the primary binding factor in society: the elite theory emphasizes the possession of force by a minority. Elite theorists are driven to examine, as the focus of study, the cohesion of the elite and, at a more general level, the source(s) of elite domination. Underlying most elite theories, then, is a concept of a relationship, albeit a rather unequal one, between the elite and the rest of the society which is not simply one of dominance and submission but one in which to some extent the actions of the elite must take into account the responses of the rest. For elite theory, purely dominant or force relationships are inadequate to explain order, and this is so for a number of reasons. For example, power relationships are by themselves likely to create conflict: '. . . this differential distribution of authority invariably becomes the determining factor of systematic social conflicts'.[6] Again, in the problem already mentioned, that of monopolistically governing a society through the armed forces, it is quite clear that since they have an effective monopoly of force they must be bought off or balanced off by creating internal antagonisms or competing power groups (secret police, party militia, etc.). This last is a poor alternative, at least in terms of power theory, since it weakens the instruments through which social order is ensured. Realizing this predicament, elite theorists focus upon three aspects of control: (1) the cohesion of the elite, (2) the relative lack of organization amongst the non-elite, and (3) the interrelationships between these two factors. A clear implication of these considerations for elite theorists is that whilst force is a necessary condition of social order it is *not* a sufficient condition.

The major point about these elite theories which concerns us is that whilst they may appear to be part of force theory, in fact they point towards other solutions to the problem of order. Again, as already pointed out, the relationships within the elite are not force-based, but are rather those of mutual interest, if only a mutual interest in resisting the greater number of the non-elite. Also elite theory stresses the corporate nature of the elite, deriving from common educational patterns, common ideological stances, common geographical or social or ethnic origins or life style. Again, all elite theories emphasize the institutional supports of elite power within key sectors of society such as business firms, parliaments and executives, armed forces, police forces and religious organizations. Finally, considerable importance is attached to the technical superiority of the elite: 'if we leave out of consideration the tendency of leaders to organize themselves and to consolidate their interests and if we leave also out of consideration the gratitude of the led towards the leaders, and the general immobility and passivity of the masses, we are led to conclude that the principal cause of oligarchy in the democratic parties is to be found in the technical indispensability of leadership'.[7]

In Pareto's version of elite theory the incumbent elite may lose its superiority by becoming soft, by failing to recruit the energetic from the masses or because of a change in material conditions, and it may then be pushed aside by a vigorous and gifted counter-elite. This process, called the circulation of elites, takes place in all societies and at all levels of society—in the band of thieves and in the government—but it does not affect the fundamental fact of elite rule, although its possibility may well make an incumbent elite scrutinize the population carefully for signs of dissatisfaction. Generally, the process does not affect social forms, which remain relatively constant, whilst the society is characterized by a stable tension.[8]

Typically, elite theory has a 'low' view of human nature, especially the nature of the led: 'The plebs of Rome, owing to what had happened to Virginia, withdrew under arms to Mons Sacer. The senate sent messengers to enquire by what authority they had deserted their officers and retired to the Mountain; and so great was the respect which the plebs had for the authority of the senate, that since they had none of their leaders with them, no one ventured to reply . . . This shows at once how useless a crowd is without a head.'[*6*] The outstanding characteristic of the masses is inconstancy of purpose and passivity except when driven to mindless fury by the incompetence of their leaders; they have no desire to lead, wanting leadership and almost bovine security. Looked at from a slightly different perspective, the mass lacks a vision of society necessary to the management of public affairs, has no organizational capacity and 'would remain passive instruments in the power struggle, however "popular" the form of local government under which they lived'.[9]

Although lacking respect for the masses, elite theorists have a well-developed sense of their potential weight if not assiduously cultivated by the leadership and to this end elite theories normally pay very considerable attention to techniques of control and the process of mass mobilization. Leadership can, in the Leninist variant of Marxism, convert the masses from atomistically separated inchoate individuals into conscious and disciplined agents of total social change.[7] Writing from a very different angle, Georges Sorel attempted to persuade the leadership of the trade union movement to abandon conciliation and negotiation and adopt the myth of a general strike against the whole of bourgeois society. Such a technique would revive the lost unity of the proletariat and bring about 'in the proletariat the noblest, deepest and most moving sentiments they possess; the general strike groups them all in a coordinated picture, and, by bringing them together, gives to each one of them its maximum intensity'.[10] *The Prince* is in the same tradition: treat the people properly, harness them to the usurper's chariot by force and guile, put them into a popular militia, etc., etc., and they are a powerful weapon in the hands of a determined leader.

It is a specific assumption of elite theory that the relationship between governed and the governors is a manipulative one and, therefore, depends not upon pure force but upon an understanding of mass psychology which normally presumes that the masses are responsive to ideologies, symbols and sentiments. Elites realizing, perhaps intuitively, the deep need felt by the mass to be ruled 'not on the basis of mere material or intellectual force, but on the basis of a moral principle',[8] respond by 'supplying' ideologies and symbols with which the masses can identify. Such symbols and ideologies serve to create emotional ties between mass and elite and to legitimate the position of the elite, in other words to transform force into authority, a change indicating a new basis of obedience and hence social order.

Elite theory appears to direct attention to a more subtle approach to the problem of social compliance or obedience than is implied in the pure force theory. It suggests a recasting of the analysis, beginning with an assumption that force is insufficient to maintain obedience over a lengthy period of time and that a further element, that of elite prudence and calculation, is a necessary factor in social cohesion. The prudential element suggests that there are limits to command beyond which it is not wise to go. The calculative element implies that elites are aware of this constraint on their freedom to command and will take it into consideration *prior* to commanding, and that obedience is not simply a consequence of command despite the appearance of a command–commanded relationship based on force. Another element in elite theory is that obedience may result from a transformation, at least in the mass, of a power relationship into a morally justified leadership based upon ideological and symbolic attachment.

2.4. Some Inadequacies of Coercion Theory

Perhaps the major inadequacy of coercion theory is that it takes too simple a perspective on the problem of obedience, and in the previous section we indicated some of its limitations. It contains no long-term solution to the problem of order; the exercise of power may itself generate conflict; in large societies the necessary process of devolution or coalition creates further problems of control and points to the need for other bases of power and hence social order.

Let us briefly discuss some further shortcomings of coercion theories. For the student of comparative institutions, and political sociology should be a comparative discipline, the most crushing difficulty is that it fails to explain the ordered nature of the so-called stateless or acephalous societies. In such societies there is no centralization of authority, no specialized and differentiated administrative machinery and certainly no central monopoly of power, and yet such societies do cohere and coherence may be seen as a result of 'a balance of opposed local loyalties and of divergent lineage and ritual ties'.[11] S. F. Nadel, writing of the organization of one such society, that of the Nupe in the centre of Nigeria to the north of the highly centralized Yoruba area, suggests that unity of the people is based upon 'a store of traditions referring to a common origin; to certain characteristic forms of social structure; to religious beliefs, to a number of seasonal rituals which give to their life's cycle its inner hold, its deeper meaning and its sacred anchorage in the supernatural . . . we have before us . . . a spiritual background rather than an organized uniformity, an idea rather than an actual machinery of co-operation'.[12] Such societies appear to hold together, and to have structure, not because of a centralized monopoly of coercion but due to some sort of common religion and mythology together with marriage outside the immediate kin group which may be used as a conflict inhibitor. Another source of conflict limitation is the need to form coalitions in order to settle a dispute by drawing in groups less and less connected with the initial quarrel.[*9*] Even if force theorists were to argue that *within* each segment of a segmentary society force is the prime condition of cohesion, this would be a far cry from the initial postulate that it is force which holds the whole society together.

A further series of difficulties centres upon the fairly obvious fact that it is in the *interest* of people to obey the law: the example most usually cited here is traffic laws in the absence of which no one would be safe on the roads. The inference here is that people obey at least some laws not simply because the consequence of failure to obey is punishment, but also because positive benefits are derived from obedience. Costs are minimized and people are able to engage in mutual effort with a consequent improvement in general welfare. A prerequisite of this improvement is that most people obey the rules for the sake of the improvement. But since any individual acting rationally would be best off if he obtained public benefits —roads, safety, police protection, etc.—without payment it follows that coercion, or at least involuntary obligations, is necessary if these are to be provided. People need and want public benefits, but equally any given individual may obtain such a benefit—if it is provided communally—without paying: hence the need for coercion.[*10*] Force may be employed to coerce a minority of the recalcitrant or deviants, but force is then a residual rather than a primary explanation of obedience.

We have previously suggested that force theories are unable to account for coherence in 'simple' acephalous societies, but it is also unlikely that such theories can help very much in accounting for at least some significant aspects of 'complex' societies, especially developed industrial states.[*11*] Let us take the case of the Soviet Union between the period 1928 and 1938 and from the early 1950's onwards. In the earlier period the problem was to rapidly increase production of steel, oil, coal and other heavy goods, whilst maintaining control over a population suffering an overall decline in living standards and, in the case of the countryside, actual starvation. The details are unnecessary, but the point is a simple one: Russia went through a period of forced industrialization which was paid for by the people in sweat, hunger and exploitation. During this crash development period a major incentive to work was terror and the fear of real physical deprivation on the part of the Russian masses, but even then incentives other than mere force were used. Thus Stalin encouraged his workers to compete for higher rewards ('Stakhanovism' and 'socialist emulation') and provided the more energetic or fortunate with opportunities to rise very rapidly through the industrial-political hierarchies: 'The task is not to discourage these comrades who show initiative, but boldly to promote them to commanding positions; to give them the opportunity to display their organisational abilities and the opportunity to supplement their knowledge'.[13]

Force in the earlier period was used to change the structure of society, to change the attitudes of the population and to control the tensions built up as a consequence of the changes. Running a more complex industrial society, with managers, scientists, economists, military technologists, etc., makes imperative at least some measure of restraint in the use of force, and, in any case, it is hopeless to attempt to direct by force a person to become an atomic physicist or a skilled machinist. Something else is needed, and no matter what it is, the force theorists cannot produce it without doing violence to the theory. That there has been a running down at least of the worst excesses of Stalinism in the USSR is obvious. It is probably, at least partially, necessitated by the growing technical sophistication of Soviet industry, by the confidence that some groups in Soviet society have in their relative indispensability and by the fact that Soviet politicians realized that force tends to turn back on its users.[*12*] Even a casual glance at the Soviet case, then, suggests that whilst Russia in the 1930's was a good example of pure force it was held together not only by force but also by incentive. During the war, from 1941, Stalin found it expedient to rely much more on patriotism, and from the 1950's force has probably assumed a much less prominent place in Soviet life, if only because a complex society cannot be organized by force.

But it is not simply a matter of technological determinism in the case of the advanced society and of custom, tradition, balance and so on in the less developed, but rather of the commonplace observation that in all societies those in positions of power 'must *persuade* inferiors to accept their rule'.[*13*] Such persuasion can take the form of ideologies teaching sacrifice of the present for the future—Stalinism, Marxism and Nazism and much modern nationalism—or of ideologies equating individual success and social progress (Benthamite and 'Darwinian' Liberalism) or of a heavenly sanction:

> 'The rich man at his castle
> The poor man at his gate
> God made them high and lowly
> And ordered their estate.'

It can also take the form of an ideology of service, as in the case in many aristocracies, or of the fear of the enemy outside the gates whom only the elect can detect, or, as in pre-1949 China, of the mandate of heaven. However the 'trick' is worked, and the list above is not intended to be anything like exhaustive, the point is that nowhere does a ruling group or class for any length of time allow itself to be thought of as ruling by force alone.

We have dwelt at some length on the inadequacies of force theory and shall now briefly look at its merits. The treatment will be brief because we return to force theory when we attempt to evaluate the other theories of social order. Its first merit is that it does not shirk the obvious fact that there *is* conflict in society, that behind judges and civil servants there are armies, police forces and prisons, thumbscrews and executioners! Force theory also, and this is a real insight, directs our attention to a much neglected factor in politics, that of time.

Even if we accept that modern Western societies are not based upon force—and many people do not accept this—but that they rely primarily upon some sort of consensus in the population, we have still to account for the growth of this consensus over a period of time. Take the case of Great Britain, which is effectively an empire beginning from England and conquering by sheer force Wales, Ireland and Scotland all of which, prior to conquest, were independent civilizations and, in the case of Ireland and Scotland, countries which looked more to Europe than England. In the course of their incorporation into a United Kingdom, force was quite deliberately employed to destroy indigenous loyalties, to destroy local power concentrations, to redirect trade towards England, to repopulate some areas, to destroy local languages and gentries, etc., etc. It was only the use of force which initially held the elements together whilst other bonds were gradually formed: bonds such as a common language, gradually a common church, famous victories over the 'foreigner' and the bonds of an interdependent economy. None of this could have been achieved without force, and that this is so can easily be demonstrated by examining those newly independent countries of the Third World where central power is absent. Lack of power corrupts!

Force theory also has the advantage that it directs our attention to one of the central dichotomies of modern European social and political thought, *viz.*, the distinction between state and society, a distinction which normally attributes to the state 'the method of coercion or compulsion', whilst society 'uses the method of voluntary action and the process of persuasion'.[14] The state is then said to have a legal monopoly of power in the sense of being the sovereign authority, the authority that makes final adjustment of societal disputes and settles them, if necessary, by employing its legal monopoly of force. That there is a dichotomy between state and society, between man and citizen, raises anew the problem of possibly diverging loyalties, a problem faced in Western societies since the birth of Christianity: 'Render unto Caesar the things that are Caesar's and unto God the things that are God's'. Legally the problem is solved by the concept of sovereignty, that the state has no legal limits on its powers; but as a matter of practice there are, of course, many limits. There is a rough analytical distinction between state and society, and a great deal of the history of political sociology is taken up with delineating the boundaries between the two (British Liberal political philosophy is founded and foundered upon making the distinction a working one) or of subsuming the one in the other.[*14*] But today it would probably be agreed that whilst legitimate monopoly of force is the defining character of the state it is in the long run unable to use this theoretical monopoly, its sovereignty, unless it has won allegiance and support from members of society through means other than force.

It is at this point that we can move to an examination of a competing or alternative explanation of social order, that which stresses social organization as an outcome of mutual interest or as a consequence of individual interest rightly understood.

2.5. The Interest Theory of Social Order

On this view the problem of order is that of reconciling individual interests or group interests so as to produce at least a minimum of harmony amongst men. In the coercion theory no reconciliation was possible in the absence of force, but in the theories to be discussed interest itself is the mechanism of reconciliation and hence of social order. The interest theories as we understand them are theories which state that men do what they want to do and that social order is an outcome of this fact. Men are not coerced by public authority nor are they understood to be doing what they want to do because public authority has trained them into certain behaviour predispositions. Interest theories seem to occupy the ground between force theories and modern sociological theories which stress consensus resting upon socialization into publicly acceptable patterns of behaviour. One can detect two broad variants of interest theory which are alike in positing an individualistic view of man, that he is primarily motivated by private goals and motives. Such goals and motives may be of various kinds, from pride, restless search for security, pleasure, avoidance of pain, to a search for profit or for public esteem. For interest theories the trick is to transmute these private matters into a social cement and it is in working this trick that the theories differ in their emphases.

2.6. Interest Theory: the Prudential Variant

Men have private interests which they wish to pursue but are prevented from so doing by the presence of natural dangers (lions and sabre-toothed tigers!). In order to provide a safe context within which such private interests can be pursued they must band together—if only to keep the fire burning: this entails an agreement, a system of rules, about wood-gathering and keeping watch. It is difficult to think of a simpler example but more complex ones spring to mind readily, such as cooperating to build a bridge, damming a river, building a tomb, etc.

Rules are established which define rights and obligations which spring from a common understanding of the necessity of a common effort. The rules simply set out a specification for the division of labour and no more is assumed than this. Order is, therefore, a consequence of private men realizing that they stand to gain in terms of safety, benefits of one kind or another, in other words there is a rational awareness of the benefits of cooperation and hence, order. Coercion is not required, it is simply that as rational, or at any rate clear-eyed individualists, men are capable of foreseeing the personal advantages of common effort.

The lynch-pin of this variant of interest theory is the concept of an equality of mutual benefit, ie that all engaged in society benefit from engagement in broadly equal rewards for broadly equal efforts. A difficulty of this variant is that it does not explain the empirically verifiable facts of social stratification and consequent inequality of rewards. It can only become a theory explaining inequality of rewards by adding further propositions stating, for example, that some jobs or tasks require more skill, training, experience, etc., which must be rewarded to be produced. An alternative additional proposition could be that the organization originally set up for mutual benefit becomes, in some manner, more powerful than originally intended and uses the power to upset the egalitarian balance. This is the alternative chosen by a considerable body of social theorists at various levels of sophistication and makes use of the distinction, previously referred to, between society and state.

No matter what the origin of the power of the state, or even its justification, such theorists understand it as a danger to individual or group interests and as a source or consequence of corruption in society: 'Government, like dress, is the badge of lost innocence; the palaces of kings are built upon the ruins of the bowers of paradise', wrote Tom Paine in January, 1776.[15] The corruption of the original innocence and equality of men by government and civilization is the theme of Rousseau's *Discourse on the Origin of Inequality*, and whilst he did not directly draw the lesson that governments were evil (merely wishing to control them) theorists in the anarchist tradition have not hesitated to do so. In this tradition inequality and corruption are *caused* by governments, by organized *political* authority; getting rid of government and falling back on the natural balance of society is a moral imperative and the fact of government is itself sufficient to explain inequalities. Order, such as it is, in the anarchist tradition is a fabrication of coercive governments and is an imposition which destroys the natural balance or order of civil society; allow this 'natural' order to re-emerge and men's 'natural' interests will ensure a just stability. This natural order in Proudhon stems from the logic of the economy: 'All concentration should be on the organisation of economic forces. The true idea of the Revolution is to base society on economic forces organised without coercion by Government.'[*15*] Similarly, in Godwin's version of anarchism the most powerful force working against human happiness is government, and 'we should not forget that government is an evil, an usurpation upon private judgement and individual conscience of mankind'.[16] Abolish as much government as possible, decentralize the rest, educate the population and order will be ensured by 'the inspection of every man over the conduct of his neighbours'.[17]

This prudential variant of interest theory like the variant to be discussed below strongly veers towards the society in the state–society dualism, politics being at best a necessary evil in the non-anarchist version and a not very necessary one in the anarchist tradition. Force, in both anarchist and non-anarchist interest thinking, is unnecessary except as a method of doing away with the institutions of political control which caused the imbalance between state and society.

2.7. Interest Theory: the Competitive Variant

The major element in this variant of interest theory is its stress upon order as an unintended consequence of human interaction, whilst in the prudential variant order was seen as a result of human intention to cooperate. The prudential interest theory really stresses cooperation—the anarchist Prince Kropotkin in his *Mutual Aid* (1902) is a case in point—whilst the second version tends much more to emphasize order as a result of competition.[*16*] Men are less well equipped than in the prudential variant to appreciate the benefits of cooperation and theorists of the competitive persuasion are much more sceptical of the likely benefits of such cooperation. Men pursue their own interests without too much regard to the interests of others, but motivated instead by self-love: 'Every man, as long as he does not violate the laws of justice, is left perfectly free to pursue his own interest in his own way, and to bring both his industry and his capital into competition with those of any other man, or order of men'. Justice is the protection from theft of the proceeds of competition and is made necessary by virtue of the fact that 'the affluence of the rich excites the indignation of the many'.[18] In this version of interest theory men are driven to compete for limited resources, the competitors being unequally endowed in terms of birth, age, fortune and ability, with the result that resources are unequally distributed throughout society. Hence, society is stratified along economic lines, but due to competition the cleavages are fluid in the sense that men of ability or luck may be economically mobile. The grand outcome of this economic competition is that 'by directing that industry in such a manner as its own produce may be of greatest value, he (the economic man) *intends* only his own gain, and he is in this, as in many other cases, led by an invisible hand to promote an end which was no part of his *intention* . . . By pursuing his own interest he frequently promotes that of the society more effectually than when he really *intends* to promote it'.[*17*]

Interest theory in Smith's version can account on purely economic criteria for economic cohesion—scarce resources plus differential distribution of human talents—and for the fact of government which protects competitive outcomes. It can also justify *limited government*, the limits being a consequence of the complexity of the economic exchange system 'which could be safely trusted not only to no single person, but to no council or senate whatever'.[19] The basis of economic order is that, given an absolute minimum of government intervention, the distribution of reward is such that human felicity is maximized. The principle of order at work in the economy is generalized to society as a whole in the sense that the driving force in economy and society is individual interest. The manner in which this competitive version of interest theory connects individual to society is a foundation principle of modern sociology. However, another foundation principle is that men *need* a stable environment and typically feel most secure in group-like associations rather than, as the utilitarian economics implies, always striving and competing for maximum physical resources. Since this competition for maximum resources leads to considerable social fluidity—changes in industrial location and in men's patterns of life—it is in conflict with the other need for a stable, predictable environment. Hence, the principle of utilitarian maximization is always partly negated by men's apparent desire for stable environments.[*18*]

The connection between individual economic interest and 'societal economic interest' is through a concept of unintended consequences, and the connection between one individual's values and another individual's values is similarly structured. In his examination of individual moral values Smith goes into very considerable detail to demonstrate that they are socially derived and that a man outside society would have no moral standards since moral judgement or behaviour depends upon a spectator's response to them. In this tradition, which derives from Locke, men adjust their behaviour so as to gain the admiration, approval or 'esteem' of their fellows: society is a type of moral mirror into which the individual looks at himself.[*19*] It may be suggested that the moral mirror begins early in childhood when 'good' behaviour is rewarded (reinforced) and 'bad' behaviour is punished. A consequence of this responsiveness to others is a moral parallel of the invisible hand: 'by acting according to the dictator of our moral faculties, we necessarily pursue the most effectual means for promoting the happiness of mankind'.[20]

It is clear that order in this version of interest theory is a product of societal interactions, with government as a coercive element confined very much to making minor interventions either when harmony is temporarily disturbed or in protecting against foreign intervention. Solidarity comes from societal factors and not from coercion applied by a centralized political authority. Very much the same is true of Spencer's version of Social Darwinism which, from an evolutionary perspective, emphasized the necessity for allowing free competition in society in order to permit the greatest scope for progress on a basis of natural selection. As in the interest theories, Social Darwinism starts with the individual, stresses society over state and equates individual interests with those of the social aggregate: 'to recognise and enforce the rights of individuals, is at the same time to recognise and enforce the conditions to a normal social life'.[*20*] Social order in industrial society is a product of individual striving for advantage and access to scarce resources, and such resources are maximally distributed under competitive conditions. In his other type of society, 'the military', integration is achieved not by consent and contract but by compulsion exercised by politico-military force. In terms of the state–society dichotomy, interest theory is heavily biased towards society as a self-sustaining order, the order being a product of processes at the *individual* level. But it is perfectly possible to demonstrate, without adding new elements to the interest model, that group conflict and not order can be an outcome of pursuit of self-interest.[*21*] This is so if one assumed that in pursuing his private and personal interest a man may join with a number of others to produce a monopoly or a legal advantage of some kind over competitors. Smith and his followers were well aware of this and necessarily had to posit that such an action would detract from the sum of social benefits.[*22*] But it is certainly possible for a group to gain at the expense of unorganized individuals who must then, if they are rational and calculating, themselves organize countervailing groups. This consideration was taken up by Jeremy Bentham in his concept of the 'sinister interest' consisting of men, banded together, who had won privileges and positions which they defended by a variety of political doctrines which equated their sinister interests with the interests of the majority. But the point is that he saw no reason to assume that it was not rational for men to combine to their advantage: 'As long as any man has the smallest particle of this sinister interest belonging to him, he will have a fellow-feeling for every other man who in the same situation has an interest of the same kind'.[21]

Three possible outcomes can be inferred from this situation when the guiding hand is arthritic. Firstly, it is a matter of definition in a Smithian universe that the maximum strategy a disadvantaged majority could adopt would be the restoration of free individual competition by removing the minority monopoly or its legislative advantage. This is, of course, the basis upon which the English utilitarians were to opt for short periods between parliamentary elections which would prevent Members of Parliament from becoming a vested interest group.[*23*]

The second outcome is the analysis of the political process in terms of group competition and alliances, that is, of the impact of organized groups on policy outputs and predispositions. This has led political scientists to look at the manner in which pressure or interest groups help weld together individuals who have a 'common interest' but are disorganized.

The third consequence of the process of group formation is that outlined by Marx, who suggested that a logical product of competition was the formation of a basically dichotomous society with no common interest in the maintenance of the prevailing order. For Marx the outcome of this competition was certainly not harmony of interests, but rather a process of growing crisis and, ultimately, of revolution.[*24*] Meanwhile, thought Marx, the order in society was maintained by a combination of coercion, ideological justifications and dividing the working-class against itself.

2.8. An Assessment of Interest Theories

Certainly the major development of the historical versions of interest theory that we have looked at is their predication upon the individual and the comparative ease with which they allow the student to move from an individual to a group perspective. We now look briefly at the implications for sociological theory of the interest perspective. Before doing so we once again emphasize that the connection between individual and social order contained in competitive interest theory is a crucial insight used in modern sociological theory. The point is a relatively simple one although the development of it is complex: social systems imply or mean predictable and ordered behaviour amongst participants, and the problem is how are participants constrained or motivated to behave in an ordered manner? Developing the concept of interaction, Parsons, in conjunction with Edward Shils, postulated an actor behaving to optimize his gratification of drives or needs in a situation with other actors. For Parsons and those of his persuasion the trick is worked by the notion of norms, rules of behaviour which people come to regard as binding or obligatory, which are commonly held in particular social contexts. '"Actors" are then in a position to make demands upon one another, to have mutual expectations (complementarily), and to view one another as sources of need gratification and controls . . . norms develop to regulate action . . . Common values, norms, and cognitions become institutionalised and interests arise for their protection and reform. When interaction becomes institutionalised and stabilised, social systems develop.'[22]

This view is derived from the proposition that when two people regularly interact this mere fact can itself create a norm about the manner and regularity of the interaction: that one will not unilaterally break off the meetings, change the venue, bring others along, and so on. And if one does do something quite unexpected within the relationship, then a slight tension might result from breaking expectations; that is, from the regular meetings a norm has developed which has weight upon individual decisions *irrespective* of that individual's dispositions. A *social fact* has been created which is an emergent property of the relationship and, as Durkheim defined it, 'A social fact is to be recognised by the power of external coercion which it exercises or is capable of exercising over individuals'.[23]

From the perspective of Parsonian action theory the weakness of interest theory is that it pays insufficient attention to the shaping of behaviour through the actors' acceptance of social norms. It is not necessary to look further at Parsons at this point except to mention briefly that in his action theory he develops a view of culture and personality. Culture is seen as a congerie of symbols, beliefs and moral values which shape the socially permissible manifestation of actors' 'drives or needs'; internalization—making culture a part of personality—through social rewards and penalties mostly in childhood is an important source of social control in all societies. The internalized culture channels and directs the 'primitive' drives into socially approved, or at least permitted, forms of action. Basically personality does not differ much from the eighteenth-century view of calculating man. It will be noticed that the Parsonian scheme is a revamping of some basic eighteenth-century views, (1) the idea of drives, (2) actors' behaviour is orientated towards other actors (in both social and economic relations), (3) the unintended consequences of interaction constitute the social order. However, the richness of detail and the provision of complex linkages between personality, social system and culture has no earlier parallel; this is particularly the case with Parsons' massive development of the idea of norms which underpins his discussion of moral consensus. (See Chapter 2.9.)

From the perspective of Parsonian action theory, then, the older interest theories are weak in their failure to consider adequately social norms. This is not to say that Parsons neglects either individual or group interests, simply that he believes that 'normative elements are more important than the "material interests" of constitutive units' in explaining social order and cohesion.[24] A further weakness is that some people might be able to affect other people's efforts to attain their ends or might even be so placed as to *determine* those ends. 'Ego' may have more effect on 'alter' in most situations than has 'alter' on 'ego', and an analysis of this possibility may take us far from interest theories. Interest theories are based upon a number of assumptions that may be implausible; for example, they appear to assume that which needs explanation: why do people agree to interact even though they may derive little or no benefit from doing so? The definition of a person is that he is a rational calculator; it follows that when interacting he obtains a benefit. Why do societies hang together? Because rational men obtain a benefit!

Empirically, interest theories also suffer from the major difficulty that as a matter of fact in most societies the conditions under which actors compete are differentially distributed in the sense that some start with huge advantages derived from social position or political power. Let us take an actual example of this fact and ask how interest theory would deal with it.

In Britain it can be clearly shown that middle-class children enjoy very considerable advantages in competing for strategic educational resources and hence eventually occupying high-status positions over working-class children. Thus, working-class children are at a definite disadvantage in competing for places in the grammar schools which are almost a prerequisite for university entrance in Britain, and this is so within groups of the same measured ability range.[25] When a working-class child gets into a grammar school he is less likely to attain high levels of educational achievement than his IQ equivalent middle-class peer and is more likely to drop out.[26] Also, the middle-class child has a better than average chance of obtaining higher education.[*25*] Recruitment into high-status occupations in Britain is also very strongly influenced by parental class, with middle-class children strongly 'over-represented' in the learned professions such as the law, accountancy, medicine, university teaching, and in positions of economic influence such as the directors of banks, insurance companies, the larger firms, etc., and also in the higher grades of the Civil Service and Parliament.[*26*] Except for some rather detailed statistical qualifications the major facts are not in dispute, nor is there much dispute that overall the working-class standard of life and income is below that of the middle-class. There is, as might be imagined, considerable argument about the policy implication of the facts: can the situation be remedied, *should* government attempt to remedy it, is the situation improving or getting worse, is poverty a self-sustaining system?, etc., etc.

Our purpose is not to answer any of these questions, but simply to enquire if they can be reconciled with interest theory. Rational interest theory is inapplicable for the simple reason that individuals are not competing on anything like equal terms and that therefore the maximal reward distribution posited by this theory cannot occur. Maximum reward distribution takes place when talents and capital are not 'artificially' constrained from seeking highest returns, but the example above, and many others could be quoted,[*27*] shows that opportunity to compete is differentially distributed and therefore in terms of interest theory must end in a maldistribution of rewards and human resources. The question then becomes, what is the response of those who are disadvantaged by their place in the social order? Because very few opt out, in the sense of attempting to restructure the system, the implications for interest theory must be that they are receiving sufficient rewards to ensure their continued commitment to the system. Thus the argument is a circular one.

Furthermore, it is probable that most working-class individuals are not competing with most middle-class individuals for status, income, prestige, etc., *nor do they aspire to do so.* (This limitation of horizons was noticed by Marx, excoriated by Ferdinand Lassalle and immortalized by George Orwell in *The Road to Wigan Pier.*) Broadly, the working-class home environment and the educational system set limits to working-class aspirational patterns such that they are as a class not motivated to compete or aspire to high-status occupations and are incapable of competing if they do so aspire.[27] What would be the consequences if the whole of society were competing for the same scarce rewards? Is it plausible to assume that they would accept a system which is structurally biased against equal competition? Might not the disadvantaged discuss their grievances amongst themselves and come to a common conclusion, a conclusion dominated by their common situation? Since the assumption is of common aims—maximizing rewards—yet the prevailing situation is systematically biased against one class, group or type of person, we have built into the situation a source of potential conflict.[*28*] In the Marxist analysis of the situation, however, the deprived eventually produce a set of counter-values and may revolt against the system as a whole, which is sustained in the final analysis by a monopoly of power. In other versions of interest theory disadvantaged or temporarily advantaged groups will struggle, within the existing order, to adjust the distribution of rewards in their favour.[*29*]

For the consensus theory, which we shall discuss in the following section (2.9), a crucial difficulty of the pure interest theory is that it is incapable of a satisfactory account of the apparently irrational elements of social life such as ritual, legal punishment, religious self-abnegation, heroism, self-sacrifice or suicide and the like. To see these as being motivated by self-interest is, to say the least, odd. A more important logical point is that to explain all behaviour as stemming from self-interest is to render the concept of interest devoid of meaning.[*30*] Behaviour such as the non-rational is held to point to elements in social life other than self-interest and in particular to value or moral constraints as possible bases of social order. Although the works of political philosophers such as Edmund Burke, Hegel, T. H. Green and F. H. Bradley examine in some detail the social role of sentiment, symbols, norms and moral values, it is the writings of Talcott Parsons that have most contemporary influence in political sociology. After an extensive and penetrating examination of power and interest theories of social order, Parsons concludes that 'the solution of the power question . . . involves a common reference to the fact of integration of individuals with reference to a common value system, manifested in the legitimacy of institutional norms, in the common ultimate ends of action, in ritual and in various modes of expression. All these phenomena may be referred back to a single emergent property of social action systems which may be called "common-value integration".'[32] We shall now examine this theory and others with it under the general heading of value-consensus theory.

2.9. The Value-Consensus Theory of Social Order

This theory and its variants attempt to explain social order by reference to the notion of general commitment to common values, and may deny the meaningfulness of referring to an individual except as a societal product: 'Without a well-defined system of values shared to some degree with other members of the community the concrete individual is not thinkable'. [*31*] Because men share common values they share a common sense of identity and also a sense of that for which it is worth while striving. Thus, as M. Levy has claimed, 'For a society to be stable at all, there must be some general agreement among its members on basic value orientations'.[29] Another component of the value-consensus theory is that there must also be agreed means through which men may attain the worth while; this is the normative element in society. Most of the time, for most interactions, people regard values and norms as given and do not question them because they are socialized into regarding them as natural. Norms are more specific than values. For example, in Victorian England, one of the most prominent social values was that of free enterprise with norms, sometimes embodied in law, determining the manner in which men acted as 'free enterprisers'. Or again, good health is a widely distributed social value but the norms governing its achievement may differ from group to group in a society or between societies. Thus in the US 'socialized medicine' is anathema and conflicts with the value of 'freedom', so the norms governing achievement of good health differ from those of Britain where 'freedom' is defined so as to accommodate a national health service. But the point is a simple one: 'The analysis of human action shows that it cannot be understood apart from a system of ultimate values'.[30]

What happens with the Parsonian value-consensus theory is that though it begins with ego and alter interacting it rapidly moves away from this towards the values and norms *structuring* the interaction from both observer and participant perspectives. The values and norms of a society give it its characteristic culture and structure and are the *necessary* ingredient of social order and cohesion. This consideration points to 'facts' which have their source not simply in individuals but in something 'external' to the individual: 'when I fulfil my obligations as brother, husband, or citizen, when I execute my contracts, I perform duties which are defined, externally to myself and my acts, in law and in custom. Even if they conform to my own sentiments and I feel their reality subjectively, such reality is still objective, for I did not create them.'[*32*] The stress here is on societal impact upon the individual, the society having certain characteristic or emergent properties which the individual does not have; functionalist theory has taken this proposition as its starting point and has focussed upon answering the question of order from a societal rather than an individual basis. (See Chapter 3.6.)

Contemporary functionalist theory with which Parsons is strongly associated starts from the question, What are the functional prerequisites of a society? What things *must* happen if *any* society is to continue to exist?[31] Since society or a social system is understood to be a moral entity composed of mutually understood and more or less integrated beliefs, norms and values *in people's minds*, the primary source of social order is to be sought in people's minds. However, minds are contained in bodies which have to be maintained. Hence, sufficient numbers of people must be maintained to produce and care for the young. The problem of order in the presence of scarcity must be solved, ie the war of all against all must be prevented.[32] Assuming that this can be somehow achieved, the final imperative is to maintain people at such a level of satisfaction (motivation) that they play their part in the system. In individualist interest theory the trick of social order was made through a concept of unintended consequences of individual actions, but in value-consensus theory social order is implied in the very notion of the values and norms (and their mutual adjustment) which are socialized into the young so that 'The normative regulation of means defines positively the means (*mostly non-coercive*) to the society's goals'.[33] Force and coercion in the value-consensus theory is therefore a residuary analytical category, which is *not* to say that proponents of the theory ignore it, merely that it is not central to their analysis of order.[*33*]

2.10. Some Difficulties of Value-Consensus Theory

Consensus concerning values and norms is central in this theory as an explanation of social order and cohesion, but a difficulty may be that of explaining how any *particular* system of values and norms was adopted in any particular society. At a trivial level, there is the problem of the sheer variety of values and norms held in 'common' by the members of different societies. Examples, taken at random, might include differential levels of toleration of murder, the infinite variety of socially acceptable sexual behaviour, and the variety of religious and moral beliefs uncovered by sociologists and anthropologists. Are they all to be understood as contributing to social cohesion in some manner or measure? If they are, then is there any limit to the value-consensus theory other than the clear collapse of a society, an indication, presumably, of some intolerable inconsistency between values and norms or socially inappropriate values?

One might also, as Parsons does, specify a value consensus for a whole society and pitch it at a very high level of generality, so that American society can be characterized as one of 'instrumental activism' which 'favours increasing the level of adaptive flexibility primarily through increase of knowledge and economic production'.[34] But what are we then to make of the relatively small growth rate of the American economy, of the non-economic exclusion of blacks from sectors of the economy, of the clash between short-run profits and maximum growth by output restriction, and so on? And what of the widely verified findings that after a certain point in consumption people rapidly exchange work for leisure? Are all of these simply unimportant exceptions?

The theory may be salvaged by arguing a type of moral Darwinism: that the possession by a society of a common value system arose through processes akin to those of natural selection in the struggle for existence in biology and botany, an intra-societal struggle between those possessing less adaptive value systems and those possessing better adapted or more cohesive values: 'only those groups survived and perpetuated their culture which developed and held in common among their members a set of ultimate ends. The important thing was not so much the particular content of the end, but rather the fact of having ends in common'.[*34*] Unfortunately, the rescue operation entails reducing the theory to a banality: we explain that those values survive which are most fitted (held in common), and how do we know this? Because they have survived, QED.

Another difficulty involved in the value-consensus theory is that it appears to lack a who/whom perspective: in whose interest is it that people accept, for example, the values implicit in Soviet Marxism or in British welfare capitalism, or the American myth of everybody being 'dealt in'? A society's values, assuming their common existence, do not simply happen, although it may be the case that when 'fixed' in people's minds they are like stones and forests, simply there. But they were not always there and, as Barrington Moore remarks when discussing Japanese merchants, 'To maintain and transmit a value system, human beings are punched, bullied, sent to jail, thrown into concentration camps, cajoled, bribed, made into heroes, encouraged to read newspapers, stood up against a wall and shot'.[35] Clearly at least the beaten and the cajoled are not sure that a value consensus exists. Similarly, although one might admit that value consensus explains societal cohesion, this cannot be taken to imply that such a consensus precludes the grossest exploitation of one group by another.

Perhaps a further problem of the value-consensus theory is the sheer difficulty of observing a value consensus, since it is inferred to be in people's minds, by observing behaviour and then inferring from behaviour a value system. But values are *not* the same as behaviour, since one is a mental state and the other an action of some sort. It was this difficulty which caused some psychologists to drop the concept of mind altogether from their intellectual apparatus and concentrate purely upon a stimulus–response model of behaviour, which does not require the notion of reflective mental activity.[*35*] Allowing, for the moment, this difficulty to lapse there is the further technical problem of measuring the extent and distribution of value consensus over whole societies. One can by some sort of massive survey find out the values people actually hold, but in so far as this has been done it is evident that a variety of values, not always compatible, are found.[*36*] Given the well-documented fact of different values in all but the most undifferentiated societies, what becomes of the value-consensus theory? It might be argued that what the surveys have discovered are not really ultimate values and that there is an over-arching value system with which the apparently incongruent or incompatible values can be reconciled. The implication of our argument is that in the search for such over-arching social values one may either become involved in an infinite regress or one might find values that are so diffuse and vague that they accommodate any factual findings.

Let us assume that in a society we have found a number of different values, an assumption strongly supported by both Parsons and Durkheim,[36] that these values are either randomly or non-randomly distributed, then we may be driven to a conflict situation which may occur in any of the following ways. Firstly, if values are randomly distributed, individuals strive to achieve their values, which brings us to the competitive interest theory (Section 2.7). This is clearly not compatible with value-consensus theory and may lead to conflict of a destructive nature. Secondly, making the more empirically likely assumption, that particular values tend to be associated with particular groups, then we once again arrive at a potential conflict as each group strives to achieve its valued ends. In the second case we can avoid disruptive competition by building into the model the notion that whilst people may not agree on values they may often agree on norms (ie the means through which values may be attained).

Agreement on some norms is the essential social binding concept of both the Hobbesian standpoint (the contract to form civil society) and of the interest theory of social cohesion, since the latter view is crucially dependent upon the proposition that men are very different in skills, values, intelligence, perseverance, interest, and so on. If men were all the same then nothing would be gained by exchange, so that the greater the diversity amongst men—or nations or regions in a nation—the greater the likely benefits from specialization in terms of comparative costs. Hence, diversity in a society can itself be a source of cohesion with respect to private goods, ie those goods of which consumption is essentially private or at least intra-familial. With respect to public goods, those which non-purchasers benefit from—roads, defence, laws, etc.—a lack of want diversity will be a source of social cohesion. Thus the greater the diversity of a society with respect to private goods and the greater its homogeneity with respect to public goods, the greater is its likely cohesion.[*37*] The problem here, however, is that the distinction between 'public' and 'private' goods is a changing one; the people paying for public goods may well wish the burden of payment to be transferred or at least altered and there may well be a collectivist movement to shift goods from the private to the public. Hence, we are again left with the problem of norms.

When we make the assumption that people agree on the norms—'rules of the game'—we are still left with the problem of why individuals do obey the rules! Coercion theory suggests that obedience arises from a fear of punishment for non-compliance whilst interest theory maintains that obedience derives from satisfaction of self-interest. Value-consensus theory argues that obedience is a consequence of a socialized commitment to the ongoing social order. We have suggested some inadequacies of taking each of these theories as sole explanations of social order, but it may be that each theory has an insight that we should not ignore. Value-consensus theory fairly adequately explains why most of the time people obey the rules without too much questioning but what it does not adequately explain, or at least clearly focus upon, is how order is maintained when some people—for whatever reasons—lose, or never get, the habit of obedience.[*38*] Interest theory can tell why people interact, which is to satisfy drives of one sort or another, but cannot adequately account for the order in the interaction, which value-consensus theory can do by supplying a social context and content to the formless individual drives. Thus with each theory or combining the two theories we are still left with the possibility of conflict, and it is at this point that we need recourse to some elements of the coercion theory. Even in a system not characterized by the regular use of force to elicit obedience it may, on occasion, be necessary since, on any reckoning, order is not inevitable. Further, force may be employed to hold together a society under stress of change—the UK from about 1790 to about 1840, or Russia in the 1930's, or China in the 1950's, may be cases in point. Again, force may be necessary to hold together societies which have the legal form of states but within which there is certainly no value consensus nor yet much agreement on the rules of the game: the Nigerian and Pakistan civil wars are obvious contemporary examples. If force does not hold them together then quite obviously any growth of general sense of nationality or agreement about the rules of the game is an impossibility.

2.11. Conclusions and Perspectives

In the previous sections we have discussed some general perspectives upon the problems of how social order is maintained, and one conclusion is that the question is best answered by utilizing insights from each perspective. But this is a somewhat lame conclusion after such an extensive discussion. What we have tried to show is that the question is itself an old one and that there are strong historical antecedents to more modern answers. In a sense the rest of the book will be an attempt to explain more contemporary accounts of social order *and* disorder, of conflict and its resolution and their sources in state and society. Even so, if such a lengthy discussion led us no further than this the effort might not have been worthwhile. We believe, however, that the discussion has at least orientated us towards some of the key questions of political sociology which centre upon the state–society distinction and the problem of social order or social control.

The state–society distinction can be drawn upon a Weberian basis, emphasizing the possession of a monopoly of legitimate force by the state which is utilized to maintain a legal order. But the foregoing discussion has strongly suggested that the power or force of the state is only one of the means of social control. Hence, one central interest of political sociology is not only how and under what conditions the state emerged but also the variety of relationships that may occur between the state and the society, varying from the almost constant use of force as a means of control through force as merely a residuary category, the final guarantee of order. For example, in those states within which force is apparently only a latent guarantee of order interest will focus on the non-force processes underlying the social order. In such a context interest centres upon the ways in which social needs are conveyed to political authority and the process of balancing or aggregating those needs through devices such as elections, political parties, interest groups, corruption, the media, etc. It follows that political sociology must also direct attention to the processes of achieving a sense of nationality within multicultural areas encompassed by the legal envelope of the state. Further, political sociology will also necessarily attend to the problem of the disintegration of order through political violence, war and revolution and apathy, etc.

If political sociologists are to study the complex social structures and processes underlying order and disorder it is plain that to do so requires models which suggest the connection between political events and social events in more detail than those we have suggested. At the very least we require these more detailed models to order research priorities, but also because the interconnections between society and state are more complex than interest, coercion or value-consensus theories imply.

It is to these rather formidable tasks that we now turn our attention.

References

1. Machiavelli, *The Prince*, Mentor Books, New York, 1952, p. 90.
2. Thomas Hobbes, *Leviathan*, Basil Blackwell, Oxford, 1955, p. 64.
3. S. M. Lipset, 'Working Class Authoritarianism', *Political Man*, Mercury Books, London, 1963, ch. 4, pp. 97–130; Geoffrey Gorer and T. Rickman, *People of Great Russia*, Cressett Press, London, 1949; Ruth Benedict, *The Chrysanthemum and the Sword*, Houghton Mifflin, Boston, 1946. For a discussion of these ideas see Margaret Mead, 'The Study of National Character', in D. Lerner and H. Lasswell (eds.), *The Policy Sciences*, Stanford University Press, 1951.
4. Karl Marx and Frederick Engels, *Selected Works*, Lawrence and Wishart, London, 1951, vol. II, pp. 365–366.
5. Gaetano Mosca, *The Ruling Class*, McGraw-Hill, New York, 1939, p. 51.
6. R. Dahrendorf, *Class and Class Conflict in Industrial Society*, Routledge and Kegan Paul, London, 1959, p. 165.
7. Robert Michels, *Political Parties*, Dover Publications, New York, 1959, p. 400.
8. A. J. Gregor, *The Ideology of Fascism*, Collier-Macmillan, London, 1969, ch. 2, p. 40.
9. H. Stuart Hughes, *Consciousness and Society: The Reorientation of European Social Thought 1890–1930*, MacGibbon and Kee, London, 1959, p. 254.
10. Georges Sorel, *Reflections on Violence*, Free Press, Glencoe, 1950, p. 145.
11. M. Fortes and E. E. Evans-Pritchard, *African Political Systems*, Oxford University Press, New York, 1940, p. 13. See also the brilliant work of M. Bloch, *Feudal Society*, Routledge & Kegan Paul, London, 1965, especially part 3.

12. S. F. Nadel, 'Nupe State and Community', *Africa*, **8**, no. 3, reprinted in R. Cohen and T. Middleton, *Comparative Political Systems: Studies in the Politics of Pre-Industrial Societies*, Natural History Press, New York, 1967, p. 296.
13. J. Stalin, *Problems of Leninism*, Foreign Languages Publishing House, Moscow, 1945, p. 367.
14. Ernest Barker, *Principles of Social and Political Theory*, Oxford University Press, Oxford, 1951, pp. 43–44.
15. 'Common Sense' in the *Selected Works of Tom Paine*, (ed.) Howard Fast, Bodley Head, London, 1948, pp. 15–16.
16. Godwin, *Political Justice*, cited in G. Woodcock, *Anarchism*, Penguin, London, 1962, p. 75.
17. ——*Political Justice*, cited in G. Woodcock, *Anarchism*, Penguin, London, 1962, p. 78.
18. Adam Smith, *An Inquiry Into the Nature and Causes of the Wealth of Nations*, vol. II, (ed.) E. Cannan, Methuen, London, 1964, pp. 194 and 203.
19. ——*An Inquiry Into the Nature and Causes of the Wealth of Nations*, vol. II, (ed.) E. Cannan, Methuen, London, 1964, p. 421.
20. —— *The Theory of Moral Sentiments*, in H. W. Schneider (ed.), *Adam Smith's Moral and Political Philosophy*, Hafner, New York, 1948, p. 194.
21. Jeremy Bentham, *The Handbook of Political Fallacies*, Harper Torchbooks, New York, 1962, p. 231.
22. W. C. Mitchell, *Sociological Analysis and Politics*, Prentice-Hall, Englewood Cliffs, 1967, pp. 28–29.
23. E. Durkheim, *The Rules of Sociological Method*, Free Press, New York, 1966, p. 10.
24. T. Parsons, *Societies: Evolutionary and Comparative Aspects*, Prentice-Hall, Englewood Cliffs, 1966, p. 113.
25. J. W. B. Douglas, *The Home and the School: A Study of Ability and Attainment in the Primary School*, MacGibbon and Kee, London, 1964.
26. Central Advisory Council for Education (England and Wales), *Early Leaving*, HMSO, London, 1954.
27. B. Jackson and D. Marsden, *Education and the Working Class*, Routledge and Kegan Paul, London, 1962; B. Bernstein, 'Social Structure, Language and Learning', *Educational Research*, **3**, 763–776 (1960–1961); H. Himmelweit, A. Halsey and A. Oppenheim, 'The Views of Some Adolescents on Some Aspects of the Class Structure', *British Journal of Sociology*, **3**, no. 2, 148–172 (1952).
28. T. Parsons, *The Structure of Social Action*, Free Press, New York, 1961, p. 768.
29. In H. Eckstein (ed.), *Internal War*, Free Press, New York, 1964, pp. 251–252.
30. —— *Internal War*, Free Press, New York, 1964, p. 391.
31. D. Aberle, A. Cohen, A. Davis, M. Levy and F. Sutton, 'The Functional Prerequisites of a Society', *Ethics*, **60** (1950), reprinted in N. Demerath and R. A. Peterson (eds.), *System, Change and Conflict*, Free Press, New York, 1967, pp. 317–331.
32. Talcott Parsons and Edward Shils (eds.), *Toward a General Theory of Action*, Harvard University Press, Cambridge, Mass., 1951, p. 180; 'Order—peaceful co-existence under conditions of scarcity—is one of the very first of the functional imperatives of social systems'.

33. D. Aberle, A. Cohen, A. Davis, M. Levy and F. Sutton, 'The Functional Prerequisites of a Society', *Ethics*, **60** (1950), reprinted in N. Demerath and R. A. Peterson (eds.), *System, Change and Conflict*, Free Press, New York, 1967, p. 327. Our italics.
34. T. Parsons, *Structure and Process in Modern Societies*, Free Press, Glencoe, 1961, p. 172.
35. B. Moore, *Social Origins of Dictatorship and Democracy*, Penguin, London, 1967, p. 486.
36. E. Durkheim, *The Division of Labour in Society*, Free Press, Glencoe, 1933, especially pp. 366–371.

Notes and Further Reading

1. Sigmund Freud, *Civilisation and its Discontents*, Norton, New York, 1961, p. 58. Freud sees the conflict between individual biological drives and the requirements of social organization in its most emphatic form. He saw few genuine compatibilities between society and individual needs: 'Civilisation has been attained through the renunciation of instinctual satisfactions, and it demands the same renunciation in each newcomer in turn', cited in P. Roazen, *Freud: Political and Social Thought*, Hogarth Press, London, 1969, p. 196.
2. The words are those of the anthropologist Sir James Frazer cited with approval by Freud in *Totem and Taboo*, Routledge & Kegan Paul, London, 1960, p. 123. See also P. Roazen, *Freud: Political and Social Thought*, Hogarth Press, London, 1969, especially ch. 4.
3. Robert Tucker, *Philosophy and Myth in Karl Marx*, Cambridge University Press, New York,1961, p. 128. But, it must also be remarked that in his *1844 Economic and Philosophical Manuscripts* Marx does attach an apparently central historical importance to greed and lust for acquisition as major social forces.
4. As a matter of fact Marx when analysing the consequences of Louis Bonaparte's coup suggests that in some respects the state stood apart from the fundamental societal cleavage, 'The 18th Brumaire of Louis Bonaparte', *Selected Works*, vol. I, pp. 221–311; see also F. Engels, 'The Origin of the Family, Private Property and State', *Selected Works*, vol. II, p. 290.
5. Anatole France, *Penguin Island.* Leo Tolstoy made the point more succinctly when he claimed that he who has not been in gaol does not know what the state is. Perhaps even more convincing is the very general legal prohibition of strikes amongst policemen!
6. Machiavelli, *The Discourses of Niccolo Machiavelli*, Routledge & Kegan Paul, London, 1950, vol. I, p. 312. Writing as a Marxist, A. Gramsci noted that for elite thinkers 'The masses are simply for "manœuvering" and are "kept busy" with moral sermons, with sentimental goads, with messianic myths of an awaited fabulous age', *The Modern Prince*, Lawrence and Wishart, London, 1957, p. 148.
7. V. I. Lenin, *What is to be Done?*, Foreign Languages Publishing House, Moscow, 1950, especially chapters IIa and IVa–e. Lenin here follows the lead of older theorists, such as Babeuf and Blanqui, who also believed that a forceable overthrow of existing and unjust societies could be followed by a

rearrangement of the educational and property system which would stifle selfishness and, hence, produce a new and lasting moral order based on 'natural' harmony; see J. L. Talmon, *The Origins of Totalitarian Democracy*, Secker and Warburg, London, 1955, pp. 167–200.

8. Gaetano Mosca, *The Ruling Class*, McGraw-Hill, New York, 1939, p. 71. Mosca also says that 'pressures arising from the discontent of the masses who are governed, from the passions by which they are swayed, exert a certain amount of influence on the policies of the ruling, the political class' (p. 51). Pareto also suggests that in a democracy 'the primary instrument of government is the manipulation of political followings', cited in P. Bachrach, *The Theory of Democratic Elitism*, Little, Brown, Boston, 1967, p. 12, fn. 9.
9. See Lloyd Fallers, 'Political Sociology and the Anthropological Study of African Politics', *European Journal of Sociology*, vol. 4, no. 2, reprinted in R. Bendix, *State and Society*, Little, Brown, Boston, 1968, pp. 73–86. These examples suggest a common value system or a calculative relationship as conflict inhibitors.
10. For further development of this point see M. Olson, *The Logic of Collective Action*, Schocken Books, New York, 1968, esp. chs. 1 and 4.
11. By 'simple' and 'complex' we mean societies within which institutional and personal differentiation are less or more developed. We shall return to this distinction in Chapter 4.
12. This is one prong of 'convergence' theory which states that industrialism by its very logic causes two industrial societies structurally to resemble one another in a long run; the argument is usually applied to the US and the Soviet Union. For a discriminating examination see Z. Brzezinski and S. Huntington, *Political Power: USA/USSR*, Viking Press, New York, 1964. See also C. Kerr, J. T. Harbison and F. A. Myers, *Industrialism and Industrial Man*, Harvard University Press, Cambridge, Mass., 1960; John Goldthorpe 'Social Stratification and Industrial Society' in R. Bendix and S. M. Lipset, *Class, Status and Power*, Free Press, Chicago, 1966, 2nd ed., pp. 648–659.
13. H. D. Duncan, *Symbols in Society*, Oxford University Press, New York, 1968, p. 53. This is an extremely subtle analysis of society as drama.
14. Thus in Marx and Marxism the state eventually dissolves into a free society, in guild socialism and anarchism the state is replaced by societal organizations like trade unions and cooperatives, in Saint-Simon by managers, bankers and engineers and in modern sociology by the socially sensitive organization. For a brilliant discussion of this point see S. Wolin, *Politics and Vision*, Little, Brown, Boston, 1960, ch. 10; B. Crick, *In Defence of Politics*, Penguin, London, 1964, and also E. H. Carr's introduction to Bukharin and Preobrazhensky, *The A.B.C. of Communism*, Pelican, London, 1969, pp. 13–37.
15. J. Hampden Jackson, *Marx, Proudhon and European Socialism*, English Universities Press, London, 1957, p. 100. Proudhon probably took this idea from the earlier work of Saint-Simon, who argued 'In a well ordered state, the government must be only an adjunct of production, an agency charged by the producers, who pay for it, with protecting their persons and their goods while they work. . . . The peak of perfection would be reached if all the world worked and no one governed'; cited by E. Halévy, *The Era of Tyrannies: Essays on Socialism and War*, Penguin, London, 1967, p. 25.

16. An early formulation, that of Mandeville, emphasizes the power of individual egoism which could be curbed in practice only by praise and flattery. Men are activated solely by selfish drives and follow their own inclinations to the exclusion of others, but an overall societal consequence was that 'every part was full of vice/yet the whole Mass a Paradise'. As with Smith, society is ordered as an unintended consequence of the individual pursuit of self-interest, Bernard Mandeville, *The Fable of the Bees: or Private Vices, Publick Benefits*, (ed.) F. B. Kaye, vol. I, Clarendon Press, Oxford, 1924, first published 1714.
17. Adam Smith, *An Inquiry Into the Nature and Causes of the Wealth of Nations*, vol. II, (ed.) E. Cannan, Methuen, London, 1964, p. 421. Our italics. Hegel's concept of the cunning of reason, the emergence of the 'Idea' through the unanticipated consequences of men's action, may well owe something to Smith's invisible hand, see R. W. Tucker, *Philosophy and Myth in Karl Marx*, Cambridge University Press, Cambridge, 1961, p. 66. Similarly, Kant remarks that personal decisions are often free and yet form part of a pattern of collective behaviour with a regularity of its own: 'Individual human beings, each pursuing his own ends according to his inclination and often one against another . . . unintentionally promote, as if it were their guide, an end of nature which is unknown to them', cited in C. J. Friedrich (ed.), *The Philosophy of Kant, Emmanuel Kant's Moral and Political Writings*, Modern Library, New York, 1949, p. 177.
18. See M. Olson, 'Rapid Growth as a Destabilizing Force', *Journal of Economic History*, **23**, 529–552 (1963), and the imaginative presentation of the point in M. Young, *The Rise of the Meritocracy*, Penguin, London, 1961, esp. ch. 8.
19. The point is neatly put by R. V. Sampson, *Equality and Power*, Heinemann, London, 1965, p. 150: 'the metaphysic of egoism predicates a society grounded on the impulse to emulation and a reverence for the principle of inequality'. It is interesting that as in other explanations of order emphasizing the priority of society over state this version also stresses public opinion as a prime control agency: all the anarchists do so, Lenin's emphasis on criticism and self-criticism is another case in point, and it is given priority in modern studies of community cohesion.
20. Herbert Spencer, *The Man Versus the State*, Watts, London, 1940, pp. 123–124.
21. It should also be remembered that it is perfectly possible to demonstrate that in the economy an equilibrium may be established which is well short of the optimum condition and that this may lead to heavy unemployment which may lead to conflict.
22. *The Wealth of Nations* is an extended polemic against any restraints on trade, but Smith was well aware that 'People of the same trade seldom meet together . . . but the conversation ends in a conspiracy against the public'. Adam Smith, *An Inquiry Into the Nature and Causes of the Wealth of Nations*, vol. I, (ed.) E. Cannan, Methuen, London, 1964, p. 130. He was also well aware that people living on rent, wages and profit might, incorrectly, see their interests as distinct from each other (vol. I, pp. 247–250).
23. This was James Mills' major contribution to the political theory of utilitarianism plus his principle of individual interest culminating in universal male franchise.

24. Prior to Marx the possibility of this outcome was noted by Sismondi, see E. Halévy, *The Era of Tyrannies: Essays on Socialism and War*, Penguin, London, 1967, pp. 1–16.
25. See A. Little and J. Westergaard, 'The Trend of Class Differentials in Educational Opportunity in England and Wales', *British Journal of Sociology*, **15**, no. 4, 301–316 (1964), who state that the daughter of an unskilled manual worker has about one in 600 chances of getting into a university, which is a hundred times worse than that of a girl with professional parents.
26. There is a huge research literature of uneven quality on this topic, see W. L. Guttsman, *The British Political Elite*, MacGibbon and Kee, London, 1963; R. Lewis and R. Stewart, *The Boss*, Dent, London, 1961; J. F. S. Ross, *Parliamentary Representation*, Eyre and Spottiswoode, London, 1948; R. K. Kelsall, *Higher Civil Servants in Britain*, Routledge & Kegan Paul, London, 1955; A. Sampson, *Anatomy of Britain*, Hodder and Stoughton, London, 1962; T. Lupton and C. S. Wilson, 'The Social Background and Connections of Top Decision Makers', *Manchester School*, **27**, no. 1, 30–46 (1959).
27. For example, *all* the American evidence suggests that black and Puerto Rican children have to battle against systematic deprivation and that given equal ability with white competitors they are systematically disadvantaged, see P. Lauter and F. Howe, 'How the School System is Rigged for Failure', *New York Review of Books*, 18 June (1970).
28. This consideration is at the basis of R. K. Merton's concept of anomie, R. K. Merton, *Social Theory and Social Structure*, rev. ed., Free Press, Glencoe, 1957, pp. 131–194.
29. This development of interest theory has become a starting point for a number of formal theories of behaviour, including game theory and exchange theory, and also of the less formal theories of pressure group pluralism.
30. This was the point of a blistering attack by Lord Macaulay in 1829, 'We gain nothing by knowing this, except the pleasure, if it be one, of multiplying useless words'. Macaulay, *Speeches on Politics and Literature*, Dent, London, no date, p. 433 and in 1876 by F. H. Bradley, *Ethical Studies*, Oxford University Press, London, 1927, in the essay 'Pleasure for Pleasure's Sake'.
31. T. Parsons, *The Structure of Social Action*, Free Press, New York, 1961, p. 399. This is a reformulation of the old Greek insight about men outside the polity being either gods or animals, the later organic analogies between parts and wholes and the 'romantic' reaction against utilitarianism in the nineteenth century. On the latter, see the able assessment by L. Bramson, *The Political Context of Sociology*, Princeton University Press, New Jersey, 1961, pt. I.
32. Emile Durkheim, *The Rules of Sociological Method*, Free Press, Glencoe, 1938, p. 1. For an illuminating discussion and illustration of the 'objective reality' of society, see P. L. Berger and T. Luckman, *The Social Construction of Reality*, Penguin, London, 1967, esp. pp. 63–146.
33. Upon this basis the authority of a political system or government is legitimate if the people routinely consider they should obey in most circumstances and, perhaps more accurately, if routinely the question of disobedience does not occur to them.
34. Kingsley Davis, *Human Society*, Macmillan, New York, 1966, p. 144. This

view was earlier advanced by T. H. Huxley in 1894 in *Evolution and Ethics*, Macmillan, London, 1894.

35. A useful introduction to behaviourism in the reinforcement/non-reinforcement mode is B. F. Skinner, *Science and Human Behaviour*, Macmillan, New York, 1953, and the stimulus–response mode is fully developed in J. Watson, *Psychology from the Standpoint of a Behaviourist*, Lippincot, Chicago, 1919.
36. See H. H. Hyman, 'The Value Systems of Different Classes' in R. Bendix and S. M. Lipset (eds.), *Class, Status and Power*, Free Press, Glencoe, 1966, pp. 488–499; I. L. Horowitz, 'Consensus, Conflict and Cooperation: A Sociological Inventory', *Social Forces*, **41**, 177–188 (Dec. 1962); and H. McClosky, 'Consensus and Ideology in American Politics', *American Political Science Review*, **58**, 361–382 (1964), reprinted in E. C. Dreyer and W. A. Rosenbaum, *Political Opinion and Electoral Behaviour: Essays and Studies*, Wadsworth, California, 1968, pp. 237–266.
37. We owe this argument to M. Olsen, 'The Relationship Between Economics and the Other Social Sciences', in S. M. Lipset (ed.), *Politics and the Social Sciences*, Oxford University Press, New York, 1969, pp. 137–162.
38. See J. Rex, *Key Problems of Sociological Theory*, Routledge & Kegan Paul, London, 1961, ch. 6, and W. C. Mitchell, *Sociological Analysis and Politics*, Prentice Hall, Englewood Cliffs, 1967, p. 39: 'Contrary to general opinion Parsons has dealt extensively with the origins or causes of conflict, *although he has been considerably less concerned about how political systems deal with the problem*'. Our italics.

3

THEORIES OF THE POLITICAL PROCESS

3.1. Preliminary Considerations

IN THIS CHAPTER we shall be concerned with setting out and examining theories of the social and political processes. One purpose of any theory is that of explanation, a concept of massive philosophical complexity.[1] Another distinct purpose of a theory is to order research, in the sense that a theory suggests relationships amongst those phenomena one is interested in with the hope that a researcher will not simply plunge into a welter of facts. He will have some more or less articulate idea as to the ordering or relationship between the facts he is interested in, and this will be the case whether or not he consciously sets out a theory or framework prior to commencing the collection of facts. Even the most a-theoretical or empiricist-minded social scientist or historian will have some sort of implicit 'imagery' of social processes, an idea of what is relevant to a problem and what is irrelevant, and will collect his facts accordingly, and this in turn is likely to affect his conclusions about social relationships.[*1*] Such raw empiricism has a number of dangers, including its technical inefficiency and its tendency to turn to 'commonsense' for explanation of relationships dredged up in the course of the research. But the point, as we suggested in Chapter 1, is really a simple one: to deserve the name of a scientific discipline political sociology must clearly set out theories and from these theories derive hypotheses which are empirically testable.[*2*] Such a process, that of deriving hypotheses from theories, is certainly one mode of explanation: facts confirm or upset hypotheses which in turn generate confidence in or destroy the theory from which the hypothesis was drawn, the facts being explained by subsuming them under the wider theory.

In the more developed physical sciences there are a number of such wider theories, for instance the laws of thermodynamics and the theory of relativity, from which strict deductions can be made mathematically; these deductions are statements of the phenomena covered by the general law.

In the less mature social sciences, where theories are both less elaborate and less precisely stated, these rigorous standards have barely been approximated.[*3*] Whether the reason for this is the social scientist's ignorance of logic and mathematics, or the sheer complexity of social life, or even the inapplicability of logical or mathematical methods to wide areas of social experience, is not for our purposes important. The fact is that very little that would satisfy the logician or the mathematician (and often the statistician) has been produced. The difficulty is that if the theories are not very rigorous why should one use them? Perhaps one cannot answer this difficulty except to say that, as Mao Tse-Tung put it, 'the longest journey starts with a single step'. Further, as Merton warns, the search for total logical purity, by those not trained as logicians or mathematicians, can be an inhibition to any investigation at all: 'A premature insistence on precision at all costs may sterilize imaginative hypotheses. It may lead to a reformulation of the scientific problem in order to permit measurement with, at times, the result that the subsequent materials do not bear on the problem in hand.'[2] An alternative approach is to start an investigation with a more or less intuitive understanding of the factors involved in a 'problem' and simply to measure the relevant relationships by appropriate statistical techniques. The hope is then that regularities of interaction, of cause and effect, will reveal themselves and from these revelations more general theoretical relationships can be inferred. Finally, the political sociologist may well rest content simply with classifying the facts he observes or even with drawing up classification schemes. In this volume it will be noted that these last two activities are much more typical of the work undertaken by political sociologists than is that of drawing up deductive theories. And those who care to look at the cited works will find that when the word 'theory' is used it normally refers to something like a model, a proposition, a generalization inferred from limited evidence, or even a system of classification.

For political sociology, it will be remembered, the major task on hand is that of answering problems posed by the central question: why do men obey? We gave three perspectives on this problem in Chapter 2. In this chapter we shall approach a little nearer the complexity of the 'real' social world by looking at the ways sociologists have found it convenient to talk about the patterning of social life as revealed in different societies. In order to do this we need to spell out further the relationships between individual and individual, the development of groups and collectivities and how these combine to form the social system. It is convenient for our purposes to begin the discussion by examining the relationships (linkages) between individuals.

3.2. Individual and Individual

It is an obvious fact that individuals live together. How is this fact conceptualized? It is conceptualized in terms of social relationships, which suggests that a considerable range of behaviour is patterned and therefore predictable. The question then arises, why is individual behaviour patterned? People's actions are largely, *not wholly*, guided or constrained by the expectations they have of other people's responses. There are then various pattern-producing mechanisms which form the basis of all social order.

Conceptually, a social relationship is an inference derived from observation of behaviour between two or more people; more specifically, this bond is between persons in roles. Roles are culturally prescribed performances of any given position within a network of social relationships. All individuals are in some measure enmeshed in the social structure through a network of social relationships, extending from small interpersonal relationships to the total society. Any role implies at least one other to which it is related, and, in practice, many more.

Let us look at the above statements using a familiar example, that of a school classroom. Within the classroom there are two major role positions defined: that of teacher and that of pupil. Attached to each role are a number of expectations about the behaviour of actual people who occupy the roles. Hence roles are *not* to be equated with the total individual but simply with one aspect of his or her behaviour. The role of teacher is partly formally defined by the school authorities—to teach at set times, to teach to a specified curriculum, to punish within formally prescribed limits, certain formally prescribed qualifications for the role, and so on. Another element in defining the teacher's role is the structure of the pupils' expectations concerning that role—a minimally interesting presentation of material, a certain amount of toleration, etc. Similarly, the counter-role of teachers is that of pupil, to which attach certain formally prescribed aspects such as attendance between five and sixteen years, regular attendance and 'good' standards of behaviour. In addition, the teacher will also expect certain forms of behaviour from his pupils—that they are attentive, punctual with homework, listen to what is said, etc. A moment's consideration of the teacher as a person rather than in the role of teacher suggests that he may also be someone's husband or lover, the secretary of a social or political club, member of a professional organization, all of which have more or less rigorously defined role definitions and expectations. Much the same is true of the pupil, who may be captain of an athletics team, member of the SDS, potential university student, son of a widow, etc., which roles in turn are more or less rigorously defined and around which cluster many types of expectations and behaviour. These multiple-role positions are the primary structural linkages between individuals and it will be recalled that roles are not simply formally defined but also have attached to them expectations about the performance of individuals in roles.

There are two features of expectations we need to consider in a little further detail. The first is the anticipatory nature of expectations. Not only will an individual expect (though normally he will not behave as reflectively as this seems to imply) that he will behave in a certain manner in particular situations, but he, along with other individuals, will have expectations of how others with whom he associates will behave. This highlights the predictable quality of most of our social life. The importance of this aspect of interaction can be stressed by recalling those situations where expectations are at a minimum, such as the first day at a new job, when one experiences feelings of uncertainty and hesitancy and tentatively explores for social cues. This kind of situation, where expectations are minimal, can be contrasted with other situations where expectations are well developed, such as the smooth and comfortable behaviour which occurs when two old and intimate friends meet, when a court of law assembles, when Parliament meets, etc., etc. This anticipatory dimension of interaction guides the behaviour of the individual. By his being able to anticipate and predict how others are likely to react to his behaviour the individual is able to shape his own behaviour accordingly. The second major feature of role expectations is their normative quality. Failure to meet expectations is likely to elicit surprise, disgust, anger or indignation, or, perhaps, even more serious consequences for the person who has failed to conform to expectations. This brings us once again to the idea of social norms which specify, in more or less detail, what men should do and are expected to do in given circumstances. They can range from the formalized rules of legal contract to the far less formal rules of etiquette, of family relations and of friendship.[*4*] It will be apparent that such norms may vary greatly from group to group in a society, between societies, and between individuals in different situations, and that since they vary in their degrees of formality they may be open to misinterpretation. But their common characteristic is that violation of them will call forth sanctions or deprivations which may vary in intensity from actual physical punishment to a derisive glance, from failure to secure a business contract to failure to be rewarded by a mother's smile of approval.

Another set of characteristics of a role is its sheer 'weight' relative to the individual playing it: in most cases it preceded him and will be there when he is gone; it is surrounded by expectations of performance which he cannot easily dismiss. Roles will vary in their flexibility a great deal. Doctors, lawyers, army officers, civil servants, are far more role-constrained than, for example, dustmen, rodent operators and politicians. Hence, entering the role of a doctor means that the weight of social expectations is great: he will dress 'respectably', treat patients with understanding, develop a bedside manner, and generally not indulge in unprofessional conduct. A great deal of the role-actor's life becomes very predictable indeed, and his attitudes, if initially they do not fit the role, will probably do so after a fairly short while. However, since for the rodent operator and the politician the role is not so rigorously defined they have greater room for manœuvre, for changing aspects of the role and for cultural innovation.[5]

Norms are related to another category of ideas, namely, the value structure of a group. Just as the members of a group share expectations with respect to one another's behaviour, generally they also share notions concerning desirable conditions or states of affairs. These are known as values. They can be ranked according to how important they are to the members of a group. Prominent values among a group of students, for example, might include the possession of *avant garde* dress taste for a girl, long hair for a boy, ownership of a sports car, intellectual ability, and so on. While individuals' value hierarchies may tend to vary, within a particular cohesive group some consensus on ranking might be achieved. The group's ranking may be seriously at variance with the rankings of other groups. A group of students is likely to rank the same values very differently from the way in which a group of parents would rank them. Norms are related to values by virtue of the fact that conforming to the normative rules of conduct is believed to foster the achievement of the state of affairs defined by the value.

3.3. Culture

Those norms and values which, to some degree, characterize a particular society or group belong to what is termed 'the culture'. 'Culture' includes within its reference not only norms and values but also knowledge, beliefs, arts, artifacts and language: 'culture is socially shared and transmitted *knowledge*, both existential and normative, symbolized in art and artifact'.[3] Its significance is that, within a culturally bounded area, most individual actions have common meanings. This point is normally illustrated by referring the reader to the man from Mars who in New York sees people obtaining goods and services in exchange for pieces of paper. In other words, the 'meaning' of these pieces of paper is culturally defined as 'money', and one has to be familiar with such cultural meanings to understand what is happening. Similarly, when one observes people showering others with expensive gifts, or destroying their own property, or spending vast resources on what appears to be entertainment, it is necessary to 'get into' the culture within which these apparently bizarre acts take place in order to understand their meaning or significance. It is culture that gives meaning to both actions and objects. If someone kills another person under one set of conditions it is actually defined as murder and the killer punished. But if the same act is committed under a different set of conditions the killer is fêted as a war hero.

Most acts within a culture are not seen by others within the same culture as being arbitrary: they may be good or bad, useful or useless, interesting or boring, but not arbitrary since they can be classified according to culturally appropriate schemes. However, this should not be interpreted to mean that culture in a single society is homogeneous, except, like values, at some very rarified level.

Culture is learned. It is learned initially within the family (or the equivalent), within schools, business firms, sports organizations, or any other kind of organizations. Just as we suggested the possibility of defining a political role in terms of a definition of the political, so we may speak of political culture within a similar definition of the concept 'politics'. Political culture gives meaning to individual political acts and to institutional and group patterns. 'For the individual political culture provides controlling guidelines for effective political behaviour, and for the collectivity it gives a systematic structure of values and rational considerations which ensures coherence in the performance of institutions and organisations.'[4]

The individual's behaviour is, then, partly determined by the culture which helps to define the various roles he occupies. It is possible to relate roles to each other since they are not randomly distributed throughout a person's lifetime but are structured into more or less coherent role sets. Each role implies a counter-role (pupil–teacher) and a role set is a clustering of roles upon a focal role: teacher implies pupils, which implies other teachers, which implies school authorities, etc. Each of these linkages is a point of potential conflict since the occupants of the counter-roles may have different expectations concerning the focal role. Thus there may well be incompatible expectations focussed upon the occupant of a focal role and the more differentiated—in terms of role—a society is, the more likely are there to be such incompatible expectations.

Individual to individual level linkage in sociology then is conceived of in terms of roles, and the expectations of a cultural nature which cluster around the roles and help to define them. It is clear that if one succeeds adequately in defining the idea 'politics' then one can begin to talk about political behaviour in terms of role, role sets and role conflict, etc., and so bring the whole apparatus of role analysis to help our understanding of political behaviour.

3.4. The Individual and the Group

People associate together for many purposes varying from amusement to companionship, robbery, pursuit of an interest, to elect MPs, and so on. Out of the association people may begin to develop a sense of identity with those whom they meet regularly or with those with whom they have characteristics or interests in common.[6] They see themselves as a part of some definable aggregate, and at its weakest the identifications may consist of recognizing and accepting that not everybody is part of the aggregate. Identifications may, however, involve a deep and perhaps enduring commitment to the group, which may involve a very strong antipathy to those thought of as non-group. Thus one defining characteristic of a group is the strength of individuals' commitment to it, and this will vary greatly from group to group, from the typically weak attachment of the tennis-club member to the typically far stronger attachment of the soldier or guerrilla to his platoon.[7]

Another dimension in which groups differ is their size, and the number of people in the group will be an important determinant of the character of group interaction. The larger the group the more irregular and diffuse are individual contacts likely to be, and this fact broadly underpins the distinction between primary and secondary groups.[8] Primary groups are characterized by intimate face-to-face contact. This means that the members of such a group develop some awareness of each of the other members as separate and distinct entities and interact with the other members as 'total personalities' rather than as specialized role occupants.

But as the group becomes larger such primary relationships become less and less likely. Individual relationships begin to assume a more specialized character and may begin to lose the strong affective meaning which is characteristic of primary relationships. In such larger, secondary groups, more formalized norms or rules of behaviour begin to emerge and the nature of the group begins to depend less and less on the kind of individuals who compose it.[9] The relationships become regularized through roles allocated within the 'emerging' or 'emerged' organization structure. However, although most formal organizations, bureaucracies, business organizations, political parties, etc., do not really emerge from primary structures, upon investigation they will be found to contain an intricate network of such primary groups bounded by the more formalized structure. These groups may exert an important influence both upon the behaviour of individuals and upon the institutions and societies within which they are embedded.

The mechanics of attitudinal reinforcement and restructuring within small groups has been very widely researched.[*10*] One example which serves to illustrate how primary groups may support attitudes is provided by an analysis of the Wehrmacht in World War II.[5] According to this study the German soldiers were able to maintain high morale even though, towards the end of the war, to an outside observer their situation looked hopeless. This was because the primary fighting group in the Wehrmacht was an emotionally self-sustaining entity within which many of the physical and emotional needs of the individual soldier were met in face-to-face contacts with fellow members of the platoon. The interactive support experienced in these units had very little to do with either official Nazi ideology or the organizational structure of the Wehrmacht. But, indirectly, it sustained the National Socialist regime and the formal command structure of the German Army. Group solidarity may also work in opposition to the larger organization within which the primary group is embedded. This is the case in many work situations where group norms emerge around an idea of a 'fair day's work'. Where such norms emerge the over-enthusiastic worker may find himself subject to severe group pressures to conform to the output norm. It was partly in order to 'crack down' upon such practices that Stalin supported so strongly the principle of Stakhanovism and socialist emulation.[*11*]

Analytically, there would appear to be two separate processes at work here. Firstly, there is the process referred to earlier on in this section whereby individuals attach themselves to groups with which they have a measure of normative resonance. Secondly, as members of groups, individuals are likely to find that their normative predispositions are channelled and may well become reinforced. The individual, then, by being a member of a group begins to develop ideas, beliefs, norms and values in common with other members of the group. Thus, the focus of the analysis moves from individual to individual linkages towards individual to group linkages. The significance of the individual to individual link and the individual to group link is that they are part of the ordered interaction that constitutes a society.

Analytically, one can conceive of a further level of linkage, that between group and group. We can take, then, groups as units of analysis, ignoring for some purposes the individuals constituting the group. The uniformities in society can be understood as a consequence of group interactions. In this sense groups are to be understood not as categoric or statistical entities, such as illiterates, age categories and demographic categories, but as entities within which there are certain interactions or relationships giving the group its moulding or guiding character.

The individual in society is, of course, implicated in many different kinds of group associations. Some of these groups will be relatively unstructured, impinging only to a small extent upon a person, whilst others may assume a focal and overwhelming importance to the individual. The depth of the individual's emotional attachment to a group is not really a consequence of any intrinsic worth, merit or structural importance of that group, but is very much a matter of individual desire. It is perfectly possible for different individuals to be as deeply committed to a group organized for playing tennis or chess as it is for others to be committed to groups dedicated to the overthrow of society or groups waiting for the end of the world. Conceptually, there is the possibility that people may belong to one group or many groups. Empirically, it is the case that most people belong to a relatively small number of organized groups, and this fact has very considerable implications for the social and political order.

It is possible to conceive of an individual's associations with groups as a cumulative or a non-cumulative chain. In the cumulative chain of group association the individual has attitudes or action dispositions reinforced at each 'level' of the chain, but the same will not be true of the non-cumulative process. In the latter case, the individual is involved in groups which operate, to some degree, inconsistent actions and values. For example, the individual may belong to a church the values of which constrain the way he practises his profession. The case of Catholic doctors asked to perform abortions would be an instance of this. These cross-cutting attachments, which involve the individual in some social ambivalence, are a constant feature of life in complex societies. This is in marked contrast to the cumulative group memberships, where such a value conflict is unlikely. Take the case of a Catholic doctor in a dominantly Catholic country, where the law may prohibit abortion and where his professional organization will be dominantly Catholic. Another supportive chain will be found in those cases where the individual belongs to a political party controlling a trade union movement with medical facilities, sports and recreational organizations, a youth wing, and an ideology. This supportive group membership may come about in several ways. It may be, for example, that the individual is a member of a relatively isolated community, such as fishermen, mining communities, timbermen, and the like, where the social structure and culture are homogeneous. Another case may be that of a minority ethnic group which in order to retain cultural identity will establish a church, a newspaper, schools, economic institutions, all of which are mutually supportive—for example in Belfast, where working-class Protestants and Roman Catholics live cheek by jowl but are separately organized for school, religion, politics and riot, so that from childhood the Catholics are spoken of as 'fenians', 'pigs', 'papishes' and 'mickies' whilst Catholic 'children are passionately bigoted and like all children in the area wear James Conally (*sic* Conolly) badges and whistle Republican songs' (*The Times*, 8 April, 1971). A further case, perhaps of even more obvious connection with politics, is that of revolutionary parties. Forced to operate in a political environment antipathetic to the parties' objectives, individual survival necessitates strong group cohesion. In such a case the basic unit of the party, the cell or guerrilla platoon, may take on many of the characteristics of a small community.

The implications of this line of analysis for those theories basing social order upon some sort of value consensus are obvious. It can be shown that an individual holds his values more strongly and is less likely to be predisposed to change them where he receives group support.[6] Laboratory experiments, for example, have shown that placing a high value on one's group is related to the power the individual has to resist communications which seem counter to the values of the group.

The process can be visualized as a selective filtering out of counter-group messages from the extra-group environment and it follows that the more homogeneous the individual's group context is, the stronger is the filtering process and the more 'restricted' is the extra-group environment from which the messages proceed. If we now envisage a state within which there are two broad group clusters mutually filtering out messages from each other, then we have a situation of mutual incomprehension or rejection. Although this simple dichotomous model of total incomprehension is not found in the real world, situations which approach it are by no means unusual. Ethnic political parties with or without strong regional attachments, religions which assume political shape, isolated communities with a pattern of single-party support, are all cases in point where the web of group affiliations can be envisaged as a cumulative chain reinforcing group identity. Examples of ethnic political parties are numerous and include the Action Group and the National Council of Nigerian Citizens in Nigeria, and the separatist parties in French Canada. Examples of religious parties include the Christian Democrats in Italy and West Germany, the Muslim League in Pakistan, and so on.

An implication of the cumulative properties of group membership is that these may constitute serious dangers to the stability of the political and social order since they may lead to non-negotiable demands, that is, demands which may not be compromised. One can envisage these demands at two levels. The first level involves emotional and possibly social separation from the wider society, the object being to practice or engage in a group-valued activity. Examples of this process are numerous and include religious communities such as the Dukhobors, the Hutterites in America and Canada, 'hippy' communities, Utopian communities, and the many communities patiently awaiting the Second Coming and/or the end of the world. On the whole these groups do not impinge very deeply upon the problem of maintaining political or social order, but the situation is, of course, fraught with tension-creating possibilities. This is the case because these communities may constitute a permanent institutionalized affront to the values and norms of the wider society: nudity in public, absence of conventional marriage ties, cooperation in place of competition, and so on. Even if these communities pose no obvious political threat their very presence may aggravate others in the environment to take 'direct' action against the separatist community, and that is a political problem. Again, it is not difficult to provide examples of cases where such communities have clashed directly with the political authorities over such matters as taxation, voting and conscription.

Falling within the same category but probably with far more serious political and social implications are those clusters of groups concerned to change in some way the major economic, social or moral configurations of the host society. The changes demanded by such groups may also involve the break-up of the host society as a geographically defined area. Such groups have, at best, a very weak commitment to the 'dominant' norms of the host society, regarding them as unfair or historically outmoded. Examples of such groups include the totalitarian political parties which attempt a major attitudinal and behavioural reorientation of their membership, ethnic separation parties in ethnically diverse societies and socialist parties during their formative years.

The second level of group demands involve a modification of the political or economic or normative arrangements of the host society but without changing the geographical context of that society. For the purposes of political sociology these 'reformist' groups may be divided into two: those whose major thrust is towards the political authorities and those whose political activities are a byproduct of other activities. An example may make the latter category clearer. Groups concerned with the collection, classification, discussion and distribution of knowledge about butterflies may become, as a byproduct of their interest, involved with the political authorities if new tax regulations or import regulations happen to affect their *raison d'être*; otherwise, acting simply as butterfly collectors such associations are politically quiescent. This type of group has been labelled 'parapolitical'.[7] Groups, one of whose major products is political persuasion, pressure or threats, may vary enormously in size, scope, inclusiveness, in the steadiness of political interest, and in their political influence. Business firms, aggregations of business firms, federations of school principals, trade unions, universities, farmers' groups, and so on, are not primarily concerned with politics, but a major interest of theirs is in ensuring that government policy pays due attention to their concerns. (See Chapter 12.)

We spoke earlier of the social and political dangers of cumulative chains of group membership but a moment's consideration will show that in many societies, especially the Atlantic States, memberships for most people are not cumulative but rather dispersed.[*12*] Within other societies it will be remembered that cumulative group membership may be thought of as constituting societal cleavages with very limited communication 'across' their cleavage, leading to a state of mutual incomprehension which may well develop into mutual antagonism. Where group memberships are not cumulative, individual loyalties lack the emotional intensity engendered in the cumulative system. The individual's energies, time and skills are dispersed among a number of different groups. No one group is able to command the individual's entire loyalty.[*13*] As suggested earlier, this situation may even involve the individual in some ambivalence, and it has been shown that the more heterogeneous the social environment of the individual the more weakly he holds his opinions, his attitudes and his beliefs and the less likely he is to act upon any unified belief system.[8]

The two 'ideal types' we have briefly examined give us fairly important perspectives on some problems of social order. For example, one would expect that in societies characterized by cumulative chains of group attachments stability would be precarious and they would display a high ratio of force to normative consensus. Further, the concept of group cohesion through group norms also points up or throws into relief the problem of group adjustments at the societal level: how are the possibly conflicting interests of groups to be adjusted without causing some dissatisfied groups to move towards attempted disruption of the society? In other words, group theory looked at from one point of view sensitizes the student to politics as an allocative process. This is the perspective of most theorists of pressure group activity. Again, group analysis of both types (primary and secondary) also helps in an understanding of the processes of value and attitude formation and their transmission or non-transmission both between and within groups. This is the problem of socialization, a process which has very significant implications for the study of political order. (See Chapter 6.)

We have looked at linkages between individual and individual and between individual and group and have suggested in the previous paragraphs that there are group to group linkages; the rest of this chapter will be concerned with theories which operate at one or all of these levels.

3.5. Some Theories of the Social Process

'Though it is part of conventional wisdom to start with the "individual" and his act, yet as Mead and many others have insisted, we cannot get to the social by way of the "individual" by simple addition or aggregation. Rather we must begin with an interactional field of interdependent organisms in an environment.'[9] Hence, as we suggested earlier, there are emergent properties of interactions, and analysis might begin either at the level of interacting dyads or with the environment in which interaction takes place as a whole, that is at the level of 'system'. We shall begin with a brief examination of individual based theories and move towards those whose major focus is upon the system as a whole. Individual based theories of social order attempt to explain order on the basis of interacting individuals out for their own benefit, which may be simply economic or political power but can also include prestige, status, social approval, and other psychic rewards. These approaches can be seen clearly in the development of exchange theory and game theory. They are also in the tradition of the utilitarian theories discussed in the previous chapter.

Exchange Theory

Behaviour in exchange theory is seen in terms of patterns individually selected from a wide repertoire of possible behaviour, the patterns being selected on a basis of the best-rewarded or least-punished behaviour emitted. Initially, behaviour is random but becomes increasingly patterned. Patterning is a consequence of two basic propositions: (1) Past situations in which a particular response has been rewarded will, if the situation frequently recurs, evoke the same response with growing frequency, and (2) 'The more often within a given period of time a man's activity rewards the activity of another, the more often the other will emit the activity'.[10] Order in society is therefore an outcome of the patterning which in turn is securely rooted in men's individual psychology and not in any system imperative.[*14*] For Homans, norms are a product of exchange: 'A norm is a statement made by a number of members of a group, not necessarily by all of them, that the members ought to behave in a certain way in certain circumstances. The members who make this statement find it rewarding that their own actual behaviour and that of the others should conform to some degree to the ideal behaviour described by the norm'.[11] The members who *do not* make this statement must choose between the costs (in terms of reward or punishment) of obedience or disobedience and, presumably, those who obey do so because there are rewards in obedience not to be gained by disobedience. The concept of authority, power or leadership (which seem to be the same thing for Homans) arises from the rewards that the few can give the many, rewards such as good advice, material and symbolic status, etc., and for which the led reward the leaders with esteem plus a share of whatever the group seeks.[12] Institutions are also maintained by rewards, but they differ in degree from groups in that institutions rely on 'explicitly stated norms and orders'.[13]

Hence, from top to bottom societies are characterized and held together by the same principle of rewarded and punished behaviour, and if the former is the dominant behaviour it must follow that, at least in the long run, most observed behaviour is rewarded. This is also the case with habit type behaviour, for example unthinking obedience is rewarding in the sense that the costs are presumably low. All actions are individual actions and are reducible to individual rewards and *all* action involves exchange.

The difficulties of Homans' version of exchange are twofold. Firstly, it appears to neglect the consideration that many relationships, except in a trivial or tautological sense, are *not* exchange relations but exploitative ones. Those with political or economic power may take the major decisions that determine the exchange; monopolies, ruling castes and dictators are cases in point and to argue that there is really an exchange of some sort (life for obedience) is trivial since the relationship between obeyers and obeyed is one dominated by the obeyed.

Homans, however, recognizes that at the institutional level direct processes of exchange do not always operate. He remarks, 'in an informal group a man wins status through his direct exchanges with other members, while he gets status in the larger society by inheritance, wealth, occupation, office, legal authority—in every case by his position in some institutional scheme, often one with a long history behind it'.[14] In the larger and more complex group, activities tend to be maintained not by the 'principle of primary reward' but by 'contrived rewards' such as money and social approval. Also, the process of rewarding exchange becomes more and more indirect as the interactional network becomes larger. In other words, out of elementary social behaviour there develop explicit rules which govern the behaviour of many people: that is, Homans does not explain all social events by psychological propositions but is driven to entities looming larger than individual interactions and which may be major determinants of those interactions.

Another possible weakness of exchange theory is that it appears ill-equipped to deal with the very diversity of customs and norms in different societies which may be in total conflict with each other. Some societies have sumptuary norms whilst others encourage saving, some encourage bravery and male aggressiveness whilst others discourage it, some societies encourage sexual 'licence', others are much less permissive, some encourage emotion, others do not, and, presumably, all come from a similar basic characteristic of man, that he will eventually, from a repertoire of behaviour, select the most rewarded. Hence, as Homans has recognized, exchange theory cannot explain any particular pattern of behaviour.[15]

Exchange Theory and Politics

Exchange theory has no distinctive subcategory called 'the political' since relationships in politics are essentially the same, governed by the same processes, as those in the other contexts. None the less it does offer an explanation of the origins and limitations of political power. Its discussion of the origins of political power is not very important nor does it show great insight; it merely specifies that some men have resources desired by others, resources such as intelligence, experience, goods and scarce abilities which they are prepared to offer in exchange for other resources such as prestige, votes, support, promises of future support, etc., etc. In this way differences of power arise, power being the ability to cause another to take a course of action which otherwise he might not have chosen. More important and interesting is the discussion of the contingent nature of political power which hinges upon a series of propositions about the conditions underlying the allocation of resources through exchange.

Men compete for resources through seeking policies which 'are the values for which the political actors bargain and compete and are distinguished from extra-polity policies by their authoritative character'.[16] In order to obtain a policy, a more desired situation than that currently obtained, men incur costs and will balance potential costs against potential benefit. Men prefer higher levels of satisfaction to lower levels and will act so as to maximize their satisfactions and will be prepared to incur costs up to the point where costs and rewards are about equal. Politicians compete for votes in terms of time, energy and money and are rewarded with prestige, power and financial resources which they allocate so as to maximize their satisfactions; they offer policies (authoritative decisions) in exchange for power, prestige and money. If one then specifies conditions for entry into the political exchange market—entry into which is either totally unimpeded, partially impeded or totally impeded—which roughly correspond to actual entry conditions, it is possible to specify very closely the probable policy outcomes using the same reasoning as in economic analysis of a free market, an oligopolistic market and a monopolistic market.[17] In political exchange the oligopolistic model is the most appropriate because it closely corresponds with reality. Political power can then be specified quite closely by examining the difference between the rewards a politician could obtain in a competitive and a non-competitive situation or, looked at from the other side, between what a policy seeker would offer in a competitive and a non-competitive political market to maximize his chances of obtaining a preferred outcome. In all types of market men act the same way, to maximize outcomes, but the actual outcomes are very different. Also, the rate of entry into politics is very different for different people since the costs of entering politics in terms of time, money, lost leisure and so on are not equal nor are the benefits and, therefore, a man may perfectly well be allocating his resources rationally by *not* entering politics at all even to the minimal extent of voting.

In this version of exchange theory the notion of normative consensus has little if any place whilst in that of Blau it has: 'the people's obligation to comply with the authority's commands does not develop in social exchange as a result of the rulers' contribution to the common welfare, but is a *moral obligation* inculcated by socializing agencies'.[*15*] However, in Blau's version individual choice initially underpins consensus since 'Social processes . . . transform the individual rationalizations into common values'.[18] And the common values arise from a common social situation, for example in a business hierarchy or a group of some sort. But whatever their genesis the values or consensus are facts and may exert an influence on the individual pulling against his obvious self-interest but not necessarily against his satisfactions as a group member. People may attach importance to the group and its values long after any rational exchange has taken place in terms of initially choosing a particular group or its values for its exchange value to the individual. Thus Geertz in an examination of the role of Balinese princes as economic innovators suggests that they are helped by 'a quantity of cultural capital in the form of traditional social loyalties' arising from their place in a social structure which has 'either been dissolved or drastically re-organised'.[*16*]

This version of exchange theory can come close to the value-consensus theories of social order, since apparently 'moral obligation' can take on an existence apart from considerations of rational exchange except in a somewhat attenuated version of exchange. Consider the case of an untouchable in the Hindu caste system; does he do all the really menial tasks on a rational exchange basis? Presumably not, except in the sense that he *believes* that in doing his job well he strengthens his chance of a better position next time he is born and therefore accepts his position within the present order on a moral basis—and because, until quite recently, there was a dearth of organizations to mobilize the untouchables' self-interest against a 'morally justified' oppression. But it is hard to believe that rational self-interest was the dominant feature maintaining the acquiescence of the untouchable to the caste system even if we accept that, in some sense, it began as a matter of individual self-interest. Thus, by injecting a normative element Blau has almost certainly strengthened his position even at the cost of a possible inconsistency since he can explain *enduring* power inequalities by reference to socialized value orientations. Homans' version of exchange theory cannot account for the persistent inequality in this manner since it has no values, but it can argue that even acceptance of inequality can be socially rewarded. This, we have previously argued, is an empty formulation. How do we know people are rewarded? Because they are behaving as they are behaving, a formulation worthy of Mr. Podsnap himself! In the more rigorous formulation of Curry and Wade, enduring inequality in exchange relations can be explained in the sense of accounting for outcomes, but it is difficult to see why people accept them—as they do in the real world—over a number of generations unless they are deceived as to their 'real' interest or the 'exploited' have not the ability to end the system and establish a more equitable one.

Another theory beginning from an individualistic perspective is game theory. This theory simply assumes the existence of conflicts of interest and of rules specifying the range of choices open to each contestant. It does not have anything to say about the derivation of the rules.[19]

Game Theory

Strictly speaking, game theory is a branch of mathematics concerned with the logic of decisions, but in this short section we shall be concerned only with a minor element of game theory. Game theory, unlike some versions of exchange theory, assumes the rationality of participants in the sense that where alternative courses of action are possible 'with differing outcomes in money or power or success some participants will choose the alternative leading to the larger pay off' and such behaviour is rational.[20] Riker uses a zero-sum game as the second condition of analysis, a zero-sum game being a situation within which losses by one person or group are exactly the same as gains by another. Individuals then compete for maximum gain and do so by making bids for support from other players, the nature of the bids being defined by the rules of the game: they may be in money, influence, battleships, promises of support, etc. The game situation is, therefore, one of conflict in which more or less information about moods, moves, motives, dispositions, and so on, are at the players' disposal: the greater the knowledge that participants have about other participants, the greater is the possibility of purely rational responses to any move. In politics it is rarely possible to have full information—it costs time and resources to obtain—so political conflict cannot be purely rational but it does, Riker suggests, approximate to a model of rational behaviour, and furthermore he suggests what he thinks of as a testable proposition from the model. This is that with a zero-sum game played by more than two rational players who can bid for each other's support publicly 'only minimum winning coalitions occur'.[21] Such a proposition is obvious when stated but its implications are interesting since, for example, it suggests that parties will in the long period shed support over and above that necessary to win elections, that winning coalitions are *always* unstable since those in the minority outside will *always* be prepared to make a larger bid than was obtained by the least committed (least rewarded) member of coalition. In the real world without perfect information coalitions are above minimum size because members can never ascertain with certainty how to obtain just enough support, so there is always a tendency to overbid for safety; competitive bidding for electoral support between political parties is a case in point. Hence, political coalitions are always unstable in the sense that the coalition when seeking power always hedges its bets by seeking a wide range of support but realizes when in office that payoffs have to be made. Hence, politicians in office seek to narrow their base; they can afford to disappoint some of their surplus support and if they succeed in detaching supporters they also succeed in creating enemies amongst the disappointed.[*17*]

If we weaken the measurability element of the rationality principle to include not only the maximization of material gain but also the 'maximization' of such things as security, spiritual welfare, social prestige, power, and so on, then game theory sets out the logic underlying the best means whereby these ends can be achieved. In other words, given certain ends and conditions game theory sets out the possible strategies. In this sense, 'game theory' is not at present helpful for the political sociologist, yet does offer considerable potential as explanatory theory. For example, if we posit that people wish for secure rewards rather than a maximum reward we are in a better position to appreciate the caution of peasants when presented by the market with an opportunity to concentrate production on a single crop which may with good luck make them much better off but which, in a bad year, may result in starvation. Spreading the risk over a number of crops, none of which is 'efficient' in terms of maximizing income, represents a rational response by people at a subsistence level to the problem of market fluctuation, and such an insight is valuable for economic and political planning, much of which has been posited upon a profit-maximizing strategy. It also strengthens our understanding of social activity in situations where information is never available in sufficient amounts, in the right place and at the right time, that is, it strengthens our analysis of *most* situations. In the example of the political party which, in principle, should hover around the point of minimally winning—given sufficient information—we can see that a rational response in the real world is one of hedging bets by attempting to attract as much support as possible even in the full knowledge that this *cannot* maximize individual payoffs: 'The greater the degree of imperfect or incompleteness of information, the larger will be the coalitions that the coalition-makers seek to form and the more frequently will winning coalitions actually formed be greater than minimum size'.[*18*]

Game theory, even at the very elementary level we have explained it, has at least one important implication, which is that in the real world which *must* consist of coalitions greater than minimum winning ones there *must* always be competition amongst contenders.[*19*] From the point of view of individual to individual and individual to group linkages it also has the advantage of specifying in some detail the processes of involvement, the benefits of such involvement and of clearly outlining the mechanics of group (coalition) formation in competitive situations. Since we can easily quantify the rewards in a laboratory situation and can also introduce new players with new resources (or without resources) game theory also has the possibility of exact testing; it is also possible to make information more or less available or more or less costly and observe the results in the laboratory and thus obtain some sort of experimental verification of the hypotheses concerning information and the size principle.

Game theory does then appear to offer non-trivial insights into some political processes, but it *may* not do the same for other problems. Barry has argued that this mode of analysis has no answer for the question, why do people vote? Clearly a game theorist must answer in terms of the advantage to the voter in voting or not voting, and the calculation as expressed by Barry is 'how much better off he would be . . . if his preferred party won the election, and he then multiplies it by the probability that his vote for that party will change the result of the election so that his party wins instead of losing'.[22] In an electorate of millions the chances of this occurring are almost infinitesimal so that the rational citizen would not vote—yet most people do vote. The decision to vote is, therefore, irrational in game theoretic terms although other considerations—strictly outside purely rational considerations—such as traditional party allegiance, support for the political system, a desire to vote, the satisfaction gained from voting, may account for the decision.

There are other major difficulties involved in game theory, beyond the complexity of the mathematics, which limit its usefulness for the social scientist. As mentioned previously, 'the game theorist starts his work only after the rules of the game, and the utilities or value hierarchies defining the payoffs, have been specified. The genesis of the conflict, its social-psychological features, and its socio-cultural setting are beyond the scope of the analysis.'[23] In order to examine some of these features of social life, and to move to a 'higher' level of analysis than the individual and his needs, we shall now turn to theories which are more system-oriented. What we attempt to do in the following section is to set out some way in which group to group connections may be envisaged.

3.6. Systems Theory

The idea of politics as a system has gained considerable currency in political science. The notion of system implies that there is a degree of interrelatedness between the units in which one is interested. Interrelatedness is assumed to operate within the system which consists of mutually constraining or conditioning units, and the system operates within an environment of some sort from which it is distinguishable. A major condition, therefore, of a system is that somehow or other the 'energy' which keeps the system together—distinct from the environment—must be maintained if the system is not to run down and merge with the environment. Within the system energy is exchanged between units such that if one unit is affected all the others will be affected in a varying degree depending upon the linkages within the system and the loss of energy in the process of transmission. Energy is also lost in the process of maintaining the system as an entity within its environment, and it must somehow be regained.[*20*]

In a general way it is quite obvious how the systems view—which is used in, for example, electronic guidance systems—can be applied to the problem of order in political sociology by simply tracing out the interconnections in society attempting to plot the transmission of 'energy' through society. If we confine our attention to those interconnections which are in some way concerned with the political, however we define it, then we have the notion of a political system; if we then apply the idea of an environment to that of a political system we have a political system acting on and reacting to its environment, the environment being the social or other systems. The focus of attention then turns to the ability or 'capacity (of the political system) to respond to the conditions under which it functions . . . political systems accumulate large repertoires of mechanisms through which they may seek to cope with their environments. Through these they may regulate their own behaviour, transform their internal structure, and even go so far as to remodel their fundamental goals.'[24] Political systems may then be seen as meeting challenges of various sorts or demands from the environment which they may cope with in ways varying from adapting the structure of the system to meet the demands, to changing the allocation of scarce resources, or to changing the character of the environment. If they do this (meet 'stress' from the environment) then they are persistent *vis à vis* the environment; hence a political system must be successful in two tasks, (1) the allocation of values, and (2) inducing 'most members to accept these allocations as authoritative'.

Coping with the environment involves 'inputs' to the system and 'outputs' from it. Inputs are the variables such as demands and supports from the environment; demands are simply 'requests' of more or less urgency for authoritative action or allocation from the political system; and supports are simply favourable or neutral states of mind or actions from people in the system concerning the allocations from the system or towards the system or elements of it. Outputs are rules, regulations, actions, laws and so on which are authoritative *vis à vis* the environment and which in turn cause a change of some sort in the context within which the political system operates and, therefore, affect the support enjoyed by the system which may increase, decrease or shift from one level of the system to another. Outputs may help to maintain support for the system and are generally directed at specific groups in order to generate their support, but over time 'rewarded' support may be transformed into a more generalized support for the system and not merely one aspect of it. In respect of support, the system may be envisaged as containing three tiers, the political community, the political regime and the political authorities. The political community, a sentiment of 'affective solidarity' which underlies 'the functioning of all systems', binds together the occupants of political roles in the system and may be more or less widespread amongst people in the system.[25] A political regime corresponds fairly closely to the major institutional arrangements of a political system—elder plus chief, a meeting under the banyan tree, Emperor plus Diet plus central authorities, Parliament plus monarch plus parties plus local authorities, and so on. The regime constitutes a 'regularized method for ordering . . . political relationships' and stems from the 'need to accept some basic procedures and rules relating to the means through which controversy over demands (is) to be regulated'.[26] In terms of role theory the regime is simply a clustering of political roles and, therefore, the authorities are those individuals occupying the roles. Various levels of enthusiasm for the three levels of the system may be experienced from the environment varying from willing support for all levels to active dislike for all through a mixture of supporting the community but disliking the regime and authorities, etc. Loss of support, that is falling away of positive enthusiasm or approval or of supportive actions, will trigger a response from the role occupants if they become aware of the loss, which will manifest itself through demand stress, and the response in terms of allocations, etc., will in turn trigger a response from those affected.[*21*] The process of channelling information about social reactions to authoritative allocations is feedback, and is essential since otherwise the authorities would have no idea how its actions are received. Feedback channels may more or less 'distort' the information according to 'noise' in the channels, as in the case of a highly ideological party or pressure group which filters out information that goes against its ideological bias, or as in the case of a caste or class recruited bureaucracy which may be incapable of understanding grievances of other classes or castes. Again, the channels may be overloaded in terms of the time necessary to process demands.

The political system copes with stress or demands from its environment by making changes either in its structure or in allocations or by changing the environment; a measure of its success in doing this is the degree of support it enjoys, and the allocations together with compliance are 'essential variables' of the system. A system persists when its 'essential variables' operate 'within what I shall call their critical range'.[27] The system is maintained, if indeed it does survive, through the feedback process which enables authorities to make responses on the basis of information rather than hunch or intuition. Maintaining the system within its critical range, which may be a very wide one, is carried out through a process of regulation of both demands and supports, and it is at this point that systems analysis attempts to utilize notions, previously discussed, of linkages between individuals, groups and now the system as a whole.

All political systems develop regulatory mechanisms. Firstly, there are structural arrangements which regulate the flow of demands into the political system and which vary from political parties to pressure groups, opinion leaders, newspapers, assemblies, and so on. Secondly, cultural mechanisms which define the range of appropriate demands that may be made for political intervention are identifiable in all systems and may vary enormously from system to system. Thirdly, demands are regulated and channelled after they have entered the system and this involves a message (information) capacity within the system such that demands may reach centres of authority. Again, the information channels may vary greatly from organizations devoted mainly to such transmissions (functionally specific) through organizations attending to a range of problems, but *inter alia* concerned with transmitting information (functionally diffuse). Examples in the first category include parties, elections and pressure groups, and the second include primary group networks. Finally, individual or group demands are reduced, compromised, made compatible with each other or aggregated and made more diffuse by conversion or compromise within political structures like—wait for it—political parties and pressure groups.

As Easton describes a system as 'any set of variables selected for description and explanation',[28] one can hardly quarrel with his decision to spell out in detail the set of variables he has selected, but the question of whether he has outlined a theory does arise. This can, however, be easily disposed of since it is obvious that he has not and, as a matter of fact, Easton has only claimed that his system is 'a conceptual framework' through which in the fullness of time a theory 'may possibly' be produced. A conceptual framework is simply a guiding language which may or may not prove helpful in thinking about a problem area. From our brief exposition it is clear that his scheme is a dynamic one in the sense of drawing attention to processes of system change and adjustment to stress at various levels in the system and its environment, but very insufficient attention is paid to revolutionary change beyond suggesting that it arises from output failure.[*22*]

A much more serious, and possibly insoluble, difficulty concerns the concept of critical ranges of stress tolerance, about which we are told nothing beyond the proposition that when they are exceeded the system is in danger and we only know this for certain when the system collapses.[*23*] The difficulty here is that in some systems—electronic, heating, guidance, etc.—we can specify exactly in advance the parameters of the system and then test for stress (overload) and observe that the fuse blows. Similarly, we can see that most people die if boiled too long in oil, but clearly the same is not possible for total political systems although in social science laboratory situations something similar can be detected by comparing bits of information fed into a group of subjects (the system) with the information output. If the parameters of the system are not given values then all one is saying is that things are interconnected, but this is not very illuminating although it may well be true. In his extremely careful analysis of economic growth in two Indonesian towns, Clifford Geertz comes up against a similar difficulty and writes, 'It is, of course, just the sort of weak and evasive conclusion all-too-typical of social scientists to say that effective growth demands just so much group-focus and just so much ego-focus, but not too much or too little of either; *but in the case of the Tabanan–Modjokuto contrast nothing more circumstantial can be said*'.[*24*]

The Easton approach to systems is specifically an over-arching attempt to describe political systems and the manner in which they cope with stress, their persistence in the face of changing and of stable environments looked at from the point of view of authoritative value allocations. It stands or falls by its ability to deal with the problem of persistence, which is explained not in terms of allocation (although this is involved) but of purposive change by members of the political system, both of the system and its environment. The approach is at a very high level of abstraction and there is, as we have already said, a problem of providing operational routines through which specific situations could be examined.[*25*] For example, it seems impossible to know when a system has persisted since, presumably, in response to intra- and extra-systemic stress everything may change except the name (UK, US), and as Easton has written: 'Thus in the society called the United States a political system has persisted over the centuries through the very fact that it has been able to change itself, radically, from a relatively decentralised federal system without extensive popular participation at its founding to one with a relatively high degree of political centralisation and universal adult suffrage'.[29] System non-persistence seems a highly elusive concept. The problem is that if everything may change and yet the system in some sense persists, what is the sense in which it may be said to persist?

From the point of view of political sociology, systems analysis has the major advantage that it enables one to incorporate less ambitious modes of analysis—coalition theory, exchange theory, role theory, value consensus, etc.,—into the broad insight that to persist systems must adapt: 'They are no longer alternative or competing modes of analysis; they represent partial theories of allocation, referring to and explaining some special part or aspect of a political system'.[30] Systems analysis, therefore, is potentially a valuable organizing frame in two senses: it enables one to 'descend' to other levels of analysis without losing sight of the wider system problems of responding to stress, and it does suggest a range of interconnected problems for analysis and research. It is also comparative in its perspective or, better, it does provide one with a number of standardized concepts into which data from very different countries can be slotted and compared.

Systems analysis is also valuable in that it does enable one to avoid difficulties associated with individualistic theories of, for example, democracy. Thus many researchers have demonstrated the low level of individual interest in politics, low motivation to participate and a lack of knowledge of the issues between parties, all of which are inimical to individual interest theories of democracy. However, looked at from the vantage point of 'requirements of the survival of the total democratic system' individual 'inadequacy' provides a positive service to the system. Similarly, low commitment to party and political beliefs by non-participants underpins compromise and system stability.[*26*]

Another advantage of the systems concept is that it can lead to a degree of classificatory clarity. For example, in the idea of a subsystem—economic, political, integrative and cultural—we may detect a corresponding set of compliance-inducing mechanisms through which social control is exercised. For the economic the corresponding mechanism is wages, salaries and rewards, in the political it is force, bargaining, compromise, in the integrative it is the pressure of group, family, friends, tribe and so on to perform a role adequately, and in the cultural it is commitment to values like nationalism, individualism and religious doctrine that motivate adequate role performance. Obviously, sanctions from one subsystem may be used to induce adequate behaviour in another, ie religious persuasion may contribute to good citizenship and efficient entrepreneurial activity and the latter may contribute resources for the polity to function more efficiently.[31]

Structural Functionalism

Another over-arching view of the political process is that covered by the term 'functionalism' which suggests that societies must meet certain individual and group needs—shelter, nourishment, replacement, a measure of security, etc.—which lead to norms, forms (language, magic, religion) and institutions which control and coordinate men in the attempt to meet these needs.[*27*] Thus rules and norms, most behaviour and so on are connected with society in the sense that they are interrelated in such a manner as to support each other and represent solutions to the functional imperatives of system maintenance. Functionalists have given lists of various lengths of these functional imperatives which every system must meet. According to Parsons the system must (1) adapt itself to an environment—adaptation, (2) achieve collective goals—goal attainment, (3) maintain control of tensions in the system—pattern maintenance or tension management, and (4) integrate the diverse actions of members of society —integration. Actions and beliefs in a society are 'explained', that is their function is clarified, in terms of the part they play in performing the functional imperatives; thus religion may be understood both as a device of tension management and as a source of societal integration. Political activity is primarily adaptive and integrative, but at various points it touches all aspects of the imperatives. The point is that the causes of the activity are the end states produced and, hence, a consequence explains a cause. Each of the functional imperatives can be envisaged as a subsystem related to the others by exchanges through subsystem boundaries. Functional analysis normally distinguishes between functions which are consequences of action which make for better adaptation of the system to its environment, and dysfunctions which have the opposite effect. One also needs to distinguish between the latent and the manifest functions of actions or institutions, with manifest functions as the recognized and intended systemic consequences of behaviour and latent being unrecognized, but having systemic consequences. Clearly there can also be both latent and manifest dysfunctions.[32] In our subsequent discussion we shall analyse the variant of functionalism that has been most used in political research, the variant known as structural functionalism.

Functional analysis sets out prerequisites for the survival of any society or system; structural functionalism sets out the related role sets which constitute the structure which performs the functions by which the political system operates. As applied to politics, structural functional analysis focusses upon those structures concerned with politics—however defined —which are seen to be embedded in an environment with which the structures have to come to terms. The functioning of the political system is at various levels of capability: (1) its capabilities relative to other systems in terms of input and output. Here we are interested in the techniques and extent of regulation, extraction and distribution of values by the political system over other systems: (2) its internal processes, referring to the manner in which the system processes inputs of demands and support into outputs. This may be divided into the way in which six political functional imperatives are performed: (a) interest articulation, ie the manner in which demands are formed, (b) interest aggregation, ie combining demands into courses of proposed action, (c) rule-making, ie authoritative rule formulation, (d) rule application, ie application and enforcement of law, (e) rule adjudication, ie applying rules to individual cases, (f) communication, ie communication of the above activities within the political and from the political to other subsystems.[33] Finally, (3) there are the system maintaining and adapting functions which refer to the learning of political roles in pre-adult and adult life and the techniques of recruiting to fill political roles. Both the capabilities dimension and the political functional dimension may be further broken down into modes of performance by use of, for example, Parsons' pattern variables. The variables are: affective and affective neutrality; self or collective orientation; universalistic or particularistic; ascription or achievement; specificity and diffuseness; instrumental or consummatory. These variables are polar opposites and refer to the range of choices available to any actor in any situation and by extension may also characterize the manner in which a functional imperative is met or may be used to describe the style of an institution.[*28*] Thus we may be interested in rule-making in terms of whether rules are made for all people equally or only for some people, and the same could be true of recruiting patterns, ie whether people with similar qualifications (education, etc.) are recruited without reference to, for example, social class or skin colour.

Structural functionalism as a mode of political analysis posits that all political systems have a political structure which is more or less clearly demarcated from other structures in the system. The political system is conceptually demarcated from other systems because it is seen as performing the 'functions of integration and adaptation (both internally and *vis à vis* other societies) by means of the employment, or threat of employment, of more or less legitimate physical compulsion'.[34] As with systems analysis so with functionalism, the political system must respond to its environment and it may do this more or less effectively by breaking down, by changing the environment or by developing instrumentalities to cope with environmental challenges. Almond and Powell see four types of challenge: (1) that of building a legal structure: state-building, (2) that of producing affective commitment: nation-building, (3) that of meeting pressure from the population for a part in political decision-making: participation, and (4) pressure to utilize the legal monopoly of force to redistribute scarce values. To each of these demands all or any of the capability levels may respond by, for example, increasing the amount of regulation, redistributing desired values, increasing the output of symbolic rewards, increasing the structural capabilities of interest aggregation or socialization techniques, and so on.[35]

Functions are met by or through structures, but it is not claimed that *only* particular structures may perform each function or that one structure may not meet more than one function. For example, interest articulation may be performed through political parties devoted mainly to this or through riots, kin groups and religious organizations which are concerned only intermittently with articulating political interests. Again, although in developed societies a degree of structural specialization may be expected, for example, assemblies make rules but courts apply them, we very frequently observe bureaucracies making rules and applying them, and courts (for example, the US Supreme Court) make what are in effect rules. In less-developed societies the political system itself may be intermittent and political roles bunched together with religious and judicial roles played by the same person possibly at the same time. The point is that functional prerequisites *must* be met and, therefore, if one looks closely enough at a system one *must* discover the structures through which the functions *are* met.

As in the system approach, structural functional analysis is apt to relegate force to a minor position in the social order, stressing much more the process of inducting people into the political culture(s) of the system; this process is called political socialization. Political culture is in people's heads and is defined as 'the patterns of individual attitudes and orientations towards politics among members of a political system'.[*29*] The culture is thought of as important 'in regulating the performance of the political system'.[36] Further, the concept of political culture, which appears to be derived from all the functional imperatives mentioned above (but mainly pattern maintenance and tension management), links individuals to the larger system *via* groups and institutions by connecting 'individual tendencies to system characteristics'.[37] Political culture, like the other concepts employed in functional analysis, can be divided into various subcategories: parochial cultures are characterized by little sense of the national system, subject cultures contain nationally orientated individuals without interest in participating in politics, participant cultures contain people interested in politics.[38] Again, we divide the categories further by asking why participants or subjects are like they are: is it because of a sense of incompetence, or because of a sense of alienation, and so on. The difficulty of this process of almost constant subdivision is that there appears to be no limit at all on the proliferation of categories for research and analysis. One begins to have faint visions of sociological angels dancing on the head of a pin!

Difficulties of the functionalist mode of analysis are legion and need not delay us here since we are only concerned with the structural functional position as we have outlined it.[*30*] Firstly, although its protagonists insist on calling structural functionalism a theory, it is not a theory in any strict sense of the word since its major term is an extremely slippery one. The difficulty is that if one can slip from meaning A to meaning A1 anything goes! Also we have no idea what constitutes the maintenance of the system other than its physical survival and we are given no idea of the relative importance in system maintenance (meeting the functional prerequisites) of various elements of the system and can only assume they all are equally necessary. Again, we are given no idea of what would constitute a definitive list of functions to be performed by the political system.[*31*] Since we have no definition of basic terms, no weighting of the functional importance of different elements in the system and no definitive list of functions, the theory as a theory is in somewhat bad shape.

Whatever its intellectual shortcomings, functionalism does provide a large set of categories of considerable scope for comparative analysis and represents an advance on any of the older typologies based upon contiguous geographical areas, upon institutions like one-, two- or multiparty systems or upon institutional similarities like bureaucracies and legislative assemblies.[39] Not only is it comparative but it does embrace a far wider range of societal types and, although rather dimly, it does incorporate a concept of political development sequences and strains of considerable value in the study of political modernization.[40] Finally, like systems analysis, structural functionalism is a wide-ranging analysis which does knit together insights drawn from interest, socialization and group analysis into a relatively coherent body of ideas.

3.7. Concluding Remarks

This has been a laborious and somewhat tedious chapter, but we would claim that it is beyond the wit of man to condense and abstract a number of arid theories and still leave them interesting. Nevertheless, the student beginning in the field of political sociology does need at least a passing familiarity with many of the 'theories' and nomenclatures discussed above since a good deal of the empirical work he will examine makes use of them. Essentially, what we have tried to do is to present a fairly comprehensive picture of the ways in which the individual is envisaged as linked to his society. It will be realized that the conceptualizations of the linkages we have presented are by no means exhaustive nor is our presentation intended to be complete. For example, we have not mentioned Marx in this chapter nor have we looked at the symbolic interactionist theory associated with Professor Goffman. Our excuse is a simple one: in the latter case very little of direct interest to the *political* sociologist has followed from the original insight and in the former most of what has followed is discussed at other points in this volume. *En passant*, we must also convict ourselves of totally neglecting the great political novels which always develop as a central theme precisely the problems we have looked at, ie the fate of man as an individual and the fate of his society.

The linkages discussed in this chapter are at the level of individual to individual and of individual to group and we have seen that they broadly fall into consensual theories and calculative theories; in the former case the concept of political culture was argued to be important. We have used linkages to mean relationships without specifying clearly the conceptual level at which these linkages operate. In political sociology the units in which we may be interested can be seen as belonging to a number of different levels of analysis. For example, we can study the properties of individuals, their attitudes, personalities, wishes and so on, or we can study them as members of groups or collectivities. Alternatively, we can study the formal structure of such things as political parties, bureaucracies, armies, etc., and the relationships between these organizations. Where we have to be careful is in making attributions drawn or investigated from one level to another. Thus, we frequently refer to unstable political *systems* and *collectivities* and this may well conjure up a picture of neurotic and unstable *individuals* composing the collectivity, but this would be an inadmissible inference to make. Because the system is unstable it does not mean that the constituent individuals are necessarily unstable. Another example is that if one characterizes a system as democratic this should not be taken to mean that it is composed of democratically minded individuals. Similarly, the reverse inference is equally inadmissible: all police spies may be efficient at their job but this fact alone does not mean that the police department is efficient at preventing crime. What all this implies is that one's research data should be gathered and one's analysis pitched at a level appropriate to the problem.[41]

References

1. E. Nagel, *The Structure of Science*, Routledge and Kegan Paul, London, 1961; R. B. Braithwaite, *Scientific Explanation*, Harper, New York, 1960.
2. R. K. Merton, *Social Theory and Social Structure*, rev. ed., Free Press, Glencoe, 1957, pp. 39–72.
3. E. K. Wilson, *Sociology: Rules, Roles and Relationships*, Dorsey Press, Illinois, 1966, p. 51.
4. L. W. Pye, 'Political Culture and Political Development' in L. W. Pye and S. Verba, *Political Culture and Political Development*, Princeton University Press, Princeton, 1965, p. 7.

5. E. A. Shils and M. Janowitz, 'Cohesion and Disintegration in the Wehrmacht in World War II', *Public Opinion Quarterly*. **12**, 280–313 (1948).
6. S. Asch, 'Opinions and Social Pressure', G. Harding (ed.), *Science Conflict and Society*, W. H. Freeman, San Francisco, 1969, pp. 52–57.
7. S. Greer and P. Orleans, 'The Mass Society and the Parapolitical Structure', *American Sociological Review*, **27**, 634–646 (1962).
8. B. Berelson and G. A. Steiner, *Human Behaviour: An Inventory of Scientific Findings*, Harcourt Brace and World, New York, 1964, p. 567. See also S. Verba, 'Organisational Membership and Democratic Consensus', *The Journal of Politics*, **27**, 467–497 (1965).
9. W. Buckley, *Modern Systems Analysis*, Prentice-Hall, New Jersey, 1967, p. 100.
10. George Homans, *Social Behaviour: Its Elementary Forms*, Harcourt Brace and World, New York, 1961, p. 54.
11. —— *Social Behaviour: Its Elementary Forms*, Harcourt Brace and World, New York, 1961, p. 46.
12. —— *Social Behaviour: Its Elementary Forms*, Harcourt Brace and World, New York, 1961, ch. 14.
13. —— *Social Behaviour: Its Elementary Forms*, Harcourt Brace and World, New York, 1961, p. 380.
14. —— *Social Behaviour, Its Elementary Forms*, Harcourt Brace and World, New York, 1961, p. 379.
15. 'Contemporary Theory in Sociology' in R. E. L. Faris, *Handbook of Modern Sociology*, Rand McNally, Chicago, 1964, p. 969.
16. R. L. Curry and L. L. Wade, *A Theory of Political Exchange*, Prentice-Hall, Englewood Cliffs, 1968, p. 3.
17. —— —— *A Theory of Political Exchange*, Prentice-Hall, Englewood Cliffs, 1968, pp. 31–96.
18. P. Blau, *Exchange and Power in Social Life*, Wiley, New York, 1964, p. 208.
19. A. Rapoport, 'The Use and Misuse of Game Theory' in G. Harding (ed.), *Science Conflict and Society*, W. H. Freeman, San Francisco, 1969, pp. 286–294.
20. W. H. Riker, *The Theory of Political Coalitions*, Yale University Press, New Haven, 1962, p. 23.
21. —— *The Theory of Political Coalitions*, Yale University Press, New Haven, 1962, p. 32.
22. B. M. Barry, *Sociologists, Economists and Democracy*, Collier-Macmillan, London, 1970, p. 14.
23. W. Buckley, *Modern Systems Analysis*, Prentice-Hall, New Jersey, 1967, p. 122.
24. D. Easton, *A Systems Analysis of Political Life*, Wiley, New York, 1965, pp. 22–24.
25. —— *A Systems Analysis of Political Life*, Wiley, New York, 1965, p. 176.
26. —— *A Systems Analysis of Political Life*, Wiley, New York, 1965, p. 191.
27. —— *A Systems Analysis of Political Life*, Wiley, New York, 1965, p. 25.
28. —— *A Systems Analysis of Political Life*, Wiley, New York, 1965, p. 30.
29. D. Easton and J. Dennis, *Children in the Political System*, McGraw-Hill, New York, 1969, p. 49.

30. D. Easton, *A Systems Analysis of Political Life*, Wiley, New York, 1965, p. 475.
31. N. J. Smelser, *The Sociology of Economic Life*, Prentice-Hall, New Jersey, 1963, ch. 3.
32. R. K. Merton, *Social Theory and Social Structure*, Free Press, Glencoe, 1968, ch. 3, pp. 73–133.
33. G. Almond and G. Bingham Powell, *Comparative Politics*, Little, Brown, Boston, 1966, pp. 28–29.
34. G. Almond and J. S. Coleman, *The Politics of the Developing Areas*, Princeton University Press, Princeton, 1960, p. 7.
35. G. Almond and G. Bingham Powell, *Comparative Politics*, Little, Brown, Boston, 1966, pp. 34–41.
36. —— —— *Comparative Politics*, Little, Brown, Boston, 1966, p. 51.
37. —— —— *Comparative Politics*, Little, Brown, Boston, 1966, p. 52.
38. G. Almond and S. Verba, *The Civic Culture*, Little, Brown, Boston, 1965, pp. 17–21.
39. R. C. Macridis and B. E. Brown (eds.), *Comparative Politics*, Dorsey Press, Illinois, 1968, pp. 34–102.
40. R. E. Jones, *The Functional Analysis of Politics*, Humanities Press, New York, 1967, pp. 76–96.
41. H. Eulau, *Micro-Macro Political Analysis*, Aldine, Chicago, 1969, pp. 1–19; J. Galtung, *Theory and Methods of Social Research*, Allen and Unwin, London, 1967, pp. 36–48.

Notes and Further Reading

1. Ranke, the great German historian, set out 'to stick to the facts' and 'to show how things actually were' but his German patriotism deeply influenced his conclusions. G. P. Gooch, *History and Historians in the Nineteenth Century*, Longmans, London, 1952, p. 74.
2. R. K. Merton, *Social Theory and Social Structure*, rev. ed., Free Press, Glencoe, 1957, ch. 4, for an extended discussion of this point.
3. See R. E. Dowse, 'A Functionalist's Logic', *World Politics*, **18**, no. 4, 607–622 (1966), which looks at functionalism from this perspective. For a recent exercise in using mathematical rigour in sociological theory, see J. S. Coleman, *Introduction to Mathematical Sociology*, Free Press, Glencoe, 1964.
4. For an excellent example, if slightly odd, see M. F. Weinberg, 'Sexual Modesty, Social Meanings and the Nudist Camp', *Social Problems*, **12**, 311–318 (1965).
5. See P. L. Berger, *Invitation to Sociology*, Penguin London, 1966, ch. 5, for a splendid introduction to role theory.
6. See W. Buckley, *Modern Systems Analysis*, Prentice-Hall, New Jersey, 1967, ch. 5, for a thorough discussion of the process of individual and group interaction.
7. For an excellent review of groups see S. Verba, *Small Groups and Political Behaviour*, Princeton University Press, New Jersey, 1961.
8. These terms were first used by C. H. Cooley. See C. H. Cooley, *Social Organization*, Charles Scribner's Sons, New York, 1937, pp. 23–28.

9. The sort of distinction that Tönnies ('Gemeinschaft' and 'Gesellschaft'), Maine ('status' and 'contract'), Durkheim ('mechanic' and 'organic' solidarity) and Redfield ('folk' and 'urban') had in mind. For a discussion of these concepts, see E. A. Shils, 'Primordial, Personal, Sacred and Civil Ties', *British Journal of Sociology*, **8,** No. 2, 130–145 (1957).
10. Anticipatory socialization has also been investigated, where the aspirant, even before becoming a full member of the group, adopts its public norms and ideas. See L. Hudson, *Frames of Mind*, Penguin, London, 1970, esp. chs. 4, 5 and 6, for a fascinating account of this process amongst young children.
11. The classic work on group norms in the work situation is F. J. Roethlisberger and W. J. Dickson, *Management and the Worker*, Harvard University Press, Cambridge, Mass., 1939, which reports on the famous Hawthorne experiment.
12. However, it would be wrong to assume that such cross-cutting affiliations are confined to the Atlantic states: '*Seka* (group) organisation, whether religious, political, agricultural, kinship, or voluntarily based, is the heart of Balinese social structure, which can, in fact, be seen as a set of cross-cutting *seka* of various types loosely adjusted to one another'. C. Geertz, *Peddlers and Princes*, University of Chicago Press, Chicago, 1963, p. 99. See also R. Dahrendorf, *Class and Class Conflict in Industrial Society*, Routledge and Kegan Paul, London, 1959, pp. 213–240, who discusses the 'superimposing' of cleavages such as occupation, wealth, religion, etc., as leading to intensification of class violence.
13. The classical statement of this view is contained in D. Truman, *The Governmental Process*, Knopf, New York, 1951, which argues that in the US the government is restrained and interest groups are restrained by overlapping group memberships and by the danger of activating the apathetic (potential groups) if their interests are violated.
14. Homans is a good example of a psychological reductionist: all social facts are reducible to statements about individual psychology, see Homans, 'Contemporary Theory in Sociology' in R. E. L. Faris, *Handbook of Modern Sociology*, Rand McNally, Chicago, 1964, p. 969.
15. P. Blau, *Exchange and Power in Social Life*, Wiley, New York, 1964, p. 212. Our italics.
16. C. Geertz, *Peddlers and Princes*, University of Chicago Press, Chicago, 1963, p. 106. See also J. A. Schumpeter, *Capitalism, Socialism and Democracy*, Allen and Unwin, London, 1943, p. 12, 'Social structures, types and attitudes are coins that do not readily melt. Once they are formed they persist'.
17. There is a difficulty here: politicans presumably *never* have all the facts and therefore *always* must form bigger coalitions than strictly necessary. However, since they never have all the facts we can never test empirically how they would behave if they had all of them.
18. W. H. Riker, *The Theory of Political Coalitions*, Yale University Press, New Haven, 1962, pp. 88–89; on the concept of information see A. Downs, *An Economic Theory of Democracy*, Harper and Row, New York, 1957, chs. 5, 6, 7, and K. W. Deutsch, *The Nerves of Government*, Free Press, Glencoe, 1966, part 2.
19. For an extensive analysis of this point see T. C. Schelling, *The Strategy of*

Conflict, Harvard University Press, Cambridge, Mass., 1960, who uses, however, the idea of mutual *expectations.*

20. For detailed discussion consult W. Buckley, *Modern Systems Analysis*, Prentice-Hall, New Jersey, 1967; J. C. Charlesworth (ed.), *Contemporary Political Analysis*, Free Press, New York, 1967, chs. 8 and 9; O. R. Young, *Systems of Political Science*, Prentice-Hall, Englewood Cliffs, 1968, chs. 2 and 3; W. J. M. MacKenzie, *Politics and Social Science*, Penguin, Middlesex, 1967, pp. 96–110.
21. Loss of support occurs for many reasons, but 'a large part of them may be summed up under one category: output failure'. D. Easton, *A Systems Analysis of Political Life*, Wiley, New York, 1965, p. 230
22. D. Easton, *A Systems Analysis of Political Life*, Wiley, New York, 1965, p. 228; this remark may be unfair since, in a sense, revolution is simply a larger than usual change.
23. Actually, Easton eventually assigns the problem of critical ranges to 'limbo', D. Easton, *A Systems Analysis of Political Life*, Wiley, New York, 1965, p. 223.
24. C. Geertz, *Peddlers and Princes*, University of Chicago Press, Chicago, 1963, pp. 127–128. Our italics.
25. Easton is certainly aware of this. D. Easton, *A Systems Analysis of Political Life*, Wiley, New York, 1965, p. 480.
26. B. Berelson, P. Lazarsfeld and W. McPhee, *Voting*, University of Chicago Press, Chicago, 1954, pp. 322 and 316. This is a contemporary version of Mandeville's private vices and public virtues.
27. This was the approach of B. Malinowski in anthropology who started with individual needs, but the analysis can well start with social structure and the ways in which it is maintained as did Radcliffe-Brown; see P. Cohen, *Modern Social Theory*, Heinemann, London, 1968, pp. 37–45.
28. See T. Parsons and E. Shils (eds.), *Toward a General Theory of Action*, Harvard University Press, Cambridge, Mass., 1951, pp. 172–183. Political scientists using these variables include W. C. Mitchell, 'Occupational Role Strains: The American Elective Public Official', *Administrative Science Quarterly*, **3** (Sept. 1958); D. Apter, 'The Role of Traditionalism in the Political Modernization of Ghana and Uganda', in D. Apter, *Some Conceptual Approaches to the Study of Modernization*, Prentice-Hall, Englewood Cliffs, 1968.
29. G. Almond and G. Bingham Powell, *Comparative Politics*, Little, Brown, Boston, 1966, p. 50. Using a schema adopted from Parsons they see individual attitudes to political culture as divisible into a *cognitive* element which is knowledge about politics, an *affective* element of emotional attachment or rejection towards political events and an *evaluative* element which involves judgement of political events in terms of values.
30. For logical critiques of the functionalist position see C. G. Hempel, 'The Logic of Functional Analysis', in L. Gross (ed.), *Symposium on Sociological Theory*, Harper, New York, 1959; R. S. Rudner, *Philosophy of Social Science*, Prentice-Hall, Englewood Cliffs, 1966, ch. 5; and F. Cancian, 'Functional Analysis of Change', *American Sociological Review*, **24**, 818–827 (1960). Sociological critiques can be found in J. Rex, *Key Problems of Sociological Theory*, Routledge and Kegan Paul, London, 1961, ch. 4, and

D. Martindale, *The Nature and Types of Sociological Theory*, Routledge and Kegan Paul, London, 1961, pp. 441–522. A specifically political science orientated criticism is contained in W. Flanigan and E. Fogelman, 'Functional Analysis' in J. C. Charlesworth (ed.), *Contemporary Political Analysis*, Free Press, New York, 1967, ch. 4.

31. Compare the lists in G. Almond and J. S. Coleman, *The Politics of the Developing Areas*, Princeton University Press, Princeton, 1960, p. 17, with G. Almond and J. Bingham Powell, *Comparative Politics*, Little, Brown, Boston, 1966, pp. 27–30, and both with W. C. Mitchell, *The American Polity*, Free Press, New York, 1962, esp. chs. 13–14.

4

THE DEVELOPMENT OF STRUCTURES OF POLITICAL POWER IN PRE-INDUSTRIAL SOCIETIES

4.1. Compliance

A GREAT DEAL of the social behaviour in which people engage is the result of habit, or is at least generally unthinkingly activitated. Other kinds of actions are the result of a careful calculation of alternatives, while yet others are the result of people being commanded to do something. All these general types occur frequently throughout social life. The class of actions in which we are at the moment especially interested, however, are those which are the result of commands, orders or directives.

It is a matter of common observation that in any social system some people give orders and some obey. In this chapter we shall be concerned with an analysis of this fact in pre-industrial societies. The ability to elicit obedience we shall call by a generic term, power. Obedience and compliance are caused by power. Power may be thought of as stemming from three broad sources, physical, material and symbolic.

Physical or coercive power rests on the application or threat of physical sanction, for example forceable removal of sources of satisfaction whether material or psychological. Material or remunerative power is based on control over resources such as salaries, services, advice and commodities which may be distributed as rewards for compliance. Symbolic or normative power rests on the withholding or allocation of socially desired and scarce rewards in the form of prestige and esteem such as medals, civic receptions, invitations to dine with the celebrated, and so on.[1] The mix in any given situation will vary greatly from individual to individual, group to group, organization to organization and time to time but it is always there. The exercise of power to obtain compliance consists in the use of one or more of these elements.

Power may be exercised in a formal institutional setting when the major sanctions for non-compliance are derived from formal roles or, in a non-formal setting, when non-compliance does not involve institutionalized sanctions. For example, if one of the authors of this book wished to work on it on a Sunday and the other refused to do so a whole range of sanctions might be applied—withholding advice, emotional blackmail, spreading malicious rumours, etc.—and the co-author might well change his mind rather than face this orchestrated exercise in personal influence. Institutionalized formal role power is much less dependent on the personalities involved and more an attribute of the office. Thus had the same request to work on a Sunday been made by a factory foreman the available repertoire would have been the same, but the whole question of salary, promotions, etc., might well have been foremost with the possibility of dismissal somewhere in the background. The mix of compliance-inducing techniques is different but the fact or regularity of compliance may well be the same; power is always present in society and serves to ensure social patterning.

In political systems some people develop, or are seen as having developed, the right to issue orders which they generally expect to be obeyed. Max Weber groups such expectations into three types of authority defined by the basis on which the legitimacy of the order or command derives. He distinguishes between rational-legal authority, traditional authority and charismatic authority, all of which are seen to legitimate commands or directives. Legitimacy refers to the feeling that people have towards those issuing orders, and people's understanding or willingness to obey (or disobey) depends upon the legitimacy of the authority from which the orders come.[*1*] All governments, Weber argued, attempt to legitimate their authority in the eyes of the governed and, therefore, legitimacy is an idea in somebody's head about the right to give an order. Traditional authority depends upon acceptance of the 'sanctity of immemorial traditions' and is the 'most universal and primitive' of the authority types. It is present in nearly all societies and is often utilized, it is argued, in modernizing countries to throw an air of prescriptive right over new institutions. Examples of this process are Dr. Nkrumah's adoption of Ashanti traditional titles when he was President of Ghana and Mr. Nyerere's formulation of socialism in terms of 'traditional' African values. Traditional authority is also present in most developed societies, for example the British monarchy.[*2*] In the case of rational-legal authority, obedience is given to the 'impersonal order' of norms and regulations which define the status of the person issuing the command. The prototype of this authority is the bureaucracy, *the* organization exemplifying Weber's idea of rationality.

Both the rational-legal and the traditional forms of authority are relatively permanent structures providing for everyday needs of the community, but in cases of new or extraordinary situations (such as crisis or strain) a new form of authority (charismatic) may emerge, one based upon the personal characteristics of an individual by virtue of which he is set apart from ordinary men and treated as one endowed with supernatural, superhuman or at least exceptional powers or qualities.[*3*] The leader's qualities and pronouncements are seen as solutions to the crisis. Associated with this authority type is the collective enthusiasm through which masses of people surrender their individual judgements to the leader. In other words, obedience to a charismatic leader involves a degree of personal commitment by the followers to the person of the leader which has no parallel in the other forms of authority. Being born of crisis, the dilemma of the charismatic leader is opposite to that of the other forms of authority. Rational-legal and traditional authority face the problem that they are weak in crisis situations, but since charismatic authority depends upon personal qualities in a crisis, if the crisis passes so may the enthusiasm for the leader. Additionally, the leader may pass away, yet the crisis remains.

Charismatic authority, if it is to persist, must be somehow transformed or at least reinforced by one or other of the alternative authority types. The leader, that is to say, needs some form of permanent institutional support for himself, and eventually, for his message. This process can be observed when religious sects based upon the teachings of one man, Christ, Mohammed, Harris, are transformed into more formal organizations called churches, or when leader-based political parties become bureaucratized.[*4*] There are many difficulties in this conception of charismatic leadership, not the least of which is the extraordinary variety of leaders to whom the quality has been attributed: Hitler, Nehru, Gandhi, Nkrumah, Lenin, Roosevelt, Mussolini, Sekou Toure, Sukarno, the Honourable Elijah Mohammed, Mahomet, Winston Churchill and De Gaulle, to mention only a few of the more prominent.[2] The developing areas, since they are almost permanently in crisis, have provided a rich source of examples of charismatic leadership. Indeed, it is difficult to call to mind *any* leader in a developing country who has not been called charismatic by an academic commentator. A concept as wide in its scope as this lacks analytical utility. Again, the stress on what have been called charismatic figures assumes far too much dependency to the followers who may well not be attracted by any personal qualities but by what the leader promises, by his programme, and it may well be the case that with a different programme the so-called charismatic leader might have remained an obscure failure. Charisma is a contextual attribution, the context being that of novel problems, and the attribution is made not simply by the leader but also by followers. Hence the phenomenon arises when novel situations occur for which the old structures or ideologies appear unsuitable and, therefore, charisma can be found in even the most rationalized of contemporary societies.[3] Whether very much is gained by calling leaders who emerge in such situations charismatic is problematical, but certainly the situation in which leaders emerge is important.[4]

Looked at in terms of Etzioni's tripartite typology, charismatic authority can best be understood as a form of nomative power resting ultimately upon 'the ability of an actor to exercise diffuse and intense influence over the normative orientations of other actors'.[5] Here the effect of leadership may be to change the orientation or value system of the led, whilst in the other forms of compliance this may well not be the case when people obey but do not change their own criteria for decision and action.[6] In both types of compliance the end product is obedience, but in the charismatic one there is thought to be an element of attitudinal change and, perhaps, personal dependence.

Up to now we have examined some of the ways in which one may analyse the concept of compliance, but there is another analytical dimension to the problem and that is access to power. This is significant because we wish to know what are the mechanisms through which people obtain access to power and also we need to know whether compliance is differentially or randomly distributed throughout societies. Closely associated with the problem of access to power is the type of social situation that may impel people to seek power.

4.2. The Development of Structures of Power

A very general starting proposition is that the widest social, geographical and human context within which people are set determines in some measure the structural mechanisms through which political power can be exercised, the degree of concentration or dispersion of power and the relative availability of access to positions of power. In the modern world the most significant and pervasive political structure is the nation-state, and it is historically a relatively recent arrival. It is significant in the sense that there are few geographical areas not incorporated into a state and pervasive in the sense that in the more developed areas there are few activities into which the state structure does not at some point impinge. Its actions are, *in the final analysis*, authoritative because it usually has a monopoly of force, or at least sufficient force to ensure that all but the most highly organized recalcitrants may be coerced into compliance or removed. Since the state has a legal monopoly, and frequently an actual monopoly, of force (armed forces, police, etc.) it follows that to control the state is to be in a strong position to ensure compliance with one's wishes, plans or aspirations. This centralization of force in the state is historically a novelty and ethnographically a political novelty in the sense that most societies have not been so organized, since coercive power appears in many primitive societies to have been dispersed or, indeed, not to be present.

It is convenient to use a distinction between those societies with a more or less differentiated governmental system and those without. The differentiated case will include a more or less centralized government, the government having sovereignty over a number of constituent units such as towns, villages and ethnic groups. In the second type, the so-called stateless or acephalous societies, there is a sense of common identity but no differentiated political authority that can be considered as the government of the entire society.

Acephalous Societies

There are a number of economic and geographical features characterizing the acephalous society. Typically, they subsist by foraging, hunting and gathering, are rarely settled in one place for as much as a year, their average size is small, their population density is low and their political organization reflects this way of life. Thus in a survey of American Indians, P. H. Lowrie writes that 'though the Plains Indians indubitably developed coercive agencies, the dispersal of authority and the seasonal disintegration of tribes precluded a permanent state of modern type'.[7] This brings us to another feature of the stateless political system, that of extremely rudimentary role differentiation. Since the societies are so poor, they lack the ability to sustain economically specialist role occupants, ie within the basic sex division all adults are expected to play a very wide range of roles.[5] An exception to this rather general point is in the emergence of leadership roles which may be *ad hoc* and transient, moving from situation to situation, ie one person may lead a hunt, another may determine the time for foraging, and yet another may act as a war leader. On the other hand, the leadership role even in stateless societies may be more temporally secure but this begins to cross over into the other categories.

Leadership in 'acephalous' societies is usually a consequence of the personal qualities of the leader as recognized by his followers, although there may be lineage restrictions on the choice of leader. The leader is not really the focus around which the acephalous society forms but appears 'as the cause of the group's willingness to aggregate rather than as the result of the need for a central authority felt by a group already constituted'.[8] Hence, the leader does not possess a formidable apparatus of coercion but must rely upon a combination of skill, luck and persuasion. Failure may well result in his replacement by another. Further, the evidence suggests that the material rewards of leadership are very slight and, indeed, may actually be economically negative; what the leader obtains in *exchange* is prestige and opportunity of displaying his gifts. Leaders appear, despite the poor material rewards, because, as Levi Strauss puts it, 'there are in any human group, men who, unlike most of their companions, enjoy prestige for its own sake, feel a strong appeal to responsibility, and to whom the burden of public affairs brings its own reward'.[*6*] In exercising leadership the chief must employ the skills of debate, persuasion, knowledge, etc., but very rarely has he any apparatus of coercion: 'the most typical American chief is not a lawgiver, executive, or judge, but a pacifier, a benefactor of the poor, and a prolix Polonius'.[9] His task of leading, is, however, made easier by two factors. Firstly, there is not a great deal of competition for the role. Secondly, there is a strong body of normative constraints to which a chief may appeal in cases where his authority, such as it is, is disputed. But it would appear to be the case that normative constraints operate in such a manner as to make a regular judicial or executive authority otiose in the sense that the consequences of not falling in with the 'general will' or 'common good' can be disastrous and are known to be so: 'if members of a band were to quarrel the most probable cause would be disagreement about when to go to this or that veld Kos (wild food such as roots, berries, etc.) area. Bitter resentment would arise and it could be a matter of life and death if some members of a band were to take advantage and consume veld Kos in excess of their share and unknown to the others who were counting on it. The people fully realise this and, in their wisdom about self-preservation and dread of fighting, they do conform to the headman's authority.'[*7*]

But the process is double-sided. Just as the members of the band are constrained by an embedded system of political norms so a leader is also constrained. He may also be restrained by the consideration that at any time band members may withdraw support from him or if he proves a real nuisance they may withdraw physically from him.[*8*] And since political authority, religious ritual kinship, education and economics are so tightly fused in such societies the chief is able to use them as control devices, but equally he is controlled and limited by the fused authority.

Another example of a society lacking a differentiated political system is that of the Alaskan Eskimo who have neither chiefs, nor an advisory council, nor regular deliberative assemblies, nor, indeed, permanent political stratification of any kind. As with the other acephalous groups we have mentioned, leadership tends to be task-specific. In, for example, whale-hunting the boat owner has dominance over the crew and primary 'rights' to the catch, but it would be imprudent to exercise this 'right' in such a manner as to alienate the crew since a boat is useless without a crew and, anyway, he may later need to share somebody else's catch. Thus he shares the catch according to mutual obligations specified by custom. Access to resources appears to be equal and undifferentiated, with an almost universal pattern of sharing catches and finds with other members of the band. The norm of sharing is not often violated, being underpinned by a system which allocates considerable prestige to generosity and by a more prudential consideration: generosity cements relationships and, since facilities for preserving food are lacking, it is better stored in a friend's stomach than wasted.

In most acephalous societies where for some reason a dispute over, for example, food or property breaks out, the whole network of mutual obligation may be brought to bear on the dispute. The disputants will, step by step, involve in the matter those with lineage or other obligations until a rough balance of power between disputants is arrived at and enough pressure for agreement from those more and more marginally concerned has been generated.[9] The point is, however, that chiefs amongst such people are not adjudicators or law-givers, but simply those to whom voluntary obedience is rendered since in a specific situation—fighting, hunting, travelling, religion—a specific person or persons prove to be abler than their fellows to solve the problems presented by an inhospitable environment. In this situation of voluntary authority, lineage and custom are normally far more important 'agencies' of social control than are the individuals to whom a little brief authority may be entrusted.

Segmentary Societies

Within the acephalous band it is not really possible to talk of inequality in the distribution of power since the maintaining of band cohesion is more a matter of value consensus inside a group lacking much interest differentiation. Again, the pressing problem of physical survival and the absence of a significant margin between survival and non-survival in an inhospitable environment militates against a leadership emerging with radically new and untried ideas. The band is so finely adjusted to the environment that the introduction of novel procedures by a leader is almost an impossibility: the leadership role is not a creative one as it may be in richer societies.

The societies we have mentioned are all very small ones, rarely attaining group memberships of above one hundred, and on the whole relationships between groups existing in geographical propinquity are wary and relatively infrequent, but we do have examples of areas with greater population densities and consequently greater potential group interaction. The change in societal scale generates organizational problems rarely found within the small band, such as 'foreign' relations, and because of the larger size the almost anarchic informality of the whole band is unsuitable for decision-making. Instead, a somewhat more complex set of institutional arrangements emerge reaching beyond the band into which one is born. Consequently, the political aspect of societal arrangements becomes slightly more differentiated and a good deal more spatially and societally extended; relationships which in the band hardly extended beyond it may, in the societies to which we allude, ramify *via* a lineage, a secret society, an age set or other institutions meeting a specific need (for example religious, economic, hunting, policing) over a wide social and geographical area.[*10*] These societies are generally segmental and within them the social and political relations rest upon a widely ramifying system of genealogical relations. Their manner of life is settled and agricultural rather than foraging and gathering, which means that people develop more permanent interests in land and herds, which in turn implies the possibility of interests extending beyond the life span of the individual. In its turn this factor can easily lead to economic inequality and its possible consequent social tensions and to the possibility of the rich man obtaining political power. Clearly, the possibility of 'economic' warfare between advantaged and disadvantaged segmentary groups is also increased by permanent settlement.[10]

The major factor, however, is that a settled agricultural life makes possible the production of a surplus which can be employed to develop a somewhat more specialized political command structure than is possible with foraging. Alongside the development of a more specialized political group there develops a system of symbols and ideology justifying the elite group often in religious or semi-religious terms. This group may or may not control access to the land but it is most likely to do so in the case of conquest. Additionally, the group may well undertake coordination of social tasks previously either neglected or left to voluntary associations. Amongst such tasks can be counted the building of pyramids and hydraulic works and public defence; in the segmentary state, which we discuss later, the political group coordinates defence and aggression, tasks previously left to local initiatives. Given that the political group has thrust upon it or seizes upon a number of large social projects, the problem of controlling people and resources requires new organizational forms, the most obvious of which is the bureaucracy.

An example of a segmented lineage system with age sets (of three years) with a relatively high degree of social and economic differentiation is the Tiv of Middle Nigeria. The people live in smallish compounds with a head who 'has definite authority over its members and he can expel any of them for continuous trouble-making or insubordination'.[11] Influence appears to be built upon one or other combination of age and general abilities (knowledge of magic and custom) or of wealth and general astuteness in using the wealth to reward people for a variety of services. The wealthy may be restrained by the elders from exercising too much political influence since influence is seen as a product of witchcraft and as such amenable to the public authority of the elders, an authority backed by opinion and custom. The complainant against the men of influence may then be awarded reparation, a form of economic redistribution.[*11*] Should the elders for some reason fail to take action or be unsuccessful, the complainants may then turn to the age set of the persons about whom the grievance is felt, which may exercise physical force against them. In cases involving theft the aggrieved may go to the compound head for redress and the compound head may act on his own initiative and intervene in disputes.

Amongst the Tiv there is no clear political leadership apart from attaining old age or influence, and 'a man's influence amounts to leadership only if he acts *for* a segment *against* its equivalent (in war, inquest, etc.)'.[12] In this sense the role of leader is strictly demarcated; he may issue safe conducts, lead in war and represent the segment at peace talks but may not interfere in the affairs of segments to which he is not related nor favour other segments rather than his own. But political leadership is not as precarious as amongst the bands since it is associated with enduring social characteristics such as wealth and age. And in the sense that politics is about the maintenance of peace through various social controls (ritual, lineage, custom, adjudications, etc.), there are no clearly delineated political agencies, but instead the process of political control is embedded in other cultural processes in what Bohannan has described as the 'intricate inter-relation of interests and loyalties through the interconnection of cultural ideology, systems of social grouping, and organisations of institutions and the consequent moral reinforcement of each by the other'. The agencies of political apportionment (allocation of desired values) are, so to speak, always available but are not activated until a political problem arises, when they are temporarily activated and differentiated from other social performances. These devices, more or less differentiated from other social devices, are agencies through which the process called by functionalists 'tension management' is performed.

At this level of organization one can, however, detect aspects of greater functional differentiation mainly amongst institutions concerned with physical constraint, to wit, police power. Thus, amongst the Tiv the market is policed by a body of men drawn from the area upon which the market is held, who are charged with maintaining market peace. Similarly, amongst the Crow Indians a body of police emerged with the regular function of punishing malefactors, a role which ended annually with the cessation of hunting. Like the Tiv market police, the Crow hunt police had authority only within the immediate context, in their case that of the hunt.[13] We can also detect signs of associations which cut across immediate lineage ties and unite people by, for example, age sets in the case of the Tiv and politico-military associations in the case of the Crow Indians. Attachments to these associations are less particularistic than the ties of kin and immediate neighbourhood and thus contribute to a wider sense of community than would lineage itself.[*12*] These associations may be seen as at a stage of political development appropriate to the more complex problems of social control in a society too large and too economically developed to be embraced simply by kinship, but which has yet to develop the more complex and differentiated institutions of what Southall termed the 'segmentary states'.[*13*] Such states have some specialized political institutions like administrative staffs and hereditary rulers combined with politically significant lineages.[14] They are segmentary states and each segmentary level has a chiefly lineage, from which a hereditary and recognizable authority is drawn.

What appears to be happening in this 'developmental sequence' is that more complex differentiated social orders emerge as a consequence of a number of factors, amongst the most important of which appear to be a relatively high population density, trade and trade routes and military challenges.[15] The level of economic development, in the sense of producing a surplus, appears also to be involved since without it the possibility of sustaining economic differentiation and a semi-specialist 'class' of 'politicians' would not be present.

That is, the economy becomes slightly more differentiated than in 'Primitive (or subsistence) economies (which) are so organised that the allocation of labour and land, the organisation of work within productive processes . . . and the disposition of produced goods and specialist services are expressions of underlying kinship obligation, tribal affiliation, and religious and moral duty'.[16] As some economic activity is, so to say, cut loose from the traditional setting which controlled it, other differentiated control devices gradually emerge amongst which one can detect the 'political'. But it is not only political control devices (chiefs, councils, secret societies) which become more specialized and differentiated but also other sectors, and most often the religious, so that religious functions become nearer full-time concerns of a differentiated family than the sporadic concern of anyone. Thus amongst the Indians on the northwest coast of America the shaman came from specialized families and 'There also tended to be collusion in the chiefdom between the secular leader (the chief) and the spiritual leader (the shaman). They usually collaborated in matters of policy'.[*14*]

The emergent problems of controlling and directing the wider range of activities of a large and geographically dispersed population also help to generate government and administrative forms more complex than the particularistic social mechanisms characteristic of the small band.[17] In the segmentary states one can detect quite clearly a number of problems recognizable in the Western state form, for example the problem of controlling the possessors of economic power, the problem of central articulation of peripheral units and the problem of ensuring coordination and control over bureaucracies and armed forces.

The Emergence of State Power in a Segmented System

A good example of such a society is that of the Akan state centred upon Kumasi in Ghana. It is also very useful for our purposes since it well illustrates the possibility of a segmentary lineage system with a number of politically significant lineages incorporating from early on in its political formation stranger lineages with no element of consanguity or myths of common ancestry.[*15*] Thus in a standard volume on the Akan it is explained that Osei Tutu, the virtual founder of the Ashanti Federation in the early eighteenth century, accepted emigrants from other areas into his state. They were settled and allowed to retain their own chiefs but always under the control of an elder from Wenchi, a part of the Ashanti kingdom. Communications from the Wenchihene (hene = chief) to the stranger villages were *via* the appointed elder and not through the elected stranger chief. However, lineage was the most significant political link with other lineage-related villages.[18]

Within the associated villages a number of lineages were juxtaposed, with some lineages being politically more significant than others since the elected head of the significant ones elected an elder who together with other significant lineage elders formed the chief's council. By custom, the chief was bound to act with the consent and upon the advice of the elders who met almost daily to discuss matters of common concern. Meeting the elders from the village, the chief was able to act as a balancing or moderating force on sectional or lineage interests. The chief could reject the elder elected and demand a new election and the chief of the Wenchi area was himself elected exclusively from one lineage, but elected only after an extensive system of consultation with elders and others had been carried out. The 'others' are significant for our purposes. They were composed of commoners who were in some respects *organized* as such rather than as lineage members and who elected a non-hereditary commoners' chief (Nkwakahene) on the basis of bravery and eloquence. The Nkwakahene arbitrated some disputes between commoners and 'on any question of importance he presented the views of the young men (another term for commoners) to the elders'.[19] This mixture of the lineage and the associational or functional appears typical and formed the basis of the Ashanti war organization, where five separate commands based on the functional exigencies of warfare were created but the commands were occupied by lineage heads. Within each command there were a number of companies few of which were lineage-based. But the military formations were gathered together only in the event of war and, therefore, the level of bureaucratization of the armed forces was minimal. Since wars were not fought over extended periods and the armaments were not complex (the Asantehene would provide lead and powder) there was no need for a military bureaucracy. Similarly, each lineage had its senior woman responsible for women in matters concerning marriage and divorce. Again, the process of election was present but particularistic criteria applied to those available for election.[*16*]

The Ashanti Federation was based upon a number of territorial divisions owing allegiance to the Asantehene (Ashanti chief) in Kumasi and each divisional organization was roughly a miniature, but a less differentiated replication, of the central one in Kumasi where division of function was extensive. Just as there were village assemblies so were there divisional assemblies from which decisions could be relayed to lower levels and through which the Asantehene could channel his decisions or rather those of his council. Thus the Wenchihene had well-understood obligations to the Asantehene such as supplying troops equipped to fight wars—he could not fight a war without central permission—he had to attend festivals in Kumasi, could not execute a death sentence without central approval and could (in extreme cases) have his judgements disputed in the Asantehene's court.[*17*] Hence, there was a measure of judicial and foreign policy centralization and specialization within the Ashanti system combined with considerable decentralization of everyday affairs upon the chiefs who were able to act upon interests articulated by the elders and, on occasion, by commoners.

An additional and highly important agency of pan-Ashanti unity was provided by the Golden Stool, which symbolized the spiritual unity of the whole people and which was kept in Kumasi. It was a religious symbol of the origins of the unity of Ashanti and hence to refuse to help the Asantehene in war, etc., was to come up against religious sanctions. Although it was by no means the sole bond between the states of the Ashanti Union—the Asantehene always had considerable armed force at his disposal—the Golden Stool did provide religious sanctions against internecine warfare. There was also a strong element of common Ashanti interest against the tribal controllers of the south through whom they had to act to trade with Europeans and similarly with the northern tribes who needed Ashanti permission to pass as traders through Ashanti territory.

Although the account given here is grossly simplified, it is apparent that the system could meet the disparate political needs of a farming community which straddled the major trade routes between the north and south and which was almost constantly at war with the southern Fanti and their British allies. For trading purposes a centralized system of standard gold weights was adapted throughout Ashanti. Thus we have in Ashanti a segmentary state in a region of higher than average population.[20] Increased population together with the exigencies of trade and warfare generated organizational forms of considerable social and political reach. These included a countrywide system of weights, a centrally articulated military complex, a judicial system with some elements of centralization, a politico-religious symbolism vested in a hierarchy of offices, a distinction in role terms between office and office-holder and a subtle system of institutionalized consultation at most levels of the polity.

Compliance with authority was infused with familial and communal sentiment, what Weber would have called traditional elements. Thus all treaties and relationships were ultimately guaranteed by an oath sworn in the name and imputed presence of an ancestor. In office the chief was not simply a secular authority but also an intermediary between the living and the dead and derived from this relationship very considerable respect as a judicial and political figure. Also, the land was seen as belonging to the ancestors, but the chief was the custodian and responsible for its proper use. Another element in the compliance pattern was that of assent mediated through a wide-reaching system of consultation. Force was certainly used to enforce compliance—witness the activities of that least engaging, but very active of the Asantehene's officials, the executioner. Certainly force was often employed to maintain obedience from the federated states of the union.

Within the Ashanti political system power was certainly more concentrated than in the acephalous society and to an extent was hereditary. Whilst it was not unknown for a non-royal commoner to achieve considerable power, especially after the introduction of cocoa as a cash crop, the tendency was almost certainly to consult as a matter of political prudence and the commoner disobeyed at his peril. Compared with any of the acephalous types public authority was institutionalized and differentiated, but as in them there was little distinction between public and private matters, and as in them political decisions were embedded in, in fact almost a part of, religious and moral decisions.

The system lacked a very clearly defined bureaucracy even in its military component, although there is evidence that from the early nineteenth century the Asantehenes were 'transferring the functions of government to a new class of officials controlled by the King', who undermined the authority of the traditional officers. Gradually there emerged a largely appointed bureaucracy in Kumasi and with it the Asantehene attempted to curb the independence of the chiefs.[21] It is important, however, to note that the political organization of the Ashanti did as a matter of fact become greatly more bureaucratized as a response to challenges first from the British in the late nineteenth century and latterly when regional autonomy was threatened under the independence regime in Ghana.[22]

Political Power in the Bureaucratic Empire

There appears to be a complex relationship between the perception of the need for extensive and constant societal management and more bureaucratic forms of organization, and an intermediate factor is the presence of an extractable surplus with which to sustain the coordinating group. It would appear to be the case that pressing and specific problems such as flood control, defence against alien invasion, governing an enormous area and the erection of major public monuments such as the pyramids of the Aztec, Inca and Egyptian civilizations necessitate large-scale and permanent administrative machinery.[*18*] For our purposes it is not important to answer the problem of *why* large-scale works were perceived as necessary or why rulers wished to control large areas, since we are only concerned with the administrative and political implications of the decision once taken. The bureaucratic and the centralized empire was one of the most widespread political forms, and only Australia of the continents has not experienced it as an indigenous form. Bureaucratic empires normally took a relatively differentiated, autonomous and centralized political form characterized by a clearly delineated bureaucracy headed by a divine ruler. Contact between the ruler and ruled was one between total unequals, the subjects having no political rights or redress beyond the vague possibility of revolt. As a traditional Chinese expression put it, 'Those who do not occupy the seats of authority should not concern themselves with the government'. The bureaucracy in its developed form sprang out of the attempt by the ruler to centralize political power by circumventing other traditional or functional would-be rivals such as the ruling groups of a conquered territory or the military commanders. At the same time, the social tasks set by the ruler necessitated a professional bureaucracy charged with regular tax-gathering, coordination of disparate groups, supply of troops and labour, etc. Needing to assure themselves of safety from potential usurpers, the rulers could adopt a number of strategies such as bureaucratizing, destroying or fusing the traditional ruling class with that of the conquerors, or it could leave the traditional rulers cut off from the emergent bureaucracy. The rulers tried as far as possible to appoint people to administrative positions who were loyal to them, politically unattached to other social groups and qualified to execute bureaucratic tasks.[*19*] Thus in the army, officers would be recruited from lower classes and promoted by merit or recruited from foreigners; civil bureaucrats might be slaves or even eunuchs, but rarely would they come from the traditional aristocratic groups.

Within the bureaucratic empire the officials were full-time both at the centre and at the periphery. Writing of Hawaii, Wittfogel explains that the ruler had a full-time war leader, a chief steward, a treasurer, land experts and a personal standing army. These professionals were not confined to the top echelons but also worked locally 'directing the regime's constructional, organisational and acquisitive operations. They kept count of the population, they supervised agriculture, they directed hydraulic enterprises, they mobilised the corvee, they gathered the tax.'[23] Hawaii was, in terms of the major bureaucratic societies, a very primitive and undeveloped system. Thus in 213 BC the Chinese Emperor Chin Shih Huong-ti employed 700,000 to build a palace, and eight hundred years later 2,000,000 people were employed building a new capital.[24] With a larger population than any of the acephalous bands or segmentary systems the ruler was in a strong position to maintain a bureaucracy which in turn left him with a stronger political control apparatus than any conceivable in the other systems.

The bureaucratic elite, mobilizing most of the adult population, also penetrated the society and affected the everyday life of people to a much greater extent than did the less differentiated ruling groups of the Ashanti segmentary state. Every aspect of the subject's life was potentially controlled and the limit to the control was one of mechanics rather than will. Conscription for labour was universal and for war widespread; the conquering Incas standardized village sizes and reassigned families as they wished, religious practices were enforced, marriage was often obligatory and idleness was punished.[25] In the segmentary societies, most of these practices were completely unknown, but to the extent that people's lives were controlled it was by the pressure of society (customs, etc.) as a whole, rather than by a section of the population.

Loyalty and attachment to the ruler of the system appears to have arisen from two sources. Amongst the bureaucrats the element of self-interest and career prospects, which were at the behest of the ruler, were probably most important. Amongst the masses of the population loyalties were much more diffuse, couched in traditional religious terms and directed towards the ruler as divine.[*20*] However, since the bureaucratic empire is always less culturally and economically homogeneous than the segmentary society, it follows that to an extent the ruler needs either to balance or bargain competing interests, or must employ military force to a greater extent than in more traditional systems. In the absence of political parties the interest aggregation process necessarily had to be conducted through the bureaucracy, yet at the same time the bureaucracy had to be detached from any particular interest. Hence, the process of recruiting slaves, eunuchs and foreigners and investing them with corporate privileges. Similarly, since the system was an exploitative one it follows that strong standing police and armed forces were necessary and these in turn had to be maintained and controlled.

There were a number of dangers for the rulers of a bureaucratic empire, the most important of which was the ever-present one that by displacing the rulers an outsider could easily seize control of the whole state and be unlikely to meet resistance from the bureaucracy and the cowed population. Such a seizure was simply not possible in the Ashanti state, at least by indigenous people, and not worth the while in the less developed band. In a sense the Ashanti system is more participatory in that it involved a much higher proportion of the population in consultation and decision-making than did the bureaucratic empire. Due to these factors, stability at the highest political level in the bureaucratic empire was not great, since the reward of a successful coup was well worth the risk: 'the state was not merely an organisation which defined and enforced the rules in the struggle for power and privilege. It was itself one of the objects of the struggle. In fact, because of the great powers vested in it it, was *the supreme prize* for all who coveted power, privilege, and prestige.'[*21*] An enormous prize, with only a very limited number of really politically significant people standing between the covetous and the coveted! A great deal of the history of such empires—China, Egypt, Inca—is precisely that of seizure of control at the top by ambitious court officials, by aunts, uncles, sons, etc., of the ruler, and by successful generals. Hence, although the difficulty was great and consequences of failure tended to be dramatic there was always somebody willing to take the risk.

Another difficulty of the bureaucratic and centralized society is the ever-present danger of the centre of power moving from the rulers to the bureaucrats since a bureaucracy is not simply a passive instrument to be wielded at will by the ruler, but rather a strategically placed contestant in the struggle for influence and resources. At one level the bureaucracy simply struggles for more of whatever is available for distribution such as pay, land, acclamation and services. Another level of potential conflict occurred around 'the bureaucracies' aspirations to attain autonomy and independence in the political status and economic fields'.[26] The bureaucracy of centralized societies tended to attempt to carve out for itself an area of professional and legal autonomy which was justified on rational-legal criteria rather than the religio-political rationale of the ruler. In response to this process the ruler could set up a personal bureaucracy independent of the state bureaucrats, or could attempt to control recruitment to the bureaucracy, or could dismiss the more important bureaucrats. Always in the long run the bureaucracy was quite indispensable and this was the ultimate source of its power. But the bureaucracy could also seek allies or be 'colonized' by social groups such as the gentry in China, or the landed nobility in Sassanid Persia, or by combinations, as in the case of France in the seventeenth and eighteenth centuries, of aristocrats, professionals, bourgeois and new aristocrats. *Vis-à-vis* the rulers these groups would form a fairly cohesive corporation.

It is evident, then, that in the bureaucratized society there was a much greater degree of social differentiation than in any we have previously examined. Most of the population remained passive and peripheral to the major concerns of the politically mobilized or involved sector, being regarded as simply a source of wealth, agricultural and military manpower. Political conflict centred upon control of the bureaucracy and armed forces together with the tendency of local gentry or nobility to try to develop or retain power independent of the centre and, if possible, to colonize the central bureaucratic apparatus and the military. To control the more differentiated society a bureaucracy, both in the civil and military branches, was a necessity. If this process of control coincided with, for example, the demands of mass irrigation, of semi-permanent warfare or of a resource-expensive state religion (such as Maya, Aztec and Pharoanic), then the scope of bureaucratic involvement in all aspects of society was greatly increased.

In such societies, functional differentiation at the political level was limited by the traditional-cum-religious legitimation of the ruler and the total limitation of the mass of the population to the role of passive spectator and beast of political burden. Since the polity was such a limited one the impact of the armed forces, or rather of the commanding echelon, was almost unlimited and certainly was never confined merely to defence and attack. Unlike the segmented societies we have discussed, the sphere of religious activity, at least in terms of religious functionaries, was differentiated from other activities and there was always the possibility of a man's religious persuasions pushing him one way and his duties as a subject another. With this possibility of a schism between 'church' and 'state' and within religious movements, and because the ruler's legitimacy was often a religious one, acts of a religious nature naturally had a political aspect, and *vice versa*. Therefore the secular ruler had the ever-present problem of controlling a church and this was usually accomplished by establishing a state religion. Since the priesthood was normally the most literate section of the community there was always a tendency to employ its members in a bureaucratic capacity. On the other hand, as a social group the priesthood had a strong interest in retaining or obtaining secular protection for its property, privileges and religious forms which secular bureaucracy had a strong incentive 'to control . . . and to incorporate . . . into the general framework of their administrative activities'.[27]

Thus, in the bureaucratized society with its greater variety of social forms and interests there was a much higher degree of conflict and tension than in the less differentiated society. Instruments of political control, given the fact of very different social, geographical and economic interests, were much more permanent, more differentiated and a great deal more visible. Additionally, the political sphere became the major means of holding together a potentially more volatile and less consensual society: the older attachments of kin, of a lineage-based religion and geographical proximity no longer sufficed to hold the society together and consequently new forms of societal administration developed. None the less, the system was by no means a rational-legal one although there do emerge elements of rational-legal combined with ascriptive and particularistic characteristics. Symptomatic of this was the tendency of the bureaucracy to become hereditary, for recruitment to be limited to certain groups, for promotion in the armed forces to be based on favouritism and for the vast mass of the population to have no organized and independent political role at all.

Compliance in the bureaucratic society was certainly more force-based than in the segmentary society: Wittfogel in a section of great eloquence enumerates the horrors of bureaucratic power (in his case 'hydraulic despotism' based upon control of flood waters and the construction associated with such control) and concludes 'from the standpoint of the commoner, the despotic apparatus remained irrationally formidable even when it employed only the standard methods of terror'.[28] Compared with any of the societies we have discussed, power in the centralized empire was far more unequally distributed in the sense that the ruler was limited simply by prudence in his dealings with the masses. Looked at from a different angle, the inequalities of power were much greater in that the society generated more physical power, and the ability to employ this power in the form of armies and police was institutionalized for the benefit of a miniscule section of the community, the bureaucratic elite. From the ruler's point of view the various elites—bureaucratic, military, territorial and religious—were functionally, but not individually, indispensable; any individual could be disposed of but the apparatus as a whole had to be retained. Non-compliance had to take the form of physical resistance, riot or rebellion because of the absence of permanent and legal channels of representation between ruler and ruled, yet since the various elites were necessary to system maintenance their institutional interests had to be accommodated. It was this feature, plus the ability of the regime to mobilize vast resources, which made it a more recognizably political and modern regime than the segmentary state.

Political Power in Feudalism

The bureaucratic empire had a number of internal difficulties the most important of which was a gradual diminution of societal resources due to the over-reaching demands of the ruler for manpower and other forms of wealth.[*22*] A further problem was the tendency for conflicts to develop between various strata and between centre and periphery. The rulers tended to tax the most available resources and conscript the most available manpower to the point of destroying them as resources, and then move on to the next most available, thus gradually eroding the economic and social basis of the society. One outcome of this destruction was a growth of subsistence agriculture, the falling-off of trade and a general localization of power, together with a decline in the effectiveness of the central bureaucracy which enabled locally based leaders to seize local power or alternatively to be granted this power in exchange for nominal loyalty to the centre.[29] The Western European variant of this process of decentralization was feudalism, a system of government characterized by a very considerable measure of local autonomy centred upon an aristocracy owing various duties (normally military) to the king. Communications between centre and periphery were poor, so that 'Forced constantly to take the gravest steps . . . every local representative of a great potentate tended only too naturally to act for his personal advantage and thus finally to transform himself into an independent ruler'.[30] Constantly at war with one another, the territorial leaders were a threat to the peace and security of the peasant villagers who, if not already reduced to dependence on the local ruler, would be willing to trade their liberty and land for his protection.[31] Although the feudal lord was initially, in principle, a life tenant only of his area, having exchanged an oath of service to the king for his fiefdom, it proved more and more difficult to ensure that the land reverted to the throne, and the military aristocracy normally became a hereditary one. Equally, the servile conditions of the rural masses became hereditary.

The granting of a fief was intended to be a purely personal arrangement between the parties involved, so establishing a system of personal loyalty between a lord and his vassals. Over time the purely personal was gradually transmuted into a hereditary status, mainly at the behest of the powerful, and in this respect the feudal nobility resemble the empire bureaucrats in their attempts to become a hereditary corporate group. Also over time the feudal nobility gradually restricted the right to bear arms to their own class so that bearing weapons became a defining symbol of the nobility; but it was the feudal aristocracy that *vis-à-vis* the peasantry was organized with armed forces and a control of the land.

Unity in the society was developed on the basis of hierarchy with each level owing obligations of a complex variety to the level above, but in general the rationale of authority was war, which 'was for many centuries to be regarded as the normal thread of every leader's career and the *raison d'être* of every position of authority'.[32] Authority in principle was central, but in fact lay locally with the aristocracy since the king or emperor was simply administratively incapable of providing the one service above all that justified feudal relationships, that of protecting his subjects' lives and property.[33] Compliance, as always, in the long run went to those with effective power. Yet even locally effective power meant military power and to a great extent the feudal overlords were not able to influence, or not interested in influencing, the everyday life of their subjects beyond enrolling them for military duty and farming their estates. Justice and the law were often decentralized in the form of feud and custom, with the local lord hardly affected by judicial dispositions amongst the ordinary tenantry. In most cases the lord simply lacked the bureaucratic apparatus to make his will felt over a whole range of everyday affairs, and where the lord was silent, custom and kinship were pervasive. Indeed, in a sense custom ruled even the lord and the king since the older legal texts and code had gradually disappeared and 'custom finally decided the fate of the legal heritage of the preceding age. Custom had become the sole living source of law, and princes, even in their legislation scarcely claimed to do more than interpret it.' This feature makes feudal law more akin to Ashanti law than to the law of the bureaucratic empire.[*23*]

Economically, the feudal system was highly dispersed and agriculturally based and consisted of broadly self-sufficient local units. Unlike the bureaucratic empire the centre of economic and political gravity had shifted from the towns and cities to the countryside. Effective control of the land, for most people the sole basis of survival, lay with the feudal lord, who also had a local monopoly of military power, and it was this fact that enabled the lord to transfer under coercive sanction the peasants' surplus to his own use.[*24*] Other than defence the lord provided the almost autarchial villages with nothing, and with the decline of Hungarian and Viking predators as a social threat he no longer provided even that since at best he was defending his villagers against other feudal lords. In short, by the thirteenth century the feudal lord was, *vis-à-vis* the peasant, almost solely an expropriator.

Compliance in feudal Europe was, in principle, an extremely simple matter: one simply complied with the commands of the person to whom one rendered homage, and this obligation was absolute but frequently disregarded by those powerful enough to disobey with impunity. However, empirically, many factors complicated this simple relationship resulting in a rather complex and cross-cutting web of affiliation. For example, it was not unusual for a man to swear allegiance to more than one lord, and kinship ties, especially in feudal relations, would often conflict with loyalty to a lord. A complicating element in the compliance equation was the presence of the Catholic Church which spanned Europe, had interests and estates in every part and its own pattern of authority, independent but linked to the secular. Not only was the king a secular ruler but he also exercised power under God, a condition of rule symbolized at his coronation by his acceptance of religious and secular symbols—the holy oil, the orb, the crown and sceptre—from the Pope or his representative, all of which pointed to the fusion of the divine and the secular. While this generalized subordination of the ruler to divine law is characteristic of most pre-industrial government, in Western Europe kingship faced an independently organized and semi-autonomous universal church continually pitting its authority against the claims of secular rulers.

The church was a secular body in that it owned property and exercised secular jurisdiction over that property, but had a totally separate legal system and was, moreover, the best organized bureaucratic body in Europe.[*25*] So long as the church was separate or separable from civil authority the possibility of conflict between the two organizations was always present, as was the case in the controversy about the origins of royal authority. The church claimed that the emperor or king derived it from the coronation ceremony—a religious service—during which the symbol of secular power, the sword, was handed to the king by the Pope, signifying a gift from God mediated by his church.[34] Hence, the dualistic nature of allegiance in feudal society was a possible source of friction: 'Render unto Caesar the things that are Caesar's and unto God the things that are God's'. In this controversy, so long as Christianity was significant in people's lives, or there was no fusion between the clerical and secular authorities, the religious authority always had the intellectual upper hand: 'in an ideological conflict it was ideology that counted, and not custom'.[35]

Another feature complicating the simple command–compliance structure of feudal society was the presence of towns and cities inhabited by a free population engaged in trade and industry and consequently requiring a more complex legal system and enjoying almost complete autonomy.[36] Within the towns, people of various legal and feudal statuses were promiscuously mixed, but as corporate entities 'the towns possessed the power, and were in a position to laugh in the faces of the territorial lords'.[37] Effectively, they were enclaves of economic and political power, almost independent of the surrounding feudal society by virtue of rendering indispensable financial and economic services to the aristocracy. Within the city or town the older feudal relationship between man and man was either not present or was attenuated and increasingly replaced by the more task-orientated guild organization which controlled the town government. Thus the leading members of important guilds by virtue of their economic power could control the town and were in a strong position to use political power in turn to defend their status in the stratification order.[38] Townsmen needing records, clerical skills, accounting methods, etc., developed centres of administration outside the context of the church and the primitive feudal bureaucracies.

The power structure of feudal society was, then, a dispersed one with a plurality of locally based units in actual or potential conflict with a weak centre which in turn had its authority disputed by the church, and the local powers often had only minimal control over church and towns. Supreme authority was precarious since it depended upon the voluntary obedience and the purely personal loyalty of an often nominal local vassal, which meant that the centre had little independent leverage upon the periphery.[39] Instability was built into the relationship since in order to coerce one element, such as the feudal nobility, the king had to form an alliance with another, for example the towns or other feudal barons.[*26*] Instability was also endemic in the dual loyalty of a powerful trans-local church, a loyalty which wavered between heaven and earth and between one local authority and another.

For the mass of the population, life was a round of almost unremitting toil interspersed with feast days and religious festivals, with hunger and deprivation an ever-present possibility, and spoliation by marauding, almost uncontrolled soldiery and bandits never far away. Their political participation was negligible even in the towns, and in the rural areas the lord possessed organized force and a virtual monopoly of the land. The rural population were regarded as little more than providers of necessities for their lord who sat on them as he sat on his horse: 'And just as one controls a horse and he who sits above leads it where he will, so the knight must lead the people at his will'.[*27*] Incursions into politics by the masses were confined to spontaneous outbursts of violence and destruction combined with demands for a more just and more equal society under a righteous and benevolent king who would superintend the restoration of old rights and privileges. The very weakness of feudal political organization made such tumults a real danger; lacking adequate communication, intelligence sources and central standing armies the polity could be very easily temporarily disrupted even by badly armed and poorly organized peasants.[*28*] Normally, the rural masses were economically and socially depressed and lacked an independent organizational framework within which revolts could be organized or which could articulate their demands when traditional forms proved incapable of doing so. Short-term difficulties, such as the famines or the depopulation of the Black Death in the 1340's, caused actual declines in standards or appeared to offer the possibility of better standards (the labour shortage in Britain in the fourteenth century caused the possibility of higher wages plus an attempt to reimpose lapsed feudal obligations). Longer-term trends such as the growth of a considerable foreign trade market in Flanders and parts of England resulted in the formation of a free-floating class of 'Journeymen and unskilled workers, peasants without land or too little land to support them, beggars and vagabonds, the unemployed and those threatened with unemployment, the many who for one reason or another could find no assured or recognised place'.[40] Such people, as well as the tumultuous city apprentices, were unorganized but ready for mobilization by religious fanatics preaching the millenium and the end of oppression on earth.

The typical form of peasant revolt was in Hobsbawn's terms 'populist legitimism'. It was a limited rising against a local grievance such as an exaction unsanctioned by usage or a harsh abuse of one sanctioned by custom. Other forms of protest included millenarian movements, religious movements enjoined by the phantasy of a salvation[41] and a belief in the imminent appearance of an age of peace and prosperity. Although manifestly religious in character, such movements had latent political implications since they constituted a religious legitimation of people's non-cooperation with the ruling power in their society.[42] A third type of social unrest was social banditry. Fundamentally, this was a secular response to physically superior powers conceived of as alien to an established way of life. As such, the social bandit found illicit support among the peasants of his native village or territory, who condoned and encouraged his outlawry as long as he adhered to their social code.[42]

Normally, the fury of the people was directed against the petty feudal bureaucrat such as the reeve or the lord's miller or lawyers who were in direct contact with the people and might expect to be roughly handled and have their houses burned. Such uprisings were sporadic, frequent, unorganized and rarely attained more than a very restricted geographical and popular involvement; they can best be understood as a violent extension of the even more usual process by which the mass showed their resentment, ie by running away, evading rents, slacking in their work on the lord's desmesne, arriving late for work, neglecting the lord's animals, etc.

In general, the best hope for the masses lay not in any form of political institution since these were totally controlled in the towns by the rich and elsewhere by aristocrats, nor in sporadic revolts which were inevitably crushed, but in a disaster of some sort which left labour in relatively short supply. Thus the Black Death in Europe was followed by a period of rising wages and attempts by the nobility to reimpose or increase feudal labour dues; decimation of the population during the Hundred Years' War had a similar effect in France and Germany. Similarly, feudal dues were sometimes mitigated in areas where for defence or other reasons it was felt desirable to attract settlers, as was the case in the eastern marches of Germany and in the Russian east and latterly in the north.[43] An occasional peasant leader might achieve a place in the sun of political power, but as a class they were helpless.

At a local level political authority was a consequence of two factors: (1) the lord's monopoly of military power and (2) his monopoly or control of the only significant economic resource, the land. It is possible that at some early stage the basis of local authority was, as Weber suggests, the lord's charisma translated later into patrimonialism, a form of routinized charisma.[*29*] But the major point is that *vis-à-vis* his own people and territories the feudal lord *did* perform an invaluable service, albeit at a very heavy price to the locals; he did protect them against others of his kind and against robbers, bandits, Vikings, Hungarians, etc., etc. This element of mutuality in exchange was, however, a very unequal one and as in most such situations a strong justification of the inequality was advanced in the form of a legitimating ideology, that of the ordered hierarchy on earth which reflected the divine order laid up in heaven. An alternative justification of political compliance was that the political order was a divine gift given by God's grace to mitigate the worst consequences of man's original sin, without which men would simply prey upon one another in a state of complete anarchy.[44] Such beliefs were propagated in a simplified and no doubt distorted form by the network of the Catholic churches spread over the whole countryside and which almost everybody attended of a Sunday to learn his duty to God and secular authority. Amongst the restricted political class compliance to the legal authority of the monarch was much more a matter of negotiation, since the taxes and other supports of what central government there was had to be channelled through the lords. Hence, medieval Europe was for the political class a consultative system with assemblies both regular and *ad hoc* at which the king would make his requests and the feudal nobility would discuss them.

4.3. Conclusions

We have briefly examined a number of pre-industrial forms of political organization and have seen that they differ very significantly in their institutional complexity and power distribution. At the simplest level, the band society, a surplus sufficient to maintain a distinct body of leaders was not generated and compliance appears to have been voluntary, customary and task-specific. The economic advantages of leadership were minimal although it is quite possible that psychological payoffs played some part in rewarding leaders, but the scope for leadership given the 'tight' fit between band organization and an inhospitable environment was seen to be very limited. Looked at in terms of games theory we have a situation of very high risk of failure and considerable odds against winning by adopting a new strategy, since the players are not able to accumulate a surplus sufficient to make losing anything other than a disaster. To risk looking for a better waterhole or neglecting a known source of nourishment for a possible but potentially better unknown is not to risk a day or so of hunger or thirst but death, and the risk is not worth while, it is not rational. All members of the band are well aware of this since it is, so to say, the definition of the situation. Departure from custom, which can be envisaged as a store of sifted wisdom, may be disastrous: 'The custom of sharing meat is so strongly established and so faithfully followed that it has all but extinguished the concept of not sharing in the minds of the Kung'.[45]

A somewhat similar point is made by Bailey who suggests that given idyllic conditions or given less than ideal conditions involving crises and their past solutions there is little scope for leadership, which 'is called for particularly in conditions of uncertainty and when there is a need to take decisions *which are also innovations*'.[*30*] At the level we are discussing there is no scope for leadership nor is there a surplus to sustain a differentiated leadership which might conceivably impose risk-taking and if successful produce a surplus. A potential leader could not make innovating decisions nor is he likely at all frequently to be called upon to mediate or adjudicate disputes since for almost all sources of potential clash between individuals or groups—food, territory and sex—custom is sufficient to ensure that all know what is acceptable.

At this level of economic development there is no formalized and very little informalized coercive agency, and compliance appears to be due to group values or consensus as expressed by parents or elders. In so far as one can talk of consensual societies these cases would appear to fit the description. Political problems in the sense of allocative criteria are embedded in the cultural fabric of the band and are impressed upon the band member during his life span; kinship, culture, personality and environment are so tightly interwoven that unless challenged by strong exogenous forces the pattern is likely to remain stable and, hence, present little scope for political or social innovation. Their technological development is minimal and in terms of relationship with the environment they are adaptive rather than adapting and make only a miniscule impact on it. That is to say, that given their technical culture 'they (Eskimos) are operating at nearly one hundred per cent of the potential of the environment' so that there literally is no 'room' for minor innovation.[46]

At a higher level of economic development, that is in situations where a surplus is fairly regularly produced, a more differentiated social order becomes a possibility and it appears to be the case that when there is an economic possibility of a stratified society that possibility is always actualized. Lenski has suggested that this fact can be hypothesized in the form: 'In the simplest societies, or those which are technologically most primitive, the goods and services available will be distributed wholly, or largely, on the basis of need'. Referring to more advanced societies he argues that: 'with technological advance, an increasing proportion of the goods and services available to a society will be distributed on the basis of power'.[*31*] These hypotheses are derived from postulates about human nature, ie that: 'most human action is motivated either by self-interest or partisan group interest'. However, as a second postulate he asserts that most selfish interests can only be met in cooperation with others, ie equally selfish others. Hence, selfish interests compel men to social activity. Higher-level propositions follow from the postulates: 'Men will share the product of their labours to the extent required to ensure the survival and continued productivity of those others whose actions are necessary or beneficial to themselves'. Thus the first law of distribution. When a surplus is produced (a surplus is that above the minimum required to sustain producers) a second law of distribution becomes operative: 'Power will determine the distribution of nearly all of the surplus possessed by society'.[47] Hence, some men will find it in their interest to group together to expropriate for their joint use the societal surplus and these men become the powerful and the rest, in various degrees, the powerless.

This process we have seen exemplified in the more advanced segmentary society. The empirical concomitant of the process—not a necessary but an existentially normal one—is the development of a justificatory system of ideas which legitimates the distribution of power and privilege. Such ideologies or legitimating rationales serve to transform what may have been initially simply the rule of might or of the better organized segment or of a conqueror into a system within which sheer power or force as the prime determinant of compliance recedes in favour of a moral component. One obeys most of the time because it is 'right' to do so. From the point of view of the elite, governing simply by force is expensive and governing through legitimated symbols and ideological expressions is cheaper.[*32*] Forms of ideological and symbolic manipulation vary greatly in their content and formal expression, from the worked out and interconnected expressions such as Marxism or classic liberalism through the theological stances of medieval political thought and the familialism of Chinese Confucianism to the quasi-mythological tales of origin of the Ashanti.

That the Ashanti people produced an economic surplus is evident from the size of the towns, the existence of slavery, the ability to produce very considerable amounts of gold and diamonds and the very extensive trade network. Social differentiations, the existence of royals and commoners and slaves, functional differentiations in economic organization—skilled workmen in gold and cloth and an almost full-time bureaucracy at the centre—are all evidence of a far more complex society than that of the acephalous band.[*33*] In addition, the complexity and relative flexibility of the emergent political system suggests the presence of a leadership quite well adapted and specialized to risk-taking and adjudication, and the trading activities of the Asantehene for gunpowder and lead to fight and incorporate neighbouring areas is further evidence of the combination of surplus sustaining a political leadership, which uses the surplus to enhance its own power.[*34*] Again, the Asantehene's initiatives in creating a Kumasi-based and personally loyal bureaucracy are evidence of a fully fledged political leadership using its power to create an apparatus of further social control. As we have seen, the Ashanti political system was by no means force-dominated since there was a consultative network, but again it is clear that the chiefly lineages had greater political power than other lineages and that although there were checks to abuse of power (de-stoolment) the failure of an attempt at de-stoolment could be disastrous. Equally, it is clear that although all Ashanti people had the right to be given the use of land it was the chief who, as guardian, determined who got what and where!

That the political lineage heads used their authority to enhance their own standards and prestige is probable from an examination of the Ashanti tax system. For example, the local chief was entitled to a share of a dead man's wealth, entitled to levy on goods moving through his area and to fine in his courts and receive gifts from all litigants. After a successful war the chief had prior claim on the booty and a number of other financial resources were at his disposal.[48] And the more important the chief the greater his financial resources, ending up with the Asantehene as the controller of very considerable economic power. Chiefs were set apart from the commoner not merely by possessions—many were not rich—but also by their role as intercessors with the ancestors of the lineage, and this was important because 'The Akan state was a sacred state in the sense that it was conceived as falling inside a world inhabited by human beings as well as spirits and gods, to whom human beings owed specific duties through appropriate rites', and in most cases the chief played a central role in the rites.[49] That is, the spiritual welfare of the people depended on the institution of chiefdom. The chief was a ritually pure man, advised by representatives of the various politically powerful lineages, heading a well-articulated religious-cum-political system symbolized by occupancy of a well-defined hierarchy of stools. The stools in turn were thought of as spiritual entities through which the soul of the natives was manifest and in the Ashanti concept of the political community there was no distinction between the state and the society, which were fused into a single emotive unity. Although of greater wealth, power and prestige than the commoner, the chiefs were nevertheless hemmed in by a very considerable weight of tradition, not the least aspect of which was a strong sense of the past encroaching upon the present: 'in Ashanti, those in power serve the present by serving the past'.[50] Hence there was little opportunity for purely political institutions and ideologies to be generated although one can detect the beginnings of such forms. Whether or not the Asantehenes would have eventually cut loose from traditional restrictions is a matter of conjecture, but certainly there were signs of such a process in the nineteenth century, and in the twentieth century the adaptation of chieftaincy to 'modern' forms (political parties, legislative assemblies, etc.) demonstrated the possibilities.[51]

Ashanti differs greatly from the lineage band in another very important respect: non-compliance was always a problem. Firstly, as a conquering state it incorporated or attempted to incorporate a number of hitherto independent entities, especially the Fanti and Ga peoples to the south, and considerable military and diplomatic energy was devoted to subduing the non-compliant elements.[*35*] Other factors encouraging non-compliance, even in the heartland of the state, were the growth of Western education amongst non-royal lineages and, more important, the possibility of alternative bases for social power, especially with the introduction of cash crops in the early twentieth century. Very large and important merchants and farmers could and did challenge the traditional authority of the chiefs or sought out positions of traditional power for themselves. Later still, the so-called young men or commoners, often Western-educated, also challenged traditional authority.

Such problems were much more acute in the bureaucratized empire where massively diverse subject peoples were controlled by an extensive centralized governmental machine ramifying into the furthest reaches of the empire. Massive road works, extensive and rapid communication networks, formalized orders of bureaucratic officials at the centre and periphery, huge defensive arrangements and public enterprises of one type or another characterized these systems. Effectively, these empires were resource-mobilizing systems covering vast areas. When the Spanish soldier Bernal Diaz entered Mexico City in the service of Cortez he did so as an open-mouthed country cousin wondering at the richness and magnificence of Montezuma: 'the great Montezuma descended from his litter, and these other great *Caciques* supported him beneath a marvellously rich canopy of green feather, decorated with gold work, silver, pearls . . . the great

Montezuma was marvellously clad . . . and the four lords who supported him were richly clad also'.[*36*] Seen from one angle these systems were simply wealth-gathering 'taxocracies' siphoning to central consumers in the enormous cities the produce of the empire, and serving to permit the elite a sumptuary standard almost beyond the dreams of avarice. But as allocative systems the bureaucratic empires were geared to more than elite consumption since they mobilized resources for genuine societal problems. For example, the maintenance of peace and commerce in the Mogul and Mongol Empires was based on very considerable social effort, and the building of hydraulic works and defensive arrangements in China were necessary tasks. Similarly, given the nature of Mayan religion, an extensive reallocation of social resources, and hearts, could not be avoided. Or again, the task of conquering adjoining territories and controlling annexed ones entailed organized governmental efforts such as those of Pharoanic Egypt.

Both the gathering and the spending or allocation of resources are costly processes and on a large scale necessitate systems of control and accounting, and such were the societal tasks of the bureaucracy. Above all, the bureaucracy may be seen as an institutional consequence of the uncertainties and vagaries of flood control, barbarian invasion and the everlasting uncertainty of the afterlife. To control all these uncertainties vast efforts were necessary and had to be coordinated, which implied systems of accounting, of regular reporting and local control, and institutionalized—not personal—knowledge of the natural and social worlds; hence, the efforts expended on astronomy, mathematics, mechanics, etc., in all of the empires and their very highly developed system of internal communication. In short, they were *innovating* empires with the first standing armies, the first formal bureaucratized public administrators, the first planned towns on the military borders, the first extensive hydraulic works, and the first 'systematized sacred ordinances, as in India, Iran or Babylonia'.[52] The empires both gave scope for leadership and enabled a surplus-expropriating leadership to innovate.

In most of the bureaucratic empires belief systems were more assorted and varied than those in segmentary states; this was a consequence of their origins in conquest, and although there were state religions this was by no means always the case. For example, in the pre-Christian Roman Empire a very high degree of religious autonomy was permitted, a situation which ended after the official adoption of Christianity. Islam, on the other hand, was a good example of an almost complete fusion between state and religion, but even here there was always the possibility of local political interests expressing themselves in schismatic terms.[*37*] In the Islamic empire, 'where no special legislation was required by the advent of Islam, long standing local custom was generally permitted to continue without question'.[53] As in other bureaucratic empires, communications such as postal services and roads were centralized and highly developed, as was the tax system, and gradually the system of military command was brought under central bureaucratic control. Significantly, the central bureaucracy achieved its greatest development in the postal system, which established a complex network of way stations and served also as an intelligence agency, using its local agents to gather relevant information for central use. The centralization of the tax system (and taxes were levied on almost everything) was an early development, with regional officers controlled by a central bureaucracy whose officials were appointed by the Caliph's personal adviser and administrative assistant, the Vizier. Taxes were used to support a large standing army, to finance large-scale public works, to sustain a considerable bureaucracy and to enrich the ruler and his entourage in splendid style. The coinage was centralized as well, justice was in principle standard, and a body of central lay officers ensured compliance with the moral precepts of the Koran.

Technically, the Caliph was divinely appointed in succession to the Prophet 'in order to defend the faith and secure the right government of the world' and the Caliph simply declared law already present in the Koran; compliance with his commands was divinely ordered: 'Obey God and His apostle and them that have command over you'.[54] Additionally, a Caliph needed also to be able to claim kinship with the Prophet and to be acceptable for election by men 'who possess real influence in the community'.[55] Compliance in the Empire was thus ensured by a complex and shifting combination of ideological legitimation, or rational legal authority, and, finally, by force which was often exercised to change the religious stance of the conquered and hence, eventually, to religiously legitimate compliance.

During the period of the Egyptian Old Empire from 2900 to 2475 BC the Pharaoh was both a god and a political ruler controlling a massive bureaucracy headed by members of his family. Literacy was necessary and schools for potential officials were established in the bureaucracy to train the next generation of full-time officers. Each department was hierarchically organized, but there was the usual ancient bureaucratic device of passing office to sons both amongst the civil and religious bureaucracy. The prestige attached to the bureaucrat was high and as a mobilizing agency the bureaucracy was efficient, as evidenced by the massive flood control schemes, the management of very large standing armies, the building of the pyramids, and the regular extraction of a surplus with which to sustain these activities.[56] Most of the higher officials of the bureaucracy were either from the royal family or from the land-owning aristocracy and thus combined traditional religious and rational legal authority. The Egyptian bureaucracy was the classical example of an organization having the construction of major hydraulic schemes and their control as its initial *raison d'être* but which later assumed the functions of religious building in the pyramids and temples. It is also a good example of the bureaucratized exploitation of a landless tenantry for the support of state works of various kinds.

Political legitimation in the empires was thus usually cast in religious terms but, compared with the Ashanti, religious institutions had a limited although significant degree of autonomy.[*38*] Possessing an organizational framework, these state religions always had at least the possibility of developing policies and goals opposed to those of the political ruler, thus opening up the possibility that intra-elite tensions and conflict would express themselves in ideological terms. Hence, non-compliance could, in its turn, have an ideological justification backed up by a religious organization, as for example in the religious opposition to the Caliph or as in Sassanid Persia where Jews, Christians and other organized religions 'were very significant in the social and political history of the state'.[57] Religious differentiation is, of course, simply one example in these empires of the far greater social differentiations (we could have used the complex economic stratification system) which presented the rulers with political problems of a much greater order of complexity than anything encountered in states comparable to the Ashanti. Although formal authority was highly centralized the greater differentiation entailed processes likely to impede the unhindered exercise of central power from what might at first glance appear to be an arbitrary and discretionary process. Rulers were able to amass enormous personal fortunes and engender awe amongst the general population, nevertheless their power depended upon their control and alliances with other powerful groups such as the aristocracy, the military, the church and the bureaucracy. Consequently, their rule was necessarily a combination of 'force, ideology and utility'[58] with the mass of the population simply ignored as political entities and thus forced to raise their discontents in the form of riot and rebellion, as in the innumerable cases of Chinese peasant uprisings and banditry.[*39*]

European feudalism developed as the successor to the Roman Empire on the basis of a greatly restricted territorial spread, with even the postcedent Merovingian and Carolingian Empires proving to be transitional political forms. Communication networks and the central bureaucracy simply crumbled away and no leader or ruler was able to amass the financial and technical resources to replace them and regain control. Beginning as a justifiable exchange of service for protection, serfdom and its variants had declined by the beginning of the thirteenth century into a system of almost unremitting exploitation of the peasantry.[59] We have no way of knowing whether feudal exploitation was more severe than under the bureaucratic empire, but it is certain that the surplus was not centralized and directed to the achievement of major social enterprises, with the exception of castles and churches. Compliance to the orders of a legal authority was far more a discretionary matter than in the bureaucratized empire, since the central authority lacked significantly greater physical, financial and bureaucratic resources than even limited combinations of the feudal lords. Consequently, political innovation by the king was dependent to a far greater degree upon an aristocratic consensus than was the case in the bureaucratic empire, and this more conciliatory style is demonstrated by the existence of various forms of aristocratic representative assemblies such as Parliament, the Spanish Cortes and the French parlementes. On the other hand, compliance by the peasantry appears to have been far more a matter of the lack of a viable alternative to obedience alternating with peasant risings, go-slows and tumults, with the church, at least in its official ideology, preaching obedience on earth and rewards in heaven.

In this chapter we have suggested that the problems of scale and expropriation and allocation of surplus are associated with the emergence of more or less specialized political institutions. This relationship is explained by the emergence and perception of problems of social management requiring differentiated and novel forms of control. In the more heterogeneous societies, conflicts of interest are much more likely than in the more homogeneous society, and this fact entails either a measure of consultation and sensitivity to conflicting interests by the rulers or the exercise of force to maintain compliance. In the following chapter we shall examine conflict and compliance in the modern industrial state.

References

1. A. Etzioni, *A Comparative Analysis of Complex Organisations*, Free Press, New York, 1961, p. 5.
2. E. Shils, 'The Concentration and Dispersion of Charisma—Their Bearing on Economic Policy in Underdeveloped Countries', *World Politics*, **XI,** 1–19 (July 1959); W. G. Runciman, 'Charismatic Legitimacy and One Party Rule in Ghana', *European Journal of Sociology*, **4,** 148–165 (1963); S. M. Lipsett, 'The Crisis of Legitimacy and the Role of the Charismatic Leader', *Transactions of the Fifth World Congress of Sociology*, Washington D.C., Sept. 2–8, 1962, pp. 310–332 and 357–361.

3. E. Shils, 'Charisma, Order and Statutus', *American Sociological Review*, **30,** 199–213 (1965).
4. K. G. Ratnam, 'Charisma and Political Leadership', *Political Studies*, **12,** 341–354 (Oct. 1963), and P. Worsley, *The Trumpet Shall Sound*, 2nd ed., MacGibbon and Key, London, 1968, appendix.
5. A. Etzioni, *A Comparative Analysis of Complex Organisations*, Free Press, New York, 1961, p. 203.
6. H. Kelman, 'Three Processes of Social Influence', in M. Jahoda and N. Warren (eds.), *Attitudes*, Penguin, London, 1966, pp. 151–161.
7. R. H. Lowrie, 'Some Aspects of Political Organisation Among the American Aborigines', in R. H. Cohen and I. Middleton (eds.), *Comparative Political Systems*, Natural History Press, New York, 1967, p. 83.
8. C. Levi-Strauss, 'The Nambikuara of North Western Matto Grosso', in R. H. Cohen and I. Middleton (eds.), *Comparative Political Systems*, Natural History Press, New York, 1967, p. 52.
9. R. H. Lowrie, 'Some Aspects of Political Organisation Among the American Aborigines', in R. H. Cohen and I. Middleton (eds.), *Comparative Political Systems*, Natural History Press, New York, 1967, p. 76.
10. L. Bohannan, 'Political Aspects of Tiv Social Organisation', in J. Middleton and D. Tait, *Tribes Without Rulers*, Routledge and Kegan Paul, London, 1958, pp. 48–49.
11. ——'Political Aspects of Tiv Social Organisation', in J. Middleton and D. Tait, *Tribes Without Rulers*, Routledge and Kegan Paul, London, 1958, p. 53.
12. ——'Political Aspects of Tiv Social Organisation', in J. Middleton and D. Tait, *Tribes Without Rulers*, Routledge and Kegan Paul, London, 1958, p. 58.
13. L. Krader, *Formation of the State*, Prentice-Hall, Englewood Cliffs, 1968, pp. 34–35.
14. A. W. Southall, *Alur Society*, Heffer, Cambridge, 1954, ch. 9.
15. R. F. Stevenson, *Population and Political Change in Tropical Africa*, Columbia University Press, 1968.
16. G. Dalton, 'Theoretical Issues in Economic Anthropology', New York, *Current Anthropology*, **10** (Feb. 1969).
17. M. Fortes and E. E. Evans-Pritchard, *African Political Systems*, Oxford University Press, London, 1964, pp. 5–7.
18. K. A. Busia, *The Position of the Chief in the Political System of Ashanti*, Frank Cass, London, 1951, ch. 1.
19. —— *The Position of the Chief in the Political System of Ashanti*, Frank Cass, London, 1951, p. 10.
20. R. F. Stevenson, *Population and Political Change in Tropical Africa*, Columbia University Press, New York, 1968.
21. D. Tordoff, *Ashanti Under the Prempehs*, Oxford University Press, London, 1965, pp. 7–8.
22. —— *Ashanti Under the Prempehs*, Oxford University Press, London, 1965; R. E. Dowse, *Modernisation in Ghana and the USSR*, Routledge and Kegan Paul, London, 1969, ch. 2; L. Fallers, *Bantu Bureaucracy*, University of Chicago Press, Chicago, 1965 gives another example of the same process.
23. K. Wittfogel, *Oriental Despotism*, Yale University Press, New Haven, 1957, p. 241.
24. —— *Oriental Despotism*, Yale University Press, New Haven, 1957, p. 40.

25. S. Andreski, *The Uses of Comparative Sociology*, University of California Press, Berkeley, 1964, pp. 314–320.
26. S. N. Eisenstadt, *The Political System of Empires*, Free Press, New York, 1963, p. 159.
27. —— *The Political System of Empires*, Free Press, New York, 1963, p. 185.
28. —— *The Political System of Empires*, Free Press, New York, 1963, pp. 148–149.
29. ——*The Political System of Empires*, Free Press, New York, 1963, pp. 300–360.
30. Marc Bloch, *Feudal Society*, Routledge and Kegan Paul, London, 1965, p. 65.
31. —— *Feudal Society*, Routledge and Kegan Paul, London, 1965, p. 160,
32. —— *Feudal Society*, Routledge and Kegan Paul, London, 1965, p. 151.
33. H. Pirenne, *A History of Europe*, Allen and Unwin, London, 1939, pp. 146–150.
34. W. Ullman, *A History of Political Thought: The Middle Ages*, Penguin, London, 1965, esp. pp. 85–115.
35. ——*A History of Political Thought: The Middle Ages*, Penguin, London, 1965, p. 143.
36. H. Pirenne, *A History of Europe*, Allen and Unwin, London, 1939, p. 221.
37. M. Weber, *General Economic History*, Free Press, Glencoe, 1950, p. 133.
38. H. Pirenne, *A History of Europe*, Allen and Unwin, London, 1939, pp. 223–224.
39. M. Weber, *The Theory of Social and Economic Organisation*, trans. by A. M. Handerson and Talcott Parsons, Free Press, Glencoe, 1947, p. 376.
40. N. Cohn, *The Pursuit of the Millenium*, Harper Row, New York, 1961, p. 29.
41. —— 'Medieval Millenarianism: Its Bearing on the Comparative History of Millenarian Movements', in *Comparative Studies in Society and History*, Supplement II, Mouton Co., The Hague, 1962, p. 31.
42. E. J. Hobshawn, *Primitive Rebels*, Norton, New York, 1965, pp. 57–92.
43. G. Lenski, *Power and Privilege. A Theory of Stratification*, McGraw-Hill, New York, 1966, p. 276.
44. W. Ullman, *A History of Political Thought: The Middle Ages*, Penguin, London, 1965; O. Gierke, *Political Theories of the Middle Ages*, Beacon Press, Boston, 1958.
45. R. H. Cohen and I. Middleton (eds.), *Comparative Political Systems*, Natural History Press, New York, 1967, p. 23.
46. P. Farb, *Man's Rise to Civilisation*, Secker and Warburg, London, 1969, p. 35.
47. G. Lenski, *Power and Privilege: A Theory of Stratification*, McGraw-Hill, New York, 1966, ch. 3.
48. M. J. Herskovitz, *Economic Anthropology*, W. W. Norton, New York, 1952, pp. 417–421.
49. W. E. Abraham, *The Mind of Africa*, Weidenfeld and Nicolson, London, 1962, p. 51.
50. D. Apter, *Some Conceptual Approaches to the Study of Modernization*, Prentice-Hall, Englewood Cliffs, 1968, p. 119.
51. R. E. Dowse, *Modernisation in Ghana and the USSR*, Routledge and Kegan Paul, London, 1969, chs. 1–4.
52. M. Weber, *The Sociology of Religion* (1920), ch. 2, reprinted in R. Robertson (ed.), *Sociology of Religion*, Penguin, London, 1969, p. 409.

53. R. Levy, *The Social Structure of Islam*, Cambridge University Press, London, 1962, p. 295.
54. —— *The Social Structure of Islam*, Cambridge University Press, London, 1962, p. 286.
55. —— *The Social Structure of Islam*, Cambridge University Press, London, 1962, p. 286.
56. W. C. Beyer, 'The Civil Service of the Ancient World', *Public Administration Review*, **19**, 243–248 (1959).
57. S. N. Eisenstadt, *The Political System of Empires*, Free Press, New York, 1963, p. 51.
58. G. Lenski, *Power and Privilege: A Theory of Stratification*, McGraw-Hill, New York, 1966, p. 179.
59. R. H. Hilton, 'Peasant Movements in England Before 1381', *The Economic History Review*, second series, **2**, 118 (1949).

Notes and Further Reading

1. In the real world authority types may be mixed, but Weber is concerned to draw out 'ideal types' which are models formed by the exaggeration or accentuation of one or more traits or points of view observable in reality. Such 'types', which do not exist in their pure form, are used as simplifying yardsticks to facilitate empirical analysis. See M. Weber, *The Theory of Social and Economic Organisation*, trans. by A. M. Handerson and Talcott Parons, Free Press, Glencoe, 1947, pp. 110–111.
2. Edmund Burke's polemic *Reflections on the French Revolution* was a hymn to this form of authority. See also W. Bagehot, *The English Constitution*, Oxford University Press, London, 1952, chs. 2 and 3 and pp. 34–35. Also see E. Shils and M. Young, 'The Meaning of the Coronation', *Sociological Review*, **1**, 63–81 (1953).
3. M. Weber, *The Theory of Social and Economic Organisation*, trans. by A. M. Handerson and Talcott Parsons, Free Press, Glencoe, 1947, p. 358. The test of whether charisma is present is 'how the individual is actually regarded by those subject to charismatic authority' and the *essence* is that the leader has to recognize he has it 'and to act accordingly' (p. 361).
4. For examples of this process, see B. R. Wilson, *Sects and Society*, Heinemann, London, 1963, and R. Michels, *Political Parties*, Dover Publications, New York, 1959.
5. M. H. Fried, *The Evolution of Political Society*, Random House, New York, 1967, p. 62. We have no space for discussion of the universal disproportionate allocation of all manifest political roles to men, but see L. Tiger, *Men in Groups*, Nelson, London, 1970, pp. 55–92.
6. C. Levi-Strauss, 'The Nambikuara of North Western Matto Grosso', in R. H. Cohen and I. Middleton (eds.), *Comparative Political Systems*, Natural History Press, New York, 1967, p. 61. In his remarkable book *Feudal Society*, Marc Bloch makes a similar point: 'To seek a protector, or to find satisfaction in being one—these things are common to all ages', p. 147.
7. L. Marshall, 'Kung Bushman Bands', in R. H. Cohen and I. Middleton (eds.), *Comparative Political Systems*, Natural History Press, New York,

1967, p. 39. But see R. L. Sharp, 'People without Politics', in V. Ray (ed.), *Systems of Political Control and Bureaucracy in Human Societies*, Washington University Press, Seattle, 1958, pp. 1–7, who suggests that amongst his group of Australian aborigines all roles were kinship except that of curer, and that the political system is even less differentiated than amongst the Kung.

8. E. V. Walter, *Terror and Resistance*, O.U.P., New York, 1969, p. 61, writes of the 'evidence that (in stateless societies) some of the most important "political" activity of the people in these communities was directed towards limiting or inhibiting actual and potential leadership'.
9. See L. Fallers, 'Political Sociology and the Anthropological Study of African Politics', in *European Journal of Sociology*, **iv**, 311–325 (1963), reprinted in R. Bendix, *State and Society*, Little, Brown, Boston, 1968, pp. 73–86. A somewhat similar point is made by L. Bohannan for the segmented Tiv people: 'The spread of war is determined by the segmentary order of the groups involved. The fighting spreads until equivalent segments are engaged and is limited to them', 'Political Aspects of Tiv Social Organisation', in J. Middleton and D. Tait, *Tribes Without Rulers*, Routledge and Kegan Paul, London, 1958, p. 46.
10. With increasing size the possibility of differentiation and probably the necessity of differentiation increases and this relationship can be demonstrated statistically:

Social Stratification and Size of Society

Approximate Size and Political Organization	Level of Stratification	
	Higher	Lower
	%	%
Larger state (10^5 and over)	100	88
Little state (10^4–10^5)	92	8
Minimal state (1.5×10^3–10^4)	75	25
Autonomous community (*XL* 1.5×10^3)	50	50
Family band (c 10^2)	22	88

Adapted from K. Svalastoga, 'Social Differentation', in R. E. L. Faris (ed.), *Handbook of Modern Sociology*, Rand McNally, Chicago, 1964, p. 535.

Higher stratification denotes one or more of the following features: complex stratification into three or more classes or castes, hereditary aristocracy, important wealth distinction, slavery incipient or hereditary. Lower denotes absence of all these features.

11. See M. Gluckman, *Politics, Law and Ritual in Tribal Society*, Blackwell, Oxford, 1965, for an explanation of witchcraft complaints as a form of social control and p. 221 'Witchcraft beliefs condemn the unduly prosperous'.
12. However, as L. Fallers points out, lineage is also an idea in people's heads, a political theory, and may be rather flexibly employed when necessary to incorporate non-lineal people into the group. L. Fallers, 'Political Sociology and the Anthropological Study of African Politics', in *European Journal of Sociology*, **iv** (1963), reprinted in R. Bendix, *State and Society*, Little, Brown, Boston, 1968, p. 76.
13. Robert Lowie suggested that such corporate groups, based on neither kinship nor proximity, might be the nucleus of state power since they trans-

cended, as in a state, the ties of blood and neighbourhood. See R. Lowie, *The Origin of the State*, Harcourt, New York, 1927.

14. P. Farb, *Man's Rise to Civilisation*, Secker and Warburg, London, 1969, pp. 143–144. Farb also mentions the presence of art specialists amongst the Indians.
15. For another good example of a conqueror state see S. F. Nadel, *A Black Byzantium*, Oxford University Press, London, 1942 and for a highly bureaucratized state, M. J. Herskovits, *Dahomey, An Ancient West African Kingdom*, Augustin, New York, 1938.
16. The point is well made by D. Apter, *The Gold Coast in Transition*, Princeton University Press, New Jersey, 1955, p. 114: 'The Ashanti Confederacy was a decentralised bureaucracy. The *Asantehene* had a large staff. He was assisted by a Queen Mother, and the *Birempon*. He had spokesmen and officials. An elaborate pattern of specific relationships existed between the chief and his principal officers in which their various performances were carefully worked out, while their functions were not. The positions were, relative to western standards, functionally diffuse.'
17. There was also a considerable measure of disassociation between person and office; for example, a chief could, with difficulty, be removed from office (de-stooled) whereupon he became of no special significance since his authority was derived entirely from his office, which was sacred.
18. C. P. FitzGerald, *Revolution in China*, Cresset Press, London, 1952, p. 10, writing of the enormous problem posed by flood control on the Yellow River suggests that the task was beyond the resources of local leaders, class or petty regional authority and that 'The King of a large Kingdom could alone command the support and control sufficient territory, Kingdoms therefore arose which were even in the earliest stage of considerable dimension'.
19. The two most comprehensive books on the process are S. N. Eisenstadt, *The Political System of Empires*, Free Press, New York, 1963, and K. Wittfogel, *Oriental Depotism*, Yale University Press, New Haven, 1957. But in China, the most lasting of the bureaucratic empires, the administrative machinery of every dynasty 'was virtually run by men who came from the landowning families', Ping-chia Kuo, *China, New Age and Outlook*, Penguin, London, 1959, p. 15.
20. S. N. Eisenstadt, *The Political System of Empires*, Free Press, New York, 1963; K. Wittfogel, *Oriental Despotism*, Yale University Press, New Haven, 1957, p. 41: 'in the Andean zone, as in most other areas of the hydraulic work, the attachment of the priesthood to the government is beyond doubt'.
21. G. Lenski, *Power and Privilege: A Theory of Stratification*, McGraw-Hill, New York, 1966, p. 210. Lenski refers to all agrarian societies, but the point remains even stronger for the bureaucratized agrarian society.
22. As W. C. Beyer puts it, 'in common with the Egyptian bureaucracy, the Roman Civil Service finally became oppressive and burdensome. It, too, engaged in excessive regulation of the economic life of the people and subjected them to heavy taxation to support a growing army of imperial agents. Under this dual frustration the Roman Citizenship suffered the same breakdown of spirit as did their Egyptian predecessors under the Ptolemies . . . In a very real sense . . . the Roman civil service which at the outset had been the Empire's chief instrument for bringing peace and prosperity to the

Roman world, in its later stages became one of the principal causes of the Empire's fall'. 'The Civil Service of the Ancient World', *Public Administration Review*, **19,** 243–249 (1959).

23. But even in the bureaucratic empire the concept of *finding* the law rather than *making* it was by no means unknown, for example in Islam the Caliph had in theory no legislative power at all, the Koran being supreme and the Caliph one amongst other interpreters of it, R. Levy, *The Social Structure of Islam*, Cambridge University Press, London, 1957, pp. 294–296.
24. R. H. Hilton, 'Peasant Movements in England Before 1381', *The Economic History Review*, second series, **2,** 117–136 (1949): 'the level of most money rents was determined primarily, as in the case of food and labour rents, by the political relationship of lord and peasant, and not by free bargaining on a land market'.
25. It is also the case that as an extensive and commercially-minded property-exploiting body the English church, particularly in its production of wool for the foreign market, developed a bureaucratic structure far more complex than that associated with most of the secular lords.
26. Under medieval conditions the ruler's power was always limited when he found it expedient or necessary to rely on a landed aristocracy.
27. M. Bloch, *Feudal Society*, Routledge and Kegan Paul, London, 1965, vol. 2, p. 319, citing the words of a medieval romance.
28. For an interesting morphology of such revolts see N. Cohn, *The Pursuit of the Millenium*, Harper Row, New York, 1961.
29. Weber understood feudal authority as a patrimonial one: M. Weber, *The Theory of Social and Economic Organisations*, trans. by A. M. Handerson and Talcott Parsons, Free Press, Glencoe, 1947, pp. 363–386.
30. F. G. Bailey, *Stratagems and Spoils: A Social Anthropology of Politics*, Blackwell, Oxford, 1969, p. 59. Italics in text.
31. G. Lenski, *Power and Privilege: A Theory of Stratification*, McGraw-Hill, New York, 1966, p. 48. Lenski uses Weber's concept of power which refers to the ability of a person or group having his/their will obeyed even when opposed by others.
32. For a useful discussion of the costs and limitations of rule by force see R. Dahl and C. Lindblom, *Politics, Economics and Welfare*, Harper and Row, New York, 1953, pp. 107–109.
33. Further evidence for this point can be found in Akan proverbs: 'Poverty has no friends.' 'A poor man's suit is summarily disposed of.' 'Poverty is madness.' 'The poor man has no anger.' 'No-one bullies another with his poverty', and many more cited in W. E. Abraham, *The Mind of Africa*, Weidenfeld and Nicolson, London, 1967, pp. 71–72.
34. In the 1820's Ashanti controlled some twenty-five native states. G. Tordoff, *Ashanti Under the Prempehs*, Oxford University Press, London, 1965, p. 1.
35. That is, in an expanding political system kinship is no longer a sufficient tie: 'kinship, as a political principle, diminished in efficiency with distance, so that in the case of certain central Ashantis and the distant Akans, force of arms had to be used to back the assumption that cultural homogeneity was a possible foundation for the construction of a greater political structure', K. Arhin, 'The Structure of Greater Ashanti (1700–1824)', *Journal of African History*, **8,** 65–85 (1967).

36. Bernal Diaz, *The Conquest of New Spain*, Penguin, London, 1963, p. 217. Earlier, in the thirteenth century, Marco Polo had similarly been impressed with the cities and communications of the Mongol empire.
37. W. C. Smith, *Islam in Modern History*, Mentor Books, New York, 1957, p. 26, but note that the word 'state' is not appropriate. Also, S. N. Eisenstadt, *The Political Systems of Empires*, Free Press, New York, Glencoe, 1963, pp. 189–191.
38. An exception to this generalization is China, where Confucianism had no organization to become autonomous: see S. N. Eisenstadt, *The Political System of Empires*, Free Press, New York, 1963, pp. 55–58.
39. In the cities the case was not dissimilar though their riots over taxes and hunger were more likely to meet the ameliorative or diversionary action—'bread and circuses'.

5

STRUCTURES OF POWER IN INDUSTRIAL SOCIETY: THE PLURALIST AND ELITE MODELS

5.1. The General Framework

WE CAN CHARACTERIZE industrialized society by a number of general processes. In the realm of technology there is a change from simple and traditional techniques employing animal and human energy to a more thoroughgoing and explicit application of machines and the growth of an increasingly highly trained class of people concerned with the application of technical innovation to production. This class itself becomes specialized into a group concerned with producing technical innovation and a group of managers—political or industrial—concerned with directing and controlling innovation and its consequences. Innovation becomes a value, a thing desirable in itself and is a process necessarily leading to tension. The introduction of technical change is not confined to industry, but rather agriculture becomes a branch of industry. In all industrialized societies the long-term trend is of rural depopulation as men move into, or are driven into, the areas of urban expansion and economic opportunity. Relationships previously based on custom and tradition, for example, just prices, the traditional and proper way of doing things, primogeniture, religiously sanctioned wage levels, etc., are gradually dissolved and replaced by market prices and bargaining.[*1*]

This process of dissolving the older social ties is accompanied by rapidly increasing rates of social mobilization as some groups ascend and others descend in the society, by the phenomenon of spectacular urban growth and of accompanying changes in values, typically of individualism and ideologies stressing achievement and cash values. It is this feature of rapid mobility and utilitarianism that Durkheim puts at the centre of industrial society when men lacking any standards other than their achievements relative to other men or their success in pursuing an elusive happiness can ultimately only resolve their predicament by suicide. In the society produced by industrialization the guiding principle for Weber was rationality, which 'invaded' all social forms which became rational-legal, ie bureaucratic.[1]

The family, which for centuries has been a semi-autarchical production unit, becomes far more highly integrated into the economy, and, hence, dependent upon structural processes over which it has no control. Generally speaking, the size of the unit of production, the farm or factory, increases and the specificity of the thing produced also increases. Thus, the farm specializes in a much narrower range of products and the factory may produce one part of a larger unit. Hence the interdependence of productive enterprise grows, and with this growth the mutual dependence of each unit increases to the point where a crisis in one section rapidly reverberates through the system as a whole. In such an interdependent system any dislocation is likely to involve more serious societal consequences than in the more discontinuous traditional economy.[*2*]

Looked at structurally, then, the industrial society involves a shift from multifunctional organizational and role structures towards several more specialized structures. Production previously located within the extended family unit typically moves to specialized economic organizations; training and medical functions previously performed in the family are devolved upon specialized units such as schools and hospitals; most individuals become more highly specialized, at least in economic relations, and the roles they do play are less likely to be mutually compatible than previously. In the pre-industrial society (to simplify greatly) the father was head of the family, the source of major economic decisions, the most powerful moral voice and in general a figure of considerable albeit diffuse authority, whilst in the industrial society he is frequently none of these or at least there is no simple transference of paternal authority as an economic entity into a moral guide. Similarly, political institutions tend to greater specificity and specialization with the emergence of a professional administration, widespread and bureaucratized party organization, a professionalized political class, and often a widespread extension of the concept of citizenship.[2]

At the attitudinal or normative level, industrial society is held to be characterized by major shifts in the orientations of people to one another and to the society within which they live. One typology of the differing orientations is that of Parsons in his work on pattern variables.[*3*] These five dichotomous extremes are said to represent the polar choices for action of actors in a situation, with an alternative set of choices characteristic of modern industrial society and the other of pre-modern or agricultural society. The first alternative pair is 'affectivity' and 'affective neutrality', which refers to the emotional loading by the actors in a situation, and in the rationally based industrial society the actor typically views his roles, especially work and political roles, from a non-emotional and calculative posture. That is, public non-familial roles are envisaged as having a low emotion-evoking quality. The second set of variables is the self-orientation *versus* the collective orientation, which refers to whether or not in the case of clash an individual acts in his own interest or in that of the collectivity.[*4*] A third variable is the universalistic *versus* particularistic value choice, which refers to whether standards of judgement of worth are meant to apply to everyone or just to limited groups. Thus, in feudal society a man is born into a particular estate and is judged by its standards, finds it difficult to change social status and his place of residence may well be fixed. Achievement *versus* ascription is another set of variables and refers to the principles by which role allocation takes place in a society, that is, whether proven and public capacity to fulfil role demands is the criterion or whether some other factor such as birth, colour or social status is paramount. Finally, specificity *versus* diffuseness refers to the social definition of roles, ie whether they are broadly or narrowly defined. Thus a peasant in an agricultural society performs all work in producing a crop, but also may build his house, produce his clothes and act as head of an economically semi-autarchical family.

The suggestion is that one cluster of these variables—affective neutrality, self-orientation, universalism, achievement and specificity—characterize relations and attitudes within industrialized or industrializing societies, whilst the other set are more characteristic of pre-modern societies.[*5*] Further, each of the clusters may not be fully realized in any society; for example, the medieval church and armies had elements of both clusters, as did the armies and bureaucracies of the bureaucratized empires, and industrial society is not by any means based purely upon achievement or affective neutrality. For example, almost all Japanese workers who are not executives are recruited into even the largest firms because members of their families already work for the firm or because they come from the same village as or are close friends of workers already employed by the firm. Nor is it necessarily the case that because public norms tend towards one cluster private attitudes necessarily do the same. Nepotism, corruption, colour or class prejudice or political favouritism are by no means unknown as recruitment criteria even in the public authorities of advanced industrial societies.

In this way Parsons, following and elaborating an older tradition, sets out the major normative elements associated with the change from traditional to industrial societies.

This combination of structural and attitudinal changes is understood to be associated with the development of industrial society, but also the combination is held to characterize the *developed* polity. The developed society is generally thought of as a nation-state and political development 'becomes the process by which communities that are nation-states only in form . . . become nation-states in reality'.[3] Reality is brought about essentially (1) by developing amongst a possible diverse population a sense of belonging and attachment to a new legal entity, for example, Ghana, Zambia, Tanzania, etc., and (2) by developing the political machinery, for example, parties, pressure groups, bureaucracies, assemblies, armies, associated with the Western industrial nation.[*6*] Political development then becomes the process of building a sense of nationhood and of constructing organizations through which the government can make its policies felt and through which it, in turn, can be influenced. An implication of this view is that the modern society is at least a potentially participatory one. In the West the political inclusion of the masses was generally quite slow, whilst in the new developing countries their inclusion has generally been very rapid, which opens up the possibility of elite manipulation of ignorant populations.[4] But whether the process of incorporating the masses is slow or fast, and whether they are more or less manipulated, the point is that the masses cannot be ignored. Unlike the societies discussed in the previous chapter, the modern society must take cognizance of the masses.

Political development may also be seen as the production of a growing capacity to respond successfully to environmental challenges by initiating or at least permitting changes to take place. Institutions become more complex, new ones are created and new political roles develop so that the polity acquires 'a new capability, in the sense of a specialised role structure and differentiated orientations which together give a political system the possibility of responding efficiently . . . to a new range of problems'. Almond suggests that *all* developing political systems have to acquire in one form or another the following four capacities: (1) capability to integrate their population, (2) capability to engage in extra-systemic intercourse, (3) capability of creating a participatory political culture and (4) a welfare or distributive capability.[5] These capabilities may be seen as responsive capacity. The more developed a system is the greater is its capability to respond to change generated in its local or international environment. Thus, Eisenstadt emphasizes that modernization necessarily implies changes and argues that political development means a growth in the 'ability to absorb varieties and changing types of political demands and organisation'.[6]

The question to which we now turn is, what implications have these innovations in attitude, value and structural processes for the character of politics in industrial societies?[7]

5.2. Compliance and Stability in Industrial Society

Contrasted with the societies examined in Chapter 4, the industrial society displays a far greater degree of social differentiation or division of labour. This means that occupations or tasks which previously were either unknown or were fused together become separate but interdependent processes. Thus factories become uniproduct entities with management tasks which may previously have been fused now broken down into personnel, production, training, forward planning, design, etc., departments each with specialized, trained managers. Occupations emerge, such as systems analysts, airline pilots, design engineers, advertising executives, which are entirely novel. The general process is one of constant and accelerating innovation, not only technologically, but also culturally and structurally.[7] From this consideration a number of problems arise from the point of view of social control.

Firstly, innovation may well place some groups at a positive disadvantage even if, in some sense, the innovation is generally beneficial. Appalachian miners are hardly helped by the expansion of oil and atomic energy, or small shopkeepers by chain stores, clerks by computers, farm labourers by machines, etc., etc. Again, with the development of new occupations there emerge possible new sources of competing and conflicting loyalties. In fine, the problem of order amidst innovation when time-sanctioned loyalty bases and attitudes have become less effective is a serious one. Typically also in industrial society the process of innovation is not an even one and the major changes take place where change has previously taken place, leaving the rest of the country disadvantaged pre-technological 'deserts'. Compare California with Appalachia, North and South Italy, England with the rest of the UK, the Ruhr with Bavaria.[8] Strain or tension is also generated in industrial societies in many other ways. Clearly, with the emergence of new professions roles cannot have been clearly defined and therefore role ambiguity is established. Migrants from the rural areas have little idea of the behaviour patterns of city life and cannot easily conform. Problems of acute poverty and inherited poverty are not solved automatically by the industrial state. Again, with the far higher degree of mutual interdependence which is characteristic of the industrial society dislocations in one sector are far more likely to reverberate through the society than in any previous system and this in turn forces political authorities to take remedial action. Obviously, these processes lead to tension and somehow the tension has to be reduced to manageable levels if the society is to persist.

Alongside the process of breaking down the older integrated but parochial structures and loyalties, there emerges another process of reintegration which normally has a wider geographical and social spread than in the older society. People are integrated into a *national* community rather than a local one. This is a multifacetted process. People are integrated into a national economy through nation-wide currency systems, banking systems and industrial organizations catering for a national and international market. Life styles, customs and consumption patterns become national with the growth of nation-wide communication networks such as roads, railways, canals, newspapers and books. Involved in this process is the discovery of the historic identification of the nation through history, mythology, music and heroic ancestors. Thus the high period of German and Italian historical writing coincided with the nationalistic upheavals of the nineteenth century, when the historians, folklorists and poets sang the praises of German and Italian heroic forebears and carriers of the national spirit.[8] Identifying with these symbolic heroes, taught the national language and heritage in schools set up and controlled by national political authority, the 'masses' were inducted into a much wider national culture.[9]

Given the greater numbers potentially involved, and pressing for involvement, organizations such as political parties and pressure groups serve to mobilize and canalize the newer participants. Such parties may be older ones like the Conservative Party in the UK or newer ones which emerge specifically to press the grievances and interests of those seeking representation. Normally, after struggle or interparty competition the industrial society responds to the major grievances of the masses by conceding representation, welfare schemes, marginal income redistributions, ameliorative factory ordinances, etc., etc.

However, all this implies that there is a viable political framework which is at once capable of controlling the tensions thrown up by societal change and which has the flexibility to incorporate new political demands. The danger here is that the new classes, ie bourgeoisie and then proletariat, will be kept out of government and their aspirations frustrated which may lead, as was the case in France and Germany and Russia, such disenfranchised groups to seek not to reform the system but rather to overthrow it. Alienation from the political system in such cases can be gauged from the ideological content of the out-group's politics and by the extent to which the out-group coincides with and coalesces with religious, party, class and possible ethnic cleavages. If the cleavages are cumulative then clearly management is much more difficult and, consequently, stability much more problematical.[9]

Government itself, responding to pressure, requests and the exigencies of national warfare, becomes more and more deeply involved in problems of societal management. As we saw in the case of the bureaucratized empire, the administrative agencies of government become larger and more bureaucratized so that the state apparatus becomes easily the largest in the nation. In America today the government employs one person in six, whilst in 1930 it employed one in fifteen; in the UK the government employs one in four, whilst in 1930 it was one in ten. As this process develops, the taxable capacity of the people increases, so that in the UK public expenditure increased by about 600 per cent and in the US by about 1100 per cent in the twentieth century. At the same time, the government appropriates a growing share of national income, thereby increasing its responsive capacity. For example, in the US there is evidence that the overall effect of governmental redistribution of its tax income favours those areas with lower than the national average income.[10] This appears to be a nearly universal characteristic of government in industrial society and enables the government and its agencies to react to the tensions endemic in a society growing more heterogeneous and innovative. This relationship appears to hold for all countries except the US and Canada and subsistence agricultural countries; but 'Where income levels are higher and the industrial and commercial sectors are larger, an expanded role of government is "normal" and would seem to be more or less expected—a modern economy cannot operate without substantial governmental activity'.[*10*]

The responsive capacity of industrial societies may be measured in economic and political terms. We may argue that stability is highly correlated with the level of economic development, which in turn is interrelated with industrialization, degree of urbanization, and education. And the reasons for the interrelations in terms of group theory are not far to seek: 'Since the more well-to-do and better educated man is the more likely to belong to voluntary organisations, the propensity to form such groups seems to be a function of levels of income and opportunities for leisure'.[*11*] Again, we may well see a connection between high levels of industrialization and a systemic capacity to ward off economic frustration and for governments to tax and redistribute in order to 'buy off' potential malcontents. In part at least the welfare policies associated with both Bismarck and Lloyd George were conscious attempts to integrate the working-class and, in this context, one should not neglect the heady delights of imperialism as a political anodyne. Nor is it likely that in both Germany and Britain the association between welfare policies and imperialism was an accidental one. Responsive capacity has also been seen as a major consequence of the development of a national communication system with a degree of urbanization, level of education and percentage of population involved in agriculture.[11] As nations develop these capacities, they also develop complex and specialized political institutions which give them a higher responsive capacity than have less developed nations.[*12*] Similarly, it can be shown that an effective bureaucracy constitutes a massively important responsive agency of government and that it is 'highly dependent upon a relatively advanced level of economic development, literacy, urbanisation and communication capacity'.[*13*] It can also be shown that there is a positive association between those polities permitting competition between parties and pressure groups and their development in terms of wealth, industrialization, urbanization and educational indices[12] Finally, political competitiveness in the states of the US—defined in terms of office rotation and closeness of voting—has also been found to be quite strongly associated with years of education of citizens, wealth, urbanization and degree of industrialization. High wealth and urbanization were most strongly associated with two-party states, whilst low wealth, low education, low urbanization and low industrialization were most strongly associated with single-party states.[13]

All of the societal configurations we have enumerated, plus the politcial agencies such as parties and pressure groups, combined with the national symbols and mythologies, constitute much of the apparatus of tension management in the industrial society. Additionally, the greater resources of the industrial state enable it to sponsor research and support professions and institutions specifically concerned with ameliorating strain. Thus the police becomes national and highly professionalized and sponsors research into suicide, drug-taking, criminality, juvenile delinquency, alcoholism, etc. Separate professions, often state sponsored, develop to detect strain and control the environment, ie town planners, youth employment agencies, and leisure leaders, juvenile officers, psychiatric social workers, industrial retraining agencies, and so on.

Tension management can be attained in two ways which are not mutually exclusive: by leaving adjustment to non-governmental agencies thrown up by society, or by governmental intervention, or by a combination of these two. The mixture differs in different industrial states. Some suggest that left to itself society is a self-adjustive mechanism or system of such complexity that even the best-willed governmental intervention is likely to prove harmful. This may well be an attractive argument to those in a societally advantaged position, but its beguiling qualities are not readily apparent to those groups who, rightly or wrongly, believe themselves to be unjustly served by the system. An adaptation of this argument is that of Durkheim who suggests that the very complexity and differentiation of industrial society constitutes the basis of its solidarity; men are interdependent and too specialized to exist without the help of others, and out of this fact of functional interdependence there develops what he calls 'organic solidarity'. However, for Durkheim, although there is mutual interdependence there is also a situation of potential clashes since interest can hold people in peace only for as long as this mutuality of interests persists and, therefore, the state has to ensure that duties attaching to positions are fulfilled irrespective of individual interests or whims.[*14*] Put slightly differently, interests and dependencies must be linked together and made mutually compatible whilst disruptive interests must be insulated or kept apart, and there must be known procedures or laws delineating the way in which interests may be defined and pursued. It is the state that is the agency in the modern industrial society which, amongst others, performs the task of regulating and defining the rules by which social interests may be pursued, thereby maintaining social cohesion.

In this version of solidarity theory although there is no logical basis for it the state is normally understood as a kind of honest broker, above the temporary conflicts and competition and the hurly-burly of competitive life. It is not an agency of social struggle but an arbiter, judging and adjusting in the light of a presumptive common interest. Similar in many ways to this version of compliance in the industrial state is the pluralist theory of democracy.

5.3. Power, Compliance and Pluralism

The major actors in the pluralist theory of compliance are groups of people with common interests arising from occupation, neighbourhood, ideology, ownership, and so on, who associate together in pursuance of that interest. State institutions are seen in theory as suppliers of authoritative rules and values for which the groups strive but which cannot, at least in the long term, act so much in one group's interest as to alienate any other considerable section of interest. Thus an assumption of the pluralists is that the groups in the struggle are able to bring pressure to bear upon the government, the pressure being in the form of votes, assents, cooperation and information. A further assumption is that politics is not dominated by a single power centre but rather power is dispersed amongst 'multiple centres of power, none of which is or can be wholly sovereign'.[14] With the growing differentiation of the society new groups enter the political arena with demands for help and offers of assistance and are, therefore, not neglected.[*15*]

The pluralist theory thus states that governmental policy is essentially a compromise between the various interest groups involved, that policy is an outcome of the pressures and shifts in the balance of social and political influence.[15] There is an assumption here that no one group is sufficiently powerful to control the 'output' of government in the face of competition from other interested groups. In this way, political power and influence is fragmented, no one group of interests being sufficiently strong to be dictator, but instead each group having a kind of veto over the policy influence of the others. An elaboration of this is contained in the concept of 'countervailing power'.[*16*] Here, the idea is that if one group of interests proves strong enough to dominate the other groups, processes are generated which cause the threatened groups to organize resources and support as a counterweight to the power and influence of the original group. Such processes can be seen in the development of consumer organizations as a response to the perceived power of the retail organization to control prices in the market. Similarly, the history of industrial relations illustrates the mutual development of employer and employee organizations specifically constructed to deal with the activities of the other. It is a crucial element in the pluralist model that societal 'disturbance', whether induced by government or by other action, may call into activity previously unorganized interests (potential interests) when such interests are affected, and that a consequence of this possibility is that when issuing policies or demanding them, government and organized interests keep this outcome in mind. This consideration necessarily moderates demands and outcomes.

Another interesting aspect of pluralist theory is the use of the concept of 'cross-cutting solidarities' as a further explanation of why interests are not pursued in such a manner as to 'overload' the system.[*17*] Here the argument makes use of the high level of social differentiation characteristic of complex societies. Individuals in some such societies are involved in many organizations and institutions not all of which involve loyalties and demands compatible with each other. As a result, the individual is more likely to be faced with the necessity of choice between alternative and incompatible lines of action, loyalties pulling him in different ways. In such cases, the individual is more likely to perceive the value of compromise and reasonableness, or perhaps be so torn as to be reluctant to make a choice.

Also, the pluralist model of compliance includes a set of rules of the political game especially, but not necessarily, those of democracy. Such rules include the proposition that opposing political forces must have access to authoritative decision-makers; violence, intimidation and fraud are barred from the political arena; participant orientations are instrumental and not ideological; and the government is not captured by any one group.[16] There are two sanctions for these rules: the present out-groups may become in-groups so it is unwise to outrage them and, secondly, potential interests may be outraged by breaking the rules and act so as to restore the rules. The condition underlying these sanctions is adult suffrage, which necessitates competition for the support of those without significant economic resources.

Compliance in the pluralistic industrial society is mediated through group affiliation with the 'masses' only indirectly involved but, presumably, requiring at least minimum payoffs from group leaders in exchange for support. The effect of the pluralistic structure of competing, semi-autonomous groups is that government is insulated from excessive demands from the masses by virtue of the muting effect of cross-cutting affiliation and moderate group leadership.[17] By virtue of group affiliations the people have a sense of social and political involvement, or at least of satisfaction, and because of this fact, as well as the payoffs, they support the system and hence the system's rules and outputs. Newton suggests that essentially, 'The importance of a pluralist political system lies not in the number or competitive nature of elites but in the extent to which elites are responsive and responsible to the non-elites'.[18] But one might add that in all pluralist theorizing it is a necessary condition of responsiveness that there is competition amongst elites for popular support.

The pluralist model is claimed to be peculiarly appropriate for the analysis of compliance in differentiated industrial societies and, as we have explained, it is not a model of direct participatory democracy but on the contrary one of mediated indirect participation with the bulk of people compliant and uninterested in direct participation. Although in most democratic systems the manifest values are claimed to be participatory and equalitarian, in fact the levels of interest and participation fall far short of the ideal. This shortfall is regarded by the pluralist as not a bad thing since direct incursion would lead to demagogic politics, violence and instability, a condition which the leaders of groups have a direct interest in preventing. 'Being more influential, they (the group leaders) are privileged; and being privileged, they have, with few exceptions, a special stake in the continuation of the political system on which their privileges rest.'[*18*] Most pluralists would regard this state of affairs as desirable, structurally conditioned and as an accurate picture of Western democratic societies; for the pluralist model the citizen is an important political resource whose energies are, and must be, canalized, mobilized and competed for by leaders of various groups in the political process, and it may be that the very success of this process keeps levels of citizen involvement relatively low since there is a mechanism through which grievances can be directed or even anticipated.[*19*] Writing specifically on American foreign policy, Rosenberg mentions his 'impression' that the 'policy elite' produces the policies it does 'due, in part, to expectations that public disapproval and indignation over conciliatory undertakings may lead to electoral losses and other imposed disadvantages'.[19] In this situation the average citizen has little incentive to trade off his energy for political payoffs since he gets them anyway, hence the generally low level of political interest and involvement in the developed industrial society. As Dahl puts it, 'politics is a side-show in the great circus of life. Even when citizens use their resources to gain influence ordinarily they do not seek to influence politicians but family members, friends, associates, employees, customers, business firms and other persons engaged in non-governmental activities.'[*20*]

Pluralism, as a mode of academic analysis, can also be understood as a response to the empirical evidence that as a matter of fact the vast majority of people are at most intermittently concerned about, involved in, or informed about public affairs, have very little interest in public affairs and seem to attach only limited possibilities to personal involvement in terms of affecting outcomes. In this sense it involves simply a description of the existing state of affairs: most people do not wish to be involved but some do, and these tend to be the best educated, best informed, and generally enlightened sections of the population, but they *are* a minority. Pluralism, unlike the older prescriptive participatory thesis of people such as J. S. Mill, claims to be a description and not a recommendation.[20] It describes how, given the undisputed facts of minimal involvement by the majority of people, the system survives and, indeed, flourishes; that is, the emphasis changes from the normative democratic theory which stressed the moralizing qualities of participation for the individual's development of civic and personal responsibility to an emphasis on system needs, which are met by limited rather than extensive and constant intervention by the 'masses'.[*21*] It also switches emphasis from individual participation to group participation and, given the fact that only a minority of people belong to any politically meaningful group, and of this minority only a minority is active, emphasis is really upon competition between oligarchs.[21] We may term this 'elite pluralism'.

Pluralism is *not an alternative* to elite theory but a development of it which insists on the central role of elites in all social life, but differs from elite theory in a number of respects. Firstly, elite theory must posit a unified elite whose ranks are broken only by superficial differences, but who are united on the issue of maintaining elite power.[22] Secondly, elite theory must depend upon the proposition that the rulers are able to manipulate the citizens by devices such as symbols, ideologies, recruitment of most able citizens and concessions so as to obtain the active or passive acceptance of united elite rule. Finally, elite theory must argue that, for example, economic wealth or social prestige can be transmitted into political influence and that these attributes tend to be cumulative, ie that the political power structure follows the other lines of social stratification.[*22*] All of these elite propositions are denied by the pluralists. Thus the major difference between the two models is that the elite model posits a unified elite responding to citizen demands as a prudential concession, whilst the pluralist asserts that responsiveness is a structural condition of the various and competitive elites' existence.

Although the pluralist model has been especially fertile in the production of monographs and articles describing pressure group activity, it has also led to very considerable attention being paid to the problems of participation and power in local politics. One such study was Dahl's empirical investigation into New Haven.[23] In this study he tested the proposition that all significant decisions were made by a unified group of people who controlled the major resources of influence in the community. He tested this idea by looking at the way in which decisions in three 'issue areas' were taken; the decisions were varied in their content in order to provide adequate evidence to test whether or not those who took one type of decision also took another. Accordingly, he selected three issue areas in which it might reasonably have been expected that those politically most significant in the community would have had some interest in influencing the outcome. A number of decisions made by ' "*political*" officials' were studied to discover involvement and participation in the community and three groups of potential leaders—politicians, social notables and economic notables—were distinguished by office, reputation and command of resources. He discovered that, for example, economic leaders did not coincide with political leaders even before he looked at his three issue areas, ie the positions were not cumulative or overlapping and, therefore, were potentially competitive. The most regularly participant group was the economic, but during the period of the study their involvement was largely confined to one of the three issue areas, that of urban redevelopment, an issue closely affecting economic interests, yet one on which there was little intra-group solidarity. Dahl concludes, 'Economic notables, far from being a ruling group, are simply one of the many groups out of which individuals sporadically emerge to influence the policies and acts of city officials. Almost anything one might say about the influence of the Economic notables could be said with equal justice of about half a dozen other groups in the New Haven community.'[24] In New Haven, although by no means 'an ideal democracy', influence is not only unequal, it is also non-cumulative; the system is 'dispersed inequalities',[25] and lack of economic power in one sector may be made up for by political power or by greater popularity or by strong ethnic support in another.[*23*]

There is considerable support for Dahl's pluralistic model of city politics in the US and wide agreement that power is relatively dispersed in city politics.[26] Moreover, there is some evidence that the fragmentation of influence is relatively recent and is associated with definite community characteristics. Many US studies have shown monolithic power structures in small one-industry towns. For example, the Lynds' study of Middletown detailed the enormous economic, political and social resources which were controlled by very few individuals (the X family), or again Hunter identified in Regional City economic institutions that were dominant over others.[*24*] Indeed, Dahl's own New Haven study, when he deals with the period *prior* to the massive influx of immigrants, and the rise of a strong Democratic Party organization, shows much the same pattern: 'the institutions and processes of industrial society produced a dispersion of political resources'.[27] Those communities characterized by monolithic power structures are typically small, lightly industrialized with locally owned enterprises, with a homogeneous ethnic population, low rates of trade unionization and one-party systems; businessmen dominate governmental offices and are members of the social elite, thus fusing the three types of political resource.[28]

In such systems, when and if industrialization comes to them, a number of changes occur which provide a basis for a more elite pluralist power structure. Professional managers in the larger corporations, although not rooted in the community, are a potential opposition to the older business elite which can no longer make demands backed by a monopoly economic power. A larger, more mobile and organized working-class also offers a challenge to the older elite and is in a strong position to mobilize votes.[*25*] Thus, responding to environmental changes the political system moves from an elite to an elite pluralistic system within which influence is dispersed, and in which the basis of compliance moves from a situation where people obey because they have few alternatives to obedience towards a situation where compliance is more a matter of payoffs and satisfaction.

5.4. Some Inadequacies of Pluralism

Let us now turn to an examination of pluralism's adequacy as an account of the political process in industrial societies.

Firstly, it is probable that the definition of the 'political' used by pluralists is too restricted. Dahl, for example, restricts his 'attention to decisions made by "political" officials', a strategy which neglects the exercise of power inside corporations and between them affecting wage levels, the types of goods and services available, the level of employment, availability of loans, and so on. Those making such decisions are, at least in the major economic conglomerates, in no meaningful sense of the word responsible, but are a small and almost certainly cohesive minority.[29] It is possible that these people do not make any more impact on 'political' decisions than any other people, but they do affect the daily lives of many and to exclude this consideration by definitional fiat may indicate a failure of the 'sociological imagination'.

Secondly, there appears to be something odd about the notion of 'non-cumulative resources', in at least the sense that Dahl suggests that those lacking in one resource may make up for it by having another: 'Though he has less money, he may have more time, more energy, greater popularity'.[30] This is certainly possible and not to be ruled out of court, but equally much of the available evidence suggests the contrary, ie that those with the most economic resources, at the very least, are not lacking some other resources. Middle-class people are more likely than working-class people to vote, join parties, hold office, have a higher sense of political competence, have greater knowledge and organizational skills, have more time to devote to politics, and so on.[*26*] These cumulative relationships are the best researched and confirmed findings in political sociology. Those lacking the above resources are envisaged by the model as exerting indirect influence by their votes and because the elite prudence will ensure that account is taken of non-elite interests.[31] Dahl himself reports that 'a large proportion of the adult population of New Haven does not even vote'.[32] But, and again this is a well-researched finding, it is just those people who do not vote who have the fewest resources of money, time, education, and so on.[33]

Thirdly, the issue orientation method used by Dahl to discover the influentials within New Haven tends to avoid those issues that never get raised or those issues that are settled with little fanfare but which cumulatively may be very significant. As Bachrach and Baratz point out, one of the basic methodological assumptions of the pluralists is that 'power is totally embodied and fully reflected in "concrete decisions" or in activity bearing directly upon their making'.[34] This presents a difficulty since the pluralist method provides no adequate decision-rule for distinguishing between 'key' and routine issues, and, as suggested above, the 'model provides no account of the fact that power may be, and often is, exercised by confining the scope of decision-making to safe issues'.[34] The 'issue area' notion of the pluralists ignores what Bentley called the 'habit background' of a community and its role in the political process, or non-process. Various values within the community will often define which issues become matters of public consideration and which issues do not reach that threshold. For example, in the United States the extent of poverty for years failed to become a major political issue, or in Britain the condition and the state of the old did not reach the political area for some considerable time.[*27*]

Finally, one might well be suspicious of the pluralist suggestion that the relative passivity of the uninvolved is in itself evidence that their interests are considered and in most cases at least partly met.[35] But, there is an alternative explanation of the passivity of relatively large sectors of the electorate which emphasizes the 'minority might become apathetic, believing participation to be fruitless. Their interests would not appear as demands for the political leaders to consider.'[36] In one study of three issue areas in Newark which were of concern to the inhabitants of the black ghetto the author concluded that, 'Since the data indicate that a lower-class group exercises no successful influence when active, I find no compelling reason to entertain the conclusion that the group wields power through unspecified means when inactive'.[37] Such withdrawal might come to be associated with feelings of political impotence, feelings of cynicism and anomia which in general have been found to be associated with a lack of resources such as education, status and ethnic pride.[38] Hence, one cannot be other than sceptical about the suggestion that the uninvolved are the satisfied. Furthermore, the long history of violent repression of the American black people perhaps suggests a flaw in the passivity equals satisfaction equation![*28*] Presumably, passivity can be a consequence of *either* satisfaction or of feelings of political inefficacy, feelings which may be expressed in 'non-political' forms such as crimes of violence, emotive religiosity and extreme sectarianism characteristic of the black ghetto in America and South Africa,[39] in an apathetic withdrawal of interest and concern, or simply in a failure to take any interest at all in the comings and goings of public figures. Whatever the cause, and it is too soon to foreclose argument by attributing disinterest to satisfaction, it is evident that the general level of interest in public affairs is low.[40]

In a pluralist democracy, such as the US is argued to be, it is perfectly possible to isolate sections of the population whose interests over a very long period are simply ignored, for example the negro, the American Indians and the rural poor. If these interests become channelled either separately or in coalition, as there is contemporary evidence that they are, this may pose a threat to the stability of the system. As Templeton puts it, 'The stability of the (American) political system seems to rest upon the absence of institutionalised channels through which discontent can be effectively expressed' rather than upon popular satisfaction with the political system.[41] It may well be the case that when such interests do finally make an impact upon the system, their influence tends to be extremely disruptive.[42] Even with groups who are inside the general political process, with a well-structured organization and access to decision-makers, there can be a tendency to reject the compromise supposedly implicit in the bargaining process. This is especially the case during periods of political or technical change which act as a disadvantage to previously powerful or high-status groups, for example, the French settlers in Algeria, the old middle-class in America, the small farmers and shopkeepers in France, and so on.[43] Such groups exist within a pluralist system, yet find that their interests either are not, or cannot be, realized and are, therefore, strongly motivated to change the system.

It is also the case that not all interests compete on anything like equality of footing. Consumer interests are notoriously badly organized and more difficult to organize than producer interests. Perhaps more important is the fact that ideas do not compete on anything like equal terms: in Britain major institutions such as the monarchy, the public schools, the military, the universities and the enormous weight of private property and enterprise embody values which are quite closely connected with those of the Conservative Party and broadly antithetical to the Labour Party. A consequence is that if there is a pluralist system in Britain it is one in which all groups are not equally placed: 'most of the major institutions are involved with values not easily made compatible with socialism (and therefore) the range of effective influence of any Labour government could be expected to be less than that of any Conservative government'.[44] Further, the congruence between the major social values and those of the Conservative Party means that the party has a built-in electoral advantage in the sense that socialism or a Labour vote represents a *deviation*, won at some considerable cost, from a structure consistently favouring the Conservative Party.

Hence, the theory of the elite points to the *systematic* disadvantages enjoyed by the great mass of the population not merely in lacking material resources, education and leisure but, more importantly, in assimilating values and personal resources conducive to social success. Thus Bernstein has shown the behavioural and psychic consequences of modes of speech which are class-linked and which have profound consequences for the child in later life in so far as they help to reproduce class divisions.[45] Other studies have shown the relatively slow development amongst working-class children from their first year of life of both verbal and motor skills.[*29*] Yet other studies have shown that a considerable section of the working-class actually *believes* that people from elite and high-status backgrounds are more fitted to rule than are the less privileged.[*30*] Other suggestive work has demonstrated the systematic engendering of feelings of hopelessness and inadequacy and of racial inferiority amongst whole populations subject to alien rule.[*31*]

What these studies indicate is that to some extent a self-fulfilling prophecy mechanism operates which defines the poor, the dispossessed, the immigrant, the black, and so on, as being apathetic, ignorant, second-class and content with their lot. Then, in accordance with the popular social definition of such minorities, they are treated as though they are apathetic, and they may then become so. A recent article demonstrates this mechanism and adds a class dimension interesting to the political sociologist. It has been known for some time that children's scholastic achievements are related to a number of factors such as intelligence, home background, the self-esteem of the child and also upon the expectations of educational achievement that teachers have about the children in their charge. If the teacher expects the child to do well, this is statistically related to the child actually doing well. In an all-black school in Washington DC it was observed that from the first days of a child's education the teacher —herself a black—*unconsciously* favoured the better dressed, the cleaner, the better speakers, and those with better educated and paid parents. She grouped these children together and defined them as her 'fast learners' within two weeks of their arrival in the school. Having so defined them she treated them in such a manner as to encourage their verbal, intellectual and social skills whilst tacitly discouraging the rest and, in the course of a year, the favoured group in turn learned 'through emulating the teacher how to behave towards other black children who came from low-income and poorly-educated homes'. The children initially defined as 'fast learners' became fast learners and, although the point is not made, probably fitted for leadership positions when they became adults.[*32*] This last point was demonstrated in a study of five schools in England which showed that children in secondary modern schools were not expected by their teachers to be interested in or have knowledge of political affairs. The teachers' expectations were largely fulfilled.[46]

The implication of these studies is very simple: the masses are not kept out of the political arena by their satisfaction with its products, but rather because they are socialized into acceptance of the existing order. It is not a matter of equally competing elites, but rather of elite competition from which great numbers of those most in need are systematically excluded from competing for the limited resources. And, given that educational qualifications are becoming more important for obtaining careers which open the possibility of social mobility and which help engender political skills, the systematic bias in the educational system has obvious long-term implications for the distribution of politically significant careers. In short, the elite case is that most advanced societies seem to act in a manner which *systematically* excludes the majority from anything like an even break over the whole range of societally significant institutions. And, although some sectors are worse off in terms of opportunity the others (what *happened* to Dahl's five hundred New Haven families who were moved to make room for redevelopment?), the majority do not have a fair chance given the self-reinforcing and interlocking cycle of economic, political, psychological, educational and cultural disadvantages.[*33*] Further, not only are many people, almost certainly the majority, systematically undermined in terms of effective participation, but issues that are potentially important to the least powerful sections of the community do not have an equal chance with those that are sanctioned by the powerful values and interests that are built into the political system.

5.5. Power, Compliance and the Elite Model

The pluralist democratic model relies, as we have previously asserted, upon a responsive elite or elites without the ultimate power to restrict entry into the political arena, whilst the ruling elite model is far more sensitive to the difficulties of the non-elite in affecting the decisions which influence the basic distribution of power and influence in the society. It is suggested, contrary to the pluralist model, that influence is concentrated, that it is cumulative and that to a considerable extent those with influence can use it to make conditions for entry to positions of political influence. Although not always the case, elite theorists are apt to distinguish between the elite and the potential elite from whom the elite is recruited. The potential elite may be seen as a bridge between the elite and the rest of society, as a channel of information, as performing lesser leadership functions and as a source of recruitment into the top echelon of influence.[47] The potential elite, or 'political class' in Mosca's terms, consists of those willing or able to compete for influence and from amongst whom the *political elite*—those actually exercising political influence—are drawn. Unlike the political elite, the potential elite is a rather disparate group or groups 'which may be engaged in varying degrees of co-operation, competition or conflict with each other'.[48] The important differences between this view and the pluralist model are that (1) resources are cumulative and potentially transferable between institutions, (2) policy preferences amongst the elite are broadly agreed, (3) these preferences will determine political and economic allocations, which the population will normally accept, and (4) the elite has very considerable powers to determine access to elite positions.

Probably the most important characteristic is the first one, that power resources are cumulative and potentially transferable, since without it the *elite* model shades off into a competitive *elites* model very similar to that of the pluralist. The other conditions appear to be more matters of judgement than of any absolute value since, for example, no elite theorist argues that a political elite is totally unanimous nor that the elite is impervious to determined outsiders.

There appear to be two broad types of evidence for the elite view of the structure of political power. Firstly, writers such as Pareto, Mosca and Schumpeter take a very low view of the capabilities of the masses for self-government or indeed of their desire for it, arguing that most people are only too eager to give the burden of making decisions to those willing to do so. Often backing this argument is the proposition that always a minority has the advantage in that it can organize more effectively than a majority: 'Its internal channels of communication and information are much simpler. Its members can be contacted more speedily'.[49] Thus in any situation calling for even a modicum of organization the minority has an advantage. Secondly, and perhaps more characteristic of modern elite theory, is the use of data based upon the social background of decision-makers. The assumption underlying the data is that a person's social background and training determines his range of sympathy and responses to problems, and that if leaders come from a particular milieu their choices of policy will be biased towards that milieu. Hence, at its weakest, if it can only be shown that decision-makers come from similar backgrounds then elite theorists presume that their behaviour and policies will favour the group from whom the decision-makers are recruited. As we have shown and shall develop below, there is a great deal of evidence supporting the elite view that some social sectors are greatly advantaged in terms of recruitment to positions of influence. Having shown this, elite theorists then attempt to demonstrate that the elite is able to set the tone of the society by developing a legitimating ideology through its control of the mass media and curricula of the schools and colleges, through the formation of law, manipulation of national symbols and the channelling of discontent into politically harmless avenues.

There is very substantial evidence indeed for the view that the people occupying 'top positions' in industrial societies are disproportionately drawn from limited sections of the population, with other sectors relatively disadvantaged in the 'competition' for top positions. The technique used is to isolate a number of important positions in the society—legislators, top bureaucrats, higher officers in the armed forces, board members of significant corporations and top institutionalized religious leaders—and then to investigate their social and educational origins. These origins are

TABLE 1. Class Structure of Cabinet Personnel 1868–1955

	1868–86	1886–1916	1916–35	1935–55	Total
Aristocracy	28	49	22	21	120
Middle-class	22	49	45	54	170
Working-class	0	2	20	21	43
Total	50	100	87	96	313

Taken from W. L. Guttsman, *The British Political Elite*, MacGibbon and Key, London, 1963 and Basic Books, New York, 1963.

then held to account for the differential recruitment since they add up to a socially structured advantage in the 'competition' for the top positions. For example, Guttsman, in one of the most thorough studies of a parliamentary elite, demonstrates the changing social composition of that elite in the last hundred years when it altered from a land-based to a commercial-cum-professionally qualified elite (see Table 1).[*34*] Similarly, the figures for MPs show the trend from the agrarian to the urbanized elite when between 1868 and 1910 landowners were reduced from 36 per cent of Conservative and Liberal MPs to 16.5 per cent in 1910, whilst the category 'Commerce and Industry' increased from 40.5 per cent to 59.5 per cent in the same period. Comparable figures for the category 'Legal and Professional' are 13 per cent in 1868 and 17.5 per cent in 1910.[*35*] It is obvious that these people are drawn from a narrow but changing catchment area reflecting the changing nature of the British economy, but it is important to note that there *has* been change.[*36*] In other words, even these few rudimentary figures show that over time the elite, assuming it wished to do so, could not entirely restrict entry of other groups.[*37*]

It can be shown that in obtaining access to elite positions a person's educational background is important. In the Conservative Cabinet of 1964 and the Labour Cabinet of the same year the educational figures are as shown in Table 2.[*38*]

TABLE 2. Educational Background of British Cabinet Personnel

	Conservative Cabinet	Labour Cabinet
Public schools	30	9
Grammar schools	3	6
Other state schools	0	9
University	16	13

Taken from R. Millar, *The New Classes* Longmans, London, 1966, p. 274.

Comparable figures for MPs were:

	Conservative MPs	Labour MPs
Public schools	297	58
Elementary and secondary grammar	39	177
Oxford and Cambridge	159	60
Other universities	33	74

Adapted from D. Butler and A. King, *The British General Election of 1964*, Macmillan, London, 1964 p. 237.[*38*]

The figures suggest that politically the nearer the centre of power—the Cabinet—the greater is the concentration of high-status origins and education.[*39*] It is not merely a matter of occupying formal roles of political import, but also of having putative political influence, and again it can be shown that those most likely to serve on government advisory bodies, members of research councils, governors of public bodies like the BBC, etc., are drawn very disproportionately from those groups most likely to obtain formal political roles.[50] Again, the bulk of British high civil servants have been recruited from the same relatively narrow section of the population; one finding reports that in 1959 nearly 70 per cent of all senior civil servants came from Oxford and Cambridge Universities.[51]

A similar pattern is detectable in military recruitment, which has changed from one dominated by rural landlords and gentry towards an urban but still predominantly upper- and middle-class dominated profession with broadly the same educational bias as the political and administrative leaders: 'toward boys from Public Schools in the southern half of England, the traditional "gentry" territory in fact'.[52]

Table 3 puts the situation very clearly:

TABLE 3. Social Background of British Senior Officers and Other Groups (% ages)

	Upper-class	Upper middle-class	Middle-class	Working-class
British army officers				
Lt. Gen. & above, 1956–60	18%	39%	43%	—
Major Gen. & above, 1956–60	10%	36%	54%	—
British company directors	2%	33%	56%	9%
British admin. class civil servants	29%		41%	27%
Population as a whole	3%		35%	62%

Reprinted from P. Abrams, 'The Late Profession of Arms: Ambiguous Goals and Deteriorating Means in Britain', *European Journal of Sociology*, **6**, 238–261 (1965).

Otley, in an examination of the social background of the three top ranks of the British army between 1870 and 1959, concludes that only 3 per cent of his sample of 330 officers came from lower middle-class backgrounds and none from the working-class. The educational milieu of this elite was similarly restricted, with 69 per cent as graduates of just ten boarding schools, and they tended to have close connections by birth or marriage to other sectors of the British elite (see Table 4).[53]

Very similar patterns emerge from studies of businessmen and of religious leaders in Britain who are disproportionately drawn from a limited social and educational milieu, and indeed every study of the social and educational background of occupants of powerful and prestigious positions (except entertainment) shows this to be the case. Further, the wealth of comparative material available from France, Germany, Italy and America shows in differing degrees the same phenomenon.[*40*]

It can be shown then that top position holders are not a social microcosm of their societies, but this is only the first step towards establishing an elite dominance model although it does, in Mosca's terms, point to the existence of a political class from which the ruling elite is predominantly drawn. These people, drawn from similar backgrounds, would presumably have been exposed to similar cultural ideas through similar educational experiences and regular contact with others in the same situation and will therefore base their actions on the same values. Further, because

TABLE 4. Connections by Birth or Marriage of the Military Elite with Other Elites

Year	Officers closely related to members of the: Economic elite A	Military elite B	Political elite C	Administrative elite D	Total elite connections E	
	%	%	%	%	No.	%
1870	33	15	30	10	41	51
1897	19	27	11	6	27	43
1913	21	24	12	7	25	43
1926	27	13	15	15	19	40
1939	27	22	11	4	22	49
1959	31	17	3	3	16	44
Averages	26	20	16	8	150	46

A, Sons or sons-in-law of great landowners, major financiers, entrepreneurs and company directors; B, Sons or sons-in-law of army officers of the rank of major-general or its naval equivalent; C, Sons or sons-in-law of peers, cabinet ministers and MPs; D, Sons or sons-in-law of senior diplomatists, civil servants, etc.; E, Some officers had multiple connections, therefore this column does not sum the four it precedes.

C. Otley, 'Social Affiliations of the British Army Elite', in J. Van Doorn (ed.), *Armed Forces and Society*, Mouton, The Hague, 1970.

they are privileged they have an interest in maintaining the broad outlines of the social structure which supports these privileges and are in a strong position to legitimate that structure in the minds of the unprivileged. Although this process of legitimating privilege can be seen as the outcome of wilful manipulation by the elite, as a matter of fact most elite theorists understand the elite to be as much convinced by the content of the ideology as the non-elite. The important point is that the very structure of privilege is seen by the population as natural, and is legitimated by the institutions of society: 'The advance of capitalist production develops a working class, which by education, tradition, habit, looks upon the *conditions of that mode of production as self-evident laws of Nature* . . . Direct force outside economic conditions is of course still used, *but only exceptionally*.'[*41*] Likewise, the elite theorist understands the educational system as, if not designed, then at least functioning to produce not radical critics of the society but rather those who accept and admire the broad structure of the society and with it the distribution of power and privilege.[54] Writing of political socialization in capitalist society, Miliband suggests 'that much of the process is intended . . . to foster acceptance of a *capitalist* social order and its values, an adaptation to its requirements, a rejection of alternatives to it'.[*42*] One could list the other techniques such as welfare schemes, attachment by symbols of the nation, ideological persuasion *via* the mass media, the general conservatism of much religious indoctrination, all of which are understood to account for the widespread passivity, obviating the need for, to use Marx's phrase, 'direct force' since the population is persuaded or dulled into accepting the *status quo* without questioning its fundamental tenets.

Thus the population is maintained in a passive state whilst the elite is cohesive because of common social, educational and career patterns. Non-passive or especially gifted individuals from the mass may rise into the elite but will be repatterned so as to suit the requirements of elite dominance. The data already examined shows that working-class boys do become officers, highranking civil servants, MPs, etc., but for the elite theorists these are bought men or men struggling against odds which will soon overwhelm them.[*43*]

Elite organization is also understood and examined from a slightly different perspective, that of the interconnections between key institutional positions. The extent to which the institutions are interlocked through top personnel and legal ties is thought of as an indicator of elite power. Although not specifically with the point in mind, elite theorists in this way demonstrate the transferability or cumulative nature of power. We have, for example, careful studies of the complicated patterns of interlocking directorships between different industrial, banking and commercial firms so that a relatively small number of people, 'a coherent group', exercise very considerable power.[55] Again, many studies have demonstrated the interchangeability of top personnel between the armed forces, the universities, the public services, legislatures, and influential pressure groups and the boardrooms of powerful public private industries. After examining the structure of the American elite, Wright Mills concluded that 'interlocking directorate is no mere phrase; it points to a solid feature of the facts of business life, and to a sociological anchor of the community of interest, the unification of outlook and policy, that prevails among the propertied class'.[*44*]

This brings us to a key consideration in elite studies, the question of what it is that is felt to hold the elite together. We have already seen that elite studies concentrate attention on a common educational and general career pattern and, in some cases, common leisure patterns which are understood to be important but not crucial. What is more important is the 'interest' the elite or elites have in maintaining the *status quo*, that is, maintaining the society in the form in which elite members continue to receive the benefits accruing to their position. They have a joint vested interest in the social arrangements supporting their position; writing of the British elite, one group explained the mechanism as follows: 'The groups may represent several interests—financial, managerial, industrial—but in any true oligarchy, the "natural competitiveness" of these elites of power has been subsumed into their greater interest—the mutual cause of corporate property'.[56] Wright Mills similarly argues that the 'top man in the bureaucracy derives his right to act from the institution of private property; he does act insofar as he possibly can in a manner he believes is to the interest of the private property system'.[*45*] Thus elite empirical studies are intended to show that the elite is drawn from a more or less narrow social area, but it is tightly enmeshed within a number of important institutions, that these institutions are interconnected in terms of legal titles and personnel and that in capitalist industrial society the function of these arrangements is the defence of the property interests of the elite. Concessions and reforms may be forced or conceded in advance of serious troubles, but such reforms do not impinge upon the major institutional configurations and interests which these institutions exist to defend.

5.6. Some Inadequacies of Elite Theory

Although important, the data and considerations we have presented do *not* constitute a crucial test of the elite theory, which also implies a strong element of consciousness or common social perspective amongst the elite. In other words, it has to be shown that in cases of conflict between elite and non-elite the former will think and act alike. This is, of course, a very difficult test for the theory because of the practical difficulty of obtaining information about the assumed manner in which elite accord is reached. Elite theorists must specify in some detail what they take to be the crucial decisions or structures upon which the elite must agree; if they do not, then we are involved in an almost infinite regress in which empirical studies demonstrate specific disagreements amongst the elite on policy but which are then held by elite theorists to be not crucial. Examples abound: the decision to drop A-bombs on Japan; the decision to invade

Suez in 1956; the current debate on Vietnam; the Roosevelt New Deal policy; Britain's entry into the Common Market; the Cuban missile crisis, and many others, all showed the elite, however defined, at odds with itself. If these were not crucial decisions then it is difficult to know what a crucial decision is. On the other hand, it is a fact that very few people indeed had any say at all in any of these decisions. There is no doubt that on the whole the political elite is rather narrowly recruited, it does occupy focal positions and in Dahl's terms has a 'high potential for control', but in all the cases mentioned above—and there are many more—the elite was in fact divided; it displayed a 'low potential for unity'.[57] Because a group *could* control if it was motivated to do so, is not the same thing as saying that it *does* control: 'The actual *political effectiveness* of a group is a function of its potential for control *and* its potential for unity'.[57]

In an interesting article Edinger and Searing succeeded in illuminating the question of elite attitudes and in relating these attitudes to background factors amongst a group of German and French leaders. Firstly, data was gathered on the background experience along 40 dimensions, including occupation, party affiliation, social class, university specialization, military rank, region of birth, religion, and so on. Then Manifest and Latent Attitude Schedules were administered to the 220 respondents. Finally, the background information was tested for its predictive capacity relative to the attitudes elicited by the schedule. They discovered that some background factors—social class, region of birth, university education, membership of voluntary organizations and military service, occupation, party affiliations—were better attitude predictors than other factors. They also discovered that the French elite was greatly less attitudinally cohesive than was the German elite. Most significantly, they found that by clustering social background data they were able to make predictions about manifest attitudes which varied between 66 per cent and 80 per cent in accuracy of assignment.[58] Hence, although the conclusions are 'admittedly tentative', it does seem quite likely that elites do have at least some attitudes in common—but this, of course, cannot be taken to mean they do not have these attitudes in common with non-elites nor that these attitudes necessarily determine their behaviour.

There is another crucial difficulty involved in elite theory: if both elite and non-elite subscribe to the same basic cultural values and norms, that is they are not ideological or symbolic manipulators, in what sense are they an elite other than in terms of people holding top positions in the society? In this sense elite theory becomes simply another way of saying that in an organization or a polity only a minority actively take decisions or are involved in taking them.[*46*] This is true but not very revealing! Dahl has suggested that before one can identify an elite it is necessary to have different policy preferences with one group, the elite, regularly obtaining its preferred position. If we could identify a group which regularly had its way, would it be sensible to refer to it as an elite? It would be if one could show that the indifference of the masses was a consequence of elite manipulation through the educational system, etc., or if the indifference resulted from regular defeats over conflicting interests with a consequent failure of popular morale. In most cases, the argument for elite manipulation is simply inferred from the fact that it does have both the opportunity and the reason, ie top positions and, by inference, the collective desire to protect these positions.

As a matter of fact in some degree all educational systems mould children towards particular cultural patterns, but the crucial question is whether or not, or to what extent, the elite determines the cultural content of the society and its pattern of education. It is the case that educational patterns and, indeed, the content of education have both been intentionally designed to meet what were seen as certain national needs for 'better' educated citizens, for more skilled workmen, for more loyal bureaucrats, for military conscripts better adapted to technical armies, and so on.[*47*] There is little doubt that such designs were deliberate, that they did produce generations of loyal citizens, soldiers, workmen and bureaucrats, but all evidence is that the ruling group was bitterly divided in every case. For example, educational reform in Britain was extremely tardy, opposed by many influential people and in many ways not really adapted to an industrial society. Or again, factory legislation was long opposed by the mass of factory owners and forced upon them by Parliament, evidence that the elite was divided. Another example: the elite was divided upon the issue of adult suffrage yet it was granted in the teeth of sectional elite opposition.

In the face of this consideration, those advocating an elite theory are apt to suggest that the opposition did not know its own real interest because the grievances of the population, which might otherwise have built up and exploded, were dispersed. Advocates of an elite theory might also argue that the concessions were necessary to make the system more efficient and to give the population a false sense of involvement. But it is difficult to discover what a person's interest is other than by asking him what his interest is or inferring it from his actions. Thus we rapidly find ourselves in metaphysical speculation about real interests *versus* declared ones and are dragged into the somewhat rarified air of counter-factual history. This is a major difficulty of elite theory: it involves one in a series of regressions, none of which is readily amenable to demonstration and empirical test.

It is for reasons such as these that Dahl has attempted to construct a rigorous formulation of the elite model based upon a view of power which stresses decision-making. Before one can meaningfully speak of an elite it is necessary, Dahl claims, to see if the following conditions are met:

> '(1) The hypothetical ruling elite is a well-defined group.
> (2) There is a fair sample of cases involving key political decisions to which the preferences of the hypothetical ruling elite run counter to those of any other likely group that might be suggested.
> (3) In such cases, the preferences of the elite regularly prevail.' [*48*]

Here the burden of proof rests on the proponents of elite dominance to demonstrate that all three conditions are met; but it should be borne in mind that Dahl is referring to 'American communities' and not, presumably, to the national system in the US or any other country nor specifically to the so-called 'totalitarian systems'.[*49*] In this sense Dahl's proposals are potentially very restricted, but in principle there is no reason why his tests should not be applied to any non-totalitarian system at any level.

5.7. Elites in the USSR

The difficulty is in applying the test to totalitarian societies, since some of the defining characteristics of such societies—the monopoly of mass communication and all means of social mobilization—can easily result in a population manipulated and controlled by an elite. This is a difficulty since in the totalitarian society the effect of monopoly control is precisely to preclude the population from forming interests and opinions contrary to those of the ruling elite. Hence, the second of Dahl's three tests for the existence of an elite is not in this case capable of fulfilment.

It can be argued that the methods of totalitarian control are distinctive in the sense that an ideologically self-conscious minority is able to utilize the technology of communication and 'persuasion' available in an industrial state to make the political and social attitudes of the population consonant with the ruling group's ideology. In Russia a tiny minority party, certainly less than 1 per cent of the population, dominantly urban, with a high proportion of non-Russian intelligentsia, seized power amidst the chaos of German invasion, Allied interventions and administrative incompetence.[*50*] Initially, there was a period of political consolidation of power with the legal banning of opposition groups, the reconquest of most of the Tsarist empire, the reformation of the armed forces under party control and the gradual establishment of a strong party bureaucracy together with the banning of factions within the party.[*51*] Party control over the population was relatively minimal in the countryside but strong in the towns, and central control *via* the party bureaucracy over party members was gradually strengthened from 1922 onwards.

Classical Marxism had stressed that the socialist society would come as a successor to a developed capitalist regime within which the problems of production had been solved. This, of course, was not the case in Russia where the technical level of the population was low and modern industry rather patchily developed. Lenin, in a major revision of Marxism, insisted that left to themselves the working-class would be unable to achieve a scientific appreciation of society—leading to its overthrow—but rather would be trapped by concessions and short-term gains into attitudes favourable to the continuation and stability of the regime.[59] The proletarian socialist consciousness which, broadly speaking, for Marx was a product of developing social and economic forces was, for Lenin, to be brought to the workers from outside the immediate milieu of working-class social and economic struggle. Bringing the socialist consciousness to the workers was the historic task of the *organized* advance guard of the revolution, the militant and self-conscious elite party. From the beginning, Lenin's faction was envisaged as a tightly ideological, well-organized, clandestine, directorate: an instrument of social control leading a possibly reluctant mass towards the new socialist society. Society in the Leninist cannon was a plastic body upon which a determined leadership could make its mark and which, with proper scientific handling, could be moulded to accord with socialist desires. How was the moulding to be achieved? What was to be the shape of the society?

Certainly the Bolsheviks in the period 1917–1922 were a fairly well-defined group and certainly by 1922 they were fairly securely in power in Russia. But it is equally certain that they could not meet Dahl's second test since in decision after decision the Bolsheviks compromised with their principles and did so with their eyes fully open. For example, the Peace of Brest-Litovsk, the retreat from workers' control of the factories, the employment of Tsarist officers and bureaucrats, the grant of land to the peasants, and most important of all, the New Economic Policy of 1922 which Lenin specifically designated 'a retreat'. It was a retreat in the face of a sullen and alienated peasantry which simply refused to produce enough to feed the urban population. Concessions were made to groups or categories such as the factory managers, the bureaucrats and the army-officers in order to gain at least overt support.

Here we must refine Dahl: an elite may be prevented from obtaining its object because of the impracticability of the objective due to the lack of appropriate resources or because 'the preferences of the hypothetical ruling elite run counter to those of any other likely group that might be suggested'. It makes a difference which of these explanations applies, for, in the former case, the elite group may still retain its preeminent position of power and influence *vis-à-vis* other groups in the society while, in the latter case, the elite's power is threatened. Eventually in Russia most of these decisions were overturned as Stalin drew to himself more and more the power-levers of Soviet society. But it was a relatively gradual process during which almost the whole of the erstwhile elite was destroyed. The problem then becomes one of time-span together with personnel continuity. Dahl does not sufficiently differentiate between what one might call elite positions or roles and the occupants of these roles. In the Soviet Union in the 1930's there was an almost total change of personnel in elite roles in the armed forces, state and party bureaucracies and in the industrial complex, yet taken together such roles were important and gave whoever their occupants were significant collective power.[*52*] It was this sort of consideration that Pareto had in mind when writing of the governing class: 'To be sure they must now and again bend the knee to the whims of ignorant and domineering sovereigns and parliaments, but they are soon back at their tenacious, patient, never-ending work, which is much the greater consequence'.[60] Equally, occupants of important roles had a common interest mediated through their membership of the Communist Party, had a strong interest in preserving common privileges and a strong incentive to hang, as Lenin put it, together lest they hang apart.

During the early period, up to about the mid-1930's, the Soviet elite was composed of the members of the Party Central Committee whose major concern was in consolidating the revolution and controlling the pre-revolutionary organizations (principally the state bureaucracy) and new organizations (armed forces and police) principally manned by previous incumbents. Hence the proliferation of control devices of one sort and another, for example, the Party Control Commission, The State Security Committee (KGB, Cheka GPU, Rabkrin, etc.), the Political Commissariat in the armed forces, and so on.[61] The higher echelons of the party in that period were 'marked by a blend of political skills and the skills of Specialists in Persuasion'.[62] No special recruitment areas can be defined except that at the top minority groups like Poles, Jews and Latvians were strongly represented and in the rank and file efforts were made to recruit from the working-class. Although it is not possible to identify, with any degree of certainty, the elite, one can be sure that the Central Committee of the party, the higher personnel of the state bureaucracy, the police and industrial management were important. But most personnel were under continuing party surveillance, with only a thin layer of trusted—if not always effective—Bolsheviks at the top directing operations.

Whole areas of social life remained relatively untouched by the party: the arts, literature, theatre, the family and education were only peripherally affected by anything other than shortages, whilst the peasant was left almost alone except for taxation and conscription. As might be expected, compliance in this early stage of Soviet development sprang from mixed sources; in the towns, Soviets controlled by the party, the lack of viable alternatives after the Civil War, famine and poverty, opportunism, patriotism and moral commitment all played a part. The countryside, containing more than 80 per cent of the population, was during most of the 1920's—except very near the towns—virtually self-governing, concerning itself mainly with survival and retaining the land, the gift which above all others maintained the peasants' benevolent neutrality towards the regime. Also, it should not be forgotten that the draconic pre-revolutionary social discipline and habit of obedience to constituted authority meant that the Bolsheviks, so long as they did not attempt to take back the peasants' land, could rely on at least passive approval.

This pattern was destroyed totally during the period of collectivization and the first two Five Year Plans when the party attacked the twin problems of control of the peasantry and growth of the industrial sector. By 1928, Soviet industrial and agricultural production was approximately back to 1914 levels, but the prospects of further development were not good since growth both in industry and, especially, agriculture had led to the rise of a 'class' of well-off people who it was feared would form the social base of a 'capitalist' revival. As is usual in agricultural production, a substantial part of the marketable surplus was produced by a relatively small sector of the larger producers and there was a danger that they might—not having read Dahl—transform economic power into political power. But without this class producing a surplus for the export and urban market the Soviet authorities were unable to finance new capital goods from abroad or to feed the urban proletariat who would work the new machinery. Collectivization was the sword used to cut that particular Gordian knot: it was both a political control operation and a technique of squeezing a development surplus from the peasantry whilst forcing peasants off the land into the new industries, ie forming the proletariat upon whom Marx had posited the success of socialism. Since the decision was made to collectivize rapidly and by force—previous efforts to persuade having failed—new mechanisms had to be employed. In the towns living standards were held at a very low level and a new urban peasantry had to be taught the discipline of the factory whistle and the regularity of factory work.[*53*]

The goals set by the elite were to industrialize as rapidly as possible. Such an objective is easily set; achieving it, however, is far more problematical in a dominantly agricultural society. Amongst the impediments perhaps the most crippling is the absence of a skilled proletariat and of a work force attuned to the rhythm of modern society. Again, resources have to be transferred from sectors considered less important to those considered essential to achieve the object, and effectively this means that those attempting the transfer are depriving the population of immediate material incentive. In the Soviet case this meant a substantial drop in rural standards and a stagnation or actual decline in urban standards of living. Given any opportunity, those affected are likely to attempt to form organizations to resist this process: in the USSR a number of techniques were developed to meet this possibility.

Firstly, although not designed with collectivization in mind, the fact is that by the early 1930's the party was a strong and unified entity within which the major oppositions to Stalin had been eliminated and in which a formidably experienced cadre of administrators—the *apparat-chiki*—had developed. Additionally, it was a party highly responsive to the policy decisions of the leadership, and the Communist Party was deeply embedded in controlling positions in the state bureaucracy, in the armed forces, in the trade unions, the secret police, the state apparatus and in the existing managerial force.[*54*] By the period 1928–1930 it was by far the most highly organized and conscious group in the USSR, forming a powerful organizational lever with which to mobilize an unorganized mass. In principle, and to a large extent in fact, dual hierarchy of organization gave the party a means by which most aspects of social life could be supervised. Within the party the member was understood to be at the disposal of his political superiors, movable from job to job and area to area.

Again, and most effectively with the young, a series of socializing agencies helped to produce loyal Communist citizens. For example, some schools were firmly under party influence, Marxist-orientated textbooks were gradually introduced, whilst the young Pioneers and the Comsomol trained promising youngsters as potential party members. Gradually in the twenties trainee teachers were brought under party influence, but for the rural areas the most important agency of sovietization of the young was the period of compulsory military service. During this service the peasant conscript was taught the elements of Marxism and inducted into the wider political life of the Soviet Union.[*55*]

It was upon these bases of support that the collectivization and crash industrial programme were initiated, but what resistance there was was destroyed by terror: that is, by the use of violence designed to make people submit out of fear, uncertainty and a developing sense of powerlessness against the forces that confront them.[*56*] Sociologically, terror involves the use of unrestrained violence to create amongst the population feelings of mutual distrust and a pervasive sense of unease. The terror descends almost arbitrarily upon the just and the unjust, the guilty and the innocent, the involved and the uninvolved alike: it abolishes social boundaries, so creating what has been termed an atomized population. No one can be sure that he is not next on the list nor why he is on it, but some measure of security lies in proving loyalty by denunciation. Hence no one can trust his neighbour, his friend or his work fellows, so no mutually sustaining organization or group to resist the elite is possible. Thus Barrington Moore writes that 'Terror ultimately destroys the network of stable expectations concerning what other people will do that lie at the core of any set of organised human relationship'.[63] Boundaries are also abolished between the real and the unreal, and the older certainties disappear to be replaced by the imposed reality of the ideological elite. Thus the individual is shorn of the supportive relationships of friendships, kinship, primary group loyalty, the linkages between self and group. However, although the authorities controlled the mass media of communication, there is some evidence to suggest that monopoly did not entirely prevent the transmission of illicit information by informal, unofficial oral communication.[64] He is also shorn of the possibility of anticipating the consequences of action and is left with no real alternative but obedience to the dictates of those in authority.[65] The complete isolation of man in totalitarian society is well brought out in the torture scene in *1984* when Winston Smith is finally terrorized into agreeing that two and two only make four when his tormentors say so. Like man in totalitarian society Winston Smith is then ready for 're-education'.

As might be expected, terror is strongest where organized resistance is potentially strongest, so the party and the armed forces and the administration in both state and economy and, finally, the terror apparatus itself are purged and repurged. The consequence of the purging is that an older generation of party and governmental functionaries is replaced by a new one which owes its promotion and education to the regime. Between 1933 and 1938 about 800,000 party members were purged, the army high command almost disappeared and the older generation was replaced by a younger group of 'plant managers, engineers, technicians and scientific personnel who played an increasingly important role in running and directing the economy'.[57] Stalin put his finger on the significance of this change when he declared that the 'Soviet intelligentsia is an entirely new intelligentsia, bound by its very roots with the working class and the peasantry'.[66] ('Working class and peasantry' is a code name for Communist Party.) In the 1930's the party was transformed from a dominantly 'persuasive' and manipulative party of agitators and political generalists or 'entrepreneurs' into a young, highly educated technical elite drawn from the ranks of the administrators, managers and technicians of the rapidly developing economic and administrative sector.

During the 1930's the social structure of the Soviet Union was dramatically altered towards an industrial urban society with a strong numerical rural sector of landless 'proletarians' organized in a variety of collective farms and controlled through a system of urban Communist outposts, the Machine Tractor Stations.[58] Millions of peasants were forced into the towns and the new industrial areas and there compelled by hunger, privation, lack of alternatives, by a fierce labour discipline and by sheer terror to adopt to the rhythm of industrial life. In this process the trade unions, dominated by the Communist Party, were employed not to defend workers' standards, but to discipline their membership.[59]

The first point to be made about this change is that the population quite certainly did not want it nor were they consulted, nor for that matter was the party; it was initiated by Stalin and a segment of the party leadership. It was not merely a process of structural change but also a massive exercise in attitudinal reorientation, a process initiated rather unsuccessfully under Lenin soon after the Revolution and continued under more 'favourable' conditions by Stalin in the 1930's and 1940's.[60] The regime aimed to produce the New Soviet Man, a loyal, work-orientated and obedient citizen displaying boundless affection for the regime and its leaders—and to a very considerable extent it succeeded.[61] Education was brought under rigid control and massively expanded, propaganda and agitation were incessant and sources of alternative information practically eliminated, the church was almost destroyed, the pre-revolutionary generation almost removed from influence and 'extraordinary opportunities for social mobility were opened up for those willing to go along with the regime or able to acquire more specialised skills'.[62] Soviet citizens abandoned traditional rural values—devotion to the land, the local community, religion and social immobility—and instead took up the values of the industrial order 'which involve a consumption ethic, social and geographical mobility and financial success. The population is proud of Soviet achievements and does not question the basic premises of the regime.'[67]

Using the apparatus of total control which they developed, a very small group of people were able to change a massive country from top to bottom and to change it *purposively* in at least its major societal and attitudinal configuration. A modernizing elite with a relatively clear ideological perspective heaved an underdeveloped society on the road to economic development and political stability.[*63*] So it would seem at first glance that the pluralist model does not fit the Soviet case and is unlikely to fit any case in which rapid political and social mobilization is a key element in the process of industrialization. The Soviet example—rightly or wrongly—has become a dominant feature for the intellectual leadership in almost every developing country, ie in most of the world.[68]

By the mid 1950's Russia had emerged as a fully fledged industrial society, and this raises the question of the extent to which the changed nature of the socio-economic system is associated with changes, if any, in the political system of the society. One view of this is that the impact of modern technology and an advanced economy on a society produces a social order in which the state comes to regulate competition between the interests which the modern economy always produces and aggregates these interests on the basis of a widely accepted 'web of rules'. Industrialization produces a population relatively more homogeneous than its predecessors in terms of wealth, status and political power. An advanced economy requires increasing numbers of well-educated and highly trained personnel, and hence the middle of the hierarchy pyramid expands while the bottom contracts so forming a diamond-shaped social hierarchy with a homogeneous and growing middle stratum.[69] In the advanced economy *efficiency* demands the consent and involvement of the expensively produced experts, technicians and professionals who have or come to have a measure of functional independence of the regime: 'a monolithic structure gives way to one in which there are a number of "strategic" elites and of different foci of power'.[*64*] Changes in the economy thus produce pressures on the political system which cannot be, in the long period at least, neglected or channelled in other directions and therefore must be given due weight in the political decision-making process. We have already seen the process at work in the changing composition of the Communist Party, but it is not simply a matter of altered composition but also of considering and taking into account in policy decisions these functionally necessary personnel. Thus, this model has a great deal in common with the elite pluralist model which also hinges upon institutional differentiation and autonomy and their political expression. In the Soviet Union such organizations and groups as the higher command of the armed forces, the top bureaucracy in state and party, the industrial management, the leading figures in the scientific establishment, are all understood to exert pressure on the political elite; acting either alone or in collusion these groups are powerful enough to constitute a system of countervailing elites.[*65*]

That there has arisen in the USSR a highly literate population, a very well-educated technical stratum, a skilled working-class, an extensive bureaucracy, a highly experienced military leadership, is beyond dispute. That the working of the economy depends upon this group is also undeniable, and certainly terror is no longer the key control device it was. But none of this means that the political elite is not still firmly in control nor that terror could not be revived: 'The arsenal of totalitarianism, its instruments of suppression, terror, and censorship are to be kept in readiness, but are to be used more sparingly while the regime bases its policies of the moment on its ability to persuade and demonstrate to the Soviet citizens that communism is a vigorous and viable way of life'.[70] The elite has to meet the expectations of the population—the so-called 'goulash socialism'—but is it a condition of meeting these expectations that the party retains control? Thus Schapiro, discussing the 1961 Party Programme, argues that it 'enunciates squarely the concrete fact that Party rule has come to stay. It calls upon the Soviet citizen to recognise and accept this fact . . . In return, it promises him great benefits and prosperity.'[71] Nor do we have much evidence that the countervailing elites are in fact able to determine or greatly affect policies in other than an instrumental sense by acting in such a manner as to make the policies work. The Liberman economic experiments in consumer choice do not challenge the position of the party since they could not be tried without political permission, but they do make distribution more efficient and help counteract the well-known bottlenecks of the Soviet economy.[*66*] Again, although the Soviet armed forces have always done quite well—in the 1930's the growth of production of war potential exceeded that of all other sectors—they have always been controlled and at the disposal of the party elite and have never attempted independent policy initiatives. On the other hand, they have also sought and gradually obtained a measure of autonomy in matters of purely professional concern, but the condition of this autonomy is that they do not 'challenge the basic policy-making powers of the Party'.[*67*]

Another putative challenge to the hegemony of the party elite is the very rapidly growing managerial class which certainly could, if it wanted, or thought it possible, take over the reins of power—gradually. But the fact is that they do not see themselves as challengers or successors; rather they appear to be technical realists whose 'realism is confined within a broader ideological orthodoxy and finds its principal expression in implementation of the established party line'.[*68*] Also, despite the massive restructuring of the state and economic bureaucracies during the 1950's, there is no evidence to suggest that the bureaucrats were either consulted or that they put up serious resistance—or that they initiated the changes. There was yet another group of presumptive heirs apparent or liberalizers, the intelligentsia, who included the artists, playwriters, poets and in general the more educated stratum which has been a traditional 'opposition' in Russia. This group can be divided into 'a new efficiency-seeking intelligentsia', with whom we have already dealt, and 'the more traditional truth-seeking intelligentsia' whose ideas 'seemed to touch some resonance in the younger generation'.[72] Possibly symptomatic of the latter groups' importance is the continuing barrage of vituperation and censorship to which they are subject by the regime, but we have no way of knowing whether the attacks are an almost conditioned response by the rulers of a country well aware of the potential impact of the arts on politics, or simply an attack on a relatively harmless but deviant group. Whatever the case, it is probable that the truth-seeking intelligentsia is a small minority without a large following so that, at least in Stalinist terms, the regime can afford to be lenient. When a group of demonstrators was brought to trial for protesting in Moscow in January, 1967 against the arrest of a number of writers the prisoners were tried by something like due process and they did have a defence lawyer and were able to appeal. Significantly, however, although technically it is now possible for a Soviet citizen to hold almost whatever views he likes, the defence lawyer in pleading against imprisonment for one of his clients suggested that 'He must be slowly and patiently re-educated, he must be helped to rid himself of his childish ideas about Rousseau and the English parliament as the ideal social order'.[*69*]

The evidence, therefore, suggests that industrialism is not incompatible with a modified form of totalitarian control and that it is perfectly possible to have groups functionally important to society and economy but unable, unwilling or culturally unaware of the possibility of trading one type of authority for another. Pluralistic structures in the economy and society are not necessarily associated with plural influences upon the polity. At best, the impersonal demands of economic and bureaucratic efficiency may involve technical concessions—a degree of professional autonomy, consultation with experts on carrying out policies, rewards for achievement, granting elements of consumer preference, cessation of the social unpredictability induced by terror—but all of this and more is consistent with a pattern of political elite tutelage or domination. One form in which this may be expressed is what Fischer calls a system of dual executives, that is of top party bureaucrats with experience and training in both political and economic sectors. These men, because they have two kinds of skill, serve to '*counteract* the proliferation of specialised activities and the very real pressures these may set up for division of labour'.[73] Thus the existence of plural elites does not necessarily imply the existence of elite competition for political influence; in the USSR the political elite was able to mobilize masses of people and to get them to accept the basic values of an industrial socialist society. Soviet citizens accept the idea of public ownership of the economy, are well disposed to the political system, but wish for 'decent treatment from leaders who take some interest in their welfare'. There is no substantial 'rejection of the system predominantly on general ideological grounds, on matters of principle'.[*70*]

Evidently the basis of compliance in the USSR has changed in the three periods just discussed. Initially, an indifferent population still retained their traditional loyalty to a central authority, still kept a pattern of almost unthinking 'rural idiocy' and lacked any sort of viable alternative with the destruction of opposition parties by 1922. In this period the old boundaries of the Tsarist empire were consolidated, the party disciplined and the towns brought under control. In the second period—from about 1938 to the mid 1950's—terror was used to destroy any actual or potential opposition to the party leadership, the countryside was brought under party control, job opportunities on a massive scale were created, education and indoctrination were tremendously expanded and rewards for specialists of all kinds were greatly increased; and the use of patriotic themes and symbols during the war, as well as a sense of bitter pride that Russia after centuries of backwardness was finally emerging, also played a part in creating a sense of loyalty to the regime.[74] But the major source of compliance was fear and its consequences: 'the complete destruction of the human personality—an absence of fixed authority, orthodoxy, stable personal relationships, in general the "atomisation" of society'.[75] In this period the distinction between the political and what in Western society is often regarded as the non-political was abolished so that everything, every activity, was politicized. No longer was there such a thing as private life or a private sphere of activity; the political was all.

During the final period, when almost all of the population knew nothing other than Soviet authority, the ruling elite was legitimated because the population had assimilated a political culture experienced in a network of institutions controlled by an ideologically aware leadership.[*71*] Having complete control of the economy and polity, this leadership was able to make significant concessions which almost certainly had the effect of further reinforcing popular loyalty. This loyalty appears to be predicated upon the ability of the system to provide satisfactions and, therefore, in part upon policies which cannot, as in the previous period, be arbitrary but rather must be an outcome of systematic considerations of interests and involved groups.

5.8. Some Conclusions

We have discussed two models purporting to represent the distribution of compliance and power in industrial societies, both of which have some measure of plausibility. Difficulties arise in both models. For example, both Britain and the US are certainly industrial countries, yet proponents of one model see them as more or less pluralist whilst the other view understands them to be elite-dominated. A number of possibilities immediately suggest themselves: both are inappropriate; one of them is inappropriate; both are appropriate, but both focus upon different aspects or levels of the political system. Which of these alternatives is the most accurate characterization is difficult to say since both, as we have shown, have their ambiguities and conceptual fuzziness. Given this, the problems of operationalizing and researching and building up an accurate picture of the distribution of power are made harder. As we have seen, Dahl has insisted upon a set of conditions for verifying the elite model which are so strict as almost to preclude the possibility of the existence of an elite but at the same time has so restricted his own model that one is not at all sure whether it applies to anywhere other than New Haven. Certainly, the evidence is that New Haven 'pluralism' is not a universal pattern in American towns, nor does Dahl claim that it is since his contention is that pluralism is associated with a relatively extensive industrial division of labour: multi-industry towns with a peripatetic executive class, a mobile working-class organized in competitive unions and competitive parties. There is a great deal of internal evidence that at most the pluralist model as constructed by Dahl fits Western industrial societies—and this is vigorously denied by elitists—and has very limited application to the Third World.

However, it is possible to imagine more or less pluralistic decisions when, as Presthus puts it, we envisage 'pluralism' as a continuum, along which the context of each of the major decisions can be regarded as being 'more' or 'less' pluralistic.[76] Measuring pluralism is then a matter of determining actual individuals' direct participation in various decisions—attending meetings, contributing money and time, voting, etc.—and mediated participation through membership of involved voluntary associations.[77] Using these indices Presthus found that participation varied between his two communities and with different issues for decision, but in other than a decision about hospital building 'few organisations participated at any stage. In fully half the decisions only one local organisation played an active role.'[*72*] Since pluralism stresses the importance of mediated involvement through groups and Presthus found both a low group membership and a very low level of group involvement in taking decisions—'only 6 per cent of 52 organisations were active in more than one decision'—he concludes 'tentatively' 'that the role of voluntary organisations in ensuring pluralist forms of decision-making has been somewhat overrated'. Of course, this is not a sufficient test of the pluralist model, which also indicates that decision-makers take into account even those groups and interests who do not become involved, yet it does suggest that the onus is upon the pluralists to demonstrate that such interests are taken into consideration in a sense other than simply accepting the decision-makers' word for it. But it is extremely difficult to envisage how operationally this could be achieved—as difficult as it is for the elite model to meet Dahl's requirements.

On the other hand, the pluralist critics have put their fingers on a number of important weaknesses in the elite model: its self-fulfilling character; its tendency to select evidence from various countries, periods and social conditions and lump it together; its failure to isolate crucial decisions; its often naïve head-counting sociologism, and so on. Yet there do appear to be systematic advantages in most stable systems for a relatively restricted social class or group to obtain access to roles of considerable social importance. This may well be the major virtue of the elite model, but it has considerable defects beyond this in explaining the relationship between a particular policy and the concrete interests of a particular group. This is problematic since there is a tendency in elite studies to define the elite interest in terms of the policy outcomes: *post hoc ergo propter hoc!* An alternative method of identifying elite interests is to explore social backgrounds, property holdings, etc., and then to define policy outcomes as the more or less subtle defence of these interests. This weakness of the elite model forms the central investigatory tenet of the pluralist model and also forms the central weakness of the pluralist model outside the US: the fact of the matter is that this view is culture-bound. In no other industrial society are so many political and economic decisions as openly arrived at, often in the glare of publicity and investigation, as in the US. This is obviously not an objection to the accuracy of the model, but it is a major difficulty in meeting Dahl's criteria for an elite.

Another problem with the elite model is that the inequalities it specifies fit every society other than the simplest and most undifferentiated, but the real issue in political sociology is *how and whether these inequalities affect political decision-making*. This is a problem to which there is no simple answer, since even in the apparently simple case of the USSR it is now not at all obvious that there is a simple fit between the political regime and the social and industrial structure. However, in succeeding chapters we shall investigate the relationships between social structure and phenomena such as voting, rates of and kinds of political participation, attitudes to the political system, the impact of groups and parties on some actual decisions, the social sources of loyalty and disloyalty, and so on. But none of this will amount to a generalized theory predicting particular policy outcomes from particular economic, social or attitudinal configurations, since there is no such theory.

References

1. I. Davies, *Social Mobility and Political Change*, Pall Mall, London, 1970, ch. 1.
2. T. H. Marshall, 'Citizenship and Social Class', in *Sociology at the Cross Roads*, Heinemann, London, 1963, pp. 67–127.
3. L. Pye, *Aspects of Political Development*, Little, Brown, Boston, 1966, p. 37.
4. E. Shils, 'Demagogues and Cadres in the Political Development of the New States', in L. Pye (ed.), *Communications and Political Development*, Princeton University Press, New Jersey, 1963, pp. 64–77.
5. G. Almond, *Political Development*, Little, Brown, Boston, 1970, pp. 159–179.
6. J. La Palombara (ed.), *Bureaucracy and Political Development*, Princeton University Press, New Jersey, 1963, p. 96.
7. H. Hart, 'Social Theory and Social Change', in L. Gross (ed.), *Symposium on Sociological Theory*, Harper and Row, New York, 1959, pp. 196–238; N. J. Smelser, 'Mechanisms of Change and Adjustment to Change', in J. Finkle and R. Gable, *Political Development and Social Change*, Wiley, New York, 1968, pp. 28–43.
8. C. S. Whitaker, 'A Disrhythmic Process of Political Change', in *World Politics*, **19**, 190–217 (1967).
9. S. M. Lipset, *Political Man*, Mercury Books, London, 1963, ch. 3.
10. W. C. Mitchell, 'The Shape of Political Theory to Come', in S. M. Lipset (ed.), *Politics and the Social Sciences*, Oxford University Press, New York, 1969, p. 116.
11. P. Cutwright, 'National Political Development: Its Measurement and Social Correlates', in N. W. Polsby, R. Dentler and P. Smith (eds.), *Politics and Social Life*, Houghton Mifflin, Boston, 1963, pp. 569–582; D. McQuail, *Towards a Sociology of Mass Communications*, Collier-Macmillan, London, 1970, ch. 1, especially p. 13.
12. G. Almond and J. Coleman, *The Politics of the Developing Areas*, Princeton University Press, Princeton, 1960, pp. 532–576 and appendix.
13. T. W. Casstevens and C. Press, 'The Context of Democratic Competition in American State Politics', *American Journal of Sociology*, **68**, 536–543 (March 1963); R. E. Dawson and J. A. Robinson, 'Inter-Party Competition,

Economic Variable and Welfare Policies in the American States', *Journal of Politics*, **25,** 265–289 (May, 1963).
14. R. H. Dahl, *Pluralist Democracy in the United States*, Rand McNally, Chicago, 1967, p. 24.
15. E. E. Schattsneider, *The Semisovereign People*, Holt, Rinehart and Winston, New York, 1960, p. 141.
16. J. R. Gusfield, 'Mass Society and Extremist Politics', *American Sociological Review*, **27,** no. 1, 19–30 (Feb., 1962).
17. W. Kornhauser, *The Politics of Mass Society*, Routledge and Kegan Paul, London, 1960; S. M. Lipset, *Political Man*, Mercury Books, London, 1963, ch. 3, and Tocqueville's classic study, *Democracy in America*.
18. K. Newton, 'A Critique of the Pluralist Model', *Acta Sociologica*, **12,** 209–223 (1969).
19. J. Rosenau (ed.), *Domestic Sources of Foreign Policy*, Free Press, New York, 1967, p. 150.
20. R. Dahl, 'Further Reflections on the "Elitist Theory of Democracy" ', *APSR*, **60,** 298 (1966).
21. R. Presthus, *Men at the Top*, O.U.P., New York, 1964, pp. 238–281.
22. R. Aron, 'Social Structure and the Ruling Class', *British Journal of Sociology*, **I,** Part 1, 1–16; Part II, 126–143 (June, 1950).
23. R. H. Dahl, *Who Governs?*, Yale University Press, New Haven, 1961.
24. —— *Who Governs?*, Yale University Press, New Haven, 1961, p. 72.
25. —— *Who Governs?*, Yale University Press, New Haven, 1961, p. 85.
26. E. C. Banfield and J. Q. Wilson, *City Politics*, Harvard and MIT Press, Cambridge, Mass., 1963, pp. 244–245.
27. R. H. Dahl, *Who Governs?*, Yale University Press, New Haven, 1961, p. 85.
28. D. Rogers, 'Monolithic and Pluralistic Community Power Structures', in B. E. Swanson (ed.), *Current Trends in Comparative Community Studies*, Community Studies Inc., Kansas City, 1962, pp. 31–48.
29. T. Gitlin, 'Local Pluralism as Theory and Ideology', in H. P. Dretzel, *Recent Sociology*, Macmillan, New York, 1969, pp. 62–87.
30. R. H. Dahl, *Pluralist Democracy in the United States*, Rand McNally, Chicago, 1967, p. 378.
31. —— *Who Governs?*, Yale University Press, New Haven, 1961, p. 164.
32. —— *Who Governs?*, Yale University Press, New Haven, 1961, p. 277.
33. L. W. Milbrath, *Political Participation*, Rand McNally, Chicago, 1965, pp. 55–66.
34. P. Bachrach and M. Baratz, 'Two Faces of Power', *The American Political Science Review*, **56,** 948 (1962).
35. N. Polsby, *Community Power and Political Theory*, Yale University Press, New Haven, 1963, p. 118; J. Walker, 'A Critique of the Elitist Theory of Democracy', *APSR*, **60,** 285–295 (1966): R. H. Dahl, *Who Governs?*, Yale University Press, New Haven, 1961, pp. 101, 140 and 163.
36. G. Parry, *Political Elites*, Allen and Unwin, London 1969, p. 126.
37. M. Parenti, 'Power and Pluralism: A View From the Bottom', *Journal of Politics*, **32,** no. 3, 501–530 (1970).
38. M. E. Olsen 'Alienation and Political Opinions', *Public Opinion Quarterly*, **29,** 200–212 (1965); S. J. Kenyon, 'The Development of Political Cynicism Among Negro and White Adolescents', paper at the 1969 conference of the

SPSA; R. E. Dowse and A. Brier, 'Political Mobilisation: A Case Study', *International Review of Community Development*, **19–20,** 327–340 (1968); B. Barry, *Political Argument*, Routledge and Kegan Paul, London, 1965, chs. 14 and 15, for a formal examination of the point.

39. R. K. Merton, *Social Theory and Social Structure*, Free Press, New York, 1968, chs. 6 and 7; M. B. Clinard, *Anomie and Deviant Behaviour*, Free Press, Glencoe, 1964.
40. B. Crick, ' "Them and Us": Public Impotence and Government Power', *Public Law*, 8–27 (Spring, 1968).
41. F. Templeton, 'Alienation and Political Participation, Some Research Findings', *Public Opinion Quarterly*, **XXX,** No. 2, 249–261 (Summer, 1966).
42. W. Kornhauser, *The Politics of Mass Society*, Routledge and Kegan Paul, London, 1960.
43. J. R. Gussfield, 'Mass Society and Extremist Politics', *American Sociological Review*, **27,** no. 1, 19–30 (1962); S. M. Lipset, 'Social Stratification and Right Wing Extremism', *British Journal of Sociology*, **10,** 1–32 (1959); M. Trow, 'Small Business, Political Tolerance and Support for the McCarthy', *American Journal of Sociology*, **64,** 270–281 (1958).
44. F. Parkin, 'Working Class Conservatives', *British Journal of Sociology*, **18,** no. 3, 281 (1967).
45. B. Bernstein, 'Some Sociological Determinants of Perception', *British Journal of Sociology*, **9,** no. 2 (1958); also 'Language and Social Class', *British Journal of Sociology*, **11,** no. 3 (1960).
46. R. Dowse and J. Hughes, 'The Family, The School and The Political Socialization Process', *Sociology*, **5,** no. 1, 21–45 (1971).
47. G. Parry, *Political Elites*, Allen and Unwin, London, 1969, pp. 33–34; T. Bottomore, *Elites and Society*, C. A. Watts, London, 1964, pp. 2–15.
48. T. Bottomore, *Elites and Society*, C. A. Watts, London, 1964, p. 9.
49. G. Parry, *Political Elites*, Allen and Unwin, London, 1969, p. 37; J. H. Meisel, *The Myth of the Ruling Class*, University of Michigan Press, Ann Arbor, 1962, p. 35.
50. W. L. Guttsman, *The British Political Elite*, MacGibbon and Key, London, 1963, pp. 319–367.
51. T. Lipton and C. S. Wilson, 'The Social Background and Connections of "Top Decision-Makers" ', *Manchester School*, **27,** no. 1, 30–51 (January 1959); R. K. Kelsall, *The Higher Civil Servants in Britain*, Routledge and Kegan Paul, London, 1955; C. H. Dodd and J. F. Pickering, 'Recruitment to the Administrative Class 1960–64', parts 1 and 2, *Public Administration*, **45** (Summer and Spring, 1967).
52. P. Abrams, 'Democracy, Technology and the British Officer', in S. P. Huntington (ed.), *Changing Patterns of Military Politics*, Free Press, New York, 1962, p. 155.
53. C. Otley, 'Social Affiliations of the British Army Elite', in J. Van Doorn (ed.), *Armed Forces and Society*, Mouton, The Hague, 1970, pp. 84–108.
54. D. Glass, 'Education' in M. Ginsberg (ed.), *Law and Opinion in England in the Twentieth Century*, Stevens, London, 1959, pp. 318–346.
55. S. Florence, *The Logic of British and American Industry*, Routledge and Kegan Paul, London, 1961, p. 193.
56. C. Wright Mills, *The Insiders*, New Left Review, London, 1958, p. 31.

57. R. Dahl, 'A Critique of the Ruling Elite Model', *APSR*, **52,** 463–469 (1958).
58. L. Edinger and D. Searing, 'Social Background in Elite Analysis', *APSR*, **61,** 423–445 (1967).
59. V. I. Lenin, *What is to be Done?*, Foreign Languages Publishing House, Moscow, 1950, first published in 1902.
60. J. A. Armstrong, *The Soviet Bureaucratic Elite*, Atlantic Books, London, 1959, p. 2.
61. M. Fainsod, *How Russia is Ruled*, Harvard University Press, Cambridge, Mass., 1963, esp. ch. 12.
62. G. Fischer, *The Soviet System and Modern Society*, Atherton Press, New York, 1968, p. 7.
63. Barrington Moore, jr., *Terror and Progress, USSR*, Harvard University Press, Cambridge, Mass., 1954, p. 176.
64. R. A. Bauer and D. Gleicher, 'Word-of-Mouth Communication in the Soviet Union', *Public Opinion Quarterly*, **17,** 297–310 (July, 1953).
65. H. Arendt, *The Origins of Totalitarianism*, Allen and Unwin, London, 1958, part 3; C. J. Friedrich and Z. K. Brzezinski, *Totalitarian Dictatorship and Autocracy*, Harvard University Press, Cambridge, Mass., 1956, ch. 13; H. Eckstein and D. Apter, *Comparative Politics*, Free Press, New York, 1963, pp. 433–483; R. J. Lifton, *Thought Reform and the Psychology of Totalism*, Penguin, London, 1967; C. W. Cassinelli, 'Totalitarianism, Ideology and Propaganda', *Journal of Politics*, **22,** no. 1, 68–95 (1960).
66. J. Stalin, *On the Draft Constitution of the USSR*, Foreign Languages Publishing House, Moscow, 1950, speech of 1936, p. 21.
67. A. Inkeles and R. Bauer, *The Soviet Citizen*, Oxford University Press, London, 1959, pp. 380–381.
68. M. Watnick, 'The Appeal of Communism to the Underdeveloped Peoples', *Economic Development and Cultural Change*, **1,** no. 1 (1952); E. Shils, 'The Intellectuals in the Political Development of New States', *World Politics*, **12,** no. 3 (1960). For a case study see R. E. Dowse, *Modernisation in Ghana and the USSR*, Routledge and Kegan Paul, London, 1968.
69. C. Kerr, J. Dunlop, F. Harbison and C. Myers, *Industrialisation and Industrial Man*, Oxford University Press, London, 1964; A. Inkeles and R. Bauer, *The Soviet Citizen*, Oxford University Press, London, 1959., esp. chs. 1, 2 and 10; T. Parsons, 'Communism and the West: the Sociology of the Conflict', in A. and E. Etzioni (eds.), *Social Change*, Basic Books, New York, 1964, and 'Evolutionary Universals in Society', *American Sociological Review*, **24,** no. 3 (1964); section 7 of P. Hollander, *American and Soviet Society*, Prentice-Hall, Englewood Cliffs, 1969.
70. A. Ulam, 'The New Face of Soviet Totalitarianism', *World Politics*, **12,** no. 3, 409 (1959–60).
71. L. Schapiro, *The USSR and the Future*, Praeger, London, 1963, p. XIV, and see his introduction 'From Utopia Towards Realism'.
72. J. H. Billington, 'The Intellectuals', in A. Kassof (ed.), *Prospects for Soviet Society*, Praeger, New York, 1968, pp. 449–470.
73. G. Fischer, *The Soviet System and Modern Society*, Atherton Press, New York, 1968, p. 14.
74. R. Bauer, A. Inkeles and C. Kluckholm, *How the Soviet System Works*, Vintage Books, New York, 1956, pp. 265–266.

75. C. W. Cassinelli, 'Totalitarianism, Ideology and Propaganda', *Journal of Politics*, **22**, no. 1, 90 (1960).
76. R. Presthus, *Behavioural Research on British Executives*, University of Alabama Press, Alabama, 1965, p. 242.
77. —— *Behavioural Research on British Executives*, University of Alabama Press, Alabama, 1965, p. 267.

Notes and Further Reading

1. Writing of this process in the West, in the sixteenth century, W. H. McNeil suggests that 'for the first time in all civilised history, an absolute majority of the population ceased to find their lives circumscribed by an immemorial round of traditional agricultural tasks. Instead, they faced the troubling ups and downs of an unpredictable market economy', *The Rise of the West*, Chicago University Press, Chicago, 1963, p. 585.
2. Equally, when the size of firms increases there is a tendency for the economic position to move from a competitive one, where demand is independent of any firm as is supply, towards oligopolistic or monopolistic competition when forces other than market ones operate and, hence, there may be a case for political intervention.
3. See T. Parsons, *The Social System*, Tavistock, London, 1952, pp. 158–167. Parsons built on the previous work of Max Weber and F. Toennies on the types of social action, i.e. the affectual, the traditional, the instrumental-rational and the absolute-value rational, see M. Weber, *The Theory of Social and Economic Organisation*, Free Press, Glencoe, 1947, pp. 115–118, and T. Parsons and N. J. Smelser, *Economy and Society*, Routledge and Kegan Paul, London, 1956, p. 33.
4. For extremely interesting accounts and rebuttals of this particular variable's appropriateness in the African context, see I. Kopytoff, 'Socialism and Traditional African Societies', in W. H. Friedland and C. G. Rosberg, *African Socialism*, Stanford University Press, Stanford, 1964, pp. 53–79, and W. J. Argyle, 'The Concept of African Collectivism', *Mawaza*, **1**, no. 4, 37–43 (Dec. 1968).
5. We have not read of Parsons making such a suggestion, but F. Riggs, *Administration in Developing Countries: The Theory of Prismatic Society*, Houghton Mifflin, Boston, 1964, ch. 1, does so. See also J. Huizinga, *The Waning of the Middle Ages*, Doubleday, New York, no date, especially chs. 1 and 3.
6. Good examples of this approach are R. Bendix, *Nation-Building and Citizenship*, Anchor Books, New York, 1969, and R. Emerson, *From Empire to Nation*, Beacon Press, Boston, 1960.
7. We are aware that in using words like 'associated' we have neglected the very interesting question of the *causes* of modernization. Those interested in this question can do no better than consult A. Diamant, 'Political Development: Approaches to Theory and Strategy', in J. Montgomery and W. Siffin (eds.), *Approaches to Development*, McGraw-Hill, New York, 1966, pp. 15–47; L. Salamon, 'Comparative History and the Theory of Modernization', *World Politics*, **23**, no. 1, 83–103 (1970).

8. See H. Maus, *A Short History of Sociology*, Routledge and Kegan Paul, London, 1962, pp. 22–35, for an account of these influences on German sociology.
9. For a general account of this process in developing areas today, see also L. Pye, *Aspects of Political Development*, Little, Brown, Boston, 1966, esp. pp. 1–112, and C. Hill, *Reformation to Industrial Revolution*, Penguin, London, 1969, esp. pp. 25–123.
10. The 'Normal' refers to statistical likelihood; B. Russett, *Trends in World Politics*, Macmillan, New York, 1965, pp. 132–133. See also J. H. Goldthorpe, 'The Development of Social Policy in England, 1800–1914', in *Transactions of the Fifth World Congress of Sociology*, **4,** 41–56 (1962), and A. V. Dicey, *Law and Public Opinion in England*, Macmillan, London, 1952, esp. pp. 211–310. For UK figures which show welfare expenditure as a percentage of national income rising from 1.2 per cent in 1850 to 10.7 per cent in 1950 see J. Stirling, 'Social Services Expenditure During the Last 100 Years', *Advancement of Science*, **8,** no. 32 (1952).
11. S. M. Lipset (ed.), *Politics and the Social Sciences*, Oxford University Press, New York, 1969, p. 67. Lipset was interested in the relationship between democracy—which is defined as a combination of legitimate institutions such as parties, free presses, etc.—and one set of leaders in office and at least one set seeking to obtain office by using legitimate institutions.
12. For an excellent analysis of why this relationship might have been expected see K. W. Deutsch, *The Nerves of Government*, Free Press, New York, 1966, esp. parts 2 and 3.
13. J. Forward, 'Toward an Empirical Framework for Ecological Studies in Comparative Public Administration', in N. Raphaeli, *Readings in Comparative Public Administration*, Allyn and Bacon, Boston, 1967, pp. 450–472. For reasons why this relationship might have been expected see J. La Palombara, *Bureaucracy and Political Development*, Princeton University Press, Princeton, 1963, chs. 1 and 2. We discuss these matters in more detail in our chapters on revolution and military intervention, but the reader interested in examining these relationships in more detail is referred to B. Russett, *Trends in World Politics*, Macmillan, New York, 1965, ch. 8, and H. A. Scarrow, *Comparative Political Analysis*, Harper and Row, New York, 1969, ch. 9, and for a general discussion of the implications of the relationships, D. Lerner, *The Passing of Traditional Society*, Free Press, New York, 1964, pp. 60–65.
14. E. Durkheim, *The Division of Labour in Society*, Free Press, Glencoe, 1960, ch. 7. This form of solidarity in a differentiated society he called 'organic solidarity', whilst the solidarity of segmented and undifferentiated societies was named 'mechanical'.
15. D. B. Truman, *The Governmental Process*, Knopf, New York, 1958, p. 44: 'The moving pattern of complex society such as the one in which we live is one of changes and disturbances in the habitual sub-patterns of inter-action, followed by a return to the previous state of equilibrium or, if the disturbances are intense or prolonged, by the emergence of new groups whose specialised function is to facilitate the establishment of a new balance'.
16. For veto groups see D. Riesman, *The Lonely Crowd*, Doubleday Anchor, New York, 1950, pp. 244–251; for 'countervailing power' see J. K. Galbraith,

American Capitalism, the Concept of Countervailing Power, Pelican, London, 1963.

17. D. B. Truman, *The Governmental Process*, Knopf, New York, 1958, ch. 16. Potential groups 'are significant not only because they may become the basis for organised interest groups but because the membership of such potential groups overlaps extensively the membership of various organised interest groups . . . it is this multiple membership in potential groups . . . that serve as a balance wheel in a going political system' (pp. 512–513).
18. D. Truman, 'The American System in Crisis', *Political Science Quarterly*, 481–497 (1959). Similarly V. O. Key in *Public Opinion and the American Democracy*, Knopf, New York, 1961, p. 588, R. A. Dahl, *Who Governs?*, Yale University Press, New Haven, 1961, pp. 311–325, and S. M. Lipset (ed.), *Politics and the Social Sciences*, Oxford University Press, New York, 1969, ch. 4; all of whom are extremely aware of the *dangers* of mass involvement and participation in politics.
19. The point here is that individuals and groups do not act in a vacuum but have some idea of other people or group reactions and therefore tailor their actions in the light of anticipated reactions, see C. J. Friedrich, *Man and His Government*, McGraw-Hill, New York, 1963, ch. 11. Writing of the widely expected social reform which would follow the Second World War, Calder suggests that in 1942 'The shrewder captains of industry likewise prepared to *reculer pour mieux sauter*' and in the Commons 'the Conservative majority . . . dared not frustrate measures which it was bound to concede were necessary'. A. Calder, *The People's War*, Panther, London, 1971, p. 292.
20. R. H. Dahl, *Who Governs?*, Yale University Press, New Haven, 1961, p. 305. This has obvious parallels with the exchange theorists discussed above who argue that the marginal costs of involvement exceed the marginal benefits for most people, see R. Curry and L. Wade, *A Theory of Political Exchange*, Prentice Hall, Englewood Cliffs, 1968, pp. 20–26; see also W. H. Morris-Jones, 'In Defence of Apathy', *Political Studies*, **II**, 25–37 (1954). When grievances are met or anticipated, political activity is likely to have a low exchange priority—and, of course, the converse is true.
21. There is a large modern literature, owing a debt to Toqueville, stemming from the Nazi and Fascist era which is clearly not simply descriptive but persuasive, cf. Ortega y Gassett, *The Revolt of the Masses*, Labour Book Service, London, 1940. For an account of the literature, see W. Kornhauser, *The Politics of Mass Society*, Routledge and Kegan Paul, London, 1960.
22. N. Polsby, *Community Power and Political Theory*, Yale University Press, New Haven, 1963, ch. 1. Polsby certainly goes too far in the opposite direction in failing to discern any connection between economic resources and political influence, see pp. 100–104.
23. R. H. Dahl, *Pluralist Democracy in the United States*, Rand McNally, Chicago, 1967, p. 378. Political assets, 'political resources', in Dahl's list include time, money, skill, energy, political office, group support, intelligence, etc., which are non-cumulative.
24. R. S. and H. M. Lynd, *Middletown in Transition*, Harcourt, Brace and World, New York, 1937; F. Hunter, *Community Power Structure, A Study in Decision Making*, University of North Carolina Press, Chapel Hill, 1953. See also R. Agger, D. Goldrich and B. Swanson, *The Rulers and the Ruled*,

Wiley, New York, 1964, and R. Presthus, *Men at the Top*, Oxford University Press, New York, 1964, both of which discern a greater spread of empirical possibilities than elite or plural theories by themselves allow. But Presthus does point out that 'Social and Economic Notables tend, in Edgewood and Riverview at least, to be important members of the power structure. One may not want to categorise them as a "ruling elite" but they are constituted a vital segment of the 1 per cent of the community who were directly active in the initiation and control of the major community decisions in our sample' (p. 421).

25. R. O. Schulze, 'The Bifurcation of Power in a Satellite City', in M. Janowitz (ed.), *Community Political Systems*, Free Press, New York 1961, pp. 19–81. It should also be noted that in the highly mobile industrial society (in Britain about 10 per cent of the population change address each year) migrants may not have time to form political attachments but they are not economically dependent on a local elite; see M. Stacey, *Traditions and Change*, Oxford University Press, London, 1960, R. Millar, *The New Classes*, Longmans, London, 1966, pp. 56–105, and W. Watson, 'Social Mobility and Social Class in Industrial Communities', in M. Gluckman (ed.), *Closed System and Open Minds*, Oliver and Boyd, Edinburgh, 1964, pp. 129–157.
26. See L. W. Milbrath, *Political Participation*, Rand McNally, Chicago, 1965. R. H. Dahl, *Who Governs?*, Yale University Press, New Haven, 1961, pp. 245 and 287, recognizes some accumulation. The non-accumulative nature of resources does, however, appear in the simplest societies where 'The prestige which even the mightiest hunter enjoys is not transferable to other areas and does not constitute a firm basis for political power'. M. Fried, *The Evolution of Political Society*, Random House, New York, 1967, p. 66.
27. For the extent of poverty in the United States, see M. Harrington, *The Other America*, Penguin, London, 1962.
28. See C. Perrow, 'The Sociological Perspective and Political Pluralism', *Social Research*, **31**, 420 (1964), 'Political pluralism is not a theory . . . which explains the behaviour of those who are outside the system—the lower classes, the unemployed, deprived minorities, etc'.
29. Writing of the British educational system and political culture, R. Rose has stressed that it 'emphasised cultural norms concerning inequality. Inequality is presented as natural, and often as desirable', in *Politics in England*, Little, Brown, Boston, 1964, p. 65. Both British and American studies of child development show, *inter alia*, that by the age of *one year* there is a significant and potentially socially disadvantaging difference in the IQs of middle- and working-class children. See also B. Jackson and D. Marsden, *Education and the Working Class*, Pelican, London, 1966, esp. ch. 3, for a rewarding analysis of the intellectual impoverishment of working-class life at least in terms of achieving academic success.
30. See E. Nordlinger, *The Working Class Tories*, MacGibbon and Key, London, 1967, esp. pp. 23–43. In a most interesting article B. Stacey and R. Green demonstrate that considerable numbers of both white and blue collar workers are attracted to support the Conservative Party in part because of its 'elitism, hierarchy and privilege', 'Working-Class Conservatism: A Review and an Empirical Study', *British Journal of Social and Clinical Psychology*, **10**, 10–26 (1971).

31. There is a very considerable literature on this subject; see F. Fanon, *Black Skin, White Masks*, Grove Press, New York, 1967; O. Mannoni, *Prospero and Caliban*, Praeger, New York, 1956; G. Jahoda, *White Man*, Oxford University Press, London, 1961.
32. R. Rist, 'Student Social Class and Teacher Expectations: The Self-Fulfilling Prophecy in Ghetto Education', *Harvard Educational Review*, **40,** no. 3, 385–451 (1970). Rist concludes, 'the system of public education in reality perpetuates . . . class barriers which result in inequality in the social and economic life of the citizenry'.
33. Although writing only of American blacks, the point made by M. Tumin that *given equality of opportunity and training* blacks and whites are 'interchangeable at random for all cultural roles' is of wider application.
34. W. L. Guttsman, *The British Political Elites*, MacGibbon and Key, London, 1963. See also R. Rose, 'Class and Party Divisions: Britain as a Test Case', Survey Research Centre, University of Strathclyde, Occasional Paper no. 1, table 2, which shows the decline of working-class members of Labour Cabinets from 55 per cent in 1924 to 9 per cent in 1967, ie from 11 to 2.
35. —— *The British Political Elite*, MacGibbon and Key, London, 1963, p. 104; by 1964 about 44 per cent of all MPs were from the professions.
36. Similar evidence is presented for the UK by J. F. S. Ross, *Parliamentary Representation*, Eyre and Spottiswoode, London, 1948; P. W. Buck, *Amateurs and Professionals in British Politics*, University of Chicago Press, Chicago, 1963.
37. Of course, elite theorists since Pareto and Mosca always stress the importance to elite stability of including amongst themselves the representatives of vigorous social interests, see J. H. Meisel, *The Myth of the Ruling Class*, University of Michigan Press, Ann Arbor, 1962, pp. 42–43.
38. There is also evidence that educational factors operate prior to the elections in the sense that public school and university educated people have a much better than random chance in both major parties of being selected especially for the more winnable seats, see M. Rush, *The Selection of Parliamentary Candidates*, Nelson, London, 1969, pp. 87 and 206. Rush also explains of all candidates 'that they are drawn from a broadly common source—*the middle class*' (p. 206).
39. Thus in the 1966 General Election 1707 candidates stood and 37 per cent were elected. In the Labour and Conservative Parties 436 candidates were university graduates and of these 356 or 82 per cent were elected. In the Labour Party 77 per cent of graduate candidates were elected, compared to 44 per cent of non-graduates; in the Labour Cabinet of 1967 81 per cent (17) were university graduates of whom 82 per cent (14) were from Oxford and Cambridge Universities.
40. The material is ably summarized for Western countries by R. Miliband, *The State in Capitalist Society*, Weidenfeld and Nicolson, London, 1969, esp. chs. 2 and 3, who concludes that 'it has remained a basic fact of life in advanced capitalist countries that the vast majority of men and women in those countries has been governed, represented, administered, judged, and commanded in war by people drawn from other, economically and socially superior and relatively distant classes' (p. 67).
41. Karl Marx, *Capital*, vol. I, Foreign Languages Publishing House, Moscow, 1954, p. 737, our italics; see also R. Bendix, *Work and Authority in Industry*,

Harper and Row, New York, 1963, for comparative study of the legitimating ideologies in management–worker relations.

42. R. Miliband, *The State in Capitalist Society*, Weidenfeld and Nicolson, London, 1969, p. 182, and see chapter entitled 'The Process of Legitimation'.
43. W. L. Guttsman, *The British Political Elite*, MacGibbon and Key, London, 1963, p. 319, writes of the British elite that 'New men have entered it, but they have generally become assimilated into the groups from which the majority of their colleagues sprang'.
44. C. Wright Mills, *The Power Elite*, Oxford University Press, New York, 1956, was endorsed for the UK in *The Insiders*, New Left Review, London, 1958, p. 30.
45. C. Wright Mills, *White Collar*, Oxford University Press, New York, 1956, p. 102. Similarly, P. C. Lloyd, writing on African traditional elites, suggests that 'holding extensive privileges, they themselves form an interest group for the protection of these privileges against the masses', 'The Political Structure of African Kingdoms', in M. Banton (ed.), *Political Systems and the Distribution of Power*, Tavistock Publications, London, 1968, p. 76.
46. For an analysis of the concept of oligarchy see C. W. Cassinelli, 'The Law of Oligarchy', *APSR*, **XLVII,** no. 3, 773–784 (Sept. 1953).
47. There is a massive literature on this theme; see, for example, A. H. Halsey, 'The Sociology of Education', in N. Smelser, *Sociology*, Wiley, New York, 1967, pp. 384–434.
48. 'A Critique of the Ruling Elite Model', *APSR*, **52,** 466 (1958). It is also the case that Dahl in insisting on the application of falsifiability criterion to judge the elite model confuses a theory and a model, since the latter is not true or false, but more or less useful. Certainly the elitist arguments look more like models than theories and very certainly the elitist would have no difficulty in treating his statements as a model; see the very interesting article by V. Dusek, 'Falsifiability and Power Elite Theory 1', *Journal of Comparative Administration*, **1,** no. 2 (1969).
49. One might also enter the *caveat* that as a matter of fact investigation into those believed to be the elite is rather difficult. Thus R. Lewis and R. Stewart in a study of British businessmen remark on the difficulty of persuading 'the subject to submit to study', *The Boss*, Dent, London, 1963, p. 273, and A. Kornhauser suggests that the same is true in the US, A. Kornhauser (ed.), *Problems of Power in America*, Wayne State University Press, Detroit, 1959, p. 195; a similar difficulty was experienced by Presthus in gaining access to British firms, R. Presthus, *Behavioural Research on British Executives*, University of Alabama Press, Alabama, 1965, p. 105.
50. The social composition of the Bolsheviks is admirably discussed in D. Lane, *The Roots of Russian Communism*, Van Gorcum, The Hague, 1968, and in M. Fainsod, *How Russia is Ruled*, Harvard University Press, Cambridge, Mass., 1963, chs. 1–4.
51. For this process see L. Schapiro, *The Origins of the Communist Autocracy*, Bell, London, 1955.
52. This view of the elite as deriving its power from occupation of 'pivotal positions' which constitute the 'strategic command posts' of the social structure was advanced by C. Wright Mills in his volume *The Power Elite*, Oxford University Press, New York, 1956, p. 4.

53. For a further discussion of this point see R. Bendix, *Work and Authority in Industry*, Harper, New York, 1956, and R. E. Dowse, *Modernisation in Ghana and the USSR*, Routledge and Kegan Paul, London, 1968, esp. ch. 3.
54. For an excellent account of this process see A. Avtorkhanov, *The Communist Party Apparatus*, H. Regnery Company, Chicago, 1966, esp. chs. 12, 13, 15 and 16.
55. For a useful account of the bases of Bolshevik support in the 1920's see P. Sorlin, *The Soviet People and their Society*, Pall Mall Press, London, 1968, ch. 3.
56. See E. V. Walter, *Terror and Resistance*, Oxford University Press, New York, 1969, for an attempt to 'develop a general theory of terrorism' with more specific references to the Zulu.
57. M. Fainsod, *How Russia is Ruled*, Harvard University Press, Cambridge, Mass., 1963, pp. 260–262; John Erikson, *The Soviet High Command*, Macmillan, London, 1962. Conditions for entry into the party by the skilled worker and the technician were relaxed in the 1934 new party statutes: 'the predominance of the manual worker ceased to be a "categorical imperative" ', A. Avtorkhanov, *The Communist Party Apparatus*, H. Regnery Company, Chicago, 1966, p. 78.
58. On Soviet agriculture see N. Jasny, *The Socialised Agriculture of the USSR*, Stanford University Press, Stanford, 1949. In 1927 about 19 per cent of the population were urban, by 1933 about 23 per cent were urban and by 1938 about 32 per cent were urban.
59. For this process see I. Deutscher, *Soviet Trade Unions*, Royal Institute of International Affairs, London, 1950.
60. For Lenin's attempts to inculcate a work ethic, see R. Bendix, *Nation-Building and Citizenship*, Wiley, New York, 1964, pp. 149–158.
61. For the techniques of manipulation used to produce the New Soviet Man see H. Cantril, *Soviet Leaders and Mastery Over Man*, Rutgers University Press, New Brunswick, 1960.
62. A. Inkeles and R. Bauer, *The Soviet Citizen*, Oxford University Press, London, 1959, p. 193, and see also ch. 16 for a favourable assessment of the regime's success in inculcating supportive attitudes especially amongst the young. For the educational system as a method of control and resocialization see G. Kline, *Soviet Education*, Routledge and Kegan Paul, London, 1957, and J. S. Coleman (ed.), *Education and Political Development*, Princeton University Press, Princeton, 1968, introduction and ch. 8 by J. R. Azrael.
63. For Bolshevism as a developmental ideology see J. H. Kautsky (ed.), *Political Change in Underdeveloped Countries*, Wiley, New York, 1962, esp. pp. 57–119, and also Kautsky, *Communism and the Politics of Development*, Wiley, New York, 1968, esp. chs. 8, 9 and 10.
64. J. H. Goldthorpe, 'Social Stratification in Industrial Society', *Sociological Review Monograph*, No. 8 (Oct. 1964). Also, on the greater numbers of potential political participatory groups and the likely consequences for the future of Soviet society, see Z. Brzezinski, 'The Soviet Political System: Transformation or Degeneration', *Problems of Communism*, 1–15 (Jan.–Feb. 1966).
65. For example, R. Pethybridge, *A Key to Soviet Politics*, Allen and Unwin, London, 1962, p. 30, writes of the possibility of bureaucratic 'collusion with one or more of the sectors it administrates'. See also C. Lindon, 'Krushchev

and the Party Battle', *Problems of Communism*, **14**, no. 5 (1963), who writes that Krushchev unlike Stalin 'operates amidst an alignment of political forces' and that his major political imperative is to produce successful policies (p. 28).

66. H. Shaffer, 'What Price Economic Reforms', *Problems of Communism*, **12**, no. 3, pp. 18–24 (1963), who concludes that 'major economic objectives were still to be determined by the central planning agency' and that the purpose of the experiments is 'the more efficient performance of tasks prescribed by the government'.
67. T. W. Wolfe, 'Political Primacy versus Professional Elan', *Problems of Communism*, **13**, no. 3, 44–52 (1964), but Wolfe does suggest that the relationship is quite tense. See also the very detailed study by R. Holkowicz, *The Soviet Military and the Communist Party*, Princeton University Press, Princeton, 1967.
68. J. Azrael, *Managerial Power and Soviet Politics*, Harvard University Press, Cambridge, Mass., 1968, p. 162. Similarly, Inkeles and Bauer suggest that managers and engineers, etc., accept 'the underlying principles of Soviet political control over the ends of economic and administrative behaviour'. A. Inkeles and R. Bauer, *The Soviet Citizen*, Oxford University Press, London, 1959, p. 389.
69. P. Litvinov, *The Demonstrations in Pushkin Square*, Harvill Press, London, 1969, p. 39. For a measure of the contrast since the 1930's see Evgenia Ginsburg's novel, *Into the Whirlwind*, Heron Books, London, 1967, ch. 29, 'A Fair and Expeditious Trial'.
70. A. Inkeles and R. Bauer, *The Soviet Citizen*, Oxford University Press, London, 1959, pp. 392–3. For a very similar conclusion see Z. Byrski, 'The Communist Middle Class in the USSR and Poland', *Survey*, no. 73, 80–92 (1969).
71. C. P. FitzGerald, *Revolution in China*, Cressett Press, London, 1952, argues that in China historical experiences in the period from the early 1900's combined with a psychological *need* amongst most of the population for a secure authority made it unnecessary for the Communist regime to use more than minimum force after it won the civil war. The ideology and authoritarianism of the CPC 'fulfils the unexpressed desire of many' and, hence, makes otiose some of the worst excesses of Stalin (p. 191). Ping-chia Kuo, *China, New Age and Outlook*, Penguin, London, 1959, p. 77, makes a very similar point, stressing that 'Marxian determinism fitted in well with the temperament of the Chinese people'.
72. R. Presthus, *Behavioural Research on British Executives*, University of Alabama Press, Alabama, 1965, p. 281. He also writes, 'Although the members of the power structure in Edgewood and Riverview do not comprise a close monolithic elite the decision-making process does indeed resemble the elitist model' (p. 283).

6

POLITICAL SOCIALIZATION AND THE SOCIAL PSYCHOLOGY OF POLITICS

6.1. The Concept and Processes of Socialization

WE HAVE PREVIOUSLY outlined the argument that in some measure all human societies depend for their cohesion upon a shared understanding of values, norms, symbols, etc., in fact, all that is contained in the idea of a culture. These shared understandings are not given at birth but have to be acquired during the life of the person. This process of acquiring social learning is known as socialization and is the means whereby 'individuals acquire the knowledge, skills, and dispositions that enable them to participate as more or less effective members of groups and the society'.[*1*] Whilst it is almost always the case that the crucial period of induction into the culture is during childhood and early adolescence, it is nevertheless a lifelong experience. Crucial and novel situations such as political revolution, social catastrophe and migration to new cultures entail the learning of new patterns. Less dramatically, but equally important, all new experiences, and especially those undergone when adopting a highly structured role such as during induction into an established profession, involve additional socialization experiences for many young adults. Looked at from the point of view of the collectivity, be it a society or a group, socialization is a mechanism whereby the relative endurance of the culture is maintained despite the essentially temporary membership of any given set of individuals. This perspective involves us in an examination of the social agencies, both manifest and latent, through which the culture is transmitted and mediated. Looked at from the point of view of the individual, socialization can be summarized as *what* the individual learns, *when* he learns it and *how* he learns it, and the personal consequences of this process for him.

There are a number of possible intellectual orientations towards the study of socialization: socialization as the intergenerational transmission of culture; as the process of acquiring socially acceptable controls of 'basic' drives; and as role-training or preparation for social participation. Whilst not discrete, these theoretical traditions do emphasize different factors.

Socialization as Enculturation

This is the perspective used mainly by the cultural anthropologists, who see the fundamental problem of social life as the preservation and transmission of distinctive cultural patterns through the generations. In its simplest form, this perspective sees the acquisition and the internalization of culture as an almost automatic process in which the individual acquires the culture by simple exposure over time. This process of cultural absorption was conceived of holistically and no particular learning mechanisms were seen as specific to it.[1] Although more complex versions of this viewpoint involve attempts to analyse the mechanisms of culture transmission,[2] none the less the following distinctive elements were retained. Firstly, the child was conceived as an almost passive recipient of the culture. Secondly, it was holistic in its idea that a stable culture provided a consistent content —one element interlocking and complementing another—to which the child was exposed. Finally, it insisted that specific cause-and-effect relationships could not meaningfully be isolated from the whole mutually reinforcing patterns of interaction and meaning within the culture.

This mainly anthropological point of view was based upon fieldwork in primitive small stable societies. (And also upon a somewhat romantic adherence to one side of the folk–urban, *gemeinschaft–gessellschaft*, status–contract, dichotomies.) Behaviour seemed very much of a piece, a consequence of unreflective following of a coherent culture within which conflict and dissension were at a minimum, and where, in consequence, if social innovation occurred it was usually disruptive and always exogenous in origin.

Socialization as Impulse Control

As we saw in Chapter 2, one tradition of social thought, going back as far as Plato, sees the problem of order as essentially one of devising means whereby man's innate drives can be controlled. The view derived from this tradition is that socialization is a process of curbing potentially disruptive drives by channelling them in socially acceptable directions. This is, of course, the view of Freud and the psychoanalytic tradition.[*2*]

Political involvement in this tradition may be understood as a transference of private and personal drives—which could take other forms—to the public realm, where they may have far-reaching effects or may be relatively innocuous. That is, the psychologist may well be interested in answering the question, how does the individual, consciously or more likely unconsciously, use political involvement—or any other involvement—to meet certain drives, release personal tensions, and so on? The political sociologist, on the other hand, is much more concerned about the possible relationship between certain personality types and social structure; he is interested in the impact of these types on the political system, the provisions available for different personalities to find political outlets (they may, of course, find other outlets). Also, one is interested at a more overt, less 'basic' level in the manner in which people are taught the 'correct' performance of more obvious political roles, irrespective of 'basic' personality, to be found in societies, for example those of chief, war leader, legislator, party activist, civil servant, etc. Finally, the political sociologist is also interested in whether or not certain personality types are *attracted* to certain political roles.

Socialization as Role-Training

This view stresses the social object of socialization, that is, achieving conformity of individuals to the normative structure of the society. Socialization is a process of training the child for participation in the society. The starting point for this view is that structural survival necessitates finding persons to fill the institutionalized roles which constitute the social order. In some versions of this theory, the socialization process is seen as a mere adjunct of the wider social process, adequate socialization being more or less taken for granted. In more complex forms, however, the relationship between socialization and role demands is seen as more problematic and the whole process of socialization envisaged as fitting, more or less successfully, the individual with the needs of society. Within this tradition, personality and social structure are seen as *separate* systems with their own requirements for system maintenance and the socialization process is concerned with creating some minimal compatibility between the two.[3]

As we have remarked above these ideas are not incompatible, but we shall lean most heavily on socialization as role-training since it offers a number of advantages from the viewpoint of political sociology. It assigns a central role to the socialization process in shaping individual behaviour and its consequences for society. Further, this perspective focusses upon a number of socializing agencies such as family, school, peer group, factory, office, etc. By allowing the possibility of interplay between socializing agencies it suggests conflict and change as an ever-present possibility in any system. The first perspective will be discussed further in Chapter 7 when we outline the idea of political culture. The second view will receive further attention later in this chapter when we examine some psychological bases of political behaviour.

6.2. Political Socialization

Directing the general study of socialization towards the study of political socialization involves a consideration of the relevance of socialization processes and patterns for the working of the polity and for the understanding of political behaviour. We are interested in the ways in which people 'structure' their political world, cognitively and affectively, in

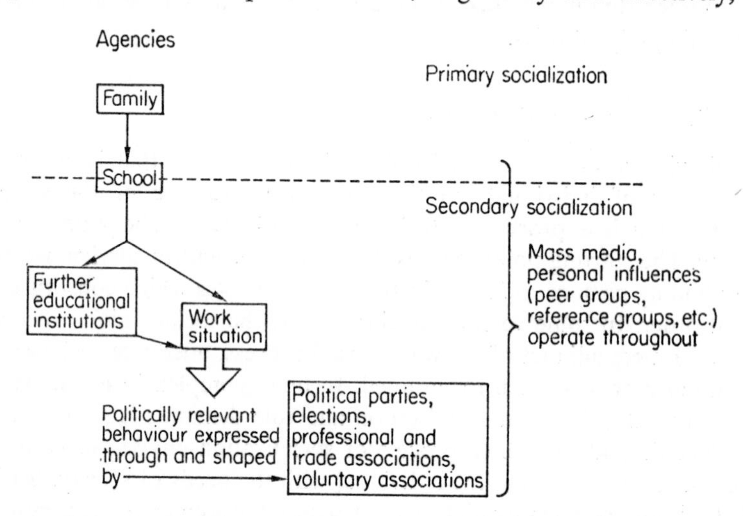

FIGURE 3. The process and agencies of political socialization in complex societies.

comparing these both within and between systems and in analysing this structuring by a consideration of agencies, process, time-span and change.[4] We are also interested in the effect of overtly non-political socialization agencies generating attitudes and behaviour which have political consequences. Thus an important element to bear in mind is that much political socialization is both non-political in its origins and latent in its process.

Diagramatically, one might illustrate the process of political socialization (at least in structurally differentiated societies) as in Figure 3. Broadly, these are the agencies of political socialization. But they tell us little about a number of important problems. Firstly, we cannot tell from the agency what the *content* of the political socialization is; that is a matter of investigation. Secondly, and more important for our purposes, the whole interest of the diagram for the political sociologist is the final stage which suggests that attitudes, opinions, ideas or whatever in some way direct or determine a person's political behaviour. This, as we shall show later in the chapter, is very problematic.[5] Finally, as political sociologists, we are interested in the relationship between the process as outlined in Figure 3 and the effect which the 'resulting' popular political behaviour has on governmental policy and stability. Again, as we shall show below, the relationship is not easily traced.

The primary stage of socialization in all societies normally takes place within the family or in kin group and peer group. In this phase the child begins to learn a language and a set of rights and wrongs as defined by the culture and certain behavioural patterns pertaining mainly to age and sex roles. Little in the way of overt and manifest political socialization takes place at this stage, but what is learned may well be transferred to the context of the political. This can be seen most clearly in the relatively undifferentiated societies where the family or kin system is almost co-extensive with the political system. Le Vine has examined authority and attitudes towards it in two segmentary lineage systems, the Nuer and the Gusii, and finds a striking contrast between them.[6] The Nuer are reluctant to accept positions of authority and the Gusii are not; the Nuer indulge in blood feud whilst the Gusii resolve conflicts in courts; the Nuer emphasize their personal independence and only very reluctantly accept direct orders whilst the Gusii are deferential towards persons of higher status. In short, the Nuer are egalitarian in attitudes and behaviour whilst the Gusii have far more authority-supporting values. Searching for an explanation of these differences, Le Vine suggests it is to be found in 'socialization into the authority structure of the family (which) leaves (the person) with values and role expectations which are adaptive in socio-political units above the family level. Because of this connection between the early family environment of the child and the political system, it is reasonable to expect differences in the early learning experiences of typical individuals in Gusii and Nuer societies'.[7]

Utilizing ideas developed by social psychologists, Le Vine proposes 'that the individual's attitudes towards authority are a function of his early relationships with his parents'.[7] Relationships with parents are then examined along three dimensions: (1) authority distribution in the family, ie is it shared or is it concentrated on one person; (2) the closeness and warmth of relationships between the child and those in authority in the family; (3) disciplinary patterns in the family, ie are they severe with frequent physical punishment or are they more indulgent and reward-centred. In all of these respects there is a consistent difference between the two cultures which is held to account for the subsequent differences in politically relevant matters. Gusii fathers do not take care of infants and are called in mainly to punish the child whilst Nuer fathers are warm and often play with the child. Further, Gusii families strongly emphasize that children should not fight but take the cause of their quarrel to adults for adjudication whilst the Nuer set a high value on childhood aggression and independence.

As these examples suggest, in the undifferentiated society, when the political system is embedded in a nexus of family and kin, family socialization has a direct impact upon the 'political' behaviour of members of the society. In the more differentiated society, at least the theoretical possibility of non-congruent influences on socialization must be considered. Potential inconsistencies arise whenever there is more than one important agent of socialization. Thus in a racially mixed or culturally varied society socialization into subcultures could well affect the ability of individuals to integrate themselves into the official or dominant political culture. For example, in Southern Italy, the family develops as the one association to be adhered to, trusted, protected and striven for, to the exclusion of all other associations through which the individual might connect up with the wider society. Within the family the child learns to distrust all outsiders—'amoral familialism'—regarding them as potential threats to individual welfare which can only be met by the united family. Thus the family systematically undermines the confidence and ability of its members to participate in the wider society even though competing agencies such as the schools, newspapers and parties are there representing the wider perspectives of a national society.[8] As we have suggested in previous chapters, heterogeneity of this type is typical of the loosely integrated developing areas where family and kin-group socialization processes may be inimical to the development of viable national institutions.

Typical of this problem of non-congruent patterns of socialization is bureaucratic inertia and corruption in developing areas. In these societies, primary social value may be deference to older people or the giving and receiving of gifts for services, and the multifarious obligations of kin towards kin. All of these values have their origins in the primary socialization phase, yet they are totally opposed to the bureaucratic forms of organization characteristic of any developed society. When the bureaucrat is presented with a case from his own kin, or with a request for a job from his kinsman, he is automatically presented with a problem of resolving a dissonant situation of value conflict. He may solve this by presenting a totally impersonal front to all clients, thereby falling into a rigid and unhelpful pattern; he may accept his 'primary' obligation, thereby negating his *raison d'être* as a bureaucrat, but whatever he does he is caught in the inevitable dilemma brought about by conflicting role demands.[9] At a psychologically more subtle level, Pye has suggested in his study of Burma that 'the family provides the unmistakable focus for all Burmese social life',[10] and that within the family the mother rapidly alternates 'between extremes of warmth and affection and disinterest and exasperation'.[11] Thus inconsistent behaviour of the mother towards her child leads him to feel that he has no control over the ways in which he is treated by others, since his mother's behaviour bears little relationship to his own behaviour. 'Thus from the time of his earliest experience the child exists in a world in which there is no rational relationship, no recognizable cause-and-effect connection between his power of action and choice and the things he most desperately wants.'[12] As a result of this experience, the Burmese child comes to feel unconsciously that the world is fickle and human relationships, even with those who seem warm and close, are essentially impermanent.

As the child matures, he is not taught in any firm fashion how to reduce the unpredictability in social relationships. He learns only that he should try to avoid becoming a nuisance, and to expect security by being subservient and yielding to all who are his superiors. Moreover, the Burmese child becomes dependent upon the opinions of others because the socialization process has left him with few internalized standards of behaviour that provide a root for any self-assured independence.

The Burmese child is also taught that his family is the centre of his existence and loyalty, and submission to parents is the ultimate test of character. So, from an early stage, 'The Burmese child is taught to be completely submissive before any form of authority and to expect that a passive and yielding attitude is more likely to please those with power'.[12] The sum effect of these early socializing experiences appears to be, according to Pye, a 'peculiar blending of a perennial capacity for optimism with a diffuse, all pervasive distrust and suspicion of others in any particular relationship'.[13] This makes it extremely difficult for the Burmese to operate effectively in any organizational context, and in a nation-building framework this peculiar combination of 'faith in the diffuse and suspicion of the particular' is the opposite of what is needed in order to 'build' a viable modern polity.

The connection between family socialization and adult political behaviour in the more industrialized and therefore more differentiated society is probably more indirect. This is the case because the social coverage of the family is a good deal narrower than in the previous societies we have mentioned in the sense that many previous family functions have been hived off to specialized social agencies. Due to this 'decline' of the family, the individual, after childhood, is involved much less in intra-familial relationships (especially extended kin relationships), hence the family's potential impact on the individual's behaviour and attitudes is arguably much weaker. More specifically, a great proportion of the individual's socialization is experienced in institutions other than the family. The family has proved inadequate in industrial society to prepare individuals at all thoroughly for specialized adult roles which involve a high degree of expertise and affective neutrality. Hence, there is the possibility of conflicting influences between the various socializing agencies.

Nevertheless, in an industrial society the young child grows up in a fairly homogeneous milieu composed of family and extended kin and neighbourhood, all of which are likely to have a cumulative impact during these formative years of the individual's life. During this period the political self begins to take shape, according to many observers even before formal schooling begins.[*3*] Looked at from the point of the political system, one of the earliest aspects of learning is attachment to the political community. This attachment is initially affective, having little cognitive or factual content. American studies suggest that such early orientations are normally positive, with political leaders regarded almost unanimously as benevolent and friendly.[14] In addition to these basic orientations towards the political community the child may also begin to identify with a political party, though again this identification normally lacks any major cognitive content, which tends to develop in the 'teens'. Similarly, the child begins to acquire awareness and identification with other significant societal groupings such as social class, religious groups, and ethnic or racial groupings. But again the cognitive element is weak and the identification amounts to rather inchoate and weakly defined categories. Thus the child develops a positive emotional attachment to his immediate milieu, especially his father and mother, and then, it is suggested, projects these feelings on to figures of political authority and political institutions such as, in the best researched case, the American President: 'attitudes toward the President of the United States are initially attitudes that have been held toward other authority figures, which are now transferred to an additional object'.[15] Hence, most of the child's initial emotive contact with the political system is mediated by and infused with his emotive familial involvements.

He sees the public authority figures nearest and most visible to him in terms of the benevolent images engendered in the familial context: 'the mayor helps everyone to have nice homes and jobs'.[16] Thus the child is brought into the political system through the transference of affective attachments, bonds which precede any real cognitive understanding of the system. Similarly, the child, certainly in American society, begins to identify with the political party most salient to him, normally that of his parents. As with his other attachments, the cognitive element is a weak one since the child knows very little about policy, etc. As the child gets older, his cognitive map becomes a more detailed one and gradually there is a diminution of the benevolent aura surrounding public authority: he becomes more 'realistic'. Roughly between the ages of seven and thirteen years the child comes to perceive the world in a more abstract manner: the image of the nation is partly separated from the political leadership, politicians lose the benevolent aura and are seen in more realistic terms, paralleling the marked increase in political knowledge.

By the early teens most American children have acquired many elements of a mature political self. Affective political attachments—to the nation, to the democratic system, to political parties and regime norms—have been established. Knowledge of the roles and functions of political life and institutions has increased and during the later 'teens' the pre-adolescent patterns crystallize and the child's opportunities for involvement increase.

However, during the period of his life from about seven years old the child is normally involved in a more formalized institution of socialization than the family, the school, in which he is presented with extra-familial friends, competitors, ideas and authorities. The pattern of school authority is less personal than in the home; monitors, prefects, school teachers, games captains and so on are chosen on achievement, or at least non-familial criteria. He comes into contact with a social system where performance is increasingly assessed on achievement, where roles are more differentiated than in the family and with a set of less personal authorities than his immediate family. For example, as an authority figure, the teacher is much more like a political authority than his parents, that is, there is a considerable element of separation in the role of teacher and the person of the teacher. The child learns to obey any incumbent filling the role of teacher.

In the classroom the child is taught the history, literature and general culture of his own society and learns to value them, and in this way the child is taught to be a 'good' citizen. Much less formally, but no less important, the actual mechanics of education may fit the child into a 'preordained' social track. In British and American studies of streaming in the classrooms the evidence is that children in the lower stream may actually deteriorate in terms of IQ and learn a great deal less than their ability levels might suggest. The children repond to what is *expected* of them and in the lower streams they are defined as failures. In both countries the evidence is that the initial streaming placement is strongly associated with, if not decided on, class and racial features: blacks and working-class in the lower streams.[17] Sometimes the school curriculum actually includes formal lessons in 'citizenship', but there is some doubt about their efficacy. In general, it appears that such programmes are most effective when not too discrepant with the child's actual observation and limited knowledge of political life. An American study of civic training in several high schools showed that the civics curriculum had its strongest impact when the course content was consonant with other specializing agencies. Specifically, it reinforced students' 'support for democratic processes', a value already strongly entrenched within the community, but it failed to make any major impact upon attitudes towards political participation.[18] A French study suggested that when in school children were taught a benevolent and trusting attitude to political authority, whilst in the home such authority was constantly denigrated and abused. The result was that formal political learning was relatively ineffective because it was not reinforced.[19]

The points we have mentioned about the classroom primarily are at the manifest level but a great deal of school socialization is more latent. The evidence is that political interest increases through school years, use of the mass media becomes slightly more politically focussed, the level of political knowledge is raised and the level of political realism is gradually increased.[20] Parsons has suggested that in America the schoolroom is a learning microcosm of American social norms within which the child internalizes regime norms 'a step higher than he can learn in his family alone'. The schoolclass exposes him to 'the fundamental American value of equality and opportunity, in that it places value *both* on initial equality and differential achievement'.[21]

This is the modal pattern of American childhood political socialization and as such ignores a number of important departures from the pattern in America, and is not necessarily typical of other 'advanced' societies. Firstly, there is the problem of subcultural socialization. For example, there are groups in the US who do not display the same benevolent attitude to the system. Children in Appalachia were dramatically less positive towards the President. Jaros and his colleagues note that for many of the children they studied 'there is no indication that a process conducive to the development of political support is operative'.[22] In this study an important influence was the father's absence or presence: when present he was often unemployed and therefore bitter and transmitted this feeling to his children. One would expect that similar disenchantment with the system is the norm amongst the urban ghetto dwellers! The norms taught to the young are regime norms and, in the US, this means that since virtually all political power is white power what the black child is taught in the schools 'are essentially white norms and behaviours'. But although young whites and blacks in one study are reported as having fairly similar scores on political efficacy, knowledge and participation rates, by the time they get a bit older blacks are well below similarly aged whites.[*4*] The lesson of this seems to be that the individual learns behaviour appropriate to particular positions, classes or neighbourhoods and not to some generalized system.

Another consideration is that in this modal pattern insufficient attention is paid to institutions other than the family within which young children find themselves and these *may* constitute non-congruent experiences. More concretely, what the child learns in one part of his environment may jar with experiences in another: the American negro hears of log cabins as way stations to the White House, of equality, liberty, opportunity, mobility, etc., in the school and over the media, but finds that life is not quite so simple for a black. Similarly, there may well be conflicting stimuli for the majority of children socialized by their parents—members of a previous generation—but facing contemporary problems and attitudes. There is an inevitable time-lag between the period when much of the basic political learning is experienced and the time when the individual performs explicit political roles. In any but the most stable, or better, stagnant societies, change does take place and the greater the rate of change the more likely is it that older socialization patterns will be incongruent with new or emergent political role demands. Revolutionary change of the institutions of the political regime is a case in point. Thus in the Weimar Republic the regime was characterized by 'unalleviated democracy' (universal suffrage, proportional representation, a plebiscitary presidency, and so on) whilst the 'society (was) pervaded by authoritarian relationship and obsessed with authoritarianism'.[23] But, of course, not all change is so dramatic as that introduced in Germany in 1920 or in Russia in 1918; nevertheless societies do change and discontinuities exist in all but the totally integrated—only theoretically a possibility—societies.

6.3. Education and Political Socialization in Britain

Education, as we have seen, is a process not only imparting specific skills and knowledge but also inducting the child into the norms and values of the culture. Of course, the culture into which the child is inducted varies from society to society and educational processes will reflect these differences. British political culture has often been described as one in which there is a marked deferential element combined with a strong sense of trust in the good intentions of the government.[24] A 'gradual political development has allowed traditional attitudes towards authority to become fused with more recent democratic values to form a governmental tradition in which leaders are expected to lead'.[25] These cultural norms are reflected in the educational systems, where selection at a (very) early age is a major feature and one which to a large extent determines the child's future (status). The bulk of British children were, until very recently, selected for a grammar school or a secondary modern school at the age of 11 and, to a large extent, this fact determined access to more advanced education. Selection for this state sector was based upon success in a competitive examination and in 1964 just 31 per cent of all children taking the examination succeeded in getting into a grammar school. The rest, if they remained in the state sector, were educated in the secondary modern schools. Grammar school children took a series of educational tests which defined their fitness for further education, tests which the secondary modern children were rarely given.

Thus from an early age British children are divided into what is virtually a potential elite and a mass with little chance of higher status. This is the system called by Turner one of 'sponsored mobility' in which 'elite recruits are chosen by the established elite or their agents, and elite status is *given* on the basis of supposed merit and cannot be *taken* by any amount of effort or strategy'.[26] Another sponsorship element is constituted by the so-called public school sector, which in 1964 composed approximately 2.7 per cent of all children in school. Selection for this sector is primarily based upon parental ability to pay school fees, these schools being mainly privately financed. Education in this sector, for reasons including the generally high quality of the education, favourable staff–student ratios, expert knowledge of university requirements, and so forth, gives the child an especially favourable opportunity for maintaining elite status.

These schools roughly replicate the class structure of Britain in that the type of school a child attends is strongly associated with the class origins of the child's parents.[5] But for our purposes the major point is that from an early age children know their place in the world and, excepting a relatively insignificant percentage of children in secondary modern schools who become influential, the pattern that is established at 11 (years) continues more or less through life. Further, it is said to be the case that 'Nearly all schools within their own school community stress a hierarchical system of authority, training youths for the different but complementary roles of leader and follower'.[6]

One finding which relates school type to students' career aspirations demonstrates clearly that children have been socialized by quite early ages to expect more or less, in terms of career, what they have been prepared for by the schools. The report shows that both middle- and working-class children in grammar schools expected to occupy non-manual jobs, whilst children in secondary modern schools were likely to expect manual jobs.[7] It is also suggested that the secondary modern student will generally lack

TABLE 5. School, Age and Political Efficacy

	Grammar			Secondary modern		
Age	High %	Low %	Total	High %	Low %	Total
15+	62.5	37.5	120	52.5	47.5	44
13–14	45.5	54.5	95	41.5	58.5	170
11–12	53.5	46.5	75	49	51	121
		Total	292		Total	335

From R. Dowse and J. Hughes, 'The Family, The School and the Political Socialisation Process', *Sociology*, 5, no. 1, 21–45 (Jan. 1971).

the ability to act successfully in politics since this is partly a function of education and partly of a feeling of general competence, and that failure to be selected for grammar school undermines this ability. In the Abramson study it was revealed that children in secondary modern schools were less interested in politics, believed people like themselves were unlikely to attain political responsibility and were marginally more deferential than grammar school boys. These findings were corroborated in another study which revealed that over all age ranges grammar school children felt more politically effective than did secondary modern children (see Table 5). It was also found that grammar school children were far more likely than secondary modern children to attain a high level of political knowledge and were more interested in politics; secondary modern children were marginally more deferential than their grammar school age equivalents.

We have already mentioned that there is a very strong association in

Britain between the social class of the parents and the school placement of the child. There is also a very strong association, of which the children are obviously aware, between career possibilities and type of school attended, so that the school tends to function as a type of anticipatory socializing and stratifying agent. The school helps to create and fix in the children ideas of what is possible and appropriate for them. If their eventual job situation is such that they exercise little autonomy and responsibility this will reinforce what has been learned in the school, and in general this is the life situation of the secondary modern child who typically enters a manual occupation. Similarly, middle-class children in the grammar schools and eventually in professional or white-collar occupations where opportunities for autonomous behaviour and responsibility are greater might be expected to feel more effective and to participate more often in political life. They might also be expected to develop in the school and in the job organizational skills, which can be transferred into political assets and which, in general, working-class people do not have as much opportunity to acquire.

There are, of course, variations on this general pattern in Britain. Firstly, there are regional variations since in Scotland the educational system differs from that of the rest of Britain, and in Wales the percentage of working-class children in grammar schools is significantly above the national average. Secondly, with the gradual abolition of the secondary modern and grammar school system in favour of the non-selective comprehensive school, one would expect the relationships between class and political attitudes, participation and so forth to be weakened. Unfortunately, no research has been undertaken in the comprehensive schools designed to tap political orientation, and also there is not yet a full generation of English comprehensive school children to study.[*8*] Two points of more general significance relate to sex differences in socialization experience and the variability of working-class participation in political activity.

One of the best researched findings in British politics is that women participate less and declare lower levels of interest in politics than do men. Fewer women occupy significant political positions at all levels than men. Women are less likely to vote than men. In general, women are more Conservative politically and are usually less politically interested than men, a finding which is, of course, not confined to Britain.[27] The role-training perspective in socialization theory would suggest that these facts are related to the different ways in which boys and girls are reared at home and educated in the schools. Robert Lane's proposition that 'A major feature of our culture's typing of the two sexes is the assignment of the ascendant, power-possessing role to the man and the dependent, receptive to the woman' is also applicable to Britain.[*9*] A study which investigated, *inter alia*, this proposition revealed that the crude political differences between boys and girls were *not* very large and conformed to no systematic pattern.[28] For example, although girls in general had lower levels of political knowledge than boys, the differences almost disappeared amongst grammar school children. Girls did not report much less interest in politics than boys nor were they less likely to discuss politics. Although the boys were 'higher' than the girls, the differences were mostly relatively trivial except that boys were always more likely to answer questions with a firmer opinion than girls, who tended to be more indefinite in their responses.[*10*] Sex differences amongst children were only relatively slight but usually in expected directions, so one might conclude that major adult sex differences, if they are to emerge amongst the sample, are likely to be a consequence of post-adolescent experiences. That is to say, early political socialization experiences may well not be the crucial determinants of the manner in which political participants behave. Adult behaviour may well be much more affected by adult experiences, including recruitment and induction into political roles. For example, the evidence is that American legislators and city councilmen, although able to recall early political experiences, were not affected by these in their role performance as elected officers.[29]

An implication of this point of view is that women, like the blacks and the working-class authoritarians, do not necessarily obtain their views of the world merely as a consequence of home and school socialization. Rather, their attitudes and behaviour are as much informed by the real situation in which they find themselves—that of powerlessness—as by socialization experiences in their past.

6.4. The Political Relevance of Adult Socialization

These considerations bring us to socialization in adult life and to the ways in which adult life may modify or reinforce predispositions created during childhood. As an illustration of the political impact of adult experiences we shall begin by looking at the problem of women's generally lower rates of interest and involvement in politics. As we have seen, the evidence is consistent with the proposition that in general girls are socialized into a more a-political role than boys. Further, our research also demonstrated that in terms of political knowledge, political interest, parental encouragement of an interest in politics, sense of efficacy, and so on, *working-class girls* were consistently below all other categories. This parallels adult findings which show the lower level of participation of women generally, and of working-class women in particular. Thus Butler and Stokes, in a study of British political life, report that 60 per cent of their women respondents were not much interested in politics as opposed to about 33 per cent of the men.[30] Writing of parliamentary candidates, Buck concludes that 'Although women have had more than forty years of participation in British politics, it is still an activity dominated by men'.[*11*] Almond and Verba discovered that British women discussed politics less than men, were less likely than men to consider participation a duty, and felt less politically competent than men.[31] The tendency of British women to vote Conservative is well documented (see Table 6).

The point is that whilst there are weak differences amongst boys and girls these differences emerge more strongly and clearly amongst adults, so

TABLE 6. Sex and General Election Vote

	Percentage distribution within each = sex		
	Percentage male	Percentage female	Percentage both
Conservative	44	50	47
Labour	56	50	53
	100	100	100

From F. Bealey, J. Blondel and W. McCann, *Constituency Politics*, 1965, p. 171. Reprinted by permission of Faber and Faber Ltd., London.

it almost certainly follows that something happens in adult life to direct women into more a-political roles than men.

One possibility is that women's extra-political roles, such as home and child management, prevent them from developing strong links with the wider network of social contacts which help maintain interest and involvement in politics. In other words, women's environments tend to act as a barrier to political stimuli, so restricting the likelihood that they will participate in politics.[32] The life experience of women generally reinforces earlier, childhood patterns although the earlier differentiation is not very strong. The foregoing discussion raises wider considerations as to the extent to which early socialization experiences determine adult attitudes and involvements. This is a problem because as an adult the person is subject to a range of experiences and social 'requirements' he does not face as a child. These experiences may, for our purposes, be divided into two groups: adult experiences congruent with childhood socialization experiences, and adult experiences that are not congruent.

An example of the second is the case of the socially mobile individual who may have been socialized in one milieu and eventually arrives at another one for which he has not been fully socially prepared. We have already suggested that such a process is by no means unusual since (1) the rate at which people move socially and geographically in industrial society is quite high, (2) rapid technological and social change cannot be anticipated for purposes of childhood training.[*13*] The significance of these processes is as follows: sociological or socio-psychological theory stresses that in such situations for which people are unprepared they experience a measure of tension and anxiety which, it is posited, most people will attempt to reduce. One tension-reducing technique is full adaptation to the terminal status group or milieu by taking on the social and attitudinal characteristics of that group or milieu, if this is possible.[*14*] This involves an element of resocialization in that the socially or geographically mobile need to learn new modes of behaviour and amongst these new modes there may well be changes in political attitudes and behaviour. Further, it may be posited that the more homogeneous the terminal milieu the greater is its likely impact upon the migrant, since the likelihood of encountering messages and situations supporting previous commitments is reduced.

Studies in Britain and America have shown that upwardly mobile individuals are very likely to take on the political attitudes and behaviour of the stratum into which they move. As Butler and Stokes show, the upwardly mobile offspring of Labour parents show a distinct tendency to become Conservative, whilst those who remain working-class are a great deal more loyal to the Labour Party.[*15*] Equally striking is the tendency of localities to become homogeneous in their political behaviour at least as indicated by voting patterns. In mining towns 14 per cent of those interviewed in the Butler and Stokes study assigned themselves to the middle-class (11 per cent were actually in middle-class occupations), whilst in resort towns 43 per cent defined themselves as middle-class (44 per cent had such occupations). But in the mining towns the Labour Party attracted 36 per cent of the middle-class vote—far above its national average—and lost only about 10 per cent of working-class votes—far less than its average loss to the Conservatives. Similarly, in the resort areas the Conservative Party actually gained a majority of working-class votes. There is a very strong relationship between class homogeneity and support for one or other of the two major parties. If the area is strongly working-class this tends to pull a section of the population away from the national average of working-class Conservative allegiance. In dominantly middle-class constituencies the Conservative losses to Labour amongst the middle-class are less than the national average.[*16*] Precisely the same phenomenon, first observed by Tingsten in Sweden, was also detected in an American study which reported that 'in precincts where blue collar workers constitute 85% or more of the population some 76% of them voted for Stevenson; where they constituted between 65% and 84% of the population some 64% voted for Stevenson; and where they were less than 65% of the population only 36% voted for Stevenson'.[*17*] Although there is no empirical evidence on this point, in Britain we would expect that an adult moving into a homogeneous political milieu which differed from his community of origin would soon begin to develop a political stance more congruent with his new milieu than his older one. The social migrant, all other things being equal, will resolve inconsistencies by adopting a behaviour pattern congruent with that dominant in the new milieu.

All of this points to the importance of institutions and groups as influences on the continuing socialization process. We shall explore this theme further in an examination of working-class Conservatism in Britain.

6.5. Working-Class Conservatism in Britain

One of the most consistently supported relationships discovered in investigation of British electoral behaviour is the very strong association between social class—however defined—and party choice. Manual workers are very likely to vote for left-wing parties and non-manual people to vote for centre and right-wing parties. It is also known that non-manual status is more strongly associated with Conservative voting than manual status is with voting for the Labour Party (see Table 7).

TABLE 7. Voting By Class in Britain

Class	% of population	Cons. %	Lab. %	Others %
Solid middle-class (non-manual workers)	15	85	10	5
Lower middle-class	20	70	25	5
Upper working-class (manual workers)	30	35	60	5
Solid working-class	35	30	65	5

From M. Abrams, R. Rose and R. Hinden, *Must Labour Lose*, Penguin, London, 1960, p. 76. Copyright © Mark Abrams, Richard Rose and Rita Hinden, 1960. The table 'roughly averages our survey findings for post-war elections . . .'.

Politically, the problem of the working-class Conservative voter is an important one in at least the practical sense that about one-third of the working-class do vote Conservative and this accounts for about one-half of the total Conservative Party votes in post-war elections. At a more abstract level, the problem of the working-class Conservative arises from Marxist-derived expectations about class and its relationship with political behaviour which suggest that over time the working-class become less and less attracted by the ideology of the ruling class and will increasingly act as a politically cohesive and conscious force.[*18*] Psephologists have been strongly interested in this expectation and hence a great deal of study has been devoted to explicating the relationship.

The starting point for an analysis is that as a matter of fact Britain is the purest example of class voting in any Anglo-American democracy.[33] None the less, the polarization is very far from complete as the figures in Table 7 show. Let us now break down the crude figures of voting support for the Conservative Party and attempt a profile of the working-class Conservative voter. Firstly, the working-class Conservative is quite likely to be a woman, and amongst them the 'older working class women vote Conservative with considerably more frequency than do other groups'.[34] Secondly, there is evidence that amongst the working-class support for the Labour Party is associated with membership of a trade union (see Table 8).

TABLE 8. Support for Labour Among Union and Non-Union Families by Occupational Grade, 1964

	Supervisory non-manual III	Lower non-manual IV	Skilled manual V	Non-skilled manual VI
	%	%	%	%
Proportion voting Labour among union families	42	56	23	80
Among non-union families	18	20	53	62

From D. Butler and D. Stokes, *Political Change in Britain*, Macmillan, London, 1969, p. 156, and St. Martin's Press, Inc., New York, with permission.[*19*]

These two findings are not, of course, surprising and clearly they are linked. Women are greatly less unionized than men and do not generally work in the large plant units that men do and therefore receive fewer left-wing reinforcements. Another element associated with working-class Conservative voters is their tendency to use the middle-class as a reference group when assigning themselves to a social class, and when they do this they take over the most obvious political coloration of the middle-class, its solid Conservative vote (see Table 9).

TABLE 9. Party Preference; By Self-Rated 'Class' within Occupational Stratum

	Non-manual		Manual	
	Self-rated middle %	Self-rated working %	Self-rated middle %	Self-rated working %
Conservative	52	23	36	16
Liberal	25	23	19	16
Labour	11	37	31	55
Other	1	0	0	1
Don't know or refuse	11	17	14	12
Total	100% (n = 365)	100% (n = 124)	100% (n = 303)	100% (n = 610)

From W. G. Runciman, *Relative Deprivation and Social Justice*, Routledge and Kegan Paul, London, 1966, p. 171. Originally published by the University of California Press; reprinted by permission of the Regents of the University of California.

Attitudinally, the working-class Conservative is more likely than the working-class Labour voter to have a poor opinion of trade unionism. Correspondingly, some working-class Conservatives frequently display an instrumental orientation to the Conservative Party; it is the party which gets things done whilst others appear to regard it as an elite which deserves deference and support.[*20*] However, the bulk of the research done on this problem demonstrates strikingly similar cultural perspectives amongst the working-class, whether Labour or Conservative voters. As McKenzie and Silver put it, 'it is hard to think of working class Conservatives in Britain as normatively deviant from working class political culture; on the contrary, they seem to express aspects of a wide national consensus'.[34]

If this consensus is one best represented by the Conservative Party and which is developed in the major institutions of British society, such as the selective schools, business and economic organizations, the monarchy, the established church and the communication media, it follows that the working-class Conservative voter is not best understood as a deviant, as implied by Marxist derived theory. He is better understood as rather well integrated into the society and the Labour voter as a deviant. The working-class Conservative is supported by most of the institutions and processes characteristic of British society and one would, therefore, expect that where the working-class is most insulated from this culture the deviance would be highest. That is, when workers are part of a normative subsystem which has structural supports which protect them against the predominant culture one would expect Labour and left-wing voting, and other political activity, to be greatest. We have already shown that in strongly working-class communities a working-class Conservative *voter* is rarer than in more socially heterogeneous communities. Other studies have shown that working-class people who assign themselves to the middle-class are likely to live in socially heterogeneous areas and that in dominantly middle-class areas working-class people are very likely to assign middle-class status to themselves.[35] We know that one of the symptoms of this tendency to use the middle-class as a reference group is voting as they do: 'The rule . . . is that the more the middle class predominates in a district the more the

TABLE 10. Plant Size and Voting Behaviour

	Size of plant workforce		
	1–10	51–300	1000+
Conservative %	62	37	25
Labour %	38	63	75
Total %age	100	100	100
Total number	37	82	160

E. A. Nordlinger, *The Working Class Tories*, MacGibbon and Kee, London, 1967, p. 205.[*22*]

working class identify themselves with it, and, incidentally, the more they vote Conservative'.[*21*] Thus, in strongly working-class areas this factor alone constitutes a support to the predominantly Labour, hence deviant, vote.

Another support for working-class Labour voters is the work situation: the size of the plant is very strongly associated with voting patterns in the sense that people in small plants tend to support the Conservative Party and those in large plants the Labour Party (see Table 10). Again, we know that unionization is strongest in the larger factories. What appears to happen is similar to the process underlying the search for congruence previously outlined, that is, the normative subculture of the unionized larger factory supports Labour voting and not Conservative voting: 'wishing not to appear "different" to themselves or others, and as a minority finding it difficult to justify their party allegiances to themselves and others, some of the Conservative workers gradually move to the Left'.[36]

We have looked at the problems associated with working-class Conservative voting to illustrate a number of points which arose in discussing tension reduction which occurred in cross-pressured or dissonant situations. We have suggested that in such situations there appears to be a tendency for people to take on the coloration of their terminal milieu, especially if that milieu is homogeneous. Ideas or attachments may be modified or changed completely if the individual is constantly exposed to situations and experiences conflicting with those of childhood. On the other hand, 'the worker who has moved to the suburbs may still receive left-wing stimuli from his shop-mates, his union leader, and his conflicts with authority in the plant, all of which may overrule any pressures to conform to the more conservative values of his neighbourhood'.[37] It is also possible that childhood patterns and attachments may be reinforced by situations and experiences congruent with those already learned, but we suggest that in a mobile and technologically developing society incongruences of experience are likely to be more frequent.

6.6. Socialization and Political Personality

A further element in the study of political socialization is that concerned with examining the effect of early processes on the formation of personality and the effect of personality on behaviour. This is an aspect of the more general and social-psychological endeavours of linking personality and the social system.

The notion of personality is chronically difficult to define. Psychologists, no less than sociologists and political scientists, have failed to reach much agreement. Allport, in a standard text, distinguishes no less than fifty different definitions of 'personality'.[38] None the less, what seems to be agreed is that the term 'personality' refers not to directly observable phenomena, but to an inferred 'entity' introduced to account for the regularities of an individual's behaviour in response to diverse external stimuli. It represents, then, an area of interest pointing to processes 'deeper' than overt attitudes.

Our interest here is to examine some of the issues and problems connected with socialization processes claimed to result in different types of personality and to look at the effect of such personalities on the political system. One of the most researched dimensions of political personality is that of 'authoritarianism'.[39] This research was stimulated by Adorno and his colleagues' investigation into the psychology of anti-semitism.[*23*] In this study it was claimed that anti-semitism was part of a personality syndrome which they termed 'the authoritarian personality'. The traits which composed this personality type included intolerance, anti-semitism, ethnocentrism, dominance–submissiveness, intolerance of ambiguity and a tendency to think of social relationships in power terms. The authoritarian has orientations towards authority that are highly ambivalent and it is this ambivalence which is central to the logic of this personality type. Such an individual, outwardly servile and submissive towards his superiors, also harbours strong negative feelings towards them. However, this hate is repressed by strong ego defences. He heaps praise on people in authority over him and represses his critical impulses towards them. It is from this repression that other elements in the personality syndrome are derived: the repressed, hostile drives seek alternative outlets and are normally channelled towards those perceived to be weak and inferior. Thus the authoritarian unconsciously seeks out weak and disadvantaged individuals or groups such as blacks, Jews and other minority groups upon whom to vent his repressed hostility towards those in authority.

An important element in this study, one derived from the psychoanalytic tradition of which it is a part, was the task of uncovering the childhood antecedents of authoritarianism and in particular the socialization processes producing the authoritarian personality. The typical early determinants of the pattern were understood to be parents who administered rigid discipline and doled out affection conditional upon the child's overt obedience. Within the family, roles were defined in terms of dominance and submission. So, 'forced into surface submission to parental authority, the child develops hostility and aggression which are poorly channelised'.[40] This development of a repressed antagonism towards authority is considered to be the source of the authoritarian's hostility towards outgroups.

There is considerable evidence that these primary socialization patterns do give rise to this particular type of personality, *but the relationship between personality and the political system is much more ambiguous.* As Smelser points out, 'We do not at present have the methodological capacity to argue causally from a mixture of aggregated states of individual members of a system to a global characteristic of a system'.[41] In primitive societies, as we saw earlier, the personality types produced by family socialization are most nearly reflected in the political structure because of the close interpenetration of family roles and political roles. But in complex societies, as we also suggested above, the connection between family and polity is much more remote and mediated by a number of institutions intervening between the family and the polity. The major implication of this fact is that the authoritarian, for example, is presented with a much wider range of opportunities to express his personality needs. As Greenstein has pointed out, people with similar psychological characteristics may entertain different political beliefs or may express their needs in, say, organizing a business rather than chairing a ward party or joining an extremist group.[42]

The authors of *The Authoritarian Personality* did little to resolve (1) the complex question of how personality traits link with actual political belief and behaviour, and (2) the relationship between the distribution of psychological dispositions in a society and its overall social and political structure.

One school of thought which attempted to deal with both these links was the early culture-and-personality school, especially that dealing with national character. The common error of this approach was to infer a single national character type from various characteristics of the social system, then to use the character type as an explanation of these same attributes of the social system. Generally, the national character approach finds a near uniformity of character which is produced by patterns of early socialization or, as in the case of Gorer's study of the Great Russians, by methods of swaddling infants, or even potty-training.[*24*]

Nor, as we have previously argued, can we simply sum the characteristics of individuals in systems in order to reach conclusions about the characteristics of the system as a whole, for example, by adding the number of authoritarians in a community in order to reach conclusions as to whether or not the system has an authoritarian structure. The reason is that aggregation does not take into account the institutional and structural context in which actors perform their roles.[*25*] Some of the very real difficulties of sorting out the relationship between personality and political behaviour can be illustrated by reference to the phenomenon of 'working-class authoritarianism'.

Turning to the problem of the link between personality type and political behaviour, many researchers have noted the great propensity for the working-class to support authoritarian, non-democratic parties, and it is perhaps tempting to try to explain this in terms of the authoritarian dispositions and personalities formed by family socialization patterns characteristic of the working-class. The original research reported in the 'authoritarian personality' study elucidated some of the childhood antecedents of authoritarianism, to wit, parents who administered a rigid and restrictive discipline. So, this conclusion, coupled with the further finding that working-class families are much more likely to make frequent use of physical punishment in an authoritarian manner,[*26*] presents a reasonably plausible explanation of the greater propensity of the working-class to support authoritarian-type political movements.

But, it would be equally plausible to argue that working-class authoritarianism is not due to personality dynamics, of the ego-defensive type as outlined in *The Authoritarian Personality*, but is the result of social learning. This type might be termed 'cognitive authoritarianism'.[*27*] In this case the syndrome of characteristics are very similar to the ego-defensive type of authoritarianism except that they have their roots in 'the learned (ie cognitive) conceptions of reality which are prevalent in certain cultures or sub-cultures, rather than on the labyrinthine process of reaction formation described in the ego-defensive typology'.[43] It could be argued that much of the working-class social world may well contribute to such learning. Thus lower levels of education, for instance, are likely to predispose the working-class to see the complicated political world in basically black and white terms and to prefer those parties which suggest quick and easy solutions to perceived social problems. There is a great deal of evidence to suggest that

TABLE 11. The Relationship between Occupation, Education and Political Tolerance in the United States, 1955. Percentages in the Two 'Most Tolerant' Categories

	Occupation			
	Low manual	High manual	Low white-collar	High white-collar
Grade school	13	21	23	26
Some high school	32	33	29	46
High school grade	40	48	47	56
Some college	—	64	64	65
College graduate	—	—	74	83

the degree of formal education an individual acquires is highly correlated with undemocratic attitudes (see Table 11).

In addition, low-status groups are less apt to participate in formal organizations, do not buy magazines and books regularly, possess less information and knowledge on public affairs, and so on; all these attributes, available evidence suggests, are related to non-democratic political attitudes.[44] In other words, the lower strata are much more likely to be isolated from the activities, conflicts and organizations essential to a democratic political system—'an isolation which prevents them from acquiring the sophisticated and complex view of the political structure which makes understandable and necessary the norms of tolerance'.[45]

In addition to the view of the world which the working-class are most likely to acquire there is an additional factor which disposes them to authoritarianism, that is, their relative lack of economic and psychological independence and security. This, it is claimed, leads them to seek immediate solutions for their insecurity, these being frequently found in venting hostility against scapegoats—Jews, capitalists, Negroes, immigrant Pakistanis. Similarly, their lack of prolonged security may lead them to search for short-term political solutions by supporting extremist groups.[46]

To sum up, the whole life experience from childhood onwards, authoritarian upbringing, low education, social isolation, restricted cultural and educational background, all contribute to the tendency of much of the working-class to view politics, and personal relationships generally, in relatively unsophisticated terms such as a desire for immediate action, impatience with discussion and a need for immediate gratification.

Similarly, in a comparative study, employing the 'F' scale, of young people in the US and Egypt it was discovered that both Christians and Moslems in the Middle East scored higher than Christians in the US (see Table 12).[47]

TABLE 12

Group	Number	Mean
Egypt		
Moslem males	443	68.2
females	301	67.6
Christian males	143	67.0
females	79	65.2
US		
Protestant males	667	55.8
females	673	57.2
Catholic males	221	59.1
females	99	59.4

From L.H. Melikian, 'Authoritarianism and its Correlates in the Egyptian Culture and in the United States', *Journal of Social Issues*, 15, No. 3, 58–69 (1959)

The higher score for the Egyptians was explained by reference to the pervasive power of the Middle Eastern family, by the very low literacy rate, because the Moslem religion emphasizes submission and because of a weakly developed sense of community with others outside the immediate group.[48] Thus, as with the working-class authoritarian in Western societies, it is quite possible that the higher authoritarianism of people in Middle Eastern countries is a reflection of the authoritarianism of their environment.

The suggestion underlying both the personality and the learning theories of behaviour is that there may well be major factors contributing to an understanding of the manner in which political systems operate. At the level of the political system the results have been somewhat disappointing since it is, to all intents and purposes, impossible to specify the psychological requirements for societal stability and change. Further, the concept of requirements, of societal demands, is a very problematic one indeed, not merely at the level of intellectual doubt about the viability of functionalism as a method, but also because 'the variety of roles and role clusters made available in institutionally diversified large-scale social systems permit effective functioning for so wide a range of personality patterns that only the most general congruence of "basic" personality with the over-all social structure is required as a minimum condition for individual participation in the system'.[49] But analysing at the level of the constituent units of the political system, psychological considerations may well prove fruitful, and we shall initially concentrate on studies of 'basic' personality and then move on to studies of the role socialization of political participants. The logic of this order is the logic of political sociology, which stresses emergent properties of interaction, and the inference from this is that institutions operate in a situation wider than that of the personality of those occupying even major roles in those institutions. A politician may be seriously disturbed psychologically and yet be constrained to act in ways very similar to other politicians because of the need to win votes, obtain enthusiastic help, maintain the approval of his colleagues and generally meet the role demands of a politician.[*28*] This may well be the case even where an institution which appears to many outsiders to attract 'cranks'—the Communist Party, the various right-wing extremist groups, the Cornish and Welsh nationalists, etc.—operates most of the time in conformity with patterns exhibited by the more political activists. They form committees, delegate responsibility, have social meetings, publish legal literature, fight elections, collect funds and account for them, hold public meetings, issue membership cards and in dozens of other ways demonstrate quite clearly that institutional demands constrain action and operate quite independently of personality.

When the emphasis is placed upon adult socialization into institutionalized roles and role sets the importance of pre-adult socialization begins to recede except in the sense that experiences, whilst young, may anticipate adult roles. We know a good deal about the social background and putative familial influences of, for example, legislators and party officials, and we can understand that, all other things being equal, a youth from a 'political' family may himself become interested and involved in politics.[50] But none of this necessarily tells us anything about the *actual behaviour* of politically involved people, even if it does tell us a great deal about those most likely to become involved since adult political behaviour, as we have insisted, is very frequently institutionally determined or at least constrained.

As we have already mentioned, the primary point about relating a person's psychological condition to political involvement is that the involvement can be understood not only in terms of its consequences for the political system—although studies of Lenin, Gandhi, Stalin, Woodrow Wilson and others do examine political consequences [*29*]—but also in terms of the consequences for the individual's psychological needs. Looked at psychologically, political involvement for the 'maladjusted' is one of a possible range of activities meeting the individual needs of the actor and it is a contingent matter that he 'opts' for politics. Such maladjustment can have different degrees of severity and hence its political expressions can be more or less dramatic and violent. In a study of badly maladjusted people, confined in mental hospitals, following threats to assassinate the American president, it was concluded that the most dangerous would-be assassins were 'socially isolated persons who adapt to stress by symbolizing their problems in a political idiom and who identify with the President in terms of violence and death'.[51] In a study of the psychology of dictators, the major factor causing the population to *need* a dictator was a 'weakening of the collective ego . . . under the impact of anxiety, fear, and insecurity'. Due to these conditions, the ego regresses to an 'infantile stage and looks anxiously for help, support, and salvation' which it finds in a leader whom it then invests with an aura of infallibility.[52] In his turn, the dictatorial leader needs his adulators since their adulation enables him to forget, or compensate for, 'feelings of weakness and inferiority often based on early frustrations and on inadequate virility'.[53] In a similar manner, Lasswell delineates a less extreme psychological type who is 'characterised by strong and ungratified cravings for deference which are displaced upon public objects' and the deference-seeking is then rationalized in terms of the public interest. The psychological origins of the craving stem from a low estimate of the self which he seeks to alleviate by eliciting deference to himself as a power-holder. The origins of the low estimate of the self are in childhood. But there is no suggestion that Lasswell's *homo politicus* will necessarily seek political power—all he seeks is deference and he may well get more in business activity or in a religious organization.[54]

One important study of membership of the American Communist Party suggests that social situation, economic situation, religious persuasion, etc., are all useful predictors of propensity to join the party, ie that membership is not random but associated with a cluster of social characteristics. Also associated with membership, however, was a 'neurotic susceptibility to communism' where the 'neurotic person will join the party in response to the pressure of internal needs'.[55] These needs, basically the needs for tension reduction, are derived from unconscious hostility, inability to relate to others, feelings of self-rejection and inferiority which in the majority of cases 'appeared to be situationally induced and in conformity with community patterns'. But for a 'substantial number of cases it appeared to be a pattern of chronic and unconscious hostility resulting from family and childhood experiences'.[56] For these latter people the party is a sort of therapeutic haven in which their psychological needs are met by the pseudo-family of the cell, by the certainties of the ideology, by the institutionalized enemy of capitalism which may be attacked and destroyed. Other things being equal, of two people, one unconsciously hostile and destructive and the other 'normal', there is a greater probability that the former will join the Communist Party and will, therefore, be projecting personal problems on to the political system.

Looked at purely in terms of political sociology, the weakness of such studies is that whilst they are useful in highlighting a mechanism behind political involvement, they do not tell us much about the distribution of such psychological types in terms useful to political sociology. We know a good deal about family background, education, marital status and so on but we do not know whether the type is *systematically produced* in one structural location rather than another.

Turning now to this problem of the relationship between psychological dispositions and social structure, we may note the attempt made to explain the rise of the extreme right-wing political groups in the US, which is seen as a reaction to the very rapid technological, economic, political and status changes of that society. Such changes have brought into being new classes of the 'dispossessed'—the lower echelon managers, the old independent middle-class, the middle-rank military—who react to these changes by political action designed to turn the clock back. This is, naturally enough, impossible and out of the impossibility comes 'the politics of frustration, the sour impotence of those who find themselves unable to understand . . . the complex mass society that is the polity today'.[*30*] First and second generation Americans, new urbanites from the countryside and all those older independent groups of traditional America—the small farmer, the garage owner, the small shopkeeper or manufacturer—find that they simply cannot understand or compete and, in the case of the immigrants, are not accepted as true Americans. From this combination of 'insecurity over social status (which) has . . . been with insecurity over one's very identity and sense of belonging' has resulted widespread status anxiety which is projected upon the task of child-rearing.[57] The children are expected to achieve what their parents were unable to and 'from the standpoint of the children their expectations often appear in the form of an exorbitantly demanding authority that one dare not question or defy. Resistance and hostility, finding no moderate outlet in give and take, have to be suppressed and reappear in the form of internal destructive rage. An enormous hostility to authority which cannot be admitted to consciousness, calls forth a massive over-compensation which is manifest in the form of extravagant submissiveness to strong power.'[*31*] The sub ject imagines that he is dominated by scheming enemies, that the country is falling under the influence of alien forces that manipulate and control him, and the demonological ideologies of the radical Right which comprehend the government to be controlled by the 'left', which see blacks and Jews as agents of Communist plots, and detect 'creeping socialism' in all government acts, perfectly suit him. They suit him the better since they enable him at once to submit to the power of America and work off his aggression against nonconformists.

A rather different type of psychological analysis concentrates on frustrations which are structurally induced but makes no attempt to relate these to patterns of early childhood experiences within the family. Here the primary notion is a simple frustration–aggression pattern in which the frustration can occur at any age, not necessarily in early childhood.[*32*] The members of those social groups badly disadvantaged in terms of career opportunities, those suffering a reduction of previously high status, those in occupations becoming technologically outmoded, and those affected by the increasing complexity of large institutions, fail to understand what is happening societally and 'feel that their social standing is now threatened by new groups and "alien conspirators" '.[58] The psychological outcome is that they feel a lack of control over their lives and react to this by stressing fundamentalist ideologies attacking intellectuals, liberals, welfare schemes, foreign countries and Communism. In their interpersonal relations 'the style of group interaction is designed, consciously or unconsciously, to satisfy simultaneously the personal motivations of the participants and relieve some of the shared feelings of alienation and frustration that have been built up by the changing social order'.[*33*] Similarly, in an analysis of the John Birch Society, the underlying cause is seen as the 'greatly accelerated alteration and realignment of its (America) social, economic and political institutions'.[59] Analysis of the extremist Front de Liberation Quebecois (FLQ) in Canada reveals its membership as falling within a syndrome of above average intelligence, emotional immaturity, substituting a secular Marxist 'religion' for the orthodox Catholicity of their upbringing and rejection of parental values. This syndrome is seen as a response to life in society where all the cards are stacked against French-Canadians: they are economically depressed, educationally disadvantaged, politically weak and little local industry is locally controlled.[*34*] Like the American Right, they are part of a society which is passing them by and which they understand—probably correctly—to be alien controlled and over whose major decisions they have little influence. In this context they adopt a violently nationalistic ideology, widely accepted by many French-Canadians minus the violence, which offers both an explanation of the depressed situation and a programme of action. A primary appeal of such extremist organizations is an ideological one with the ideology providing an anchor of logic-tight and argument-proof certainty and also giving the dispossessed a sense of direction denied them socially.[*35*]

Another analysis, this time of the Black Muslim church in the US and its attraction for the 'Negro masses', stresses that they are 'trapped in negro ghettoes' by their economic status, moral habits and their acceptance of the white man's image of them.[60] Rejected both by the white world and by the black middle-class which has accepted white definitions of reality, politically helpless and ethnically despised, 'they become over-whelmed by a feeling of total powerlessness'.[61] In one of his letters from Harlem, James Baldwin put the point with sustained anger: 'They work in the white man's world all day and come home in the evening to this fetid block. They struggle to instil in their children some private sense of honour or dignity which will help the child survive. This means, of course, that they must struggle, stolidly, incessantly to keep this sense alive in themselves, in spite of the insults, the indifference, and the cruelty they are certain to encounter in their working day. They patiently browbeat the landlord into fixing the heat, the plaster, the plumbing; this demands prodigious patience; nor is the patience usually enough. In trying to make their hovels habitable, they are perpetually throwing good money after bad. Such frustration, so long endured, is driving many strong, admirable men and women whose only crime is colour to the very gates of paranoia'.[62] In this situation of powerlessness which can develop into self-rejection, the American black may be attracted to a counter-ideology in which the virtue of 'blackness' is stressed, the eventual formation of a black nation in the US predicted, and an emotional attachment to a 'black' power centre such as Egypt, Ethiopia, Morocco or the Sudan formed. Thus the aggression which is potential in all people when frustrated is produced amongst American blacks by their situation in US society where they are denied opportunities for legitimate tension release 'by the callous and hostile white society'.[63] By these means black nationalists may cope 'with the material, cultural, moral and psychological problems which are purported to impede the advancement of the negro masses'.[*36*]

The Black Muslims are especially interesting since they also illustrate a point made earlier, that *political* activity is simply one amongst a range of possible outlets for displacement of socially induced aggression. The Black Muslims have a great deal in common with religious sects which so often spring up amongst the societally disadvantaged and which can be alternatives to political action to put the situation 'right', or which can temporarily precede organized political activity, or which can eventually drift or be driven to take political action.[64] Again, in such religious organizations people may also learn organizational and oratorical skills which can be used in the political arena for more purely secular ends.[*37*]

6.7. Socialization Into Political Roles

The problem about the application of psychology to politics is that it suggests people move towards or seek out political roles as a source of displacement for psychological needs on to the public arena. If this means that overall the politically active or successful are more likely to have serious psychological problems then it is simply false.[*38*] If it means that politicians are quite normal in seeking displacement but happen to opt for politics rather than another displacement target then the problem still remains of why they choose politics rather than the other options available.[*39*] It also does not explain the regularity of behaviour observable amongst political actors in their institutional settings, nor does it explain the differential recruitment to political roles from strategic social groupings. In an attempt to clarify the complex problem of the interconnection between psychological factors and the institutional setting of political action, Greenstein offers a number of propositional suggestions, including the following:

(1) 'Ambiguous situations leave room for personal variability to manifest itself.' For example, in newly formed political groupings such as parties or pressure groups, where no framework of expectations has emerged, there is more room for personal psychological variability to determine behaviour. Such a loose framework can be crucial, as it was in the case of Lenin who was able to manipulate the RSDLP, and when this failed and 'he realised that he was psychologically unfit to share power, he set up his own organisation'.[65] Similarly with Hitler's decision to join the German Workers Party, 'the decisive turning point of my life', a party with 'nothing, no programme, not a leaflet, nothing at all in print, not even a miserable rubber stamp'.[66] Such situations are characterized, initially at least, by

the absence of specific and fixed expectations about the occupant's behaviour in the position and therefore allow considerable freedom of behaviour.

(2) 'The impact of personal differences on behaviour is increased to the degree that sanctions are not attached to certain of the alternative possible courses of behaviour.' An example of this might be the extremely predictable Lobby behaviour of Members of Parliament in the same party but, presumably, of different psychological dispositions. Sanctions, both formal and informal, against maverick political behaviour in the Lobby are so strong that in spite of personal variability most MPs eventually conform.[67]

(3) '. . . to the degree that individuals are placed in a group context in which their decision or attitude is visible to others personal variation is reduced'. This factor is demonstrated in the studies of group pressures mentioned earlier.

(4) '. . . intense needs to take one's cues from others will tend to reduce the affects of variation' of other psychological traits. For example, data from the South of America hints that susceptibility to conform, more than other usually noted psychological correlates of prejudice, is an important determinant of prejudicial behaviour in regions where cultural norms positively sanction intolerance.[68]

Another set of considerations relates to the possibility of routinized behaviour such as voting where there is, especially in countries with a relatively limited number of parties, only a very restricted opportunity for personality to express itself in other than the most trivial fashion. Nor, when the party choice is restricted, would one expect any very deep psychological differences to be displayed in voting for a party or in support for it. At this level, then, other factors are evidently far more strongly, and certainly obviously, associated with the behaviour. Amongst these factors are peer and reference groups, the family, socio-economic status, work situation and so on, with personality, at best, a rather attenuated possible intermediate variable.[*40*]

Whilst these considerations are important, it is also the case that a major emphasis of the bureaucratized society is on fitting the individual to a routinized pattern of behaviour. This is not to say that individuals in organizations have no opportunity for expressing personal variability in styles of interpersonal behaviour or that the formal specification of official role and role hierarchy corresponds with actual behaviours. There are, of course, informal norms and expectations in opposition to, or complementary with, the formal norms and roles and this duality may allow the individual some room for expressing personal variations. However, unlike the generalized socialization process spoken of earlier, joining an organized group—whether a firm, a religious sect or church or a political party—involves the learning of skills, attitudes and norms much more specific to the institution. Here we come up against the problem of *types* of institution and the *types* of goals of these institutions because organizations appear to differ systematically in the amount, intensity, duration and content of socialization required by their recruits. For example, socialization into prisons involves, to a great degree, elimination of social behaviours and expectations formed outside so that the inmate is better suited to the highly depersonalized routine of prison life. This is less true of socialization into a business firm or a political party. Thus, the new prisoner is stripped of possessions, put in a dull uniform, has his hair shorn to regulation length and in general is forced both through the official and unofficial pressures exercised by warden *and* other prisoners into a common and regimented behaviour pattern.[*41*] Similarly, where it is functionally desirable to disassociate the actor from the act, the action may be dramatically depersonalized as in the case of judges surrounded by the apparatus of the majesty of law, and less dramatically by doctors and other professional groups with their rigid codes of professional behaviour. An analogous process may occur in bureaucracies, which require their personnel to maintain a restricted range of behaviour in their role as bureaucrats.

Bureaucracies, whether part of private industry, public service or voluntary organizations, act so as to break complex processes into simpler constituent parts so that they can attain maximum efficiency. This is merely an element of the division of labour observed in all advanced societies and is the root cause of the organizational limitations placed on individual behavioural variation. That is, the bureaucracy is the 'ideal type' of the formal organization with its emphasis on precision, rationality, continuity and so on which leads to, or approaches, 'the complete elimination of personalized relationships and non-rational considerations (hostility, anxiety, affectual involvement), etc'.[69] Naturally, the amount of resocialization required will be related to the degree of formal bureaucratization and to the kind of socialization experienced *prior* to joining the organization. An example was provided in a study of Appalachian workers employed in an anti-poverty organization. These workers attached low value to hierarchical authority and were committed to much more individualistic and levelling values which are supposed to be antithetical to the working efficiency of bureaucracy. As an organization the bureaucracy has to ingest these people and resocialize them into acceptance of the hierarchical authority characteristic of all bureaucracies. In the study cited, 'participants were found, in relation to deference to authority, to become socialised through their membership in the organisation' but at the same time the bureaucracy was found to have accommodated to its social surroundings by integrating 'certain of the values of the local culture into its operations'.[70]

For the psychologist, the bureaucracy is likely to *attract* the 'compulsive' type who 'seeks orderly procedures . . . treats people as objects to be manipulated . . . avoids situations involving many "unknowns", and presents himself to others as blandly as possible'.[71] He is characterized by a need to impose order which springs from a fear of ambiguous or uncertain situations, all of which bureaucracies exist to eliminate. The bureaucracy, from the psychological stance, may not be primarily a socializing agency since many of those attracted to it already fit attitudinally: it is rather a collecting or concentrating agency for those compulsives who rely 'upon rigid, obsessive ways of handling human relations'.[*42*] Although the approach does not preclude an element of intra-bureaucratic reinforcement of compulsive attitudes, the emphasis is on the bureaucracy attracting people who fit best because of their psychological predisposition. Presthus found that in the two business organizations he studied the most successful bureaucrats were significantly more likely to score higher on an authoritarianism scale than the less successful. He adds that such successful executives were disproportionately recruited from 'upper-class and upper middle class groups, members of which have usually been found to rank low on authoritarianisms'.[72]

Socialization into roles within a political party may well be a more diverse process than into other more formally structured roles or role sets. There are many different positions at various levels of the party, with various degrees of possible individual autonomy in the positions, and very little indeed is known about the process of fitting the recruited individual to the roles.[*43*] It is probable that for most mass-member political parties the degree of socialization into the role of party member is minimal since role expectations are non-demanding and the member can make almost anything he likes of it: he can be active or passive, he can attend branch meetings or not, read the 'literature' or listen to the radio, and so on. Hence, it is improbable that he will differ from the rest of the population in any marked way except that his levels of interest and political knowledge will be higher, he will be more likely to vote, more likely to have a higher than average social status, etc. None of this requires much from the political party and, indeed, his joining the party may be a consequence of these characteristics rather than cause them. Again, it is unlikely that the professional bureaucrat in the party differs in any dramatic way from the bureaucrat in the state or private sector although his commitment to the organization may well be higher. However, for the legislator it is probable that a period of relatively intensive resocialization occurs in most cases since 'the individual legislator accepts a set of severe limitations on his discretion to act for whatever purposes he pleases'.[*44*] These limitations are the rules of the legislative game and exist independently of any individual legislator and if he is to play successfully he simply must learn them and to a considerable extent must abide by them.

Wahlke and his colleagues delineated the task of the legislator in terms of a number of roles which, although not allowing one to predict the legislator's behaviour in all situations, 'are effective indicators of behavioural possibilities'.[73] The role set for an American legislator includes that of lawmaker, representative of constituency and geographical areas, pressure group roles, and so on, and the legislator may bring to these a set

TABLE 13. Distribution of Purposive Role Orientations

Role orientation	New Jersey $n = 79$	Ohio $n = 162$	California $n = 113$	Tennessee n = 120
	%	%	%	%
Ritualist	70	67	58	72
Tribune	63	40	55	58
Inventor	49	33	36	30
Broker	33	48	27	15

From *The Legislative System* by John C. Wahlke, Heinz Eulau, William Buchanan and Le Roy C. Ferguson. Copyright © 1962, John Wiley & Sons Inc. New York. By permission of John Wiley & Sons Inc.[*47*].

of expectations and attitudes. Out of the interaction of his self-expectations and the role set there emerges the actual role types in the legislature, which include the 'ritualist' concerned to master rules and procedures of the legislative process, the 'tribune' who perceives himself 'as the discoverer, reflector, advocate or defender of popular needs and wants', and the 'inventor' who sees his primary role as the formulator of the general welfare or of particular policies. The 'inventor' directs himself to what he considers the creative aspects of his job. Finally, there is the 'broker'. The broker is concerned with compromise, and integration of conflicting interests and demands.[*45*] Such role types were discovered to be differentially distributed in the four state legislatures studied although the ritualist appears more frequently than any of the other types.

Wahlke and his colleagues go into some detail about the pre-adult socialization patterns of their legislative sample, exploring dimensions such as early interest in politics, influence of primary groups such as parents, early voluntary association membership, etc., but no attempt is made to explore the personality sources of political involvement. Nor do they attempt a longitudinal study of the process of learning the various role types a new legislative politician may adopt.[*46*] But they do delineate the role types of legislators, and since these types in four such widely disparate states have almost the same rank order the supposition must be that the role types are dependent more upon the socio-political characteristic of the states and the nature of the legislative process than upon the basic personality or childhood socialization of the legislators (see Table 13).

6.8. Conclusions

It seems, then, that in most societies political socialization of the future political generation begins early, if unsystematically. Most children begin to structure their political world from an early age, first by developing affective attachment to salient political symbols, such as the President, the flag, the Queen, or whatever, and then, with age, gaining some cognitive understanding of the 'reality' underlying these attachments.

While much is known of the modal developmental pattern that Anglo-American children follow in their induction to the political culture, there remain a number of problem areas. Firstly, the political socialization of cultural subgroups has been relatively unexamined, as well as the political socialization process in societies other than the Anglo-American. A second problem area is that of evaluating the consequences of early political learning for the functioning of the political system. In pre-industrial societies the relationship between what is learned in early socialization and the character and process of the social system is quite direct. But, in the more complex, faster changing industrial societies other institutions, groups and organizations intervene between early socialization experiences and adult life. This fact alone increases the possibility that attitudes and values formed early in life may be modified at stages throughout the life cycle. Such changes in individual orientations need not be cataclysmic and it may be that in relatively stable political societies, complex or otherwise, early political learning is subject to little modification, going beyond change of party preference or of political interest, but rarely leading to a basic questioning of the political system itself. Of what happens in more rapidly changing societies, very little is known. This is more or less directly tied up with the question of *what* and how much is learned in early life and, of this, how much can be related to adult political behaviour. As we saw, it is very difficult indeed to trace out connections between child socialization and adult political behaviour and, indeed, the great mass of research evidence 'examining both personal and situational influences on overt behaviour has shown that predictions of overt behaviour can be made more accurately from a knowledge of the situation than a knowledge of individual differences'.[74] The 'basic personality' school, derived as it is from the Freudian tradition, argues that what we learn in childhood has a great deal to do with our behaviour as adults. The contribution of this kind of thinking to an understanding of political behaviour is difficult to evaluate even though it is not a new mode of political analysis.

An early error (or sociological heresy) of this school of thought was to underestimate the role of structural and institutional factors in social behaviour. Today, the problem is focussed much more on the issue of *how* much and in what context does personality as opposed to other variables affect behaviour. What we have tried to show in the last section is that bland assumptions about the relationship between psychological characteristics and political behaviour need to be treated with extreme caution and scepticism.

References

1. For example R. Benedict, 'Continuities and Discontinuities in Cultural Conditions', *Psychiatry*, **1,** 161–167 (1938).
2. M. Mead, *Continuities in Cultural Evolution*, Yale University Press, New Haven, 1964.
3. T. Parsons, *The Social System*, Tavistock, London, 1964; T. Parsons and E. Shils (eds.), *Towards a General Theory of Action*, Harvard University Press, Cambridge, Mass., 1951; A. Inkeles and D. J. Levinson, 'National Character', in G. Lindzey (ed.), *The Handbook of Social Psychology*, vol. ii, Addison-Wesley, Cambridge, Mass., 1954.
4. G. J. Bender, 'Political Socialisation and Political Change', *Western Political Quarterly*, 390–407 (1967).
5. D. Marsh, 'Political Socialization: The Implicit Assumptions Questioned', *British Journal of Political Science*, **I,** 519–531 (1971).
6. R. A. Le Vine, 'The Internationalization of Political Values in Stateless Societies', in R. Hunt (ed.), *Personalities and Cultures*, Natural History Press, New York, 1967, pp. 185–203.
7. —— 'The Internationalization of Political Values in Stateless Societies', in R. Hunt (ed.), *Personalities and Cultures*, Natural History Press, New York, 1967, p. 195.
8. E. Banfield and L. Banfield, *The Moral Basis of a Backward Society*, Free Press, Glencoe, 1958.
9. R. Harris, 'The Role of the Civil Servant in West Africa', *Public Administration Review*, **25,** 308–313 (1965).
10. L. Pye, *Politics, Personality and Nation Building*, Yale University Press, New Haven, 1966, p. 181.
11. —— *Politics, Personality and Nation Building*, Yale University Press, New Haven, 1966, p. 182.

12. —— *Politics, Personality and Nation Building*, Yale University Press, New Haven, 1966, p. 184.
13. —— *Politics, Personality and Nation Building*, Yale University Press, New Haven, 1966, p. 185.
14. D. Easton, R. Hess and J. Torney, *The Development of Political Attitudes in Children*, Aldine Publishing Co., Chicago, 1967; F. Greenstein, 'The Benevolent Leader: Children's Images of Political Authority', *APSR*, **54**, 934–945 (1960).
15. R. Hess and D. Easton, 'The Child's Changing Image of the President', *Public Opinion Quarterly*, **24**, 632–644 (1960).
16. F. Greenstein, *Children and Politics*, Yale University Press, New Haven, 1965, p. 39.
17. P. Lauter and F. Howe, 'How the School System is Rigged for Failure', *New York Review of Books* (18 June, 1970).
18. E. Litt, 'Civic Education, Community Norms and Political Indoctrination', *American Sociological Review*, **28**, 69–75 (1963).
19. L. Wyle, *Village in the Vaucluse*, Harvard University Press, Cambridge, Mass., 1957, pp. 206–207.
20. M. Kent Jennings and R. Niemi, 'Patterns of Political Learning', *Harvard Educational Review*, **30**, no. 3, 443–467 (1968).
21. T. Parsons, 'The School Class as a Social System', *Harvard Educational Review*, **24**, 297–318 (1959), reprinted in A. H. Halsey, C. J. Floud and C. A. Anderson, *Education, Economy and Society*, Free Press, Glencoe, 1961, pp. 434–455.
22. D. Jaros, H. Hirsch and F. J. Fleron, 'The Malevolent Leader: Political Socialisation in an American Subculture', *APSR*, **62**, no. 2 (June 1968).
23. H. Eckstein, *Division and Cohesion in a Democracy*, Princeton University Press, Princeton 1966, p. 248.
24. R. Rose, *Politics in England*, Little, Brown, Boston, 1964, ch. 2; E. Nordlinger, *The Working Class Tories*, MacGibbon and Kee, London, 1967, ch. 1; G. Almond and S. Verba, *The Civic Culture*, Little, Brown, Boston, 1965, pp. 360–362.
25. E. Nordlinger, *The Working Class Tories*, MacGibbon and Kee, London, 1967, p. 14.
26. R. Turner, 'Sponsored and Contest Mobility and the School System', *American Sociological Review*, **25**, 855–867 (1960).
27. G. Almond and S. Verba, *The Civic Culture*, Little, Brown, Boston, 1965, esp. pp. 324–335; L. W. Milbrath, *Political Participation*, Rand McNally, Chicago, 1965.
28. R. E. Dowse and J. Hughes, 'Girls, Boys and Politics', *British Journal of Sociology*, **22**, 53–67 (1971).
29. K. Prewitt, H. Eulau and B. Zisk, 'Political Socialisation and Political Roles', *Public Opinion Quarterly*, **30**, 569–582 (1966).
30. D. Butler and D. Stokes, *Political Change in Britain*, Macmillan, London, 1969, p. 50; M. Abrams, 'Social Trends and Electoral Behaviour', *British Journal of Sociology*, **13**, 228–242 (1960), reprinted in R. Benewick and R. Dowse, *Readings on British Politics and Government*, University of London Press, London, 1968, pp. 61–77.

31. G. Almond and S. Verba, *The Civic Culture*, Little, Brown, Boston, 1965, pp. 324–335.
32. L. W. Milbrath, *Political Participation*, Rand McNally, Chicago, 1965, p. 39.
33. R. Alford, *Party and Society*, Murray, London, 1964, pp. 123–171; but see also S. Lipset and S. Rokkan (eds.), *Party Systems and Voter Alignments*, Free Press, New York, 1967, pp. 95–112 on New Zealand.
34. S. Lipset and S. Rokkan (eds.), *Party Systems and Voter Alignments*, Free Press, New York, 1967, p. 119.
35. P. Willmott and M. Young, *Family and Class in a London Suburb*, Routledge and Kegan Paul, London, 1960.
36. E. A. Nordlinger, *The Working Class Tories*, MacGibbon and Kee, London, 1967, p. 209.
37. S. M. Lipset, *Revolution and Counterrevolution*, Basic Books, New York, 1968, p. 169.
38. G. Allport, *Personality*, Holt, New York, 1937, pp. 24–54.
39. R. Christie and P. Cook, 'A Guide to Published Literature Relating to the Authoritarian Personality Through 1956', *Journal of Psychology*, **45**, 171–199 (April 1958).
40. T. W. Adorno, E. Frenkel-Brunswick, D. Levinson and R. Sanford, *The Authoritarian Personality*, Harper and Row, New York, 1950, p. 482.
41. N. J. Smelser, 'Personality and the Explanation of Political Phenomena at the Social-System Level; A Methodological Statement', *Journal of Social Issues*, **24**, no. 3, 123 (1968).
42. F. I. Greenstein, 'Personality and Political Socialisation: The Theories of the Authoritarian and Democratic Character', *Annals of the American Academy of Political and Social Science*, no. 361, 81–95 (1965), and also N. Glazer and S. M. Lipset, 'The Polls on Communism and Conformity', in D. Bell (ed.), *The New American Right*, Criterion Books, New York, 1955, pp. 141–166.
43. F. I. Greenstein, *Personality and Politics*, Markham Publishing Co., Chicago, 1969, p. 109.
44. M. Komarovsky, 'The Voluntary Associations of Urban Dewellers', *American Sociological Review*, **11**, 686–698 (1946); H. Hyman and P. Sweatley, 'Some Reasons Why Information Campaigns Fail', *POQ*, **11**, (1947); S. M. Lipset, *Political Man*, Heinemann, London, 1969.
45. S. M. Lipset, *Political Man*, Heinemann, London, 1969, p. 112.
46. G. Almond, *The Appeals of Communism*, Princeton University Press, Princeton, 1954, p. 236; H. Cantril, *The Psychology of Social Movements*, Wiley, New York, 1941, chs. 8 and 9; W. Kornhauser, *The Politics of Mass Society*, Routledge and Kegan Paul, London, 1960.
47. L. H. Melikian, 'Authoritarianism and its Correlates in the Egyptian Culture and in the United States', *Journal of Social Issues*, **15**, no. 3, 58–69 (1959).
48. G. H. Gardner, 'The Arab Middle East: Some Background Interpretations', *Journal of Social Issues*, **15**, no. 3, 20–27 (1959).
49. A. Inkeles, 'Some Sociological Observations on Culture and Personality Studies', in C. Kluckholn, H. Murray and O. Schneider, *Personality in Nature, Society and Culture*, Knopf, New York, 1967, p. 587.
50. A. Kornberg, J. Smith and D. Bromley, 'Some Differences in the Political Socialisation of Canadian and American Party Officials', *Canadian Journal*

of Political Science, **2,** 64–88 (1969); L. W. Milbrath, *Political Participation*, Rand McNally, Chicago, 1965, ch. 2.
51. E. Weinstein and O. Lyerly, 'Symbolic Aspects of Presidential Assassination', *Psychiatry*, **32,** no. 1, 1–11 (1969).
52. G. Bychowski, *Dictators and Disciples*, International Universities Press, New York, 1969, p. 242.
53. —— *Dictators and Disciples*, International Universities Press, New York, 1969, p. 242.
54. H. Lasswell, 'Power and Personality', in H. Eulau, *Political Behaviour*, Free Press, Glencoe, 1956, pp. 90–103; this basic account was first published by Lasswell in *Psychopathology and Politics*, Viking Press, New York, 1930.
55. G. Almond, *The Appeals of Communism*, Princeton University Press, New Jersey, 1965, p. 236.
56. —— *The Appeals of Communism*, Princeton University Press, New Jersey, 1965, p. 261.
57. R. Hofstadter, 'The Pseudo-Conservative Revolt', in D. Bell (ed.), *The Radical Right*, Anchor Books, New York, 1964, p. 88.
58. M. Chelser and R. Schmuk, 'Participant Observation in a Super-Patriot Discussion Group', *Journal of Social Issues*, **19,** 18–49 (1963).
59. J. Broyles, 'The John Birch Society: A Movement of Social Protest of the Radical Right', *Journal of Social Issues*, **19,** 51–62 (1963).
60. E. U. Essien-Udom, *Black Nationalism*, Dell, New York, 1962, p. 16.
61. —— *Black Nationalism*, Dell, New York, 1962, p. 66.
62. J. Baldwin, *Nobody Knows My Name*, Corgi, London, 1965, p. 56.
63. C. E. Lincoln, *The Black Muslims in America*, Beacon, Boston, 1961, p. 249.
64. D. Apter, 'Political Religion in the New Nations', in C. Geertz (ed.), *Old Societies and New States*, Free Press, Chicago, 1963.
65. S. Possony, *Lenin: The Compulsive Revolutionary*, Allen and Unwin, London, 1965, p. 469.
66. Hitler, *My Struggle*, Hurst and Blackett, London, 1935, p. 100.
67. R. E. Dowse and T. A. Smith, 'Party Discipline in the House of Commons', *Parliamentary Affairs*, **16,** 159–164 (1963).
68. T. F. Pettigrew, 'Personality and Socio-Cultural Factors in Inter-Group Attitudes', *Journal of Conflict Resolution*, **2,** 29–42 (1958).
69. R. Merton, *Social Theory and Social Structure*, Free Press, New York, 1968, p. 250.
70. R. B. Denhardt, 'Bureaucratic Socialization and Organisational Accommodation', *Administrative Science Quarterly*, **13,** 441–450 (1968).
71. E. V. Wolfenstein, *Personality and Politics*, Dickenson Publishing Company, California, 1969, pp. 36–37.
72. R. Presthus, *Behavioural Research on British Executives*, University of Alabama Press, Alabama, 1965, pp. 105–112.
73. J. C. Wahlke, H. Eulau, W. Buchanan and L. Ferguson, *The Legislative System*, Wiley, New York, 1962, p. 243.
74. A. Wicker, 'Attitudes versus Actions: The Relationship of Verbal and Overt Behavioural Responses to Attitude Objects', *Journal of Social Issues*, **25,** 41–78 (1969).

Notes and Further Reading

1. O. G. Brim, Jr., 'Socialisation Through the Life Cycle', in O. G. Brim Jr. and S. Wheeler, *Socialisation After Childhood*, Wiley, New York, 1966; similarly I. L. Child in G. Lindzey (ed.), *Handbook of Social Psychology*, Addison-Wesley, Cambridge, Mass., 1954, vol. 2, p. 655, defines socialization as 'the whole process by which an individual, born with behavioural potentialities of enormously wide range, is led to develop actual behaviour which is confined within a much narrower range—the range of what is customary and acceptable for him according to the standards of his group'.
2. See S. Freud, *Civilisation and its Discontents*, ed. James Strachey, Hogarth Press, London, 1963, and J. W. Whiting and R. L. Child, *Child Training and Personality*, Yale University Press, New Haven, 1953, and for an application of the tradition to politics see H. Lasswell, *Power and Personality*, Norton, New York, 1948; see also the careful chapter in P. Rieff, *Freud: The Mind of the Moralist*, Viking, New York, 1959, pp. 220–256.
3. As D. Easton and R. Hess say, 'Every piece of evidence indicates that the child's political world begins to take shape well before he even enters elementary school . . .', in 'The Child's Political World', *Mid-West Journal of Political Science*, **6,** 231–235 (1962).
4. Joan Laurence, 'White Socialisation: Black Reality', *Psychiatry*, **33,** 174–194 (1970); young = 8 to 11 years, old = 12 to 15 years.
5. See the Report of the Minister of Education's Central Advisory Committee (The Crowther Report), *Fifteen to Eighteen*, HMSO, London, 1959, and J. W. B. Douglas, J. M. Ross and H. R. Simpson, *All Our Future: A Longitudinal Study of Secondary Education*, Davies, London, 1968.
6. R. Rose, *Politics in England*, Little, Brown, Boston, 1964, p. 71. In 1966–1967 each grammar school pupil cost £150; each secondary modern pupil cost £114 to educate, *The Times*, 9 March, 1970.
7. P. Abramson, 'The Differential Political Socialization of English Secondary School Students', *Sociology of Education*, **40,** 246–269 (1967). This finding supports earlier reports by H. T. Himmelweit, A. Halsey and A. Oppenheim, 'The Views of Adolescents on Some Aspects of the Social Class Structure', *B.J.S.*, **25,** 148–172 (1952); M. D. Wilson, 'The Vocational Preferences of Secondary Modern School Children', *British Journal of Educational Psychology*, **23,** 97–113 (1953), and G. H. Elder, 'Life Opportunity and Personality: Some Consequences of Stratified Secondary Education in Great Britain', *Sociology of Education*, **38,** 173–202 (1965).
8. As a matter of fact in 1970 about 30 per cent of school-age children in Britain attended comprehensive schools.
9. R. Lane, *Political Life*, Free Press, New York, 1965, p. 213; R. Rose, *Politics in England*, Little, Brown, Boston, 1965, p. 63, suggests 'In national political activity a woman finds that her sex is a handicap, because national political activity is not considered a woman's role'.
10. This finding is similar to an American one to the effect that '. . . there are more girls than boys who say they are uncertain about what the word "government" means at every age', D. Easton and J. Dennis, *Children and the Political System*, McGraw-Hill, New York, 1969, p. 338.

11. P. W. Buck, *Amateurs and Professionals in British Politics*, University of Chicago Press, Chicago, 1963, p. 35; for evidence of this in local political candidacies see L. J. Sharpe (ed.), *Voting in Cities*, Macmillan, London, 1967, pp. 317–319.
12. See also R. S. Milne and H. C. MacKenzie, *Straight Fight*, Hansard Society, London, 1954, pp. 38–39; W. G. Runciman, *Relative Deprivation and Social Justice*, Routledge and Kegan Paul, London, 1966, p. 172.
13. On these points see A. Rose, 'Incomplete Socialisation', *Sociology and Social Research*, **44,** 244–250 (1960).
14. For a good general discussion of this concept, see L. Festinger, *A Theory of Cognitive Dissonance*, Harper and Row, New York, 1957.
15. D. Butler and D. Stokes, *Political Change in Britain*, Macmillan, London, 1969, p. 98. Incidentally, the evidence also suggests that the downwardly mobile are far less likely to vote Labour than the upwardly mobile to vote Conservative (p. 100). On this general point see also B. Stacey, 'Inter-General Mobility and Voting', *Public Opinion Quarterly*, **30,** 133–139 (1966).
16. ——*Political Change in Britain*, Macmillan, London, 1969; see also the very interesting study by H. Pelling, *The Social Geography of British Elections*, Macmillan, London, 1967, especially pp. 420–421 on 15 English mining constituencies 'where the mining vote was probably in excess of 40 per cent' and in which median support for Unionist and Conservative candidates was 38.1 per cent, well below the English median of 50.8 per cent.
17. D. Katz and S. Eldersveld, 'The Impact of Local Party Activity Upon the Electorate', *Public Opinion Quarterly*, **25,** 12–15 (1961); see also I. Foladare, 'The Effect of Neighbourhood on Voting Behaviour', *Political Science Quarterly*, **83,** 516–529 (1968), who provides further verification.
18. On this point, see J. H. Goldthorpe, F. Bechhofer, and J. Platt, *The Affluent Worker in the Class Structure*, Cambridge University Press, London, 1969, ch. I.
19. But, as the authors suggest, it is quite possible that people who support the Labour Party *join* trade unions rather than supporting the Labour Party because they are trade union members. Using a different sampling frame R. McKenzie and A. Silver, *Angels in Marble*, Heinemann, London, 1968, p. 98, suggest 'union membership (amongst their working class informants) is only moderately linked to voting choice: 23 per cent of members . . . vote Conservative as against 35 per cent of non-members'.
20. But at least one study suggests that working-class Labour voters are increasingly calculative in their support for the party and would abandon it if the Conservative Party could or would 'deliver the goods' to the working-class. See J. H. Goldthorpe, F. Bechofer and J. Platt, *The Affluent Worker in the Class Structure*, Cambridge University Press, London, 1969.
21. P. Willmott and M. Young, *Family and Class in a London Suburb*, Routledge and Kegan Paul, London, 1960, p. 115; see also F. Bealey, J. Blondel and W. McCann, *Constituency Politics*, Faber, London, 1965, p. 183, who note a similar finding.
22. See also G. Ingram, 'Plant Size: Political Attitudes and Behaviour', *Sociological Review*, **17,** 235–249 (1969).
23. T. W. Adorno, E. Frenkel-Brunswick, D. Levinson and R. Sanford, *The Authoritarian Personality*, Harper and Row, New York, 1950, and for a

critique, see R. Christie and M. Jahoda, *Studies in the Scope and Method of the Authoritarian Personality*, Free Press, Glencoe, 1954.

24. G. Gorer and J. Rickman, *The People of Great Russia*, Cressett Press, London, 1959. But see R. Lynn, *Personality and National Character*, Pergamon, Oxford, 1971, for a statistically sophisticated study of the distribution of anxiety in a number of countries.
25. For some of the literature on this general problem of 'structural' and 'individual' effects, see P. Blau, 'Structure Effects'; A. S. Tannenbaum and J. C. Bachman, 'Structural Versus Individual Effects', *American Journal of Sociology*, **69**, 585-595 (1964); J. S. Coleman, *Introduction to Mathematical Sociology*, Free Press, New York, 1964, pp. 84–90.
26. See, for a summary of this literature, V. Bronfenbrenner, 'Socialisation and Social Class Through Time and Space', in E. E. Maccoby, T. M. Newcomb and E. L. Hartley (eds.), *Readings in Social Psychology*, Dewey Holt, New Yo:k, 1958, pp. 400–425.
27. See, for an excellent discussion of this and other matters relating to personality and politics, F. I. Greenstein, *Personality and Politics*, Markham Publishing Co., Chicago, 1969. Much the same kind of conclusion has emerged in studies of prejudice. Pettigrew in a study of racial prejudice in South Africa and in the southern United States concludes that 'In areas with historically imbedded traditions of racial intolerance externalizing personality factors underlying prejudice remain important, but sociocultural factors are unusually crucial and account for the heightened racial hostility'. T. Pettigrew, 'Personality and Sociocultural Factor in Intergroup Attitudes: a Cross-National Comparison', *The Journal of Conflict Resolution*, **II,** 29–42 (1968).
28. A very similar point is made by D. Easton, *The Political System*, Knopf, New York, 1953, p. 196, writing of party leaders whose personalities were dissimilar but who 'confronted with the existence of powerful social groups' will tend to converge in their 'decisions and actions'.
29. See, for a general survey, E. V. Wolfenstein, *Personality and Politics*, Dickenson Publishing Company, California, 1969.
30. D. Bell, 'The Dispossessed', in D. Bell (ed.), *The Radical Right*, Anchor Books, New York, 1964, p. 42. But see R. and B. Wolfinger, K. Prewitt and S. Rosenhack, 'America's Radical Right: Politics and Ideology', in D. Apter (ed.), *Ideology and Discontent*, Free Press, New York, 1964, pp. 262–293, who show that the right wing Christian Anti-Communism Crusade has a membership better educated, of higher occupational status and higher income than the area they operate in.
31. —— 'The Dispossessed', in D. Bell (ed.), *The Radical Right*, Anchor Books, New York, 1964, p. 89. I. Rohter, 'The Genesis of Political Radicalism: The Case of the Radical Right', in Roberta Sigel (ed.), *Political Socialization*, Random House, New York, 1970, pp. 626–651, emphasizes the connection between holding radical right opinions and a fundamentalist religious upbringing which appears to inculcate self-doubt, aggressiveness and deep feelings of dependency.
32. Unlike the psychoanalytic theories which are biased towards the full complexity of the individual life, the frustration–aggression mode of analysis lends itself well to aggregate data treatment as we shall show in Chapter 9.

33. M. Chelser and R. Schmuk, 'Participant Observation in a Super-Patriot Discussion Group', *Journal of Social Issues*, **19**, 27 (1963). R. Hofstadter, 'The Pseudo-Conservative Revolt', in D. Bell (ed.), *The Radical Right*, Anchor Books, New York, 1964, p. 81, refers to this sort of situation as 'probably one of the most perverse forms of occupational therapy known to man'.
34. *The Sunday Times*, 18 October, 1970; see J. Porter, *The Vertical Mosaic*, Toronto University Press, Toronto, 1965, for a detailed examination of the Canadian elite system and the great under-representation of the French-Canadians on the national level.
35. On this point see M. B. Smith, J. S. Bruner and R. White, *Opinions and Personality*, Wiley, New York, 1956; R. Lane, *Political Thinking and Consciousness*, Markham, Chicago, 1969, both of which examine the relationships between psychological needs and acceptance of ideas, and H. Toch, *The Social Psychology of Social Movements*, Methuen, London, 1966, ch. 3, 'The Benefit of Perceiving Conspiracies'.
36. C. E. Lincoln, *The Black Muslims in America*, Beacon, Boston, 1961, p. 71; see also the chapter on Malcolm X in E. V. Wolfenstein, *Personality and Politics*, Dickenson Publishing Company, California, 1969, pp. 40–68.
37. On this point see K. Little, *West African Urbanisation*, Cambridge University Press, London, 1965, for a comprehensive account of voluntary associations as 'bridging' devices for the integration of West African urban conglomerates; see also E. Wallerstein, *The Road to Independence*, Mouton, The Hague, 1964, pp. 83–134.
38. This is an even more curious position, given the comparative finding that only about 20 per cent of the population are entirely free of measurable psychopathological tendencies; see B. M. Rutherford, 'Psycho-Pathology, Decision-Making and Political Involvement', in *Journal of Conflict Resolution*, **10**, 387–407 (1966). The evidence is that by various different standards the prevalence of psychopathological traits amongst general populations is rather high, see J. Manis, J. Bravver, C. Hunt and L. Kircher, 'Estimating the Prevalence of Mental Illness', *American Sociological Review*, **29**, 84–89 (1964). See also, J. B. McConaughty, 'Some Personality Factors of State Legislators in South Carolina', in J. C. Wahlke and H. Eulau (ed.), *Legislative Behaviour*, Free Press, Glencoe, 1959, pp. 313–316, who state that 'political leaders were decidedly less neurotic than the general male population'. However, J. D. Barber, *The Lawmakers*, Yale University Press, New Haven, 1965, p. 217, states that three of his four categories of legislators 'resemble . . . the political figures Harold Lasswell described as suffering from marked feelings of personal inadequacy or inferiority'.
39. An empirical study of 550 US legislators and councilmen shows that 125 (22.5 per cent) of them were routed into political office through activity in non-political groups of a civic, vocational and religious nature; K. Prewitt, H. Eulau and B. Zisk, 'Political Socialisation and Political Roles', *Public Opinion Quarterly*, **30**, 569–582 (1966). In an article of very considerable interest, R. Browning, 'The Interaction of Personality and Political System in Decisions to Run for Office', *Journal of Social Issues*, **24** (1968) suggests that 'several' business leaders matched the politicians he was studying on a particular psychological dimension ('need to achieve' and 'need to affiliate')

but that the politicians were more likely to have politically active parents.

40. It is this consideration which appears to account for L. Froman's use of socialization or 'learning of certain relatively stable traits, and the resultant behaviour' although he does stress 'the importance of personality as a link between the "environment" and "behaviour"', 'Personality and Political Socialisation', *Journal of Politics*, **23**, 341–352 (1961).
41. For a discussion of socializing patterns in prisons and similar 'total' institutions see E. Goffman, 'The Characteristics of Total Institutions' reprinted in A. Etzioni (ed.), *A Sociological Reader on Complex Organisations*, 2nd ed., Holt, Rinehart and Winston, New York, 1969. See also M. Janowitz, *The Professional Soldier*, Free Press, Glenoe, 1964, esp. part 3.
42. Lasswell, *Personality and Politics*, cited in E. V. Wolfenstein, *Personality and Politics*, Dickenson Publishing Company, California, 1969, p. 37. See also A. Inkeles, 'Sociology and Psychology', in S. Koch (ed.), *Psychology: A Study of Science*, McGraw-Hill, New York, 1963, p. 354, 'there is a great deal of evidence to indicate that particular statuses often attract, or recruit preponderantly for, one or other personality types'; again R. Browning and H. Jacob, 'Power Motivation and the Political Personality', *Public Opinion Quarterly*, **28**, 75–90 (1964), interviewing both defeated candidates and successful political office incumbents, were strengthened in their belief that particular offices attract some psychological types since both groups were of similar psychological disposition. See also D. Schwartz, 'Toward a Theory of Political Recruitment', *Western Political Quarterly*, **22**, 552–571 (1969), who compares personality schedule profiles of a group of American politicians with that of a national sample and finds that the former were consistently higher on need to achieve, autonomy, dominance and aggression. Unfortunately the study is not concerned with whether or not these traits are produced by office.
43. The problem is that of time: we know something about social background and role perceptions of legislators, etc., because the information is relatively cheap to acquire, but the changing behaviour patterns of political recruits undergoing role socialization is a problem that extends over time and is therefore expensive to observe.
44. J. C. Wahlke, H. Eulau, W. Buchanan and L. Ferguson, *The Legislative System*, Wiley, New York, 1962, p. 135. See also C. Price and G. Bell, 'Socialising California Freshmen Assemblymen', *The Western Political Quarterly*, **23**, 166–179 (1970), who go into detail on the formal and informal agencies, the personal contacts, seating arrangements and eating arrangements through which the new member picks up the *mores* of the legislature.
45. See also J. D. Barber, *The Lawmakers*, Yale University Press, New Haven, 1965, who generates a fourfold typology of legislators—Lawmakers, Advertisers, Spectators and Reluctants—gives an extremely thorough list of psychological characteristics of each type, indicates their likely socio-political background and demonstrates each type's adjustment to the work of the legislature.
46. The study by K. Prewitt, H. Eulau and B. Zisk, 'Political Socialisation and Political Roles', *Public Opinion Quarterly*, **30** (1966) focusses upon the period of the legislators' and councilmen's lives when they became interested

in politics, ie pre-adult and adult. They expected this to be strongly associated with their respondents' political role orientations, but concluded that 'early political socialization is apparently unrelated to major aspects of incumbent orientation' whilst 'institutional considerations and pressures undoubtedly provide direction' for the people in them.

47. Of course, an alternative explanation is, as usual, possible: legislatures *attract* those with the psychological orientations of the role types found in legislatures, so that the 'ritualist' may correspond with the 'compulsive' mentioned earlier.

7

POLITICAL CULTURE

7.1. Culture and Politics

WE HAVE PREVIOUSLY suggested that as individuals interact with one another they generate ideas, expectations, attitudes and beliefs about their common activities; in short, they create a culture although, of course, the vast majority of people are born and socialized into a culture which they take as given. These cultural ideas come to be associated with particular patterns of social behaviour so that, for example, golf clubs or, to pick a more obvious case, hippy communities, develop a semi-private language, a distinctive dress and, perhaps, a distinctive moral code. And in the communal context, the adoption of these languages, modes of behaviour and so on symbolizes and expresses the group's solidarity against elements of the culture of the wider community. This expression of solidarity or association may take any number of more or less trivial forms—pet names in a family, slightly different departmental routines in an office or factory, minor dress variations, etc.—but in other cases the associational variance may be more consequential, as in the case of criminal gangs or revolutionary groups. However, the point is that these are understood to be variations from a more general culture in which they are embedded.

Such subcultures may be politically consequential, as in the case of the American South or of the tribal subcultures of many African states and the religion or regional subcultures characteristic of the Asian developing areas. They are significant politically since they may well operate in a direction opposed to that of the developing 'national' culture so that the stability which is widely understood to result from a common and internalized culture may be lacking. People may well be subject to cross-pressures between subcultural patterns of behaviour and those demanded by the larger national culture. But as we shall see when discussing public opinion, other less important subcultures may actually serve to insulate the members from potentially damaging national pressures.

For an individual the culture gives meaning to the actions and objects of social life; in one context a killer is a brutal murderer, in another he is fêted as a hero. In one context a golf club is simply a place to drink, meet one's friends and play golf, but in another it may be a focus of anti-Semitic solidarity—and a place to meet one's golf-playing, drinking, non-Jewish friends. Further, even if one is not an anti-Semitic golf player the chances are that continued membership of the club, through group pressure, will encourage the development of some conformity with anti-Semitic values. Similarly, 'The preacher finds himself believing what he preaches (and) the soldier discovers martial stirrings in his breast as he puts on his uniform'.[1] Generally, this process is an unreflecting one, the role, rules or culture having been automatically internalized so that 'in a sociological perspective, identity is socially bestowed, socially sustained and socially transformed'.[2]

We suggested earlier, when discussing Parsons and the consensus theory of social order, that widely accepted common cultural values and norms may be thought of as an important element in maintaining social order amongst physically discrete individuals, and one of the sociological perspectives derived from this is the study of the political culture as a source of ideas and propositions about the functioning of the political system. As two leading authorities define it, the term 'refers to specifically political orientations toward the political system and its various parts and attitudes toward the role of the self in the system'.[3] This is to say, that in any political system there is 'an ordered subjective realm of politics which gives meaning to the policy, discipline to institutions and social relevance to individual acts'.[*1*] For the individual the political culture provides guides for political behaviour, and for the society as a whole it constitutes a structure of values and norms which helps ensure coherence in the operation of institutions and organizations.

The focus of 'political culture' studies, then, is less on the formal and informal structures of politics, governments, parties, pressure groups and so on, or on the actual pattern of political behaviour observed within a society, but rather on what people *believe* about those structures and behaviours. It is these beliefs that give the behaviours of men meaning for them and others. These beliefs can be of several kinds, such as cognitive beliefs about what the state of political life is, or they can be values concerning the desirable ends of political life, or attitudes towards some perceived state of the system.

The political culture is the product of the history of both the political system and the individual members of the system, and, thus, is rooted in public events and private experience. In this sense, the development of the concept of political culture is an attempt to bridge the gap between psychological interpretations of individual political behaviour and macro-sociological analysis. It therefore represents an effort to return to the studies of the total political system without losing sight of the benefits of knowledge of individual psychology. During the outset of the 'behavioural movement' in political science the focus of analysis tended to become the single act or decision. But in the desire to uncover the psychological basis of human behaviour there was a danger of ignoring the political community as a collective entity. There was a need, then, to develop a means of relating individual psychology and action to the social aggregate. It is out of this need that the concept of political culture was adopted from social anthropology. For example, in studying the origins of a political society through the ideas embodied in the political culture approach it is necessary to treat both the historical development of the society as a whole and the life experience of the individuals who eventually embody the culture of the society. From the historical study of the evolution of the institutions and values which compose the political culture and from studying the political socialization process through which individuals are inducted into the culture, it can be seen how the institutions impinge on the members of the society. This specification of the relationship between the private individual socialization process and the operation of public institutions provides crucial insights into continuity and change in societies. This approach, which defines political culture as a 'psychological orientation toward social objects', differs from the childhood socialization theories in that it relates attitudinal differences 'to characteristics of the social environment and patterns of social interactions to specifically political memories and to differences in experience with political structure and performance'.[4] The authors then suggest that a typology of political cultures can be drawn up by a combination of (1) kinds of internalized personal orientations, and (2) the objects or targets of these orientations. There are three internalized orientations, and all derived from the work of Parsons: (1) cognitive orientations, made up of knowledge about the rules, roles, outputs, etc., of the system, (2) affective orientations, which refer to feelings about the system, its rules, roles and outputs, and (3) evaluational orientations which include judgements of political objects involving the use of values, information and feelings. These orientations are directed towards political objects classified as (1) specific roles or structures such as legislatures, bureaucracies, etc., (2) the incumbents of political roles and (3) the outputs of the role structures such as policies and legal enforcements. In turn these three objects may be dichotomized as 'input' and 'output', the former referring to the flow of demands from the societies to polity and the latter to the conversions of these demands in the polity into authoritative declarations. Profiles of individual political orientations can then be drawn up by filling in the cells of a matrix constructed from the dimensions of orientation and objects of orientation (see Table 14).

TABLE 14. Dimensions of Political Orientations

	Political systems as object	Input objects	Output objects	Self as object
Cognition				
Affect				
Evaluation				

From G. Almond and S. Verba, *The Civic Culture: Political Attitudes and Democracy in Five Nations* (Copyright © 1963 by Princeton University Press, published for the Center of the International Studies, Princeton University) and reproduced by permission.

These combinations, in turn, enable one to produce types of political culture by substituting the dimensions along the vertical in Table 14.

Following the procedure outlined above, the authors then go on to generate a series of political cultural types. These are as follows:

(1) *The parochial.* Here the orientations of the citizen towards political objects are extremely weak and he does not relate himself in any positive way to national political institutions, to national questions and policies, nor does he see himself as affecting them. Although the authors do not make the point, in the parochial system the citizen whilst not relating himself to national objects may, nevertheless, be intensely involved in 'local', 'tribal' or village politics, as is frequently the case in areas cited by the authors as most likely to contain parochial systems, ie African tribal societies and other societies within which institutional and role differentiations are relatively simple.

(2) *The subject culture.* Here the citizen is strongly aware of the political system and its outputs, and he may like or dislike them, but he has only a weakly developed sense of the institutions through which societal demands are channelled and only a limited sense of personal political efficacy. In this culture the input institutions are likely to be only weakly developed, for example as in the hydraulic societies previously discussed.

(3) *The participant culture.* Here the citizen has a high awareness and, possibly, involvement in political objects and is orientated towards a politically activist role.

The three types outlined above are akin to Weber's ideal types in the sense that they are very rarely found in their pure form, whilst the three mixed types below are more likely to be found in the real world. The three mixed political cultures are defined as follows:

(1) *The parochial–subject.* Here the citizen is moving away from the purely local political attachments of the parochial culture and begins to develop allegiance towards more specialized government institutions. In this cultural system a sense of self as a political force is still relatively weak and political parties and pressure groups are relatively poorly defined. This type is classically found in the early stages of kingdom-building.

(2) *The subject–participant.* Here the citizens are divided into a significant number of politically aware and active people and the rest who are relatively passive. The politically aware are sensitive to all types of political objects and may have a developed feeling of political efficacy. Such cultures are typically found in France, Germany and Italy from the nineteenth century onwards.

(3) *The parochial–participant.* Here the input institutions are relatively local—tribal or caste associations—whilst the national output institutions are fairly well developed and there is 'official' encouragement to popular political participation in the form of mass rallies, nationalistic appeals, national elections, etc. However, both the input and the output organizations may be 'colonized' by parochial interests, so impairing their performance as national participatory organs. Examples of this can be found in the armies, civil and economic bureaucracies and the parties in developing areas.

A political culture is not, as the above discussion implies, necessarily homogeneous but may be heterogeneous along the dimensions mentioned above with one or other of the dimensions dominant. This means also the possibility of orientational clustering amongst segments of the population, ie that the existence of political subcultures, more or less insulated from the dominant political culture, cannot be ruled out as a possibility in even the most developed nation-states.[*2*] And certainly, as we shall show later, these subcultures may be enormously significant and it may well be the case that the *officially dominant political culture* is actually the subculture of a modernizing minority. In Almond and Verba's terms a subculture may accept the major *structural* arrangements of the society but 'differ persistently . . . on the whole range of domestic and foreign policy issues'.[5] If the system or the system's operators have sufficient available resources—as is usually the case in industrial societies—this source of cleavage can often be mitigated by value reallocations. On the other hand, where the basic structural arrangements of the society are called into question by a cleavage—such as that found in many developing countries where a whole segment of the population does not accept the basic state structures as including or catering for them—the possibility of reallocation is more limited. In such a situation the state may have to use force to compel compliance.

Almond and Verba's final category of political culture, a mixed one, is called the 'civic culture' and includes the notion of participation in structures widely regarded as legitimate but in which, for most people at least, life offers a range of opportunities for commitment to parochial and a-political institutions, a commitment which helps to develop both a sense of potential personal competence and a sense of trusting other people. The sense of competence *and* trust allows the citizen to feel at ease with the government, in that he will not feel it necessary to oppose the government on all issues but does feel competent to associate in opposing it on issues he feels to be important. Similarly, the norm of participation—which is rarely acted out behaviourly except in general elections—allows the government to act fairly freely but it is also a constraint on government abusing its freedom to act; citizens are both capable of associating and willing to associate when they perceive the government acting against their interests. The citizen in a civic culture has a 'reserve of influence': he is a potentially active citizen whose interest in political life is not necessarily high but whose general rate of extra-political association is high.[6]

The general research strategy of this approach is to relate the combinations of psychological orientations and actual behaviour to structural features of society. In this particular study the authors chose five countries —the US, Italy, Britain, Mexico and West Germany—and, by using a similar questionnaire on respondents in the five countries, were able to draw up national political culture profiles. We have no space to go into anything like the detail of *The Civic Culture*, but will concentrate on just one variable—that of citizen competence or, as it is sometimes called, political efficacy—and will outline the five national profiles on this dimension.

Efficacy or competence is, as we pointed out in the previous chapter, the feeling that some people may have that their environment is a malleable one in that it can be changed in desired directions by acts of personal will, and the sense of political competence is the feeling that political 'inputs' and 'outputs' can be affected by the citizen. The sense of political efficacy involves the feeling by the citizen that the system is responsive to demands, and in the study the authors asked respondents whether they thought they could do something about an unjust local or national regulation. In all five countries people were more apt to think they could influence the local decision. Asked how they would go about influencing outputs, 59 per cent of Americans, 30 per cent of British, 28 per cent of Mexicans, 21 per cent of Germans and 9 per cent of Italians said they would attempt to enlist the support of other people and groups, but very few (about 1 per cent in all countries) mentioned a political party as the group from which help would be sought, but rather stressed informal groups such as friends or neighbours. This is thought to be a significant orientation since it suggests people look on informal groups as an important political resource and, moreover, 'It means that some of the most basic building blocks of the social structure have been incorporated into the political system'.[7] Educational attainment is strongly positively related to sense of competence although the impact is different among the five nations: the better educated a person is the more likely he is to consider himself politically competent, and in all countries males were considerably more likely to feel competent than females.

A sense of political competence was found to be strongly associated with political activity and with self-exposure to political communications through the radio, TV, news media and face-to-face discussions. Here the point is that participation in a responsive system is likely to develop in the participant a sense of system legitimacy which in turn produces a degree of system stability. In all countries except Germany and Italy, those with a sense of competence also felt pride in the political aspects of their country.[*3*] A relationship between having a sense of competence and belonging to voluntary organizations was hypothesized as an element of the civic culture and this association was explored in the study. In all cases the males had the greatest percentage of memberships and in all cases the higher the educational attainment the greater the likelihood of a person's belonging to a voluntary organization. Further, in all the nations there was a positive relationship between high education, sense of political competence and membership of a voluntary organization, with the association highest for membership of a political organization, and in all cases the more active members of organizations felt more competent than the non-active members.

The authors then relate civic competence to patterns of pre-adult socialization but insist, correctly, 'that later experiences have a more direct political implication'.[8] When respondents were able to recall memories of participation in family decisions this was associated by nation with the distribution of civic competence. Intra-nationally, it was discovered that the highest rates of familial 'democracy' in decision-making were associated with higher-status families. Similarly, those with higher education were more likely to have participated in school debates and discussions than those of lower education. Again, there were significant inter-nation differences on whether or not people were consulted about job decisions, and the rate of consultation increased with higher status intra-nationally. Hence, there is a congruence between experiences with authority in home, school and occupation which is associated with socio-economic status and which is also associated with sense of personal efficacy or, as the authors put it, 'Non-political experiences with participation increase the individual's availability for an active political role and increase the likelihood that he will believe in his political influence'. If the experiences are congruent then they are likely to be mutually reinforcing and cumulative. This is a major conclusion of the intra-country political cultures and it holds true, with relatively insignificant exceptions, for all five countries.

The profiles which emerge from the study centre upon the categories outlined above:

(1) *Italy*. Family socialization is more authoritarian than in the other four countries: Italians are reluctant to take part in politics, have a low sense of competence in politics, do not feel proud of national political institutions and have a low propensity to join voluntary organizations. The social environment is regarded as threatening and alien, sustaining very little allegiance. In short, the political culture of Italy is one of relatively high alienation.

(2) *Mexico*. In Mexico in 1910 a group of political revolutionaries came to power stressing the role of the poor in politics and creating opportunities for their political involvement, yet in many respects the government is bureaucratic and corrupt. Generally, government performance is not highly regarded, but Mexicans combine a high sense of competence with political inexperience and non-participation. Mexico is an excellent example of *political* forces working on the *society* to produce attitudinal changes—norms of civic participation—which can, in turn, have an impact upon the political structure.

(3) *West Germany*. Here, once again, political events—Nazism and defeat in war—have had substantial social impacts. Germans are well educated, well informed about politics and have high voter turnouts and feel a developed sense of competence in dealing with the administration. They are satisfied with both input and output objects but evince 'a detached practical and almost cynical attitude towards politics'.[9]

(4) *The US*. America is nearest the civic culture: participant roles and norms are widespread both in social and political life and there is a high level of satisfaction with the political system. Social trust is highly developed and levels of emotional partisanship are low. Citizens have adequate opportunity for parochial involvement and can, if they wish,

quite easily adopt a passive subject stance. An element of unbalance in America stems from a perhaps overdeveloped participant orientation.
(5) *Great Britain*. Like America, the UK approximates to the civic culture with widespread participation norms and roles but, unlike the US, the British political culture has a strong deferential element which allows those in authority to rule with relatively little participatory hindrance.[10]

A study such as that just outlined has some virtues. It does direct attention in a disciplined manner to the proposed normative context within which political behaviour is thought to take place and potentially offers concepts and techniques useful for inter-nation comparisons. It also directs attention to a problem discussed in some detail earlier, that of linking the individuals to the macro-levels of society. In other words, uniformities in behaviour are seen in part as deriving from commonly held expectations, many of which have been internalized through the process of socialization. Looked at in the context of political development the concept, and, possibly, the investigators' method, may be especially illuminating in looking at the relationships between politics and society. However, there are very serious problems indeed associated with the Almond and Verba study, some of which the authors acknowledge.

Firstly, there is a technical-cum-political problem. The survey method favours, from the researchers' angle, the 'officially' sponsored research programme, which is unlikely to probe the politically sensitive problems of the host country. Surveys are enormously expensive and, apart from those supported by the largest private foundations, are most likely to be government sponsored and this fact alone may vitiate the whole enterprise amongst potential hosts unless the project is acceptable to the host.[*4*]

The problem is compounded in societies where there is rapid change, since one then needs not merely a single survey but a battery of surveys through time in order to chart the path of cultural change.

Secondly, because the survey presupposes some kind of verbal interaction it is confined to those sectors of the social structure where such interaction is feasible. For one thing, it presupposes a sufficient level of literacy, a condition often not realized in certain areas of the world. This means that if one has made the decision to use the survey method of data collection then one's sampling must be confined to those sectors of the population able to cope with interview schedules or available to cope with them. That is to say that those interviewed may not be the politically important section of the population and an image of the 'political culture' based on such data may be seriously misleading. In other words, the survey method faces considerable constraints in dealing with the 'social periphery', the illiterates, the aged, the non-participant, the destitutes, the geographically isolated or the revolutionary guerrilla. It is true that to some extent those problems can be overcome by adequate and informed sample design, for example, by making sure that significant cultural and geographical subgroups are well represented in the sample. Yet one is baffled by the problem of administering questionnaires to the Viet Cong, to the Bolivian guerrillas, the Weathermen, and so on; it might also prove a trifle expensive in research assistants.

Thirdly, there is a more general difficulty associated with questionnaire surveys. They are predicated upon the assumptions that verbal responses are accurate reflections of mental states and that these mental states give rise to behaviour patterns. It has long been recognized that this relationship is not so simple in practice since all kinds of influences may affect the verbal responses of the individual. For example, questions about 'satisfaction' with political activity, 'pride' in one's country and so on may well be strongly influenced by what the respondent perceives to be socially desirable. Clearly, the possibility that verbal behaviour is influenced by social norms and expectation is an argument that culture exerts some pressure on the individual, but the implications of this kind of verbal behaviour for the individual's actions are more difficult to isolate. This is because surveys are often not designed to 'pick up' the structural location of the respondent except in rather aggregated and possibly remote terms. A man prejudiced against blacks may find it very difficult to act out his prejudice if his occupational role is such that discrimination involves severe personal costs. Similarly, the unprejudiced man in a multi-ethnic area may have to act as if prejudiced in order not to alienate significant but prejudiced associates. Bringing this back to the civic culture we can see a possible source of difficulty: the study provides an aggregate picture of some elements of the proposed political culture, but this *may* tell us very little about the *actual* working of the society. Given that we know that x per cent of people in society Y approve of that society the problems still remain: (1) is this mere verbal behaviour and, equally significant, (2) what are the structural locations of x minus the total. It may well be that even if x minus the total is only small, some of them may occupy crucial strategic positions so that their disapproval can outweigh, by their actions, the opinions of the majority. It can be the case that a highly active minority who do not share a supposed political culture might also by virtue of their activity, for example, as guerrillas, have greater significance than a more passive majority. In this subject at least the survey method is too democratic since it gives equal weight to possibly unequal individuals.

An important and related point is that it may be the case that 'collective

	Working-class perspective	Middle-class perspective
General beliefs	The social order is divided into 'us' and 'them': those who do not have authority and those who do.	The social order is a hierarchy of differentially rewarded positions: a ladder containing many rungs.
	The division between 'us' and 'them' is virtually fixed, at least from the point of view of one man's life chances.	It is possible for individuals to move from one level of the hierarchy to another.
	What happens to you depends a lot on luck; otherwise you have to learn to put up with things.	Those who have ability and initiative can overcome obstacles and create their own opportunities. Where man ends up depends on what he makes of himself.
General values	We ought to stick together and get what we can as a group. You may as well enjoy yourself while you can instead of hoping to make yourself 'a cut above the rest'.	Every man ought to make the most of his own capabilities and be responsible for his own welfare. You cannot expect to get anywhere in the world if you squander your time and money. 'Getting on' means making sacrifices.
Attitudes on more specific issues	(on the best job for son)	
	'A trade in his hands.' 'A good steady job.'	'As good a start as you can give him.' 'A job that leads somewhere.
	(towards people needing social assistance)	
	'They have been unlucky.' 'They never had a chance.' 'It could happen to any of us.'	'Many of them had the same opportunities as others who have managed well enough.' 'They are a burden on those who are trying to help themselves.'
	(on trade unions)	
	'Trade unions are the only means workers have of protecting themselves and of improving their standard of living.'	'Trade unions have too much power in the country.' 'The unions put the interest of a section before the interests of the nation as a whole.'

images' of groups in the society may well differ quite radically along dimensions not sufficiently explored by *The Civic Culture*. Studying this possibility, Goldthorpe and Lockwood outline what they call a dichotomous or power model of society and a hierarchical or prestige model.[11] In the former, society is characterized as divided into two contending classes one of which is greatly more powerful than the other. In the latter model, society is open and differentiated minutely in terms of prestige. The power model is that most used by wage-earning manual workers and the prestige model that of the salaried or the independent professionals. Schematically the differences are set out on page 236.

The point is not that this perspective is better or worse than that suggested by Almond and Verba, but rather that although they mention the possibility of subcultural variation they do not explore the hint at all thoroughly and do not admit the possibility that these variations may be class-based.[5]

The final difficulty, and it is one that by now the reader will be thoroughly accustomed to, is the possibility of a false attribution of causality after an association has been found. Is it the case that because the civic culture is associated with democracy the former *causes* the latter? In the study the authors note that men are more confident politically than women, that women equal men in expecting reasonable treatment from the police and that the better educated people are confident of reasonable behaviour towards them by civil servants. This could be a consequence of political culture, 'but the alternative explanation that the differences express reasonable expectations founded on common experience has the great virtue of parsimony'.[12] The implication of Barry's argument is that at best the 'political culture' is second to the 'facts' of a situation in explaining people's actual behaviour. The 'facts' concern the structural location of the act and the actor.

An important point to get hold of is that those who write on political culture do *not* insist that there is a one-to-one relationship between general political forms—democracy, dictatorship, totalitarianism, authoritarianism, etc.—and a particular cultural pattern whether mixed or unmixed. This can be illustrated in the case of the political culture of democracy.

7.2. The Political Culture of Democracy

In the language of political culture analysis the major characteristic of democratic government is that it combines 'a proper balance between governmental power and governmental responsiveness'.[13] Involved here is the idea that the government must have room to manœuvre and the power to implement its decisions, but at the same time its decisions must, at the very least, be taken in the light of the known wishes and aspirations of the citizens. There should also be formal and informal channels of communication through which the government can ascertain the actual wishes and aspirations of the people. The institutional framework within which governmental decisions are taken may vary from polity to polity: a presidential system or a cabinet system, a single- or multi-party system, unicameral or bicameral legislatures, a unitary or federal arrangement, strong or relatively weak local government, all are seen as, in a sense, epiphenomenal or at least only part of the picture. The proposition here is that 'good' constitutions are not sufficient to ensure democratic governments, that underlying these various arrangements of government there *must* be an appropriate political culture. According to Almond and Verba, the most appropriate political culture for a democratic system of government is the civic culture and to the extent that a country's political culture deviates from the ideal mix to that extent does it lack an effective and stable democratic government. Thus, although Italy, Germany and Mexico *are* formal democracies, they deviate from the political culture most congruent with democracy and thus are not fully effective or stable.[14]

Behind the idea of political culture is the implicit, sometimes explicit, assumption that societies require for their stability some consensus on values and norms. For example, Almond and Verba state that 'In general this management of cleavage is accomplished by subordinating conflicts on the political level to some higher arching attitudes of solidarity'.[15] In Eckstein we find that in a strongly competitive democracy it may be a condition of stability that it contains a sentiment of 'higher, over-arching solidarity'.[16] Sociologically this is not a novel idea, but as we have argued previously, these over-arching values cannot be detected by any known process of social investigation.

Eckstein in dealing with the problem of the relationship between cultural ideas and democracy focusses upon a narrower set of orientations, those which people hold towards the exercise of authority. His basic proposition is that a government will be stable to the extent that its authority pattern is congruent with other authority patterns of the society in which it is embedded.[17] He uses authority to denote relationships of superordination and subordination among individuals in social groups and organizations. Another crucial concept in Eckstein's hypothesized relationship between culture and political forms is that of 'congruence'. Authority patterns are congruent when they closely resemble each other; for example, the authority patterns which characterize the British Government and British political parties are congruent in that both patterns consist of 'a curious and very similar mixture of democratic, authoritarian and . . . constitutional elements'.[6]

But, as we have previously argued, it is difficult to imagine such close resemblances of authority patterns in any complex society; some social relationships cannot very easily be conducted democratically, ie care of infants, prisons, military organizations, economic organizations, and so on. However, Eckstein maintains, one can still speak of congruence if authority patterns 'fit' with one another.[7] One way in which this may be achieved is by partial imitation of the governmental authority patterns by other non-government structures, for example, in allowing worker representatives on the boards of economic organizations or in introducing trade union systems into the armed forces. A more common method of achieving congruence amongst dissimilar authority patterns is by a system of graduated resemblances. To grasp this idea we may think of societies as composed of segments more or less distant from governments—families are more distant than pressure groups, which are more distant than major political parties. Social authority patterns are congruent if similarity to governmental pattern increases as distance from the government decreases.

There is an important cultural element within Eckstein's theory which centres upon his use of the concepts 'anomie' and 'strain'. Anomie refers to a complete breakdown of the normative guidelines governing or restraining behaviour; and strain, on the other hand, refers to ambivalent expectations arising from different or even contradictory norms. Most societies have within them strains and anomic behaviours but the problem is their extent.

Incongruity between authority patterns is a possible source of strain and anomie and, therefore, conducive to behaviour potentially inimical to governmental stability. So, given the likelihood of structurally complex societies producing varying patterns of authority within different sectors of that society, it follows that incongruity will be reduced if the governmental system of authority replicates or, at least, has itself 'balanced disparities' which reflect the types of authority found in the society. Governmental balanced disparities therefore reflect the varieties of authority to be found in the society and to the extent that this reflection does not take place the relationship is an unstable one. Thus, in the more structurally complex society the most appropriate form of political authority is the mixed one, ie democracy.

Eckstein illustrates his argument with reference to the Weimar Republic and Great Britain. In Weimar there was a serious incongruity between a highly authoritarian social system 'shot through with large and petty tyrants in every segment of life' and the parliamentary level characterized by 'unalleviated democracy'.[18] Had there been 'interposed between (the authoritarian society) and government certain institutions having mixed authority relations'[19] these might have mitigated the stark contrast and have given people the chance of exposure to a culture having something in common with the official or constitutional culture. As it was, both the political parties and the other association groups 'were extraordinarily authoritarian in structure' and the same was true of the civil service and the armed forces. Ultimately the incongruity was resolved by Hitler, who repatterned the formal governmental structure to make it more congruent with the rest of society.

In Britain, on the other hand, authority patterns between the government and political parties are similar and it is only when the distance from the government is relatively great that resemblances are smaller. Thus in pressure groups there is normally an honorific figurehead, then a council often dominated by relatively few people and, in turn, the powerful people on the council act as chairmen of other committees which advise the council. The generality of members of the pressure group may meet annually, but normally this annual conference is little more than a ratifying body. Finally, there is a body of paid officials who are experts and work more or less closely with the active members of the council. Such a structure is typical of Britain and allows a fairly well-insulated elite to make policy, but gives the non-elite an opportunity to participate, criticize and, in some circumstances, to affect policy changes. Such a pattern is typical of a wide range of voluntary associations but in economic organizations there is a much wider scope for authoritarian patterns to emerge. Authoritarian patterns are also found in schools, although less so in the grammar and public schools than in the secondary modern and technical schools. No abrupt and discontinuous patterns of authority separate segment from segment or government from any other segment.

It is not necessary to criticize these findings in detail since they suffer from the weaknesses already adumbrated for the more general political culture. But it must be mentioned that disproving Eckstein is impossible, since at one point 'congruence' appears to explain stability (for Britain); at another where there is congruence at all points except for a constitutional document (Weimar Republic) this was not enough for stability; and at another point (p. 76) 'higher over-arching solidarity' seems to explain stability in competitive democratic states. But since we are not told, nor can we be told, how much congruity or fit is necessary for stability nor when, in the absence of congruent patterns, higher over-arching attitudes of solidarity are enough for stability we have no way of testing the theory.

Political culture studies normally focus upon the modal values and norms of a political society, but may also pay attention to subcultures, and a typical procedural feature is the use of the survey. For most people the political culture is an unreflective and internalized set of more or less unrelated ideas and beliefs or, at least, a set of ideas and practices which they do not bother to order into any sort of coherence, and the very process of investigating them through surveys may give a somewhat false appearance of behavioural and attitudinal coherence.[*8*] However, some individuals do have much more formally structured attitudes and ideas and this fact may be politically consequential, and it is to this possibility that we turn in the following chapter.

References

1. P. Berger, *Invitation to Sociology*, Penguin, London, 1966, p. 113.
2. —— *Invitation to Sociology*, Penguin, London, 1966, p. 116.
3. G. Almond and S. Verba, *The Civic Culture*, Little, Brown, Boston, 1965, p. 12.
4. —— —— *The Civic Culture*, Little, Brown, Boston, 1965, p. 34.
5. —— —— *The Civic Culture*, Little, Brown, Boston, 1965, p. 27.
6. —— —— *The Civic Culture*, Little, Brown, Boston, 1965, p. 347.
7. —— —— *The Civic Culture*, Little, Brown, Boston, 1965, p. 154.
8. —— —— *The Civic Culture*, Little, Brown, Boston, 1965, p. 267.
9. —— —— *The Civic Culture*, Little, Brown, Boston, 1965, p. 315.
10. D. Kavanagh, 'The Deferential English: A Comparative Critique', *Government and Opposition*, **6**, no. 3, 333–360 (1971).
11. J. Goldthorpe and D. Lockwood, 'Affluence and the British Class Structure', *Sociological Review*, **11** (July 1963).
12. B. Barry, *Sociologists, Economists and Democracy*, Collier-Macmillan, London, 1970, p. 51.
13. G. Almond and S. Verba, *The Civic Culture*, Little, Brown, Boston, 1965, p. 341; see also H. Eckstein, *Division and Cohesion in Democracy*, Princeton University Press, Princeton, New Jersey, 1966; and E. Nordlinger, *The Working Class Tories*, MacGibbon and Kee, London, 1967, pp. 219–252.
14. G. Almond and S. Verba, *The Civic Culture*, Little, Brown, Boston, 1965, p. 364.
15. G. Almond and S. Verba, *The Civic Culture*, Little, Brown, Boston, 1965, p. 492.
16. H. Eckstein, *Division and Cohesion in Democracy*, Princeton University Press, Princeton, New Jersey, 1966, p. 76. He quotes Almond and Verba.
17. —— *Division and Cohesion in Democracy*, Princeton University Press, Princeton, New Jersey, 1966, pp. 225–287.
18. —— *Division and Cohesion in Democracy*, Princeton University Press, Princeton, New Jersey, 1966, pp. 248–249.
19. —— *Division and Cohesion in Democracy*, Princeton University Press, Princeton, New Jersey, 1966, p. 249.

Notes and Further Reading

1. L. W. Pye and S. Verba (eds.), *Political Culture and Political Development*, Princeton University Press, Princeton, New Jersey, 1965, p. 7; note that they refer to '*an* ordered *realm*' and 'meaning' rather than 'ordered realms' and 'meanings'.
2. As Pye and Verba state, '. . . in no society is there a single uniform political culture, and, in all politics there is a fundamental distinction between the culture of the rulers or power holders and that of the masses, whether they are merely parochial subjects or participating citizens'. L. W. Pye and S. Verba (eds.), *Political Culture and Political Development*, Princeton University Press, Princeton, New Jersey, 1965, p. 15.
3. The lack of this feeling in Germany and Italy is attributed by Almond and Verba to 'sharp historical discontinuities'. G. Almond and S. Verba, *The Civic Culture*, Little, Brown, Boston, 1965, p. 201.
4. For a classic summary and account of this type of difficulty see I. Horowitz (ed.), *The Rise and Fall of Project Camelot*, MIT Press, Cambridge, Mass., 1967.
5. Similar dichotomies have been detected in the US by Miller, who writes of a considerable section of society 'whose way of life, values, and characteristic pattern of behaviour are the product of a distinctive cultural system'. For West Germany one student remarks that the middle- and working-class 'constitute separate populations which have, for the most part, independent and relatively autonomous values'. W. Miller, 'Lower Class Cultures as Generating Milieu of Gang Delinquency', *Journal of Social Issues*, **14,** 5–19 (1958) and P. Hamilton, 'Affluence and the Worker: The West German Case', *American Journal of Sociology*, **71,** 144–152 (1965–66).
6. H. Eckstein, *Division and Cohesion in Democracy*, Princeton University Press, Princeton, New Jersey, 1966, p. 234. By democracy Eckstein means an authority pattern denoted by a high degree of popular participation in decision-making; regularized choice between competing elites and elite responsiveness to popular demands. Authoritarianism refers to limited mass participation in political decision-making plus a high degree of elite autonomy. Constitutionalism is the subjection of the elite to a broad, explicit framework of procedural and substantive rules operating as a main limitation on elite autonomy.
7. This concept is not defined.
8. For an excellent short account of the major points and difficulties of political culture see D. Kavanagh, *Political Culture*, Macmillan, London, 1972.

8

POLITICAL IDEOLOGY AND PUBLIC OPINION

8.1. Political Ideology

WE HAVE PREVIOUSLY hinted that at a minimum political ideology can be distinguished from political culture by its clarity, coherence and greater internal articulation or consistency. Because of its relatively greater coherence, its restraint on actual political behaviour is sometimes thought to be more potent than that of political culture. By consistency, one means that having discovered a person holds one idea we may reliably predict that he will also hold another idea which appears to be 'logically' connected, although, to the outsider, the logic may not conform to any notions of the rules of classical logic. Thus one would be surprised to come across a Nazi who hated Jews and liked blacks. Additionally, the ideology contains a set of political values, states to be desired and, if possible, striven for, attained and, in some cases, to be maintained. These political values generally are posited upon assertions about the nature of man—he is egoistic, cooperative, rational, etc.—which in turn lead to 'deductions' about the forms of society best suited to that nature. These elements form the basis of the immediate tactics and programme of the ideological group or party in the sense that tactics and programme are, in principle, derived from the basic values of the ideology.

Bound up with the idea of ideology as a potential source of restraint upon the political behaviour of the ideologue are its functions of insulating the ideologue from sources of criticism and of alternative intellectual perspectives on society and social problems. This consideration leads us to the point that the ideologue is notoriously impervious to argument and criticisms which, to the non-committed, appear important or significant. For example, it is not very obvious that Britain is dominated by the Jews or the Communists, but for a Nazi this very fact itself is evidence that cunning and wily Jews or Communists command—from behind the scene—their non-Jewish puppets. Who would expect such cunning practitioners of the art of manipulation to reveal themselves, since then they would be discovered and overthrown? Hence, evidence that a disproportionate number of Jews are not on the boards of all big companies, newspapers, and so on, far from disproving the Jewish conspiracy, is actually evidence of that conspiracy. In Marxism a somewhat similar function is met by the concepts of false consciousness and *real* interests and, indeed, by the Marxian interpretation of the role of ideology. Arguments are not met with counter-arguments but with assertions that, for example, working-class Conservatives are unaware of their real interests or that the counter-argument is simply a verbal smokescreen for the protagonists underlying class or economic interest. As Gregor puts it, 'the Marxist or quasi-Marxist analyst is driven into a conspiratorial interpretation of history in which he maintains that the big capitalists of Argentina were "really" directing the proletarian fascism of Peron and capitalists of Rumania "really" created the peasant fascism of Cornellu Codreanu'.[1] Thus, the ideologue normally denies the existence of alternative criteria of truth.

Another reason why the ideologue is incapable of reasonable argument with his ideological opponents, and is driven to hidden conspiratorial explanations, is that he claims his view of world processes is not only truly scientific and correct but *obviously* so. Failure to realize this can have only two sources. His opponents are misled by cunning propagandists, by bad education and influences which, given time and a modicum of intelligence, may be countered and the erstwhile opponent shown the light of truth. On the other hand, his opponents may be evil or their social position may not permit their acceptance of the truth. In such cases they may be eliminated by destroying their social base (broadly the Marxist intellectual technique), by destroying them (broadly the Nazi technique), or both, as with Stalin and the Kulaks.[*1*] Whatever the solution adopted, the ideology, often by reducing the opponents to a beast-like level (*untermensch*, running-dogs, hyenas, apes, etc.), distances the ideologically motivated from his deeds, or deeds done in his name, which may vary from discrimination to genocide.

The ideology also specifies in more or less detail desirable end states and the methods of achieving these. Hence, ideologies are often seen as sources of a very high degree of political activity amongst the ideologically committed. But approached from another perspective, it may be the case that ideological commitment is derived from personality needs and in this case the ideology may determine the focus of activity but it does not explain the activity itself. In other words, the ideology directs and gives content to personality drives which, in other circumstances, could be met by other forms of activity. Freud, for example, claimed that ideologies were elaborate mental fictions, protecting the individual personality: a form of personal rationalization. In this tradition, Erikson, in his study of Luther, establishes a theory linking ideology and personality based on a stage in the development of a person's psychological constitution which he calls 'the search for identity'. Because this search for identity coincides with a period of role-searching, youth and others who have yet to form or establish an identity are particularly vulnerable to ideologies.[2]

Somewhat akin to this perspective is the more sociological one which views ideology as clustering around major social cleavages which are understood to condition people to search for an explanation. In this situation, understood to be tension-creating, the ideology serves as a manner of comprehending the disturbing situation and as a guide to the action necessary to alleviate the source of societal disturbance, and, therefore, ideological commitment is a tension-reducing attachment for the committed. At a less dramatic level, discontinuities, seen as an inevitable part of any complex society, between polity and economy, discrepancies between profit and product beauty in industry, between different roles, are all seen as sources of strain and hence cause individual disturbance. Since the present is, for the ideologist, a time of disorder and cleavage, a period when things fall apart, it is usual for ideologies to incorporate either an archaic element looking back to a time of order, nobility and simplicity or strong futuristic components. Fascism had a strong archaic element, and Marxism fuses the two, as, apparently, do the ultra-activist young radicals of contemporary Japan.[3] Ideology provides for such people a release from strain by providing symbolic enemies—the Jews, the Reds, etc.—and by enabling them to accept, for example, the long hours and competition endured by the small businessman in the US in the name of American economic progress.[4] Around such disturbances counter-ideologies may develop. For example, in Britain during the 1930's both the Communists and the Fascists were able to make their maximum political impact and the same was true in the Weimar Republic. Both made an impact because they offered coherent explanations of circumstances the majority found mysterious and incomprehensible and, therefore, threatening. The appeal was not simply at the contemplative level of understanding, but also at the more activist level of changing and controlling. Ideology thus gave men the hope of controlling their fate, a hope denied them by the more conventional political philosophies and creeds. In this sense, ideology is, in the words of Daniel Bell, 'the conversion of ideas into social levers'.[5] Involved in this perspective on ideology is its capacity to move men to take action and, therefore, its impact is primarily emotive and only secondarily an intellectual one. That is to say, assuming that men are liable to be rational calculators in most situations, an ideology *may* be a device to transcend this fact by appealing to them so emotionally that they temporarily forget immediate self-interest and become absorbed in the ideological movement. Looked at in this manner, it is not really a question of the truth or falsity of the ideology that is important, but rather its apparent solution to the major social problems of the day and its capacity to galvanize men into activity in order to achieve the ends laid down in the ideology. 'Action', as Eric Hoffer puts it, 'is a unifier.'[6] The ideology gives content and explanation of the tensions individual men must endure during periods of social strain or at points of social cleavage and, for this reason, Bell suggests that 'the most important, latent, function of ideology is to tap emotion'.[7] This may be a slightly passive interpretation of ideology, since it is quite possible to understand ideology not simply as 'tapping' but also as *creating* emotion, as in Sorel's case of the myth of the general strike. The Sorelian myth, which inspires the working-class with a sense of mission and nobility—which previously it lacked—creates amongst a demoralized working-class a sense of class *cameraderie*. Sorel's myth is a creative thing which produces amongst believers something not present without the common belief, an urge to action, out of which springs a class unity or solidarity. Hence for Sorel ideology (the myth) *produces* solidarity amongst believers, a solidarity conjured up '*by intuition alone*' and, hence, impervious to the niggling criticism of middle-class rationalists and parliamentary compromisers.[*2*]

The Marxian perspective on ideology differs from that of Sorel. For Marx there is a much stronger historical element in his analysis of ideology in the sense that historically, for example, bourgeois ideology (roughly Benthamite Liberalism) was, in its day, initially revolutionary and then, with the development of capitalism, a partially accurate description of economic and political reality. Social structure changes, broadly independently of ideology, and bourgeois ideology remains the same. When this happens bourgeois ideology serves a double purpose. It rationalizes the class interest of the bourgeoisie by its insistence that the interests of the middle-class are identical with those of the society as a whole. Within the logic of Marx this was only true of the earlier period when capitalism was a revolutionary and economically progressive force.[*3*] It also serves to deceive the working-class—by suggesting to them that with hard work and disciplined saving they can become capitalists—and to split sections of that class away from their real class interest; this is the phenomenon of 'false consciousness' which is ultimately dissolved by the more and more obvious contradictions between bourgeois ideology and reality. But meanwhile ideology serves to conceal from the proletariat its real interests which are best represented in the ideology of Marx. Writing of German philosophy, Marx explained that his task 'has the aim of uncloaking these sheep . . .; of showing how their bleating merely imitates in a philosophic form the conceptions of the German middle class; how the boasting of these philosophic commentators only mirrors the wretchedness of the real conditions in Germany'. Ultimately, since 'Life is not determined by consciousness, but consciousness by life', the disparity between life and the now unreal reflection of it in bourgeois ideology will be revealed to all, and the now conservative ideology of the bourgeois displayed as a mere cloak for a minority interest.[8]

As the 'material production' of a society develops and men develop their 'material intercourse', so they 'alter, along with this their real existence, their thinking and the products of their thinking'.[9] So, as the processes of production become more cooperative, the fact of private ownership of the means of production becomes technically unimportant and ownership develops from being initially a spur to production and rationality into a rather irrelevant nuisance, a hindrance to further progress.[*4*] Recognizing this developmental direction, which is not yet fully mature, Marx insists that Communism is incipient in developing capitalism —it will emerge one day in the future—and it follows that 'Communism is not for us a *state of affairs* which is to be established, an *ideal* to which reality (will) have to adjust itself. We call communism the *real* movement which abolishes the present state of things. The conditions of this movement result from the premises now in existence.'[10] Hence, in the end the focus for Marx is not ideology, which is a derivation, but rather the economy. Knowledge and ideology are important since 'In order to abolish the *idea* of private property, the *idea* of communism is completely sufficient.' But, 'It takes *actual* communist actions to abolish actual private property'.[11]

Ideologies are for Marx, then, historically rooted and may, therefore, become out of date, but nevertheless bourgeois ideology even if out of date in terms of the technical development of the forces of production (roughly, the economy) is presented as though it had a validity independent of a particular class interest. Marx's point is that it does not, but both bourgeoisie and proletariat may believe that an ideology is universal and always true. The essential point of Marx's interpretation of ideologies, then, is that they are in some sense derived from men's social location, and most importantly from men's class position, which itself is determined by man's relationship with the forces of production. Ideologies may become out of date, irrelevant survivals from a previous economic system, but they may still retain their persuasive and emotional appeal, albeit in an attenuated manner.

However, although Marx has presented a powerful intellectual critique of other ideologies, it is difficult to believe that his highly intellectual and detailed criticisms account for the success of attack. In other words, one needs also to ask why a particular ideology gains support. Marx himself seems to have believed that ideologies gained adherents when initially they could in truth be thought of as representing 'the whole of society', when its supporters appeared 'as the whole mass of society confronting the one ruling class'.[12] The difficulty with this idea is that it seems to assume a level of general intellectual attainment and sophistication that no one has yet been able to detect.

An explanation of the 'success' of Marxism that does not depend so critically upon intellectual comprehension posits that as an ideology Marxism has a special resonance in societies within which a strong trade union movement has not developed but in which industrialization has made the idea of anarchism an anachronism. In such a situation Marxism can effectively preempt the *protest* element against the excesses of early industrialism but it can also turn that protest into a more *organized* form than the anti-authority bias of anarchism permits. As an ideology Marxism has also the major advantage of accepting many of the basic liberal tenets, especially the propositions that man can control his environment by science. This enables Marxism to tap similar sentiments to those of the early Liberal: 'uncomplicated materialism, belief in economic "laws" and passion for industrialisation'.[*5*] At the same time, the anti-state bias of Marxism—the state as the executive organ of the bourgeoisie—appeals to the everyday experience of the worker in the early stages of industrialization, who is often prevented by the state from forming unions, lacks political power, except as a rioter to be put down by the state police, may find that the military intervenes in industrial disputes, and so on. In this analysis Marxism is seen as 'a synthesis based not only as theories and movements, but also (as an) intuitive appraisal of the social and political *psychology* of various classes'.[*6*] The suggestion here is that Marx's appeal is only secondarily as an exponent of a coherent ideology and that his primary resonance is at the level of psychological needs engendered by societies as they endure the strains of early industrialization. For example, a very typical response to early mechanization is Luddism in one form or another. Marxism can capture the Luddite by explaining the place of the machine in economic development, by holding out the prospect of transcending the machine and controlling it for men's good and by offering the organizational form (the political party) through which the social order can be changed.[7]

8.2. Ideologies and the Developing Areas

In this section we shall simply assume, possibly incorrectly, that as social structures change inevitably there are pressures to explain, control and understand these changes at a cultural level and many of these attempted explanations take on an ideological form. In the developing areas, structural change typically takes the form of making a nation-state out of a number of only weakly associated groupings.[8] The weakness of the association arises because a common language may be absent, because of competing subcultures, divided allegiances, lack of nation-spanning institutions, sparse communications, and so on. Even if there is legally a national government, the chances are that support for it is very limited and highly conditional. In such a situation the sense of national identification is extremely limited and the attention of the population is confined to village or tribal affairs.[13] It is almost a part of the definition of a developing area that its central government lacks the almost automatic obedience that governments in many developed areas enjoy, and in many cases the government also lacks administrative structures through which such obedience can be won. Developing areas lack the traditional organizing principles which are gradually eroded by contacts with the West—and the East—and their people are, at least in the 'modernizing' sector, subject to strain and tension.[9] As well as these political shortcomings, the government also presides over a country in which economic development is normally very limited but in which, partly through diffusion of expectations from outside, the population desires higher standards of living. There is also a desire, especially amongst the Westernized sector of the population, for rapid economic development, a process involving almost endless social dislocation and widespread misery in exchange for which those pressing for economic development can offer only future gratifications.

But whatever the precise nature of the structural and institutional changes in developing areas, inevitably changes are induced in the traditional values and normative structures of that society. These traditional values can be looked at from the point of view of whether or not they support attitudes functional to economic and political development. Robert Bellah has suggested that value systems characteristic of traditional societies are inimical to development whilst others, David Apter and R. A. Le Vine, are more discriminating. In his discussions, Bellah claims that traditional societies tend to be characterized by prescriptive value systems.[14] These systems are highly specific and embrace almost every situation in life. They are always integrated with ultimate religious values and, therefore, even the most apparently mundane activities have a religious implication so social innovations may well come up against the charge of heresy. Hence, according to Bellah, such systems are intrinsically conservative and inflexible. The modern society, on the contrary, requires flexibility and a more pragmatic or instrumental value system so that change is not resisted simply because it offends an all-embracing set of religious values. Hence, Bellah's point is that for a society to develop it needs to move on or be moved at the level of its religions; in other words, '*only* a new religious initiative, *only* a new movement which claims religious ultimacy for itself, can successfully challenge the old value systems and its religious base'.[15] Any political movement in such a traditional society, where the political has no independent legitimacy, *must* take on a religious coloration.

Bellah illustrates his argument with reference to Turkey and Japan. In Japan, the Emperor as a symbol of government was invested with a sacredness under the Meiji Restoration which enabled the young Samurai reformers to 'legitimize the immense changes they were making in all spheres of social life'.[16] Essentially, the Meiji Restoration was a political movement to modernize the country against the threatened Western incursion, but in order to succeed and make the population willingly accept the tax burden necessary to develop a modern army, administration and economy, the process had to be presented in a traditional religious guise which focussed upon the religious status of Emperor. Thus, Japan's rapid movement from a 'feudal' to a modern society was achieved by the utilization of traditional values. The leaders of the Meiji period (1868–1912) utilized 'values meaningful to the Japanese that could serve both as mainspring of motivation for the people to support modernisation and as sanctions for necessary social changes entailing sacrifices and painful adjustments'.[17] Thus, according to Bellah, 'the mainspring of motivations' and the 'sanctions' were religiously derived, and this religious derivation is a necessary element in ideologies of modernization.

A number of points arise from this discussion. Firstly, is it the case that *all* effective ideologies in developing areas are religiously based? On the face of it this claim would seem hard to justify unless religion is so broadly defined that almost any commitment to change becomes religion. There is nothing obviously religious, and much overtly anti-religious, about nationalism, Marxism or fascism as developmental ideologies. Even so, the problem still remains of why they appear to attract, initially at least, some sections of the population and not others; thus in the case of Japan, the young Samurai rather than the old warriors. Further, and this brings us to Apter's refinement, it is not the case that all value systems in traditional societies are inimical to political and economic development. For example, it was apparently the case that the traditional Japanese family system displayed elements of 'the universalistic relations (found) in modern bureaucracies and industries' and, as Saniel makes clear, this was of crucial importance since 'Japan's family system was the core of its social structure. A cohesive model for other basic social units'.[18]

Apter suggests a dual division of traditional value systems and employs the terms *consummatory* and *instrumental*. The former system is very close to Bellah's concept of traditional values, in which 'society, the state authority and the like are all part of an elaborately sustained, high-solidarity system in which religion as a cognitive guide is persuasive'. Such systems have been hostile to innovations.[19] Instrumental systems have religions, but religion is 'decidedly secondary' and amongst office holders there is heavy reliance upon performance; such systems are generally receptive to innovation, which tends not to bring severe dislocations of the social and cultural order. Hence, if Apter is correct, it is the case that modernizing ideologies need not necessarily be cast in a religious form. This opens up the possibility that innovation in the one society would be best cast in a religious form whilst, in the other, a more secular ideology might be more effective in producing changes. In his study of the social derivations of different levels of 'need to achieve' amongst the three major ethnic groups in Nigeria, Robert Le Vine produces evidence that (1) the Ibo political culture was an instrumental one which 'placed a premium on occupational skill, enterprise and initiative' and that these virtues were important in determining status allocation, and (2) that Ibo achievement strivings took on ideological forms, especially in the writings of Dr. Chike Obi.[20] It is also the case that much of the initial impetus for Nigerian independence came from the Ibos and Ibo dominated parties such as the NCNC, which, given the greater mobility and higher educational standards of the Ibo, meant that they stood to gain, in terms of 'Nigerianization of all the political institutions of the Nigerian state'.[*10*]

Thus the Ibos' indigenous belief system was conducive to modernization without the necessity of religious intervention, and the nationalist ideology served to legitimate modernizing aspirations, which in turn can be understood as rationalizations of Ibo interests. Hence, in this case at least, ideology served one of its classical functions—that of interest rationalization—and also, the Ibo case does illustrate the 'fit' between ideology and political culture.

Ideology is also thought to have a solidarity function in the developing areas, where it is understood to be used to help develop a sense of nationhood and national community amongst a highly varied population. Here the elements of racial pride, as in negritude, and 'historical' roots, as in the very names of Ghana and Mali, all combine with an explanation of economic backwardness and proposals for economic advance, fuse together into an ideological kaleidoscope. The resultant ideology in the developing areas can be looked at from at least two perspectives:

(1) Who are the ideologists, and does the ideology serve as a rationalization of their own group or individual interests?

(2) Who are the consumers of ideology?

The first point to be made is that ideologists need at least a minimum level of literacy and this minimum is a fairly high one since it nearly always involves a real understanding of an alien language. In its turn this usually involves an education abroad, which means that (1) often the ideologist is not from the masses (although extended family financing of education in Africa mitigates this factor), (2) the person educated abroad is in danger of becoming the 'man of two worlds', not really at home in either, since his alien education may have taught him to reject traditional values and norms, but his emotional links may well not have been severed. Hence, the ideologist may be seeking a sense of personal identity through the eclectic or mixed ideology which combines both traditional and modern values. But leaving this possibility aside, it is still true that whatever function ideology plays for the intellectual personally, the intellectuals as a group have played a vital role in the formation and government of the undeveloped areas.[*11*] And, as we have previously remarked, the ideologist is necessarily an intellectual.

In at least one important sense the typical ideologies of the developing world can be seen as a rationalization of group interests. Both the ideologies of nationalism and of economic development—whether in the form of socialism or of Marxism—place focal importance on the intellectuals. It is the intellectuals who are employed on the newspapers, who are the politicians, who man the rapidly expanded educational apparatus, who will take over the colonialists' jobs, who will man the massively expanded bureaucracy of the new states and who, in general, become the directorate of the country. Thus, ideologies stressing the imperative of independence and of directed development are quite certainly rationalizations of the interests of the intellectuals as a social group, but this is *not* the same thing as saying it is *only* their interests that are served. Although in a country like Dahomey it is hard to imagine what other interest is served by the government.

The question of ideological consumption is a much more vexed one, since there is considerable evidence that even in high-literacy countries the mass of the population does not think politically in ideological terms. In the developing areas there is also the fact that much of the physical and economic burden of development is borne not by the ideologists and the elite but rather by the masses and, given the incidence of popular political violence it is hard to believe that ideological and symbolic satisfactions are all that general. In one form or another ideology in African countries is called socialist, with precedent qualifications such as 'African', 'Nkrumaist', 'Arab', and so on. Nearly always the major stress of the ideology is upon economic development, but this development has to be African in the 'romantic' sense that community and African identity must be preserved. That is to say, the 'traditional'—and often mythical—African sense of dignity in work, of looking after the old, of spontaneity, of common possessions, must be maintained alongside economic development, which is normally seen as inimical to such virtues.[*12*] Further, economic development is very rarely understood to be possible or desirable as a spontaneous outcome of individual initiatives. Not desirable, since the industrial history of the West is seen as a bad example of the destructive impact of *laissez faire* upon the community,[*13*] and not possible, because for various reasons individuals in Africa do not have capital accumulations sufficient to finance large-scale enterprises. This is true also because no individual could finance the economic infrastructure—higher literacy rates, better roads, better health services, better banking facilities—without which economic development necessarily is painfully slow. The economic segment of the ideology also stresses the imperative need for *rapid* development and this element reinforces the need for directed economic change. Together, these segments of the ideology constitute a very different focus from that of European socialism, which is based, however loosely, on the idea that the problem of production has been solved and that the major problem is one of distribution. African socialism, on the other hand, is universally about production and how to increase it rather than how to distribute what already is produced.[*14*]

The implication of this is that the government can only allow at best rather limited increases in popular living standards and will tax the population relatively heavily; in short, it can only give the population limited physical increases but can dole out almost unlimited rations of ideological and symbolic satisfactions. The justification of present sacrifice for future benefit, of the individual to the collectivity, the glory of the nation, the pride of national participation in foreign affairs, the excitement of the political rally, the new head on the national currency, and, let it be said, the new road, school, clinic or water-well, are designed to demonstrate and forge loyalty—and to persuade the masses to forget present discontents. In explaining the intense ideological and symbolic components of Indonesian politics under President Soekarno, one authority points to its use as 'creating a manipulated but still quasi-voluntary acceptance of authority'. And when the government controls the media and there is no organized ideological alternative to that of the political authorities, 'members of the political public who are not schooled in any such alternative way of looking at the world are almost obliged to take the view that "There is something in what the government says".'[21]

Evidence is scanty on whether or not the regimes actually succeed in obfuscating the basic facts of the situation, but what there is demonstrates clearly that 'the overwhelming majority of peasants appear to be ignorant of the modern meaning of use of Ujamaa'.[22] Again, the evidence from Tanzania is that peasant farmers are more interested in individual profits from their crops than in collectivist ideals of Ujamaa, and that when the latter clash with the former it is the ideals—the ideology—that are ignored by the peasants.[23] Similarly, in Ghana, where the ideological apparatus the CPP, Ideological Institute, the ideological press, was quite well developed, all the evidence suggests that people preferred immediate gratification to deferred ones. Hence the failure to stamp out corruption, the constant demands of MPs on behalf of their constituents for roads, schools and clinics, and the absence of any protest when Nkrumah—certainly an ideologue—was destroyed by the army and police in February, 1966.

Thus the answer to our question 'Who are the consumers of ideology?' is not the mass of the population, who appear relatively untouched by it. Unfortunately, the more obvious answer, that the producers of ideology are also its consumers, does not admit of such an unequivocal negative, at least in the sense that it is by no means obvious that once in power the ideologists derive their day-to-day politics from ideology. Firstly, no ideology is cast in a purely predictive form so that its policy outcomes cannot be precisely deduced and therefore the ideologist in power *always* has room for argument, manœuvre and interpretation. 'Bogrov advocated the construction of submarines of large tonnage and a long range of action. The Party is in favour of small submarines with a short range. You can build three times as many small submarines for your money as big ones. Both parties have valid technical arguments . . . but the actual problem lay in quite a different sphere. Big submarines mean: a policy of aggression to favour world revolution. Small submarines mean: coastal defence—that is, self-defence and postponement of world revolution. The latter is the point of view of No. 1 and the Party.'[24] Bogrov was discredited and executed.

In part, at least, it is this factor which accounts for the ideological antagonisms usually surfacing soon after an ideological party has assumed office. Such was the case in the 1934 Roehm Purge of the German National Socialist Party, which followed from Roehm's much more radical attitude to the German Army and his belief that the 'Socialist' part of the party label should not be ignored when power had been won. Hitler, on the contrary, was prepared to conciliate the High Command. Similarly, after 1917 Lenin fought a series of ideological battles against the 'left' in the Social Democratic Party, and always he had to stress the contingent nature of Bolshevik rule and the necessity for practical consideration to take priority over, for example, workers' control of factories or democratic control of the army. There was a general ideological difference; partly the ideology was used as a stick by the out-group to belabour the in-group (this was evident in Roehm's case), but another factor is that those having the responsibility for taking practical decisions were always restrained by their greater knowledge and immersion in the facts of the situation. Hitler was not strong enough, and knew it, to rule without extra-party support. Lenin knew that, as a productive enterprise, factories which were controlled by workers would be inefficient; the same would have been true of a democratic army faced by the German Army or by the White armies. Thus, a second reason for scepticism about the existence of ideological politicians is that, when in power, the ideologue is faced with a constellation of considerations and pressures which drastically limit his ability to implement the ideology. The ideologue in office has to be a politician since he has to compromise with powerful and entrenched interests and to meet problems of an everyday nature which do not concern the ideologue out of office. In short, the ideologue in office is almost a contradiction in terms: he is, as Lenin put it, 'not a revolutionary but a chatter-box'.

This is not to say that the ideologue in office cannot use ideology as a sort of smokescreen behind which to operate, but rather what appears to happen is that the audience is responding to slogans and symbols rather than to any coherent set of ideas and beliefs, the audience for the latter being very limited. But, and the evidence is clear, slogans and symbols have only a limited currency and whilst, possibly, they may have a limited effect in directing popular attention away from shortcomings and failures, in the longer period the system has to deliver more tangible rewards. Failure to do this entails either a collapse of the regime or the regime becomes more and more authoritarian.

8.3. Political Ideology in Industrial Societies

As we have seen, in the developing areas, ideology has been understood to be intimately concerned with fundamental changes from tradition to modern and from politically dependent to politically independent nation-states. There the ideology is concerned with 'understanding', directing and supporting the changes, thus bridging the gap between the old and the new. An implication of this imputed association between ideology and fundamental change is that where the latter is absent the former is unlikely to be present, at least as a very significant social phenomenon.[*15*] This is one of the themes in the current debate on the place of ideology in present industrial societies where, it is claimed, the society is broadly integrated, and where standards of living are such that the working-class—the class most likely to revolt in the nineteenth century—now has a stake in social stability. Sometimes this process is thought to have accelerated since 1945, with the frequent electoral victories by the 'left' parties, which have resulted in '*the entrenchment of the working class parties in local and national government structures*' and their consequent 'domestication' with the established system.[*16*] Again, the sheer complexity of the industrial society is thought to necessitate not the simplicity and certainty of explanations as found in the typical ideology, but rather the more sophisticated and contingent multicausal explanations to be found in modern social science.[*17*] Developed societies, in short, develop social science and provide conditions adverse to ideological prosperity. In such societies the matters of controversy are relatively minor—a little more pay, a bit more or less for basic social services, more or less nationalization—and are not the stuff out of which revolutions are made. Further, in such societies the new working- and middle-class is thought of as adapting an instrumental attitude to life and work, concentrating on improving private standards and comfort.[25] It follows from this that the Social Democratic parties whose support is dominantly from the working- and lower-middle-class will, in order to retain their allegiance, dilute their ideology.

Another factor, claimed to undermine the appeal of ideology, has been 'such calamities as the Moscow Trials, the Nazi-Soviet Pact, the concentration camps, the suppression of Hungarian workers' which now are seen as necessary outcomes of the ideological mentality.[*18*] Closely associated with this point has been the evident failure of Marx as a social and economic prophet, a failure which has undermined confidence in his ideas.[*19*]

A combination of structural changes, historical disappointment with ideological politics and the intellectual conviction that ideologies cannot encompass the complexity of actual societies is therefore seen to undermine the basis of ideology as an operative ideal. Of this combination of factors the most important in the literature on the 'decline of ideology' in the West is undoubtedly the structural one; as Lipset puts it, 'Intense ideologisation, sharp conflict, is characteristic of polities in which new emerging classes or strata denied political, social, or economic rights, are struggling to achieve these rights, but declines when these classes are admitted to full citizenship'.[*20*] Clearly, as Lipset himself notes, this is a factual proposition, one which is true or false, and should be treated as such.

There is also another dimension to the issue, a more problematic one which concerns whether or not there is a sense in which, in the name of scientific objectivity, *those claiming the end of ideology are themselves ideologists*. This accusation hinges upon a proposition, previously mentioned, that generally one's location in the social structure means that one has only a limited perspective on 'total reality' but that people will take this limited perspective for the whole, thereby distorting it in the interests of those similarly located: 'the ideological element in human thought . . . is always bound up with the existing life-situation of the thinker . . . human thought arises, and operates, not in a social vacuum but in a definite social milieu'.[*21*] One implication of this idea, known as the sociology of knowledge, is that at least all social knowledge is relative, although Mannheim himself attempted to escape from this predicament by suggesting that the 'socially unattached intellectuals' are trained 'to face the problems of the day in several perspectives and not only in one'.[26]

The substantial implication of this mode of criticism is that the end-of-ideology school is itself ideologically informed and that its members 'write not as sociologists or social scientists but as journalists and as an anti-totalitarian ideological cabal. Their work is ideology, but like almost all Western ideologies since the 18th century, with a heavy scientific component to give respectability and a sense of truth'.[27] From this perspective, whether personally conservative or liberal, protagonists of the 'end of ideology' serve their own interests derived from their position in Western society. They can be seen as comfortable members of a society in which major dislocations would disadvantage them and hence, ideologically, they display 'a positive commitment to the values of the present, historically specific system of Welfare Capitalism'.[*22*] Their espousal of piecemeal social engineering is, as has been suggested of the pluralists, an ideological defence of the *status quo*, and, moreover, a defence of the *status quo* in the context of a Cold War within which the enemy is identified with Marxism.

What we have here is a debate in which each side accuses the other of being ideological in the sense that each side finds difficulty in accepting the arguments of the other at face value and instead clashes at the level of motives and interests. The level of argument is more rarified than in mutual slanging matches between Nazis and Communists but the logic of the argument is not dissimilar, since it appears that both sides deny each other's criteria of truth.[*23*] The philosophical ramifications of the sociology of knowledge need not concern us here except to say that in scientific terms the debate can only be resolved by formulating and testing hypotheses concerning the empirical relationship between ideology, social behaviour and social configurations. As a matter of fact, Lipset has advanced one very loose but potentially testable proposition already mentioned: 'Intense ideologisation, sharp conflict, is characteristic of polities in which new emerging classes or strata denied political, social, or economic rights, are struggling to achieve these rights, but declines when these classes are admitted to full citizenship'. Clearly, as it stands the hypothesis is not tight enough, since we have no specification of 'intense ideologisation' or of 'sharp conflict' and it also appears that there is an unspecified relationship between 'intense ideologisation' and 'sharp conflict'.[*24*] In one sense, if the terms are interchangeable, ie that *whenever* there is the one there is *always* the other, the task of testing is made simpler since sharp conflict is more easily observable and quantifiable than is intense ideologization. But this assumption needs further empirical support. The same is true of other hypotheses contained in his formulation, ie those relating to ideologization and the *three* separate factors, 'political, social or economic rights'.

Reformulating one aspect of Lipset's propositions into more manageable form we offer the following hypotheses: (1) The greater the percentage of a population denied the vote the greater is the percentage of the population that is ideologically aware;[*25*] (2) The greater the percentage of a population that is ideologically aware the greater is the incidence of political violence.[*26*] Provided that we then specify what we mean—in this context, give indices—by 'ideologically aware' and 'political violence' we can then test the hypotheses. Naturally, since the hypotheses are not derived from a theory, testing the associations posited tells us nothing about causes of the relationships although it may prove possible to provide a link, preferably a deductive one, between the hypotheses and the level of economic development which Lipset sees as closely connected with democracy.[*27*] However, the fact of the matter is that in the stringent form we have suggested Lipset's propositions have not been tested. It is almost impossible to prove in any serious manner that there has been a decline of 'ideological awareness' within the populations of those stable democracies which have solved the major problems posed by industrialization. Impossible because ideological commitment and awareness is something that goes on in people's heads and the heads needed to provide a starting point for a historical analysis are long since dust.[*28*] Thus we assert that the thesis of the decline of ideology is extremely difficult if not impossible to test unless it can be demonstrated somehow that intense conflict is *nearly always* a consequence of growing ideological awareness and that both are *nearly always* associated with structured frustrations. This is so because, as a matter of fact, it is possible to roughly ascertain the dimensions of popular involvement in political violence. It is also possible to locate sources of structured frustrations. However, there are a number of counter-instances. We know that, for example, the denial of female suffrage in Switzerland has not caused sharp conflict or intense ideologization of women. Also, we know that during the eighteenth century in France and the French Revolution popular participations and violence were motivated not by any ideological fervour but by 'the compelling need of the *menu peuple* for the provisions of cheap and plentiful bread and other essentials, and the necessary administrative measures to ensure it'.[28]

A further point is that possibly the 'end of ideology' school has mistaken what may be a trend towards ideological homogeneity in advanced industrial societies for the *absence* of ideology. In fact, it can be argued that what has emerged in such systems is an official ideology of pragmatism which celebrates the *status quo*, rules out political violence, defends pluralism, is scientific and in which politics is understood as a process of mutual adjustment rather than as a challenge to the structure of the society. All of these may be good things, and certainly few in Britain or America are inclined to reject them, but this does not provide an end to ideology but simply an ideology which is widely accepted and widely disseminated.[29]

Converse's Constraint Conception of Ideology

Up to this point we have accepted one of the assumptions of both the contending parties to the debate on the end of ideology, which is that a significant number of people actually think in the structured and 'logically' coherent mould of the classical ideologies. That even if most people are incapable of writing *Das Kapital*, *Mein Kampf* or the *Rights of Man* they are capable of understanding the broad thrust of the argument and of relating it to their situation. This is an assumption that needs to be cast in an empirical form and tested, and a preliminary task is to define ideology in a rigorous manner. Hitherto, one of the problems in using the concept of 'ideology' has been that its very complexity and intricate intellectual structure means that most people may be incapable of fully absorbing it. For Converse, who has explored these limitations, a political ideology is a belief system of high 'constraint' and 'inter-dependence' which gives 'centrality' to political objects and covers a wide range of social, moral, political and philosophical matter.[30] The idea of constraint is a crucial one and characterizes a set of ideas where 'a change in the perceived status, (truth, desirability, and so forth) of one idea-element would *psychologically* require, from the point of view of the actor, some compensating change(s) in the status of idea elements elsewhere in the configuration'. This means that the ability to develop, retain and hold ideological belief systems entails the skill to discern logical connections between ideas, '. . . an act of creative synthesis characteristic of only a miniscule proportion of any population'; roughly speaking, this means the more educated and intelligent sector of the population.

Although large proportions of the population may well display signs of ideological thinking at an overt level, this is likely to be due to the fact that the elements of an idea system are presented and are socially diffused in 'packages' which are very often socially presented in close juxtaposition and which, therefore, people come to see as 'natural' wholes. That is, the connected ideas are held by people as a matter of social learning, but from this is does not follow that such people are capable of discerning the logical connection between idea-elements nor that they understand the action imperatives of the connected ideas they may hold. As Converse illustrates, the large proportion of the American population know that Communists are atheists but this perception 'represents nothing more than a fact of existence'. Few would be able to justify and explain the links, since they lack what Downs has called 'contextual knowledge' relevant to a piece of information. Again, the possession of such contextual knowledge is confined to only a small proportion of any population. For these reasons Converse claims that as the ability to use and receive information declines so does the level of ideological thinking. In an analysis of American survey data Converse claimed that only 3 per cent were in a rigorous sense ideologues and a further 12 per cent were able to achieve something near this level of ideological conceptualization.[*29*] Ideological rigour declines as information declines, and Converse uses this association to explain findings of other investigations. Prothero and Grigg, for example, in a study of a cross-section sample of the American electorate, show that while there is widespread support for the principle of freedom, democracy and tolerance, this support becomes less apparent when it concerns specific and direct application of principles.[*30*] Thus, many people do not discern the action implications of holding an idea nor do they discern that the specific application and the general principle belong to the same belief system and are logically connected. Converse also uses his theory to explain the fact, noted in a previous chapter, that historically a higher percentage of the upper social classes have supported conservative or rightist parties than lower strata have supported reformist or leftist parties. This is because the upper strata are better educated and, therefore, more likely to hold to the constraints of ideological belief systems. One might also add of Britain that a similar explanation probably holds for the more liberal attitudes of the educated Labour supporter as contrasted with those of the less well-educated Labour supporter.

Similar findings are reported in another American study which clearly demonstrates that, on a national sample attempting to discover the behavioural consequences of holding certain attitudes, there is a lack of consistency and that there 'is almost no correlation between a general disposition that we would expect to be of prime political relevance (an ideology) and variations in issue attitudes or partisanship'.[31] As with Converse, when ideology does appear—'islands' of ideology—it does so amongst the politically active, the better educated and the better informed. 'The closer the individual stands to the sophisticated observer in education and political involvement, the more likely it is that the observer's analytic construction will bear fruit.'[32] Explaining the absence of a link between attitudes—that is, an ideology—and between attitudes and party preference, the authors suggest that the emotional and social linkage between a person and a party is formed early in life prior to full knowledge of the party programme and ideology. Thus, amongst the more informed and educated those who have made an incongruent linkage early in life are likely to change towards a party more congruent with present attitudes. This expectation, although not overwhelmingly endorsed, was met in the case of people with conservative attitudes who moved towards the Republican Party from the Democratic Party.

That these results were not accidental can be shown in yet another study of American opinions which set up an operational spectrum and an ideological spectrum and compared responses to them.[33] The operational spectrum consisted of a number of questions about the role the Federal Government should play in reducing unemployment, in subsidizing teachers' salaries, on Medicare, on the anti-poverty programme, and so on. About 65 per cent of the sample answered indicating that the Federal Government should play an *active* role in these matters, and these people were classified as 'Liberal'. The ideological spectrum was constructed of five general items such as one on initiative, whether or not the poor are to blame for their poverty, the unemployed to blame for their lack of employment, and so on. On the ideological spectrum only 16 per cent of the sample came out 'Liberal'; in a large majority of cases there was little correspondence between general ideas and their ideas about concrete cases and the authors conclude that the discrepancy is 'almost schizoid'.[34] However, as with other reports, congruence between ideology and specific opinions was greatest amongst college educated (86 per cent) and the richer (83 per cent), professional and business people (87 per cent) and, interestingly, amongst Jews and blacks (88 per cent).[*31*]

One implication of Converse's extremely rigorous definition of ideology is that only a tiny minority are true ideologues, that a larger minority approach this condition and that the majority hold their beliefs in a much less structured manner and these beliefs have less predictable behavioural consequences than those of the ideologue. If we take the rigorous view of ideology, then it is probably true that the whole end of ideology debate is lacking in precision in defining ideology and the scope of ideological appeal. Although Converse researched in the US, there is no reason to believe that he is wildly inaccurate for, say, the Third Reich or Mussolini's Italy. People may have belonged to the Fascists or the NSDP, but this does *not* mean they were ideologues in Converse's sense of the word.[*32*] In both cases the parties expanded massively in membership *after* they achieved power, and almost certainly the people who joined them did so for reasons other than ideological appeal. Certainly, the evidence is that voting for an ideological party is not a clear sign of intellectual commitment to the ideology, since in the Weimar Republic the Nazi vote fluctuated very significantly from election to election and, moreover, it attracted a very large vote from previously apathetic non-voters, always the least informed and least ideological segments of the community. 'The mass vote for Hitler was not motivated by ideological commitments or by endorsement of a programme but by an articulate desire to register a protest of general discontent on the part of the voters who were uncommitted ideologically and non-committal politically.'[35]

Given that in a rigorous sense ideological thinking is confined to a very small minority, the question arises of its significance as a determinant of political behaviour. Firstly, as we suggested in the previous chapter, it may well be the case, especially in the developed industrial society, that 'social structure commits behaviour to certain channels quite independent of specific cognitions and perceptions of the actors themselves'.[36] To take a trivial example, in an industrial democracy the voting choice is limited by the number of parties so that in voting the ideologue is most unlikely to have this opportunity of expressing the full ramifications of his ideological posture. Yet, this is too simple since it takes no account of relative strength of commitment to an ideology which, if it coincides with party choice, is likely to lead to a greater range of intense activity on behalf of the party.[*33*] Converse has shown that there is a significant increase in correlation between occupation and voting amongst ideologues when contrasted with the rest of his sample.

Secondly, and this too is a consideration raised in the previous chapter, even if it is the case that ideologues are relatively thin on the ground this does not mean that they are politically insignificant. We know that they cluster amongst the more highly educated and it is, therefore, quite possible that they gain access to positions of influence which demand a highly educated entry. Bound up with this is the possibility that if such people cluster around educational media organizations they *may* have an impact upon people, not by making them into ideologues but by disseminating intellectual categories or idea elements consonant with their ideology. Indeed, something like this has been suggested of the BBC and the newspapers in Britain. Similarly, it seems quite clear that a fairly small ideologized minority can have a political impact which extends well beyond their numerical significance, as is the case with the student movement in France, Germany, Britain and the United States. They do not create other ideologues, although this is by no means a rarity, but rather convert what Milbrath has called 'spectators' into active participants on issues which had previously caused little impact. Military founding of academic research grants in the US cannot now be seen in isolation—simply as a fact of nature—apart from the issue of ROTC, of university independence from the 'military industrial complex', of student involvement in areas of university administration hitherto considered sacrosanct, and US involvement in Vietnam. If most students do not see the issues through a clear ideological glass it is, nevertheless, almost certainly true that they now regard them not as discrete events but as somehow bound together and have been taught to do so by the ideologues.[37] Similarly, there is evidence from a typical radical right organization, the Christian Anti-Communist Crusade in Oakland, California, which is composed of people who are well educated, of high status, politically active and with a high sense of political efficacy, who have a developed ideology. They are well placed to influence their milieu and 'They appear to have had some success' in pursuing their 'goals in the internal politics of the Californian Republican Party'.[38]

What appears to be neglected in Converse's formulation is that the ideological minority, consciously or unconsciously, employs in the language of its ideology a whole range of symbols and emotive terms which does help a greater number of people to respond to the message. Some of the language of ideology is cool, instrumental and flat, but a great deal is emotion-laden and expressive. Words like blood, vampire, cannibal, shackles, exploitation, traitor, alien, rootless, hyena, dog, scab, sick, ancestor, battle, struggle, revolution, democracy, imperialism, motherland and many others are employed to evoke a wider response than the technical language of the ideological code.[39] Symbols such as the flag, the black star, the Gandhi cap, the dashiki, the fly whisk, the airline, the afro cut, the Zapata moustache, similarly convey an emotional burden and resonance that no barebones ideology can achieve. Cantril, in an investigation into Soviet official language as a control device used by a leadership to inculcate elements of the official ideology, demonstrates that 'freedom' was defined in a standard Soviet dictionary as 'the recognition of necessity' and 'individual' is always referred to in his relation to a collective.[40] Further, he suggests that, although without 'real conviction or enthusiasm', 'Soviet ideology is generally accepted' by the population.[41] In the US many very evocative symbols cluster around the economic order so that ' "Free Enterprise" and "Private Property" are practically unquestionable symbols, even when they are not properly used'.[42] These symbols constitute a potential leverage for the ideologist who can appeal to them and evoke a response in an audience even if they do not follow or understand the total ideology. They can also be used to foreclose debate on policies which might otherwise have an appeal, for example creeping socialism, bureaucratic, un-American, alien, cosmopolitan.[43]

This symbolic component is the link between the ideologue and his main audience, if he has one, and between the social directives implicit in the ideology and the emotive energy necessary to translate the directives into action.[*34*] Although the majority may not answer questionnaires as ideologues, they *may* respond to the ideological message if it has, or can be presented as having, answers to questions thrown up by cultural, economic or political transformations.[*35*] Although it is the case, as the 'end-of-ideology' party suggests, that such questions arise in their most acute form in the developing areas, it is also true that racialism, the problem of Vietnam, of private affluence and public squalor and of ecological death are not only problems of the developing areas. It is only the last which has not yet been ideologized, and if a prediction is not out of place in a textbook, it is probable that the next ten years will see this happen!

We have said that ideology is a belief system incorporating moral, political, economic and philosophical ideas, more or less tightly organized and logically interrelated. Ideologies contain idea elements and symbolic contents of a rather unspecific nature (the flow of history, man is in chains, the nation's historic mission, and so on) from which the ideologist derives more specific assertions and propositions (capitalism is in crisis, the state is the executive of the bourgeoisie, the betrayal of Versailles, the stab in the back). These latter, unlike the more generalized values, can be specifically related to concrete issues and events. Thus, Lenin's formulation of the role of the party has as its immediate background the efficiency of the Russian secret police, but the wider background is that of Marx's ideas about social development. More specifically still, the Bolshevik attitudes to strikes were positive but always the wider lessons and organizational precepts had to be drawn and brought to the attention of the masses. As we have suggested, most people do not achieve this degree of intellectual and behavioural integration or congruence but they do have ideas and opinions about the world around them, and it is to this fact that we now turn.

8.4. Public Opinion

Ideologies, as we have seen, connect generalized beliefs with more specific opinions and behaviours towards definite contemporary issues, and most people appear not to operate at this level of consistency. None the less, people do hold opinions and attitudes concerning the political world in which we live and this fact is important, since government policy is often thought of as 'shaped by the opinions of the political communities involved'.[44] An opinion may be thought of as a verbal response given by a person to a particular question, or held by him about a particular event, person or object. In principle, opinions may be totally random and inchoate, having no discernible connection each with the other, but it is usually only psychiatrists who come into regular contact with such people. An individual's opinions, in short, tend to cluster in a more or less regular manner and we have seen that this clustering can be accounted for by cultural factors, by personality needs, by the 'logic' of an ideology and because socially ideas are presented in juxtaposition so that many people holding one opinion are likely to hold a socially juxtaposed one.[*36*]

In cultural factors we include the rather loose constraints that values and norms, previously discussed, impose upon people. There is also another enormously important element to cultural constraint likely to be more immediately significant in the formation or reception of an opinion and that is a person's social milieu. People belonging to the same profession, class, occupation, religion, region, tribe, trade union, etc., do tend to have similar opinions although, obviously, their influences may be 'cross-cutting' rather than mutually reinforcing.

Personality needs, as we saw when discussing the concept of the 'authoritarian personality', may also help to determine the clustering of ideas and opinions though not necessarily the particular content of such clustering. Although we have discussed this previously, the point is important and can be demonstrated in another way using Eysenck's concepts of 'tough' and 'tender' minded personalities which, he explains, are, respectively, projections of extraverted personality and introverted personality traits.[45] 'Tough mindedness' was associated—although relatively weakly—with both fascist and Communist supporters.[*37*] They have similar personalities (dominance and aggression were strongly associated with both groups) but their opinions on most subjects are different. Hence, such people will adopt and use their opinions as ego defences or as expressions of other frustrations.[*38*]

By the social communication and presentation of clustered ideas and juxtapositions of ideas and opinions we mean such things as black, devil, bad, crime, darkness;[*39*] white, pure, virgin, unsullied, good, clean; red, danger, Communism, anarchy and rape. These clusterings are at a fairly naïve level of emotive association. At a more sophisticated level opinions also tend to be packaged together; that Communists are atheists is, in many people's minds, as closely associated as grass and green; capitalism and freedom; God and America; Russia and the future. These packages are still rather general and it is easy to think of more specific juxtapositions: the Labour Party and the working man and the welfare state; universities and protest and long hair; democracy and elections and parties.

Some people, as we said, have purely random opinions, but the mechanisms we have outlined generally ensure that most opinions are not purely ephemeral and *ad hoc*. These relatively stable clusters of opinions which we find a person holds concurrently we may call 'attitudes'.[*40*] People have attitudes about many things, but what is of political interest is the distribution of these attitudes and their related opinions, their foundation and change and their influence in affecting public policy. Just as we saw that opinions are not randomly scattered in the individual, so we might expect that opinions are not randomly distributed amongst populations, and this possibility might be a factor in the reception of governmental policies. Public opinion is often understood as some sort of aggregate of the opinions of a whole national population, such as 'British public opinion demands the retention of the death penalty'. This rarely means that, say, 60 per cent of the population has been polled and has requested the retention of hanging, and much more often represents the social pleading of an interested group. At other times it seems to mean some sort of nebulous group mind with all the ambiguous metaphysics normally associated with that idea. By public opinion we mean the end products of a 'process of public discussion leading to the formation of one or more widely shared opinions as to the advisability or desirability of a public policy or mode of action by government'.[46]

People are not born with opinions, they arise in interaction with others, not with random others but rather in structured interaction within families, schools, factories and other such institutions. Through these groups and institutions, the individual acquires general cultural perspectives and may acquire opinions. We have already discussed the fact that consensus of opinion tends to emerge within groups, and essential to this consensus is the process of communication within the group. Communication patterns may be more or less complex depending on such things as the degree of hierarchy within the group, level of social technology and also the distribution of power within the society. As societies develop socially and politically so have their communication systems developed. By a communication system we mean the techniques a society employs to send and receive information between individuals. Without communication any government or social relationship is impossible.

In a modern society there emerges a whole network of more or less formalized institutions dealing with communications of all types. Normally this requires considerable technical knowledge and considerable funds of capital, as is the case with radio, TV, publishing and printing. Necessarily, this means they cater for a mass audience and for this reason those who control the media are often seen as formers and manipulators of mass opinion because, for most people, the major source of social information is the mass media. The underlying suggestion here is of manipulation, with a powerful elite controlling the media and, through this control, selecting out information to conform with elite interests and feeding the mass a diet of diversionary pulp in order to keep the population passive. As Wright Mills puts it, 'the media, as now organised and operated, are even more than a main cause of the transformation of America into a mass society. They are also among the most important of those increased means of power now at the disposal of elites of wealth and power'.[47]

From the communication side this is often justified as giving the population what they want. Those who believe that the media are extremely powerful in setting, forming and changing people's ideas and opinions are probably also committed to the idea, in one form or another, of the mass society which consists of more or less 'atomized' individuals. Within the mass society the attenuation of primary social relationships, under the impact of industrialization, has left a population lacking in a firm sense of individual or group identity and in which, due to the cracking of the 'cake of custom', men lack traditional standards and become available and amenable to manipulation and persuasion. This view of modern society was reinforced by a whole spate of volumes on the mass society, on the soulless suburb, the bureaucratized and routinized work situation and the growth of the modern corporation.

One result of this 'massification' of society, it is claimed, is that the foundations are laid for the advent of totalitarianism. Mass man, unrelated to the primary and intermediary networks which could furnish his support and integrity, is available for manipulation by the elite who control the media. Another claimed result is the progressive deterioration of cultural taste. The economics of mass communication demands that a successively broader audience be reached and, inevitably, the content of the media accommodates more and more to the common denominator of taste.[*41*]

Unfortunately for the mass society theorists the bulk of modern research on mass communication and opinion formation gives little support to the thesis. What the research demonstrates is that society is not massified, that most of the so-called bureaucratic situations are honeycombed with informal groups, that the soulless suburb contains neighbours, trusted friends and networks of face-to-face informal relationships. It is in the context of an intervening 'nexus of mediating influences' that the mass communications operate.[48] The model is not one of the isolated individual facing the mass media, but rather of mass-media use being absorbed through the group. Audience research, for example, shows that visiting the cinema, watching TV or even reading a newspaper is not a private but a group activity.[*42*] It is known that group membership plays a large part in forming and influencing a person's perception and evaluation of his milieu, and part of his milieu consists of media messages, and for this reason group membership is a vital aspect of opinion formation.

In other words, the implication of the mass society thesis, that the mass is not only a large number of people but is also a mass in the sense of being socially disorganized, is not borne out. Even cinema-going, once accepted as the prime example of isolated, individualized communication behaviour, is very much a social phenomenon. The decision to see a film is normally arrived at after social discussion and attendance is normally in the company of others.[*43*]

There are other reasons for believing that people are more resistant to media messages than was once believed. The evidence is that people, in using the media, filter out or select mainly on the basis of what they already believe, or what they find useful to them. As Berelson and Steiner suggest, 'people tend to see and hear communications that are favourable or congenial to their predispositions'.[49] For example, Lazarsfeld and his colleagues, in an early study of a presidential election, concluded that exposure to media such as press and radio had little measurable effect on individual voting decisions because those most exposed to the media were already well informed and already committed to a party.[*44*] Merton's study of a marathon series of radio broadcasts by a popular singer, Kate Smith, designed to increase sales of war bonds to Americans during the Second World War, showed the success of the appeals to be mainly due to the medium's effect in channelling existing behaviour and activating predispositions and intentions already present.[50] What appears to happen as a result of media campaigns is that the general level of awareness and of information about the subject increases, but that deeply held political or social attitudes either do not change or change only very slightly.[*45*] This can be illustrated with reference to electioneering, when it might be thought that the barrage of propaganda to which the electorate is subject might have an impact in changing preferences, but party preferences reflect the gradual accumulation of predispositions and loyalties through an individual's lifetime. Many important influences upon voting behaviour —parents' party loyalties, parents' social class, childhood experiences, the influence of spouse, friends and fellow workers—link party loyalties with the face-to-face groups. Again, during the 1964 Goldwater campaign for the Presidency, when he attempted to arouse public feeling about a number of Supreme Court decisions he succeeded, if at all, only on the civil rights and prayers in public schools issues about which there was already considerable media exposure.[*46*]

Campbell has argued that in the late 1920's and 1930's the vast increase in radio coverage enabled the less educated to gather more political information and that radio did have the effect of making more people vote. But TV has not had the same impact since. Between 1952 and 1960 coverage massively increased, but neither turnout nor interest increased. He concludes that 'Television has shown a capacity to catch the public eye but it has yet to demonstrate the unique capacity to engage the public mind'.[51]

The evidence is, then, that audiences for the mass media are not as responsive to messages as one might have thought, and this is the case even with quite young children, who might be thought to be more responsive than adults.[52] Existing attitudes are reinforced (and this could be significant) and cognitive awareness increased. As might be expected, the evidence also suggests that when the same message comes from many different quarters it is more likely to be effective than is the case with competing messages. The major weakness of the media appears to be what at first sight might be taken for their strength, their very size and indifference, which makes them unable to cater to the subtly dissimilar characters of their audience. This audience uses the media, as we said earlier, in the context of an existing network of social relationships which may be seen as insulating the individual from the media. The bulk of empirical evidence suggests that the role of personal influence is much more important than the mass society theorists have allowed. If we see society as highly differentiated, then we might hypothesize that the broad message of the media needs to be interpreted and made relevant to the specific situation of the *differentiated audiences*. We can see this process of adjustment and relevance taking place at two levels. Firstly, we may allude to trade and professional journals, local newspapers and radio stations. The press is maintained by the interest and pressure organizations; they break down the broader messages, interpreting and suggesting their relevance to particular audiences, and provide special knowledge, information and interests.[*47*] Secondly, and this is a more researched area, a similar but less organized process takes place at a more personal face-to-face level in the social order. Here individuals—called 'opinion leaders'—interpret, transmit and discuss media messages by talking to their fellow workers, union branches, friends, drinking companions, at informal tea parties, and so on. Knowing intimately their immediate milieu they are able to relate media messages more effectively and meaningfully to local issues and interests than any impersonal media organizations could hope to do. Looked at in this perspective, the relationship between media and audiences is described as a 'two-step flow' in which messages are mediated, perhaps subtly 'corrected' and interpreted before they are to reach their 'targets'.[*48*]

A subsequent elaboration of the term 'opinion leader' was made by Merton who classified them into 'locals' and 'cosmopolitans'. The former group is 'preoccupied with local problems' and the latter group is 'orientated significantly to the world outside Rovere, and regards himself as an integral part of that world'.[53] Locals are likely to have lived in the same town for a long time, are not interested in moving, are interested in meeting many townspeople and are also interested in local politics, and, like the cosmopolitan, regard the information they glean from the media not as an article of consumption but as a 'commodity for exchange, to be traded for further increments of prestige'. Both groups belong to more voluntary organizations than the average citizen but differ in their attitudes to them and satisfactions gained from membership. Cosmopolitans are better educated, read more news magazines but fewer local newspapers. An important point, resembling that of the pluralists' analysis of local political power, is that 'although the top influentials individually have a large measure of interpersonal influence, they are likely to be so few in number that they *collectively* have a minor share of the total amount of interpersonal influence in the community'.[*49*]

8.5. Government and Public Opinion

As the public becomes better educated, more aware of public affairs and more directly affected by government action, it might also be thought likely that increasingly larger sections of the public will take a greater interest in what the government does. Information, explanations and answers will be demanded of government and political leaders with ever greater frequency and intensity. This is reflected in the burgeoning of government information services. In the United States as early as 1862, the Department of Agriculture began to acquire and diffuse information about its activities to the public and was soon followed, in 1867, by the Office of Education. Other departments assumed similar responsibilities before the end of the century. The First World War and the New Deal gave further impetus until, at the present time, most government departments, military and civil, have extensive 'opinion management' personnel.

This trend may reflect a greater sensitivity on the part of the government to public opinion. But apart from providing the public, or sections of the public, with information another equally important task is shaping and moulding public opinion. The action President Kennedy took, in April 1962, on the occasion of a price rise by United States Steel illustrates this. Immediately after the announcement by the steel company, President Kennedy took steps to induce the company to rescind its actions; these steps included investigation into steel manufacturers' practices, direct pressure on officials and also appeals to the general public. After constant pressure, the company withdrew its increase. This event underscores the role of political leadership in moulding public opinion. An estimated 65 million people watched, or listened to, President Kennedy's press conference on April 8, when he explained and justified government action.

Of course, this kind of appeal is not always successful. The increase in information and discussion in an attempt to influence public opinion may well increase the intensity of opinion differences. Again, in the United

States, as the public became better informed about Medicare and the implications of government proposals, it became more and more cautious and discriminating. In late May 1961, 67 per cent of the public favoured Medicare, but by March 1962 only 55 per cent favoured it and by May of the same year 48 per cent were of the similar opinion, declining still further, in August, to 44 per cent. This decline paralleled a growth in discussion and information on the issue of Medicare.[54]

Nor need the government always listen to the voice of public opinion, as is shown by the passing of the Homicide Act in Britain in 1957 which effectively abolished capital punishment. From 1945 onwards a small group of abolitionists had waged an uphill fight against majority public opinion until, in 1957, they more or less achieved their aims. It was a victory of a small minority who, because of their better organization and persistence, managed to persuade the government to allow time for Parliament to consider appropriate legislation, in spite of the majority of the public being against such a move.[55]

So, government responsiveness and influence is a variable relationship. In spite of their relatively greater resources of information and communication, the political leaders do not always succeed in persuading public opinion to their side. For, after all, there are tremendous resistances to opinion change. For one thing, opinion is often a habit learned through childhood and adulthood. It may also be reinforced through group attachments, highly valued by the individual and where giving up or changing opinion threatens some part of what he values in these group attachments. Opinions often serve a social function in helping the individual to make friends and aiding his incorporation into groups into which he desires entry. His opinions may also serve his interests. The businessman, in opposing what to his eyes is heavy taxation, is holding an opinion rationally designed to serve his interest in retaining as much of the profits of his enterprise as possible. Or, as we have mentioned previously, the opinion may serve some intra-psychic function beyond the reach of rational argument.

However, the situations we have described up to now are ones in which there are competing and alternative sources of opinion and information which the various publics may employ as they wish. But should the sources not be competing, but rather mutually reinforcing and reaffirming, it is quite likely that their impact upon the public will be greater, and if a government can control all media then it might well be able to control the opinions of the population. The facility with which it could control opinion would be increased if it also controlled the educational system and the content of education so that media messages were congruent with those disseminated *via* the schools. The nearest approach to this situation obtained in Nazi Germany, and the USSR today. The Third Reich lasted only twenty years and only for about fifteen years did the government control all education and all the media, yet one who did live under the system insists that 'No one who has not lived for years in a totalitarian land can possibly conceive how difficult it is to escape the dread consequences of a regime's calculated and incessant propaganda'.[56] Similarly, in Fascist Italy the regime utilized, so far as it could, 'the family, the educational system . . . physical and military training, leisure time, sports and other voluntary and compulsory associations . . . in addition to the control of the mass media'. Both regimes were able to bring two generations through the schools and confine the messages received through the media to fit regime policies and ideologies, so that for the young 'calculated and incessant propaganda' was probably not experienced as a novelty but rather 'the totalitarian way of life was perceived as *normal*'.[57] In the Soviet Union the situation is comparable except that with the total disappearance of the pre-revolutionary generation there is no large-scale body of people educated within a different cultural and educational milieu. Within such countries it is probable that public opinion has no influence at all on the government.

Up to this point we have looked rather hastily at some of the factors affecting the formation of public opinion and we now turn to the problem of the effect that public opinion has on the formation of public policy and the ways in which political leaders react to public opinion. This is an important issue, even in non-democratic societies, since it is easier to rule with a measure of consent than without it. Despite the many problems attached to the notion of consent, the idea is none the less crucial to the idea of democratic government which, at a minimum, means 'that governors shall seek out popular opinion, that they shall give it weight, if not the determinative voice in decision, and that the persons outside the government have a right to be heard'.[58] Political authorities can gauge and assess public opinion on issues in many ways: by visits to constituents, by reading the press, by listening to interest group representatives, through the political parties, by elections, referenda, polls, and so on. Essentially, the authorities are attempting to gauge the level of support and convey information to the population in order to win support. As government and society become more complex, so political authorities need more and more sensitive instruments to enable them to judge popular reactions. Thus, in the 1962 American elections, two-thirds of the senatorial candidates, three-quarters of the gubernatorial candidates and one in ten seeking a place in Congress had opinion research conducted for them.[*50*]

On radio and television increasing use is made by political authorities of the opportunities to present and define issues.

It is difficult to present a concise and systematic account of the influence of public opinion on governments because little work has in fact been done on it. But considerable research has been done on the effect of pressure groups on specific government policies and, of course, this is a consequence of the fact that many people interested in a particular issue will join a pressure group or party. Moreover, it is technically much simpler for a government to consult with organized opinion than with a nebulous general public. Indeed, at what Almond has called the 'level of general opinion on public policy' where a 'consensus of mood, of shaped emotional states' is said to exist, it is very difficult to see that such opinion can have any impact on any specific issue.[59] But at a general level it has been claimed that the US Government was actually prevented from adopting a more conciliatory and flexible attitude towards the Soviet Union, during the high period of the cold war, by its 'apprehensions about the domestic mass public'.[60] When we come down to the level of more specific issues, what we find is that people appear to take many of their opinion cues from the parties or pressure groups which they already support. When the UK invaded Egypt during the Suez crisis of 1956—without any form of prior consultation with the electorate—it was eventually revealed that most people's opinion of the affair clustered around those of the party they supported prior to the intervention. Rather than changing party preferences or opinions, it appears that 'the effect of Suez was more often to intensify existing partisan commitments—to give activists in particular, but ordinary voters as well, an additional reason for their (party) identification'.[61] Consequently, the electoral fortunes of the Conservative Government were probably not affected. Another study, this time of public opinion in the US about the Supreme Court, demonstrated that generally people had very little knowledge about the Court but held it in high esteem. The factor most strongly associated with esteem was party affiliation. Democrats were more favourable than Republicans and this reflected the more positive attitude of the Democratic Party leadership to the Court.[62] It is possible, however, as Key has suggested, that causality runs the other way and that people adjust their voting intention to fit their opinions. Key reports from a US poll in 1960, when people were asked what they thought was the most important issue of the election and which party was best equipped to deal with it. There was a distinct tendency for the answer to match.[63] However, the stronger possibility, given the evidence of quite weak cognitive appreciation by very considerable sections of the people, is that people take their leads from the party of their choice.

What appears to be the case is that for most people politics does not have a high visibility or salience and they are not especially concerned to trade leisure or pleasure for personal political expertise and knowledge. As we saw in the chapter on socialization, party identification is learnt quite early in most people's lives and people use this attachment as a substitute for an often laborious process of intellectual deliberation. Party attachment is a short cut to a conclusion that otherwise might be arrived at by a more intellectual process.[*51*]

Downs has argued that this procedure is a perfectly reasonable one given that most people are not willing to make the exchange of something they desire—leisure, money, peace of mind—for the information necessary to hold an 'informed' opinion.[64] But it does open up the possibility that people will simply drift along taking the party or group opinion as their own until a crucial issue—usually a highly emotional one—crops up. They then must either accept the party but not the particular party stance, change party, abstain, change their opinion consistent with the preferred party opinion, or work to change their initially preferred party. In general, the first four options are easiest, involving least expenditure of effort. Abstention appears to be a short-term strategy with abstainers drifting back, and changing party is not very frequent even on such an issue as civil rights as shown by continued high level of Democratic Party support in the American South. Thus, even in such an issue as race the evidence is that people's opinions are *not* so effective in changing party policy stances as might have been thought likely.

An important effect of taking opinions from the party one supports is that this leads to a clustering of opinions, so that the person's opinions scale, ie if he holds one opinion he is likely to hold another closely associated one. In an American study on domestic policy issues, this relationship was discovered to be strongest for those who called themselves 'strong' Democrats or Republicans. But on foreign policy issues, where the two parties differences are more confusing, less clear cut, the same association was not observed. On domestic policy, the authors conclude that parties 'provided the party followers with cues that facilitate the structuring of his opinions'.[65] In an American study which omitted *the variable of party adherence* but used other variables, it was confirmed that there was no relationship in aggregate between holding liberal domestic opinions and liberal opinions on international affairs. Even on domestic affairs amongst those groups that one might have expected to have a high clustering of opinions—the participants, the wealthy, college graduates, etc.—the clustering was well below anything statistically acceptable (see Table 15).[*52*]

Even at the level of more specific opinions on particular issues, we find other significant factors. Firstly, that most people on most issues do not in any very meaningful sense have any opinion—although an answer can be wrung from them by pollsters. In this case one can expect curious results, as Converse discovered on analysis of data obtained from the same sample of people in the US employing the same question in each of three interviews at two-year intervals. When he analysed the results it was revealed that individual answers to policy and attitude questions were almost random, ie that most people, in any meaningful sense, did not have opinions.[66] More important, even if a political authority is, in some sense,

TABLE 15. Coherence of Liberalism Scale for Each of the Publics

Public	Average scale coefficient
Participants	0.44
Wealthy	0.42
College graduates	0.39
Concerned	0.37
Informed	0.35
Total population	0.32
Peer	0.32
Uneducated	0.28
Non-voters	0.25

influenced by the opinion of the politically informed or relevant public, the government will always leave itself 'wide discretion in the determination of whether to act, in the timing of the action and in the choice of measures that it takes'.[67] In no society will political authority be content to regard itself as simply a *responsive* tool, but will, as previously mentioned, attempt also a *responsible* attitude by trying to adopt policies that are consistent, prudent and far-sighted, none of which are necessarily consequences of taking possibly ephemeral and badly informed opinion as the *sole* guide to policy formation.[*53*]

Closely connected with these considerations is the now widely accepted fact, that, at least within the framework of capitalist democracy, people in political offices of various kinds, community and business leaders, are more tolerant in many respects than the rest of the population, at least in their expressed opinions. Party leaders in the US have been shown to be more deeply attached to democratic procedures than their followers; business and political leaders are more likely to allow Communists and

Socialists free speech than are non-leaders and, in general, the association between high levels of education and 'liberal' beliefs about democracy is clear.[68] Since this is the case, it is evident that public opinion is unlikely to be fully effective in many situations so that, in a sense, if there is to be reformist legislation it is very likely to be in advance of public opinion.

There is another group of issues regarding which party attachment appears to exercise a weaker influence upon people's opinions—issues such as fluoridation, birth control, race and capital punishment. Although the word is unsatisfactory, we shall call these 'moral' issues and on them public opinion is normally less strongly related to party preference than is usual with the more mundane topics. Also, parties fight shy of adopting strong lines on these topics since they have such a high affective loading.[69] On the race issue, in both the US and Britain, it has been found that, in the one case Democratic voters, and in the other Labour voters, can be swayed from their traditional allegiances and either abstain or vote for the party associated with tougher racial attitudes. However, even on this most explosive of issues, the evidence for Britain is that a very large section of the electorate vote for the same party all their adult lives and, anyway, the possibility of a racialist party winning an election is so remote that effectively the racialist elector's choice is between abstaining and voting for one of three parties, none of which endorses his views. This became apparent in the British General Election of 1964 when, in 24 seats in which immigration could have been an issue, the swing to the Labour Party was 3.2 per cent, precisely the average national swing to Labour.[70] In the US the evidence suggests that in the South many whites disapprove of what they regard as the too liberal attitude of Democratic federal administrations towards civil rights. There is also evidence that the old hold of the Democratic Party on the South is being gradually eroded and that the Republican support is growing, but 'if individual partisan conversion is occurring in a manner which systematically favours one party over the other in the South, the phenomenon is so weak that it very nearly eludes any sample analysis for the 1956–60 period'.[71] Although the Democratic Party in the South is shedding support, it still continues to hold the vote of many who do not support its national stance on civil rights.

An issue upon which party preference proved to be equally unrelated to opinion was that of the abolition of capital punishment in Britain when, in 1956, 30 per cent of Conservatives, 38 per cent of Labour and 39 per cent of Liberal voters approved of a trial period of suspension. The opinion on suspension was also unrelated to newspaper reading, to church affiliation, to age of leaving school or to sex.[72] As a moral issue, the question was one upon which expert advice was not as salient as it is on more technical questions and probably most people felt competent to hold 'firm' opinions even when their level of factual knowledge was extremely rudimentary. Both Conservative and Labour governments trod warily and 'showed themselves to be extremely sensitive to both the state and the trend of public opinion surrounding the dispute'.[73] Although there was never a popular majority in favour of abolition, the House of Commons eventually —on a free vote—elected for a trial period of abolition. In this situation it appears that when party opinion is not solid a relatively small and well-organized body of people, with a firm opinion, can be extremely influential. [*54*]

Hence, on a wide range of issues, most people tend to align their opinions with those of the political party they support or vote for. On moral issues they often do not, but this does not appear to affect their voting preference. Further, as we have seen, political agencies themselves have well-organized facilities for attempting to shape political opinion, but the evidence does strongly suggest that, for many reasons, people are far less easily influenced than might have been thought. Again, it is not at all clear that either in fact, or in theory, governments do or should follow public opinion or, more accurately, the opinion of the informed public. Nor is it clear at what point, if at all, in its policy formation a government should consult the electorate. Finally, it may well be the case that policy decisions taken by a public authority on matters of controversy actually affect the way people think about the matter, or that, when the authority acts, the matter is then removed from public opinion and controversy to technical argument and adjustment. Such a process clearly occurred with some nationalization in the UK, with the foundation of the National Health Service, with adoption and abolition of compulsory military service, and so on.

8.6. Conclusions

No general conclusion is really possible on the topic of public opinion and public policy, but a number of limited and tentative conclusions may be drawn. Firstly, the extent to which a public authority should be responsive to the opinions of the electorate is a matter of dispute. Secondly, it is not the case that public authorities are always responsive; this seems to depend on the issue, the division of opinion and the organization of the opinions. Thirdly, on most matters of public policy most of the electorate does not have an opinion in the sense of having thought about the issue, or having any consistent body of information about it. Instead, most people are prepared to take a party line rather than invest time and effort and are prepared to trust public authorities. However, public opinion does seem to 'determine the outer limits of permissible government action and . . . decide(s) certain crucial issues which goverment experts and elites avoid until public opinion has crystallised'.[55]

Fourthly, in the section on influences on public opinion, we noticed that face-to-face opinion leaders appear to exert a very considerable influence in relating and tailoring information to suit the needs of a specialist clientele, and of those people Key remarked that their activities explain a considerable amount about 'how democratic regimes manage to function'.

Finally, public authorities are not passive recipients of opinion but consciously try to shape, organize and even control it. They do this by propaganda and also by making decisions which add a new dimension to the situation.

The problem of the relationship between political culture, political ideology and public opinion is a vexed one, but not nearly so tangled as that between the three entities and the behaviour of the individuals acting in a political role, or roles. Political ideology is probably best defined in the Converse manner and may be regarded as the concern of a very restricted minority of the population who may, however, be able to use it symbolically. In terms of political behaviour, the ideologist in office may *initially* operate within the 'imperatives' of the ideology, but the evidence suggests that either the 'imperatives' are open to interpretation or that the practical exigencies of political survival soon operate to make the ideology simply a symbolic referent, as is almost certainly the case with African Socialism and 'Marxism' in the USSR. Public opinion or, better, the opinions of the various publics are certainly not derived from any philosophic notions about the nature of man or historical processes, nor does holding an opinion have anything like the behavioural consequences that holding an ideology does. It is also not envisaged as having the range that political culture does which, as we saw, is generally understood to refer to attitudes, beliefs and cognitions which support or do not support the broad institutional arrangements of the political society. Public opinion operates more at the level of Easton's authorities and their policy outputs and is seen as less stable than culture; after all, we do talk of opinions changing *rapidly* whilst culture is seen as more enduring.

The major problem associated with all these subjects is their relevance for various forms of government and political behaviour, although with public opinion the angle of approach may be 'what notice *should* a political authority take of public opinion?' A relevant consideration is that most people may have attitudes, or opinions, which may be related to the concepts of political culture, opinion and ideology but, in fact, for the vast majority of people—except in periods of revolutionary turbulence—their attitudes and opinions about politics have little cognitive content and politics has only a limited relevance for them. In the following chapter, we shall explore the extent of political participation and shall examine the electoral process, a process which marks the limit of most people's political involvement and participation.

References

1. A. J. Gregor, *The Ideology of Fascism*, Collier-Macmillan, London, 1969, p. 12.
2. Erik H. Erikson, *Young Man Luther: A Study in Psychoanalysis and History*, W. H. Morton, New York, 1958.
3. R. J. Lifton, 'Patterns of Historical Change in Modern Japan', in S. Eisenstadt (ed.), *Comparative Perspectives on Social Change*, Little, Brown, Boston, 1968, pp. 160–175.
4. C. Geertz, 'Ideology as a Cultural System', in D. Apter (ed.), *Ideology and Discontent*, Free Press, New York, 1964, pp. 47–76.
5. D. Bell, *The End of Ideology*, Collier Books, New York, 1961, p. 394.
6. E. Hoffer, *The True Believer*, Mentor Books, New York, 1958, p. 111.
7. —— *The True Believer*, Mentor Books, New York, 1958, p. 395.
8. Marx and Engels, *The German Ideology*, Progress Publishers, Moscow, 1964, pp. 1 and 38.
9. —— —— *The German Ideology*, Progress Publishers, Moscow, 1964, p. 38.
10. —— —— *The German Ideology*, Progress Publishers, Moscow, 1964, p. 47.
11. Marx, *Economic and Philosophic Manuscripts of 1844*, Foreign Languages Publishing House, Moscow, p. 124.
12. —— *Economic and Philosophic Manuscripts of 1844*, Foreign Languages Publishing House, Moscow, p. 62.
13. D. Lerner, *The Passing of Traditional Society*, Free Press, New York, 1958.
14. R. Bellah, 'Religious Aspects of Modernisation in Turkey and Japan', *American Journal of Sociology* (1964), reprinted in J. L. Finkle and R. W. Gable, *Political Development and Social Change*, Wiley, New York, 1966, pp. 188–193.
15. J. L. Finkle and R. W. Gable (eds.), *Political Development and Social Change*, Wiley, New York, 1966, p. 189. Our italics.
16. —— —— *Political Development and Social Change*, Wiley, New York, 1966, p. 192.
17. J. M. Saniel, 'The Mobilisation of Traditional Values in the Modernisation of Japan', in R. Bellah (ed.), *Religion and Progress in Modern Asia*, Collier-Macmillan, London, 1965, p. 125.
18. —— 'The Mobilisation of Traditional Values in the Modernisation of Japan', in R. Bellah (ed.), *Religion and Progress in Modern Asia*, Collier-Macmillan, London, 1965, p. 126.
19. D. Apter, *Some Conceptual Approaches to the Study of Modernisation*, Prentice-Hall, New Jersey, 1968, p. 116.

20. R. Le Vine, *Dreams and Deeds*, Chicago University Press, Chicago, 1966, pp. 35 and 76–77.
21. H. Feith, 'Indonesia's Political Symbols and their Wielders', *World Politics*, **16**, 84–96 (1963).
22. F. G. Burke, 'Tanganyika, the Search for Ujama', in W. Friedland and C. Rosberg (eds.), *African Socialism*, Stanford University Press, Stanford, 1964, p. 201.
23. D. Feldman, 'The Economics of Ideology: Some Problems of Achieving Rural Socialism in Tanzania', in C. Leys (ed.), *Politics and Change in the Developing Countries*, Cambridge University Press, London, 1969, pp. 85–111.
24. A. Koestler, *Darkness at Noon*, Four Square Books, London, 1959, pp. 111–112.
25. J. Goldthorpe, D. Lockwood, F. Bechhofer and J. Platt, *The Affluent Worker*, Cambridge University Press, London, 1968.
26. K. Mannheim, *Essays on the Sociology of Culture*, Routledge and Kegan Paul, London, 1956, p. 105.
27. W. Delany, cited in T. La Polombara, 'Decline of Ideology; a Dissent and Interpretation', *APSR*, **60**, 5–16 (March 1966).
28. G. Rude, *The Crowd in the French Revolution*, Oxford University Press, London, 1959, p. 200; C. Tilly, *The Vendee*, Arnold, London, 1964.
29. R. Haber, 'The End of Ideology as Ideology', printed in E. Lindenfeld (ed.), *Reader in Political Sociology*, Funk and Wagnalls, New York, 1968.
30. P. Converse, 'The Nature of Belief Systems in Mass Publics', in D. Apter, *Ideology and Discontent*, Free Press, New York, 1964, pp. 206–261.
31. A. Campbell, P. Converse, W. Miller and D. Stokes, *The American Voter*, Wiley, London, 1964, p. 211.
32. —— —— —— —— *The American Voter*, Wiley, London, 1964, p. 214.
33. L. Free and H. Cantril, *The Political Beliefs of Americans*, Simon and Schuster, New York, 1968.
34. —— —— *The Political Beliefs of Americans*, Simon and Schuster, New York, 1968, p. 33.
35. W. Simon, 'Motivation of a Totalitarian Mass Vote', *British Journal of Sociology*, **10**, 338–345 (1959).
36. P. Converse, 'The Nature of Belief Systems in Mass Publics', in D. Apter, *Ideology and Discontent*, Free Press, New York, 1964, p. 231.
37. K. Keniston, 'Becoming a Radical', in E. S. Greenberg (ed.), *Political Socialization*, Atherton Press, New York, 1970, pp. 110–150 and esp. pp. 133–135.
38. R. Wolfinger, B. Wolfinger, K. Prewitt and S. Rosenback, 'America's Radical Right: Politics and Ideology', in D. Apter (ed.), *Ideology and Discontent*, Free Press, New York, 1964, p. 288.
39. D. Lane, *The Roots of Russian Communism*, Van Gorcum, The Hague, 1969, esp. pp. 119–122, for analysis of Bolshevik symbols in 1905.
40. H. Cantril, *Soviet Leaders and Mastery Over Man*, Rutgers University Press, New Jersey, 1960, pp. 8–9.
41. —— *Soviet Leaders and Mastery Over Man*, Rutgers University Press, New Jersey, 1960, p. 84.
42. H. Gerth and C. W. Mills, *Character and Social Structure*, Routledge and Kegan Paul, London, 1954, p. 281.

43. T. Arnold, *The Symbols of Government*, Harbinger Books, New York, 1962, and especially the new preface and ch. 1.
44. R. Lane and D. Sears, *Public Opinion*, Prentice-Hall, New Jersey, 1964, p. 1.
45. H. Eysenck, *The Psychology of Politics*, Routledge and Kegan Paul, London, 1954.
46. J. McKee, *Introduction to Sociology*, Holt, Rinehart and Winston, New York, 1969, p. 568.
47. C. Wright Mills, *The Power Elite*, Oxford University Press, London, 1956, p. 315.
48. J. T. Klapper, *The Effects of Mass Communication*, Free Press, New York, 1960, p. 8.
49. B. Berelson and G. Steiner, *Human Behaviour, an Inventory of Scientific Findings*, Harcourt, Brace and World, New York, 1964, p. 529.
50. R. K. Merton, M. Fiske and A. Curtis, *Mass Persuasion*, Harper, New York, 1946.
51. A. Campbell, 'Has Television Reshaped Politics', in E. Dreyer and W. Rosenbaum (eds.), *Political Opinion and Electoral Behaviour*, Wadsworth, Belmont, California, 1968, pp. 318–323.
52. H. Himmelweit, A. Oppenheim and P. Vince, *Television and the Child*, Oxford University Press, London, 1958, esp. chs. 3 and 4.
53. R. Merton, *Social Theory and Social Structure*, Free Press, New York, 1968, p. 447.
54. H. Child, *Public Opinion; Nature, Formation and Role*, Van Nostrand, Princeton, 1965.
55. J. B. Christoph, *Capital Punishment and British Politics*, George Allen and Unwin, London, 1962.
56. W. Shirer, *The Rise and Fall of the Third Reich*, Pan, London, 1964, p. 308.
57. G. Germani, 'Political Socialization of Youth in Fascist Regimes', in S. Huntington and C. Moore (eds.), *Authoritarian Politics in Modern Society*, Basic Books, New York, 1970, pp. 339–379.
58. V. O. Key, *Public Opinion and American Democracy*, Knopf, New York, 1961, p. 412.
59. G. Almond, *The American People and Foreign Policy*, Praeger, New York, 1960, p. 158.
60. M. Rosenberg, 'Attitude Change and Foreign Policy in the Cold War Era', in J. Rosenau (ed.), *Domestic Sources of Foreign Policy*, Free Press, New York, 1967, p. 148.
61. L. Epstein, *British Politics in the Suez Crisis*, Pall Mall Press, London, 1964, p. 172.
62. K. Dolbeare and P. Hammond, 'The Political Party Basis of Attitudes Towards the Supreme Court', *Public Opinion Quarterly*, **33**, 16–30 (1968).
63. V. O. Key, *The Responsible Electorate*, Harvard University Press, Cambridge, Mass., 1966, p. 132.
64. A. Downs, *An Economic Theory of Democracy*, Harper and Row, New York, 1957.
65. A. Campbell, P. Converse, W. Miller and D. Stokes, *The American Voter*, Wiley, London, 1964, p. 202.
66. P. Converse, 'Attitudes and Non-Attitudes; Continuation of a Dialogue',

in E. Tufte (ed.), *The Quantitative Analysis of Social Problems*, Addison-Wesley, Reading, Mass., 1970, pp. 168–189.
67. V. O. Key, 'Public Opinion and Democracy', in E. Walker, J. Lindquist, R. Morey and D. Walker (eds.), *Readings in American Public Opinion*, American Book Company, New York, 1968, pp. 358–367.
68. H. McClosky, 'Consensus and Ideology in American Politics', *APSR*, **68,** 361–382 (1964); S. A. Stouffer, *Communism, Conformism and Civil Liberties*, Wiley, New York, 1955; J. W. Prothro and C. M. Grigg, 'Fundamental Principles of Democracy: Bases of Agreement and Disagreement', *Journal of Politics*, **22** (1960); S. M. Lipset, *Political Man*, Mercury Books, London, 1963, esp. ch. 4.
69. A. Brier, 'The Decision Process in Local Government: A Case Study of Fluoridation in Hull', *Public Administration*, **48,** 153–168 (1970).
70. N. Deakin (ed.), *Colour and the British Electorate 1964*, Pall Mall Press, London, 1965, p. 158.
71. A. Campbell, P. Converse, W. Miller and D. Stokes (eds.), *Elections and the Political Order*, Wiley, New York, 1966, p. 225; D. Mathew and J. Prothro, 'Southern Images of Political Parties', in A. Leiserson (ed.), *The American South in the 1960's*, Praeger, New York, 1964, pp. 82–111.
72. J. Christoph, *Capital Punishment and British Politics*, Allen and Unwin, London, 1962, pp. 118–121.
73. —— *Capital Punishment and British Politics*, Allen and Unwin, London, 1962, p. 172.

Notes and Further Reading

1. In the case of the Chinese Communists it appears that the authorities believed that a major source of error was failure of *intellectual* comprehension by at least the intellectuals, hence the attempts to convince by 'reason'—and threats, see R. J. Lifton, *Thought Reform and the Psychology of Totalism*, Penguin, London, 1967.
2. G. Sorel, *Reflections on Violence*, Free Press, Chicago, 1950, p. 140, italics in original; on this point see also D. Apter (ed.), *Ideology and Discontent*, Free Press, New York, 1964, introduction.
3. In this sense Marx's concept of ideology, after it has served as a social beneficial expression of a *wide* social interest and becomes merely a rationalization of a class interest, is similar to that of Mosca's 'political formula' or Pareto's 'derivations' which prevent men from seeing the objective facts of class or elite dominance. Ideologies, looked at from this angle, make it possible to rule more effectively and economically than by force and are, therefore, functional to the ruling elite or class.
4. 'The conditions of bourgeois society are too narrow to contain the wealth created by them', *Communist Manifesto*, Lawrence and Wishart, London, 1948, p. 20.
5. A. Ulam, *The Unfinished Revolution*, Vintage Books, New York, 1960, p. 107; this section is freely adapted from Ulam. As with Liberal ideology Marxism is optimistic in that it posits men can affect their environment to their own ends and, again, they have in common that the end posited by the ideology is an earthly not a heavenly paradise. For a discussion of this point see

C. Becker, *The Heavenly City of the Eighteenth Century Philosophers*, Yale University Press, New Haven, 1955.

6. —— *The Unfinished Revolution*, Vintage Books, New York, 1960, p. 132, our italics. A somewhat similar point is argued by R. C. Tucker who suggests that Marx was a moralist who made his major appeal at the psychological level of alienation, a concept owing nothing to Marx's economic studies, *Philosophy and Myth in Karl Marx*, Cambridge University Press, London, 1961.
7. See E. Hobsbawm, *Primitive Rebels*, Norton Library, New York, 1965, for an interesting study of protest movements which were weak organizationally, failed to link immediate discontents with the social and economic changes causing them and which, crucially, lacked a perspective of historical development.
8. We, of course, recognize that prior to the last few decades the major problem of such areas was not nation-building but colonialism, but the point still holds since the colonial government also attempts to impose unity upon diversity; see P. Worsley, *The Trumpet Shall Sound*, MacGibbon and Kee, London, 1957, for an excellent study of cargo cults as producing a form of political integration in a highly segmented society.
9. C. Geertz, 'Ideology as a Cultural System', in D. Apter (ed.), *Ideology and Discontent*, Free Press, New York, 1964, p. 64, puts it as follows: 'It is the confluence of socio-psychological strain and an absence of cultural resources by which to make (political, moral, or economic) sense of that strain, each exacerbating the other, that sets the stage for the rise of systematic (political, moral, economic) ideologies.'
10. N. Azikwe, 'Political Blueprint of Nigeria', reprinted by R. Emerson and M. Kilson (eds.), *The Political Awakening of Africa*, Prentice-Hall, New Jersey, 1965, pp. 55–61; for an example of the Ibo advantage in competing purely on academic grounds with other Nigerians see W. Gutteridge, *The Military in African Politics*, Methuen, London, 1969, pp. 60–95.
11. See E. Shils, 'The Intellectuals in the Political Development of New States', *World Politics*, April, 1960, reprinted in J. Kautsky (ed.), *Political Change in Underdeveloped Countries*, Wiley, New York, 1962, pp. 195–234; Shils defines the intellectuals in developing areas simply as 'all persons with an advanced modern education' (p. 198). See also M. Matossian, 'Ideologies of Delayed Industrialisation', in the same volume, pp. 252–264.
12. On this point, see J. Nyerere, 'Ujamaa: the Basis of African Socialism', T. Mboya, 'African Socialism', in *Africa's Freedom*, Allen and Unwin, London, 1964; 'The Cabinet of Kenya', in P. Sigmund, *The Ideologies of the Developing Nations*, Praeger, New York, 1968, pp. 269–278, especially pp. 269–272; and also the brilliant account by L. S. Senghor, *On African Socialism*, Pall Mall, London, 1964; and for a general account see W. Friedland and C. Rosberg (eds.), *African Socialism*, Stanford University Press, Stanford, 1964.
13. On this point see L. Bramson, *The Political Context of Sociology*, Princeton University Press, Princeton, 1961, chs. 1 and 2; and R. A. Nisbet, *The Sociological Tradition*, Heinemann, London, 1967, ch. 3; and also P. Laslett, *The World We Have Lost*, Methuen, London, 1965, chs. 1, 2 and 3.
14. It is this factor that accounts for the wide interest in Russian and Chinese industrial growth.

15. A fascinating parallel to this suggestion of ideological changes corresponding to changes in structure can be found in various studies of managerial ideologies. Thus, R. Bendix in *Work and Authority in Industry*, Wiley, London, 1958, contrasts the 'entrepreneurial ideology' of early industrializers and the 'managerial ideology' of mature industrialists. Similarly, R. Dahrendorf, *Class and Class Conflict in an Industrial Society*, Routledge and Kegan Paul, London, 1959, suggests that with the divorce of ownership from control in industry the most appropriate form of ideological legitimation of the manager is 'some kind of consensus among those who are bound to obey his commands'. Thus, 'the "human relations" movement is nothing but a symptom of the changing basis of the legitimacy of entrepreneurial authority once ownership and control are separated' (p. 45).
16. S. M. Lipset and S. Rokkan (eds.), *Party Systems and Voter Alignments*, Collier-Macmillan, London, 1967, p. 22. Italics in original.
17. See, for example, K. Popper, *The Poverty of Historicism*, Routledge and Kegan Paul, London, 1957, although he does not advocate social science explanations. M. Oakeshott, *Rationalism in Politics and Other Essays*, Methuen, London, 1962, also attacks ideological techniques of social understanding.
18. D. Bell, *The End of Ideology*, Collier Books, New York, 1961, p. 397; see also J. Talmon, *The Origins of Totalitarian Democracy*, Secker and Warburg, London, 1952, esp. vol. I, ch. 1, and Introduction; and see also H. Arendt, *The Origins of Totalitarianism*, Allen and Unwin, London, 1958, esp. pp. 305–479.
19. Although it should be noticed that there has been an upsurge of interest in Marx as an analytical historian and a moral philosopher, see for example D. McClellan, *The Young Helegians and Karl Marx*, Macmillan, London, 1969; J. Hyppolite, *Studies on Marx and Engel*, Heinemann, London, 1969; and two selections from Marx's and Engel's works, R. Freedman, *Marxist Social Thought*, Harcourt Brace, New York, 1968; S. Avineri, *Karl Marx on Colonialism and Modernisation*, Doubleday, New York, 1969.
20. S. M. Lipset, 'Some Further Comments on "The Decline of Ideology"', *APSR*, **60**, 17–18 (1966); see also Lipset, *Political Man*, Mercury Books, London, 1963, pp. 403–417. 'This change (the "end of ideology") in Western life reflects the fact that the fundamental political problems of the industrial revolution have been solved' (p. 406).
21. K. Mannheim, *Ideology and Utopia*, Routledge and Kegan Paul, London, 1960, p. 71, chs. 2 and 5, contain the classic statements of this view of the sociology of knowledge, but see also W. Stark, *The Sociology of Knowledge*, Routledge and Kegan Paul, London, 1958; P. Berger and T. Luckmann, *The Social Construction of Reality*, Penguin, London, 1967; and H. Speier, *Social Order and The Risks of War*, M.I.T. Press, Cambridge, Mass., 1969, 'The Social Determinations of Ideas'.
22. R. Haber, 'The End of Ideology as Ideology', printed in F. Lindenfeld (ed.), *Reader in Political Sociology*, Funk and Wagnalls, New York, 1968, pp. 555–576; see also I. L. Horowitz (ed.), *Power Politics and People: the Collected Essays of C. Wright Mills*, Ballantine Books, New York, 'The Social Role of the Intellectual', pp. 292–304. See also the very interesting article by J. Petras, 'Ideology and United States Political Scientists', *Science and*

Society, **29**, 192–216 (1965), which very clearly outlines the ideological stance common amongst leading US political scientists.

23. Thus, in a dispute with Lipset, Professor La Polombara states, 'I am convinced that the issue I am posing here will not be readily or convincingly resolved by asking merely which of the above "findings" is more "scientific" or what kinds of questions are or are not researchable'; the dispute was one on the end of ideology! *APSR*, **60**, 111 (1966).
24. Nor do we have an explicit formulation of the possibility that the relationship between a decline in sharp conflict, intense ideologization and admission to full citizenship may be one in which there is a threshold beyond which the relationship may change or even reverse.
25. Obviously 'the vote' can be replaced by other factors such as education, a specific cubic footage of accommodation, a minimum calorific intake, and so on.
26. We shall discuss the concept of political violence and the techniques of operationalizing it in Chapter 13.
27. Since in his volume, *Political Man*, Lipset defines democracy purely in institutional and participatory terms (p. 45), the link between economic development and having the vote is clear, but the link between voting and ideology is not at all clear.
28. Even if one undertakes a content analysis of books, pamphlets and newspapers this only gives us a clue about the ideological attitudes of the tiny minority writing them.
29. See the similar finding in D. Butler and D. Stokes, *Political Change in Britain*, Macmillan, London, 1969, who eliminate the 70 per cent of their sample demonstrating no response connection between 'ideologically' connected political propositions and still find that amongst the 'elite' 30 per cent the degree to which such items were tied in people's minds was very low; see especially p. 199.
30. T. Prothero and C. Grigg, 'Fundamental Principles of Democracy: Bases of Agreement and Disagreement', *Journal of Politics*, **22**, 776–794 (1960). When people are presented with the opportunity, possibly embarrassing, of acting on expressed general opinions they may not do so. In a classic study La Piere accompanied a Chinese couple to a large number of restaurants, hotels and motels in the US and the couple were only once refused service. But when the proprietors were subsequently polled by La Piere about accepting Chinese people as customers, more than 90 per cent indicated they would refuse; R. La Piere, 'Attitudes v. Action', *Social Forces*, **13**, 230–237 (1934).
31. Congruence amongst Jews may be explained since they tend to be well educated, but that of the blacks is a very different matter; unfortunately the authors do not go into this question.
32. K. Newton, *The Sociology of English Communism*, Penguin, London, 1969, p. 155, states that 'Most Communist Party members are not Communist ideologists at the time of serving and, indeed, few become so even after a considerable time in the party'.
33. If the commitment is really intense, as in the case of the Jehovah's Witnesses in Soviet and Nazi concentration camps, it may leave the believer impervious to even the most extreme pressure to change his behaviour and act like other

citizens, ie allow himself to be conscripted; see B. Bettelheim, *The Informed Heart*, Paladin Books, London, 1970, p. 115.

34. The ideologist may, however, lack an audience: 'We were right,' Dwight MacDonald is reported as claiming, 'but they (the masses) wouldn't listen', in L. Feuer, 'What is Alienation?', in M. Stein and A. Vidich, *Sociology on Trial*, Spectrum Books, Englewood Cliffs, 1965, pp. 127–147.
35. Such language and symbols are especially important to the ideologist outside the official structures of power since they are virtually *all* he has to oppose the police, army, and legal structures and official symbols of the regime he opposes; they are, initially at least, his total stock-in-trade. He can offer his followers understanding, control and hope for the future and the excitement of commitment, but he demands from them sacrifice, possible death and probable discomfort. The rewards *must* be high and an important ideological reward is the symbolic assurance that the future beckons. If and when the ideologist attains power he will then usually make his symbols the official ones to replace the older, although the older may also be employed to legitimate a new regime.
36. One might add that Festinger's concept of cognitive dissonance or rather its reduction also helps to explain relative consistency.
37. But subsequent research seems to suggest that Communists in *democratic countries* do not produce high scores on the F scale (authoritarian personality); M. Rokeach, *The Open and Closed Mind*, Basic Books, New York, 1960. Also, there is considerable doubt whether Eysenck's scale was adequate since it contained a number of items testing religious feeling which meant that Communists scored high, but on other items they were quite low and liberal.
38. For an excellent example of this point see R. Cohen, 'What Segregation Means to a Segregationalist', in J. D. Barber (ed.), *Readings in Citizen Politics*, Markham Publishing Co., Chicago, 1969, pp. 127–139.
39. For an account of this collection in Shakespeare see P. Mason, *Prospero's Magic*, Oxford University Press, London, 1962, ch. 2.
40. H. Eysenck, *The Psychology of Politics*, Routledge and Kegan Paul, London, 1954, p. 112. However, social psychologists use 'attitudes' to mean a disposition on the part of the individual to respond, positively or negatively, to social or physical objects or behaviours, whilst opinions is reserved for beliefs about such objects which may, or may not be, accompanied by positive or negative feelings.
41. A representative selection of essays on this theme is to be found in B. Rosenberg and D. Manning White (eds.), *Mass Culture*, Free Press, Glencoe, 1957.
42. A typical summary of this position: 'It needs stressing that the communicating act is but one part of a total ongoing social interaction process within a given network of social relationships', J. D. Halloran, *The Effects of Mass Communication*, Leicester University Press, Leicester, 1964.
43. For a discussion on this point see E. Freidson, 'Communications Research and the Concept of the Mass', *American Sociological Review*, **18**, 313–317 (1953).
44. P. Lazarsfeld, B. Berelson and H. Gaudet, *The People's Choice*, Duell, Sloan and Pearce, New York, 1944. It would be odd if they did not since, presumably, some information is dissonant with positions already held; see G. Stempel, 'Selectivity in Readership of Political News', *Public Opinion Quarterly*, **25**, 400–404 (1961).

45. Evidence for this assertion is ably summarized in D. McQuail, *Towards a Sociology of Mass Communication*, Macmillan, London, 1970, esp. ch. 3. See also J. Blumler and D. McQuail, *Television in Politics*, Faber and Faber, London, 1968, p. 281: 'even in a critical election, the mass media would be impotent to effect major changes in voters' attitudes toward the leading parties and personalities'.
46. W. Murphy and J. Tannenhaus, 'Public Opinion and the Supreme Court: The Goldwater Campaign', *Public Opinion Quarterly*, **33**, 31–50 (1968). In a UK study people were asked whether there was anything the other party could do to make them change their allegiance: 69 per cent said that nothing the other party did would cause them to switch, R. Rose, *People in Politics*, Faber, London, 1970, p. 73.
47. See D. Truman, *The Governmental Process*, Knopf, New York, 1962, ch. 7, for a study of the function of interest group communications, and ch. 8 for a study of group propaganda to the extra-group public.
48. See E. Katz and P. Lazarsfeld, *Personal Influence*, Free Press, New York, 1955; A. Campbell, P. Converse, W. Miller and D. Stokes, *The American Voter*, Wiley, New York, 1960, p. 271, report that about 25 per cent of respondents taking part in an election engaged 'in informal attempts to convince someone else to support a given party or candidate', but doubtless at other times the percentage decreases significantly. The concept of the opinion leader was first enunciated in the 1944 volume by P. Lazarsfeld, B. Berelson and H. Gaudet, *The People's Choice*, Duell, Sloan and Pearce, New York, 1944.
49. R. Merton, *Social Theory and Social Structure*, Free Press, New York, 1968, p. 465, italics in original; also in an addendum (p. 477) Merton argues that there is only a limited correlation between being high on 'class, power and prestige hierarchies' and being an opinion leader.
50. L. Harris, 'Polls and Politics in the U.S.', *Public Opinion Quarterly*, **27**, 3–8 (1963), but Harris also writes that 'No poll I have ever been witness to has made the candidate a different man, has changed his position on an issue, has made him into what he is not'.
51. But see B. Barry, *Sociologists, Economists and Democracy*, Collier-Macmillan, London, 1970, esp. pp. 126–136.
52. R. Axelrod, 'The Structure of Public Opinion on Policy Issues', *Public Opinion Quarterly*, **31**, 51–60 (1967), reprinted in C. Larson and P. Wasburn (eds.), *Power, Participation and Ideology*, David McKay Co., New York, 1969. In Table 15 the column 'Average scale coefficient' indicates the likelihood of a particular 'public' agreeing with one liberal statement and then agreeing with a similar one, ie it is a measure of opinion clustering.
53. On this point see A. H. Birch, *Representative and Responsible Government*, Allen and Unwin, London, 1964, esp. pp. 14–22.
54. For a somewhat similar case see R. E. Dowse and J. Peel, 'The Politics of Birth Control', *Political Studies*, **13**, 179–197 (1965).
55. H. L. Child, *Public Opinion; Nature Formation and Roles*, Van Nostrand, Princeton, 1965, p. 311. R. Lane and D. Sears, *Public Opinion*, Prentice-Hall, New Jersey, 1964, p. 49, write of public opinion as a 'considerable restraint upon the ability of a leader successfully to advocate measures which do not accord in some degree with public opinion'.

9

POLITICAL PARTICIPATION

9.1. Political Participation

IT SHOULD NOW be obvious that people participate in politics in many different ways, with different degrees of emotional involvement and at different levels of the system. Traditional democratic theory generally regards participation by the individual in political activity as a virtue in its own right. Participation has been seen as a civic duty, as a sign of political health, as the best method of ensuring that one's private interests are not neglected and as a *sine qua non* of a democracy. Generally, this perspective was predicated upon a Greek view of the private man as an animal, or an idiot, or the more calculative eighteenth-century view of participation as being caused by a deliberate weighing of the alternatives to involvement—tyranny or oligarchy. In any event, an important factor in this view of democracy was that it implied and encouraged a high level of popular involvement.

Today, except at a value level—people should be encouraged to participate—it is difficult to sustain a proposition to the effect that in democracies people actually do display high rates of political participation and interest, except in general elections. Even here, the rates of political participation as voters are quite variable between democracies: in the US presidential elections 58 per cent of the electorate vote, in Norway about 79 per cent do so, in Italy 90 per cent vote, in the UK about 80 per cent vote and in France about 78 per cent vote in general elections. Thus, even at the minimal level of voting, there is considerable national variation, but the overall level in democracies is quite high. When we come to participation in local elections, however, the rate drops to about half, or below, that usual in the national elections. Invariably, the rate of expressed interest in politics and in the level of knowledge about political institutions and events amongst the electorate—although variable between countries and within countries—is far below that implicit in the classical models of a democracy. Hence, as has been suggested elsewhere in this volume, another model of the political processes associated with democracy is necessary.

Following McClosky, let us define political participation as 'those voluntary activities by which members of a society share in the selection of rulers, and directly or indirectly, in the formation of public policy'.[1] At its widest, this definition includes casual political conversations such as one might have in a club, and the intense activity of the member of the fringe political group. Such activities can be classified into various categories and we shall employ the typology suggested by Milbrath.[*1*]

Below any of the activities set out in Figure 4 are the apathetics who, in the US, constitute about one-third of the population and are 'unaware,

Holding public and party office Being a candidate for office Soliciting party funds Attending a caucus or strategy meeting Contributing time in a campaign	Gladiatorial activities
Attending a political meeting or rally Making a monetary contribution Contacting a public official or political leader	Transitional activities
Wearing a button or showing a sticker Attempting to influence another into voting in a certain way Initiating a political discussion Voting Exposing oneself to political stimuli	Spectator activities

FIGURE 4. Political involvement. (From Lester Milbrath, *Political Participation*, © 1965 by Rand, McNally & Company, Chicago, Figure 3, p. 18)

literally, of the political part of the world around them'. Some 60 per cent of the population play spectator roles and only about 1 to 3 per cent are fully active, leaving about 7 to 9 per cent in a transitional stage from which they may ascend or descend.[*2*] Milbrath suggests that his ordering involves 'a kind of internal logic, a natural progression of becoming involved in political activities' and that persons involved at one level are also likely to involve themselves at 'lower' levels.[2] Central to this logic is the idea that ascending the hierarchy involves increasing costs in terms of time, energy and resources, and at each level fewer people are able or prepared to make the necessary investments. So one of the interests of political sociology is in accounting for the positions that people occupy on the hierarchy of involvement, and this will bring us to a consideration of participation as a consequence of the social, psychological and political circumstances associated with involvement.

However, prior to doing this it is necessary to ask the question, why participate in politics at all? As Lane puts it, 'of what use to a man is his politics?'. Lane suggests a number of broad reasons, one of which is rational and calculative, the rest having their origins in other aspects of personality.[3] In the following sections we shall examine the *correlates* of this involvement whilst here we shall look at some suggested explanations of why people become involved at all in politics.

Economic Explanation of Political Involvement

'Men seek to advance their economic or material well-being . . . through political means.' It should first be pointed out that there are more direct ways of advancing economic interests—by working, by buying cheap, by saving—than by engaging in politics, although men of property may be driven to defend it when it is attacked by those without property who, in a democracy, are most numerous. Again, it is the men who already have economic resources who are most likely to participate[4] and it is quite likely that although there may be an economic component in this participation there is also a seeking of other gratifications such as the approval of others, feelings of power, symbolic assertions of self-worth and success, and so on. In short, Lane reduces the economic imperative to a cultural and psychological one in which economic success is invested with other values such as worldly success, pride and achievement.

Participation as Meeting Psychological Needs

Some men need to win the approval of themselves and of others and some men need to reduce in themselves tensions which are not necessarily political in origin. This orientation corresponds very closely to that discussed in the section of Chapter 6 concerned with projection. Men engage in politics only secondarily for its allocative consequences; although reallocation of income, prestige, approval and status may occur, the origin of participation is found in personal psychological needs. The reallocations overtly sought are sought because they symbolize to the actor in his milieu, whatever that milieu may be, that he is powerful, that he can dominate, that his father was wrong in calling him a failure, that his wife is wrong to refuse him connubial bliss, that he can win the love and respect of those who support him. This psychological need to participate may, however, be differentially distributed, for example people in the 'American culture are more likely to employ their participation as an aid to social adjustment than persons socialized in other Western cultures'.[3]

Similarly, some psychologists posit the existence of an instinctual drive on the part of people which manifests itself in the need to understand their environment, and part of the environment they need to understand is, of course, the political. The need to understand is based upon curiosity, which is instinctual, and may manifest itself in sexual curiosity, in exploration, in philosophy, literature and in politics. In politics the need to understand may take more or less activist forms, from simply attending to the media, going to meetings, reading political material, testing one's views against others, to seeking office and the opportunity of further understanding.

None of these explanations is understood to be exclusive either in the sense that some people may not be both economically motivated and, for example, also seeking to understand, or in the sense that some political events may not elicit a stronger component of one than the other. But they are set out by Lane as being more than a mere classification, or a typology of participation such as that suggested by Milbrath. The difficulty is that except for the economic explanation they do not enable one to answer the question, why do some men project their needs—for approval, understanding, attention, to understand and so on—on to the political, whilst others do not? In this respect the economic argument is more self-contained since, as a matter of fact, men can advance and defend their economic concerns very well indeed in politics whether the interest is understood to be personal, group or class. The other two explanations are not self-contained in this sense. However, if we add to them the factors to be considered below, most of which stress that the opportunity and resources to become politically involved are not equally or randomly dispersed, we are in a better position to answer the question. We shall return to this topic again, but meanwhile we turn to the correlates—the opportunities and resources—of political participation.

9.2. Opportunities and Resources of Political Participation

Some of the most researched findings in the study of political behaviour concern the association between political participation and various social characteristics such as sex, age, occupation, length of stable residence, education, religion, and so on. One of the reasons for this is that data on these variables are cheap to obtain since they are usually available at public cost, but only very rarely have public surveys enabled the researcher to conduct the more sophisticated analyses that contemporary surveys have been able to achieve. This state of affairs is partly the result of the legal framework of elections. While elections represent a kind of mass experiment on a strictly defined population in which all members of the population are asked to choose among the same basic alternatives, and each choice is registered, the fact is that individual decisions are 'counted as anonymous acts cut from their origins'.[5] The rules of electoral secrecy mean that the social scientist's analysis of election data must confine itself to aggregate data, such as counts by locality or constituency, and is barred from direct analysis at the individual level. All of which means that those who attempt to explain political behaviour employing data made available in the election labour at a disadvantage. They can only approach many questions about social meaning of the vote indirectly. Due to the absence of data concerning individual electors, various 'indicators' must be used instead of more direct evidence which makes any interpretation problematic. But the extensive activity since the 1920's has meant that a large body of material has been assembled, and a great deal of this relates various aspects of social class to political behaviour. The most general finding is that high social status—whether measured by occupation, education or prestige—is strongly but variably associated with high turn-out, high information, conservatism, higher than average rates of political involvement and a high sense of political efficacy, and such high-status people are placed in a milieu of extensive political stimulation. They can be envisaged as well located and well disposed to receive political communications, whilst those of lower status are not so well located nor so highly disposed to receive such communications. They are well disposed because of their education and quite possibly because they come from a family with a high level of political awareness; they are well located because their occupation brings them into contact with the politically relevant and because their occupational skills are themselves politically pertinent. Another locational aspect is that such high-status individuals are generally able to maintain wide community contacts with people such as officials, teachers and political and economic leaders. Their situational location and personal backgrounds can be summed up by saying that they are at the political centre, whilst those not so well equipped are further away from the centre, nearer the periphery where political communications are sparser, and, in any case, such people are less predisposed to receive political communication.

It is the centre–periphery distinction and the factors underlying the distinction that explain the finding that 'higher class persons are more likely to participate in politics than lower class persons'.[6] But it should be clear that this higher participation in politics is only an aspect of the greater general involvement of high-status people in their milieu (see Table 16).

TABLE 16. Community Participation Rates and Status

Status indices and categories	Community participation Inactive %	Active %
Family income group	(N = 212)	(N = 278)
Lowest income	53	22
Middle income	37	36
Highest income	10	42
	100	100
Grades of school completed	(N = 255)	(N = 336)
Eight or less	63	24
Nine to eleven	18	13
Twelve	14	37
More than twelve	5	26
	100	100
Occupation of male respondents or husbands of female respondents	(N = 271)	(N = 338)
Professional	2	13
Farmer	39	36
Proprietors	4	21
Clerical	1	9
Skilled and semiskilled	35	18
Unskilled labourer	19	3
	100	100

Taken from D. Krech, R. Crutchfield and E. Ballachey, *Individual in Society*, McGraw-Hill, New York, 1962, p. 376. Copyright 1962 McGraw-Hill Book Company. By permission of McGraw-Hill Book Company.

However, not all people remain in the same class or status position all their lives but are mobile between status categories and classes. Indeed, in complex industrial societies social movement is characteristic of large segments of the population (see Table 17).

Such movements, as Table 17 makes clear, are common in industrial societies. There is evidence that the upwardly mobile are more participatory than the downwardly mobile, as a study of members' involvement in Dutch trade unions demonstrates (see Table 18).[7]

TABLE 17. Comparative Indices of Upward and Downward Mobility (Percentages)

Country	Non-farm populations Total vertical mobility across line between working- and middle-class
	%
US	30
Germany	31
Sweden	29
Japan	27
France	27
Switzerland	23

Table adapted from S. Lipset and R. Bendix, *Social Mobility in Industrial Society*, University of California Press, Berkeley, 1967, p. 25. [*3*] Originally published by the University of California Press; reprinted by permission of the Regents of the University of California.

TABLE 18. Social Mobility and Participation

Status compared with father's occupation, in own view	Participants	Non-participants
	%	%
Lower	7	40
Same or higher	93	60
	(100% = 38)	

Taken from M. Van De Vall, *Labour Organisations*, © Cambridge University Press, London, 1970, p. 162.

However, the political involvement and its direction—left or right—is more problematic. In the US and Great Britain, both upward and downward mobility tend to be associated with the development of more conservative social attitudes and voting. The first relationship is generally explained by reference to social pressures to conform to a new milieu or by anticipatory socialization. The second is explained as compensating for loss by a strong identification with a symbol of the lost status. That is, any resocialization of downwardly mobile persons into their new class may be mitigated by a desire to emulate behaviour that gives them a sense of superiority over others, in this case, the political orientation of their class of origin.[*4*] However, sometimes downward mobility may be associated with political radicalism; in other words attitudes become consonant with those prevalent in the terminal status. This appears to be the case in Italy, a society where individualization and the claims of an 'economic miracle' have been accompanied by inequalities of reward, public scandals and graft, inflexible bureaucracy and other abuses, and the downwardly mobile, particularly eager to ameliorate these conditions, are especially frustrated by the privations and strains of their situation and are readily attracted to parties of the left.

We may look at social status as consisting of a number of social attributes—education, occupation, income, race, religion—and in accordance with the theory of status consistency suggest that when a person has these social attributes in some sort of *inconsistent* arrangement he may well be 'predisposed toward participation in social movements'.[8] This predisposition is understood to follow from the psychic tension engendered by the inconsistency of being, for example, of high income but low ethnic prestige or high in political status but low in occupational status. Participation at a relatively high level on the involvement hierarchy can be understood as tension-reducing (especially in ideological movements) because the involvement provides an opportunity to change or attack the structures producing the inconsistency.[9] However, not all types of inconsistency, in fact only those of underreward—high ethnicity but low education, and high occupation and low income—have been 'found to participate in social movements attempting to bring about extensive societal change'.[10] Status inconsistency has also been found to affect not only participation but also type of participation, as in the case of occupational and religious clashes when inconsistents were revealed as disproportionately supporters of Liberal and Socialist parties.[11]

Although this type of analysis is suggestive, it does have a number of operational difficulties. One could argue that in a complex and highly differentiated industrial society almost no one exhibits consistency, so that if one looks at participants at all thoroughly one will inevitably find non-consistent elements which can then be held to explain the participation. This is especially the case if one takes into account the possibility of status rankings other than those normally employed in participation analysis. For example, what is the participation outcome of high occupational prestige and low ranking on sexual attractiveness? Are American legislators unattractive ex-lawyers? The problem is one of selecting out the salient status hierarchies and, cross-nationally, this problem may be almost insuperable, especially between nations of very different cultures. For example, Lenski in his cross-national study of status inconsistency found that the Catholic religion counted for very little in Britain, so that discrepancy between religion and occupation had no effect in determining party preference, whilst in Australia, Canada and the US it did have an effect.[11]

Up to this point we have presented two typologies of participation—the gladiator–transitional–spectator breakdown and the centre–periphery dichotomy. We have also employed the theory of status consistency but have suggested that it is relatively weak. However, even if explanations of political participation do not lack difficulties, it is nevertheless true that a good deal of information is available about social factors associated with political participation. Some of these findings are tabulated below:

INVENTORY OF SOME SOCIAL CORRELATES OF POLITICAL PARTICIPATION

Education

Those with higher education are more likely to participate.

Confirmed for: United States, Finland, Mexico, Britain, France, Italy.

In Norway, the relationship holds for voting but not for gladiatorial activities. In Norway, the fact of vigorous, status-polarized parties means that each party must actively recruit workers from within its own supporting status group.

Urban–rural

Farmers are less likely to become active in politics than city dwellers.

Confirmed for: United States, Finland, Britain, Norway, Denmark, Sweden.

Some contradictory evidence in US; in Japan, this relationship does not hold, presumably because rural Japanese are no further from social centre than are urban Japanese.

The larger the constituency, the higher the rate of participation.

Confirmed for: United States, UK.

Social Involvement

Trade union members are more likely to take an interest in politics, to have a stronger stand on issues and to vote than are non-union manual workers.

Confirmed for: United States (with some exceptions), Britain, Sweden.

Higher voluntary association participation is associated with higher political participation.

Confirmed for: United States, Britain, France, West Germany.

Persons in group cross-pressures are less likely to participate than those not cross-pressured.

Confirmed for: United States, Britain.

That is, high group involvement is not unequivocably associated with a correspondingly high rate of political participation. Group memberships may 'pull' in contrary ways, and this tends to be associated with a withdrawal from political activity.

Residence

The longer a person resides in a given community, the greater the likelihood of his participation in politics.

Confirmed for: United States, Finland, Britain.

This is especially true of gladiatorial activities. Apparently it takes some time before a community is ready to entrust office to a newcomer.

Life cycle

Participation gradually ripens with age, but after 50 or 60 begins to decline.

Confirmed for: United States, Britain, France.

The most apathetic group are the young unmarried citizens who are only marginally integrated into their community.

Confirmed for: United States, Finland, Norway, Britain.

Highest participation rates are for married persons with no children.

Confirmed for: United States.

Sex

Men are more likely to participate in politics than women.

Confirmed for: United States, Britain, Italy, France, Germany, Mexico, Sweden, Norway, Japan.

Relationship disappears when factors such as social class and education are concerned, although in terms of gladiatorial activities the relationship still holds.

Religion, race, ethnicity

Negroes participate less than whites.

Jews participate more than Catholics, who, in turn, are more active than Protestants.

Confirmed for: United States, France, Belgium.

As our inventory shows, considerable knowledge has been accumulated concerning the various social factors associated with participation in politics at various levels and in various countries, but the problem still remains of organizing the information in the context of a general theory of participation. There are no very satisfactory accounts of political participation. We know that participants differ systematically in their social characteristics from non-participants and we can see that participants—especially at the upper reaches of the spectator hierarchy and above—possess resources which facilitate their greater involvement. But we do not have a theory capable of explaining *why* they expend these resources politically rather than in another way. Even Milbrath's suggestive concepts of 'centre' and 'periphery' only go so far. The factors associated with high political participation such as high levels of education, urban location, high social involvement, high socio-economic status, and so on, represent advantageous locations within the social system for receiving political information, having a better leverage on politics, a greater contact with political life, and so on. But such concepts do not explain, except in a negative way, the periodic involvement, both legitimate and illegitimate, of the 'social periphery' in politics. They do not, for example, give much guidance in the explanation of the rise of the Black Panthers, the emergence of 'grass roots' pressure groups such as tenants associations, or the sporadic disturbances which often typify peasant life. Part of this deficiency is due to the dependence of much political participation research on a particular mode of investigation: the survey. The big expansion of research into political behaviour, especially voting behaviour, came with the developments in survey designs, a type of investigation which has particular implications for the theory based upon such data. For one thing, the survey tends to treat the individual as the basic social unit. It is the individual who is normally selected by probability sampling procedures and the individual who is interviewed or given a questionnaire to complete. Moreover, analysis is done on the basis of individual attributes.

So, in an important sense, the individual is torn out of his social context and the processual, immediate character of much of social life is lost. Even if, in the analysis stage, individuals are grouped together on the basis of their attitudes or some other social characteristic, 'the extent to which individuals may suddenly act together in groups, because new groups are formed or old ones are reinforced, is easily lost sight of and predictions are made on the basis of so and so many per cent of the sample have this or that attitude'.[12] What is missing, in other words, is information on the processes such as the development of group consensus which help translate attitude into action.

There are ways which attempt to overcome this excessive individualism: one such technique is purposive sampling, in which individuals are selected according to their position within the social structure. Another

TABLE 19. Vote Intention in October

Actual vote in November	Republican	Democrat	Didn't know	Don't expect to know	Total
Republican	215	7	4	6	232
Democrat	4	144	12	0	160
Didn't vote	10	16	6	59	91
	229	167	22	65	483

From P. F. Lazarsfeld, B. Berelson and H. Gaudet, *The People's Choice*, Columbia University Press New York, 1948, p. xi.

method is the panel type of design, developed in voting studies by Lazarsfeld and his colleagues. In this design, a group of individuals are studied over a period of time in order to examine the effect time-related variables may have on their behaviour. For example, this kind of design enabled Lazarsfeld and his colleagues to use a 'turnover' type of analysis to identify changeover rates in party preference throughout the period of the campaign. (See Table 19.)

If the study had interviewed different groups of people in October and November rather than the same people, the findings would have read as follows: in October 41 per cent (167 out of 396) of those who had intended to voted for the Democrats, in November 42 per cent (160 out of 392) voted for the party. This would have indicated a great constancy in political attitudes throughout the campaign. But, in fact, only the people in the main diagonal of Table 19 remained unchanged: 418 out of 485 respondents did in November what they intended to do in October, while 13 per cent changed their minds one way or another. This kind of technique offers to the researcher a finer net in which to catch the dynamic and processual quality of social life. In other words, theories based on survey data often appear too static and deal with variables remote from any more tangible social process.

Most of the explanations offered in this area are *post hoc*. The only rigorous general theory available is that put forward by Downs, who concentrates his attention on the decision to vote, but the theory can in principle be extended to higher levels of participation.

The economic theory is basically an exchange theory positing a rational calculative actor. A man acts rationally when he minimizes his costs for any desired end. Hence, a man votes—expends energy—for the party which is nearest his ends. His calculation involves the following: how much better off (or less well off) would he be as a result of his preferred party winning (or losing) the election. He must then calculate the possibility that *his* vote will be the crucial one without which his preferred party would lose the election. If his party will win or lose as a consequence of his voting or not voting, he acts rationally in not voting because his expenditure of energy does not affect the result, ie his preferred party will win without his incurring any cost. The victory of his party is a collective good—like a road or a park—in that if it wins he will obtain a share whether he votes (pays) or not, and clearly most *individuals* are better off not voting (paying). Parties may attempt to reduce the voter's costs of acquiring information by acting in a predictable manner and by producing ideologies. He may also be uncertain of the electoral situation, ie of the exact chances that his vote will decide the issue, and, therefore, the almost infinitesimal chance of his voting when he has perfect information becomes slightly greater. In any case, the point is, 'Even low turnouts of say 25% are, on this analysis, clearly inconsistent with rationality'.[13] Hence, the economic theory cannot account for high turnouts and one needs different types of explanation to discern why people vote as they do, for example group pressures to vote, non-rational processes such as identifying with one's parents, friends, etc. The difficulties of adopting this procedure are legion. Firstly, we have slipped from one theory to another. Secondly, even if we assume that one's costs are reduced by following one's parents, this does not explain the parents' actions, or if held to explain one's own voting, what then is the explanation of the parents' behaviour? Clearly, we are involved here in a regression to Adam and Eve. Again, if we assert that in voting the voter is acting rationally by affirming his loyalty to a party, to democracy or to his group, we seem to be coming very close to the proposition that everything a person does he does because he gains some sort of benefit.

Downs, not altogether successfully, attempts to meet this difficulty with his concept of 'free political information' which, although differentially available, may be available in some measure to all and, therefore, an absolute minimum of participation—voting—is reasonable since the costs are extremely low. There is also a hint—no more—of an alternative solution when he writes that 'some citizens also seek straight political information *purely for its entertainment value*'.[*5*] This suggests that political participation is simply not regarded as a cost by most people but rather as, in itself, a pleasure or, weakening the point, the *act* of voting is below the threshold of any calculated cost–benefit, although the *choice of party to support* may well be a more calculated one. If participation is regarded as a pleasure, however, this still implies the possibility that to obtain it other competing pleasures must be foregone. Probably a more reasonable explanation is that the pleasure–pain calculation is so sub-threshold that for most people other factors—group, family, work situation, a feeling that one has a duty to vote, and so on—operate almost to the exclusion of personal calculation except in the attenuated sense that group–family–work interests may be held to subserve personal interest.

However, leaving this difficulty aside, Downs' model is a powerful one on other aspects of participation. One can deduce that in marginal seats people are more likely to affect the outcome of the election, and this expectation is confirmed for a large number of local government seats in the UK.[*6*] Another deduction one would make is that in the seats with the most electors the cost of acquiring information about the likely impact of one's own vote would be higher than in seats with fewer votes, hence, *ceteris paribus*, the larger the seat the smaller the turnout. This inference is quite strongly supported in Britain for turnout in local elections: 'the average turnout in wards with contested elections ranged from 46%, in towns with populations of less than 50,000, to 32.3% in towns with more than half a million inhabitants . . . average ward turnout is also very strongly correlated to size of ward, ranging from 54.4% in wards with less than 2,000 electors to 34.3% in wards with electorates of 10,000 or more'.[14] Similarly, it can be inferred that the closer people perceive the election will be, ie the narrower the margin between the parties, the more likely it is that the turnout will be high. This is because the marginal vote then has a better chance of being the deciding vote. Equally, in such a situation one would expect the parties to decrease information costs to the electorate by increasing their canvassing, propaganda and offers to help electors to the polls, etc.

It can also be inferred from Downs' model that as the size of the electorate increases *over time*, ie as the lower social echelons are enfranchized, the turnout will decrease since the opportunity cost of acquiring political information is higher for these groups. This brings one to the consideration of the sort of explanation that a model such as Downs' can offer for the known facts of differential participation between the sexes, the social classes, between levels of education, and age. As a matter of fact, the immediate consequence of an increase in the electorate is a decline in turnout, but this appears to be made up in subsequent elections. In Norway, for example, in 1898 all men over 25 were given the vote, so increasing the electorate from 238,000 qualified and 196,000 registered in 1897 to 440,000 qualified *and* registered in 1900. But it took some time before the newly enfranchized exercised their rights. At the first national election, after the introduction of manhood suffrage, there was a 16 per cent drop in turnout, and it was not until 1924 that the percentage level for men reached the pre-1900 level.[15]

The lower figures require no comment, but the upward trend does, and this can be explained in two ways both of which are compatible with the model. Firstly, the political parties appear to respond to increases in the electorate by cheapening the costs of acquiring information by expanding their publicity, by personalizing the election and establishing symbolic-cum-ideological rallying points. Secondly, from the side of the electorate, it is arguably the case that the payoffs of participation are only apparent after a delay. Arguably, the non-participant may find that the costs of non-participation *after* the election, when policies may begin to affect him detrimentally, are higher than appeared likely before the election.

The Downs model is also useful in accounting for the known facts of lower participation by women and higher participation by older people and by the better educated. Downs does not take the case of women, but it is known that they are less exposed to political discussion, since those that work tend to do so in smaller units and in non-union situations; and their social role, especially in working-class life, is often defined as non-political. Hence, the chances of accidentally acquiring political information are greater in the case of males. An inference is that for women to acquire the same amount of political information as men they must make greater sacrifices. Hence, their lower participation is explained by the theory, and the tendency to follow the husband's lead in voting also acquires a new significance. They are acting rationally when they do so because this way minimizes costs. Similarly, the higher participation by older people—up to the age when physical effort is too great—can be explained, in part, by reference to Downs' concept of accidentally acquired free information. The older one is, the more likely one is to have acquired much more free information and, *ceteris paribus*, the lower is the cost of voting. Turning to education, a factor Downs does not comment on, we find that higher education is associated with (1) the desire to obtain and assimilate information (education is associated with 'better' jobs) and (2) the educated person acquires a stock of free political information as a byproduct of his education. This gives him a free context within which to assess new information. Hence, the costs of participation for the educated are lower and therefore the rates of participation are likely to be higher.

In a sense, all of these relationships are trivial ones since by far the most significant finding about political participation is that, in all countries where it has been investigated, social class has been found to be the single most important general determinant of party preference: 'Persons in professional and business occupations, persons of upper income levels, persons with more than high school education are more likely to vote for a party that stands for protection of business interests and little welfare legislation than persons in low-prestige occupations, with low incomes or with little education'.[16] Religion, regional ties, ethnic factors, etc., disturb but do not wipe out the relationship. The question, of course, is whether the association can be explained by Downs' model. The answer is that although Downs does not deal directly with the problem it can be easily inferred that those voting for no change are voting for the minimum of income, prestige, status redistribution *via* taxes, benefits, etc., and those voting for change are voting for redistribution of some sort. Each group is voting to maximize its own income and, hence, acts rationally.

This consideration brings us to what may be a very important weakness in Downs' argument. It appears that people act rationally when they act to maximize benefits and minimize costs. This may be 'true' (1) in the short period and (2) for an individual. But this does not mean to say that it is the case that individual benefits are social benefits nor that what is advantageous in the short run is necessarily so in the long run. Take the case of the profit-maximizing entrepreneur. He acts to maximize his profit, which is not the same as, and indeed may be incompatible with, socially desirable innovation. Take also the case of the politically astute elite willing to make considerable concessions to non-elites in order to dampen down non-elite solidarity. They may do this at their short-term expense but it is clearly in the elite's long-term interests to make concessions.

This discussion of Downs on participation and the weaknesses of the analysis we have outlined suggest that a more satisfactory analysis of political participation may be found in a consideration of possible intervening psychological variables.

9.3. The Psychological Correlates of Political Participation

The most fundamental difficulties in discussing psychological correlates will be familiar to the reader, but they bear reiteration: (1) it is very difficult to disentangle cause and effect: are those more psychologically involved active because of their psychological needs, or are they psychologically involved because of satisfactions derived from political activity? (2) how does one measure psychological traits other than by eliciting behavioural—in this case verbal—responses from the subjects? This opens up the possibility of the respondent lying, of inappropriate questions, of socially approved responses, of eliciting answers where none really exist and, most important, of inferring what is going on in people's heads from what they say. Since we discussed, in some detail, in a previous chapter the problem of sorting out the 'basic' personality from the socially derived or the socially learnt personality traits, we shall ignore the problem here, but it should be borne in mind. As a matter of fact, the evidence is that such basic personality traits as rigidity, guilt, intolerance of ambiguity, manic depression and manifest anxiety do not correlate highly with political participation.[17] Participation is a complex social act, so that it is not a matter of surprise that any one basic personality trait is of only very limited significance in explaining it. For many people, psychological investment in politics is so slight that it is unlikely that overall importance can be attached to any given political activity as meeting deep-seated psychological needs. But this does not mean that for some people such involvement is not enormously important.

Other psychological traits, which owe their origin to social learning, appear to be more correlated in the aggregate with political participation than does basic personality. Amongst these learned traits the following have been researched: sense of efficacy, sense of civic responsibility, sociability, sense of alienation and authoritarianism.

Quite clearly politicians (in Table 20 they are people who 'aspired to or occupied some national office') are more deeply involved in politics than electors, and it is clear from the table that they are less politically alienated and have a higher sense of political efficacy than the sample of voters. But, in turn, the sense of efficacy and of alienation is strongly related to personal social status.[18] Probably what happens is that the middle-class resources of time, education and opportunity give a person an initial sense of efficacy and if he then participates he is likely to be successful, which

TABLE 20. Sense of Political Efficacy and Political Alienation of Politicians and Electors

	Sense of political efficacy		Sense of political alienation	
	Politicians	Electors	Politicians	Electors
	%	%	%	%
Low				
Score 0	0	20	66	15
Score 1	0	32	21	18
Score 2	4	24	9	23
Score 3	34	20	2	18
Score 4 or more	62	4	2	26
High				

Taken from Ian Budge, *Agreement and the Stability of Democracy*, Chicago, Markham Publishing Company, 1970, p. 125.[7]

reinforces the feeling. However, the association is a strong one since (1) people who belong to an organization are more likely than those who do not to feel a sense of political efficacy, (2) the better educated belong to more organizations than the less well educated and (3) there is a strong connection between belonging to an organization, being well educated and having some sense of efficacy.[19] Finally, there is a strong connection between all of these and a person's social class, however defined. Within the British working-class, participation in voluntary associations discriminates between those who feel they could influence a political decision if they wanted to from those who feel they could not. Membership of a voluntary organization is also positively related to frequency of political conversations and to the amount of political information possessed.[20]

Again, people with a high sense of civic duty tend to be more participant than those with a lower sense, and the former are more likely than the latter to be of upper socio-economic status. However, this feature is more strongly related to the level of education than to general socio-economic status.[8] Similarly, it is a well-researched finding that anomic and alienated people are less likely than the rest of the population to participate in politics. Anomic people tend to lack social direction, feel ineffective and often lack a central value frame of reference. They are politically detached and indifferent, whilst the alienated displays 'suspicion, distrust, hostility and cynicism'.[21] As with all the other relationships, there is also a strong association between socio-economic status and both anomie and alienation in that people who display these conditions are most likely to be low on socio-economic indices (see Table 21).[22]

However, the problem is not merely to find relationships nor, in the cases we have outlined, to explain them since the Downs theory and the centre–periphery distinction are adequate for this purpose. The problem is rather to investigate whether the relationships discovered between social class and social status and the other participatory characteristics are improved by *adding* the psychological characteristics while controlling for

TABLE 21. Status and Alienation (in per cent)

Status indicators	Alienation High	Low	Total	(*N*)
Race				
Negro	76	24	100	(25)
White	39	61	100	(140)
Occupation				
Manual	60	40	100	(40)
Non-manual	31	69	100	(106)
Education				
0–12 years	57	43	100	(51)
13–15	32	68	100	(31)
16 plus	25	75	100	(64)
Class identification				
Working plus lower	58	42	100	(38)
Middle plus upper	32	68	100	(100)

social class and status.[*9*] A presumption is that the association will either increase or diminish since the association between each set of variables is not perfect, for example not all the alienated people are working-class and non-participant. Thus if we add a psychological variant to a social variable we would expect the former to increase or decrease the association between the social variable and political participation and this will demonstrate the independent effect of psychological conditions. Table 22 shows the relationship between certain psychological characteristics and political beliefs.

It is clear that conservative beliefs (at least on this American sample) have quite definite associations with clinical psychological traits. In

TABLE 22. Comparison of Conservatives and Liberals. By Personality Traits—Clinical

Psychological variable	Liberals (*N* = 190)	Moderate liberals (*N* = 136)	Moderate conservatives (*N* = 331)	Extreme conservatives (*N* = 245)
Hostility				
% low	59	38	26	9
% high	18	37	46	71
Paranoid tendencies				
% low	56	42	28	13
% high	16	27	37	62
Contempt for weakness				
% low	61	33	21	5
% high	8	18	29	55
Rigidity				
% low	58	43	29	14
% high	18	32	41	60
Intolerance of human frailty				
% low	52	30	17	6
% high	8	16	23	54

Taken from H. McClosky, 'Conservatism and Personality', *APSR*, 52, 27–45 (1968), slightly abridged.

addition, McClosky also shows the relationship between sense of social responsibility, anomie, self-confidence, alienation, and so on, and being a conservative. However, when *social* variables are introduced—status and education—these 'factors account, by themselves, for a significant share of the total variance found in our data'. Nevertheless, McClosky concludes that 'while the *range* and scores varies as occupation, education or knowledge varies, the *direction* and *magnitude* of the differences between the liberals and the conservatives remain very much the same for all status and educational levels. In short, personality factors seem to exercise a fairly uniform influence on the formation of conservative or liberal outlooks at all social levels.'[23] Thus, personality seems to exert some independent effect.

Campbell and his associates have demonstrated that even holding the *social* variable, education, constant, political involvement and turnout are increased as the person's sense of personal effectiveness increases (see Table 23).[24]

The implication of Table 23 is clear, although due to small numbers it is not conclusive: holding education constant, sense of personal effectiveness exerts an independent effect in increasing propensity to vote and to become involved. But at the higher education level this particular variable exerts no independent effect. Campbell concludes that at the higher status milieu the pressure from the environment supports high voting and involvement levels, but 'at lower levels, the individual is more dependent on

TABLE 23. The Relation of Sense of Personal Effectiveness to Political Involvement and Vote Turnout by Education

	Sense of personal effectiveness			
Education	Low	Low medium	High medium	High
Grade school				
% voting	43	47	72	82
% involved	32	34	48	41
N	47	47	60	22
High school				
% voting	67	79	80	82
% involved	48	45	62	57
N	67	61	136	34
College				
% voting	0	90	90	88
% involved	0	76	73	86
N	*	29	52	22

* Figures for this column merged with adjacent column

From *The American Voter*, by Angus Campbell, Philip E. Converse, Warren E. Miller and Donald E. Stokes, Copyright © 1960 by John Wiley & Sons Inc. By permission of John Wiley & Sons Inc.

personal motivations, and hence personality becomes a more visible discriminant'.[25] Similarly, Agger and his colleagues found that political cynicism exerted an independent effect on political activity such as discussing politics with people, even controlling for education.[26]

In a study of voting for, and against, a proposal to consolidate the government of Nashville, Tennessee, the psychological dimensions of anomia and alienation were tested against the social characteristic, education, and these were related to participation in the political activity surrounding the proposed change. It was discovered that the psychological variables were associated with the decision to vote but more strongly associated with voting for and against the consolidation proposal: 28 per cent of anomic people voted, whilst 50 per cent of non-anomic did so, but of anomic people only 46 per cent voted in favour, whilst 68 per cent of non-anomic people voted in favour. Education was the factor which most accounted for the decision to vote (see Table 24).

TABLE 24. Voting Behaviour by Education and Anomia

	Less than high school education		High school or above		A	B
	Anomic	Non-anomic	Anomic	Non-anomic		
Voting	20%	37%	46%	58%	0.24	0.15
No. of cases	82	41	39	78		
In favour of proposal	19%	60%	56%	67%	0.21	0.24
No. of cases	16	15	18	45		
Favourable attitudes	40%	62%	55%	71%	0.12	0.19
No. of cases	45	26	29	62		

Column A, the proportion of variation in each dependent variable explained by education *independent* of the effect of anomia; Column B, the proportion of variation in each dependent variable explained by anomia *independent* of the effect of education.

Table adapted from E. McDill and J. Ridley, 'Status, Anomia, Political Education and Political Participation', *American Journal of Sociology*, **68**, 205–213 (1962). Copyright 1962 by the University of Chicago Press and reproduced by permission.

But, as Table 24 shows, even holding education constant, anomia does explain some of the relationships both of the decision to vote and of a favourable attitude to the proposal. The authors conclude that 'at the affective level political participation may be viewed in terms of a negative *weltanschauung* (as measured by the anomia and political alienation scales); at the cognitive level it may be viewed in terms of lack of education with its resultant paucity of understanding of community problems.[*10*]

Yet another study of the relationship between social and psychological variables of political participation also produced positive results. In this study 'sociability', 'a feeling of ease, graciousness and confidence in social situations and a willingness to accept the responsibilities that attend effective social relations', was tested against various types of participation, holding SES (defined as income) constant.[27] People ranking high on sociability were significantly more likely than those ranking low to participate politically (see Table 25). But when income level (defined as high = above $5000 pa and low = below $5000 pa) is added, the association

TABLE 25. Sociability and Participation

	Low participation	High participation
Low sociability	48	16
High sociability	33	36

drops quite steeply (see Table 26). Milbrath, however, concludes that 'the sociability factor itself, aside from the relationship to SES, seems to be a significant intervening variable leading to greater political participation'.[*11*]

The evidence is, then, that although psychological variables do seem to account for some of the relationships outlined above, not enough multivariate analysis has been done to make a firm conclusion possible. Further, the connection between the sociological variables and the psychological

TABLE 26. Sociability, Income and Participation

	High income		Low income	
	Low participation	High participation	Low participation	High participation
Low sociability	20	10	28	6
High sociability	24	31	9	5

variables tends to be close. This is what one would expect given the existence of a subject such as a *social* psychology. Disentangling the relative weights that the sociological and psychological elements contribute to participation is a complex problem, and this only adds to the difficulties mentioned earlier in this section.

It is easy for the political sociologist to confine his attention almost entirely to the social and psychological aspects of the problem in hand, ignoring the legal and constitutional framework within which the problem is frequently embedded. The political parameters of participation, however, cannot be so easily ignored since participation in some senses is a function of legal and constitutional rules and it is to these that we now turn.

9.4. The Political Context of Participation

Perhaps the most obvious sense in which participation is influenced is by legal enactments, such as literacy tests, adequate provision for absentee voting, residence requirements, and the like. By such tests as these the American black, especially in the Southern US, was effectively barred from legal participation and so withdrew into apathy. Equally obviously, the law can admit wider or narrower sections of the population to the franchise and can make it more, or less, difficult for the population to associate together in political or social organization: witness the French and British laws in operation in the nineteenth century curtailing the legal existence of trade unions and the different rates at which the American, British and French citizens were admitted to the franchise. Naturally this does not mean that the formally disenfranchised did not participate in other ways nor that their interests were necessarily ignored. The British theorists, such as Edmund Burke, argued that the people without a legal vote were virtually represented by those with it. Methods of participation in such situations vary considerably and it is worth noting that, in 1812, during the Peninsular Campaign, more troops were stationed in Britain than in Spain. It is also worth noting that, even in Britain, traditionally taken as a peaceable polity, over the last one hundred and fifty years, mobs, riots, plots and violent industrial disputes have been frequent.[28] Again, and more peaceably, the unenfranchised were drawn into agitations for the reforms of the electoral law in the nineteenth century, for the repeal of the Combination Laws, repeal of the Corn Laws and for factory legislation.[29] Today, in industrial societies, universal suffrage is almost complete although there is some variation in the age at which the vote is granted, in the difficulty of getting on the register, and so on.

When suffrage is universal it is plausible to imagine that, besides the social and psychological factors, already discussed, party structures may affect relative turnout rates and participation. There are two ways in which this might occur. Firstly, it may be the case that turnout is a function of the number of parties realistically competing for national political offices. Certainly, the evidence seems to suggest that the turnout varies independently of the number of major competing parties. The lack of any clear association is brought out in Table 27.

The table shows that there is no association: in New Zealand with two major parties the turnout averages about 90 per cent, whilst in the US and Britain turnout is a good deal lower, being 58 per cent and 78 per cent respectively. Again, in multi-party systems, with or without a dominant party, turnout is 79 per cent; whereas in Italy, with a similar structure,

TABLE 27. Turnout and Party Systems

A Party system	B Turnout %age
Two-party system	
US	58
New Zealand	90
UK	78
Austria	90
Two and a half parties	
W. Germany	87
Luxemburg	71
Canada	80
Belgium	87
Eire	71
Multi-party with dominant party	
Denmark	84
Sweden	83
Norway	79
Italy	90
Iceland	86
Netherlands	92
Multi-party without dominant party	
Switzerland (male suffrage only)	28
Finland	73
France	80

Column A compiled from J. Blondel, *An Introduction to Comparative Government*, Weidenfeld and Nicolson, London, 1969, p. 157; column B compiled from B. Russett *et al.*, *World Handbook of Social and Political Indicators*, Yale University Press, New Haven, 1964, pp. 84–85.

turnout is about 90 per cent; in Finland, a multi-party system without a dominant party, turnout is about 73 per cent, whilst a similar structure in Israel reveals about 80 per cent. Thus, there is no simple relationship between turnout and party system. Secondly, it might be thought that where there are more parties competing for political office these would perforce provide a greater opportunity for people to become officers and activists in the parties. But the number of parties does not seem to affect the percentage of people who participate in a more activist fashion than simply voting. It would seem that in most populations there is only a very limited reservoir of people willing and able to do more politically than merely vote.

Since voting participation is nearly always high in a democratic industrial, or simply democratic system it follows that, at best, the nature of the electoral campaign (noisy or quiet, one in which 'important' or 'unimportant' issues are discussed, where many or few parties are involved) does not very significantly affect the turnout. It might be thought that ideological polarization between the parties would affect turnout since, presumably, those not supporting one ideology would have a strong incentive to vote for the other. Norway is a country with such a degree of 'ideological polarization', yet its turnout is about the same as that of the UK where the parties, although different, are certainly not ideological. Also, the rate of participation, above that of voting, is strikingly similar to non-polarized countries at about 2 per cent–3 per cent taking on gladiatorial activities, about 7 per cent attending meetings, 19 per cent claiming to have read some electoral material, and the rest relatively uninvolved.[30] On the other hand, there is evidence that during a crisis, when the election is regarded as important, the turnout will marginally increase.[31] The following generalization is probably very near a universal law in politics: in all democratic countries voter turnout is generally above 70 per cent in general elections, while more strenuous forms of participation fall below 1–2 per cent. It has been suggested that this is a sign of generalized satisfaction with the state of affairs in the country. This conclusion is almost certainly too narrowly based in that it ignores a whole range of other activities such as strikes and mob violence, which may show intense dissatisfaction with other than 'obviously' political elements. Moreover, it ignores the very real possibility that the lack of interest in becoming deeply involved is a sensible adaptation, by most people, to their relative helplessness to change matters; as we saw when discussing the elite model, most people simply do not have the resources with which to intervene politically to any serious effect. Finally, most of the aggregate data on which these generalizations are based ignore (1) the possibility that it is not through electoral participation that most people's political requirements are met but through organizations and pressure groups and (2) the possibility that even if people do not become involved in national politics they may be sporadically involved on certain issues which flare up and then flicker away. The Campaign for Nuclear Disarmament and SANE in the US are examples which span both possibilities, but here we shall briefly describe a small sporadic incursion into politics by a group of hitherto uninvolved people who were activated by a single complaint which, when partly met, resulted in the demise of the organization. We do this because such sporadic involvement is probably very widespread, it engages people who are not normal activists and because neglecting this type of participation leads one to overstress the apathy of the average voter.

Early in 1965 The Exeter Council Tenants Association was formed following the introduction of a new scheme which would have involved some tenants in paying higher rents and would have made it obligatory for all tenants to provide evidence of income. The tenants were not consulted about the new scheme by either the local parties or the ward councillors, and both councillors and parties were taken by surprise when the Association was formed. The organizers of the Association differed in almost every respect from the classic picture of political activists: of the twenty-two members of the executive only three were formally educated after the age of fourteen years, only twelve of the twenty-one eligible for trade union membership had joined one, and of these only five claimed to attend trade union meetings. However, eight claimed to have politically active friends and ten were members of various kinds of voluntary organization, but only four claimed any sort of previous committee experience on a union, a social voluntary organization or a political party. Finally, not one member of the executive could recall having noticed any sort of political activity—other than voting—amongst their parents. They were, in short, not untypical of the average non-involved citizen.

Yet this group of people *organized* a series of deputations, marches and consultations with the local press, local parties and councillors, and a few months after they were formed they contested five seats for the city council and averaged 23 per cent of the vote. They recruited 53 per cent of all council tenant households to the Association and were known to 99 per cent of the council tenant households. As a consequence of their involvement, this group of people met very frequently and a strong group consensus soon emerged about, for example, the motives of councillors in meeting them and in making concessions and, very significantly, they developed a highly structured and coherent point of view about local politics which differed sharply from the very much less structured views of the less involved general membership.[32]

Such a community may be regarded as a field of social interaction, with relatively frequent meetings in pubs, clubs, car-parking lots, etc. Also, the milieu is necessarily fairly socially homogeneous and the major defining characteristic—in this case being non-householders—constitutes a common interest which is potentially a basis for common action when that interest appears threatened in some way.[*12*] In the case of tenant associations—which have developed very rapidly in Britain—the initial common interest is established by the political decision, taken by public authorities, to set up such housing estates. When the interests of the inhabitants are apparently in jeopardy, any defence of these interests becomes automatically a matter of political concern. But not, be it noted, of active and public concern to all affected. Only a minority get involved, but a minority previously classifiable—at least in terms of political activity—as spectators or peripherals. Unfortunately, we have no study of such groups which focusses upon their sense of efficacy, anomia, sociability, and so on. However, as we have seen, the electorate cannot be envisaged as a homogeneous mass. This, of course, suggests that those acting relatively passively at one level may be mobilized to a higher level of activity by direct and particular events rather than indirect and general ones. Thus, those politically inactive electors whom Budge identified as having a sense of potential effectiveness very close to that of politicians may well be available for higher levels of participation should the appropriate political stimulus occur.[33]

A consideration that should not be neglected when thinking about political participation is the possibility that a similar action in one set of circumstances would have political repercussions and in another set would not. Consider the same sort of circumstances as those discussed above but in this case on a private estate. In the altered circumstances it is much more likely that public authorities would not be drawn into the issue. In the one case the organization attempts to influence authoritative allocations of values, whilst in the other it does not; yet basically the actions taken are similar although the council tenants are, by virtue of their public tenancy, impelled to take overtly 'political' action.

This consideration suggests that 'political' involvement is a fairly arbitrary category and that the same activities may in one case be classified as political, whilst in another they would come under another category, such as economic or social. It appears that the context of the action rather than the action itself is important since, in the case mentioned, the activities of the tenant associations produced responses from local parties and councillors, whereas in the private case this is less likely as the interests of the councillors may be less threatened. Further, political participation is itself a contextual category in that an activity which in Britain has a strong political tone does not in the US. For example, in the UK since nearly all doctors are paid by the state it follows that a demand for higher salaries necessarily involves political arbitration, whilst in the US this is not necessarily the case. Or, as in the case of New York and Newark, teachers' pay is a political issue as it is in Britain, but because of the racial composition it is a symbolic, emotive and power issue in the US to an extent unlikely in Britain. Writing a literary essay has usually very little significance politically and is not regarded as a political intervention in the UK, whilst in France it may well be, in Russia it very often is and in China it always is. What this means is that in a comparative perspective political activity—being, for example, a gladiator or being at the political centre—does not necessarily mean the same thing. Electoral and other forms of 'political' activity which may have one meaning in Britain or the US have very different meanings in the USSR and Africa.

9.5. Political Participation: Some Conclusions

It is apparent that there is little in the way of coherent and systematic theory relating social, psychological and political variables to the act of participation in politics. The one systematic theory suffered from the major difficulty that on its own premises it could not easily account for high rates of participation and the concept of sub-threshold had to be introduced and the rather curious notion that voting is itself a pleasurable act had to be made. What we are left with is a mass of correlated data which is explained by *ad hoc* theorizing. This is itself a major step forward but what is needed is a theory which relates the data in a consistent fashion. The difficulty is that without such a theory one can, almost indefinitely, spin out associations between, say, turnout and, say, rate of illiteracy, domestic mail *per capita*, government intervention, number of parties, and so on. One can always 'explain' the relationship in terms of a partial sociological theory. Thus, if we found, as well we might, that low electoral turnout is associated with a high illegitimacy rate, it would not be unreasonable to attempt an explanation in terms of anomie, which not only affects the moral life of the community but also leaves people cross-pressured, so inducing them to abstain from voting. Or take the case of the effect that downward mobility is said to have on voting behaviour. Where the vote changes this is said to be adaptation to terminal status: if it remains 'appropriate' to the status of origin this is said to be a consequence of symbolic status maintenance. In other words, much of the theorizing in this area (and, we might add, other areas of political sociology) is *post hoc* and incremental—a little bit of theory is added to explain each empirical deviation from the pattern originally found. This is a technique which Ptolemaic astronomers would have found familiar.

When we turn to comparative research on turnout and participation, the problems are compounded by the absence of statistics and by the fact that cultural and political differences make adequate comparisons more difficult to achieve. Take the example of political efficacy, for which there are standard measuring instruments available which have been tested in many different societies. In a society where the culture stresses the norm of participation, low efficacy may represent a serious estrangement from the political system, but in a more subject political culture low efficacy may simply represent what the citizen conceives as his normal role. Would finding a general distribution of low citizen efficacy in the USSR represent a social norm, or serious estrangement from the system? Looked at in a slightly different perspective, we also have the problem of comparing the modes of participation between countries. Clearly, as we suggested earlier, elections do not mean the same to people in all countries despite the fact that turnouts are generally high and more important opportunities for participation are variously structured. What looks like a strike over wages and conditions in Spain may be a structurally determined mode of participation which in another country might take the form of mob rioting or a higher rate of electoral abstention or the formation of pressure groups.

Given these difficulties, however, have we been able to move any closer to an understanding of political participation? We have in two ways. Firstly, it has proved possible to demonstrate that political participation has both a social and a psychological component. Secondly, we have seen that the resources and opportunities for such participation are not equally distributed and, *vide* Lane, this does give us a possible explanation of the question: 'Given that all people have the need to be approved, to dominate, to win approval, to reject/accept parents, to understand themselves and their milieu, why do some choose to do so politically whilst others choose some other way?' Although it is foolish to be dogmatic, it is quite probable that it has something to do with resources. It is not the case that all on the periphery lack opportunity for meeting psychological needs by political activity but that they have less. Moreover, it is the case that these resources or opportunities are *not* distributed randomly between the social classes—however defined—but rather that the middle-classes, or stratum, of the population have the distribution quite markedly skewed towards them. Hence, a proposition such as Dahl's that 'people are less likely to get involved in politics if they place a low valuation on the rewards to be gained from political involvement relative to the rewards expected from other kinds of human activity' is true but not very helpful.[34] It is not helpful precisely because it seems to be the middle-class—other things being equal—who *consistently* place a high value on participation. Towards the centre they have greater opportunity and, given Downsian rationality, they would probably be acting sensibly to meet their needs by seizing opportunities which involve relatively small sacrifices of effort. Incidentally, this suggestion that participation is functionally related to needs may enable one to overcome the difficulty implicit in the Downs model of getting an explanation for high rates of participation.

References

1. H. McClosky, 'Political Participation', *International Encyclopedia of the Social Sciences*, Collier-Macmillan, New York, 1968.
2. L. Milbrath, *Political Participation*, Rand McNally, Chicago, 1965, p. 19.
3. R. Lane, *Political Life*, Free Press, New York, 1959, pp. 101–111.
4. F. Lindenfeld, 'Economic Interest and Political Involvement', *Public Opinion Quarterly*, **28**, 104–111 (1964).
5. S. Rokkan, *Citizens, Elections, Parties*, David McKay Co., New York, 1970, p. 173.
6. L. Milbrath, *Political Participation*, Rand McNally, Chicago, 1965, p. 116.
7. M. Van De Vall, *Labour Organizations*, Cambridge University Press, London, 1970, p. 162.
8. T. Geschwender, 'Status Inconsistency, Social Isolation, and Individual Unrest', *Social Forces*, **48**, 477–483 (1968).
9. I. Goffman, 'Status Consistency and Preference for Change in Power Distribution', *American Sociological Review*, **22**, 275–288 (1957).
10. T. Geschwender, 'Status Inconsistency, Social Isolation, and Individual Unrest', *Social Forces*, **48**, 483 (1968).
11. G. Lenski, 'Status Inconsistency and the Vote: A Four Nations Test', *American Sociological Review*, **32**, 298–301 (1967).
12. J. Galtung, *Theory and Methods of Social Research*, George Allen and Unwin, London, 1967, p. 150.
13. B. Barry, *Sociologists, Economists and Democracy*, Collier-Macmillan, London, 1970, p. 15.
14. P. Fletcher, 'An Explanation of Turnout in Local Elections', *Political Studies*, **17**, 495–502 (1969).
15. S. Rokkan, *Citizens, Elections, Parties*, David McKay Company, New York, 1970, pp. 183–184.
16. R. Alford, 'Class Voting in Anglo-American Political Systems', in S. Lipset and S. Rokkan (eds.), *Party Systems and Voter Alignments*, Free Press, New York, 1967, pp. 67–93; S. Lipset, *Political Man*, Heinemann, London, 1963, ch. 7.
17. H. McClosky, 'Political Participation', *International Encyclopedia of the Social Sciences*, Collier-Macmillan, New York, 1968.
18. L. Milbrath, *Political Participation*, Rand McNally, Chicago, 1965, pp. 56–57; B. Lazerwitz, 'National Data on Participation Rates Among Residential Belts in the U.S.', *American Sociological Review*, **27**, 691–696 (1962).
19. Almond and Verba, *The Civic Culture*, Little, Brown, Boston, 1965, p. 261.
20. E. Nordlinger, *The Working Class Tories*, MacGibbon and Kee, London, 1967, pp. 111–136.
21. A. Campbell, 'The Passive Citizen', *Acta Sociologica*, **6**, 9–21 (1962); M. Clinard (ed.), *Anomie and Deviant Behaviour*, Free Press, Glencoe, 1964, esp. pp. 1–56.
22. F. Templeton, 'Alienation and Political Participation', *Public Opinion Quarterly*, **30**, 249–261 (1966).
23. H. McClosky, 'Conservatism and Personality', *APSR*, **52**, 44 (1968).
24. A. Campbell, P. Converse, W. Miller and D. Stokes, *The American Voter*, Wiley, New York, 1960, p, 519.

25. A. Campbell, P. Converse, W. Miller and D. Stokes, *The American Voter*, Wiley, New York, 1960, p. 518.
26. R. E. Agger, M. Goldstein and S. Pearl, 'Political Cynicism: Measurement and Meaning', *Journal of Politics*, **23**, 477–506 (1961).
27. L. Milbrath, 'Predisposition Toward Political Contention', *Western Political Quarterly*, **13**, 5–18 (1960).
28. B. Crick, 'The Peaceable Kingdom', *Twentieth Century*, **173**, 51–60 (1964/5); C. Tilly, 'Collective Violence in European Perspective', in H. Graham and T. Gurr (eds.), *The History of Violence in America*, Praeger, New York, 1969, pp. 4–45.
29. C. S. Emden, *The People and the Constitution*, Oxford University Press, London, 1933, esp. chs. 3 and 4.
30. S. Rokkan, *Citizens, Elections, Parties*, David McKay Co., New York, 1970, ch. 11; A. H. Birch, 'England and Wales' and G. Dupeux, 'France', in a special issue of the *International Social Science Journal*, 'Citizen Participation in Political Life', **12**, 15–26 and 40–52 (1960).
31. L. Milbrath, *Political Participation*, Rand McNally, Chicago, 1965, p. 104.
32. A. Brier and R. E. Dowse, 'Political Mobilisation: A Case Study', *International Review of Community Development*, **19–20**, 327–340 (1968), and 'The Politics of the A-Political', *Political Studies*, **17**, 334–339 (1969).
33. I. Budge, *Agreement and the Stability of Democracy*, Markham, Chicago, 1970, pp. 130–144.
34. R. Dahl, *Modern Political Analysis*, 2nd ed., Prentice-Hall, New Jersey, 1970, p. 79.

Notes and Further Reading

1. L. Milbrath, *Political Participation*, Rand McNally, Chicago, 1965, p. 18; his list does not include violent activities, which we deal with in Chapter 10.
2. See D. Butler and D. Stokes, *Political Change in Britain*, Macmillan, London, 1969, p. 25, for very similar figures.
3. See also T. Fox and S. M. Miller, 'Occupational Stratification and Mobility', in R. Merrit and S. Rokkan, *Comparing Nations*, Yale University Press, New Haven, 1966, pp. 217–237.
4. See E. Maccoby, 'Youth and Political Change', *Public Opinion Quarterly*, **13**, 23–39 (1954); this finding is confirmed for the UK also.
5. A. Downs, *An Economic Theory of Democracy*, Harper and Row, New York, 1957, p. 223, our italics. We were sensitized to this point after discussion with our colleague J. Stanyer. For a development of the point that political activity is a form of play see H. Kariel, 'Expanding the Political Present', *APSR*, **63**, 773–774 (1969).
6. See the statistical appendix by P. Fletcher to L. J. Sharpe (ed.), *Voting in Cities*, Macmillan, London, 1967, pp. 290–336. In the UK general election of 1964 the same relationship was not observed, see D. Butler and A. King, *The 1964 General Election*, Macmillan, London, 1965, appendix 2, but for 1966 'In marginals, apathetic voters were much more likely to turn out', D. Butler and A. King, *The British General Election of 1966*, Macmillan, London, 1966, p. 284.

7. Scores indicate assent or dissent with a series of questions taken to tap efficacy and alienation.
8. See L. Milbrath, *Political Participation*, Rand McNally, Chicago, 1965, pp. 61–64, for the evidence.
9. For example, when considering the somewhat dramatic level of participation discussed under the heading 'Assassination Attempts Directed at the Office of President' the authors explain that 'neither socio-economic class nor employment seem to establish a common thread', in J. Kirkham, S. Levy and W. Crotty, *Assassination and Political Violence*, Bantam Books, New York, 1970, p. 79.
10. The authors also have a table which demonstrates that alienation, independent of education, also helps to explain both decisions to vote and direction of vote.
11. Milbrath gives x^2 tests for his data; Table 25, $x^2p < 0.001$ and Table 26, $x^2p < 0.05$ and the second is barely acceptable. Using his figures we calculated the gamma associations for both tables: Table 25, gamma = 0.6, and Table 26, gamma = 0.44, ie the association drops.
12. For a fuller development on this perspective, see S. Greer, 'The Social Structure and the Political Process of Suburbia', *American Sociology Review*, **25**, 514–526 (1960).

10

THE PLACE OF ELECTIONS IN THE POLITICAL PROCESS

10.1. Elections and the Political Process

ELECTIONS ARE ONE type of social mechanism, amongst others, for aggregating preferences of a particular kind. An election is, therefore, a procedure recognized by the rules of an organization, be it a state, a club, a voluntary organization or whatever, where all, or some, of the members choose a smaller number of persons to hold an office, or offices, of authority within that organization.[1] As such, the first function we shall mention is to provide the opportunity for a peaceful succession and transfer of office. An election is not, of course, the only way in which this can be met, since it is perfectly simple to achieve a peaceful succession by direct appointment, a rule of primogeniture or by applying other rules of inheritance or of physical or spiritual or mental fitness for office. It is quite usual for such other techniques of transference of authority to be mixed up with the purely elective, as is the case with age, sex, or criminal or mental bars to putting oneself forward for election. However, formally at least, in contemporary political systems elections of one sort or another seem to be the established manner of rotating and transferring office, although it is the case that there is considerable variation in what is considered to be an office suitable for election. For example, in the US many judges and legal officers are elected, whilst in Europe the system is appointive; in Yugoslavia important factory officials are elected whilst elsewhere this is comparatively rare; in the US the Cabinet is not selected from amongst elected politicians whilst in the UK it is. The point is that, although there is considerable variation in the scope of elections, most contemporary political systems have elections of one sort or another. The Yale Data Programme reports that of the hundred different nations for which information was available ninety-two had held elections in the preceding six years.[2]

In the West, development of electoral systems can be analysed employing an ideal type of five successive stages. The first stage—the pre-revolutionary phase—was characterized by marked local variations in franchise practices, with citizenship being largely determined by membership of an estate, whether of nobility, clergy, artisan, merchant or freehold peasantry. The American and French Revolutions mark the beginnings of a second stage, when the franchise rules became more standardized. By and large, access to the political arena was restricted, and there was a formal equality of influence amongst the citizenry. This is the classical era of the political philosophy of formal equality, that of utilitarianism and its variants. Citizenship in this era was in practice dependent upon legal requirements, such as property or income, since it was still widely believed that economic dependence necessarily implied a lack of the independence without which (reasonable) political judgement would be impossible. Such restrictions are abolished in the third stage with the emergence of the mass electorate, although residual individual inequalities still persisted, often in the form of multiple votes for holders of university degrees, businessmen, and so on. Similarly, in this stage there is considerable variation in the ratio of votes to representatives. The process of mass mobilization continues into a fourth stage, when all signs of significant economic and social criteria as a requirement for the vote, for men over a certain age, are abolished but marked differences in the vote–representation ratio still persist. The fifth, and current, phase is one of continued 'democratization' by extending the franchise to all adults, lowering the age of voting, lowering the age at which one may become a representative, abolishing property and educational qualifications for representatives, making concerted efforts to equalize the vote–representation ratio—and paying representatives in order to increase the number of 'lower-class' legislators.[*1*]

Only Britain, Belgium and Sweden have passed through these five stages in anything closely resembling a regular evolutionary sequence, as contrasted with the abrupt and frequently violent changes in, say, France. Countries have also varied in the length of time taken to arrive at the fourth and fifth stages. In Britain, it took more than a hundred years from the passing of the Reform Bill of 1832 to the abolition of multiple votes in 1948 and the lowering of the age of franchise in 1969. In France, the transition from the first to the fourth stage took only four years, but most European countries by the end of World War I had opted for universal male suffrage and many for female suffrage also. With the ending of World War II and the subsequent dismemberment of the colonial empires, the principle of one man one vote gained worldwide currency, not only in countries with low levels of literacy but also in countries lacking a tradition of national government.

As a means of bringing the political periphery into the political arena, elections may be understood to reflect changing opinions and social conceptions about citizenship and equality. All are now equal before the ballot box, even if they are not equal in other respects, and this equality is symbolized by the secrecy of the ballot. By bringing the periphery into politics, elections may also serve to help form a sense of political community, or of a shared interest in the polity. As Shils has argued, 'The drawing of the whole adult population periodically into contact with the symbols of the centre of national political life must . . . have immeasurable consequences by stirring people up and giving them a sense of their own potential significance and attaching their sentiments to symbols which comprehend the entire nation'.[3] In this way it can be argued that elections serve to integrate an organization or polity by maintaining the legitimacy of the entity. Thus, it is suggested that in a number of developing nations, where legitimacy is poorly developed, electoral participation can lead individuals to become mobilized and more involved in, and receptive to, regulation, with or without party competition. On the other hand, elections may also serve in such countries to exacerbate ethnic or religious cleavages especially when there are ethnic or religious parties, as the case of the Congo illustrates; and, as the very recent phenomenon of the one-party state clearly shows, elections by themselves, without any underlying agreement by those involved to adhere to the 'verdict', are not likely to prove integrative. In short, a peaceful and meaningful election is almost certainly a consequence of, not a cause of, political integration.

Elections may also be seen as one method amongst others whereby the actions of the governors may be influenced by the governed. Normally, this process is understood to take place in the following ways. Firstly, elections provide an opportunity for the aggrieved to put forward candidates of their own and, hopefully, to become governors themselves. Secondly, elections provide an opportunity for the aggrieved to bring their grievances to those seeking office, who are likely to be especially sensitive at such a time. Thirdly, governors in anticipation of the first two possibilities may be the more disposed to cut their policies to suit their constituents. From this perspective the essential role of the election is to act as a mechanism whereby the governors are circumscribed and made aware that their position is a contingent one, at least where there is a real possibility that they may be ousted from office. This is, of course, an essential element in the democratic 'myth', the idea that the rulers are chosen by and rule with the approval of the people and that when this approval is withdrawn the rulers are likely to face defeat—and accept it—at an election. In a sense, if elections are more than a simple ritual of solidarity it is necessary that in some way they allow the translation of at least the majority interests into public policy. Various methods have been tried and suggested to make this possibility more obvious to the rulers: the mandate, the recall, the referendum, the popular initiative, are all devices which have the basic function of making the office-holders sensitive to their constituents' wishes. Equally, the various proposals for electoral reform are based upon, amongst other things, the idea that, through an electoral device which makes the representative assembly in some sense a microcosm of the electors, the assembly will be more sensitive to the electors. Again, the shortening of the legal period between elections, the old Chartists' demand for annual Parliaments, the Guild Socialist concept of the trades Parliament, were similarly intended to reduce the distance between governors and governed, through legal electoral devices.[2]

Elections can, therefore, be understood as one weapon in an armoury by which the governors are controlled; others include violence such as riots and political assassination and the exercise of inter-election influence through pressure groups, informal contacts, public opinion polls and, at a more rarified level, the democratic political culture, or just plain prudence. But it is much easier to assert in a general way that because a ruler can be replaced by election he is more likely to be responsive, to act in a non-arbitrary fashion, than it is to demonstrate that elections actually do restrain governors.[3] The difficulties involved in demonstrating the independent impact of elections in restraining governors are legion. Firstly, it is necessary to demonstrate that, in fact, without elections rulers are likely to act in an arbitrary manner: that is, we need to know what a ruler would have done had there not been an election. Assuming (heroically) that this can be done, we have next to show that, independently of the whole arsenal a population may have at its disposal, the election does help to restrain the ruler, and this task is probably impossible. It is probably impossible for any of the totalitarian or authoritarian countries, where elections are regularly held but are ritualistic, although one cannot be certain that the leadership does not use them to gauge popular feelings. Thirdly, in order to assess the restraining effect of an election it is necessary to know what an election is supposed to be about and what people think it is about. Although this is a relatively well-researched area, it is the case that data from the area can only be of limited value in answering the question. This for two reasons: (1) as we shall see, people generally have only the vaguest notions of what the issues are and what the party differences on them are, and (2) it is by no means clear that the electoral victor(s) is/are committed to anything very specific.

The evidence that people's level of political awareness is very low is almost overwhelming. We have already given very considerable evidence indicating that one's voting preference is determined by or at least strongly associated with factors such as social class, parents' voting preferences, reference groups and religious behaviour. Of itself, this fact does not undermine the idea that people are acting in a reasonable, or even rational, manner when allowing these considerations to influence them. Nor does it mean that elections do not act as perfectly satisfactory transmission belts of voters' preferences, provided it is possible to demonstrate that even if people do have the habit of voting they are also aware of what they are voting for and what they are voting against. It is just at this point that the connection is weakest, although, using the concept of party 'image', it may be possible to demonstrate that even if people are uninformed about electoral issues, nevertheless generally the 'image' of the party which attracts them corresponds broadly with its legislative record and that record is generally favourable to its supporters. However, the evidence from both the US and Britain is that loyal party supporters often have little idea of the party programmes or are actually opposed to them, and are only slightly better at correctly attributing policies to parties than they would be if they attributed them randomly.[*4*]

In a Greenwich survey it was found that a majority of the Labour and Conservative supporters were in substantial disagreement with many important aspects of their party's programme, whilst 21 per cent of the Labour supporters were actually more in agreement with Conservative than with Labour policies.[4] Summing up the British evidence, Blondel writes that 'Electors hold views which are not those of their party and still vote for that party'.[5] As our previous discussion of opinion suggested, people actually seem more prepared to change their opinion to that of their preferred party than they are to change their party preference. Hence, we conclude that private opinion is only one of a number of factors behind a voting preference, so that we cannot make the claim that people consistently use elections to transmit their policy opinions, or preferences, since a substantial number of people have neither. In this sense, anyway, it is hard to see how elections act as either a spur or a brake on governors.

Yet it may still be the case that even if for most of the population elections do not loom large, nevertheless for those who govern they do, since, as a matter of fact, incumbents are frequently defeated and there is no reason to suppose that they court defeat. For example, in the UK the easy pre-election Budget is hardly a novelty. This suggests that the incumbents may well be made more sensitive to the fear of losing office. Unfortunately, hard evidence on this point is extremely rare; although it is by no means unusual to come across assertions that politicians do bend with the electoral winds, it is equally usual to come across proud references, by politicians, to their consciences which will not allow them to bend to every passing whim of the public. Although the electoral defeat of an incumbent is not rare, it is nevertheless the case that the incumbent is much more likely to win an election than he is to lose it. In the UK, about 75 per cent of MPs from the two major parties are elected more than once and over 50 per cent of the MPs from the two major parties are elected between three and five times.[6] It is quite rare for a seat to change allegiance even once in a decade, so that in the UK about 87 per cent of seats contested between 1950 and 1959 remained with the same party.[7] In the US the comparable figures are even higher.[*5*]

Much more tenuous than this is the evidence demonstrating that elections do affect politicians' behaviour. Jones, in an attempt to measure this dimension, divided a batch of US Congressmen into three groups, (1) those who lost 5 per cent of their votes in a previous election, (2) those who lost less than 5 per cent and (3) those who increased their margins. He then compared these groups by correlating their pre-election behaviour on a range of economic and political issues. One might have predicted that those with the greatest losses would have changed their behaviour most, but he observed no statistically significant change of behaviour in any group and concluded that 'there is support in these data for the notion that a representative will not change his policy making behaviour because of the result of his own election'.[8] However, it is almost certainly true that the American legislator is more responsive to constituent opinion than is the British MP, if only because the latter does not have the protection of a strong party machine in the legislature or a national party to insulate him from strong local interests.[9]

It is massively difficult in any election campaign to know what is being discussed by most people and, more important, no one really knows what a general election actually decides. It is fairly clear, in recent British elections, that a decision is made about which party leader is to form an administration and the same is true of most Atlantic states, but it is by no means clear to what substantive issues that leader is committed. Since no one can tell what the issues may be until after the Government assumes office, it is quite obvious that elections cannot bind a Government. But since politicians are not as a corporate body known for the crystal clarity of their promises, ambiguity being the tribal totem, it becomes very difficult to say, with any certainty, what an electoral victor is pledged to, other than doing his best in difficult circumstances.[*6*] Writing of the 1956 presidential election in the US, during which the questions of nuclear bomb testing and the draft arose, Kelly explains that 'nothing was said by either candidate that would not have permitted him with consistency and political decorum to (a) ask for the end of the draft, or (b) not to ask for the end of the draft'. On all the policy issues which arose, 'Each candidate defined his position in terms so general that it became almost impossible to distinguish it from that of his opponent'.[10] Even assuming that the issues are presented with unusual clarity at an election, one still cannot unambiguously argue that the winning party has a mandate to go ahead with certain issues because, as we suggested above, people very often vote for a party *despite* its programme.

It probably follows from the above discussion that it is best not to regard elections as having very much to do with specific issues nor with giving a ruling group anything more concrete than general approval of its record. In many countries, even this would be too strong a formulation. In countries such as the USSR it is better to see an election as a ritual 'public display of personal re-affirmation of the Soviet way of life and the party leadership' rather than a technique of choosing rulers.[7] Indeed, although this is rather speculative, it is not unlikely that, to a greater or lesser extent, this ritual element is present in most elections. The street-corner meetings which nobody attends, the 'literature' which nobody reads, the parades, flags, rallies of the faithful, reiteration of the emotive slogans, all point to the ritual element involved in elections. Looked at from this angle, MacKenzie has argued that elections are 'rituals of choice', their binding character being derived from the participation of the individual as a chooser in a social act which confers legitimate authority on the person chosen.[11] The act of voting then becomes a symbolic expression of the voter's identification with his party, community, group, or whatever. From an anthropological angle Gluckman, discussing the part played by ritual in a tribal society, suggests that it is a relatively harmless way of releasing the tensions which have their source in social order. All individuals have to recognize competing demands on their time and resources; group loyalties conflict, self-interest may conflict with group interest and groups have conflicting interests, so that 'separate interests develop in which several loyalties conflict with the moral unity of the major group'.[12] In this situation of endemic conflict, 'Reconciliation of quarrelling persons is explicitly sought through celebration of ritual . . . Furthermore, rituals are celebrated which often explain and revive sentiments which sustain a moral order; they induce certain moods and sentiments, they teach men to feel and teach them what they ought to feel about.'[*8*]

In a similar way, it can be argued that in the more industrialized societies there are a number of major cleavages—between the haves and the have nots, between town and country, between regions, between religions, between ethnic groups and even between generations—and these are sources of tension. Probably the major cleavage is that between lower-income groups and the higher, and it is quite normal for this basic cleavage to find its expression in elections, with the lower-income groups voting for the parties of the left and the higher-income groups the right. As we have seen, this simple picture is clouded by religious, regional and ethnic factors but, as a generalization, it is an accurate one. Leftist parties represent the economic or social interests of the poor, which are greater equality, more satisfying work and higher status, whilst rightist parties represent the desire for the better off to remain better off.[*9*] This fact is a possible source of conflict and has, of course, historically been a very usual cause of civil strife. By projecting this potential source of conflict into the open, and developing a quasi-ritualized set of rules and the operations of an electoral situation, the possibility of open conflict is muted. Elections are, therefore, as Lipset puts it, 'the expressions of the democratic class struggle', where class conflict becomes institutionalized and the election is not only a method of choosing a leadership but also a ritualistic expression of the common moral order.

A major problem arises at this point. Do elections have more substantive consequences than simply affirming the national order, which may well be an order systematically working to the disadvantage of quite considerable sectors of the population? Put slightly differently, does the fact that one party, rather than another, wins an election produce significant changes in the distribution of national resources or is it the case, as some have claimed, that elections are merely devices by which ruling groups seduce the masses with illusions of power and influence.

> And thus, whichever way I vote,
> I get into the same old boat,
> And my Mr Brown and Mr Grey
> Are rowing it in the same old way.
>
> *E. M. Forster*

It is difficult to dispute that in almost any substantive sense of the word the distribution of resources in industrial societies is extremely unequal and there is little evidence that, overall, there has been a major amelioration of this situation in the twentieth century. Surveying the evidence for the UK, one book points out that 'Britain today is not a significantly more equal society than when the Labour Party was brought into existence by the unions over sixty years ago'.[*10*] For the US, Kolko claims that between 1910 and 1957 'no significant trend towards income equality' could be detected.[13] John Strachey, generalizing about modern capitalist societies, writes that 'it has taken the utmost efforts of 90 per cent of the population to prevent their share of the national product from falling . . . capitalism has, in fact, an innate tendency to extreme and ever growing inequality. For how otherwise could all the culminatively equalitarian measures, which the popular forces have succeeded in enacting over the last hundred years done little more than hold the position constant?'[14] Additionally, there is the immense accumulation of evidence that in many other ways—access to education, to positions of influence, possession of wealth, length of life expectancy and so on—although the conditions of the have nots have immeasurably improved in all industrial societies overall, there has not been any very significant change in the distribution of resources.[*11*] Parkin, in a comparative survey of the effect that socialist parties have had on bringing about a redistribution of resources in capitalist countries, concluded that 'all this must raise serious doubts on claims concerning the ability of parties or governments based on the underclass to redistribute material rewards in an egalitarian manner'. Rather, what has apparently happened is that the countries which have electorally successful socialist parties are also the countries which have the highest rates of upward social mobility from the working-class and the highest percentage of working-class pupils in grammar schools. The inference Parkin draws is that in countries with a record of socialist rule the effect of that rule has been to 'broaden the social base of recruitment to privileged positions (rather) than to equalise rewards attached to different positions'.[15]

This rather limited survey serves to cast doubt on the efficacy of elections as instruments in the democratic class struggle, at least if that struggle is seen as being about the possession of resources. Although it is the case that most people are better off, this is almost certainly, in the main, as a result of factors other than electoral policies: between 1870 and 1950, in the UK, the share of wages in the national income varied between 38.6 per cent and 41.9 per cent.[*12*] What this suggests is that if people think that by engaging in elections they are working effectively to alter the distribution of national resources between haves and have nots they may well be mistaken. It may also be taken as inferential evidence that those who believe elections to be rituals rather than effective means through which the majority of the population can alter the distribution of resources towards themselves may well be correct. However, if elections are not especially satisfactory as devices in effecting redistribution they may well be the best way of choosing rulers, they may also be a useful source of tension reduction through the provision of 'ritualized pseudo-conflicts' and they may in addition be important factors in shaping the character of party systems. It is to this latter consideration that we now turn.

10.2. Elections and Party Systems

Electoral systems differ widely in their rules, but broadly they may be divided into two major types according to how the number of votes cast is related to the number of representatives. One type, the proportional system, emphasizes the importance of a given number of votes electing a given number of representatives whilst the other, the plurality system, divides the country into constituencies each electing a single member, this being the candidate obtaining the most votes. It has been argued that this division is the major variable affecting the number of parties in a country. This idea is most strongly associated with Duverger, who has claimed that it is 'most nearly perhaps to a true sociological law' that there is an 'almost complete correlation between . . . the simple majority single-ballot system and the two party system: dualist (two party) countries use the simple majority vote and the simple majority countries are dualist'.[*13*]

On the other hand, the large number of proportional techniques favour multi-party systems. Exceptions to the 'true sociological law' are held to be rare and are as a result of special conditions (which are, nevertheless, very numerous). Even when the third parties do appear in single ballot simple majority systems, the system operates in such a manner as to return to the 'natural' dualistic conditions.[*14*] The forces producing this result are twofold. Firstly, a mechanical factor which inevitably leads to the under-representation of the third party, and secondly, a psychological consideration which leads voters to see that if they vote for the weakest of the three parties, in a simple majority single ballot system, their votes are wasted 'whence their natural tendency to transfer their votes to the less evil of the two adversaries'.[*15*]

Let us first examine whether, as a matter of fact, the relationship posited by Duverger's law exists in the real world. Blondel has shown that, in general, those countries with simple majority systems are likely to be two-party systems, whilst those with proportional techniques are more likely to be multi-party systems (see Table 28).

Using a larger sample than that of Blondel, Rae in another study of the relationship suggests that party systems are quite strongly associated with electoral systems and he advances the proposition that 'Plurality formulae are always associated with two party competition except where strong local minority parties exist'.[16] Hence, the empirical evidence does suggest that there is a relationship between electoral systems and party systems,

TABLE 28. Electoral Systems and Numbers of Parties

	Number of countries			
Atlantic area	Single-member majority one ballot	P.R. (any system)	Other	
No. of parties				
2	4	1	1	
2½	1	4	0	
Multi-dominant	0	5	0	
Multi	0	3	1	
Total	5	13	2	
Whole world				Unknown
No. of parties				
2	10	4	1	6
2½	5	8	1	5
Multi-dominant	1	8	0	2
Multi	0	5	1	1
Total	16	25	3	14

Table taken from J. Blondel, *An Introduction to Comparative Government*, Weidenfeld and Nicolson, London, 1969, p. 202.

but that it certainly is not as strong as Duverger implies since there are a number of important intervening variables.

The most important of these variables is the existence of strong and continuing local minority parties where plurality systems are operative. Such minority parties may be based upon religion, linguistic and ethnic sentiments, as is the case in Canada, where minority party candidates regularly win when competing with the candidates from the two major parties. Again, as in the case of Austria, proportional representation goes hand in hand with two-party legislative competition, because divisive forces are too few and too weak to support minority parties, which receive only about 10 per cent of the popular vote and about 5 per cent of the seats.[17] In both Germany and Italy before 1919, when plurality systems operated, this did not divide parliamentary representation into two homogeneous bodies of opinion. In Italy, plurality systems resulted in a tendency to elect a deputy for his local influence, and the deputy had no fixed party allegiance. When a proportional system was introduced in 1919, there was no substantial increase in the number of parties.[18] We conclude that whilst electoral systems are significantly associated with party political systems, there are other intervening variables such as social heterogeneity and the possible conflicts engendered by it, the extent to which a country is geographically divided, skill of minority organizers and the whole complex of historical, geographical and social factors influencing party formation and continuity. Hence, it may well be the case that 'only (social) systems which can inherently produce structural balance can "afford" the (plurality) system and consequently that those (social) systems which over a period do not come to be structurally balanced do not find this plurality system politically satisfactory'.[19] Writing of the social division in France, Campbell concurs in this judgement and explains that the introduction of plurality voting would be most unlikely to affect either the party system or the legislature.[*16*] Exactly the same point was emphasized by Grumm, who examined five electoral systems which changed from plurality to proportionality and concluded 'that it may be more accurate to conclude that P.R. is a result rather than a cause of the party system in a given country. Experience has shown that . . . plurality elections produce glaring inequalities and are inappropriate when associated with the multi-party systems . . . The election gamble becomes one in which the odds are almost completely determined . . . On the other hand some parties, due to the geographic distribution of their votes, and the apportionment of the districts, become almost permanently under-represented or over-represented. Eventually, one or more parties begin to demand P.R. as a means of reducing the inequalities . . . When they grow strong enough . . . they then put their demands for P.R. into effect'.[20] Hence, it is more than likely that the association between plurality systems and two parties and between proportional systems and multi-parties is caused by the parties themselves.

Let us now examine the evidence that third and subsequent parties are necessarily under-represented due to the mechanical and psychological factors adduced by Duverger. This can be done by looking at countries which have changed from plurality to a proportional system, and there are five examples—Belgium, Denmark, Norway, Switzerland and Germany—where this is possible.[21] In none of these countries does the evidence suggest that Duverger's law operates, and in Germany 'P.R. was *more* effective in denying representation to very small splinter parties than the former electoral system had been'. In Denmark the introduction of proportionality, in 1920, did not increase the number of parties although it did adjust the party representation to correspond with its electoral support. Similarly in Belgium, the downward trend of the Liberal Party preceded the introduction of proportionality in 1900 and was not prevented by it. The most obvious effect of the proportionality system is that it allocates seats in the legislature more in accord with the votes cast, but it does not appear to affect in any very direct way either the number of votes cast for a party or the number of parties capable of winning seats.

Once established, a two-party system appears to have a momentum of its own and the parties, as we have previously seen, become the major organizing foci of most people when they act politically. On the other hand, if a two-party system is not established, as was the case in France—where local interests, historical memory, pro- and anti-revolutionary tendencies, the clerical issue and so on prevented its emergence and provided a basis for a multi-party system—no amount of electoral rules will easily create a dualistic system. Also, in multi-party systems it may be the case that the child does not have the same opportunities as in two-party systems to learn his parents' affiliation and attach to it, so that 'flash' parties can more easily gain adherents in the former where the emotional bond with a party is weaker.[22] Leys, in an important critique of the Duverger model, has gone beyond a detailed historical and empirical refutation and has demonstrated that, as it stands, the model is actually one which 'predicts' *immobilisme* but which cannot predict the number of parties.[23] Using Duverger's psychological hypothesis—in plurality systems the voter realizes that voting for a third party is a waste and transfers to one of the other two parties—Leys shows that this implies that 'all those parties will be established permanently in the field which are initially in first and second place in any constituency'. It follows that whatever the number of parties initially winning a seat in the legislature that will be the number which will always win seats in the legislature. From this it follows that, in the Duverger model, the actual rules of electoral procedure—proportionality or plurality—cannot affect the number of parties winning seats. If this suggestion is tied in with the previous suggestions about local, regional, ethnic and religious factors, we have, perhaps, a stronger explanation of multi-party systems than previously. That is, if a party appealing to these sentiments does succeed in winning there is no reason to assume that, in a plurality system, the wasted vote proposition it likely to operate against it. If such smaller parties or even declining parties can then somehow succeed in forming a coalition, it is not unlikely that they will turn to a proportional system in the hope of improving their electoral fate, but they are unlikely to do more than marginally increase their representation in the legislature.

10.3. Conclusions

A major implication of this section on elections and the political order is that, by themselves, elections have very little direct influence on the policy and decision-making of government. Probably of more importance are such things as the pressures which the parties and the groups are likely to exert continuously, the politicians' own preferences, external factors such as the state of the economy and foreign relations, prudential consideration, and so on. Perhaps it is the case that elections have a strong mythic or ritualistic element. As is obvious, elections do have a central place in the democratic credo, but it is not easy to justify this central place empirically. So even though the idea of electoral influence on government has something of a mythical status, as any anthropologist well knows, myths and rituals are not to be disregarded. For one thing, when myths are incorporated into people's minds they become part determinants of social reality and hence, to some extent, order mass behaviour. Thus, politicians may well behave as if the democratic myth was reality in at least the sense of taking what they see as electoral opinion as one reference in their decision-making. Certainly a good deal of the campaign rhetoric of politicians suggests this as a possible interpretation. At least one survey of Congressmen implies that although the electorate has almost no idea of the legislative record of its representatives, nevertheless the Congressmen themselves 'feel that they and their records are quite visible to their constituents'. [*17*]

Looked at more ritualistically, the election may serve as a morally binding form of social interaction—provided it can be demonstrated that people do believe that they are an integral part of the democratic creed. Certainly, the very high rates of participation, which we did not succeed in explaining on purely rational grounds, might have something to do with this consideration. It is difficult to explain Soviet and Chinese elections on other than these grounds. Fairly commonplace observations about politicians breaking election pledges suggest that, whatever the objective picture, people do see 'promises' made during elections as somehow binding and to break them as being somehow discreditable. People are aggrieved when the 'rules' of elections are broken, they do interest themselves in the confrontation of politicians during elections and politicians themselves are concerned to preserve the riutal forms, as is evident from the whole paraphernalia of elections in the one-party states of Asia, America and Europe.

References

1. W. J. M. MacKenzie, 'Elections', *International Encyclopedia for the Social Sciences*, Collier-Macmillan, New York, 1968.
2. B. Russett, H. Alker, K. Deutsch and H. Lasswell, *World Handbook of Social and Political Indicators*, Yale University Press, New Haven, 1964, Table 24, pp. 84–87.
3. E. Shils, *Political Development in the New States*, Mouton, Gravenhage, 1969, p. 38.
4. M. Benney, A. Gray and R. Pear, *How People Vote*, Routledge, London, 1956, pp. 145–146.
5. J. Blondel, *Voters, Parties and Leaders*, Penguin, London, 1963, p. 80.
6. P. Buck, *Amateurs and Professionals in British Politics*, Chicago University Press, Chicago, 1963, p. 40.
7. C. O. Jones, 'Inter-Party Competitions in Britain, 1950–9', in R. Benewick and R. E. Dowse, *Readings on British Politics and Government*, London University Press, London, 1968, pp. 78–87.
8. —— 'The Role of the Campaign in Congressional Politics', in M. Kent Jennings and L. H. Zeigler, *The Electoral Process*, Prentice-Hall, New Jersey, 1966.
9. E. Shils, '*The Legislator and His Environment*', in S. Ulmer (ed.), *Introductory Readings in Political Behaviour*, Rand McNally, Chicago, 1961, pp. 85–94.
10. S. Kelly, 'Policy Discussions in Political Campaigning', in J. D. Barber (ed.), *Readings in Citizen Politics*, Markham, Chicago, 1969, pp. 79–81.
11. W. J. M. MacKenzie, 'Elections', *International Encyclopedia for the Social Sciences*, Collier-Macmillan, New York, 1968.
12. M. Gluckman, *Politics, Law and Ritual in the Tribal Society*, Blackwell, Oxford, 1965, p. 247.
13. G. Kolko, *Wealth and Power in America*, Praeger, New York, 1962, p. 13.
14. J. Strachey, *Contemporary Capitalism*, Gollancz, London, 1956, pp. 150–151.
15. F. Parkin, *Class Inequality and Political Order*, MacGibbon and Kee, London, 1971, p. 121.
16. D. Rae, *The Political Consequences of Electoral Laws*, Yale University Press, New Haven, 1967, p. 95.
17. —— *The Political Consequences of Electoral Law*, Yale University Press, New Haven, 1967, pp. 94–95.
18. E. Lakeman and J. Lambert, 'Voting in Democracies', reprinted in H. Eckstein and D. Apter (eds.), *Comparative Politics*, Free Press, New York, 1963, pp. 281–305.
19. J. Blondel, *Voters, Parties and Leaders*, Penguin, London, 1963, p. 32.
20. J. Grumm, 'Theories of Electoral Systems', *Midwest Journal of Political Science*, **2,** 357–376 (1958).
21. —— 'Theories of Electoral Systems', *Midwest Journal of Political Science*, **2** (1958).
22. P. Converse and G. Dupeux, 'Politicization of the Electorate in France and the United States', *Public Opinion Quarterly*, **26,** 1–23 (1962).
23. C. Leys, 'Models, Theories and the Theory of Political Parties', in H. Eckstein and D. Apter (eds.), *Comparative Politics*, Free Press, New York, 1963, pp. 305–315.

Notes and Further Reading

1. For a fuller account of these stages see S. Rokkan, *Citizens, Elections, Parties*, Scandinavian University Books, Oslo, 1970, ch. 4.
2. For an examination of the idea behind these various proposals see Robert Dowse, 'General Elections, Representation and Democracy', in *Parliamentary Affairs*, **15**, 331–346 (1962).
3. Lipset claims that 'The electorate does have *access* to government decisions whenever politicians worry about the electorate's reactions and whether they might not vote for an opponent who favours a different measure', in *Revolution and Counter Revolution*, Basic Books, New York, 1968, p. 404; R. Dahl, *Who Governs?*, Yale University Press, New Haven, 1961, p. 164, states categorically that 'elected leaders keep the real or imagined preferences of constituents constantly in mind in deciding what policies to adopt or reject'.
4. R. Milne and H. MacKenzie, *Marginal Seat*, Hansard Society, London, 1958, p. 121. But J. Blumler and D. McQuail, *Television in Politics*, Faber and Faber, London, 1968, ch. 9, do demonstrate that the ability to make correct attributions increases during elections.
5. C. O. Jones, 'The Role of the Campaign in Congressional Politics', in M. Kent Jennings and L. H. Zeigler, *The Electoral Process*, Prentice-Hall, New Jersey, 1966, pp. 21–41. But see W. Crane, 'Do Representatives Represent?', *The Journal of Politics*, **22**, 295–299 (1960), who shows that 84 of 99 Wisconsin legislators voted in the same way as their districts had voted in a referendum. He also reports that the legislators argued that this did no violence to their conscience since they agreed with their districts on the issue. H. Ingram, 'The Impact of Constituency on the Process of Legislating', *Western Political Quarterly*, **22**, 265–279 (1969) argues that the more active a representative is as a legislator the *less* likely he is to respond to constituency considerations.
6. See M. Edelman, *The Symbolic Uses of Politics*, University of Illinois Press, Urbana, 1964, esp. chs. 6–7, for an extremely interesting discussion of political language.
7. W. Swearer, 'The Function of Soviet Local Elections', *Midwest Journal of Political Science*, **5**, 149 (1961). E. Jacobs, 'Soviet Local Elections', *Soviet Studies*, **22**, 61–76 (1970), endorses this and adds that they also provide the opportunity to 'involve a huge number of people in the workings of the state, both as electors and as candidates for office'.
8. M. Swartz (ed.), *Local Level Politics*, Aldine, Chicago, 1968. The words quoted are part of Swartz's summary of a number of papers on political and ritual in 'simple' societies.
9. For a survey of the evidence for this claim see S. Lipset, *Political Man*, Heinemann, London, 1963, ch. 7.
10. R. Blackburn and A. Cockburn (eds.), *The Incompatibles*, Penguin, London, 1967, p. 16. But see A. Carr Saunders, D. Caradog Jones and C. Moser, *A Survey of the Social Conditions of England and Wales*, Clarendon Press, Oxford, 1958, ch. 11, which does show quite considerable redistribution of *earned* income.
11. It is quite likely that governmental intervention to improve the health and

general conditions of the masses has more to do with the needs of martial efficiency and political stability than with elections!

12. E. Phelps-Brown and E. P. Hart, 'The Share of Wages in the National Income', *Economic Journal*, **62,** 253–277 (1952), but the percentage earning this relatively stable percentage of national income was dramatically reduced.
13. M. Duverger, *Political Parties*, Methuen, London, 1954, p. 217. A difficulty is that Duverger actually claims a little later (p. 223) that the 'true effect of the simple majority system is limited to local bi-partism' so that he is presumably committed to the proposition that his sociological law is a statistical 'happenstance'.
14. —— *Political Parties*, Methuen, London, 1954, pp. 226–227; see p. 215 for his claim that 'the two party system seems to correspond to the nature of things'.
15. —— *Political Parties*, Methuen, London, 1954, p. 226. As a matter of fact to the extent that it is possible to isolate the psychological—or rational—factor the evidence is that it did *not* operate in Britain during the period 1892–1966; see W. Shively, 'The Elusive Psychological Factor', in *Comparative Politics*, **3,** 115–125 (1970).
16. P. Campbell, *French Electoral Systems and Elections Since 1789*, Faber, London, 1968, p. 32. It is fair to add here that Duverger has in fact 'repealed' his law and now believes that 'The influence of the electoral system is . . . minor compared with that of socio-economic factors and even cultural factors', *The Idea of Politics*, Methuen, London, 1966, p. 116.
17. W. Miller and D. Stokes, 'Constituency Influence in Congress', *APSR*, **57,** 45–56. This is also confirmed in C. Cnudde and D. J. McCrone, 'The Linkage Between Constituency Attitudes and Congressional Voting Behaviour', *APSR*, **60,** 66–72 (1966).

11

POLITICAL ORGANIZATIONS I: PARTIES

11.1. Introduction

POLITICAL SCIENTISTS have been one-sided in their approach to the study of political parties; many eminent scholars have furnished us with descriptive, historical, anecdotal and normative studies, but few have attempted consistently to explain the prevalence of the two-party system in modern Western democracies. Similarly, although a large proportion of the world's population live under a one-party system, this phenomenon has been relatively neglected by political scientists. In this chapter we shall discuss the origin and development of political parties, and then investigate some structures and processes of political parties in both competitive and non-competitive systems.

As a society increases both in population and extent, so the organizational problems of feeding and coordinating such a society become increasingly complex. In a tribe, the chief and his aides are perfectly capable of making and executing organizational decisions on behalf of the whole community. In a bureaucratic empire, the leader's household is considerably bigger as it is responsible for the coordination of more people stretched over a wider area, but decisions are still made by the leader and his followers. In the modern state, however, authority is diffused and the organization of the society is done by complex, specialized and formalized bureaucratic administrations. An integral part of this mass of decision-making is done by the political parties, influenced by another form of political organization we shall discuss in the next chapter, pressure groups.

The role of the political party in the modern state more specifically involves the practice and justification of political authority, the recruitment and removal of leaders, the mobilization of opinion, the ordering of public policy and the balancing of group interest. In short, the political party 'provides the major connective linkage between separate formal agencies and officials of government and between official and non-official (extra-governmental) holders of power'.[1]

Before discussing the various factors that have led to the rise of political parties it is necessary to examine the various definitions that have been put forward.

La Palombara and Weiner, putting forward a functionalist characterization, assert that in whatever type of political society a party is found it appears to perform some common functions. Firstly, 'it is expected to organise public opinion and to communicate demands to the centre of governmental power and decision'; secondly, 'it must articulate to its followers the concept and meaning of the broader community'; and thirdly, the party 'is likely to be intimately involved in political recruitment—the selection of the political leadership in whose hands powers and decision will in large measure reside'.[2]

The difficulty with this and similar formulations is that it comes dangerously close to ruling out most of the organizations we would call political parties. For example, one may assess how well certain parties perform these functions, and one can gauge whether certain functions are being emphasized at the expense of others. It would seem preferable to conceive of these so-called functions as variables to be explained and explored. Although the capacity a party has to mobilize public opinion and to give its followers a sense of the broader community and its suitability to be involved in political recruitment are all factors associated with the behaviour of political parties, they do not stand up alone as a definition of parties.

Coleman and Rosberg provide a better formulation when they assert 'political parties are associations formally organised with the explicit and declared purpose of acquiring and/or maintaining legal control, either singly or in coalition or electoral competition with other similar associations over the personnel and the policy of the government of an actual prospective sovereign state'.[3]

The stress on electoral competition practically rules out 'one-party' states in this definition, but it is an improvement on the functionalist definition because it begs fewer questions and it includes most of what we would want to discuss under the term 'party'.

The definition 'any organisation which nominates candidates for election to a legislature'[4] includes not only the traditional European parties but also those one-party states where the party at least goes through the motions of legislative representation. It also includes those parties which for one reason or another are not permitted to nominate candidates, but would do so otherwise. Hence, by omitting a competitive element, the definition of a political party can embrace those parties in one-party states as well. The definition does, however, exclude interest groups, parliamentary cliques and revolutionary movements that do not nominate candidates.

11.2. The Origin and Development of Parties

It has been suggested that the political party is the creation of a particular kind of political society. The term 'political party' itself emerged in the nineteenth century with the beginning of representative government and the expansion of the suffrage in Europe and the United States. Then it designated a group of people whose aim was to capture public office in electoral competition with one or more other such groups. Later, of course, the term was extended to include organizations not directly engaged in electoral competition, such as minor parties with virtually no hope of providing serious electoral rivalry, revolutionary parties working outside an elective framework and the governing parties in totalitarian and dictatorial societies.

The political party, then, is a type of political organization which emerges when the activities of a political system reach a certain degree of complexity which requires the development of new and wider political forms. In particular, the requirement encouraging the emergence of parties is when those who seek to win or maintain political power, within a large-scale and complex political system, need to seek the support of the larger public. The influence of social crises is argued to be crucial, especially crises of *legitimacy*, *participation* and *integration.* Here the suggestion is that the development of political systems often involves crises characterized by such systemic experiences as movements from a traditional to a more modern polity, changes in demographic patterns, modes of production, stratification systems, and the like, which involve a recasting of existing institutions or the development of new institutions. So far as the political system is concerned, the three types of crises mentioned above seem the most crucial. In practice, each of these crises, while analytically distinct, may well be compounded. This is especially true of late-modernizing societies.

In Europe, *legitimacy* was the issue around which some of the earliest parties were created. As the demands for popular participation and a devolution of centralized authority began to threaten the legitimacy of the existing structures of authority, as in late eighteenth-century France, revolutionary groups began to assume a popular character, seeking much of their support from the population hitherto excluded from having an autonomous political role, the peasantry, the artisan and the bourgeoisie.

Similarly, nationalist movements are often the result of legitimacy crises. They frequently begin as small groups of men concerned with increasing their influence on colonial governments by opening up the opportunities for indigenous political participation. If the colonial administration refuses to allow the demands, the nationalist group finds it necessary to broaden its support among the people, and, in the process, develops a political party organization.[*1*] Of course, once the active electorate becomes larger and national parliaments have evolved, the tasks of political recruitment, of bringing the new citizenry into the process of policy formation and decision-making can no longer be handled by a small coterie of men but instead necessitates new modes of political organization. So, what hitherto had been simply fairly loose coteries of legislators began to see the need to organize the new electorate. In Britain, for example, the major phases of party development are associated with the electoral reforms of 1832, 1867 and 1885. In Europe, as a whole, as the electorate expanded in size, so legislators felt the need for local committees or organizations to broaden and organize their support in the country. Thus, many of the earliest parties were formed on the initiative of the legislators themselves. Such were the Conservative and Liberal Parties in Britain, the Democratic and Republican Parties in the United States, and the Liberal and Progressive Parties in post-Tokugawa Japan. The early history of such parties is often associated with factions centring around a notable politician. In Britain, Walpole and Fox, Peel and Canning, Disraeli and Gladstone, and in the United States, Jefferson and Hamilton were all the cause for faction and crucial for the development of party tradition. This personalistic and factional character of the early history of these legislative-formed parties is typical, being firmly rooted in the exigencies of legislation rather than programmatic action.

Not all political parties owe their origins to what one might call the legislators' 'need' to control their constituencies. Others, and here the classic examples are the socialist parties in Europe, were externally created. Such parties are often, though not exclusively, associated with the crises of participation: the demand of new or existing but excluded groups for a more participatory role in government. As we have said earlier, the classic European examples of externally created parties are the socialist parties that emerged in the late nineteenth and early twentieth centuries; and the Christian Democratic parties created as a response to the success of these socialist parties. In the developing societies of Africa and Asia, more of the now functioning parties were formerly based on nationalist movements that arose outside the governing framework. While mass parties evolved slowly in Europe and the United States, they have been characteristic of many new states from the beginning. Where a nationalist movement is struggling to achieve independence, its natural focus is a mass party which attempts to unite all the elements of the society in a common demand for self-rule. Of course, when independence is achieved strains may appear based on traditional groupings such as tribal, ethnic or commercial loyalties. In India, for example, the religiously infused Moslem League refused to work with the more secular Congress Party which was largely Hindu supported. The result was that the subcontinent had to be partitioned. In the years immediately preceding independence, the middle-class, and tribally recruited groups in the Gold Coast, combined against Kwame Nkrumah's Convention Peoples Party.

Participation crises brought about by new group demands being placed on the system nearly always, additionally, involve a legitimacy crisis, and a threat to the position of the ruling group, especially if the ruling group proves insensitive to the demands of those seeking greater participation. In other words, externally created parties are often born of a situation out of which they derive less commitment to the existing social, political and economic institutions. Moreover, this revolutionary or reforming zeal is often associated with greater ideological coherence, more membership discipline and less influence by the legislative wing of the party on policy and other internal party matters. But, the longer the party is able to survive in this uneasy tension with the political system, the more likely it is to become integrated into the existing political framework, and begin to assume the character of more traditional parties. This has certainly occurred with many of the larger socialist and social democratic parties in Europe.

Finally, crises of *integration*, that is, the problem of territorial integrity plus the process by which divided ethnic communities come to accommodate themselves to each other, have also provided the context in which parties have first emerged. In Europe, parties in Germany, Italy and Belgium emerged during such crises. In Belgium, the struggle between the Flemish and the Walloons created ethnic parties, and in present-day Canada, French separatist parties are trying their wings. In India, the Muslim League expanded into a mass party with the integration crises associated with the partition of the subcontinent. Elsewhere in Asia, religious, linguistic and tribal groups have often organized political parties in opposition to the predominant political group.

Thus, the occurrence of political parties is related to the crises experienced by extensively developed polities, although, of course, the particular historical situation in each society continues to condition the pattern of relationship between the party and society.

Existing studies of party organization often seek to establish a typology of parties. Now, as with any typological endeavour, the criteria one uses to generate the types depend on the focus of interest of the study. Neumann, for example, lays stress on the goals sought and social posture as a basic criterion of classification.[5] Here he suggests the value of distinctions between parties which stress patronage and expediency and those which insist on ideological purity; between parties which are dominated by personalities and those more programmatic, and so on. Duverger, on the other hand, points to the basis of membership as the distinguishing criterion.[6] By this stipulation, those parties which have direct memberships he calls mass parties, while cadre parties do not. Duverger also gives considerable emphasis to the basic organizational units of political parties, the caucus, the branch, the cell and the militia. The caucus consists of *ad hoc* electoral committees of notables, the branch of local membership, the cell of occupationally orientated membership groups and the militia is the armed units of parties.

The first, almost defining aim of the political party is to achieve power. This is its rationale. The social context is largely responsible for the means that the party must use, thus providing it with its organization. In order to discuss matters here it is convenient to divide parties according to the type of polity in which they are found: whether they are in electoral systems with other competing parties, or whether they are to be found in systems where they are the only legal party. The electoral system is an important structural feature of a political system. The stability and regularity of the electoral system are firm expectations which condition the behaviour of political parties. The fact, for example, that in the United States there is a presidential election every four years and that no president may serve for more than two successive four-year terms has an obvious part to play in such things as leadership selection, effectiveness and political strategy of the party. Again, the method of electoral scoring, whether single-member constituencies, plurality system or whatever, can influence such factors as party solidarity, electoral alliances, concentration of party support, and so on.[7]

In this chapter we shall examine political parties in competitive systems and we shall then turn to single-party states. Traditionally, the academic emphasis has been upon competitive systems, but even a cursory glance will serve to convince that numerically this emphasis is misplaced. In most of the states with the highest population—China, USSR, Indonesia, Pakistan—there is either an authoritarian regime based on the military or a one-party state. Furthermore, irrespective of size of population or territory the one-party state is not deviation from a statistical norm. Hence, prior to examining the structure and process of parties in competitive and non-competitive systems we shall glance briefly at some attempts to account for the emergence of the two systems.

The Bases of Competitive and Non-Competitive Party Systems

There is a strong association between the level of economic development and the existence of a party competitive system.[8] This association can also be shown geographically (see Table 29).

TABLE 29. Party Systems By Area

	Non-party	One party	More than one party	Total
Atlantic	1	2	20	23
Eastern Europe and North Asia	0	13	0	23
Middle East	10	6	5	21
South and South-East Asia	9	3	7	19
Africa, South of Sahara	9	20	9	38
Latin America	2	5	17	24
Total	31	49	58	138
Percentage	23%	34%	43%	100%

From J. Blondel, *Introduction to Comparative Government*, Weidenfeld and Nicolson, London, 1969, p. 40.

The one-party system may be a consequence of a legal rule of some sort which simply prohibits an opposition party, or of a more or less violent repression of the opposition; usually there is a combination of these factors. A second cause of the one-party system may lie in the structure of the society. Two almost contradictory arguments are advanced. Some African leaders have argued that their societies lack the developed social classes which they suppose support the two- and multi-party systems found elsewhere. African society, Nyerere has claimed, is based upon the family and not the class, so its basic unity necessarily expresses itself through supporting a single party. Writing from a Marxist perspective, Madeira Keita explains that although there are divisions in African societies, nevertheless the *Union Soudonaise* of Mali is 'agreed on the essentials and pursued the same objectives'. What other parties and groups there were in Mali 'have voluntarily sacrificed themselves for the sake of Unity'.[9] This view approaches the contrary one which suggests that it is the cleavages and divisions of a developing society based upon varying languages, religions, regions and tradition which are the most salient aspect of those societies. In order to bring some sort of order and uniformity to this variety a one-party state is necessary. The new nations are not solid, their traditional patterns of authority are seriously weakened, so that one-party regimes 'are necessary in Africa precisely because the nation rests on such shaky foundations'.[10] In short, in most African states the choice is not between a one-party or a multi-party regime but between 'one party states and either anarchy or military regimes or various combinations of the two'.[11]

Huntington argues that one-party systems result *either* from an accumulation of mutually reinforcing cleavages so that society is bifurcated, *or* from a multiplicity of non-reinforcing cleavages which are not spanned by secondary associations. In these situations, the one-party system may be produced not spontaneously but by an effort of will: 'the product of the efforts of a political elite to organise and to legitimate rule by one social force over another'.[*2*] In common with others who concentrate on the social background of single-party systems and of democracy, Huntington is arguing that the developing society often does not throw up the possibility of a moderately competitive system. But if the opportunity to develop a moderately competitive system does occur and the elites seize the opportunity then it may become institutionalized so that peaceful competition is widely acceptable.

However, this explanation, although it does tell us a good deal about the relationship between economic and social development and competitive polities, does not explain much about the actual number of competing parties. We have seen in our examination of Duverger in Chapter 10 that the attempt to relate the number of parties to the method of electoral scoring was deficient. Again, it is hard to take very seriously those who believe that two-party systems arise when people are moderate and reasonable in their politics whilst one- and multi-party systems are products of politically immoderate societies. Other explanations which emphasize that a party out of office can make more attractive promises than one in office or that party strength varies with the business cycle fail to account for systems of more than two parties.

Similarly, arguments that political decisions are basically divisible into 'yes' and 'no' or 'left' and 'right' or that there are just two sides to political office—inside and outside—fail to account for the fact that there are established party systems consisting of more than two parties.[12] Such arguments do help to explain the enormous difficulties under which third parties labour. Looked at slightly differently, although it is the case that proportional voting systems are initiated *because* more than two parties exist, nevertheless, 'Once proportional representation is established, it helps not only to perpetuate the parties that establish it, but also to facilitate the emergence and continuance of other non-sectional minority parties. At least proportional representation makes it easier for such parties to exist.'[13] In an explanation of the *persistence* of the two-party system in the US it is demonstrated that the narrow range within which the votes for their respective presidential candidates varied could not be accidental but must result from equilibriating forces in the system.[14] The forces acting to restore and maintain equilibrium (no party wins more than 15 per cent beyond an equal share of the vote) were identified as follows.[*3*] Firstly, about 75 per cent of adults are firmly fixed in their voting allegiance to one or other of the major parties so that third parties have to break through this crust of familiarity. And since *the* prize of American politics—the Presidency—is indivisible it follows that a third party which cannot quickly win it is crippled as a national entity. Secondly, and partly compensating for the first factor, is the consideration that even in a massive defeat the defeated party still always retains a number of state bastions and Congressional seats, so losing an election does not destroy the party in a temporary minority. Thus, one party is always poised for an electoral comeback whilst the other is in office.

When a party is in office it does not gain strength: 'it may preserve for a time its electoral majority, but the next marked *change* in the party vote will issue from a negative response of the electorate to some aspect of the party's conduct in office'.[15] If and when things go wrong in the country, the electorate responds by *blaming* the party in office rather than rewarding it for success, so that there is no long-term trend towards a growing vote for a successful incumbent party.[*4*] If this were the case, then obviously the result would be eventual one-party dominance at a national level. Since it is not, then we have a combination of psychological, sociological and institutional explanations for the two-party system in the US.[*5*]

11.3. Political Parties: Some Structures and Processes in Competitive Systems

We have stated that the party's main defining characteristic is that it nominates candidates for legislatures. It may well, and usually does, do other things, but this is its main organizational rationale. In polities where nomination is mediated through electoral competition with other parties, certain structural styles began to emerge which are inherent in this type of party organization. The degree of political party competition is an important factor influencing the behaviour of the parties. Competition, of course, varies in level, quality and durability. As far as levels are concerned, some parties are unable to nominate candidates for all public offices. In the United States, for example, many more public offices are open to party nomination than there are in Britain and other European states. Competition varies qualitatively. Some small intensely ideological parties nominate candidates only intermittently, yet compete ideologically with some vigour. In some systems, the failure of a party to win a majority means only a lesser role in some governing coalition, while in others, electoral loss is virtually tantamount to exclusion from the political system. Take the example of the British Liberal Party which has, since World War II, consistently fought general elections with a comprehensive slate of candidates and yet its success rate has been very low. This has had considerable effect on its political impact: an impact which might have been somewhat greater if its political representation were in closer accord with its national votes. The degree of competition and monopoly has a bearing on such things as party recruitment and ideology. A permanent minority party may tend to choose a leadership more for its glamour than for its experience. Such a minority party may also be able to preserve any ideological purity it may have, being less concerned to win or appeal to a broad spectrum of popular support. A party with good expectations of winning an election will have to take more care with the candidates it selects and the appeals it makes.

The first element of this 'structural state' is that the party is a 'clientele-orientated' organization.[16] That is, in an electoral situation where the number of votes the party can command is the coinage with which to 'buy' power, the party, as Michels pointed out, becomes 'an organisation ever greedy for new members'.[17] In other words, the party is ever open for new members, supporters and voters. It might make a direct appeal for new recruits and workers in order that its electoral advantage is enhanced. As Michels went on to say, 'the party no longer seeks to fight its opponents, but simply to out-bid them'.[17]

'Openness' of party structure seems to be related to the electoral marginality of a party. In Eldersveld's study of the structure and activity of the Democratic and Republic Parties in Detroit, it was found that in 'electorally doubtful precincts both parties adapted, and allowed socially deviant leadership where the power-winning requirements of the situation demanded or permitted it'.[18] In other words, where parties were competing on more or less equal terms, they tended to have fairly open recruitment practices.

This organizational permeability poses a number of problems for internal cohesion of the party organization. One of these is that if the party is in strong competition for voters and supporters, then, because it may have to appeal to a wider range of interests and groups, it must operate with a much diluted political philosophy. To quote Michels once again, the party, because of its need to go out and win voters, 'sacrifices its political virginity, by entering into promiscuous relationships with the more heterogeneous political elements . . .'.[19] Of course, this ideological dilution is a severe problem only to those parties which claim or espouse anything like an ideologically bound set of principles. Michels himself was writing of socialist parties of over 50 years ago. But in parties where ideological purity is not valued this dilution is less of a problem. In the Conservative Party of Britain, for example, the mass of party members do not expect the leadership to be subservient to its wishes.

A further consequence of the open-endedness of parties is that it creates difficulties for managerial control. Because the party is a voluntary association in that no one is forced to join, its members will remain within the party and contribute to its affairs only so long as they receive sufficient satisfactions from their participation. Thus, the party leadership cannot simply command compliance, but must make suitable appeals to the interest or to the loyalty of the members. Parties, then, are not bureaucracies in the classic sense of that term.

These considerations lead to the image of the political party as a grouping of socio-economic interests, each seeking political recognition and advantage. As such, the party can be conceptualized as an alliance of substructures or coalitions. The elements of the coalition can clearly vary from party to party, polity to polity. They may be geographical, economic, religious, ethnic or whatever, or even various functional wings of the party, such as the legislative or executive wings. On this view the party is simply a group representing and exploiting multiple interests that it may achieve direct control over the government of the society.

An interesting consequence of this view is that, as an organization in a conflict system, the party must somehow manage internal conflict and stabilize the groups in the coalition so that the goal of attaining power is more likely to be realized. In fact, this tension between the goals of office and what one might term the goals of interest or policy is a typical dilemma of parties in competitive systems. In this regard, students of political parties have often observed that the rank and file are more militant and more extreme than are the legislative leaders who must take due concern of the party's electoral chances. As Duverger, when writing of the French Socialists, put it: 'the militant are more revolutionary than the electors, who are scarcely revolutionary at all. And the deputies are naturally more prone to follow the electors than the militant.'[20] The very attitudes which produce the necessary sacrifice and devotion of party workers reflect an intensity of conviction not shared by the bulk of the population. Further, this intensity of conviction is unmodified by the practical vote-getting considerations which affect those who seek public office under the party label.

One of the ways in which parties differ is the manner in which their leaders avoid becoming too influenced by the mass membership. As far as the British Conservative Party is concerned, the leadership can depend upon its followers appreciating their own limited role in determining the party policy and action.[*6*]. The British Labour Party leadership, on the other hand, has less of an elitist tradition on which to depend. Tensions between the leadership and the mass membership are regular features of party conferences. In fact, the security of the Labour leadership is often due to the support of the votes commanded by trade union leaders, themselves cognizant of electoral effect.

Yet it may well be the case that many party members are not at all deeply and continuously interested in politics and political activity, but rather are attracted because their husbands or wives are members, because of the social life or simply for the company in the party club. Branch meetings are notoriously badly attended and members are happier with generalities than with practical politics. Hence, on most issues the branches may fairly easily be swayed by a small but impassioned and/or informed minority, and it is generally these that attend annual conferences to discuss party policy and criticize the leadership. Knowing this the leadership can, except in the gravest cases, regard the annual conference not as a source of policy but rather as an opportunity to harangue the faithful and as a sounding-board for policy.[21]

This ability shown by many party leaders to avoid full responsibility to the wishes of the membership led Michels to formulate his famous 'iron law of oligarchy'.

The Iron Law of Oligarchy

Michels, writing early in this century, was concerned to reconstruct and update the insight of Marx. While accepting Marx's position on the importance of economic development for social change, Michels demurred at accepting the idea that democracy and socialism were the inevitable results of the economic forces at work in industrial societies. Instead, he claimed there were other forces operating which were sufficiently strong to preclude the further democratization of industrial society. These forces were, briefly, the nature of the human individual, the nature of the political struggle and the nature of organization. The consequences of these tendencies, according to Michels, were that democracy inevitably leads to oligarchy, the central thesis of his work *Political Parties*.

To test this idea, Michels made a study of the Social Democratic parties of Europe. He reasoned that if oligarchic tendencies could be found 'in the very bosom of the revolutionary parties' which claimed to represent opposite tendencies then this would constitute 'conclusive proof of the existence of imminent oligarchic tendencies in every kind of human organisation which strives for the attainment of definite ends'.[22] Michels begins his thesis with a psychological assumption that it is man's inherent nature to crave power, and, once having attained it, to seek its perpetuation. The second consideration refers to the technical and practical problem of involving large numbers of people in the democratic decision-making process. If democracy is taken to mean the *direct* involvement of the mass membership in decision then democracy, as mass democratic theorists since Rousseau have understood it, is indeed impossible. So, according to Michels, the very size of party membership makes it technically impossible for all members to govern their affairs directly. Unavoidably, then, a division of labour becomes necessary. The organization begins to require specialists, men trained in the details of organizational administration. The result is the emergence of a 'class of professional politicians, of approved and registered experts in political life'.[7] This expertise possessed by the party functionaries frees them from being servants of the party membership, and the organization becomes increasingly hierarchic and bureaucratic. Soon, the men originally appointed to serve the interests of the collectivity develop interests of their own opposed to those of the collectivity. Of course, once the 'experts' have attained their positions they begin to legitimize their role by an appeal to their functional indispensability. Whenever their decisions are challenged, the offer of resignation, apparently a fine democratic gesture, is in reality a reminder to the followers of the leaders' indispensability.

Leadership positions are further reinforced by the political indifference and incompetence of the masses and the gratitude and veneration they feel towards their leaders. The result is a growing *social* gulf between leaders and masses. Michels explains:

> 'Whilst their occupation with the needs of daily life render it impossible for the masses to attain a profound knowledge of the social machinery, and above all of the working of the political machine, the leader of working class origin is enabled, thanks to his new situation, to make himself immediately familiar with all the technical details of public life, and thus to increase his superiority over the rank and file'.[23]

Thus, for Michels the dilemma of democratic socialist parties is that in order to bring about their ideological aims it is necessary to organize, and organization inevitably results in the establishment of the very oligarchy and inequalities the parties were established to destroy.

While Michels' observations are extremely important to an understanding of political parties, his 'iron law of oligarchy' is not as 'iron' as he claims.[*8*] McKenzie's study of the British Labour and Conservative Parties presents evidence of revolts against party leaders which have resulted in their overthrow. In other words, though all political parties are more or less oligarchic (Michels is right here; how else can parties operate?), this does not mean that party leaders can ignore with impunity the aspirations and demands of the rank and file. Blind appeals to party loyalty may often achieve their purpose, but 'they are rarely successful in bridging a real gulf when one does develop between the leaders and their followers'.[24]

Also, at one level, Michels' thesis can be rendered trivial: that is, if we mean by oligarchy merely that minorities rule, then not only is the law irrefutable, it is also virtually tautological. This is a simple point. More seriously, Michels' thesis could be taken to mean that elites rule in their own interests, which are counter to those of the rank and file. This is a more complicated problem. First of all, we have the partly normative question about the 'real' interest of the groups involved. Do elites consistently act in a manner to subvert the 'real' interest of the rank and file? In other words, the proof of oligarchy domination lies in answer to questions such as, are the leaders always unified in their action? Are they virtually unaccountable and irremovable? To what extent can they ignore 'popular opinion'? And so on.

In addition, the oligarchy thesis seems to fall into the fallacy we mentioned in an earlier chapter, that social origins determine political preference. Numerous studies have shown that upper- and middle-class elements are over-represented among the membership of all parties, including working-class ones. This is often taken as evidence of elite control. But, as we have seen, social origins do not directly determine political sympathies. Evidence of oligarchy is needed other than social background.

Michels' analysis belongs to a particular European tradition which sees the party primarily as an organization designed to further the interest of its members, especially in class or economic terms. In other words, it is assumed that the party needs to be responsive to its members, and to find that it is not, as often happens, means that there has been a betrayal of the party's primary purpose. A few years prior to Michels, Ostrogorski, the first to make a systematic study of parties, pointed to a danger which political parties themselves represented to the political system.[9] Ostrogorski argued that the combination of large electorates and the difficulties of governing an industrial country necessitated the growth of nationwide political parties. Because the mass of the citizenry was politically indifferent, these political parties were able to act almost without fear of being checked. A monster had been created, making both citizenry and most politicians dependent on the services the organization could provide. This he saw as being to the detriment of the common good and of the substance of democracy. Ostrogorski's analysis misses a number of important considerations amongst which are some we have previously mentioned. Firstly, given electoral competition it is perfectly reasonable to assume that a consequence will be competitive bidding by the parties for voters' support. Unless one assumes a radically sceptical posture, the outcome must be that to some extent the preferences of the electorate will determine policy. Secondly, for the reasons we have outlined, he probably overemphasized the influence of organizational minorities (the 'caucus') within political parties. In Britain, the evidence is that the parliamentary leadership in all three major parties is well able to control the mass membership and the professional organization. On the other hand, his fear that parties, which begin as popular instruments, degenerate into particular organizations concerned primarily with their own interests is probably a reasonable statement of the situation. The problem is whether or not party organizational interest coincides with that of a more general interest. As we have seen, it is usual to argue that in a competitive party system this coincidence is an outcome of the search for an electoral majority. Whether or not this is the case, it is difficult to imagine how preferences, interests and opinions can be conveyed and aggregated without an organization which may not be called a party but which is one.

An alternative view to the oligarchic model of Michels and Ostrogorski is that which stresses that party structure is based upon coalition.[25] In this view, each individual or subgroup within the party is considered as possessing its own set of goals ('preference orderings'). The party organization then 'bargains' with these groups and 'for the purposes of the political game' enters into a coalition agreement with them, and thus a 'joint preference ordering' of organizational objectives develops. This is the result of 'side payments' to the elements of the coalition on a calculation of reciprocal strengths, needs and contributions to the total party structure. Once the 'bargain' has been consummated, the party is able to move ahead, goal-setting having been finalized, and it can operate as a single 'entrepreneur'.

While this view of the party can be overstressed, it does point to the essentially pluralistic nature of party organization. Policy and action are the result of processes of compromise and bargaining within the party. Even in the more carefully structured American party machines, for example, a reciprocal pattern of influence operates between the 'boss' and his precinct captains.[26] Eldersveld's analysis of the Democrat and Republican Parties in Detroit showed that both parties consisted of moderately self-conscious subgroups. In the Republican Party, the business-managerial and white-collar groups were sufficiently well orientated and politically self-conscious to exhibit a measure of autonomy and stability. The Democratic Party was a collection of seven to nine major subgroups—including Negroes, Poles, blue-collar immigrants, and so on—who also showed evidence of party substructural identity and integrity.[27]

If this image of the party as a 'collection of communities, a union of small groups'[28] is an accurate one, then this has clear implications for the control structure of parties. Because of the 'open-ended' character of parties in competitive systems, and the plural character of its internal structure, it is difficult to see how the control structure can be a simple bureaucratic hierarchy. On paper, party organization may correspond to the Weberian bureaucratic model: an ordered system of authority from the leaders to the meanest party worker. In practice, because of the scarcity of voluntary workers, the limited rewards for party work, and the irregularity of loyalty, the party must usually tolerate a considerable degree of autonomy, local initiative and local inertia. Also, the strong drive for voting support, the lack of effective managerial sanctions and the election-mindedness of leaders further encourage decentralization of control and influence.

One does not want to deny that a hierarchy exists, but as far as competitive parties are concerned, this cannot be a simple monolithic hierarchy. Party organizations vary not only in the scope or amount of control membership implies, but also in the way control is distributed among the various roles comprising the organization. One model which generally states the character of hierarchy in parties is the notion of 'stratarchy'.[29] The general features of a stratarchy are the proliferation of the ruling group and the diffusion of power in the form of 'strata commands' which operate with varying degrees of independence throughout the party organization. As we have said before, the very heterogeneity of membership, coalition relationships, make centralized control not only difficult but politically suicidal. Thus, 'the party develops its own hierarchical pattern of stratified devolution of responsibility for the settlement of conflicts, rather than jeopardize the viability of the total organisation by carrying such conflict to the top command levels of the party'.[30] Further, because the party must accommodate to local and particularistic milieux of opinion and tradition, this encourages the acceptance of local leadership, strategy and influence.[31]

Although this model is more plausible than that of the centralized hierarchy model in its characterization of the authority structure of the political party, we would expect, none the less, considerable variation between parties. There is some evidence to suggest that parties in a favourable competitive position, for example, will be dominated by their legislative office-holders. McKenzie's study of the British Labour and Conservative Parties suggests that, on balance, on matters of issue the locus of power rests with the parliamentary leadership.

But again, it is not a simple 'either/or' question as to whether leadership is paramount or not. The answer is sometimes 'yes' and sometimes 'no'. For one thing, a great deal depends upon the issue. To take the British Conservative Party once again, national headquarters does not limit the candidate choice of constituency associations.[32] This is a task primarily the responsibility of the local association. In other words, study of a particular party structure may well reveal devolution of responsibility on certain matters, if not on others. That is, considerable autonomy might be given to local units in their selection of candidates, but less local initiative is allowed in respect of election platforms, or parliamentary strategy.

Duverger's distinction between 'internally' and 'externally' created parties provides one dimension upon which elite authority could vary. 'Internally' organized parties, for example, give greater weight to the legislative wing of the party, while 'externally' created parties give more weight to the party functionaries. But this must not be overworked. As we suggested earlier, many 'internally' created parties have created mass organizations in response to universal suffrage and to the success of the organization of the 'externally' created parties. In other words, the nationalization of politics created the need for electorally orientated parties to develop mass organizations. Convergent with this tendency, 'externally' created parties have, once they approach possibilities of office, become looser in organization. The necessity of coalition, compromise and office-seeking required a degree of discretionary authority for legislative leaders. This decreased the authority of party segments outside the inner legislative circle. Thus, the differences between 'internally' and 'externally' created parties have decreased.

In addition, the fact of a party being in office may well increase the influence of the legislative as against the other sectors of the party, whereas in opposition the differences between sectors may be less obvious. But, again, examples can be found to counter this idea.

It is a commonplace, but none the less an important observation that political elites do not act in a vacuum, and perhaps the best way to assess the influence of a party elite is to examine how far their position gives them a hold on the political system compared to other elites. In other words, how important are party channels as opposed to other channels for reaching, affecting or replacing those in positions of political influence. In relatively stable competitive societies with long-established parties, the party is crucial in the recruitment of political elites, either as avenues of political careers or as agencies legitimating attainment of leadership positions. In systems where parties have only a precarious position *vis-à- vis* other groups, then their role in the recruitment of the political elite is correspondingly more limited.

However, even in societies where the reach of the party system is wide it could be erroneous to conclude that party elites thereby have a monopoly of political influence. Although the party's commanding position may be stable, there could well be a reasonably rapid turnover of elite personnel. Again, no political leadership in a competitive system can afford to ignore the claims of other sectors of society, industry, military, education, trade unions, or whatever. In principle, the President of the United States is the most powerful man on earth, but it would be foolish to pretend that he can make unrestricted decisions.[*10*]

Stated simply, the problem of the party operating in a competitive party system is to bring together individuals and groups of diverse interest into voluntary cooperation so that collective goals of the party may be attained. What we have argued is that for various reasons it is theoretically arid to regard political parties simply as the bureaucratic extension of the leadership. Moreover, we have argued that *vis-à-vis* the electorate it may well be incorrect to regard party elites as being in a necessarily dominant position. In the following section, we shall attempt to outline a more theoretical justification for those empirical assertions. This is the theory advanced by Mancur Olsen.

The Logic of Collective Action

This theory is an attempt to build a formal theory of individual behaviour within large collectivities.[*11*] The theory begins with the assumption of classical economics that man is a rational, calculating creature and, in addition, in large collectivities he will always act in this manner. The theory goes on to make a further assumption that 'unless the number of individuals in a group is quite small, or unless there is coercion or some other special device to make individuals act in their common interest, rational, self-interested individuals will not act to achieve their common or group interest'.[33] That is, a rational man will make an effort in proportion to the expected return. In the case of collective goods (for example, parades, health services, political freedom, etc.) the contribution of any one individual to their achievement is not crucial, yet, because of the nature of collective goods, all individuals will profit if the good is provided, even if only some individuals have contributed towards its provision. Thus, since an individual member gets only part of the benefit of an expenditure he makes to obtain more of the collective good, he will discontinue his purchase of the collective good before the optimal amount for the group as a whole has been obtained. So 'the larger the group, the further it will fall short of providing an optimal amount of a collective good'.[34] If applied to political parties and these are viewed as organizations primarily oriented towards collective benefits, then, accepting the logic of collective action, most party duties will be performed by those seeking selective, non-collective benefits. That is, although most people feel they would be better off if the party they supported were in power, they recognize that if their party is going to win, it will as likely win without their individual contribution, and they will get the benefit in any case. The average person will not be willing to make a significant contribution for his party, since victory brings a collective good. On the other hand, there are many people with personal political ambitions of one sort or another, and for these people the party can provide the opportunity for non-collective benefits, such as public office.

In other words, the political machine is an organizational structure that works for specific incentives such as patronage, and collective goods emerge, if at all, as byproducts. 'Political machines are able to develop well articulated organisational structures . . . because they strive mainly for benefits that accrue to particular individuals, rather than for the common interest of any large group.'[35] There are a number of other interesting implications in this theory. For one thing, the theory contradicts many of the assertions of the group theory school of Bentley and Truman, that latent groups will mobilize simply because they have common interests to pursue. This, claims Olsen, is the 'anarchistic fallacy', an assumption that 'the need of incentive for organised or coordinated cooperation . . . would ensure that the necessary organisation and group action would be forthcoming'.[36] In fact, according to the logic of collective action, latent large groups are disadvantaged in competition with pre-existing small groups because of the high initial costs of organization. How then do such groups arise? How and why are political parties, lobby and pressure groups created? Olsen's answer to this is that they are often a byproduct of other activity. The existence, for example, of a trade union or a business concern can reduce the costs of political organization.

The theory also provides us with a perspective on party elite behaviour. Party office-holders do not seek a collective end. What they seek instead are personal gains which balance the investment they make in party activity. Such ends may be status, monetary rewards, and so on. But, in a mass party, part of their investment must be to make an appeal to the rank and file. They must compete for the support of the membership, and this forces the leaders to sublimate the non-collective aspects of their struggle and, perhaps as a byproduct, seek collective ends as the price of achieving their own specific goals. Additionally, if they are to achieve their private, non-collective ends such as office patronage, personal status, and so on, they must win elections. In order to win elections they must seek the voting support of at least enough voters to give them access to these goods. Barnes' study of the Italian Socialist Party (PSI) illustrates this well.[37] Within this party there were two distinct factions: one group, the Autonomists, who favoured independence from the Communist Party and cooperation with the centre parties (Christian Democrats, Social Democrats and Republicans); and a second group, the Leftists, who, fearing a loss of revolutionary fervour that would result from cooperation with the centre parties, preferred to continue the alliance with the Communists. The PSI party system rested on these two leadership sets, and the personal interests of the leaders of the factions were tied to the divisive policy considerations that underlay the fight for dominance between the two groups. The minority Leftist group was intensely concerned with party policy and feared that a move towards the centre would jeopardize the faction's good relations with the trade unions from whom the leaders received extra-parliamentary posts. The Autonomists, on the other hand, wished to preserve their governmental posts. In this case, party democracy was preserved as a byproduct of different leaders pursuing their individual non-collective benefits.

Thus the theory of collective action explains why, *vis-à-vis* party members and the electorate, the party leader is constrained from the uninhibited pursuit of his own self-interest. Or rather it shows how—as in economic theory—a collective benefit is derived from the pursuit of individual benefits. In consciously moderating his own self-interest in favour of the electorate, the party leader is constrained by the logic of his situation. This theory, whilst not providing us with a complete theory of political parties, does suggest that the personal motivations of party office-holders may have, amongst other things, organizational consequences for the political party. An office-holder with discrete ambitions, not intending to stand for re-election or to make a career out of public service, may well have only ephemeral organizational needs. Then, one would expect party organization to be weakest around such individuals.[38] Those with more far-reaching ambitions must pay greater attention to the organization and its relation to their private goals. Perhaps an example of the former was the campaign for the Democratic nomination by Senator Eugene McCarthy a man, by all accounts, of discrete ambition. The cursory attention he gave to organization was notorious, compared with, say, the organizational effort expended by the more ambitious Kennedys. Again, it appears that legislators who had progressive ambitions of moving to higher office were more sensitive to political considerations and had a more sophisticated view of the complexities of office-seeking.[39]

However, while the main office-holders may be motivated primarily by the desire for office and its benefits, it is unlikely that such ambitions would attract sufficient members to form an effective organization. The very nature of organization precludes the majority from holding office; only a few can entertain realistic possibilities of accession. That is to say, office-holders must offer inducements to non-office-holders if the latter are to sustain a level of activity sufficient to ensure the satisfactory performance of a basic minimum of tasks connected with mobilization of popular support and willing elections. Since inducements the office-holders could offer can hardly be their own offices, it follows that another range of satisfactions must be offered to the numerous rank and file workers. In the United States, patronage has been an important source of incentive for party workers. By far the largest number of government jobs are dispensed at a local level. As a result, local party units were often able to develop as patronage systems when government jobs were held at the discretion of party leaders. These material incentives meant that the local machine enjoyed great flexibility in defining goals and objectives. As long as the patronage remained and the party workers depended upon its material incentives, it could operate almost independently of party policy and remain flexible in reacting to public problems.[40] Studies in the United States revealed that many precinct workers were drawn to party work by the attraction of economic reward, and a high proportion of them were on the public payroll.[41]

Of course, not all political parties have such a leverage on public offices as American parties. Even in the United States, there is evidence that the patronage system is on the decline.[42] In any case, it is unlikely that material incentives are crucial. Other types of incentives include status incentives and satisfaction derived from participation itself. The identification of party workers with a successful candidate, sense of participation and involvement with political activity, and so on, are often rewards party workers may derive from their activity.

Finally, one cannot ignore the policy or 'purposive' incentives. In other words, party leaders, even if entirely self-interested or calculative in their actions, must appeal to the interests, aims, ideas, aspirations and so on of the party activists upon whom they rely.

Thus we conclude that there are compelling theoretical reasons for arguing that individual interests are important in understanding the operation of political parties. It might also be suggested that at least in competitive political situations the possibility is that the fact of competition drives leaders to become sensitive to social interests located both inside and outside the party. Furthermore, looked at in the theoretical perspective of the logic of collective action, we can see how the system operates to constrain leadership and provide collective goods out of private behaviours. Parties with little chance of winning public office lack one of the more obvious private goods to distribute; they must either make a highly specialized appeal, which means they are very unlikely to win elections, or they can offer broader ideological appeals.

Since small parties are, in effect, remote from public office, the prime motivations of the membership are likely to be ideological, and if the organization is to survive then it has the problem of maintaining this ideological commitment in the face of conflicting demands. From this point of view the 'exclusive' organization has rather an easier task given the initial commitment, but it certainly has a harder time recruiting membership because of the heavier demands of time and effort placed on the member.[*12*] Once recruited, the member is more insulated from competing social values and movements. In other contexts this type of organizational exclusiveness is often pronounced, involving almost a complete withdrawal from the host society. Examples are many, ranging from convents and monasteries to whole communities such as the Oneida Community, the Hutterites and, of late, 'hippie' communes in the United States.[*13*] In the case of the 'inclusive' organization, while it is relatively easier to become a member, it is also easier for the member to become exposed to cross-pressures of various kinds because he is free to interact in a less guided, more exposed manner. If, for example, an individual is a member of a minor 'inclusive' socialist party and also a member of a trade union which is not entirely composed of other individuals of the same political persuasion, then we might expect cross-pressures to be more likely to operate in this case. To take an example from the United States, during the McCarthy era the Socialist Party suffered a more rapid decline in membership than did the more 'exclusive' Socialist Workers Party, despite the fact that the latter's ideology was more left-wing, hence more open to charges of 'anti-Americanism'.

In a sense, then, the 'exclusive' oriented party is a more viable type of organization in a context where its ideas and values are threatened. It can, in other words, constitute an 'organizational' weapon, and its mode of organization and commitment represent not only a weapon aimed at revolution, but also a measure of mutual support and protection for its membership.

However, the 'exclusive' type suffers from problems of its own. Given the highly committed, purposive nature of its membership, the history of such an organization is often marked by internal factional conflict and schisms. This is especially true of those organizations concerned with doctrinal purity and truth which often lead to the questioning of authority within the movement.

The extent to which 'exclusiveness' operates among the members poses problems for any organization, large or small. But, for a minor party with at least some foothold in the electoral system, the consequences are, perhaps, a little more severe. If the party seriously wishes to maintain a challenge it must attempt to win the voting support, at least, of a significant portion of the electorate. As Downs has shown, this kind of situation is likely to lead to a watering down of party ideology. But, if the party contains a large proportion of people deeply committed to ideological, highly principled perspectives, then this poses a problem for the leadership. Does the leadership sacrifice its electoral chances by maintaining doctrinal purity, and then preserve the support of its most active and energetic supporters, or, does it attempt to maximize its appeal to the electorate, thus jeopardizing the support of its committed membership? Thus Howe and Coser report that the internal political life of the American Communist Party displayed divisions based in large part on styles of commitment:

> 'Two kinds of political orientation could be distinguished among the members at this point—and in turning to this fact we . . . approach one of the most persistent and difficult problems of radical (as perhaps any other kind of) political action: the relationship between doctrine and conduct, between eventual ends and immediate methods, between the pressure for ideological exclusiveness and the pressure of political actuality. In the Worker's Party which by 1922 was still far from being a Leninist organisation, there were first the confirmed Communists and second those radicals who had recently come from the Socialist Party and whom the Communists sneeringly called "centralists". Between these two tendencies, whose ultimate incompatibility

lay equally in politics and temperament, there was at best an uneasy alliance'.[43]

This is less of a dilemma in a larger party which can perhaps afford to lose the minority of those not office-orientated. The British Labour Party, for example, could afford to axe its radical youth movement with little harm to its electoral performance, whereas the Liberal Party is finding it difficult to resist the pull of its significant and increasingly radical youth movement.

The dilemma is a hard one, and there is no simple equation specifying its result, since it is dependent upon so many factors in the social-political situation in which the party finds itself. One such factor is the success or failure of the movement. A movement which is becalmed or in a slow decline is likely to lose members and be subject to periodic bouts of apathy. All this could well increase the power of the leaders, and the organization will then begin to approximate to the oligarchic party model. However, an organized movement enjoying success is perhaps more prone to the leadership dilemma of trying to reconcile office-seeking goals with ideological purity.

But success itself solves a number of problems. In a competitive system, office-seeking goals and bureaucratization become essential. Simple increases in size will ensure the latter. The leaders begin to adopt a more 'articulating' style of leadership, trying to link the organization and its tactics to the larger society, and the uniqueness of the organization is toned down in favour of tactics of compromise. This development often leads to the loss of more radical members but may be balanced by the new supporter brought in by ideological diffuseness. As Lorwin summarizes the fate of a number of European socialist movements:

> '. . . the bearded prophets gave way to the smooth-chinned organisers, parliamentarians, and planners. Socialist militancy was a victim of Socialist success, itself made possible by economic growth . . . Along with socialist militancy, socialist certitudes faded. The motto of "socialism in our time" was amended, at least sotto voce, to Socialism . . . but not in our time. Socialism became less than ever a doctrine and more a political temper'.[14]

This is the pattern followed by most of the political parties which began as radical movement organizations, such as the British Labour Party and the French and Italian Communist Parties. The conditions which gave them success pose organizational dilemmas for the party and the selection of alternatives tends to become restricted as the party grows and becomes virtually institutionalized within the system.

11.4. Political Parties: Some Structures and Processes in Non-Competitive Systems

Political parties are not an essential feature of a political system. We have already suggested that they may begin to emerge when certain social preconditions are present. However, even when these are present, parties may still not materialize for one reason or another. For one thing, they may be repressed and enjoy only a sporadic and clandestine existence. There are many examples of authoritarian states ruled by military or civilian bureaucracies which deny a place to political parties. In some ex-colonial areas this has occurred because the dominant elite managed to maintain its power and keep political parties from coming into existence, as in Vietnam under Diem. In others, the first post-colonial regimes were formed only to be displaced by military coups or revolutions. This occurred in Pakistan when the military regime under Ayub Khan outlawed political parties, claiming that they intensified the nation's problems. The implication was that a formal opposition party would only accentuate existing differences and divisions, and that there was no place for a Westminster-type parliamentary battle when existing skill and experience were so limited, especially when what available talent there was needed to be concentrated on national development.[44]

But, even though parties may be suppressed, this does not necessarily terminate their activities. Outlawed parties often continue to operate underground. They begin to take on a clandestine and conspiratorial character which affects the party's style and view of society, which, when such parties re-emerge, can have a strong, long-term effect on the society. Classic examples here are, of course, the Bolshevik Party in Russia and the FLN in Algeria and the CPC in China. Their orientations to society were strongly moulded by their long history of suppression and the need to fight for recognition and power.

As a matter of fact, oligarchical or dictatorial regimes may find that they cannot function adequately without the existence of at least one party through which the regime can operate. This is nicely illustrated by Egypt.

It had been an assumption of the free officers in their coup of 1952 that the act of removing King Farouk would be sufficient to rally the population behind the revolutionaries and support the reforms thought necessary. But, of course, Egyptian society was not to be transformed overnight. Instead, what was required was a way to mobilize support by breaking down the mass indifference of the population. It was also realized that the poor economic state of Egypt was not solely due to exploitation by its previous rulers, but also due to lack of resources and socio-structural factors that needed massive 're-engineering'. The gradual realization by the new rulers of this fact is reflected in the slow growth of the ideology of Arab Socialism, and the formation of instruments of political organization for implementing the new policies. The revolutionary government felt that in order to achieve development it needed to increase the political participation of certain groups, especially the peasant masses, and restrict the participation of the urban political elite who were major influences during the previous regime.

Three successive political organizations were formed to achieve these ends. The first, the Liberation Rally, was established after all political parties had been banned. It was intended to fill the gap left by the previous political parties and to mobilize support for Nasser after his victory of Neguib. The second organization, the National Union, was organized following the Anglo-French-Israeli invasion and was an attempt at unifying the Egyptian population behind the regime. It was a more positive organization than the Liberation Rally, and not merely concerned to block the formation of other parties. The third, the Socialist Union, and the adoption of a more explicitly socialist ideology, corresponded to the growing realization by the elite that mass cooperation and mobilization were necessary if the goals of development were to be achieved.

Each of these organizations was arranged as a pyramid of committees paralleling the governmental levels of village, district, province and nation. The tensions displayed within the organizations reflect the dilemma facing all populist regimes bent on development: the need to mobilize the population and to prevent diversion of resources in compliance with popular demands for immediate satisfaction. Overlaying this dilemma is often a participation crisis brought about by the demands of relatively modernized groups for participation. In the case of Egypt, the participation crisis has yet to reach great intensity, so the prime purpose of the mass parties has been a 'means of mobilizing sentiment for the regime and . . . means of rendering the masses unavailable to alternative leaders'.[45] When the regime was better established, additional uses for the mass party were found. Mass education for hygiene, agricultural cooperation, 'interest group articulation' and the redress of individual grievances were all additional functions attempted by the mass organizations. But the requirements of legitimacy and national integration made it advisable to organize a mass party with a structure of leadership and to create a greater impression of popular involvement in policy-making. This is represented by the Socialist Union, one of the activities of which was to bring members to Parliament. The activities of Parliament were mainly supportive and had little or no role to play in decision-making.

Thus, the case of Egypt affords an example of a regime establishing a party to help with the tasks of national development. The Republic of Turkey during the period 1923–1945 under Kemal Ataturk's Republican People's Party also falls into this pattern. Such parties are rarely, certainly in the early stages, independent or autonomous groups able to act with a measure of independence from the state.

Many other factors are, of course, responsible for the development of one-party states. In a number of colonial societies, nationalist movements, almost from the beginning, had to be clandestine. This often necessitated the formation of 'armed parties' able to act as guerrilla forces against the colonial regime. Examples here are the FLN in Algeria, the Communists in China and the Viet Minh in Indo-China. Such parties, after independence, are likely to view opposition or rival parties with little enthusiasm.

There are two types of single-party systems, the totalitarian and the monolithic. Of these two types much the most frequent in existence is the monolithic single-party which has the basic characteristic of being the sole legal party in a state. The totalitarian party is, of course, empirically no novelty but the totalitarian party in power is quite rare.

The Totalitarian Party

Totalitarian parties are concerned with the total restructuring of the society. But, of course, success brings problems for the party as we can see in the case of the Soviet Union and some Eastern European states. The Soviet Communist Party was created in the autocratic Tsarist regime. At this period it was denied any legitimate place in the political system. Threatened by the Tsarist secret police it had, naturally, to operate as a clandestine political group. In ideology it aimed at a revolution, the ultimate goal of which was the total destruction of Tsarist society. Its organizational structure reflected the conditions under which it had to operate. At the bottom of the hierarchy were the small 'cell' organizations, uniting members within one workplace. Because the 'cell' was workplace based, the members had more or less daily contact with each other, thus strengthening party solidarity. Its daily contact with workaday problems was also an excellent context for political education and agitation.[46] It enabled party members to operate through other workplace organizations, such as trade unions. It is fairly easy to see that the 'cell' structure was ideally suited to clandestine political action. There was no necessity to call meetings, since 'cell' members were in daily contact and it was only rarely necessary to call them together as a group. It was easy to pass party orders on and coordinate action. Notice the different concept of political party that is implied by 'cell' organization. As Duverger points out, the size and nature of the 'cell' does not make it a suitable weapon for fighting an election.[47] It is designed for action at the workplace, not for electoral participation. Not intended for winning votes, for selecting representatives, or for maintaining contact between representatives and the electors, it is, instead, an instrument of agitation, propaganda, discipline and, if necessary, for clandestine action. Cells do not communicate with each other except through the next echelon—the section—which also acts on the same principle.

We can see the suitability of this mode of organization for clandestine action. Since the units at each level do not communicate directly with one another, contamination by factions and schisms, and infiltration by agents, is minimized. Relationships between the levels are described by the 'democratic centralism'. This, in principle, allows free discussion within each unit before a decision taken by the centre, but strictest discipline is to be observed after the decision has been reached. Local leaders are responsible to the centre for transmitting the views of the rank and file and for the task of conveying to the base the reasons behind the decisions of the centre. This organizational principle, known as democratic centralism, provides for very careful control by the centre of the implementation of its decisions.

In principle, this mode of organization gives strong central direction, with some participation of the rank and file in decision-making. But, of course, this is an uneasy balance to maintain. Even as early as 1905, Rosa Luxemburg warned against the power the central committee would have over the party.[*15*] This fear was realized when Stalin, largely through his control of the party apparatus, managed to oust his fellow claimants as Lenin's successor. In 1922, when Stalin assumed the post of Party Secretary, he began to convert this position from a technical into a political job by his control of appointments to key positions and through them control of the essential party apparatus.

While such centralization of control may be less of a problem in revolutionary conditions, conditions of stability present other factors which effect changes in party organizations and process. The totalitarianization of Soviet society under Stalin vastly broadened the scope of the party. All life was increasingly organized, coordinated and politicized. The party, in other words, acted as the agent guiding Russian society towards the industrial goals set by Stalin. Organizationally, the party extended its apparatus in order to parallel the state bureaucracy responsible for implementing the goals set by the party leadership. Thus a totalitarian party, such as the Soviet Communist Party, differs in its relationship to the state from parties in competitive systems. For one thing, since there are no opposition parties, any differences of opinion, if they are to be heard at all, must be heard within the party itself. A great deal of party activity is concerned with formulating and communicating doctrine and 'right thinking'. For the party member, commitment involves more than passive support. He is continually involved in party work so that the distinction between party and non-party activities is eroded. He is immersed in a constant process of education and re-evaluation. Because of this high investment required of party members, the party is selective and small, unlike most parties in competitive systems, which try to have as high a membership as possible with the minimum criteria for membership. In Soviet Russia, control from the centre is intensified by measures designed to increase the dependence of the member on the party. Party membership gave access to many privileged positions of power, responsibility and material reward and these, coupled with secret police surveillance and the terrorized, created a membership almost totally dependent on the will of the leadership. Under Stalin, the regime evolved a system of internal checks and balance, to prevent state and party bureaucrats from straying too far from the line promulgated from the top leadership. Thus, the bureaucrat was subject to three performance criteria: the classic bureaucratic criterion of efficient, disciplined loyalty to administrative procedure; secondly, conformity to current party line; and, thirdly, the exigencies of the situation resulting from his concrete task.

However, the very success of the party in gaining control and legitimacy created other strains within the organization. The tasks of societal management, of creating an industrial society and facing the external threats of war with Germany, meant that the party could not ignore the requirements for skills not automatically provided by party membership or doctrinal excellence. Engineers, managers, economists and scientists were needed in large numbers. While the party, through the educational system, attempted to maintain ideological purity, the inevitable differentiation of a complex society created the basis for interests other than purely party ones. Engineers and factory managers, for example, began to develop instrumental perspectives more concerned with their roles as engineers or managers than with their roles as representatives of a revolutionary party. There is evidence to suggest that of the three criteria of bureaucratic performance spoken of earlier, efficiency is becoming the most powerful criterion of success or failure. It appears that a degree of casualness towards ideology and a certain measure of extra-legal operations are tolerated for the sake of substantive results. The result has been the emergence of leaders at the top of the various bureaucratic hierarchies who are effective bureaucrats rather than great devotees of ideological or revolutionary vigour. Under Stalin, the terror and feelings of national loyalty prevented these potentialities for conflict becoming too real, but after his death, in 1953, these were some of the issues on which the struggle for power was fought. What had happened was that within the party a 'technocratic' element had intruded, having inevitable consequences for the operation of the party apparatus. A tension had been created between those whose interests were the party and those whose interests were more concerned with the economy, the military or other institutions in a way not necessarily consonant with party policy.

In other words, the problems of government changed the character of the revolutionary party. After some years, the party membership was composed of people who had little or no memory of the revolutionary period. The result is a loosening of centralized control in favour of greater devolution which gives greater initiative to local and functional units.

The Monolithic Party

The monolithic party is nearly always associated with the name of one man—Nkrumah, Houphouet-Boigny, Mussolini, Nyerere, Bourguiba, Castro, and so on. Their rise is associated with a cause—national unity—and generally their ideological stance is a nationalistic one. Such parties may be elected to power—the Convention Peoples Party, the Democratic Party of the Ivory Coast—or they may win power by armed struggle, as with Destour and the Italian Fascists. But however they achieve power it is quite unusual for them then to be voted out of office.

States within which monolithic parties arise are normally badly integrated both socially and politically so that the party achieves power and by using an umbrella ideology it encapsulates the demands of disparate sectors of the population. Historically, these parties arise when the country is only partly modernized, which consideration itself means a highly divided population stratified in terms of religion, ethnicity, economy and education. For this reason, a particularly effective ideology is that of nationalism, which attributes all present discontents and sectionalisms to the perfidious foreigner or imperialist. To combat this threat to the nation it is necessary to unite behind the leader and his party. Hence, the natural diversity of interest and ideas which characterize any society, but which run deepest in the mal-integrated country, must be dealt with in order to ensure national security. Basically there are two techniques through which this objective can be quickly achieved: (1) by destroying the social foundations upon which the diversity is based and (2) by integrating and assimilating the diversity into the framework of the party. Broadly, the first technique is that of the totalitarian party in power whilst the second is more typical of the monolithic party when it achieves power. Initially, the monolithic party claims to represent the interests of the nation or the nation-to-be and bids for the support of all but the most recalcitrant 'anti-national' elements in the society; and this 'tradition' continues after the party achieves power. Thus the African one-party states were initially dominated by parties which stressed the unity of the society against the colonialists, and after independence, when nationalism as a philosophy was otiose, the parties began to emphasize socialism of one variety or another. What all of these socialisms had in common was their non-exclusive nature. As Julius Nyerere said: 'It is therefore up to the people of Tanganyika—the peasants, the wage earners, the students, the leaders, all of us—to make sure that this socialist attitude of mind is not lost'.[48] Similarly, in Ghana the Convention People's Party gradually incorporated a host of previously independent organizations such as the trade unions and marketing concerns, whilst 'socialism' was transmuted into Nkrumaism.[*16*] Whilst the CPP incorporated more and more disparate organizations, so a parallel process of adopting a vacuous socialist ideology took place. At the same time, the party may also absorb members of the opposition by giving its leadership jobs, arresting and harrying them, and simply by being a majority party which enables the government to starve opposition areas of resources.

In the African states, when independence had been gained under the guidance of a dominant party the role of that party usually changed considerably. As we have seen, nationalism was often replaced by socialism as the official ideology, whilst incorporating the community into the party and very often attempting to act as a coordinator of the society to build economy and nation. Presented with the enormous problems of nation and economy building, the party became overinvolved or overabsorbent, either through force or persuasion, so that it ceased to have a separate identity from the society. Surveying the African evidence in the mid-1960's, Wallerstein concluded that 'In effect the one-party state in Africa has become in many places the no-party state'.[49]

Thus the monolithic party, since it does not destroy its social environment, must needs come to terms with it, and this means a process of accommodation with the major social forces of the society. For example, in Italy the Fascists had to work with the existing bureaucracy and were not powerful enough to control the Catholic Church, even supposing they wished to do so. Similarly, in Ghana the CPP regime attempted to control the bureaucracy but failed, and attempted to control the chiefs and was only partially successful. This process also takes place at a local level when the branches of the party are 'captured' by the social structure rather than dominate it, so that one account of the Convention People's Party in a town outside the capital of Ghana concludes that 'even the powerful CPP

. . . emerges as a Larteh rather than a national institution'.[59] Failing to control they necessarily have to compromise, and this immediately opens up the possibility that those in the party who take the ideology seriously are likely to become disillusioned with the regime. The spectacle of the disillusioned ideologue bitterly attacking the regime he has suffered to produce is one of the standard features of the societies within which the monolithic party has established itself; the Military Opposition and the Workers' Opposition in Russia in 1918–1920, the Falange in Spain from 1946, the Socialist Boys in Ghana from 1961, all provide examples of this tendency. The regime has then to decide whether or not to take the ideological criticisms seriously. Normally, practical considerations rule out of court the possibility of implementing an ideology and, anyway, the regime in office begins to shift its political base from its mass support towards the state bureaucracy. At this stage, the party usually attempts to penetrate the civil bureaucracy and armed forces, but the normal consequence is failure to infiltrate the army whilst influence seems to run from bureaucracy to party rather than *vice versa*. Here the danger is that the older emotional ties with the mass are destroyed so that the regime becomes both bureaucratic and necessarily authoritarian. At the same time, the party begins to degenerate from a nationally articulated party into a series of local cabals headed by a national committee consisting of the leaders of these cabals, as in the case of the PDCI of the Ivory Coast or the Italian Fascists.

The party fails to deliver the goods; heaven is not found on earth and *someone* must be to blame. Sectionalism, which plagues all underdeveloped countries, but which during the independence struggle or national crisis recedes into the background, becomes a primary political factor once again. To counteract this the leadership may attempt to divert the popular attention towards the foreigner who is accused of fanning 'the fires of sectional interests, of personal greed and ambition among leaders and contesting aspirants to power'.[51]

Thus the party, having incorporated at an institutional level the diversity of the host society, responds to this by diluting an already amorphous ideology. It becomes more dependent upon bureaucratic support to control the country and is, therefore, fairly readily overthrown by the armed forces who act with the civil bureaucracy to govern the country. Such a fate is always avoided in the totalitarian society, which acts from the beginning to destroy the social basis of opposition, and, equally important, reforms the educational system too so that it inculcates values and ideals corresponding to those espoused by the leadership. Having compromised with vested social interests, the monolithic party is in a much weaker position as regards enforcing conformity with regime norms, since the schools may actually be controlled by religious institutions, as in Italy and Spain, or by teachers trained in non-regime traditions, as in the African one-party states. Thus what tends to happen is that the monolithic party either degenerates and merges into the bureaucracy and army, as in Italy, Spain and the Ivory Coast, or it is overthrown by the military.

The monolithic party state is also quite unstable for another reason already hinted at: the party is very closely associated with the name and personal appeal of its leader who is nearly always a mortal. If he dies or is exiled there is a very strong chance of his party collapsing, as in the case of the CPP, of the Italian Fascists, or of the Argentinian Peronist party.

As we have seen, the monolithic party which dominates a country may well be quite unstable, but a monolithic party may also be in power within the state subunit of a stable federal country or, for that matter, in an unstable federation. Thus in the US there are a number of states, nearly all Southern, where one party (the Democratic) has for many years dominated the state legislatures and governors' offices and regularly obtains a majority of votes cast.[*17*] In Canada, the Liberal Party from 1896 up to the late 1950's dominated the Quebec electoral scene and in Australia the Labour Party dominates the electoral politics of New South Wales. Similarly, in Nigeria between 1959 and 1966 the constituent units were dominated by single-party systems whilst the central authority was based upon a shifting coalition. Almost certainly the explanation of the one-party dominance in Nigeria's regions was the ethnic basis of the different parties, which made it very difficult for them to capture the support and loyalty in other regions. Explanations of the single-party enclaves in more politically developed countries generally centre upon socio-economic variables such as level of urbanization, *per capita* income, level of industrialization, level of religious cleavage, and so on. What seems to happen is that the one-party dominant enclave in the federal state occurs when *per capita* income is low, when urbanization is low and when the percentage of the population engaged in manufacturing is low. Thus, reviewing the American evidence, Dawson claims that 'The competition of party systems, at least since the early 1930's, has been closely associated with higher levels of socio-economic development'.[*18*]

These associations between party competition and social developments will come as no surprise to those who noted the similar associations between high economic and social development and literacy, education, political stability, low alienation, political tolerance, sense of efficacy, toleration of ambiguity, and so on. Unfortunately, although these associations are sufficient to account for, or at least underpin, explanations which we have previously examined of democratic competition, they do not explain why the competition has taken a two-party rather than multi-party form.

11.5. Conclusions

Despite the ample body of literature on political parties, there are many questions left untackled or too quickly passed over, whilst other fields, particularly descriptive and historical accounts of particular political parties, seem to have suffered from over-exposure.

The political sociologist should perhaps be concentrating less on political parties as organizations in their own right, and more on the relationships between parties and, for instance, elections, political culture, political participation, ideology, doctrine and pressure groups, so as to discern more clearly the role of parties in general and in specific cases in the complex network of interrelationships called government. Political scientists, because of their background, often tend to be institutionalized in their approach to phenomena such as political parties, hence the failure to view parties as a unit in a web of relationships. The political sociologist is perhaps better equipped to deal with this topic.

In the next chapter we hope to rectify this situation to a certain extent by looking at pressure groups, and, in particular, their relationship with political parties.

References

1. A. Leiserson, 'The Place of Parties in the Study of Politics', *APSR*, **51,** 943–954 (1957).
2. J. La Palombara and M. Weiner, *Political Parties and Political Development*, Princeton University Press, Princeton, 1966, p. 3.
3. J. S. Coleman and C. G. Rosberg (eds.), *Political Parties and National Integration in Tropical Africa*, University of California Press, Berkeley, 1966, pp. 4–5.
4. F. W. Riggs, 'Comparative Politics and the Study of Political Parties: A Structural Approach', in W. J. Crotty (ed.), *Approaches to the Study of Party Organisation*, Alyn and Bacon, Boston, 1968.
5. S. Neuman (ed.), *Modern Political Parties: Approaches to Comparative Politics*, Chicago University Press, Chicago, 1956.
6. M. Duverger, *Political Parties*, Methuen, London, 1954.
7. J. Grumm, 'Theories of Electoral Systems', *Midwest Journal of Political Science*, **11,** 357–376 (1958).
8. S. M. Lipset, *Political Man*, Heinemann, London, 1963, pp. 45–76.
9. Madeira Keita, 'The Single Party in Africa', in P. Sigmund (ed.), *The Ideologies of the Developing Nations*, Praeger, London, 1967, pp. 232–233.
10. R. Emerson, 'Parties and National Integration in Africa', in J. La Palombara and M. Weiner (eds.), *Political Parties and Political Development*, Princeton

University Press, Princeton, 1966, p. 296; S. Rothman, 'One-Party Regimes: A Comparative Analysis', *Social Research*, **33** (1967).
11. I. Wallerstein, *Africa: The Politics of Independence*, Vintage Books, New York, 1961, p. 96.
12. D. Smiley, 'The Two-Party System and One-Party Dominance', *Canadian Journal of Economics and Political Science*, **24,** 312–322 (1958); F. Sorauf, *Political Parties in the American System*, Little, Brown, Boston, 1964, pp. 27–30.
13. L. Epstein, *Political Parties in Western Democracies*, Pall Mall, London, 1967, p. 39.
14. D. Stokes and G. Iversen, 'On the Existence of Forces Restoring Party Competitions', *Public Opinion Quarterly*, **26,** 159–171 (1962).
15. A. Campbell, P. Converse, W. Miller and D. Stokes, *The American Voter*, Wiley, New York, 1964, pp. 552–558.
16. S. J. Eldersveld, *Political Parties: A Behavioural Analysis*, Rand McNally, Chicago, 1964, p. 5.
17. R. Michels, *First Lectures in Political Sociology*, University of Minnesota Press, Minneapolis, 1949, ed. by Alfred de Grazia, p. 145.
18. S. J. Eldersveld, *Political Parties: A Behavioural Analysis*, Rand McNally, Chicago, 1964, p. 70.
19. R. Michels, *Political Parties*, Free Press, Glencoe, 1949, pp. 374–376; A. Downs, *An Economic Theory of Democracy*, Harper and Row, New York, 1957, pp. 96–141.
20. M. Duverger, *Political Parties*, Methuen, London, 1954, p. 192.
21. R. T. McKenzie, *British Political Parties*, Heinemann, London, 1955, pp. 188–199 and 485–615.
22. R. Michels, *Political Parties*, Free Press, Glencoe, 1949.
23. —— *Political Parties*, Free Press, Glencoe, 1949, pp. 81–82.
24. R. T. McKenzie, *British Political Parties*, Heinemann, London, 1955, p. 644.
25. R. M. Cyert and J. C. March, 'A Behavioural Theory of Organisational Objectives', in M. Haire (ed.), *Modern Organisation Theory*, Wiley, New York, 1959, pp. 76–89; S. J. Eldersveld, *Political Parties: A Behavioural Analysis*, Rand McNally, Chicago, 1964.
26. E. C. Banfield, *Political Influence*, Free Press, New York, 1961, pp. 235–262.
27. S. J. Eldersveld, *Political Parties: A Behavioural Analysis*, Rand McNally, Chicago, 1964, pp. 88–89.
28. M. Duverger, *Political Parties*, Methuen, London, 1954, p. 17.
29. S. J. Eldersveld, *Political Parties: A Behavioural Analysis*, Rand McNally, Chicago, 1964, ch. 5; H. Lasswell and A. Kaplan, *Power and Society*, Yale University Press, New Haven, 1950, pp. 219–220.
30. S. J. Eldersveld, *Political Parties: A Behavioural Analysis*, Rand McNally, Chicago, 1964, pp. 9 and 98–117.
31. —— *Political Parties: A Behavioural Analysis*, Rand McNally, Chicago, 1964, pp. 98–117.
32. L. Epstein, 'British Mass Parties in Comparison with American Parties', *Political Science Quarterly*, **71** (1956); R. T. McKenzie, *British Political Parties*, Heinemann, London, 1955.
33. M. Olsen, Jr., *The Logic of Collective Action*, Harvard University Press, Cambridge, Mass., 1965, p. 2.

34. —— *The Logic of Collective Action*, Harvard University Press, Cambridge, Mass., 1965, p. 35.
35. —— *The Logic of Collective Action*, Harvard University Press, Cambridge, Mass., 1965, p. 165.
36. —— *The Logic of Collective Action*, Harvard University Press, Cambridge, Mass., 1965, p. 131.
37. S. Barnes, 'Party Democracy and the Logic of Collective Action', in W. Crotty (ed.), *Approaches to the Study of Party Organisation*, Allyn and Bacon, Boston, 1968, pp. 105–138.
38. J. A. Schlesinger, 'Political Party Organisation', in J. G. March (ed.), *Handbook of Organisations*, Rand McNally, Chicago, 1965, pp. 764–801.
39. J. Wahlke, H. Eulau, W. Buchanan and L. C. Ferguson, *The Legislative System*, Wiley, New York, 1962, pp. 121–124.
40. J. Q. Wilson, *The Amateur Democrat*, University of Chicago Press, Chicago, 1962.
41. E. Banfield, *Political Influence*, Free Press, Glencoe, 1961, and summary by J. A. Schlesinger, 'Political Party Organisation', in J. G. March (ed.), *Handbook of Organisations*, Rand McNally, Chicago, 1965, p. 770.
42. F. J. Sorauf, 'The Silent Revolution in Patronage', *Public Administrative Review*, **28,** 20–28 (1960).
43. I. Howe and L. Coser, *The American Communist Party: A Critical History*, Praeger, New York, 1962, pp. 104–105.
44. Robert E. Dowse, 'The Military and Political Development', in C. Leys (ed.), *Politics and Change in Developing Countries*, Cambridge University Press, London, 1970, pp. 213–246.
45. L. Binder, 'Political Recruitment and Participation in Egypt', in J. La Palombara and M. Weiner (eds.), *Political Parties and Political Development*, Princeton University Press, Princeton, 1966, pp. 217–240.
46. M. Duverger, *Political Parties*, Methuen, London, 1954, p. 29.
47. —— *Political Parties*, Methuen, London, 1954, p. 35.
48. Julius Nyerere, *Africa's Freedom*, Unwin Books, London, 1964, p. 73.
49. I. Wallerstein, 'Decline of the Party in Single Party States', in J. La Palombara and M. Weiner (eds.), *Political Parties and Political Development*, Princeton University Press, Princeton, 1966, pp. 201–214.
50. D. Brokensha, *Social Change at Larteh, Ghana*, Oxford University Press, London, 1966, p. xix; M. Owusu, *Uses and Abuses of Political Power*, Chicago University Press, Chicago, 1970, chs. 9 and 10.
51. Kwame Nkrumah, *Africa Must Unite*, Heinemann, London, 1963, p. xvi.

Notes and Further Reading

1. In societies where the nationalist elite is relatively satisfied with the steps taken by the colonial power to improve participation, a mass party may not develop. For example, in Ceylon, the Ceylon National Congress was moderately content with the steps taken by the British to increase opportunities for self-government, and no mass movement developed until elections had been established after independence. See J. La Palombara and M. Weiner, *Political Parties and Political Development*, Princeton University Press, Princeton, 1966, p. 16.

2. S. Huntington in S. Huntington and C. Moore, *Authoritarian Politics in Modern Society*, Basic Books, New York, 1970, p. 11. Similarly, M. Pinard writing of one-party dominance in Canadian provincial politics argues that 'One-party dominance is itself produced by structural attachments, not by class homogeneity', in *Canadian Journal of Economics and Political Science*, **33**, 358–373 (1967).
3. A. Campbell, P. Converse, W. Miller and D. Stokes, *The American Voter*, Wiley, New York, 1964, pp. 552–558. In an extremely interesting article Rose and Urwin demonstrate that for 19 countries with competitive elections in Western Europe, Scandinavia and Anglo-America for a total of 142 elections since 1945 'the electoral strength of most parties in Western nations . . . had changed very little from decade to decade or within the lifespan of a generation'. They include only parties which had fought three elections and obtained at least 5 per cent of the vote once, so that one can conclude that once a party system is established, whether two- or multi-, it is not easy for another party to break in. 'Persistence and Change in Western Party Systems Since 1945', in *Political Studies*, **18**, 287–319 (1970). See C. Landé, *Leaders, Factions and Parties*, Yale University Southeast Asia Studies, Monograph 6, 1966, for a fascinating account of 'functional bifactionalism' and the social mechanisms producing it in the Philippines.
4. In a UK survey it was actually discovered that some people believed that it was undesirable for one party to dominate the government and they were more likely than those who did not believe this to vote against an incumbent party, D. Butler and D. Stokes, *Political Change in Britain*, Macmillan, London, 1969, pp. 431–437.
5. But note this explanation is couched in terms of *persistence* so that it does not explain why in the first place a party system took the shape it did. See S. M. Lipset, *The First New Nation*, Heinemann, London, 1964, pp. 286–317, and S. M. Lipset and S. Rokkan, *Party Systems and Voter Alignments*, Free Press, New York, 1967, Introduction, for analyses of historical origins.
6. See L. Epstein, 'British Mass Parties in Comparison with American Parties', *Political Science Quarterly*, **72**, 97–125 (1956). The fullest account of the complexities of internal party relationships of the major British parties is in R. T. McKenzie, *British Political Parties*, Heinemann, London, 1955.
7. R. Michels, *Political Parties*, Free Press, Glencoe, 1949, p. 29. Michels is subscribing to a classical theory of democracy which, in fact, bears little relationship to the way in which the democratic process has evolved in Europe and the Anglo-American democracies. See, for example, J. Schumpeter, *Capitalism, Socialism and Democracy*, Allen and Unwin, London, 1943. But see G. Hands, 'Roberto Michels and the Study of Political Parties', *British Journal of Political Science*, **1**, 155–172 (1971), who detects three different usages of the term 'democracy' by Michels.
8. For an excellent critique and evaluation of Michels as a sociological theorist, see I. M. Zeitlin, *Ideology and the Development of Sociological Theory*, Prentice-Hall, Englewood Cliffs, 1968, ch. 14.
9. M. Ostrogorski, *Democracy and the Organisation of Political Parties*, 2 vols., Macmillan, London, 1902. The best short account is contained in S. Lipset, *Revolution and Counter-Revolution*, Basic Books, New York, 1968, pp. 362–411.
10. This is not claiming that his decisions are always, or even occasionally,

democratic in the sense of following the 'will of the people', only that he cannot do what he pleases, but is subject to the process of compromise and reconciliations of competing values and means.

11. M. Olsen, Jr., *The Logic of Collective Action*, Harvard University Press, Cambridge, Mass., 1965; see also S. M. Barnes, 'Party Democracy and the Logic of Collective Action', in W. J. Crotty (ed.), *Approaches to the Study of Party Organization*, Allyn and Bacon, Boston, 1968, pp. 105–138.
12. Of the group interviewed by Almond, 29 per cent cited pressure on personal relationships as a reason for defecting from the party. See G. Almond, *The Appeals of Communism*, Princeton University Press, Princeton, 1954.
13. For an account of these 'Utopian' communities, see T. Caplow, *The Principles of Organisation*, Harcourt, Brace and World, New York, 1964, ch. 8.
14. V. R. Lorwin, 'Working-class Politics and Economic Development in Western Europe', *American Historical Review*, **LXIII**, 338–351 (1958). For an account of such a process in the UK see Robert E. Dowse, *Left in the Centre*, Longmans, London, 1966.
15. Mentioned in F. C. Barghorn, 'The U.S.S.R.: Monolithic Controls at Home and Abroad', in S. Neumann, *Modern Political Parties*, University of Chicago Press, Chicago, 1956, p. 222.
16. On this process in Africa generally see J. S. Coleman and C. G. Rosberg (eds.), *Political Parties and National Integrations in Tropical Africa*, University of California Press, Berkeley, 1964, pp. 318–443.
17. See Chapter 1 of A. Heard, *A Two-Party South?*, University of North Carolina Press, Chapel Hill, 1952, for details.
18. R. Dawson, 'Social Development, Party Competition, and Policy', in W. Chambers and W. Burnham (eds.), *The American Party Systems*, Oxford University Press, Oxford, 1967, pp. 203–237. P. Cutright, 'Urbanisation and Competitive Party Politics', *American Political Science Review*, **25**, 552–564 (1963) supports this finding as does T. Casstevens, 'The Context of Democratic Competition in American State Politics', *American Journal of Sociology*, **68**, 536–543 (1963).

12

POLITICAL ORGANIZATIONS II: PRESSURE GROUPS

12.1. Introduction

THERE ARE basically two kinds of organizations formally concerned with politics. The first kind, political parties, we have discussed in the previous chapter: they are interested in governing, and in most advanced societies, where there is more than one party, they compete for the governing position. However, the other group of organizations, while not attempting to govern, attempts to influence those that do govern. Interest groups, lobbies, pressure groups and so on all come under this heading. They vary enormously in their strength, size, amount of influence and scope of interest. While the political party is directly concerned with nominating candidates for political office, the interest group eschews candidate nomination in favour of the strategies of persuasion, lobbying and the devices of public relations.[1]

In practice, as might be expected, the distinction between the governors and those who attempt to influence the governors is often difficult to operate.

In the first place, some interest groups develop into political parties. The trade unions in late nineteenth-century Britain, for example, were important interest groups that in 1900 helped form the Labour Representation Committee in order to promote working men to Parliament. In 1906 the LRC became the Labour Party. At what stage, if any, interest groups cease to be interest groups and become political parties is difficult to say, as is also the case with the small minor parties that compete in American presidential and British general elections. Are these parties or interest groups? The line is further blurred by interest groups which have a particular working relationship with a political party; that between the trade unions and the British Labour Party is a case in point. Similarly, the Anti-Saloon League achieved its alteration of the United States constitution by working through existing party organizations.[2] Other examples of this close working liaison between interest groups and particular political parties abound. In some political systems, the claims of major groups are put by organized interest groups working through the major parties. In Sweden, the claims of manual workers are formulated by the Federation of Labour and channelled through the Social-Democratic Party. Similarly, farmers reach up through the Centre Party and white-collar workers through the Liberal and Conservative Parties.[3] In Italy, the situation is more complex because one of the unions, the Confederazione Generale Italiana del Lavaro, works through two political parties, the Partito Communista Italiano and the Partito Socialista Italiano, and all three bodies are run by what amount to interlocking directorates. In addition, the flow of influence is not only from interest groups to party, but from party to interest group.[4] In one-party states, of course, the identification problem is even more pronounced. It appears that here the political party itself is the arena within which contending interests struggle for influence.

Though in practice it may be difficult to separate what we are calling interest groups from political parties, we do need to give some consideration to what it is we are referring to by the term 'interest group'. An interest group we take to be an association of individuals, which is not a political party as we have defined it, concerned to influence the government in a manner favourable to the interests of the group. We are here speaking of formally organized and constituted groups not with simple categories such as occupational strata, women, immigrants, etc. These may be the basis of interest groups but are not themselves interest groups as understood here.

Another difference between political parties and interest groups is that the latter tend to have a rather narrower set of objectives than political parties. Since they do not intend to win a majority of votes, interest groups have less need to develop anything like a comprehensive policy platform. They are more concerned with promoting the interests of a particular sectional group, whatever it may be. As is to be expected, in some cases this distinction presents a number of problems. An interest group may reach the stage where it becomes closer to a political party by developing a more open, less restricted platform. The classic case here is that of trade unions, especially in Europe, which espouse issues and causes relevant to the society as a whole rather than maintaining a narrow concern with occupational interests. British trade unions, for example, have often tried to influence Labour Party policy on such matters as foreign affairs, nuclear disarmament, racial discrimination, general social and economic policy, and so on. Perhaps a further illustration of this point is the example of the military as a corporate group with its own specific professional interests but also with wider interests which may cause it to move from the position of a pressure group to that of ruling group following a *coup d'état*. In other words, when we speak of a narrow set of concerns we are referring to a general tendency rather than a definitive characteristic.

The academic study of 'interest groups' is historically derived from the 'group theory' of politics we discussed earlier, which, briefly, argues that politics is the process by which social values are allocated and one which is to be understood by examination of the groups which play a part in effecting decisions. To some writers, government was conceived as the adjustment or balance of group interests.[5] While certain ambiguities were involved in the notion of 'group', the theory did serve to direct empirical attention to the important role played by what we are calling 'interest groups' in the political process. In other words, it widened the scope of the attention of political scientists and bade them look beyond the formal machinery of legislatures and political parties to organizations which seemed at first sight peripheral to the proper business of politics.[*1*]

12.2. Typologies of Interest Groups

Here, as with political parties, we do not want to get too deeply involved in discussions of typologies. None the less, to pay some attention to typologies may also give some idea of the problems and areas of interest in the study of interest groups.

The very term 'interest group' suggests the usual conception of them: they are organized groups pursuing fairly clearly defined goals, hence an obvious way to categorize them is in terms of the goal characteristics. Thus, we have the distinction between the 'protective' and the 'promotional' groups, the former defending a section of society, the latter promoting a cause. Usually classified in the first category are trade unions, professional associations, trade associations, and so on; all the thousands of associations which defend the interests of a particular sector of society. The second includes groups such as the Campaign for Nuclear Disarmament, the Royal Society for the Prevention of Cruelty to Animals, and so on. This at least has intuitive merit in that it is fairly simply grasped. The difficulties become only too apparent on closer inspection. Part of the trouble is that there is no clear line between defending and promoting an interest. Trade unions, for example, may wish to promote a minimum wage law as a means of defending the interests of their members. Motoring organizations, often claimed as associations protecting the motorist, may well promote a campaign for better roads. But even accepting for the moment these ambiguities, it is not clear how the distinction serves to say very much more about the behaviour or the structure of such groups. The claim is that protective groups are rooted only in a narrow sector of society, say, workers in a particular industry or the members of a particular profession, while promotional groups have no such restriction but potentially draw on all members of society. The trouble with this is that a number of characteristics are being confused here. True, a so-called protective association may draw only on the members of a defined industry or trade and thus has a formally prescribed membership, but it is difficult to see the precise link this has with it being a protective group. Many promotional groups may, in other ways perhaps, restrict their membership. An animal sadist would no doubt be quietly rooted out of the RSPCA and there would not seem to be much point in a convinced warmonger being a member of CND. There are differences here, but they are not conveyed precisely by the idea of being 'protective' and 'promotional' or by the simple notion of restriction of membership. Interest groups do differ in terms of clientele. Some groups do try to represent the interests of a fairly well-defined group or section of society, while other groups have no comparable clientele other than the whole body of citizens. Instead, they seem to attract members because of consensus on a specific issue or because they have a set of general dispositions about events. Another point here is that source of membership needs to be separated from scope of appeal. As far as promotional groups are concerned, they want to appeal not to a special group but to everybody. Thus, CND, to take it as an example of a promotional group, was not solely concerned with group maintenance but also with trying to convert or educate non-members to its point of view. Unfortunately, a protectional group which neglected to sway public opinion may find itself so much the weaker. Protection often involves education of public opinion, as the propaganda of trade unions and of trade associations will attest.

Though other authors use different terms for what we have called 'interest groups', the distinction just discussed seems to be the predominant one. However, as we have said previously, typologies need to be geared to a particular problem and providing we, here, have reasonably well specified what the phenomenon is we are looking at, there seems little need to pursue the discussion further. Instead, we shall address the discussion to questions about the performance and operation of interest groups, how they arise, and their relation to the political system.

12.3. The Social Basis of Interest Groups

There are two questions here: firstly, the origin of interest groups as a phenomenon of political society and, secondly, the origin of particular interest groups. As far as the first question is concerned, we have already sketched the lines of an answer when speaking of political parties. Then we spoke of parties emerging as societies grew more complex and *gesellschaft* in character. In other words, society becomes more differentiated and a person's life more and more segmented between the various differentiated structures. One outcome of this process is the emergence of a great number of secondary structures or associations. Some of these associations begin to attempt to exert influence on the government—and in so doing become 'interest groups'. This contact between state and other associations is facilitated by the greater reach government has in large-scale societies which makes inevitable its contact with those associations. This is especially true of its economic role. Industrialization brings with it an increased spread and frequency of governmental participation in economic and social affairs. This is illustrated by the fact that in under-developed societies only about 10 per cent of the gross national product is spent by the government, whereas in highly industrialized societies it tends to be of the order of 30 per cent.[6]

As society becomes more complex and specialized, it will tend to form additional associations:

> 'With an increase in specialisation . . . the proliferation of associations (in the technical sense of the term); as they grow more complex, ie as highly differentiated institutionalised groups increase in number, societies evolve greater numbers of associations'.[7]

This increase in the number of associations will inevitably have its impact on government whenever government is important to the group in question.

Nevertheless, as might be expected, interest groups, even if not so numerous, are certainly present in developing countries, but their social basis is not so thoroughly universalistic as is the case in the more developed countries. It is certainly the case that functional groups such as the state bureaucracy, the armed forces and police together with the larger private traders are organized and self-conscious of their collective interests. Since the state is enormously more important in the undeveloped world as a source of career, economic opportunity and status than any private sector, it follows that access to the state decision-making location is absolutely crucial. Hence, those outside necessarily organize themselves in order to obtain access and those inside tend to use the state apparatus to their own advantage. The most blatant example of the organizing outsiders are the trading 'Syrians' of West Africa who, as non-citizens, lack votes but have finance and organization with which they attempt to circumvent legislation undermining their economically advantageous positions. Again, most African political parties historically sprang out of self-improvement organizations, literary societies and tribal associations of one kind and another so that pressure groups utilized existing formations to influence the colonial rulers. That is, the basis of interest group formation in the developing countries is what Almond has called 'non-associational interests' such as kinship, lineage, ethnicity and region rather than the purely associational interests of occupation, education and other non-ascriptive characteristics.[8] On the other hand, this basis, although probably the most significant for a majority of the people, is not the only one upon which interests may develop.

A massively important structural location of interest in the developing country is the organization of the state itself, which may well be the major employer of skilled manpower. In Africa, this may take the form of a mutually reinforcing system of ministerial bureaucracies, universities and armed forces upon which a very large percentage of the total tax income of the country may be spent. Attempts to bring this burden down or to shift the allocation of benefits from one sector of the bureaucratized elite to another are a major source of political instability which does not stop short at the military as a pressure group assuming political control.[*2*]

What we have argued is that as a society begins to approach the *gesellschaft*-type, then associations begin to emerge which may try to influence legislation or other types of government action. The basis of such groups in principle is any socially meaningful category or status. The universally ascriptive statuses, for example, age, sex and ethnicity, may well be the basis of interest group formation if they assume a political significance. An increase in the number of people of pensionable age may encourage an increase in associations devoted to the interests of older people. Once an association has been formed, it is likely to begin to attempt political influence if and when it perceives that the interests it is presumably proclaiming are challenged. What sparks this off it is difficult to say with any generality. It may simply be an increase in the size of the group in which the association is anchored. In Britain, the League of Coloured Peoples made little impact on the public for nearly twenty years of its existence from the early 1930's.[9] But, when the number of coloured people in Britain increased from 100,000 in the 1950's to nearly a million in the later 60's, most of them concentrated in the great conurbations, many more 'interest groups' based on ethnicity emerged. There arose the

National Federation of Pakistani Associations, the West Indian Standing Conference, the Caribbean Association, the Indian Workers Association, and so on. In other words, 'race' became an issue as the size and density of coloured immigrants increased. Coloured people perceived themselves as a group having interests as coloured people over and above their other statuses as husbands, fathers, workers, or whatever. They became noticed as a meaningful social category to be accounted for either as a threat or as contributors to the established order. It is this self-consciousness of a section of society as having needs and interests as a group which is crucial to the emergence of associations to further those interests. The kind of factors which encourage this self-consciousness are, of course, varied. Size has, perhaps, something to do with it, though it is unlikely that this is a necessary or sufficient condition. Intercommunication within the status group is another factor. Trade unions did not begin to emerge with any force until sufficient numbers of industrial workers began to realize they had common interests. But, again, things are not all that clear cut. There have always been large numbers of women but, until the late nineteenth century, few women's associations. So, in addition, we have to explain why suddenly an aggregate of people begin to develop this self-consciousness. Size and a high degree of intercommunication within the aggregate are more likely to be favourable contexts for the emergence of an interest group rather than the actual catalyst creating it. Many of these kinds of associations are born in conditions similar to those associated with social movements, where a group perceives itself as threatened or deprived in some way. This threat or deprivation may not be material, of course; other factors such as a sense of status loss, of rights being neglected, or protection against other powerful groups encroaching upon a group's social territory are equally important.

When groups undergo the sort of experiences we have described they are similar to nascent political parties or social movement organizations. The path the organization takes after this is a matter very much dependent upon the character of the political system. Here the crucial matter is the extent to which a group can gain access to the governmental apparatus and the extent that it has influence. If it is unable to achieve either of these then it may well develop into a political party. Once again, British trade unions are a case in point. During the nineteenth century they strove for legitimacy and a place within the political system. At this stage they were very political bodies espousing more than simple wage increases and improvements in working conditions. This activity culminated in the formation of the Labour Party. But, once they had achieved a legitimate status and point of contact with the governmental system, trade unions then began to assume a more limited character, losing much of their ideological and reforming fervour, and, instead, approximating more closely to a typical interest group. Thus, if the political system can accept the status of the interest group as legitimate, then, once it has emerged, it will remain thus. But, again, none of this is automatic. There are many cases of potential interest groups which rarely become actual or, at least, take many years before realizing their potential. We cannot accept, as Truman does, the idea that associations will arise spontaneously out of the social process. He took a benign view of the natural wisdom of society in that competing groups would spontaneously arise and the 'invisible hand' of this competition would ensure social checks and balance, stability, reasonable shares for all, and the prevention of special sectional interests being met at the expense of other interests.[10] If a large industry started to charge an exorbitant price to the consumer, presumably the consumers would organize a lobby to oppose the corporation's actions.[11] Indeed, he goes so far as to say that the very existence of potential groups, and the fear that they would organize, keeps the organized interests from making excessive demands.

However comfortable this arrangement may seem, unfortunately it contains a number of difficulties. It is based on premises which are untenable, namely, that large groups can attract membership and support as easily as small groups. But, because of the difference between small groups and large latent groups, there is no reason to suppose that as problems small primary groups cannot handle emerge, large voluntary associations will arise to deal with them. In other words, the idea that the outrageous demands of one group will be counterbalanced by the demands of other groups is not to be entertained.[12] Since relatively small groups will frequently be able to organize themselves voluntarily and act in support of their common interests and large groups would normally be unable to do so, the outcome of the political struggle will not be symmetrical. The small oligopolistic industry will sometimes succeed in securing favourable tax legislation even if the vast majority of the population loses as a result. That is, smaller groups, because they are generally organized and active, can often defeat the large latent groups that are, according to democratic theory, supposed to prevail.

What is missing from the view of Truman and others is an agreement as to *how* damage to a large group's interests would provide an incentive or stimulus for the members of that large group to sacrifice their individual interests on behalf of the large group goal. That is, they fail to show *why* the individual member of the large latent group will voluntarily support the group goal when his support will not in any case be decisive in its achievement, and when he would be likely to receive the benefits from the goal's attainment whether he had worked for it or not.[13]

So, if the individuals in a large latent group have no incentive to organize an interest group to obtain a collective benefit, how can the fact that some such groups are so organized be explained? According to Olsen, the significant feature of those groups is that they are generally organized for some *other* purpose.[14] The large and powerful economic lobbies, for example, are byproducts of organizations that obtain their strength and support because they perform some function in addition to lobbying for collective goods. The lobbies of the large economic groups are the by-products of organizations that have the capacity to 'mobilize' a latent group with 'selective incentives'. They are able to do this either because they have the authority and the capacity to be coercive, or because they have a source of positive inducements they can offer the individuals in a latent group. Clearly, purely political organizations cannot legally coerce people into becoming members. But if an organization, because of some other function it performed (for example selling private or non-collective goods, providing social and recreational benefits to individual members), had a justification for having a compulsory membership, or could offer other inducements to individuals to become members, it might then create resources for a lobby. 'Only such an organization could make a joint offering or "tied sale" of a collective and non-collective good that could stimulate a rational individual in a large group to bear part of the cost of obtaining a collective good.'[15] For this reason, then, there are many organizations which not only have lobbying functions but also have economic, social and recreational functions.

It is essential to note that this theory applies only to large latent groups. It does not apply to smaller groups since these can often provide a lobby, or any other collective benefit, without any *selective* incentives. This is because in some small groups each of the members, or at least one of them, will find that his personal gain from having the collective good exceeds the total cost of providing some amount of that collective good; there are members who would be better off if the collective good were provided (even if they had to pay the entire cost of providing it themselves) than they would be if it were not provided. Thus, in a very small group, where each member gets a substantial proportion of the total gain simply because there are few others in the group, a collective good can often be provided by the voluntary, self-interested action of the members.[16] However, in large latent groups the individual has no incentive to sacrifice time, money or effort voluntarily to help obtain a collective good, because he alone cannot be decisive in determining whether or not this collective good will be obtained, but if it is, through the efforts of others, he will enjoy it anyway. Thus, as said above, he would support the organization to obtain collective goods only if he was coerced into paying dues, or if he had the support of the organization to obtain some other non-collective benefit which he desired. For example, the American Medical Association, by providing individual incentives to members alone, such as defence against malpractice suits, publishing medical journals, and so on, is able to mount an impressive lobbying organization.[*3*] Thus, according to this theory, the impressive political power of groups such as the AMA is a byproduct of the non-political activities of such groups, and the weakness of other groups is due largely to their inability to offer the individual non-collective benefits as incentives for membership.

In the United States, and one would suspect most large-scale industrial societies, the largest group of lobby organizations is the business lobbies.[17] By the side of the high degree of organization of businessmen, the level of organization of other groups is small indeed. For example, in 1960 it was estimated that 'only one sixteen hundreds of one per cent of consumers' were members of the National Consumers' League. Only 6 per cent of American motorists were members of the Automobile Association, and only about 15 per cent of veterans belonged to the American Legion.[18] In Britain, by the 1950's, trade associations were virtually all-embracing in their membership: 90 per cent of the larger firms and 76 per cent of the smaller belonged to one or more of the 1300 trade associations. By 1957, more manufacturing firms were directly or indirectly affiliated with the Federation of British Industries, which represented some six-sevenths of all industrial concerns employing more than ten workers. In addition, other trade associations developed to represent a complete industry, such as the Society of British Aircraft Constructors, the Association of British Chemical Manufacturers, the British Iron and Steel Federation, the Society of Motor Manufacturers, and so on.[19] Furthermore, this high level of organization among businessmen is associated with considerable power and influence, despite the paucity of their numbers. It appears that the secret of the high degree of organization and power of business interests is due to the very smallness of their numbers. In other words, the business community is divided into a series of 'industries' each of which contains only a fairly small number of firms. Thus, instead of being subject to the constraints operating on large latent groups, industries are often small enough to organize themselves voluntarily into an active lobby. So, whereas almost every occupational group involves thousands of workers, the business interests of the society are normally congregated in oligopoly-sized groups or industries. It follows, then, that the labouring, professional and agricultural interests make up large latent groups that can only organize and act effectively when their latent power is crystallized by some organization which provides political power as a byproduct. In contrast, generally, business interests can organize action to further their interests both voluntarily and directly, without the need for such assistance.

The major type of business association is the trade association representing small, specialized interests. Schattschneider quotes figures for the metal products industry, which has 421 trade associations as listed in the *National Associations of the United States*. One hundred and fifty-three of these have a membership of less than 20, and the median membership is somewhere between 24 and 50. Much the same scale of memberships is to be found in the timber, furniture and paper industries, where 37.3 per cent of associations listed had a membership of less than 20 and a median membership somewhere around the 25–50 range. This pattern is representative of nearly all other types of industry.[*4*] Trade associations are, therefore, normally small, and this smallness must be the principal reason that so many of them exist. Many of them also provide other non-collective services—trade information, references, debt collection, advisory services and the like—which offer a further incentive to membership.

It should not be concluded from the disproportionate power of the 'special interests' of particular sections of the business community that the business community as a whole has disproportionate power in relation to other groups in the society, especially when dealing with issues of broad national concern rather than on questions of particular importance. In fact, the business community *as a whole* is a large latent group and has the same problems of organization as other similar groups in society.[*5*] To support this, Olsen quotes the case of the two major organizations in the United States which claim to speak for business as a whole, the National Association of Manufacturers and the Chamber of Commerce of the United States. Neither of them has disproportionate power in relation to similar labour organizations, such as the AFL-CIO or the American Medical Association or the American Farm Bureau Federation.

The principal members of the Chamber of Commerce of the United States are the many local chambers of commerce throughout the country. These local chambers are normally small groups which can organize themselves with ease. Through them businessmen are able to make useful contacts and exchange information and, in general, forge the informal links appropriate to their activities. The Chamber of Commerce of the United States is a federation of these local associations, and for them it provides information and organization services. But, nevertheless, individual members, even local associations, are essentially only individual units in a large latent group and can make no decisive contribution to the success of the national organization and will benefit whether they have participated or not.

The National Association of Manufacturers is really a single small group of very large businesses. Though nominally the NAM has a few thousand members, in practice it is supported and controlled by a handful of really big businesses which contribute by far the bulk of its monetary resources.[20] In other words, they are still a small group by no means any more powerful than those organizations representing labour, the professions or farming. The NAM has not always been successful in preventing the passage of legislation it opposes.[21]

The business community as a whole, which is certainly a large latent group, is not fully organized. Though it has two organizations which attempt to represent it, these draw much of their support from a small group of large businesses: they do not, in other words, attract the support of the whole business community. A small group is powerful in matters relating to a particular industry, because in this case it is usually the only organized force. It is less formidable when national issues are involved, for in this situation it must take on organized labour and other large organized groups. Thus, the business community, in the aggregate, is not a uniquely effective pressure group. For example, though it seems that particular interests are able to win specific concessions, tax loopholes, favourable tariffs and the like, the business community as a whole has not been successful in its attempt to stop the trend towards social welfare legislation and progressive taxation.[22]

Now, although this theory would seem to cover most if not all of the main economic interest associations, it does not cover so easily those interest groups which have social, political, religious, even philanthropic objectives. Its applicability to associations composed of rational individuals interested in a common goal seems obvious in the case of economic groups. But, although in principle this theory of large groups is not limited to situations of self-interested economic behaviour, or where only monetary or material interests are at stake, its helpfulness in non-economic cases needs to be carefully assessed.

True, many of these non-economic associations provide a number of incentives to the member. Veterans' organizations, for example, are not primarily economic or political in tone, but social. That is, they attract most of their members because of the social benefits they offer: comradeship, recreational facilities, recognition as a veteran, insurance, and so on. All of these benefits go only to those who join, and thus provide selective incentives to the individual member. Of course, any benefits the organization is able to win from the government for veterans go to any veteran, member or not. Accordingly, the political power of the veterans' lobbies is a byproduct of the social and economic services provided.

Part of the difficulty in applying this theory to other non-economic groups is the ambiguities which can be attached to the notion of rationality. It is tempting, in order to preserve the theory, to broaden the notion of rationality, in the sense that objectives are 'pursued by means that are efficient and effective',[*6*] to include all kinds of human behaviour in whatever context. Thus, whenever a person acts it is assumed that he acted rationally to further some 'interest' he had. Even if the action is what we would call philanthropic it is assumed that the individual obtained more utility by acting in this way rather than another. While the theory outlined here does not require such broadening of the notion of rationality, its application to some non-economic organization might encourage it. Thus, the individual who made a small contribution to a national charity would do so, not under the mistaken belief that his contribution would noticeably augment the resources of the charity, but rather because he got a non-collective satisfaction by doing so, a sense of personal worth, public praise, or whatever. But the trouble is that when all action is assumed to be rational, then the theory is correct simply by virtue of its logical consistency, not because it is empirically verifiable or true.[23] Nor is the theory useful for looking at those groups which seek 'lost' causes. Here, more powerful suggestions derive from social psychology and sociology rather than from economics. People, apparently irrationally, support and give great energy to hopeless causes because they derive other 'satisfactions' or because their crusade fulfils some 'need'. This kind of involvement is 'irrational' because there is no deliberate purposeful relating of ends and means. In other words, the members of the Prohibition Party still support its activities because they *believe* in the programme, even though, by economic criteria, such support is 'irrational'. To them, of course, their commitment to the goals, policies and programmes is by no means nonsensical. Morally and religiously, they believe this is what they must do. Thus, the mainspring of their activities is to be understood in terms of the motivations and orientations that characterize moral, religious and often political behaviour.

It will be recognized, of course, that this category of 'non-rational' involvement is probably a very large one indeed. But, on the other hand, it is probably the case that for involvement in promotional groups such as the Campaign for Nuclear Disarmament, the various animal welfare associations and humanitarian organizations the rational, calculative element is almost certainly fairly low. Nevertheless, although we are not aware of evidence on this point, promotional associations are likely to consist of a core of highly dedicated enthusiasts, totally beyond calculative allocation of their time and effort, and a body of members of relatively rapidly changing composition. This latter sector can be seen as, in a sense, more rational in that their expected expenditure of effort is proportionate to the end product.

12.4. Determinants of Group Influence

In looking at the patterns of interest group influence we are predominantly concerned with two problems: the amount of influence a group is able to exercise on relevant decision-makers, and the ways in which that influence is used and where it is directed. Clearly, these are relevant to the success or failure of a group's attempt to influence. Increased potential power, for example, as we have seen earlier, needs to be used and directed through appropriate channels to have an effect on decision-makers. Also, it may be that ease and privilege of access to decision-makers is able to counterweigh lack of other power resources. In any event, what need to be considered are the resources enjoyed by an interest group which enable it to have some influence on the process of decision-making.

Although it cannot be quantified, doubtless an important factor or recourse for success is whether or not a group's aspirations fit in with or do not conflict with the dominant values of the society. Here the example that comes most readily to mind is that of business interests in the US which operate and pressurize government in an atmosphere conducive to business. Businessmen enjoy greater prestige than politicians and trade union leaders, private business is seen as dynamic and government as a dead hand, and it is quite widely believed that what is good for General Motors is good for America. Business lobbies enjoy ready access to decision-makers and can expect to be sympathetically received. In the UK, on the other hand, it has been argued that 'business . . . lacks a social identity of its own' and what identity it has tends to be a lumpy mixture of aggressive Joe Lampton and the bland public benefactor. Influence runs from the civil service to the businessman and not *vice versa*, a process Nettl illustrates with the example of the joint stock banks acting as the *agents* of Whitehall: 'With little discretion or authority of their own, their job is to pass on applications, to sniff out transgressions . . . and to process inward demands for obvious irrelevance and unlikelihood of eventual acceptance'.[7]

An interest that seems in every industrial society to tap some deep-rooted ruralism—and obtain considerable financial support—is agriculture. For Britain, at least, it is the case that the electoral strength of the farm vote is quite negligible, yet over the period 1954–70 Exchequer support for agriculture totalled £4204 million and one analysis concludes that 'agriculture's political strength lies in its less tangible influences'.[24]

As we have already discussed, the political culture refers to that aspect of social life which to an extent structures behaviour by setting goals for legitimate activity, by making available a cognitive picture of the political world, and by defining appropriate ways and means of attaining political goals. Examples of this are the different conceptions of a representative in Britain and in the United States. A congressman is more responsive to local influence than a British MP, partly because his constituents expect him to be so and partly because he thinks it is his duty. The British MP, on the other hand, is more likely to feel that his duty is to present his judgement on an issue and not simply to be a delegate for his constituents' opinions. So, from the point of view of interest group activity, this particular illustration might indicate the greater responsiveness of a congressman to interest group pressure when compared with his British counterpart. Certainly, there is a great deal of evidence to suggest that the congressman is susceptible to considerable pressure from both national lobbies and constituency associations. But whether he is more susceptible than representatives in other polities is difficult to answer.[*8*] We would hazard the proposition that in any advanced society where the government is deeply involved in economic management and social welfare interest group activity will arise as a matter of course. However, the particular pattern of this activity will, to a degree, be structured by the political culture. To mention perhaps an obvious point, the extent to which the interest group accords legitimacy to the government will affect the range of activity. If it accepts the regime as legitimate, it will tend to fight antithetical government decisions mainly by constitutional means. On the other hand, if the group attaches low legitimacy to the regime it will feel freer to make use of extra-legal facilities such as bribery of government officials, or give support to dissident political groups.[25] An example of the latter is the financial support given to the National Socialist Party and other parties in Germany by certain sectors of German industry in an attempt to counter the growing power of the Social Democratic Party and its associated trade union movement.

The first concrete factor which helps determine the style and amount of influence of an interest group is the nature of the group itself. We have already discussed when talking of the 'logic of collective action' how some groups are able, because of their other activities, to divert some of their gross resources towards influence activities. Resources do not only include willingness of people to support and take part in influence activities, but also money, manpower, public sympathy, level of organization, and so on. To some extent, the use of resources is limited not only by the group's other commitments but also by the laws of the political system. In Britain, for example, an MP's contributions to a campaign are limited and this limits the opportunity for interest groups to directly finance his political activities, and business donations to political parties must be included in the company accounts. True, there are ways and means of overcoming this limitation, but, by and large, it does act as a constraint on the unlimited pressure activities of interest groups. None the less, there are many other channels groups can use. Business organizations as a part of their normal everyday activities spend a great deal on advertising and public relations, and it is no hard matter to divert some of this activity to influencing not only consumer behaviour but governmental decision-making.[26] It has been estimated that in the United States in 1955 there were some 5000 firms each running public relations departments at an average annual cost for supervisory staff alone of well over 400,000 dollars.[*9*] Thus, on this scale the marginal cost of embarking on political influence activities should be very low. The use of public relations activities was graphically illustrated in Britain during 1967 over the contract for an aircraft for BEA. Both aircraft manufacturers concerned, Hawker Siddeley Aviation and the British Aircraft Corporation, undertook extensive lobbying and advertising in an attempt to sway the government to support their particular project.[*10*] For both firms, attempts to influence the government's decision were almost standard extensions of the normal economic activities of advertising and public relations, except that the larger group in this case was the government, not the potential consumer.

Of course, not all groups have either the resources or the inclination to mount such extensive influence campaigns. Professional bodies, for example, rarely go in for advertising of the sort we associate with business firms. Most professional bodies, such as solicitors, accountants and the like, entertain certain inhibitions about the use of mass advertising for overtly political and economic purposes. This is not to say, however, that such bodies do not attempt to influence the government in other ways. Often the representatives of such bodies hold a consultative relationship with the government so that, in a real sense, they are already part of the governmental decision-making machine. This state of affairs is a product of the increased specialization of governmental activities. The government, because of its greater involvement in so many aspects of society, is forced to make use of specialized expertise to advise it on appropriate policy. It is difficult for any government department to possess the necessary information and expertise relevant to *all* the problems with which it comes into contact, and it needs to rely on the advice and, to a degree, the judgement of the expert in the sector concerned. As S. E. Finer has written of Britain: 'The form and functioning of British Government are predicated upon the assumption that it will be advised, helped and criticised by the specialist knowledge of interested parties'.[27] There are well-documented cases of this relationship between government and parties concerned.[28] In other words, we see here an explicit recognition of the pluralistic structure of interests within the community. This does not imply that the advice offered will always be accepted by the government, but it will almost always be sought. That this is so can perhaps be demonstrated by the experience of the Minister of Health, John Wheatley, in the first Labour Government (1924) in drawing up a new Housing Bill. Beginning with no special predilection for private enterprise, he very soon realized that the cooperation of the building trades was essential, and asked representatives to serve on a committee of the Ministry in order to draw up a report of housing and make recommendations for increasing the rate of building for the poor. Acting on its report, Wheatley then consulted with representatives of local government units to draw them in and smooth out anticipated difficulties. By consulting, he was able to ensure support for his ideas, criticism of them by those with specialist knowledge and, therefore, able to claim, when criticized in Parliament, that the interested parties supported him.[29] Thus a group is in a position of very considerable potential influence if its non-cooperation would cause the government some difficulty, as in the case of farmers' unions, which generally play a considerable part in administering government policy. And if non-cooperation could be a crucial problem for a government, then it is likely that the group will have open to it a permanent place on governmental advisory committees, of which in Whitehall there are some five hundred.[30] However, the Wheatley situation is probably not typical. It is probable that at least for major policy the broad lines of government policy are not fluid, as the BMA found when Bevan was formulating his National Health Bill and it 'stood by, waiting to negotiate. But there was no negotiating to be done'.[31] Bevan already knew BMA views and did not agree with them, and he negotiated on details only after the BMA accepted general principles.

It is appropriate here to mention a qualification to the assertion that professional bodies are inhibited about the use of full-blown advertising and campaign activities. There are at least one or two well-known exceptions to this rule. One of them is the American Medical Association (AMA) and the separately organized American Medical Political Action Committee (AMPAC). The typical American doctor is predominantly apolitical, and his main interest is the care and treatment of disease and securing a reasonably high standard of living, and this professional interest is probably stronger than in any other professional group.[32] The AMA for many years limited its activities to maintaining and increasing professional standards. However, as the government began to look as if it might extend its operations in the medical field, the AMA began to take a wider and more virulent political stance in an attempt to protect the medical economic *status quo*. Doctors were urged to support and participate actively in defeating proposed changes. Emotion-filled phrases like 'You can't socialize the black bag', 'The keystone to the arch of Communism is socialized medicine', all aided in encouraging political activity.[33] As a result, the AMA now undertakes direct political activity by supporting candidates through contributions, by public education of the role the doctor plays in the community and by lobbying within the legislature. So, even a professional group when it is threatened in some way often has little compunction in overcoming its inhibitions about political activity.

A further factor affecting the influence that a group may bring to bear on decision-makers is the intensity of their concern with influencing political outcomes, since intensity of concern *can* lead to expertise, and expertise is an important political asset. For example, about twenty people organized in various committees seem to have determined a great deal of the detail of the Race Relations Bill after the Labour Party had accepted the need, when in opposition, for legislation protecting racial minorities from discrimination.[34] But it should be noted that the Labour Party and its leadership had accepted that *something* needed doing, but it was not quite sure what the something was or how best to achieve it, and in this situation those with expert knowledge are likely to be especially effective. Similarly, when a government has no firm policy about a given problem or problem area it follows that it may be open to influence from those interested and knowledgeable at the stage of arriving at a policy; but, far more usually, the government will be concerned to consult within the framework of an already broadly defined policy. The implication is that normally pressure groups can affect matters of detail and administration but not the wider issues of policy. A notable counter-example to this generalization is the case of the commercial television lobby in the 1950's which persuaded a Conservative government, almost certainly initially antipathetic to commercial television, to pass legislation establishing independent television. A relatively small group of people, many of whom stood to benefit personally, had direct access to Conservative MPs, to the Cabinet and to the Conservative Central Office and were therefore able to influence legislation because they were focally situated for pressure activity.[*11*]

A classic case of intensity of concern being transformed into expertise and influence is that of the organized birth control movement in Britain, which began with the founding of the Malthusian League in 1877 by C. R. Drysdale. Interested primarily in the population question—the rising population was held to cause *every* social misery and catastrophe—the League was concerned to spread contraceptive knowledge to the working-class and to do this established a number of family planning clinics whilst propagating the idea that the government should allow contraceptive advice to be given within local authority maternity services. In 1924, two Labour-controlled local authorities actually permitted birth control clinics to be established within the local maternity clinic and in consequence the Minister of Health threatened to withdraw their Exchequer grant. A number of well-known Labour women went on a delegation to the Minister, who refused to move. They then formed a Workers' Birth Control Group which pressured the Ministry through the Labour Party Conference and cooperative guilds. Thus, on the birth control side there were two well-organized and articulate bodies, whilst the mass of uninformed opinion was probably apathetic. The House of Lords in 1926 (at the instigation of a vice-president of the Malthusian League—Lord Buckmaster) and the Women's National Liberal Federation in 1927 both passed resolutions calling on the government to permit child welfare centres to give contraceptive advice. During the 1929 General Election, a questionnaire was administered to all candidates asking their likely response to a proposal that medical officers at maternity and child welfare centres be permitted to give contraceptive advice; 182 of those elected were in favour, 88 were opposed and 130 MPs replied they would decide on the merit of any legislation when introduced. Questions by interested MPs were asked and in April 1930 a massive conference, organized by the Workers Birth Control Group and the successor to the Malthusian League, passed a resolution calling on the Ministry to permit medical officers in maternity and child welfare clinics to give contraceptive advice to married people. In July, 1930, the Ministry of Health issued a circular permitting such advice to be given, and from this point the various organizations concerned with birth control were interested to press for the extension of contraceptive advice and the provision of contraceptives on various technical grounds.[35]

12.5. Conclusions

We have been discussing some of the features of non-party political groups and their role within the political process. Such groups, we have said, arise as a response to the increase in 'distance' between centres of societal decision-making and the individual. Thus, an interest group association may become a way, for some individuals at least, of bridging this distance by allowing the officers of interest groups to meet, consult and represent their interest in the government. Secondly, the greater involvement of the government in regulating and coordinating much of social life is obvious. One consequence of this is that civil servants, because of their relatively greater technical knowledge and experience, their role as conflict resolvers and their continuity of office, have been entrusted with more political and administrative discretion than previously.[36]

Thus, the interest group–bureaucracy relationship becomes an important point of contact between extra-parliamentary influence and the formation of public policy. The administrator by consulting with outside bodies potentially affected by a new ruling, for example, can learn a great deal about its likely impact. In addition, the administrator can gain useful information from interest groups which may not be available in the normal course of events. In some cases, the administration may go so far as to delegate responsibility, in some way, to outside bodies, as is common in the field of labour relations and social insurance.[37] Naturally enough, this state of affairs can have considerable dangers for the principles of democratic representation: under what circumstances is the relationship between a bureaucracy and an interest group one of consultation, negotiation or subordination? Clearly, this would depend upon the variety and strength of the administrative, political and judicive controls the legislature can use. The situation is extremely complex. The extent to which the bureaucracy has a tradition of autonomy, the degree of similarity in the social origins of administrators and interest group leaders, the degree of personnel transferability from public to private administration, are among the factors to be considered here.[38]

Yet if there are aspects of the relationship between governments and interest which are complex and even problematic this is not to even hint that such a relationship is unnecessary. Given that governments are elected—if they are elected—only once every three to seven years it is obvious that without some sort of organized liaison with social interests the system would be open to Rousseau's taunt about being free once every five years. Put somewhat dramatically and simplicistically, interest groups constitute a continuous mandate for the government and without them no government could conceivably be regarded as democratic. More to the point, no government could begin to operate without the assistance of interest groups.

Going beyond these general points to more particular points, we have seen that not all latent groups actually do form interest associations. Among the reasons for this are the large size of the latent group and a consequent lack of individual incentives to encourage activity on behalf of the group, lack of suitable contexts which facilitate the communication of common interests and, in less developed states, lack of a political culture which is conducive to the development of these kinds of organization. In addition, we have discussed some of the factors which shape the pattern of interest group activity. Among these are the political culture and the constitutional rules of the country, the degree of legitimacy the group accords to the regime, and the particular ethics and values of the group concerned.

Clearly, while interest groups have a key role in the political process of complex parties, they are not, as some would have it, central to an understanding of decision-making. Interest groups do not act upon an unresponsive or inert government, even though the group might have a favourable relationship with the government. Governments are subjected to influences other than interest groups, such as their estimation of electoral effect, their own long- or short-term strategy, their own supporters' interest, and so on. It would be tempting to conclude, however, that governments tend to be more responsive to those groups which provide them with resources by way of money and support. The fact that business in both Britain and America gives money to the Conservative and Republican Parties respectively might be taken as evidence that governments of these parties, on the whole, give greater weight to attempted influence by business.

However, no such easy conclusion can be made. For one thing, the idea assumes that business always acts as a block fighting for a common interest. As we have seen, no such assumption can always be justified. The interests of car manufacturers are not necessarily those of shipbuilders, expecially when both are competing for scarce government resources. Moreover, an attempt at influence by any interest group is quite likely to evoke a response from other groups concerned with the issue. The government, then, may well have to compromise, conciliate, or at least seriously consider competing claims lest it alienates significant sections of the society.

References

1. H. Eckstein, *Pressure Group Politics*, Allen and Unwin, London, 1960, pp. 9–11.
2. P. Odegard, *Pressure Politics: The Story of the Anti-Saloon League*, Columbia University Press, New York, 1928, p. 80.
3. G. Wootton, *Interest Groups*, Prentice-Hall, Englewood Cliffs, 1970, p. 22.
4. J. Palombara, *The Italian Labour Movement: Problems and Prospects*, Cornell University Press, Ithaca, N.Y., 1957, pp. 82–91.
5. A. Bentley, *The Process of Government*, Principia Press, Evanston, 1949, pp. 258–259; R. E. Dowling, 'Pressure Group Theory: Its Methodological Range', *American Political Science Review*, **54**, 944–954 (1960).
6. K. Deutsch, 'Social Mobilization and Political Development', *American Political Science Review*, **55**, 493–514 (1961).
7. D. Truman, *The Governmental Process*, Knopf, New York, 1951, p. 87.
8. G. Almond and J. Coleman (eds.), *The Politics of the Developing Areas*, Princeton University Press, Princeton, 1960, p. 33.
9. G. Wootton, *Interest Groups*, Prentice-Hall, Englewood Cliffs, 1970, p. 41.
10. D. Truman, *The Governmental Process*, Knopf, New York, 1951, pp. 506–516.
11. J. K. Galbraith, *American Capitalism*, Penguin, London, 1963.
12. M. Olsen, *The Logic of Collective Action*, Harvard University Press, Cambridge, Mass., 1968, p. 127.
13. —— *The Logic of Collective Action*, Harvard University Press, Cambridge, Mass., 1968, p. 129.
14. —— *The Logic of Collective Action*, Harvard University Press, Cambridge, Mass., 1968, p. 132.
15. —— *The Logic of Collective Action*, Harvard University Press, Cambridge, Mass., 1968, pp. 133–134.
16. —— *The Logic of Collective Action*, Harvard University Press, Cambridge, Mass., 1968, pp. 33–34.
17. E. E. Schattschneider, *The Semi-Sovereign People*, Holt, Rinehart and Winston, New York, 1960, p. 31.
18. —— *The Semi-Sovereign People*, Holt, Rinehart and Winston, New York, 1960, pp. 35–36.
19. S. H. Beer, *Modern British Politics*, Faber and Faber, London, 1968, p. 333; S. Finer, *Anonymous Empire*, Pall Mall, London, 1958, p. 9.
20. D. D. McKean, *Party and Pressure Politics*, Houghton Mifflin, Boston, 1949, p. 489.
21. R. W. Gable, 'NAM: Influential Lobby or Kiss of Death', *Journal of Politics*, **XV**, 253–273 (1953).
22. M. Olsen, *The Logic of Collective Action*, Harvard University Press, Cambridge, Mass., 1968, pp. 147–148.
23. —— *The Logic of Collective Action*, Harvard University Press, Cambridge, Mass., 1968, p. 160.
24. R. Howarth, 'The Political Strength of British Agriculture', *Political Studies*, **17**, 485–469 (1969).
25. F. G. Castles, 'Business and Government: A Typology of Pressure Group

Activity', *Political Studies*, **XVII,** 162 (1969); F. G. Castles, *Pressure Groups and Political Culture*, Routledge and Kegan Paul, London, 1967.
26. G. Wootton, *Interest Groups*, Prentice-Hall, Englewood Cliffs, 1970, p. 50.
27. S. E. Finer, 'The Political Power of Private Capital', Pt. II, *Sociological Review*, **4,** 14 (1956).
28. S. H. Beer, *Modern British Politics*, Faber and Faber, London, 1965, p. 322.
29. R. Lyman, *The First Labour Government*, Chapman and Hall, London, 1958, p. 116.
30. PEP, *Advisory Committees in British Government*, Allen and Unwin, London, 1961.
31. P. Jenkins, 'Bevan's Fight with the B.M.A.', in M. Sissons and P. French (eds.), *The Age of Austerity*, Penguin, London, 1964, p. 245.
32. W. Glaser, 'Doctor and Politics', *American Journal of Sociology*, **61,** 231 (1960).
33. R. Joseph Mousen, Jr., and M. W. Cannon, *The Makers of Public Policy*, McGraw-Hill, New York, 1965, pp. 38–43.
34. K. Hindell, 'The Genesis of the Race Relations Bill', *Political Quarterly*, **36,** 390–405 (1965).
35. R. E. Dowse and J. Peel, 'The Politics of Birth Control', *Political Studies*, **13,** no. 2, 179–197 (1965).
36. H. W. Ehrmann, 'Interest Groups and the Bureaucracy in Western Democracies', in R. Bendix (ed.), *State and Society*, Little, Brown, Boston, 1968, p. 258.
37. —— 'Interest Groups and the Bureaucracy in Western Democracies', in R. Bendix (ed.), *State and Society*, Little, Brown, Boston, 1968, p. 260.
38. —— 'Interest Groups and the Bureaucracy in Western Democracies', in R. Bendix (ed.), *State and Society*, Little, Brown, Boston, 1968, p. 269.

Notes and Further Reading

1. We are not asserting that so-called 'group theory' is solely concerned with the activities of 'interest groups', only that its historical effect has been to encourage their study. See H. Eckstein, 'Group Theory and the Comparative Study of Pressure Groups' in H. Eckstein and D. Apter (eds.), *Comparative Politics*, Free Press, New York, 1963, pp. 389–397.
2. For the growth of the state apparatus in Latin America see S. Andreski, *Parasitism and Subversion*, Weidenfeld and Nicolson, London, 1966, ch. 3, and for Africa see R. First, *The Barrel of a Gun*, Penguin, London, 1970, pp. 61–121. For a synoptic view see P. Worsley, *The Third World*, Weidenfeld and Nicolson, London, 1964, ch. 5.
3. On the AMA see O. Garceau, *The Political Life of the American Medical Association*, Harvard University Press, Cambridge, Mass., 1941.
4. E. E. Schattschneider, *The Semi-Sovereign People*, Holt, Rinehart and Winston, New York, 1960, p. 32; he concludes: 'Pressure politics is essentially the politics of small groups' (p. 35).
5. M. Olsen, *The Logic of Collective Action*, Harvard University Press, Cambridge, Mass., 1968, pp. 145–146. S. E. Finer, 'The Political Power of Private Capital', *Sociological Review*, **3,** 279–294 (1955) concurs in this judgement: 'There is in short no political power of private capital as such.

There is the political power of British businessmen, during a particular period and in particular circumstances: and likewise of American businessmen, German, French, Latin American and so forth'.

6. M. Olsen, *The Logic of Collective Action*, Harvard University Press, Cambridge, Mass., 1968, p. 65. Olsen contends that the 'easily calculable relationships and objective standards of success and failure in economic life' means that the rational faculties are better developed in these contexts than in others. Thus, this theory would fit economic groups rather better than non-economic ones (p. 161, footnote).
7. J. Nettl, 'Consensus or Elite Domination: The Case of Business', *Political Studies*, **13**, no. 1, 22–44 (1965). A similar estimate of the role of some pressure groups in Communist countries—'writers and journalists, the workers and the youth'—which act simply as official transmission belts is made by H. Skilling, 'Group Conflict and Political Change', in C. Johnson (ed.), *Change in Communist Systems*, Stanford University Press, Stanford, 1970, pp. 215–234.
8. Certainly the American representative more than the British MP is an effective legislator in the sense that the American executive is considerably less important than the British executive in promoting legislation. Hence in the US pressure groups are more likely to concentrate on legislators, whilst in the UK the more effective pressure groups operate upon the civil service departments.
9. *Fortune* (November, 1955), cited in G. Wootton, *Interest Groups*, Prentice-Hall, Englewood Cliffs, 1970, p. 50. For details of the British situation see R. Rose, 'Money and Election Law', *Political Studies*, **9**, 1–15 (1961).
10. Details in G. Wootton, *Interest Groups*, Prentice-Hall, Englewood Cliffs, 1970, pp. 51–52. Clearly, exactly the same is true of the American aerospace industry, see I. F. Stone, 'In the Bowels of Behemoth', *New York Review of Books* (11 March, 1971).
11. For details see H. H. Wilson, *Pressure Group: The Campaign for Commercial Television*, Secker and Warburg, London, 1961.

13

POLITICAL VIOLENCE

13.1. Violence

DURING the eighteenth and nineteenth centuries it was widely believed by enlightened people that a concomitant of social progress was the diminution of violence both within and between polities. Violence was understood to be a characteristic of the childhood of nations, as filling a vacuum left internationally by the absence of an agreed system of international law and arbitration. Given goodwill and clear sight, the causes of civil strife and war could be cleared up, since they arose from a childish inability to stand above immediate interests and gratification so that a long-term view of common interests could be taken. This view of violence as a kind of intellectual error is at the heart of Cobdenism in international politics and *laissez-faire* in national politics. International economic speculation and the division of labour intra-nationally would eventually force men to realize that they had more in common than they had apart. With this realization would end the period of childhood and men would enter a mature adulthood of social peace; at the worst, war would be the consequence of peripheral contacts with barbarism: 'Wars and the destruction they cause, are now usually confined in almost every country, to those distant and outlying possessions at which it comes into contact with savages'.[1] In this view of progress the basic idea is that as a civilization develops so it will become more and more pacific both internally and externally. Acts of political violence are the acts of political children without the patience or understanding to operate the constitutional machinery, and it is this view which underlies reporting of black violence in the US where 'most of the American media and the American public share essentially the same view of the violence—as being meaningless, purposeless, senseless, irrational'.[2]

Although views such as these were more or less orthodox, there were various opposition strands of thinking. Marx and Engels showed the reverse of the coin of *laissez-faire* with its degradation of the poor and argued that doctrines of social peace were simply the ideological expressions of ruling-class interests. Rejecting violence, Engels suggested, was the 'Parsons' mode of thought—lifeless, insipid, and impotent'. Tennyson pointed out the dual nature of social peace:

VII

But these are the days of advance, the works of men of the mind,
When who but a fool would have faith in a tradesman's ware or his word?
Is it peace or war? Civil war, as I think, and that of a kind
The viler as underhand, not openly bearing the sword.

IX

Peace sitting under her olive, and slurring the days gone by,
When the poor are hovell'd and hustled together, each sex, like swine.
When only the ledger lives, and when not all men lie;
Peace in her vineyard—yes!—but a company forges the wine.

X

And the vitriol madness flushes up in the ruffian's head,
Till the filthy by-lane rings to the yell of the trampled wife,
And chalk and alum and plaster are sold to the poor for bread,
And the spirit of murder works in the very means of life.

The implication of Tennyson, as of Marx, is that the violence of the society is a matter of perspective. For the prosperous middle- and upper-classes the policeman—the newly founded 'Peeler'—was the guardian of property and custodian of a socially neutral legal system, but for the poor he was an agent of oppression, just as today he is a 'pig' to some and a benevolent uncle to others. As Oscar Wilde reminds us, the law permits the rich and the poor alike to dine in the Savoy Hotel. Between nations, the opposition was by no means clear that free trade worked to the benefit of all countries; 'a child or a boy wrestling with a strong man can scarcely be victorious or even offer strong resistance', wrote the German economist List in his justification of German industrial protectionism.[*1*] Also, the urban hand-loom weaver of India, as well as his British counterpart in the 1830's, suffered severely from the consequences of a *laissez-faire* economy over which he had absolutely no control but which was sanctioned by law and defended by the armed forces of law and order. What was order, progress and the onward march of industrial civilization from one perspective was chaos, misery and legally sanctioned oppression from another.

Today, the tradition of the nineteenth century continues, since we generally tend to think of acts of violence as illegitimate or pathological and as alien to a civil polity. At most, the inheritors of this tradition will intellectually sanction violence as a political weapon when the 'normal' processes of compromise and adjustment work so as to exclude systematically whole segments of the population from successfully claiming reasonable demands, as in the case of colonialism, of apartheid and sometimes of internal racism. However, as in the previous period there is today an opposition to treating this tradition of violence as pathological. For example, Fanon argues that the whole colonial experience is one of physical, psychological and social violence exerted by the imperialist nation upon the subject people, whose indigenous social structure is destroyed and, more importantly, whose men are psychologically emasculated. To counter this an act of creative violence by the colonized is imperative. Such violence not only weakens the political will of the colonizers but it also strengthens the moral will of the colonized. Their subjection to the common experience of actually struggling for emancipation helps to forge what had been simply a collection into a national community.[3] Similarly, Mao Tse-tung stresses the psychologically liberating effect that the armed struggle by the oppressed peasants of Hunan had, and gives numerous examples of the way in which previously unorganized people had become organized for the purpose of countering the violence inflicted upon them on the part of the strong by, in their turn, resisting legally sanctioned violence.[4] Although neither Soviet nor classical Marxism emphasize this 'therapeutic' component of violence, they do direct one's attention to another consideration, the implications of which are nearly always neglected, that is, of the class state as itself a 'violent' organization.

Even in the non- or anti-Marxist view of the state, the means of violence are seen as central to the very idea of a state. Weber, for example, wrote that 'the right of physical violence is assigned to all other associations or individuals only to the extent permitted by the state; it is supposed to be the exclusive source of the "right" to use violence'.[5] Thus, violence can be exercised by a state, can be used by agencies sanctioned by the state's legal order and can be employed by citizens against the state and its apparatus. Therefore, following Nieburg, we define political violence as 'acts of disruption, destruction, injury whose purpose, choice of targets or victims, surrounding circumstances, implementation, and/or effects have political significance, that is tend to modify the behaviour of others in a bargaining situation that has consequences for the social system'.[6] For our purposes the significant element in the definition is the stress on modification of others' behaviour, which implies that there may well be techniques for such modifications other than the use of violence. That there are such techniques is quite clear. The rulers in many societies can usually rely upon habituated habitual obedience, the sheer difficulty of disobedience, the socialization process, organs of rational and emotional persuasion, techniques of discovering what the people want, and the enormous facilities that rulers have *vis-à-vis* non-rulers for meeting these demands. From the side of the ruled, it is equally clear that violence is only one of a range of methods of making their feelings known. Political organizations such as parties and pressure groups, letters and informal meetings with representatives, peaceful demonstrations, elections and the need, experienced by all, for governments for at least minimal cooperation by the ruled, are all sources of influence on the government that obviate the recourse to violence. This implies that both governments and the governed may, under some circumstances, resort to violence, but before considering these circumstances further, we shall look a little further into another distinction related to violence.

Acts of violence can be judged morally good, bad or neutral depending upon who engages in them, who they are directed against and who is making the judgement. Terms often used to make these judgements are 'loyalty' and 'legitimacy'. If the members of a group or society regard acts of violence as in some way justifiable, then we can speak of them as legitimate. For example, the entirely illegal acts of violence committed by the colonists in America against the British Crown seem to have enjoyed widespread local support, and, in this sense, the acts were legitimate. Again, the people who in 1968 demonstrated outside the Democratic Convention in Chicago doubtless thought their actions were legitimate and certainly some of the demonstrations were technically legal. The legality depended upon local laws established by the municipal authorities, but the majority of American citizens believed that whether the demonstrations were legal or not they were illegitimate.[7] This factor is important in that it constitutes a significant source of support for the 'legal' harrying in American courts of various minority protest groups; had the protestors or their methods been widely regarded as legitimate, it is quite likely that such short-circuiting of fully legal processes would be far more difficult. Extending this factor of the believed legitimacy of violent acts, we ultimately arrive at the well-known guerrilla axiom: 'The people are like water and the army is like fish'. However, no government wishes to encourage a situation where acts of illegal violence are committed against it, so to say, with the tacit or active approval of even a large minority of the population. Hence, in its turn, the government will act in such a manner as to make this possibility a remote one. Obviously, a first step is to make unapproved acts of violence illegal and to obtain for itself a monopoly of the major means of violence. As Engels pointed out, with the rise of industrialism the major means of violence become more expensive and technically sophisticated so that only governments can afford them and have the available skills to operate them.[8] So violence, far from being the prerogative of dissident groups, is also used more or less frequently by the state and its agencies.

13.2. Violence and the State

Broadly, there are two major conceptions of the place of violence in the state. One school of thought emphasizes that politics is about power and its distribution and that, as Wright Mills put it, 'the ultimate kind of power is violence'.[9] Punishment and legally sanctioned violence is an ever-present reality and is the ultimate binding agent of the state. The other school emphasizes that legal acts of violence are possible but places far more emphasis on the voluntary assent, won by persuasion and concession, of the population. Governors normally gain *authority* by winning the voluntary consent of the population and it follows that the successful polity can be judged 'by the extent to which violence is avoided and other substitutes discovered'. McIver, putting the same point more positively, argues that 'The force of government is but an instrument of authority, vindicating the demands of an order that force alone never creates'.[*2*] However, even those most insistent on the residual nature of force or violence do accept that violence has a place, even if it is a small one, since they do concede that the state may have on occasion, albeit reluctantly and temporarily, to exercise coercion. But, as we saw in Chapter 2, there are very few who insist from the other side that to rule is simply to exercise force or coercion. Hence, the question of interest for the political sociologist is not whether states do act violently towards their citizens, but under what conditions they are likely to do so.

It seems to be widely agreed that the exercise of violence by political authorities stems from the problems associated with political integration and is often associated with the process of economic development. Political integration refers initially to the process of amalgamating distinct cultural groups into a single political unit with a single central authority, and often has associated with it the possibility that such a process also involves the creation of a national political consciousness.[10] Historically, this process has, with very few exceptions indeed, been one of extreme violence which has varied from the physical murder of whole sections of cultural minorities to their forced deportation, their forced religious and cultural conversion, and large-scale population transfers. Most significant for our purposes, however, is that this violence has been exercised by states upon its citizens—or those it claims are its citizens—and the violence has been employed as an instrument of policy, the policy being the extension of the influence of the political authorities upon those who for one reason or another do not accept the authority as legitimate. Looked at in this perspective, the modern state is built upon the violent demise of locally autonomous entities—feudal or tribal—and is, in fact, a concentration and monopolization of the means of violence. As Professor Stone writes of this process in Britain, 'The greatest triumph of the Tudors was the ultimately successful assertion of a royal monopoly of violence both public and private'.[11] When this process had been accomplished in Western societies, the next state was the attempt to set limits upon the arbitrary exercise of this violence potential by curbing the instruments of violence, police and armies, and their immediate controllers—kings, legislators, bureaucracies—by means of constitutions, balances, separations of power, bills of rights, courts of law, and so on. Latterly, the attempt has been made to curb the exercise of this violence not merely intra-nationally but also internationally through the League of Nations, the UN, the Court at The Hague, treaties, and so on. But whatever name we give to the latter stages, control of violence or its gradual elimination, the fact is that violence is the normal process by which states are initially integrated.

In an already classical exposition of this process, Walter has demonstrated that in a number of African societies terror and violence 'were used to solve crises of social integration' by crushing the sources of actual and potential resistance to the emergent political centre. The amount of violence employed differed, and sometimes the variegated groups integrated under one central leadership were organized 'in a constitutional order that balanced, mediated, and stabilized conflicting forces'.[12] But even in these cases, the exercise of violence, although devolved upon subordinate authorities, was rarely far in the background. In the case of Shaka, who took over the Zulu state in about 1818, violence was deliberately kept right in the foreground because 'Terroristic despotism depends on the impact that violence makes on the consciousness of witnesses and on the communication of their fear to others more remote'.[13] In uniting a previously diverse state, Shaka struck at all 'individuals and groups who, if left unchecked, would naturally act to limit or challenge his power'. He slaughtered the old and redefined their status from one of honour to that of being nuisances, countered the potential influence of his higher officers by terrorizing them and prohibiting their meeting outside his presence, and executed anybody whose loyalty was in any way suspect and many who were by no stretch of the imagination guilty of anything.[*3*] All this to weld a politically diverse people into a remorseless machine of military conquest supported by a completely controlled and restructured polity and an economy whose major function was to supply the army.

Shaka, then, employed terror to fulfil his political purposes, and terror is a type of violence characterized by its completely arbitrary and capricious character. All can, at any moment, incur the despot's wrath, all are potential victims and all are potential victimizers. Terror is the extreme case of the instrumental employment of violence for political ends. Normal violence, if one may employ the term, can also be used instrumentally but is deployed against categories of the objectively 'guilty' who stand in the way of the state's hegemony. As we have said previously, in the new state there are quite likely to be just such objectively guilty groups whose language, religion, culture, economic interests, and so on, do lead them to form 'anti-national' political parties. Normally, such groups are violently integrated or violently disintegrated, but as the case of Shaka shows, there is another way, that of terror.

Another classical occasion for the state to employ violence or to threaten violence is during the early period of economic development from a handicraft system, based on agriculture, to a relatively labour-intensive factory system. During the period, which is always one of suffering for the great majority of the population, the state will exercise or threaten to exercise violence in two ways. If the economic development is mainly directed by private initiative, then the state will normally act so as to minimize the revolutionary capability of the masses by making trade unions illegal or semi-legal, by introducing effective national police systems, by outlawing radical propaganda and often by stationing troops in or near the new industrial complexes.[*4*] During the 'Captain Swing' troubles in rural England in 1830 when agricultural machines were destroyed, animals killed, crops destroyed and ricks burned, 1976 people were arrested, 481 of them were transported and 19 executed.[14] As well, it should be added, governments frequently and *belatedly* interfere in a more ameliorative fashion by passing wage legislation, by enforcing better conditions in factories, by child protection laws, and so on. What happens with this mode of economic development is that the government provides a system of *explicit* coercion which protects the *implicitly* coercive emergent social structure. A system is implicitly coercive 'when the structure of and the values symbolised by, social institutions restrain the behaviour of individuals'.[*5*] Of course, the whole emergent ethos and structure of the new factory system was implicitly coerced, the new working-class having to change its leisure, consumption and working patterns almost totally.

However, when, as is so frequently the case in the economically underdeveloped countries, the government itself assumes the major 'burden' of forced economic development, one must assume that it is carrying through a policy that, although possibly of long-term value to the country, entails immediate sacrifice by very considerable sectors of the population.[*6*] Looked at simply as a problem of economics, and of course forced economic development is a great deal more than that, the government must somehow extract a surplus. Transportation, imprisonment, the knout and the lash, and even death were the lot of those agitating against the inhumanity of the early factories and mines. And this political violence was exercised against a usually unenfranchised peasantry or working-class to protect 'the scarce savings created by the new economy at the expense of the standard of living of the population'[15] from a population already at a low standard. If the state is serious, it must restrict consumption not only amongst the masses but also amongst the elite, upon whose skills the enterprise of economic development depends. The process of extraction is a formidable one and must exceed population increase by *four times* before anything is available for industrialization.[16] Or, as W. Rostow has estimated, the rate of capital formation has to *double* from about the 5 per cent of national income usual in non-industrial states to about 10 per cent before economic take-off is possible.[17] In order to achieve this increased rate of investment consumption has to be restrained, and this always involves the state in explicitly coercive actions which may vary from the Stalinist model to that of the Japanese, who obtained by a land tax about 85 per cent of the total government income.[*7*]

This relationship can be explored by relating acts of governmental coercion to levels of economic development. Coercion is defined for this purpose as the degree of political competitiveness permitted, and the amount of protection afforded to free speech.[*8*] Economic development is a level on or above a threshold of 90 per cent adult literacy, 65 radios and 120 newspapers per 1000, 2 per cent of population with telephones, 2525 calories of food a day, not more than 1900 persons per doctor, a GNP of 300 per annum, per capita and with 45 per cent of people living in an urban setting. At very low levels of economic development, in fact in traditional societies, the level of coercion is generally low, but in transitional societies the levels of governmental coercion are highest of all, as is the level of non-governmental political violence.

Between the directed and unplanned models of economic growth the mix of explicit and implicit coercion may vary, and even in the directed the 'amount' of explicit coercion will differ—contrast Japan and the USSR—but the evidence does suggest that always there will be a mix and that coercion is almost inevitable.[*9*] Although the rapid growth of national armies and national police forces in industrializing countries and in the new states of Africa and Asia is a result of more than the need to control a population undergoing the strains of political integration and economic growth, there is little doubt that this factor is also involved.[*10*] Lee has published the figures set out in Table 30 for the growth rate of a number of security forces in Africa following independence.

If civil repression was not the only reason for the expansion it was certainly an important one, as in the case of Uganda, which feared 'the growing security threats caused by refugees', but also, as Lee claims,

TABLE 30. Estimated Growth Rates of Security Forces

Country	Army Rate of growth in %age	Police Rate of growth in %age
Kenya	18.9	0
Uganda	48	5.4
Tanzania—disbanded and reformed		
Malawi	13.1	4.9
Zambia	13.3	6.0
Ghana	10.4	8.5
Sierra Leone	3.1	6.6
Nigeria (before coup)	7.0	4.6

From J. M. Lee, *African Armies and Civil Order*, Chatto and Windus, 1969, p. 105.

needed security forces 'to provide protection against possible open rebellion in Buganda'.[*11*] If we look at it in terms of a Military Participation Ratio (MPR = the percentage of adults in military service between the ages of 15 and 64) we find further evidence for the relationship between economic development and government coercion. Russett categorizes societies into five groups—traditional primitive, traditional civilization, transitional societies, industrial revolution societies and mass consumption societies. In the first two, economic development is low and there is little change; in transitional societies the old is beginning to break up and the economy is developing. In his statistical analysis of the association between MPR and his five-group breakdown the 'role of the central government . . . in military mobilisation, seems to increase sharply at this point', the point being the transitional society. It should be noted that the level of government spending—looked at from the other side, its extractive capability—also increases sharply at the transitional stage.[*12*] Hence, as

Huntington has argued, the association between poverty and political violence is a spurious one since the level of violence in traditional societies is statistically low. It is rather that the attempt to achieve higher economic standards produces violence: 'If poor countries appear to be unstable, it is not because they are poor, but because they are trying to become rich'.[18]

In this section we have argued that historically the formation of the state was and is a violent process, and that the state apparatus has been and is being deployed against considerable sections of the citizenry to hold down levels of consumption in order to finance economic development. This is the case whatever technique of resource reallocation is adopted. When the two processes—of national integration and forced economic development—are contemporaneous it is quite likely that the level of violence will be especially high, and when the one precedes the other it is likely to be lower, as in Western Europe and in Japan, where the political unification of the state territory occurred well before rapid economic development began. When, as in most of the currently developing countries—and the USSR in the twenties and thirties—the national territory is not fully united ethnically, religiously and culturally, the process is very likely to be typified by extreme state violence against minorities and against the working majority. When and if these crises are overcome, the regime is then in a position to adopt a wide range of ameliorative techniques which may obviate the need for violence by incorporating the previously exploited into the national fabric thereby creating a new basis of compliance.

But even though the state has a very considerably greater potential for internal violence than has its citizens, it is still the case that acts of political violence are not uncommon amongst the people. In the following section we shall explore the conditions associated with such popular violence.

13.3. The Causes and Origins of Popular Violence

'Violence,' Mr. Rap Brown is reported to have said, 'is as American as cherry pie', and, he might have added, as British as treacle tart, as French as frogs' legs and as German as sauerkraut! Aggression and violence have been part of human history since its beginnings, and probably because of this the idea that such behaviour is inherent in human beings has considerable plausibility. We have already examined some aspects of this in the works of Hobbes and Freud, and it is an idea which still commands widespread support. Recent work in the study of animal behaviour regards aggressive or violent behaviour as conducive to survival under certain conditions. For example, many animals and birds are thought of as possessing a territorial instinct by which they establish an area of living space which supports a 'family' or group but in which the incursion of other animals of the same type poses a challenge which elicits aggressive behaviour. When the territorial instinct is not challenged the normal state is one of 'peace', and occasional incursions are unlikely to lead to more than ritualized pseudo-aggression.[19] Others take a different stance and argue that aggression is not instinctive but rather that it is learned behaviour. On this view man learns aggression as a useful part of his behavioural repertoire which will be employed when thought suitable, by, for example, a child to gain attention, an adult to obtain domination, by a group competing for scarce values, and so on.[20] A third orientation, by far the most widely explored in the social sciences, is the frustration–aggression theory deriving from the work of Dollard and his colleagues. The basic postulate of the theory is that interference with goal-directed behaviour creates frustration which, in turn, leads to aggressive responses usually directed against the reputed frustrating agent.[21] More recent work suggests that aggressive behaviour is only one of a range of responses to frustration which may also include regression, apathy, submission and avoidance.[22]

The frustration–aggression theory assumes that individuals and groups have goals of some sort, that much of their behaviour is purposive in the sense of goal-seeking and that if this behaviour is not prevented in some way the group or individual is likely to behave quite peaceably. Since this condition is unlikely to be regularly or at least always fulfilled in the human condition of scarcity, the theory predicts that the result is likely to be aggressive behaviour, this aggressive behaviour being elicited by frustration. The frustrated individual or group is likely to attack the believed source—which is not necessarily the 'real' source—of the frustration, and if the attack fails to remove the frustration the aggression is likely to recur. Even if the attack does succeed the attacker will then have reinforced a tendency to attack if future frustrations occur.

It is those ideas which form the basis of current explanations of political violence. A person thwarted in the attempt to reach a goal is made angry and likely to strike out at the imputed source of frustration. In social life men come to value many things: wealth, status, power, security, equality, freedom, the nation, and so on. When they cannot achieve these values, or when achieving one value means losing another, dissatisfaction, anger and often aggression occur. This type of situation is a quite usual one in any complex society and is termed 'relative deprivation', which may be defined as 'The tension that develops from a discrepancy between the "ought" and the "is" of collective value satisfaction'.[23] The 'ought' refers to the conditions of life men come to believe they are entitled to and the 'is' to their perception of the possible. Crucial to the idea is the perception of deprivation: the ideas that people have of the gap between what they believe they are entitled to and what they receive or believe they can attain, whether or not objective observers would consider the deprivation real or apparent.[24] But it is perfectly possible that an objective observer might see considerable actual deprivations whilst the deprived might or might not regard this deprivation as being the natural order of things against which protest or violence is merely futile. This can come about either because people simply have never considered that their conditions can change, hence the relative passivity of the really poor and deprived, or people may be aware of poverty and so on, but might persuaded that, as Burke put it, 'Patience, labour, sobriety, frugality and religion are their natural lot'.[25] Jane Eyre's educational experiences perfectly exemplify the Burkean virtues: ' "I should wish her to be brought up in a manner suiting her prospects", continued my benefactress; "to be made useful, to be kept humble" . . . "Your decisions are perfectly judicious, madam", returned Mr. Brocklehurst. "Humility is a Christian grace, and one peculiarly appropriate to the pupils of Lowood: I, therefore, direct that especial care shall be bestowed on its cultivation amongst them." '

In effect, then, relative deprivation is the degree to which the individual feels deprived, and, as such, is related to anger and aggression. The basic proposition is that 'the potential for collective violence varies strongly with the intensity and scope of relative deprivation among members of a collectivity'.[26] Thus, if a group feels an intense sense of relative deprivation with respect to a class of values important to it then it has considerable potential for collective violence. If the group feels that collective violence is a legitimate response to its anger, and that violence is the only means to alleviate the discontent, then the likelihood of violence is the greater. Alternatively, should the group feel violence to be illegitimate, or that it is unlikely to succeed, or if it has other channels for ameliorating its discontent, then it is more likely to restrain itself, so minimizing the potential for violence.

Whether or not deprivation eventually culminates in violence depends on a number of factors, among them the intensity and scope of the deprivation. Most people at some time experience deprivation of one sort or another, but this rarely leads to collective violence. The deprivations then must be sufficiently intense and experienced by a sufficiently broad sector or a strategically located sector of the society in order to create a potential for civil violence. As a corollary, the intensity of the perceived deprivation is related to the intensity of the violence. Thus Zeitling in a study of the Cuban revolution found that those most likely to have supported Castro prior to 1959 were those who had experienced the greatest unemployment.[27] A whole series of studies of direct military interventions demonstrates the importance of their strategic locations in society as virtual monopolists of organized violence. Determinants of the intensity of relative deprivation include strength of commitment towards a goal or to the maintenance of a given level of values. The more committed a person is to a particular value the more frustrated he will feel if thwarted in the attainment of that value and the greater the consequent propensity for violence. Similarly, a violent response is likely to be greater the nearer a group is to the attainment of its goal. Further, a restriction of the number of opportunities available for the attainment of values is likely to be associated with a greater intensity of conflict. There is considerable evidence for this point. To cite one

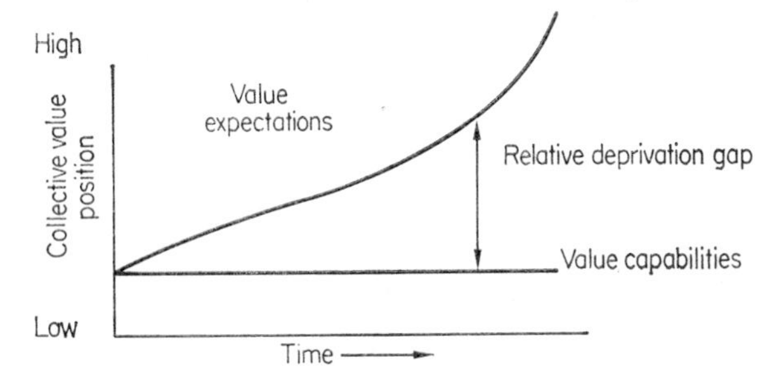

FIGURE 5. Aspirational deprivation. (From Ted Robert Gurr, *Why Men Rebel*, copyright © 1970 by Princeton University Press; Princeton Paperback, 1971, written under the Auspices of the Center of International Studies; Princeton University: Fig. 2, p. 51. Reprinted by permission of Princeton University Press)

example, by the mid-nineteenth century the English working-class had, in marked contrast to the French working-class, largely given up revolutionary methods in favour of friendly societies, cooperative societies, trade unionism, self-help, self-education and peaceful petitioning for reform.

The sources of deprivation lie in social processes which create the gap between what people believe they are entitled to and what they receive, and the general patterns have been identified as follows. A first type is where people's aspirations increase whilst their capacity for attaining the aspirations remains constant; this type is known as aspirational deprivation (see Figure 5) and is associated with the so-called revolutions of rising expectations taking place in the developing world. What happens here is that education and the learning of new skills together with exposure to the consumption patterns of the West may well create aspirations for more educational facilities, for better employment and higher living standards which the economic and political systems are incapable of meeting. Hence frustration, which may lead to violence. Groups typically in this situation are the urban unemployed, the semi-educated and the well educated in many developing areas.

A second type of deprivation, called decremental deprivation (see Figure 6), refers to situations within which value capabilities decline whilst aspirations remain constant. Frustration and anger are induced by the loss of a value once possessed.

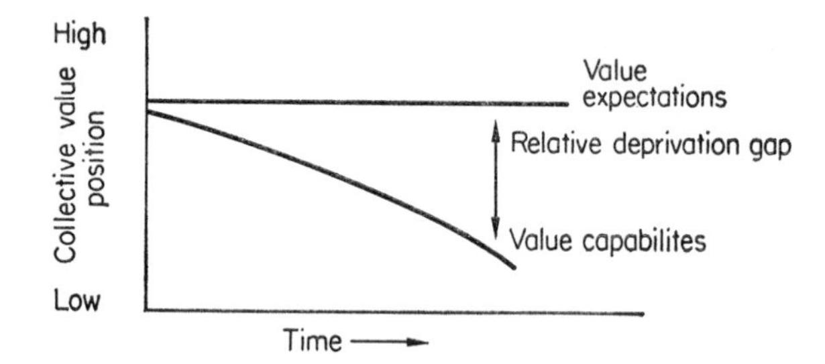

FIGURE 6. Decremental deprivation. (From Ted Robert Gurr, *Why Men Rebel*, copyright © 1970 by Princeton University Press; Princeton Paperback, 1971, written under the Auspices of the Center of International Studies; Princeton University: Fig. 1, p. 47. Reprinted by permission of Princeton University Press)

This type of deprivation is typified by the downwardly mobile, by those losing long-held rights and by people with stable incomes during periods of inflation.

A third and final variety of deprivation is that experienced by those who, having experienced short- or long-term gains, find that these will not continue, although on the basis of past experience they had assumed that such incremental gains would persist. This form is called progressive deprivation (see Figure 7).

Progressive deprivation has been called upon by Davies to explain Dorr's Rebellion in the US, the Russian Revolution of 1917 and the Egyptian Revolution of 1952, whilst Brinton in his study of the Puritan, American and French Revolutions also stressed the same factor.[28] All of these events were preceded by longish periods of growing prosperity and, in some cases, of civil liberty which caused people to consider that such incremental benefits would continue—they did not. On the contrary, immediately preceding the revolutions were periods of economic crisis sometimes accompanied by political repression. Hence, the expectations were frustrated and anger resulted.

Frustration–aggression analysis, then, emphasizes the socially produced violence of the governed; aggression is an outcome of frustration which for one reason or another the government will not or cannot alleviate. The theory, then, can be put in the form 'if social want formation exceeds social want satisfaction then the consequence will be social frustration which may lead to violence'.[29] The process of want formation is generally more rapid in industrializing societies than want satisfaction, due to exposure to high consumption possibilities through radio, TV, films, magazines, advertising, etc. Indeed, as we said earlier, initially, economic growth may actually lead to a decline or at least a halt in the rise of consumer satisfactions. This theory has been tested in part by investigating the association between acts of political violence and levels of economic development. The formation of wants has been argued to be a consequence of literacy and city life, both

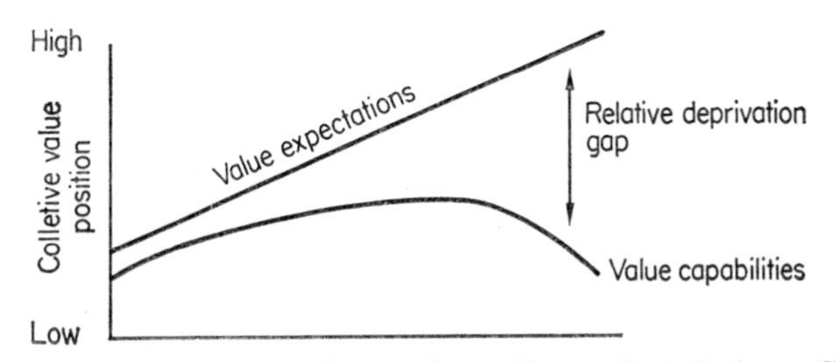

FIGURE 7. Progressive deprivation. (From Ted Robert Gurr, *Why Men Rebel*, copyright © 1970 by Princeton University Press; Princeton Paperback, 1971, written under the Auspices of the Center of International Studies; Princeton University: Fig. 3, p. 53. Reprinted by permission of Princeton University Press)

of which expose people to new consumption possibilities, whilst want satisfaction or ability to meet growing wants is seen as reflected in an index of economic capabilities. The index of want satisfaction is constructed of the following six items: GNP, caloric intake, telephones, physicians, newspapers and radios. As the theory suggests, failure to meet wants is likely to engender violence, hence an index of violence was also constructed consisting of three composite variables: (1) turmoil, which consists of mass participatory demonstrations, strikes, mass arrests and riots, (2) palace revolt with elements of limited elite participation consisting of coups and arrests of prominent men, and (3) an instability dimension denoting purges, depositions, arrests and power struggles within ruling cliques.[30] Using these indices, the authors are able to demonstrate a clear association between them, indicating that when people are exposed to a want-forming milieu their expectations increase, and that if these are not met violence is likely to increase. They also confirm that it is in societies of economic transition that violence is most prevalent (see Figure 8).[31]

The relationship can also be demonstrated employing a political modernity index, where the underlying thesis is that the association between political modernization—to be defined—and high levels of economic development is a strong one. Because modern polities are defined as flexible

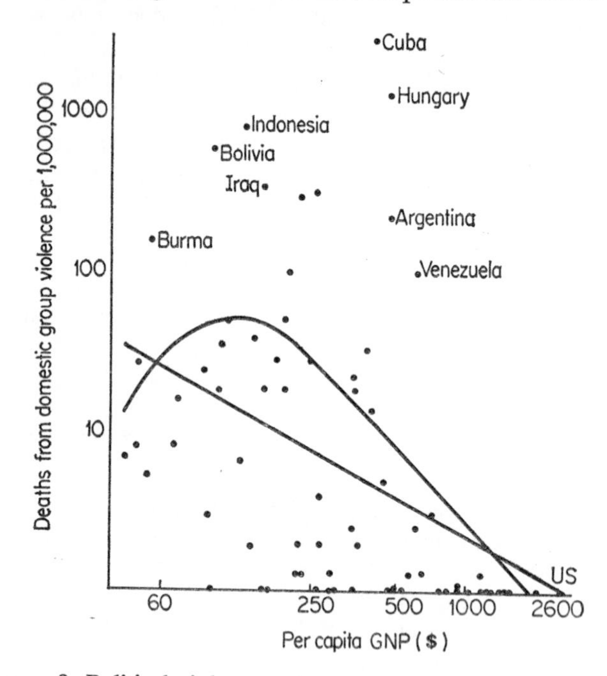

FIGURE 8. Political violence and economic development. Political violence is associated with economic development, at least in the early stages. From B. Russett, *Trends in World Politics*, Macmillan, New York, 1965, p. 137. Copyright © 1965 by The Macmillan Company and reproduced by permission.

and responsive, and because they are embedded in strong economies, they will have the capabilities of meeting the incremental generation of wants and therefore will be able to maintain frustrations within tolerable limits. The capability of a political system refers to its ability to make appropriate responses to popular wants by extracting and distributing resources and developing structures such as parties and interest groups to convey demands, together with parliaments, executives, bureaucracies and so on to process them.[*13*] Political modernization can then be understood as a process of developing such agencies and structures. Thus Forward has shown that 'it is effective bureaucracy which is the pre-condition for representative and stable government'.[32] Cutright shows that a stable legislative and executive is strongly associated with high levels of communication potential—indexed as newspaper and newsprint consumption, telephones and domestic mail per capita—with an urbanization index and an educational-cum-literacy index.[33] Tanter demonstrates that a high level of minority representation in legislatures, together with inter-party competition in electing the executive, are associated with urbanization and economic development.[34]

Thus, the evidence is relatively clear that there is a strong association between levels of economic development and the exercise of political violence, and there is also a threshold of economic development when political violence begins to decrease. Further, there is a relationship between economic and political development in the sense that in the economically more developed countries the polity is likely to acquire a capability of extracting resources and of communication with likely sources of tension which may need resources channelled to them. It is plausible to explain this link between levels of violence and levels of economic-cum-political development by the concept of relative deprivation leading to frustration–aggression.

13.4. Factors Inhibiting Political Violence

However, by themselves, the concepts of relative deprivation and frustration–aggression do not explain everything in which one is interested. They do not tell us anything about the actual form that the violence may take—insurrection and civil wars, sporadic violence, coups, and so on. Nor do they tell us much about the variety of possible system responses to the possibility of violence, whether employed by the elite or the masses, or whether or not the violence is highly organized. Mobs, riots and other sporadic outbursts of hostility are relatively short-lived events, exhibiting few clearly defined long-term aims. However, other responses to deprivation include social movements having more clearly defined goals aiming, by collective action, to change or influence the existing social order. Some of these may resort to violence while others become pressure groups working within and largely accepting the legitimate order. This is illustrated by the current black movement and protests in the United States which reflect many different kinds of protest: from urban rioting, to the relatively peaceful NAACP, to the violent philosophy of the Black Panthers. Which of these outcomes is likely depends not only upon the deprivation but also upon the actual context and the response, status and strength of the regime.[35]

In a sense these two problems are bound together since the response or lack of it by the political elite to mass behaviour is a crucial determinant of the form that such behaviour may take. For example, if the regime in response to strikes or demonstrations hits out with extreme violence, in the long term this may intensify conflict. Again, if the political elite commands the loyalty of armed forces and police, any dissident group, assuming lack of alternative channels, if it is to seize power must embark on a protracted struggle.

Up to a point we have discussed some of the extant ideas about the origins of political violence, but although one may envisage a set of preconditions which *may* be necessary it does not follow that they are sufficient conditions, since it is perfectly possible that societies may possess certain mechanisms inhibiting political violence. Furthermore, it is almost certainly the case that internationally such inhibiting agencies are differentially distributed. Amongst the most important of such inhibitions the following appear to be most significant: cultural, diversionary including reform, and state repressive capabilities.

In a previous chapter we have discussed how the cultural milieu of a society helps to define the course, meaning and desirability of different human activities and amongst these, of course, are violent acts. Examples of this are legion. Thus Bateson on the Balinese detects 'a strong normative inhibition against overt aggression', Benedict writes of the culturally sanctioned 'uses of violence to the individual psyche' in Russia, and Kling has explored the consonance between 'the values and styles imparted by non-political institutions' in Latin America and the prevalence of political violence.[36]

Intra-nationally, subcultures of violence have been identified. Analysing the different political cultures of Ulster, Rose has noted that 'The ideal-type Protestant, from his birth into a strong Unionist family into adult membership of the Orange Order, is differentiated in his regime outlook from an ideal type Catholic, moving through the local Catholic school to an adult participation in Gaelic sports and Republic parades on Easter Monday'. Asked to recall their earliest political memories, 36 per cent of Rose's sample, both Catholics and Protestants, made reference to violent events, from which he concludes that 'the modal Protestant or Catholic was first introduced to politics in explicitly violent terms'.[37] A better-known case is that of the American black ghetto, where intensive research has revealed a violent way of everyday life where 'quick resort to physical combat as a measure of daring courage or defense of status appears to be a cultural expectation'.[38] Survey evidence suggests that this 'social' violence can also spill over into politics, as, for example, when 29 per cent of Oakland residents believed that the riots were a justified manner of bringing grievances to public attention.[*14*]

Although he does not make an explicit connection between cultures in which 'a-political' violence is normatively sanctioned and the incidence of political violence, Finer does suggest that the level of political culture is the major independent variable in explaining the ability of the military to seize political power or influence politicians. He divides countries by their political culture—mature, developed, low and minimal—and the tests for these levels are twofold: a psychological dimension and an associational

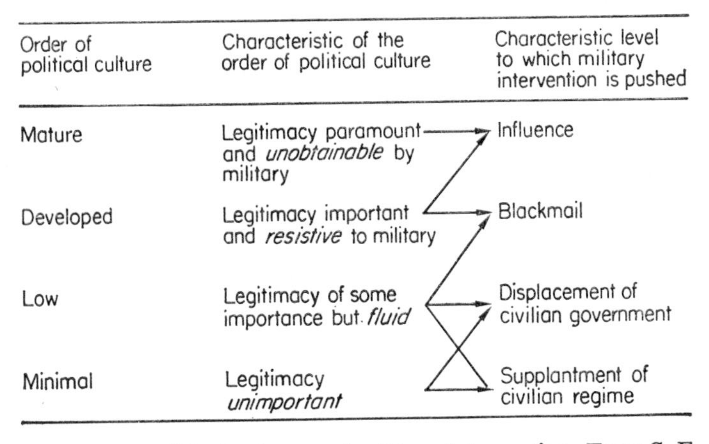

FIGURE 9. Political culture and military intervention. From S. E. Finer, *The Man on Horseback*, Pall Mall, London, 1962.

one. The psychological dimension incorporates the belief that the exercise of power outside recognized channels is illegitimate combined with a belief that a sovereign authority exists and that 'no other persons or centres of power are legitimate'. His associational test is the extent to which the population is freely organized into secondary associations such as churches, clubs, industries, trade unions, and so on.[39] Finer is then able to demonstrate that there is a close connection between these levels of political culture and the ability of the military to affect civilian policies; he sets this out schematically in Figure 9.[40]

As might be expected from the previous discussion, the levels of political culture are quite intimately related to levels of industrialization.[41] However, even given this, it does appear to be the case that political culture does act as an inhibitor upon the military at the mature and developed levels, whilst at the low and minimal levels the military can exercise violence against the regime more or less unimpeded. The incidence and types of violence are then associated with political culture in the sense used by Finer, and further, it is not unlikely as we have already suggested that there is an association between social definitions which condone interpersonal aggression and the incidence of political violence.[42]

Another set of responses can be classified as diversions and concessions. These involve in the first case a rechannelling of frustrations and aggressions on to secondary objects, and in the second case the regime responds by a partial meeting of social wants. From a regime point of view, the first technique is relatively 'cheaper' in the short term. A classical example of diversionary tactics is that mentioned by Halévy in his account of the function of English Methodism as a social anodyne at the worst period of popular suffering during the Industrial Revolution. Religion provided a source of emotional compensation for physical deprivation, and diverted energies which otherwise might have been directed against the system. Religion acted, in the well-known aphorism of Marx, as the 'opium of the masses', but it was, as Marx also saw, 'the heart of a heartless society'.[*15*] Similarly, a study of the relationship between falls in economic activity and the lynching of negroes in the American South shows a strong correlation.[43] Again, it has been found that anti-Semitism is strongly associated with general economic and political dissatisfaction, so that the more dissatisfied a person or group is with their economic and political position the more likely they are to be anti-Semites.[44] This diversionary technique can be used quite cold-bloodedly by regimes—'bread and circuses'—as the example of anti-Semitism during the Third Reich makes clear when it was used to blame Jews for 'low farm prices, high retail prices, adulteration of goods, onerous tax burdens for reparation payments, low wages, unsatisfactory labour conditions, and many other crimes against the Aryan people'.[45] It would be easy to proliferate examples of this diversionary tactic since the scapegoat is one of the more familiar figures of history, but the point is clear that what happens in this situation is that tension is diverted from possibly dangerous areas toward surrogates.

A rather more sophisticated diversionary technique consists of infiltrating the organizations of those opposing or most likely to oppose the policies and objects of the regime. For example, it is highly likely that the US Communist Party is riddled with government agents; Lenin's secretary, Malinovsky, was an Okhrana agent as were almost half of the central committee of the Russian Socialist Revolutionaries. The Fenian invasion, by 500 armed men, of Canada in 1870 with the object eventually of blockading Britain from Canada was organized by an agent of the British Intelligence

Service. As has been made clear in the US by police agents who had posed as radicals and have then come forward as prosecution witnesses, the technique is by no means moribund. Such is probably true, though the ultimate form of diversion—invented, as might be expected, in Russia, where the police actually formed and encouraged semi-legal organizations and actually helped to engineer strikes, riots and more than one assassination—no longer flourishes.[*16*]

Such diversionary tactics can be employed alone, or what is more usual, as part of a cocktail along with concessions. The ability of a regime to concede reform depends upon a number of factors: knowledge that people want reform, capability to achieve reallocation and a willingness to make the concessions. Regimes differ in their capacities to receive and act upon 'messages' received from their environment and we can posit that, other things being equal, the better the channels of communication between regime and population, and *vice versa*, the more likely there is to be reform and the less likely there is to be political violence.[46] Capabilities to reallocate can be seen as a function of ability to extract resources from the community and, as might be expected, governments of richer states have a greater capacity to obtain resources than those of the poorer countries (see Figure 10). Clearly, such governments also have a greater capability to meet demands for reform than poorer governments, but such governments are also able to improve their machinery for searching out potential sources of tension through welfare agencies, through more efficient bureaucracies, opinion surveys, and so on.[*17*] The willingness of the regime to concede reforms is a more hazy concept than the others, but is dependent upon knowledge and capacity. However, it will additionally include factors such as whether or not political incumbents are themselves the major economic group of the society. Thus, land reform or redistribution is usually a reform introduced by non-land owners, and the initial factory reforms in the UK came from a dominantly landed Parliament. Willingness to reform will also depend upon the nature of the demands made and whether they involve changing major social structures or not.

Finally, we may turn to the ability of the regime simply to repress all forms of opposition, and this, in most regimes, depends upon its ability to detect the leaders of protesting groups and, at the same time, maintain the loyalty of its repressive agencies. Detection and elimination may be more or less difficult according to the degree of support the protester can muster. Maintaining the loyalty of the armed forces and police can be managed but the trick is not easy. They can be counterbalanced, their loyalty can be won by concessions—which may leave less for the rest of the population—they can be drawn or officered from the dominant regime-supporting class, or

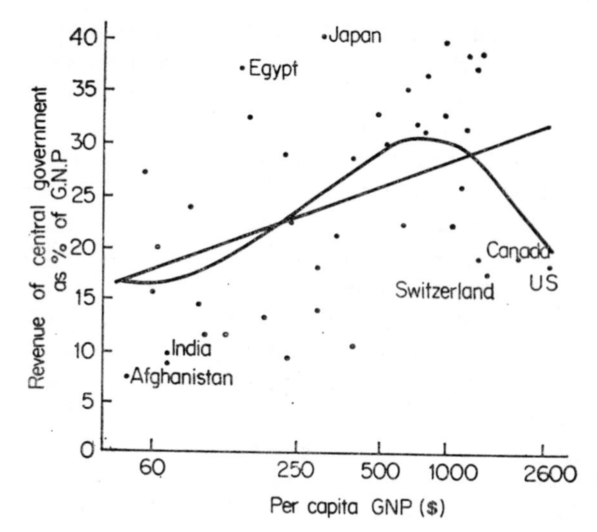

FIGURE 10. Economic development and extractive capacity. The role of the central government increases with economic development, but may diminish at very high development levels. From B. Russett, *Trends in World Politics*, Macmillan, New York, 1965, p. 133. Copyright 1965 by The Macmillan Company and reproduced by permission.

they can somehow be imbued with a purely professional ethic which does not countenance political intervention.[47] Any one or a combination of these techniques is possible, but once again it is the case that in the developing countries the capacity to maintain loyalty to the regime by police and armed forces—judged by the comparative incidence of military *coups d'état* —is very considerably below that of the more developed countries.[*18*] Repression can also be counter-productive since it may generate hatred where a concession might have won support; it also teaches the repressed the need to organize (*vide* Lenin, *What is to be Done?*) and it rapidly becomes ineffective when it initially fails.[48]

13.5. The Forms of Political Violence

Turning to the problem of the variety of forms of political violence, the following forms have been identified. The basis of the classification depends upon who participates, whether elite or mass, and whether or not the violence is highly organized.[*19*]

(1) *Turmoil*, which may be defined as relatively spontaneous and un-

organized violence with quite widespread popular support and participation which includes strikes, riots and localized rebellions. This form of violence is associated with relatively intense deprivations among the mass of people or a particular mass of people, who tend to be rather badly organized, lacking highly articulated political parties, lacking access to state bureaucracies and who are generally badly integrated into the society. Typically, this form of violence is associated with economic transition when economic and social forms of deprivation are intense, but as the ghetto violence of America demonstrates, this is not always the case. During the 1960's after protracted legal and quasi-legal attempts to relieve the generally unfavourable social and economic position of the American blacks they turned to violence, especially in the ghetto. A strong sense of relative deprivation, of being excluded from the promise of American society, the limited concessions wrung from a generally antipathetic society and the arrival of beliefs countering white racism all combined to create a potential for violence. The actual violence would then be precipitated by events which previously had met with only resignation—the arrest of a black, a shop refusing a black customer or treating him badly, rumours of police brutality, and so on. Lacking control over the political machines and access to the decision-makers in their localities, the blacks began to organize their own small parties, to attack the local political machines as in Cleveland, to demand control of school boards as in New York and to riot, shoot back and burn.[49]

(2) *Conspiratorial violence* is exercised in a highly organized manner usually, but not necessarily, by segments of the elite such as the army and the bureacracy. It manifests itself normally in minimal violence, which may include small-scale but directed terrorism, *coups d'état*, palace revolts and organized political assassinations. It is associated with intense dissatisfaction by elite groups about their lack of political influence, and normally the masses are bypassed and their degree of involvement extremely limited.[50] Conspiratorial violence may, however, have a mass reference, as was the case in Russia where the attempt was to isolate the government by terror which would 'demoralize, disorganize and weaken' the autocracy so that it became 'powerless to take any kind of measures to suppress ideas and activities directed towards the people's welfare'.[51] But, even with a popular reference, the weakness of the conspirator is that having no popular roots or support he can be eliminated by his own methods without evoking widespread outrage unless he can provoke the authorities into indiscriminate repression. If he succeeds in provoking the legal authorities into excessive or indiscriminate counter-violence (Brazil is a case in point) then this alone may help to convince the people that only active opposition to the

authorities can succeed. As with other forms of violence, this one is also strongly associated with transitional economies. The masses are not so much deliberately excluded as not even considered; nor are they capable of intervening since they play no normal part at all in governing. The masses are normally passive objects of government and 'will accept any change in government, whether legal or not'.[52]

When the coup is attempted in the more economically and politically advanced polity its success is greatly more problematic and, indeed, is unlikely to be even attempted unless the country has been seriously weakened in a war (as in the Kapp *putsch* of 1919), or has a weak party system and suffers a period of economic crisis, or any combination of these (as in the abortive generals' plot in France in 1958). In such countries the population is likely to be politically integrated and to be politically organized, most of the military and police loyal to the state and the population may well resist, as in the Kapp *putsch*, or can be mobilized: '*Français et Française, aidez-moi*'.

(3) *Internal war*, which, if successful in replacing a regime, is always associated with a high degree of organization and with at least the tacit approval of wide sections of the population. It includes large-scale terrorism, civil wars and revolutions. Internal war is generally associated with progressive deprivation of many conditions of social existence and also with struggle against foreign occupation. If the dissidents are able to concentrate in a geographically peripheral area or areas outside effective regime control, and if foreign support is available, this may strengthen the possibility of civil war. Internal wars, such as guerrilla-type insurrections, often develop, as for example in Cuba, from a conspiracy. If a regime possesses a loyal and reasonably efficient military force and is confronted by a dissident group with no corresponding assets, then, if the latter is to succeed in overthrowing the regime, necessarily it must find other sources of strength. Whether this is possible depends upon the amount of institutional support it can generate among the mass of the population. In other words, to circumvent the military superiority of the regime the guerrilla tries to win the support of the people. As that successful guerrilla leader Mao Tse-tung wrote, 'The mobilization of the common people throughout the country will create a vast sea in which to drown the enemy, create the conditions that will make up for an inferiority in arms and other things . . .'.[53] Here the guerrilla enlists the aid of an ideology offering interpretations of people's deprivations and ways of alleviating them: land reform for the landless, regional autonomy for ethnic minorities, political equality, and so on. The failure of the Greek insurgents, 1945–50, to win such popular

support, or of the Hukbalabap in the Philippines, illustrates the importance of the insurgent being able to focus on discontent and thereby generate popular loyalty. In China, in insurgent controlled areas the peasants were organized into local soviets where the poor and landless peasants were given a voice for the first time. Land was equitably distributed and attempts made to increase the efficiency of farming methods. Education and industry were started and there is little doubt that the Chinese Communist Party's synchronization of reform and the revolutionary pursuit of power was a great source of strength. This close cooperation between the guerrilla and a sympathetic population provides the guerrilla with means to overcome the military superiority of the regime's forces—near perfect intelligence, extreme mobility, freedom from fixed logistic bases and surprise.[54]

The typology we have outlined is derived from the extent of the support for those taking violent actions and the degree of organization involved. But it would be perfectly possible to use other bases such as the scale of the violence, its duration and its intensity.[55] Or one might categorize by examining the objectives of those employing violence. From the government side, it might be holding things stable, destroying an opposition, political or economic mobilization, and so on. From the other side, it might be possible to classify according to whether a simple change of elite, a reform of institutions without any necessary change of incumbents or, as in the cases of the great revolutions, whether a change of basic social power and institutions was sought or, at least, occurred.[56] Again, one might classify according to whether the violence is, so to say, segmented as in the case of Marx's analysis of revolution, the Bolivian tin-miners or, perhaps, the American blacks. When group interest, social isolation and cultural and religious cleavages combine to divide a population, the chances of violence increase.[*20*] Or one might, as Hobsbawn does, attempt to connect the organizational form of the violence with the degree of industrial development of the society so that, for example, industrialization produced 'the industrial working class, whose very being is organisation and lasting solidarity' which makes the disorganized city mob otiose.[*21*]

A great deal of this chapter has accepted the implicit assumption that political violence is primarily a transitional phenomenon of economic and political development, so that in some fully developed societies politics might be carried on in a manner similar to that of a university seminar. Unfortunately, the tone of university seminars has changed and, anyway, there is in the literature a tendency to assume that the fully 'integrated' modern society will definitionally be non-violent. In the following sections we shall look a little more closely at this assumption.

13.6. Violence in Economically Developed Societies

Economically developed societies are strongly associated with political stability in at least the sense that political violence very rarely takes the form of a conspiracy to change the regime, or internal war, but they do experience considerable turmoil. This is the case whether such countries are electorally democratic or not.[57] The form that violence takes in such countries is turmoil which, it will be remembered, includes demonstrations, strikes, riots and other relatively unorganized forms; violence may also take the form of quite highly organized attacks by 'fringe' political groups upon their various 'bogeymen'. This form of violence in Europe and America is not a prerogative of the lower social classes, but rather a form of protest likely to mobilize people whatever their social status. The objectives of violence in these countries are usually quite specific and rarely involve displacement of the regime but rather are attempts to induce policy changes in areas such as civil rights, housing, education, and so on. Normally, the majority of participants in such events are interested primarily in achieving a specific and limited end: equality before the law, economic benefits, better education, local control of affairs, etc. And it is this lack of an integrated ideological perspective which differentiates the turmoil element from the classical model of the Marxist revolution.

The turmoil dimension may, on the other hand, develop into a revolutionary situation if somehow the specific grievances can be shown and come to be understood by large numbers as somehow connected together. This is, of course, the Marxist view and, indeed, that of any other revolutionary organization. Thus, for Lenin, the role of the organized party is to press for reform, to support those who are pressing for specific reforms and, most important, to teach the masses that the reforms are ineffectual within the context of capitalism. Again, there are groups in Northern Ireland who insist that the economic and political disabilities of the Catholic minority are not adventitious but spring from the very nature of the social structure of Northern Ireland and will remain until that structure is changed. Or take the case of the Black Panthers in the US who arrived on the scene only after the 'failure' of more 'moderate' negro organizations to win significant concessions from the society. They claim that the oppressed blacks *and* oppressed whites are subject to the same forces, that the war in Vietnam is intimately associated with the repression of blacks in the US and that only concerted action against a total machinery of repression would bring worthwhile results. Recently, they have been reported as setting out ideas for a new US constitution which would include 'decent housing for all, an end to police brutality, an end to conscription, and an education programme which would "tell our children the truth about this decadent society" '.[58] In France, Pierre Poujade was able to unite in one movement discontented peasants, shopkeepers, cafe and bar owners, a section of the working-class in declining textile areas and some wealthier traders by finding a common source for their discontent in 'the high and powerful, the technocrats and officials'.[*22*]

Against this attempt to integrate various strands of discontent into a mass movement the modern regime has been able to amass very considerable forces. As we have seen, it can make concessions, as in the US and in the reforms in Northern Ireland; it can wield force, as has occurred with the harrying of the Black Panther leadership and the police actions by British troops in Northern Ireland; and it can employ the whole weight of the state to isolate the leaders of such integrating movements. At the same time, given the multifarious points of access for influence available to those with something to offer the politician or the administrator, it follows that a good deal of the political violence will be used as a political resource by the relatively powerless minorities—the very poor, the religious or ethnic minorities, the technologically dispossessed. Moreover, they are likely to be unpopular minorities who are incapable of winning widespread support and sympathy from the majority and, therefore, cannot easily gain a hearing by normal political activity and cannot win their case by revolutionary activity either. So, in the modern state the possibility of successful conspiracies or widespread insurrections is minimal. But, none the less, there are sources of strain and tension within modern societies which do lead to many acts of political violence; broadly, such sources are ethnic and religious minorities, particular issues which sometimes take on an ideological overtone, and technological innovation of various kinds.

Ethnic and Religious Violence

There are few countries in the developed world which do not have either significant ethnic or religious minorities, and where such minorities are present the possibility of violence is also present. Since the religious or ethnic minority may well also be an economically deprived group—Walloons in Belgium, Catholics in Northern Ireland, non-whites in the US and UK, Bretons in France—it is difficult to sort out the relative influences of each factor. What appears to happen is that such groups historically have either opposed the formation of the nation in its present form—Belgium, Northern Ireland and France—or, as in the case of

CND, the student protesters, the French farmers, the squatters, protesters against the South African cricket tour, the demonstrators against US involvement in Vietnam, the Communist and Fascist street-fighters, the radical nationalist groups, and so on.

For these people the normal bargaining processes may simply not work because the demands they make are so total that they cannot get an audience, or the government itself has a strong commitment to alternative courses of action, or because they are initially so politically immaterial that their grievances are neglected. In the first category one might place the British Union of Fascists, the Communist Party, the various nationalist groups, the far left and right student revolutionaries, and so on. In the second group the most obvious examples are the American and British campaigns for unilateral nuclear arms reductions. Finally, the third category includes squatters, rent strikers and protesters against events occurring in foreign countries, for example, anti-apartheid protests, anti-Greek demonstrations, pro-Biafran marches, etc. Such people usually come to regard, or begin by regarding, the processes associated with democracy as either attenuated or shams. Thus the British fascists regarded 'Parliamentary democracy as . . . outdated and inadequate' and as diverting attention from important to insignificant issues, and a recent defence of direct community action argues that the 'system we have is anti-democratic. It consists of electing a "representative" from a limited choice of options pre-selected by small cliques and who, once elected, loses touch with those who elected him'.[61] For these people violence is an instrument used to draw attention to their demands, an instrument which, by shocking people, forces the government to take notice and also enlists the support of people who hear of the demand through the publicity the violence gets. The ball is then in the authorities' court.

The protesters do not necessarily display any emotional need for violence. The object is not to provoke violence but rather to gain support. However, violence may easily erupt. It may erupt because opposition groups oppose the demonstrators, as in the case of the battles between fascists and anti-fascists in the streets of London in the 1930's. Violence may also arise when the demonstrators are attempting to undermine the authority and morale of the police, as in the cases of American student campus revolts. Or again, as with the squatters in the UK, the authorities can either accept a *fait accompli* or resist it, in which case violence is a likely outcome.

The protesters are threatening violence, and violent results are by no means unknown, as in the case of the anti-Greek demonstrators. They attempt to draw attention to causes they consider to be neglected and which

We shall discuss two types of technological innovation: political innovation and, so to say, purely technical innovation. Political innovation includes events like entering new supra-national organizations such as the Common Market, various treaty organizations, and expansion of the national role in international politics. Technical innovation speaks for itself, but we should stress that we simply mean the introduction of new, cheaper and quicker ways of doing things rather than the process of replacing tradition, folkways, the sacred by the rational, the scientific and the secular which is held to be a central process of modernization during which 'the imperatives of technology come to require no other justification but themselves'.[62]

Political innovation affects different social groups in different ways. For example, in France, entering the Common Market has meant the expansion of export opportunities for French industry, but a dramatic increase in competition for the French farmer. New treaty organizations are often the occasion for student rioting and widespread unrest in the developing areas but less so in the modern states, although violent riots against membership of NATO have occurred in Britain, Italy, Germany, Holland and France. More important sources of violence in modern societies are changes in the degree of commitment that a country experiences in international politics. For example, very considerable violence has been generated in America over the gradual expansion of the US sphere of international political engagement. In France, a civil war nearly burst out over the disengagement from Algeria and in the UK the most widespread political violence of the 1950's was associated with the Suez invasion.

The consequence of technical innovation is that skills and traditions which may have served generations gradually or rapidly become otiose. Clearly, if this happens with individuals whose work situation is isolated their organizational focus is likely to be weak and violence is not likely to occur. But when whole integrated communities are deprived or threatened the case is different. A classical example of this is the British miners during the inter-war years, when a combination of higher British costs and increasing foreign competition forced technical innovation both in the structure of management and in the pits: this was the so-called process of rationalization. A consequence was that considerable pressure was exerted for lower wages, the labour force declined and, with mechanization, old work patterns were destroyed; during this period the miners were in the forefront of industrial and political militancy. This is an extreme example, although comparable with France, Belgium and the US, but the point is that this process of innovation is a constant one and, if not dealt with by governments, can be a potent source of violence.

13.7. Some Conclusions

We have argued that violence in politics is not quite as irrational as is sometimes assumed and we have suggested that it plays a central role in state formation, in the process of industrialization and, although less prevalent in the developed country, is none the less an ever-present possibility. We have at times hinted that there are other approaches to violence other than that of statistical analysis and moral condemnation of the violent. For example, we mentioned Fanon's explicit 'approval' of violent acts committed against colonial oppressors as a form of social therapy, and in an earlier chapter we saw that Sorel thought in similar terms and many theorists of revolution endorse this view.[63] Somewhat akin to this idea is the Durkheimian notion that society *needs* its deviants and criminals as objects upon which the hatred of the conforming majority can focus. By hating the criminal the community reasserts its solidarity: 'Thus the criminal, the scapegoat, the mentally ill, in their diverse ways allow the group to re-affirm not only its social but also its moral identity, for they establish signposts which serve as normative yardsticks'.[64]

Political violence, especially the turmoil type, may also be interpreted as an early warning to the authorities that at least a segment of the society feels a sense of exclusion and is nursing grievances that have escaped the attention of the other 'normal' political processes, and from these signals the authorities may glean otherwise unobtainable information. This aspect may be especially significant for discovering the grievances of groups who lack the skill, the opportunity, the legal right to participate, or the possibility of winning an election. We have cited the cases of the Catholics in Northern Ireland and the black minority in the US, both of whom have gained more by violence than by pacific means. We might also have cited the innumerable cases of countries in the Third World—both before and after independence—where 'minor' infringements of the law which in retrospect were clearly early warnings were treated by the police rather than as proto-political events. An interesting example of treating an outbreak of violence as a political early warning system occurred in Uganda in 1945 when following riots the Commission of Inquiry concluded that 'these disturbances may prove to have been a blessing in disguise, as having in good time brought to light some of the troubles which require to be remedied'.[*26*]

It is also possible to widen the analysis and see violence as one method of overcoming what Schattschnieder has called the mobilization of bias, that is, bringing to the front issues previously ignored or considered beyond political attention.[*27*] Such bias may or may not operate against the interests of the weaker section of the community, but, to take a current example, the whole question of pollution did not become a serious political issue until the middle-classes were seriously affected by it, just as drainage did not become an issue until cholera affected the people in the 'better' part of the towns. It would appear likely that the grievances of the weak are not, as is the case with the politically stronger, *routinely* a matter of concern to the authorities so that it is quite possible that these interests are routinely ignored or at least do not become issues until dramatized in some way. The rules of the political process in developed societies are in many respects valuable and deserve support, but nevertheless such rules 'are also a means of winning the game, if some of the players can, as in fact they do, write the laws'.[65] If, as is invariably the case, the rules exclude the threat of violence by those who do not have a say in the determination of policy, then in effect the rules hinder the weak more than the strong. Thus the rules exclude actions such as the occupation by the homeless of empty buildings, the occupation of buildings by protesting students, the seizure of empty sites for children's playgrounds, and so on, but as a matter of fact these actions have caused authorities to take a second look at their policies. They have sensitized the authorities to do something about the grievances. There would be no ghetto problem if there were no ghetto violence, and it is not unlikely that in Britain today there would be no urgency about the major problem of homelessness without the sit-ins, nor would students be playing the role in universities that they are without the advent of threatened and actual violence.

References

1. J. S. Mill, cited in M. St. John Packe, *The Life of John Stewart Mill*, Secker and Warburg, London, 1954, p. 303.
2. T. A. Knopf, 'Media Myths on Violence', *New Society* (12 November, 1970).
3. F. Fanon, *The Wretched of the Earth*, Penguin, London, 1967, especially Sartre's introduction and chs. 1 and 4; D. Caute, *Fanon*, Fontana, London, 1970, ch. 6.
4. Mao Tse-tung, *Selected Works*, Foreign Languages Press, Peking, 1967, vol. I, 'Report of an Investigation of the Peasant Movement in Hunan', pp. 23–59.
5. M. Weber, cited in E. V. Walter, 'Power and Violence', *APSR*, **63**, 35–360 (1964).
6. H. Nieburg, *Political Violence: The Behavioural Process*, St. Martin's Press, New York, 1969, p. 13.
7. H. Graham and T. Gurr (eds.), *The History of Violence in America*, Praeger, New York, 1969, p. xxxiii.
8. F. Engels, *Anti-Duhring*, Foreign Languages Publishing House, Moscow, 1959, pp. 224–240.

9. C. Wright Mills, *The Power Elite*, Oxford University Press, London, 1956, p. 171.
10. M. Weiner, 'Political Integration and Political Development', *Annals of the American Academy of Political and Social Science*, **358**, 52–64 (1965).
11. L. Stone, *The Crisis of the Aristocracy*, Oxford University Press, Oxford, 1965, p. 200.
12. E. V. Walter, *Terror and Resistance*, Oxford University Press, New York, 1969, p. 291.
13. —— *Terror and Resistance*, Oxford University Press, New York, 1969, p. 132.
14. E. Hobsbawn and G. Rude, *Captain Swing*, Lawrence and Wishart, London, 1969, p. 262.
15. A. Organski, *The Stages of Economic Development*, Knopf, New York, 1965, p. 78.
16. C. Clark, 'Population Growth and Living Standards', in A. Agarwala and S. Singh (eds.), *The Economics of Underdevelopment*, Oxford University Press, New York, 1963, pp. 33–53.
17. W. Rostow, 'The Take-Off into Self-Sustained Growth', in A. Agarwala and S. Singh (eds.), *The Economics of Underdevelopment*, Oxford University Press, New York, 1963, pp. 154–186.
18. S. Huntington, *Political Order in Changing Societies*, Yale University Press, New Haven, 1968, p. 41.
19. K. Lorenz, *On Aggression*, Harcourt, Brace and World, New York, 1966; R. Ardrey, *The Territorial Imperative*, Atheneum, New York, 1961; G. M. Carstairs, 'Overcrowding and Human Aggression', in H. Graham and T. Gurr, *The History of Violence in America*, Praeger, New York, 1969, pp. 751–763.
20. A. Bandura and R. Walters, *Social Streaming and Personality Development*, Holt, Rinehart and Winston, New York, 1963.
21. J. Dollard, L. Doob, N. Miller, O. Mowrer and R. Sears, *Frustration and Aggression*, Yale University Press, New Haven, 1939.
22. H. Himmelweit, 'Frustration and Aggression: A Review of Recent Experimental Work', in T. H. Pear (ed.), *Psychological Factors in Peace and War*, Hutchinson, London, 1950, pp. 161–191.
23. T. Gurr, *Why Men Rebel*, Princeton University Press, New Jersey, paperback edition, 1971.
24. —— *Why Men Rebel*, Princeton University Press, New Jersey, 1970; W. Runciman, *Relative Deprivation and Social Justice*, Routledge and Kegan Paul, London, 1966.
25. Cited in E. Thompson, *The Making of the English Working Class*, Penguin, London, 1968, p. 61.
26. T. Gurr, *Why Men Rebel*, Princeton University Press, New Jersey, 1970, p. 24.
27. M. Zeitling, *Revolutionary Politics and the Cuban Working Class*, Princeton University Press, New Jersey, 1967; B. Wedge, 'A Case Study of Student Political Protest: Brazil 1964 and Dominican Republic 1965', *World Politics*, **21**, 183–216 (1969).
28. J. C. Davies, 'Toward a Theory of Revolution', *American Sociological Review*, **27**, 5–19 (1962); C. Brinton, *Anatomy of Revolution*, Prentice-Hall, New Jersey, 1938.

29. I. and R. Feierabend, 'Aggressive Behaviours Within Polities, 1948–62: A Cross-National Study', *Journal of Conflict Resolution*, **10,** 249–271 (1966); R. Tanter and M. Midlarsky, 'A Theory of Revolution', *Journal of Conflict Resolution*, **11,** no. 4, 264–280 (1967).
30. ——— 'Aggressive Behaviours Within Polities, 1948–62: A Cross-National Study', *Journal of Conflict Resolution*, **10,** 249–271 (1966).
31. M. Olsen, 'Rapid Growth as a Destabilising Force', *Journal of Economic History*, **23,** 529–552 (1963); R. Tanter, 'Dimensions of Conflict Behaviour Within Nations, 1955–60', Peace Research Society, Chicago, 1965.
32. J. Forward in N. Raphael (ed.), *Readings in Comparative Public Administration*, Allyn and Bacon, Boston, 1968, p. 459.
33. P. Cutright, 'National Political Development: Measurement and Analysis', *American Sociological Review*, **28,** 253–264 (1963).
34. R. Tanter, 'Toward a Theory of Political Development', *Midwest Journal of Political Science*, **11,** 145–172 (1967).
35. M. Lewis, 'The Negro Protest in Urban America', in J. Gusfield (ed.), *Protest, Reform and Revolt*, Wiley, New York, 1970, pp. 149–190.
36. G. Bateson, 'The Frustration–Aggression Hypothesis and Culture', *Psychological Review*, **48** (1941), cited in T. Gurr, *Why Men Rebel*, Princeton University Press, New Jersey, 1970, p. 167; R. Benedict, 'Child Rearing in Eastern European Countries', in R. Hunt (ed.), *Personalities and Cultures*, Natural History Press, New York, 1967, p. 344; M. Kling, 'Violence and Politics in Latin America', in P. Halmos (ed.), *Latin American Sociological Studies*, Keele, Sociological Review Monograph, no. 11, 1967, pp. 119–131.
37. R. Rose, *Governing Without Consensus*, Faber, London, 1971, pp. 328 and 334.
38. M. Wolfgang, *Patterns in Criminal Homicide*, University of Pennsylvania Press, Philadelphia, 1958, p. 188, cited in Hans Toch, *Violent Men*, Aldine, Chicago, 1969, p. 191.
39. S. E. Finer, *The Man on Horseback*, Pall Mall, London, 1962.
40. —— *The Man on Horseback*, Pall Mall, London, 1962, p. 139.
41. —— *The Man on Horseback*, Pall Mall, London, 1962, pp. 136–137.
42. L. Pye, *Politics, Personality and Nation Building*, Yale University Press, New Haven, 1962, pp. 164–166; C. W. Anderson, F. von der Mehden and C. Young, *Issues of Political Development*, Prentice-Hall, New Jersey, 1967, pp. 98–108.
43. B. Berelson and G. Steiner, *Human Behaviour*, Harcourt, Brace and World, New York, 1964, p. 268.
44. D. Krech, R. Crutchfield and E. Ballachey, *Individual in Society*, McGraw-Hill, 1962, pp. 183–185.
45. R. Brady, *The Spirit and Structure of German Fascism*, Gollancz, London, 1937, p. 66; see also F. Neumann, *Behemoth*, Gollancz, London, 1942, pp. 85–100.
46. K. Deutsch, *The Nerves of Government*, Free Press, New York, 1966, esp. part 2.
47. M. Janowitz, *The Military in the Political Development of New States*, Chicago University Press, Chicago, 1964; J. Johnson, *The Role of the Military in Under-Developed Countries*, Princeton University Press, Princeton, 1962; S. E. Finer, *The Man on Horseback*, Pall Mall, London, 1962.

48. H. Eckstein, 'On the Etiology of Internal War', *History and Theory*, **4,** 133–163 (1965).
49. R. Connery (ed.), *Urban Riots: Violence and Social Change*, Academy of Political Science, New York, 1968.
50. E. Luttwak, *The Coup d'Etat*, Penguin, London, 1969; S. E. Finer, *The Man on Horseback*, Pall Mall, London, 1962.
51. N. Morozov, a populist theoretician cited in J. Kirkham, S. Levy and W. Crotty, *Assassination and Political Violence*, Bantam Books, New York, 1970, p. 528.
52. E. Luttwak, *The Coup d'Etat*, Penguin, London, 1969, p. 32.
53. Mao Tse-tung, 'On Protracted War', *Selected Works*, Foreign Languages Publishing House, Peking, 1965, vol. 2, p. 154; C. A. Johnson, 'Civilian Loyalty and Guerrilla Conflict', *World Politics*, **14,** 642–661 (1962).
54. M. Osanka (ed.), *Modern Guerrilla Warfare*, Free Press, Glencoe, 1962; L. W. Pye, 'The Roots of Insurgency and the Commencement of Rebellions', in H. Eckstein (ed.), *Internal War*, Free Press, Glencoe, 1964, and *Guerrilla Communism in Malaya*, Princeton University Press, Princeton, 1956; C. Johnson, *Peasant Nationalism and Communists in Power*, Stanford University Press, Stanford, 1962.
55. C. Tilly and J. Rude, *Measuring Political Upheaval*, Centre of International Studies, Princeton, 1965.
56. S. Huntington, *Political Order in Changing Societies*, Yale University Press, New Haven, 1968, pp. 264–396.
57. H. Graham and T. Gurr (eds.), *The History of Violence in America*, Praeger, New York, 1969, p. 581.
58. *The Times*, London (7 September, 1970).
59. S. M. Lipset, 'Religion and Politics in the American Past and Present', in R. Lee and M. Marty (eds.), *Religion and Social Conflict*, Oxford University Press, New York, 1964, pp. 69–126; R. Alford, *Party and Society*, Rand McNally, Chicago, 1963.
60. M. Lipsky, 'Protest as a Political Resource', *APSR*, **62,** 1144–1158 (1968).
61. R. Benewick, *Political Violence and Public Order*, Penguin, London, 1969, p. 135; A. Lapping (ed.), *Community Action*, Fabian Society Pamphlet no. 400, London, 1970, p. 35.
62. R. Nisbet, *The Social Bond*, Knopf, New York, 1970, p. 246.
63. R. Debray, *Revolution in the Revolution*, Grove Press, New York, 1967; E. Cleaver, *Soul on Ice*, Penguin, London, 1971.
64. L. Coser, *Continuities in the Study of Social Conflict*, Free Press, New York, 1967, p. 116.
65. H. Nieburg, 'The Threat of Violence and Social Change', *APSR*, **56,** 865–873 (1962).

Notes and Further Reading

1. C. Gide and C. Rist, *A History of Economic Doctrines*, Harrap, London, 1923, p. 275. Today this proposition is quite widely acknowledged as true by economists concerned with development in the Third World where

economic specialization—in bananas, coffee, rubber, cocoa, food, oil, etc.—has almost certainly done little to narrow disparities between the less and more developed countries.

2. Both of these quotations, the first from C. Merriam, are taken from E. V. Walter, *Terror and Resistance*, Oxford University Press, New York, 1969, p. 43.
3. This arbitrary violence is very reminiscent of that described by H. Arendt in *The Origins of Totalitarianism*, Allen and Unwin, London, 1958.
4. In an important article by L. Spengler, 'Economic Development: Political Preconditions and Political Consequences', *Journal of Politics*, **22,** 387–416 (1960), the author heads a list of what the state must do if economic development is to succeed with the condition 'Maintains law, order and security'.
5. For this distinction see K. De Schweinitz, 'Economic Growth, Coercion and Freedom', *World Politics*, **9,** 166–192 (1956–7).
6. For a very useful and concise account of the political attitudes leading to the governments' assumption of the planning of economic development see H. Myint, *The Economics of Developing Countries*, Hutchinson, London, 1964, pp. 165–177.
7. P. Baran, *The Political Economy of Growth*, Monthly Review Press, New York, 1957, pp. 151–162. In nineteenth-century Japan about 50 per cent of all investment was by the government, W. McCord, *The Springtime of Freedom*, Oxford University Press, New York, 1965, p. 60.
8. See H. Graham and T. Gurr (eds.), *The History of Violence in America*, Praeger, New York, 1969, pp. 660–663. The analysis in the chapter cited is in terms of political modernization, but since this is very highly associated with economic development the point still holds.
9. But see W. McCord, *The Springtime of Freedom*, Oxford University Press, New York, 1965, esp. pp. 247–288. For a very useful comparison between Western European experiences and those of the contemporary developing areas see W. Fischer, 'Social Tension at Early Stages of Industrialization', *Comparative Studies in Society and History*, **9,** 64–83 (1967).
10. For the growth of the police in the UK as a response to the strain of industrialization see T. A. Critchley, *The Conquest of Violence*, Constable, London, 1970, esp. pp. 55–140; for the expansion of the military in Africa see J. M. Lee, *African Armies and Civil Order*, Chatto and Windus, London, 1969, chs. 3 and 4; and for a general analysis of the military in developing areas see J. J. Johnson (ed.), *The Role of the Military in Underdeveloped Countries*, Princeton University Press, New Jersey, 1962.
11. See J. M. Lee, *African Armies and Civil Order*, Chatto and Windus, London, 1969, p. 105. See also M. Janowitz, *The Military in the Political Development of New Nations*, Chicago University Press, Chicago, 1964, and M. Lissak, 'Modernization and Role Expansion of the Military in Developing Countries', *Comparative Studies in Society and History*, **9,** 233–255 (1967), for accounts of the assumption of tasks other than civil repression.
12. B. Russett, H. Alker, K. Deutsch and H. Lasswell, *World Handbook of Political and Social Indicators*, Yale University Press, New Haven, 1964, p. 299. He also shows (p. 319) that as the MPR increases deaths from domestic group violence decrease 'suggesting that the motive behind the creation of many large military establishments may well be the suppression of domestic dissent'.

13. For a useful analysis of the concept see G. Almond and G. Powell, *Comparative Politics*, Little, Brown, Boston, 1966, pp. 190–212.
14. W. McCord and T. Howard, 'Negro Opinions in Three Riot Cities', *American Behavioural Scientist*, **11,** 26 (March, 1968). In this study 51 per cent of respondents thought that 'riots have helped' and in a study of Watts 58 per cent of respondents believed riots had helped the negro cause, T. Tomlinson, 'The Development of a Riot Ideology Among Urban Negroes', *American Behavioural Scientist*, **11,** no. 4, 27–31 (1967–1968).
15. See ch. 2, 'Christianity and Apollyon', of E. Thompson's splendid book, *The Making of the English Working Class*, Penguin, London, 1968; J. Morgan, writing in the *New Statesman* of 23 April, 1971, suggests that two million Poles are alcoholics.
16. However, in an account of US internal intelligence activities F. Donner claims that 'Convincing evidence of provocation has emerged in a number of recent cases', 'The Theory and Practice of American Political Intelligence', in *New York Review of Books*, **16** (22 April, 1971).
17. In a study of redistribution in the US, W. Mitchell generalizes that governments do little to affect basic income distribution in a society, but that 'to the extent that redistribution takes place it is from the rich to the poor', in S. M. Lipset (ed.), *Politics and the Social Sciences*, Oxford University Press, New York, 1969, p. 17.
18. For a critical survey of the literature and a case study (Ghana 1966) of military intervention see R. Dowse, 'The Military and Political Development', in C. Leys (ed.), *Politics and Change in Developing Countries*, Cambridge University Press, London, 1969, pp. 213–246.
19. This typology is taken from T. Gurr, *Why Men Rebel*, Princeton University Press, New Jersey, 1970.
20. See R. Dahrendorf, *Class and Class Conflict in an Industrial Society*, Routledge and Kegan Paul, London, 1959, p. 239, 'The intensity of class conflict decreases to the extent that class conflicts in different associations are disassociated'.
21. See the very interesting volume by E. Hobsbawn, *Primitive Rebels*, Norton, New York, 1965; the quote is from p. 124.
22. P. Williams, *Crisis and Compromise: Politics in the Fourth Republic*, Anchor Books, New York, 1966, p. 174; see also L. Noonan, *France: The Politics of Continuity and Change*, Holt, Rinehart and Winston, New York, 1970, p. 127, who cites Poujade as realizing that it is 'impossible to defend small enterprises without attacking the technocrats of the regime, who wish to make distribution in France exclusively the property of the great trusts'.
23. See H. Bienen, *Violence and Social Change*, Chicago University Press, Chicago, 1968, ch. 1, 'Violence in the Ghetto' for this and other accounts.
24. It is important to remember that some authorities are reluctant to embark upon violent collision courses and in this case they can be very vulnerable in the face of those determined to air a grievance, for example, the British and the non-violent resistance in India. See C. Cross, *The Fall of the British Empire*, Paladin, London, 1970, chs. 2 and 8.
25. This should not be interpreted to mean that the economically more prosperous are averse to violence as a political technique. Thus one rather inconclusive survey of the anarchist weekly, *Freedom*, in 1960 revealed that

the largest occupational categories 'were education and the printed word' and these people reject the politics of modern democracies as shams; see D. Stafford, 'Anarchists in Britain Today', *Government and Opposition*, **5**, no. 4, 480–500 (1970).

26. Cited in D. Apter, *The Political Kingdom in Uganda*, Princeton University Press, Princeton, 1961, p. 229.
27. Schattschnieder's concept is very similar to that of Bachrach and Baratz on 'non-decisions'—'The practice of limiting the scope of actual decision-making to "safe" issues by manipulating the dominant community values, myths, and political institutions and procedures', 'Decisions and non-Decisions: An Analytical Framework', *APSR*, **57**, 632–642 (1963).

INDEX

Page numbers shown in italic refer to pages where the author or subject is discussed in detail. For further references to authors see the end of the chapter in which they are mentioned; each chapter is followed by References, and a list of Notes and Further Reading.